D0078170

Measurement of Audition and Vision
in the First Year of Postnatal Life:
A Methodological Overview

Fourth Row: Krasnegor   Kavanagh   Salapatek   Jusczyk   Johnston
Third Row: Spelke   Vietze
Second Row: Yonas   Gottlieb   Teller   Cardenas Kuhl Muir Hecox Bornstein
First Row: Aslin Gray Norton Blake Schneider Dooling Rubel Banks

NICHD Conference on The Measurement of Audition and Vision in Infants
Belmont Center, Elkridge, Maryland, September 21–24, 1982

MEASUREMENT OF AUDITION AND VISION IN THE FIRST YEAR OF POSTNATAL LIFE: A METHODOLOGICAL OVERVIEW

Edited by

GILBERT GOTTLIEB

Psychology Department
University of North Carolina at Greensboro
Greensboro, North Carolina

and

NORMAN A. KRASNEGOR

Human Learning and Behavior Branch
Center for Research for Mothers and Children
National Institute of Child Health and Human Development
Bethesda, Maryland

Ablex Publishing Corporation
Norwood, New Jersey

Printed in the United States of America.

Library of Congress Cataloging in Publication Data
Main entry under title:

Measurement of audition and vision in the first year of postnatal life.

Based on a conference sponsored by the National Institute of Child Health and Human Development in Sept. 1982 and held at the Belmont Conference Center in Elkridge, Md.
Includes bibliographies and index.
1. Audiometry—Congresses. 2. Vision—Testing—Congresses. 3. Infant psychology—Congresses.
I. Gottlieb, Gilbert, 1929–   II. Krasnegor, Norman A.   III. National Institute of Child Health and Human Development (U.S.)

BF720.A92M43   1985   155.4'22   84-28222
ISBN: 0-89391-130-5

Ablex Publishing Corporation
355 Chestnut Street
Norwood, New Jersey 07648

CONTENTS

v

16534

17661

SECTION 3. BEHAVIORAL RESPONSE MEASURES OF HIGHER PSYCHOLOGICAL PROCESSES

16539

16538

16537

16536

6535

LIST OF CONTRIBUTORS

Richard N. Aslin, Psychology Department, University of Indiana, Bloomington, Indiana (now at the University of Rochester, New York)

Martin S. Banks, Department of Psychology, University of Texas at Austin, Austin, Texas

Marc H. Bornstein, Infancy Studies Program, Department of Psychology, New York University, New York, New York

Rachel Keen Clifton, Department of Psychology, University of Massachusetts/Amherst, Amherst, Massachusetts

Donald M. Deegan, Waisman Center, Department of Communicative Disorders, University of Wisconsin, Madison, Wisconsin

Gilbert Gottlieb, Psychology Department, University of North Carolina at Greensboro, Greensboro, North Carolina

Carl E. Granrud, Institute of Child Development, University of Minnesota, Minneapolis, Minnesota

Lincoln Gray, Department of Otolaryngology, University of Texas Medical School, Houston, Texas

Kurt E. Hecox, Waisman Center, Department of Neurology, University of Wisconsin, Madison, Wisconsin

Timothy D. Johnston, Psychology Department, University of North Carolina at Greensboro, Greensboro, North Carolina

Peter W. Jusczyk, Department of Psychology, University of Oregon, Eugene, Oregon

Patricia K. Kuhl, Department of Speech and Hearing Sciences and Child Development and Mental Retardation Center, University of Washington, Seattle, Washington

Darwin Muir, Department of Psychology, Queen's University, Kingston, Canada

Charles A. Nelson, Department of Psychological Sciences, Purdue University, West Lafayette, Indiana

Edwin W Rubel, Department of Otolaryngology, University of Virginia Medical School, Charlottesville, Virginia

Philip Salapatek, Institute of Child Development, University of Minnesota, Minneapolis, Minnesota (deceased)

Bruce A. Schneider, Center for Research in Human Development, University of Toronto, Erindale College, Mississauga, Ontario, Canada

Elizabeth S. Spelke, Department of Psychology, University of Pennsylvania, Philadelphia, Pennsylvania

Davida Y. Teller, Departments of Psychology and Physiology/Biophysics, Child Development and Mental Retardation Center, and Regional Primate Research Center, University of Washington, Seattle, Washington

Sandra E. Trehub, Center for Research in Human Development, University of Toronto, Erindale College, Mississauga, Ontario, Canada

Albert Yonas, Institute of Child Development, University of Minnesota, Minneapolis, Minnesota

ACKNOWLEDGMENTS

Permission has kindly been granted by the publishers to excerpt material from the following works.

Chapter 1

Miller, D. B. (1980). Maternal vocal control of behavioral inhibition in mallard ducklings (*Anas platyrhynchos*), Table 1 and Fig. 12, 13, 14, and 15. *Journal of Comparative and Physiological Psychology, 94,* 606–623. Copyright ©1980, the American Psychological Association.

Chapter 2

Banks, M. S., & Salapatek, P. (1978). Acuity and contrast sensitivity in 1-, 2-, and 3-month-old human infants, Fig. 1, p. 362. *Investigative Ophthalmology and Visual Science, 17,* 361–365.

Fantz, R. L., & Fagan, J. F. III. (1975). Visual attention to size and number of pattern details by term and pre-term infants during the first six months, Fig. 1, p. 6. *Child Development, 16,* 3–18. Copyright ©1975, The Society for Research in Child Development, Inc.

Fantz, R. L., & Nevis, S. (1967). Pattern preferences and perceptual-cognitive development in early infancy, Fig. 1, p. 81. *Merrill-Palmer Quarterly, 13,* 77–108. Copyright ©1967, Wayne State University Press.

Chapter 3

Anson, B. J. (1969). The labyrinths and their capsule in health and disease, Fig. 2, p. 18. *Transcripts of the American Academy of Ophthalmology and Otolaryngology, 73,* 17–38.

Brugge, J. F., Javel, E., & Kitzes, L. M. (1978). Signs of functional maturation of peripheral auditory system in discharge patterns of neurons in interoventral cochlear nucleus of kittens. *Journal of Neurophysiology, 41,* 1557–1579.

Gray, L. (1982). Developmental and experiental changes in dendritic symmetry, p. 362. *Brain Research, 244,* 360–364.

Lippe, W., & Rubel, E. W (1983). Development of the place principle: Tonotopic organization, Fig. 1. *Science, 219,* 514–516. Copyright ©1983, the American Association for the Advancement of Science.

Northern, J. L., & Downs, M. P. (1974). *Hearing in Children.* Baltimore, MD: Williams & Wilkins. Copyright ©1974, Williams & Wilkins Co., Baltimore, MD.

Rubel, E. W , & Ryals, B. M. (1983). Development of the place principle: Acoustic trauma, Fig. 1. *Science, 219,* 512–514. Copyright ©1983, the American Association for the Advancement of Science.

Smith, Z. D. J., Gray, L., & Rubel, E. W (1983). Afferent influences on brain stem auditory nuclei of the chicken: n. laminaris dendritic length following monaural acoustic deprivation. *Journal of Comparative Neurology, 220,* 199–215.

Chapter 4

Johnston, T. D., & Gottlieb, G. (1981). Development of visual species identification in ducklings: What is the role of imprinting?, Figs. 3, 4, 7, and 8. *Animal Behaviour, 29,* 1082–1099.

Pyke, G. H. (1981). Hummingbird foraging on artificial inflorescences, Fig. 1. *Behaviour Analysis Letters, 1,* 11–15.

Chapter 7

Fay, R. R. (1974). Auditory frequency discrimination in vertebrates, Fig. 1. *Journal of the American Acoustical Society, 56,* 206–209.

Gray, L., & Rubel, E. W (1981). Development of responsiveness to suprathreshold acoustic stimulation in chickens. *Journal of Comparative and Physiological Psychology, 95,* 188–198. Copyright ©1981, the American Psychological Association.

Hienz, R. D., Sinnott, J. M., & Sachs, M. B. (1977). Auditory sensitivity of the redwing blackbird (Agelaius phoeniceus) and brown-headed cowbird (*Molothrus ater*), Fig. 7. *Journal of Comparative and Physiological Psychology, 91,* 1365–1376.

Robinson, D. W., & Dodson, R. J. (1956). A re-determination of equal-loudness relations for pure-tones, Fig. 8. *British Journal of Applied Physics, 7,* 166–181. Copyright ©1956, The Institute of Physics.

Chapter 8

Muir, D. (1982). The development of human auditory localization in infancy, Fig. 3, p. 288. In R. W. Gatehouse (Ed.), *Localization of Sound: Theory and Applications.* Groton, CT: Amphora Press.

Chapter 9

Williams, L., & Golenski, J. (1978). Infant speech sound discrimination: The effects of contingent versus noncontingent stimulus presentation, Fig. 1. *Child Development, 49,* 213–217. Copyright ©1978, The Society for Research in Child Development, Inc.

Chapter 11

Caron, A. J., & Caron, R. F. (1969). Degree of stimulus complexity and habituation of visual fixation in infants. *Psychonomic Science, 14,* 78–79.

Fantz, R. J. (1964). Visual experience in infants: Decreased attention to familiar patterns relative to novel ones. *Science, 162,* 668–670. Copyright ©the American Association for the Advancement of Science.

McCall, R. B., & Kagan, J. (1970). Individual differences in the infant's distribution of attention to stimulus discrepancy. *Developmental Psychology, 2,* 90–98. Copyright ©1970, the American Psychological Association.

Miller, G. A., Galanter, E., & Pribram, K. (1960). *Plans and the Structure of Behavior.* New York: Holt, Rinehart & Winston.

Chapter 14

Ladefoged, P. (1962). *Elements of Acoustic Phonetics,* Fig. 4.1, p. 35. Chicago: University of Chicago Press. Copyright ©1962, The University of Chicago.

Chapter 15

Aslin, R. N. (1981). Development of smooth-pursuit in human infants, Figs. 2 and 3, pp. 40–41. In D. F. Fisher, R. A. Monty, & J. W. Senders (Eds.), *Eye Movements: Cognition and Visual Perception.* Hillsdale, NJ: Erlbaum.

Teller, D. Y. (1982). Scotopic vision, color vision, and stereopsis in infants, Fig. 7, p. 208. *Current Eye Research, 2,* 199–210.

Chapter 16

Atkinson, J., Braddick, O., & French, J. (1979). Contrast sensitivity of the human neonate measured by the visual evoked potential, Fig. 2. *Investigative Ophthalmology and Visual Science, 18,* 210–213.

Barnet, A. B., Friedman, S. L., Weiss, I. P., Ohrlich, E. S., Shanks, B., & Lodge, A. (1980). VEP development in infancy and early childhood. A longitudinal study, Fig. 2. *Electroencephalography and Clinical Neurophysiology, 49,* 476–489.

Courchesne, E., Ganz, L., & Norcia, A. M. (1981). Event-related brain potentials to human faces in infants, Fig. 2. *Child Development, 52* 804–811.

Goff, W. R. (1974). Human average evoked potentials: Procedures for stimulation and recording, Fig. 3-1. In R. R. Thompson & M. M. Patterson (Eds.), *Bioelectric Recording Techniques. Part B. Electroencephalography and Human Brain Potentials.* New York: Academic Press.

Goff, W. R., Allison, T., & Vaughan, H. G. Jr. (1978). The functional neuroanatomy of event-related potentials, Fig. 7. In E. Callaway, P. Tueting, & S. H. Koslow (Eds.), *Brain-related Potentials in Man.* New York: Academic Press.

Harris, L., Atkinson, J., & Braddick, O. (1976). Visual contrast sensitivoty of a 6-month-old infant measured by the evoked potential, Fig. 2. *Nature, 264,* 570–571. Copyright ©1976, Macmillan Journals Limited.

Hoffman, M. J., & Salapatek, P. (1981). Young infants' event-related potentials (ERPs) to familiar and unfamiliar visual and auditory events in a recognition memory task. Fig. 1. *Electroencephalography and Clinical Neurophysiology, 52,* 405–417.

Sokol, S. (1978). Measurement of infant acuity from pattern reversal evoked potentials, Fig. 4. *Vision Research, 18,* 33–39. Pergamon Press Ltd.

Sokol, S. (1982). Infant visual development: Evoked potential estimates, Figs. 7 and 10. In I. Bodis-Wollner (Ed.), *Annals of the New York Academy of Sciences.* New York: New York Academy of Sciences.

Sokol, S., & Jones, K. (1979). Implicit time pattern evoked potentials in infants: An index of maturation of spatial vision, Fig. 6. *Vision Research, 19,* 747–755. Pergamon Press Ltd.

Stevens, J. (1974). The electroencephalogram: Human recordings, Fig. 2.4. In R. F. Thompson & M. M. Patterson (Eds.), *Bioelectric Recording Techniques. Part B. Electroencephalography and Human Brain Potentials.* New York: Academic Press.

PREFACE
MEASUREMENT ISSUES IN THE ASSESSMENT
OF AUDITION AND VISION

This book is based upon a conference organized and sponsored by the National Institute of Child Health and Human Development in September of 1982. The meeting, which was held at the Belmont Conference Center in Elkridge, Maryland, brought together a group of leading developmental researchers to assess the state of the art of methodology for measuring audition and vision during the first year of postnatal life. The conferees included scientists from the disciplines of psychophysics, sensory physiology, ethology, experimental psychology, and perception. This mixture of expertise was assembled because the measurement problems inherent in assessing the capacity to see and hear in infants necessitate an interdisciplinary approach. Of particular interest, as is evident from the topic chapters included, is the commonality of problems shared by researchers who measure sensory and perceptual phenomena using animal models, and those who study developing infants. The interchange of communication across disciplines within the context of the meeting was lively, productive, and materially helpful in shaping the final contents of this volume.

METHODOLOGY IN BEHAVIORAL RESEARCH

At the risk of greatly oversimplifying the enterprise, one can conceptually reduce all scientific endeavor to the following two queries: (a) What are the right questions to be asked? and (b) How do you ask the right questions? Scientists who, through a combination of creativity, knowledge, and serendipity, successfully identify the former are lionized by their colleagues and achieve a deserved, meaningful place in history. Those who contribute to the development and solution of the latter aspect of scientific inquiry provide the necessary and sufficient approaches to make significant incremental advances possible. Operationally, the dichotomy described above is not so neat. Therein, though, lies the strength of research.

More frequently than not, those who identify salient questions also devise appropriate methodological breakthroughs. Conversely, methodological innovators succeed in stimulating questions within a discipline which were not framed prior to the advent of the new approach. While it is true that the best of behavioral science is characterized by methodological rigor and excellence of experimental design, it is also fair to observe that it lags behind the physical and biological sciences in the level of quantification possible for dependent measures. Several authors in this book address the measurement of stimulus parameters. One cannot help but be impressed by the level of specificity described. The degree of variance inherent in the specification and quantification of response measures, by contrast, is several levels of magnitude greater. This state of affairs greatly complicates the interpretation of experimental results, and contributes to the uncertainty concerning sensory and perceptual capacities during the first year of life.

One can identify factors especially pertinent to the first year of postnatal life which exacerbate problems associated with measurement of behavioral indices of sensory capacity. An obvious issue is knowing where one's subjects are on the developmental baseline. Different species develop their repertoires (sensory capacity or behavior) at different rates from other species. Within a species, individual organisms reach the same endpoint at different rates. Thus, experimental subjects at the same chronological age may be on different parts of the developmental continuum for either sensory capacity or behavior development, or both. Such dispersion is attributable to the normal variance one would expect along the continuum from precociousness to developmental delay. Ignorance about such factors surely contributes to between-subjects variance. To address this problem, many workers pool data across subjects. This strategy helps mitigate the problem somewhat, but it raises the objection that the psychophysical functions constructed reflect an idealized subject rather than the performance of a psychophysical observer.

In adult and animal psychophysical experiments, N is the number of observations and its value at each point along the abcissa and ordinate of the function. Each subject is measured repetitively at all points. In human infant research, N is typically the number of subjects measured at each point. Individual subjects are often not measured at all points, and the number of observations per subject is small. This approach greatly complicates the estimation of absolute and difference thresholds in human neonates. (See Teller, this volume).

Some of the reasons for the differences in measurement tactics alluded to above reflect the degree of control possible in studies of neonatal animals versus human babies. Clearly, students of animal psychophysics can impose more stringent controls on the experimental testing procedure, use more invasive procedures, and have access to their subjects in accordance with the dictates of their experimental protocols. By contrast, those who study human babies are constrained by the ethics of human experimentation to minimize invasive procedures. They do not have total access to their subjects, and are frequently required to adhere to schedules dictated by the settings in which the subjects are recruited (hospitals, clinics, etc.). Such constraints reduce the opportunity for repeated measurements, within-subject replications, and longitudinal assessment of sensory development.

Another class of variables must also be mentioned in connection with measurement of sensory function in neonates. The state of the organism (asleep, transition, awake, alert awake) greatly complicates the reliability of measurement. Experimenters must control for this organismic variable, which undoubtedly contributes greatly as a source of inter- and intra-subject variability. Ideally, one should control this variable experimentally. That is, state should be assessed throughout each experimental session and trials presented only when the organism is awake and alert. Such state variables are particularly difficult to deal with in studies of human neonates. Experimenters who have scheduled their subjects for a particular time frequently find that the baby is asleep or drowsy. They are forced to drop such subjects from the study or, if possible, to reschedule the session. While neonatal animal subjects have changes in state similar to those of human babies, students of animal psychophysics can more easily reschedule their subjects and thereby insure continuity of state.

One alternative to holding state constant is to identify response measures that are not affected by the organism's arousal level. Such an approach is currently being studied in several behavioral development laboratories in the United States. Preliminary work suggests that unconditioned reflexes (e.g., the glabella) can be quantitatively altered in amplitude by pairing an exteroceptive stimulus with the eliciting stimulus. Reliable changes in reflex intensity, using such procedures, have been reported to occur in sleeping infants. These observations are supportive of the idea that state-independent measures may provide new approaches for assessing sensory capacity. The potential for the use of reflex measures lies in the fact that such behavioral responses can be observed from birth. This may allow accurate measurement of sensory capacity in the neonatal period, a time during which the methods described in this volume have been less than satisfactory.

The advances made during the past decade in perinatal medicine have greatly enhanced the chances of saving the lives of premature infants. Unfortunately, many of these children are born at risk for a variety of behavioral disorders. Early assessment of such children for sensory capacity can provide pediatricians and psychologists with the necessary information to determine what interventions are required to help maximize normal development. It is our hope that the work presented in this book will stimulate further research which will lead to practical tests for assessing sensory function in the neonate. Such tests will materially aid clinicians and provide a scientific basis for intervention strategies.

Norman A. Krasnegor

ACKNOWLEDGMENTS

The editors gratefully acknowledge the assistance of Richard Aslin and the late Phillip Salapatek for their aid in planning the conference. Their recommendations of participants and methodological issues contributed materially to the success of our understaking.

In addition to being subjected to the editors' scrutiny, each chapter was reviewed anonymously by other readers, whose names we make known here by way of grateful acknowledgment: Richard N. Aslin, Martin A. Banks, Randolph Blake, Marc H. Bornstein, Anthony J. DeCasper, Robert J. Dooling,

Lincoln Gray, M. Russell Harter, Kurt Hecox, Gregg Irvin, Peter W. Jusczyk, William R. Lippe, R. Bruce Masterton, David B. Miller, Thomas T. Norton, Cynthia Owsley, Edwin W Rubel, Bruce Schneider, Davida Y. Teller, and Albert Yonas.

We are grateful to Sarah Johnston, Robin Panneton, and Carolyn Schmonsees for their conscientious editorial assistance.

Finally, we thank Thomas T. Norton for the group photograph of the participants at the Belmont Conference Center.

INTRODUCTION TO SECTION 1

General Issues in the Analysis of Auditory and Visual Perception in Infants: Research Strategies, Psychobiological Constraints, and Experiential Requirements for Normal Development

One of the most prominent issues in the study of human auditory and visual perception concerns the nature of the stimuli to be used in such investigations. While there is unanimous agreement that, at some point, it is both necessary and desirable to use artificial stimuli, there is not good agreement on whether or when to use natural or ecologically relevant stimuli. In the first chapter, Gottlieb opts for beginning any investigation with ecologically relevant stimuli, and then proceeding by degrading (or otherwise altering) such stimuli to get at their critical components. In the second chapter, Martin Banks presents a case for using natural stimuli only with certain "higher level" perceptual functions, and using simple, non-natural stimuli with lower level functions for which it is assumed that the naturalness of the stimulus complex is irrelevant. Banks is clear that such inferences are problematic and are rarely if ever empirically examined, so that the best approach might be to use both artificial and natural stimuli, at least where presumptively higher psychological functions are concerned. Tradition weighs heavily in some areas such as psychophysics, so that only simple, artificial stimuli are always used without question: It is simply part of the procedure.

Two important developmental themes that are relatively neglected in the present volume's preoccupation with methodological matters have to do with psychobiological constraints (anatomical and physiological maturation) and sensory-experiential requirements for normal or species-typical development. A cardinal feature of developing systems is that they are *epigenetic* in the sense of exhibiting the serial maturation of abilities or competencies: All of the goods are not in the shop window early in development. Edwin Rubel documents this key aspect of development in his detailed review of the maturation of the auditory system and the role of auditory sensory experience in fostering normal neural and behavioral development. One of his main points concerns the difference between the organism's experiential requirements for normal perceptual or behavioral functioning versus the sensory cell's experiential requirements for normal neural maturation.

In the final chapter in this general introductory section to the book, Timothy Johnston joins the issue of the ecological choice of stimuli by showing how non-ecological choices may either overestimate or underestimate the young organism's perceptual and learning capabilities. He further goes on to show that the not-always-obvious experiential requirements for normal perceptual development may escape detection if a non-ecological approach is adopted at the organismic as well as even the molecular level of analysis.

As the remainder of the volume will attest, getting experts to agree about these important matters is well-nigh impossible, and in fact may not be the most fruitful approach at this relatively early stage of inquiry into the auditory and visual competencies of infants. So, we strive here only to induce a cautionary point of view in our readers by introducing the volume with issues that lie behind, or under the surface of, much of the measurement and methodological treatments to follow.

1

ON DISCOVERING SIGNIFICANT ACOUSTIC DIMENSIONS OF AUDITORY STIMULATION FOR INFANTS

Gilbert Gottlieb

University of North Carolina at Greensboro

INTRODUCTION

The task of this review is to determine how we can best go about specifying the acoustic (physical) basis of significant auditory perceptual functions in the human neonate and infant in the first year of life. Since the strategy of such research is all-important, I shall approach the task by first describing experiments with nonhuman animals (birds), where we have been successful in delineating the acoustic cues or features that mediate the auditory perceptual identification of other members of the species, particularly the mother. This example is not as remote as it may seem from the human case in that, first of all, we must use behavior to infer the ingredients of the perceptual process in both animals and infant humans. Secondly, as will be documented, the auditory component (maternal voice) plays a paramount role in the human infant's early social tie to its mother, beginning at birth if not before, as it does in the nonhuman species to be described. Finally, it seems likely that the human infant's early experience with the maternal voice may have significant ramifications for the learning that goes on as familiar voices eventually begin to be perceived in the speech (i.e., semantic) mode, which, in our society, seems to occur rather abruptly about the end of the first year (Thomas, Campos, Shucard, Ramsay, and Shucard, 1981). So, for these reasons, the research strategy involved in the dissection of the auditory perceptual cues that mediate the young bird's early tie to its mother can be of some relevance for a similar pursuit in human infants.

NATURAL SOUNDS, MULTIDIMENSIONALITY, HIERARCHY

Certain important orienting attitudes have emerged from the avian research, and these should perhaps be mentioned at the outset because of their methodological and conceptual significance. Since we wanted to understand the perceptual basis of the young bird's (duckling's) social tie to its maternal parent, it was pertinent to make field observations of the interaction of hatchlings with their mother. In the several species that were observed, it became apparent that two uniquely species-specific, context-specific calls that each mother emits play a prominent role in controlling the behavior of her young. One of these calls is an "assembly" call that causes the young to approach and follow their mother. The other call is a reconnaissance or "alarm" call that causes the young to behaviorally "freeze" and cease vocalizing.

So, we began the laboratory experiments utilizing natural calls recorded in nature to see if we could duplicate the behavioral effects observed in the field. Only subsequently did we systematically degrade the calls and make synthetic versions to tease out the critical acoustic features that were responsible for controlling the behavior of the young. The degradation and synthesis experiments were always done with an eye toward understanding the effectiveness of the known ingredients of the natural calls as they were uttered in the field. The parallel strategy for research with human infants would entail the use of recordings of actual maternal voices, at least as the first step. Subsequent analytic study using degraded or artificial auditory stimuli would be based on the known acoustic dimensions of actual maternal voices. The successful conclusion of such a program of research would allow one to specify the acoustic features of most relevance in actual maternal-infant auditory interactions. It hardly needs saying that the elegant fruits of classical psychophysical studies often seem remote from an understanding of the perception of natural sounds, and that the latter aim does not seem really central to most, if not all, psychophysical approaches.

The second general point that emerged from the animal research concerns the multidimensional nature of the effective auditory stimulation and the hierarchical organization of these dimensions. That is, not only are multiple features of the maternal call operating together in a kind of synergistic way, but these cues also differ in their import in a systematic pattern.

The reason for emphasizing these features (i.e., that natural calls have multiple dimensions that are hierarchically organized vis-à-vis the avian infant's perception) is that one of the main themes of the present monograph is the desirability of taking a methodologically "psychophysical" approach to the study of infant perception. To many psychophysically oriented researchers (e.g., Davida Teller's article in this monograph), psychophysics, by definition as well as procedure, involves highly impoverished, simple, non-natural stimulation. While I am here opting for a research strategy that seems at variance with usual psychophysical approaches, I do not share the complete skepticism which some hold for classical psychophysics as a way of understanding perception (e.g., J. J. Gibson, 1966). My insistence on the import of ecological validity, natural stimuli, and multidimensionality lies, conceptually speaking, somewhere between the emphasis of classical psychophysical approaches and the holistic approach to perception of theorists such as J. J. Gibson. I hope to show in the present article that one can be highly analytic even when utilizing features of normal stimulation, and that it is possible to put Humpty Dumpty back together again in a meaningful way at the end of the analysis. I see this pursuit as being in the spirit, if not in the actual mold, of conventional psychophysical approaches to perception.

CRITICAL ACOUSTIC FEATURES OF AVIAN MATERNAL CALLS

When domestic mallard (Peking) ducklings that have been hatched in incubators in the laboratory are placed in a simultaneous auditory choice test situation where they have the opportunity of approaching the maternal assembly call of their own species and those of other species, they invariably approach the mallard call in preference to the other call (Gottlieb, 1971a). Since the incubator-hatched young of other species also selectively respond to the maternal assembly call of *their* species in such tests (Gottlieb, 1981), there must exist a species-specific code of auditory cues that each species produces, and selectively attends to, when showing such a preference. In order to begin to "crack" such a code, one would want to know the acoustic features that are common to the maternal assembly calls of a number of hens recorded in nature. (If one wanted to develop hypotheses about the acoustic basis of *individual* auditory recognition, one would look for consistent individual differences or stable individual peculiarities that could reliably serve as a "signature" for a given hen [Beecher, 1981]. This approach will be exemplified in the final section of this review, in discussing the human neonate's perception of its own mother's voice.)

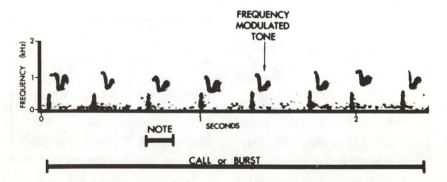

Figure 1. Narrow-band, scale-magnified sound spectrogram of a mallard assembly call depicting parts of the call. (The absence of harmonics is atypical. From Miller, 1980.)

By way of introduction to some necessary technical terms, Figure 1 shows the referents for words like call or burst, note, frequency modulated tone. (There are no harmonics in that particular mallard assembly call.)

Mallard Maternal Assembly Call

In order to search for commonalities among mallard maternal assembly calls, David Miller and I (1978) submitted the recordings of seven mallard hens to an extensive acoustic analysis. Since a species-typical, descending form of frequency modulation (FM) had already been shown to be a perceptually important feature of the wood duck maternal assembly call (Gottlieb, 1974; Miller & Gottlieb, 1976), that feature was the first to be scrutinized with the mallards. As can be seen in Figure 2, there is a modal FM for the mallard assembly call, and it takes a descending-ascending form. In order to test whether this characteristic shape is highly important for the attractiveness of the assembly call, mallard ducklings were given a simultaneous auditory choice test with a call composed of notes of this shape versus a call composed of notes of another shape. In this sort of experiment, it is of course necessary to hold all other acoustic features as constant as possible (repetition rate, number of notes or length of bursts, frequency band, etc.), while varying only that feature which one is interested in. The test calls are shown in Figure 3.

As can be seen in Table 1, the birds did not show a preference for the calls with the species-characteristic FM (I). In fact, two very different kinds of FM (IV and VI) are actually preferred over the modal FM. So, while the species-typical or modal FM of the maternal assembly call is a highly important feature of the wood duck maternal call (data presented below), that is not so for the mallard assembly call.

Other typical acoustic features of the mallard assembly call can be seen in Table 2. Repetition rate of the assembly call also showed a rather narrow range of dispersion over the seven hens, so that this is the next feature that was examined. This was done by pitting the same call against itself at various repeti-

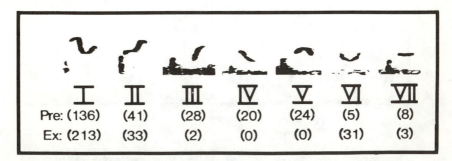

Figure 2. Seven types of frequency modulation (FM) in notes of the mallard assembly call and their actual numerical incidence in the sample studied. "Pre" signifies pre-exodus period prior to departure from the nest; "Ex" indicates exodus period itself. FM I is the modal type in both periods. (Modified from Miller & Gottlieb, 1978.)

VARIOUS MALLARD MATERNAL ASSEMBLY CALLS

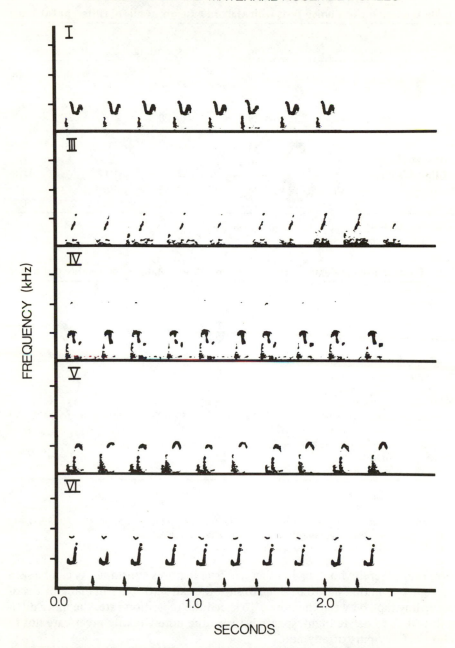

Figure 3. Mallard assembly calls coinciding with five of the FM types shown in Figure 2. Ducklings were given simultaneous auditory choice tests with these calls to determine if the modal FM type (I) or some other type is a preferred feature of the mallard assembly call. (On the frequency axis, the marks refer to 1, 2, and 3 kiloherz for each of the calls.)

Table 1. Outcome of Choice Tests with Mallard Assembly Calls of Different FM Types

Test Calls	Age (hr)	N	No. Responding	Preference		
				I	III	Both
I vs III	24	39	26	11	15	0
				I	IV	Both
I vs IV	24	41	28	1	27**	0
				I	V	Both
I vs V	24	40	21	12	9	0
	48	53	45	22	23	0
				I	VI	Both
I vs VI	24	39	35	2	32**	1
	48	41	31	7	24*	0

Note: Results of previously unpublished experiments.
*$p = .004$, **$p < .00006$, binomial test.

Table 2. Typical Features of Mallard and Wood Maternal Assembly Calls

	Mallard	Wood Duck
Frequency modulation		
Repetition rate (notes/sec)	$4.1 \pm .5$	8.8 ± 1.3†
	$3.5 - 4.7$*	$7.6 - 10.6$*
Note duration (in msec)	108 ± 24	45 ± 8
Frequency range (in Hz)	728 ± 288 to 1973 ± 685	994 ± 169 to 1375 ± 71
Harmonics (discrete bands of energy above fundamental)	$2 - 3$	1
Notes per burst during exodus from nest	12.8 ± 10	18.9 ± 14.6

Mean $\pm$ standard deviation.
* Range.
† Repetition rate for wood duck recalculated by formula described in Scoville and Gottlieb (1978) rather than formula in Miller and Gottlieb (1976, Fig. 3, p. 266).
   Data from Miller and Gottlieb (1976, 1978).

tion rates, thereby holding all other acoustic features constant. As can be seen in Figure 4, all that has to be done to slow the call is to splice in blank pieces of recording tape between the notes. To speed the repetition rate, the more difficult task is to delete blank spaces between the notes, taking great care not to chop off any part of any note.

As can be seen by comparing Table 2 with Figure 4, the natural call that was used in these experiments had a typical repetition rate (3.7 n/s), a modal FM, a typical frequency range, and the usual number of higher harmonics. To determine whether the repetition rates within the typical range are behaviorally

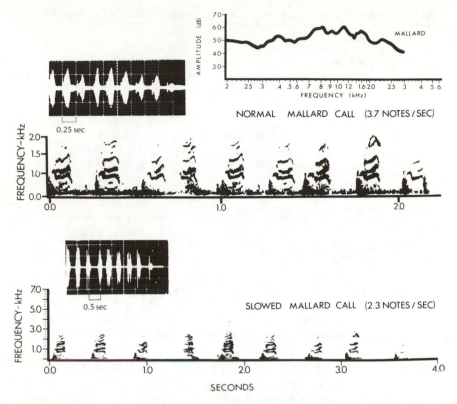

Figure 4. Normal mallard assembly call and its slowed equivalent. (The notes in the slowed version appear smaller because of the necessity of photographic reduction.) (Minor modification from Gottlieb, 1980.)

(functionally) equivalent to each other, the natural call at 3.7 n/s was placed in competition with itself at 4.7 n/s and at 4.2 n/s.[1] As can be seen in Table 3, while 3.7 n/s and 4.2 n/s are equivalent, the 3.7 call is preferred over the 4.7 call, which lies at the upper edge of the normal range of repetition rates recorded in the field (Table 2). With respect to preferences at the lower end of the range, as shown in Table 3, the 3.7 call is preferred over the 2.8 and 2.3 n/s call. Thus, it can be concluded that repetition rate is an important perceptual dimension of the mallard maternal assembly call, and that the range of preferred rates approximately matches the range uttered by hens in the field (3.3 to 4.2 n/s, and 3.5 to 4.7 n/s, respectively).

----

[1] To unencumber the presentation, all the test data presented from here on involve 48-hr-old birds, at which time the keenest perception of the various acoustic attributes of the mallard assembly call has developed (Gottlieb, 1975). It is of the highest developmental significance that the birds' perception of the key feature of the maternal call is less fully developed at 24 hr than it is at 48 hr, but that important aspect of the results is not presented here in order to make a simpler and clearer exposition of the research strategy delineating the chief acoustic features of the call.

Table 3. Outcomes of Choice Tests with Rate-Altered Mallard Maternal Calls

N	No. Responding	Preference		
		Mallard 3.7	Mallard 4.7	Both
24	24	21*	2	1
		Mallard 3.7	Mallard 4.2	Both
40	40	20	15	5
		Mallard 3.3	Mallard 4.2	Both
40	40	21	17	2
		Mallard 3.7	Mallard 2.8	Both
23	22	22	0	0
		Mallard 3.7	Mallard 2.3	Both
50	36	30*	2	4

Note: Results of previously unpublished experiments except for mallard 3.7 vs 2.3 n/s, which appeared in Gottlieb, 1978, Table 3.
* $p < .00006$, binomial test.

The next feature of the mallard assembly call listed in Table 2 is note duration (individual note length), which appears not to be very tightly bound but must, of course, be constrained by its necessary interaction with the more global variable of repetition rate of the call or burst in which the notes are uttered. So we will proceed to the next feature on the list, frequency range, which in the present case interacts with the following feature, harmonics, as can be appreciated by looking at the Sonagram of the mallard call in Figure 4. Note that there are several discrete bands of energy in the call corresponding to higher harmonics. (Since it is possible to generate artificial higher harmonics on the Sonagram by increasing the amplitude too much during analysis, the more exact harmonic peaks can be ascertained by the frequency analysis in the upper right of Figure 4—this particular call has little or no energy above 2300 Hz.)

To determine if the higher harmonics are perceptually (behaviorally) significant for mallard ducklings, the normal 3.7 n/s call in Figure 4 was passed through a high-frequency filter, and high-Hz attenuated versions of the call were recorded to test against the normal version. As shown in Figure 5, two high-frequency attenuated versions of the normal call were obtained, one with frequencies over 825 Hz reduced or eliminated, and the other with frequencies over 1800 Hz reduced. If the higher harmonics of the mallard assembly call are important, in choice tests the duckling should favor the normal call over the attenuated calls. As can be seen in Table 4, that was the case, even when the normal call was pitted against the >1800 Hz attenuated call. So it can be concluded that the higher harmonics of the mallard assembly call, when present, are an important perceptual feature, even extending up to the very highest harmonics (>1800 Hz), which are not as pronounced as the lower harmonics (cf. Figures 4 and 5).

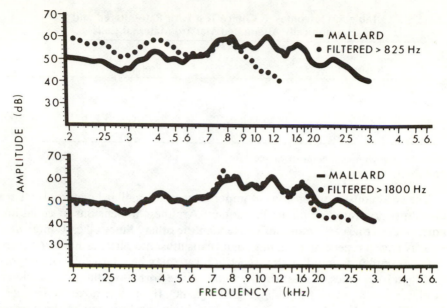

Figure 5. Peak frequency bands in normal and attenuated mallard assembly calls. The normal call was pased through a frequency filter to make the attenuated calls, so the calls differed only in the extent of higher frequencies present. (Modified from Gottlieb, 1975.)

Table 4. Outcomes of Choice Tests with High-Frequency Attenuated Mallard Maternal Calls

N	No. Responding	Preference		
50	47	Normal call 42*	>825 Hz attenuated 4	Both 1
51	49	Normal call 38*	>1800 Hz attenuated 7	Both 4

Note: Data from Gottlieb, 1974, Tables 2 and 4.
* $p < .00006$, binomial test.

The final item on the list of features of the mallard assembly call (Table 2) is notes per burst. As can be seen, there is a great deal of variability in the number of notes per burst across hens; such a complete lack of stereotypy indicates that this feature cannot serve as an identifying acoustic dimension signifying a maternal call of the mallard species.[2]

---

[2] Length of bursts can be a methodologically important variable in choice tests in the laboratory in cases where the two altered calls are closely matched in attractiveness: Under such circumstances, it is sometimes possible to bias the birds' preference by adding or reducing the number of notes in the calls, with the result being the choice of the longer call. However, as can be seen in the test result in Table 3 with mallard 3.7 and mallard 2.3, the birds do not necessarily choose the longer call (2.3) when the calls differ on a significant perceptual variable such as repetition rate.

Table 5. Outcomes of Choice Test with Rate-Altered and Harmonically Attenuated Mallard Maternal Calls

N	No. Responding	Preference		
		>825 Hz attenuated Mallard 3.7	Mallard 2.3	Both
45	32	27*	4	1

Note: Previously unpublished experimental result.
* $p < .0001$, binomial test.

The two acoustic dimensions of importance in the mallard maternal call are thus repetition rate and higher harmonics. Are these dimensions of equal import, or does one carry more influence than the other? Since all calls must necessarily have a repetition rate, but not all calls must have harmonics (see Figure 1, for example), it could be that repetition rate may be relatively more important than harmonics. To test this hypothesis, the normal mallard call depicted in Figure 4 was passed through a high-frequency filter to remove the frequencies above 825 Hz (Figure 5). This severely attenuated version of the normal 3.7 n/s call was then placed in competition with a nonattenuated version of itself pulsed at the unattractive repetition rate of 2.3 n/s. If harmonics are more important than repetition rate, the latter call would be favored, since it contains all the harmonics that were removed from the 3.7 n/s call. As can be seen in Table 5, the high-frequency attenuated call at 3.7 n/s was preferred over the 2.3 n/s call with the harmonics intact, suggesting that repetition rate takes precedence over harmonics in the perceptual hierarchy of critical acoustic features of the mallard maternal assembly call. The key importance of repetition rate for mallard ducklings is further supported by the results with rate-altered maternal alarm calls reported below.

In addition, another bit of converging information comes from experiments with the perceptual deficiencies of mallard ducklings that have been deprived of hearing their own voice and that of sibs. These birds do not distinguish between the mallard maternal call and the chicken maternal call (see Sonagrams in Figure 6). Notice that in the Sonagrams the chicken call has the normally unfavorable repetition rate of 2.3 n/s *and* an absence of harmonics above 1000 Hz. Yet the aurally deprived (devocal-isolated) birds fail to show a preference for the mallard call over the chicken call in a choice test (Table 6). From earlier experiments with aurally deprived birds, we know that their high-frequency (>825 Hz) sensitivity is as intact as in normal birds (results in Table 7). Thus, it follows that the dimension of repetition rate may be controlling their response in the mallard-chicken test. Namely, it seems possible that, in the absence of hearing their own and sib calls, their species-typical range of repetition rate preferences has broadened to include 2.3 n/s, so they are ignoring the absence of high frequencies in the chicken call. To test this hypothesis, aurally

14   *Gilbert Gottlieb*

Table 7. Outcomes of Choice Tests Indicating High-Frequency Sensitivity of Aurally Deprived Mallard Ducklings

Group	N	No. Responding	Normal mallard 3.7	>825 Hz attenuated mallard 3.7	Both
Vocal-communal	50	47	42*	4	1
Devocal-isolated	58	39	36*	3	0

(Preference)

Note: Data from Gottlieb, 1975, Table 2.
* p < .00006, binomial test.

deprived ducklings were given a choice test with the normal mallard 3.7 vs. the same call at 2.3 n/s. As can be seen in the middle sector of Table 6, they failed to show the normal preference for 3.7. If it is true that repetition rate is controlling their response in the mallard 3.7 vs. chicken 2.3 test, *and* their high frequency sensitivity *is* intact as shown in Table 7, then when the chicken call is made equivalent to the mallard call in repetition rate, the aurally deprived birds will no longer ignore the absence of higher harmonics in the chicken call and thus will favor the mallard call over the chicken call. That prediction was borne out; these very encouraging results are shown at the bottom of Table 6.

Thus, we are able to conclude that there is a strict hierarchy of perceptual dimensions controlling the aurally mediated behavior of mallard ducklings vis-à-vis the maternal assembly call of their species, with repetition rate being a primary dimension and harmonics playing a lesser though still influential role. Although we were unable to demonstrate a role for the species-typical FM, I would guess that some or almost any form of modulation would be preferred to, say, a pure tone or a band of white noise. But that would place FM at best as a tertiary feature in the hierarchy.

Mallard Maternal Alarm Call

The overriding perceptual significance of repetition rate in the mallard duckling's responsiveness to maternal auditory stimulation has been further demonstrated in David B. Miller's integrated field and laboratory study (1980) of the ducklings' response to the maternal reconnaissance or alarm call. This is a brief call which the hen utters when a potential predator is in the vicinity of her brood. It causes the young to become instantaneously silent and motionless, which presumably makes them less conspicuous to a would-be predator.

A comparison of the acoustic features of the mallard maternal alarm and assembly calls as uttered in the next situation is shown in Table 8. These calls differ most sharply on FM, dominant frequency, and repetition rate, with no overlap at all on the latter dimension. Given this fact and the import of repetition rate in the assembly call, Miller decided to examine the effect of exchanging the repetition rates of the two calls and keeping all other acoustic features the

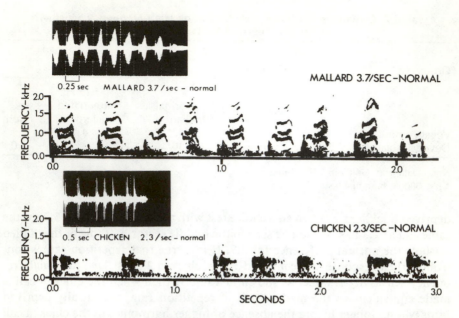

Figure 6. Narrow-band, scale-magnified sonagrams of unaltered mallard and chicken assembly calls. Note differences in FM and repetition rate, and the absence of higher harmonics in the chicken call. (Minor modification from Gottlieb, 1978.)

Table 6. Outcomes of Choice Tests with Mallard Maternal and Chicken Maternal Calls by Aurally Deprived Mallard Ducklings

Group	N	No. Responding	Preference		
			Normal mallard 3.7	Normal chicken 2.3	Both
Vocal-communal	30	24	24*	0	0
Aurally deprived (devocal-isolated)	83	43	26	15	2
			Normal mallard 3.7	Slowed mallard 2.3	Both
Vocal-communal	50	36	30*	2	4
Devocal-isolated	63	38	20	16	2
			Normal mallard 3.7	Quickened chicken 4.1	Both
Vocal-communal	53	50	49*	1	0
Devocal-isolated	48	26	24*	2	0

Note: Data from Gottlieb, 1978.
* $p < .00006$, binomial test.

13

same. Sonagrams of the two test calls are shown in Figure 7. Notice that, among other differences, the alarm call has only three notes, whereas the assembly call has nine notes. Miller's acoustic manipulation is depicted in Figure 8, where oscillograms of the four test calls are shown: Normal reconnaissance 1.4, altered reconnaissance 3.7, normal assembly 3.7, and altered assembly 1.4. Miller examined the ducklings' vocal behavior and approach response to each one of the calls in a test situation that otherwise provokes a good deal of distress calling on the part of the young (bottom, Figure 9). The 6-minute test begins with 2 minutes of silence, followed by 2 minutes of alarm or assembly call, ending with 2 minutes of silence.

As can be seen in Figure 9, when either the alarm call or assembly call is played at 1.4 n/s, the distress calling on the part of the young is completely inhibited, not merely for the 2 minutes the call is broadcast, but for the follow-

Table 8. Modal Acoustic Features of Mallard Maternal Reconnaissance and Assembly Calls

Acoustic Feature	Maternal Call	
	Reconnaissance	Assembly
Frequency Modulation		
Dominant Frequency	676 ± 77 Hz	970 ± 337 Hz
Note Duration	161 ± 39 msec	112 ± 27 msec
Repetition Rate	1.1 ± 0.4 notes/sec	3.7 ± 1.1 notes/sec

Note: From Miller, 1980.

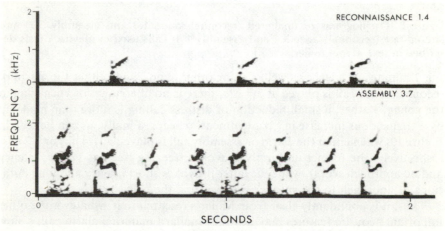

Figure 7. Narrow-band, scale-magnified spectrograms of unaltered reconnaissance and assembly calls used in playback tests described in text. These calls came from a single hen. The numbers refer to the repetition rate of calls, 1.4 notes/sec and 3.7 notes/sec, respectively. (From Miller, 1980.)

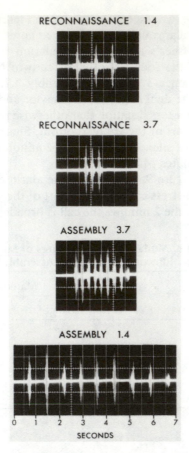

Figure 8. Oscillograms of unaltered (reconnaissance 1.4 and assembly 3.7) and altered-rate (reconnaissance 3.7 and assembly 1.4) calls used in playback tests described in text. (From Miller, 1980.)

ing 2 minutes of silence as well. On the other hand, when either the alarm or reconnaissance call is played at 3.7 n/s, there is no abatement of vocalizing in the young. Rather, a small reduction of distress calling is more than made up by a tremendous increase in "contentment" cheeps. Finally, as can be seen in Figure 10, when either the alarm or assembly call is played at 1.4 n/s or 3.7 n/s, respectively, the former uniformly provokes freezing (seen as 120 sec latency and no approach score), while the latter provokes short latency and long durations of approach to the speaker broadcasting the call.

Thus, it is abundantly clear from Miller's research that, whatever the other important acoustic features may be in the mallard maternal alarm call, a slow repetition rate is the dominant aspect. In his most recent research on the alarm call, Miller (1983) has found that the acoustical upper boundary for the production of behavioral inhibition and excitation is in the region of 2.6-2.8 n/s, which coincides nicely with the lower boundary found with the assembly call (Table 3).

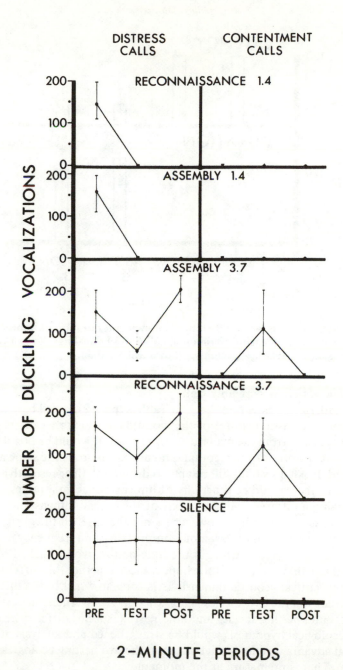

Figure 9. Number of duckling vocalizations (distress calls and contentment calls) uttered before (pre), during (test), and after (post) the broadcast of each experimental call (and of the silence control group). (Plotted values are medians and interquartile ranges, based on 30 ducklings per condition. From Miller, 1980.)

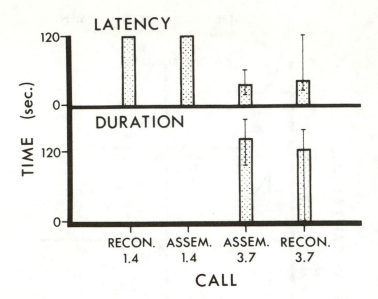

Figure 10. Median (± interquartile range) latency and duration of approach scores of ducklings exposed to each experimental call (*n* = 30 ducklings per call). (RECON. = reconnaissance; ASSEM. = assembly.) (From Miller, 1980.)

Wood Duck Maternal Assembly Call

If the reader will kindly refer back to Table 2 (page 8), it will be seen that the species-typical acoustic features of the wood duck assembly call are different on each dimension from the mallard assembly call. It would be possible, therefore, that the hierarchy of perceptual dimensions could be the same and wood and mallard ducklings would still be able to distinguish their respective maternal calls. That is, there could be generality of dimensions across species, with each species having a different value on each of the crucial dimensions. That aesthetically pleasing possibility, however, is not the case. In the ground-nesting mallard, repetition rate is of paramount importance and frequency modulation of at best tertiary import, while in the hole-nesting wood duck, FM is paramount and repetition rate is of little importance. Whether this difference in the hierarchy of critical acoustic dimensions is somehow tied to the difference in nesting ecology in the two species is not known. If the critical acoustic dimensions in ground-nesting species and hole-nesting species differ systematically, then the ecological hypothesis would be strengthened and analysis of auditory perceptual advantages and disadvantages in the two nesting ecologies would be called for. That is premature at the moment.

We learned that repetition rate was not very important in the wood ducklings' perception of their maternal assembly call by altering the rate of the maternal call shown in Figure 11 so that various versions of the same call could be pitted against one another: The modal rate of 8.8 against 6.9, and 6.9 against 4.0 n/s. No preferences were shown among these rates, even though 6.9 n/s is

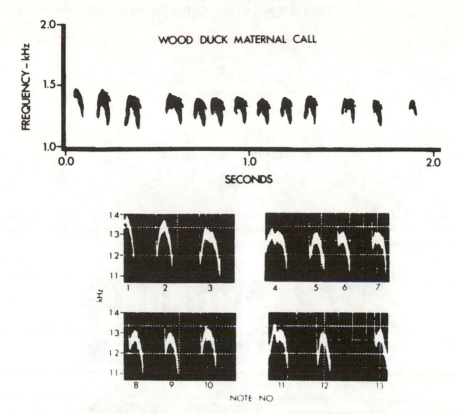

Figure 11. Narrow-band, scale-magnified spectrogram (top) and frequency chronogram (bottom) of a wood duck maternal assembly call used in the tests described in the text. (Modified from Gottlieb, 1981.)

well below the range of repetition rates recorded in the field, and 4 n/s is less than half the mean rate (Table 2). Although we have not pitted 8.8 n/s against 4.0 n/s, if 8.8 were favored it would be akin to the hypothetical outcome of pitting a frequency modulated tone against a pure tone in the mallard, suggesting at best a subsidiary role for repetition rate in wood ducklings. These data are presented in Gottlieb (1981) and, for the sake of space, will not be repeated here.

The next feature (Miller and Gottlieb, 1976) examined in the wood duck assembly call was frequency modulation. We scrutinized 661 notes in the calls of 11 hens, and discovered that 70% (462) had a pronounced descending modulation, as shown in Figure 12. In order to determine if this characteristic shape was of perceptual significance to the ducklings, we made some artificial notes which were either descending, ascending, or symmetrical in FM (Gottlieb, 1974). As shown in Figure 13, we then made three calls that otherwise shared the characteristics of the natural call in Figure 11. The strategy was, first, to determine if the synthetic descending call was favored over the other synthetic calls, and, if it was, to see if it was as attractive as the natural call in a simul-

FREQUENCY MODULATION

DESCENDING

 462

ASCENDING

148

ASCENDING-DESCENDING

51

Figure 12. Three variations in FM found in the notes of assembly calls of 11 wood duck hens recorded in nature. The numbers refer to the total notes in each classification. (Modified from Miller & Gottlieb, 1976.)

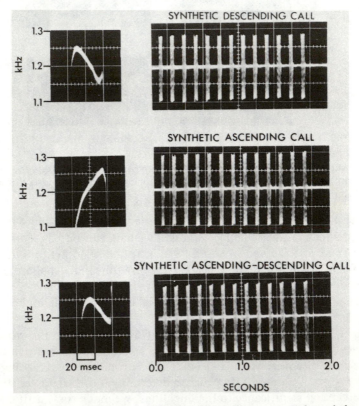

Figure 13. Frequency chronograms (left) and oscillograms (right) of the synthetic wood duck maternal call notes described in text. Each call was composed of 13 notes of equal length and equal burst durations, so the calls differed only in FM. (From Gottlieb, 1974.)

**Table 9. Outcomes of Choice Tests Indicating Favored Form
of Synthetic Frequency Modulation in Wood Ducklings**

N	No. Responding	Preference		
		Descending	Ascending	Both
26	26	13*	5	8
		Descending	Ascending-Descending	Both
38	31	20**	5	6
		Descending	Natural call	Both
35	30	10	16	4

Note: Since a relatively large proportion of birds went to Both in the first 2 tests, it is important to note that, when the absolute latency and duration scores to the calls are utilized, the birds as a whole (including those under Both) showed a statistically significant shorter latency and longer duration to the descending call compared to the other call in both tests. Likewise, the same sort of analysis bore out the absence of a preference in the synthetic descending call vs. natural call test. Data from Gottlieb, 1974, Tables 1 and 2.
* $p = .05$, **$p < .01$, binomial test.

taneous choice test. If the synthetic call was as attractive as the natural call, that would indicate that we had synthesized one of its most critical features.

As can be seen in Table 9, the synthetic descending call was favored over the other synthetic calls and, further, it was as attractive as the natural wood duck call in a simultaneous choice test. Thus, the species-typical descending frequency modulation of the wood duck maternal call is a critical acoustic feature of that call. So, in striking contrast with the mallard, FM is an important perceptual dimension in the wood duck, whereas repetition rate is relatively unimportant. The other dimensions of importance to the wood duckling remain to be determined.

CRITICAL PERCEPTUAL DIMENSIONS OF THE MATERNAL VOICE FOR HUMAN INFANTS

As a way of making a bridge between the avian experiments and those with human neonates, in Table 10 I have made a non-exhaustive list of some common acoustic features of animal and human voices and their related psychoacoustic attributes in those cases where they are known or can be reasonably inferred. Although there is some inevitable oversimplification (and thus some possible distortion) in trying to relate complex psychological (perceptual) processes to individual acoustic features, at the very least Table 10 can serve as a lexicon of important terms that often go unspecified or undefined in the experimental literature.

Two phenomena of particular relevance in the current context are (a) the perceptual basis of the human newborn's apparent "recognition" of its own

Table 10. Some Important Acoustic Features
and Their Related Psychoacoustic Dimensions*

Acoustic Feature	Related Psychoacoustic Dimension
Intensity; amplitude	Loudness** (variations contribute to "stress" in speech)
Amplitude modulation	Sequential change in perceived loudness
Frequency (Hz)	Pitch
Frequency modulation	Intonation; "quality"; pitch "contour", pattern or sequence
Note or tone duration	Length (variations contribute to "stress" in speech)
Rate and pattern of acoustic elements	Rhythm; tempo
Fundamental frequency (Hz)	Pitch of complex sounds (including speech)
Spectrum (amplitude x frequency)	Quality or timbre
Formant frequencies (peaks in speech spectrum-resonances of vocal tract)	Phonetic quality (variations in formant pattern specify phonetic segments [consonants and vowels] in speech)

* In practice it is of course not possible to isolate a single acoustic feature, in the sense that any sound has at least frequency, amplitude, and temporal dimensions. By appropriate experimentation, the relative importance of individual acoustic features can be determined as described in the text.

** Here and elsewhere in table, it should be recalled that perceived loudness is frequency-dependent, so that, for example, 500 Hz sounds louder than 200 Hz at the same intensity.

mother's voice soon after birth, and (b) the perceptual basis of the older human infant's preference for "baby talk" or "motherese" (the acoustic characteristics peculiar to infant-directed speech) as opposed to adult-directed speech. Since we have more analytic information about (b) than (a), I shall first describe the experimental results bearing on the key acoustic features underlying the infant's attraction to the so-called motherese or baby talk mode of speech.

Baby Talk

It has often been observed casually that adults speak in distinctly different modes when addressing infants or young children in contrast to adults. This baby talk phenomenon is rather general in that it seems to occur across a number of languages (Ferguson, 1964), and, recently, it has come in for especially searching and systematic analysis in both German and English (Fernald & Simon, 1984; Stern, Spieker, & Barnett, 1983). For a convenient shorthand, I will here refer to this peculiar speech mode as the BT intonation pattern. A conspicuous and recurrent finding in these studies is the use of a highly exaggerated FM, or expanded pitch intonation pattern, and slow rhythm and tempo when speech is directed to infants. Ferguson (1978) has termed this mode of speech a *simplified register,* and Sachs (1978) has suggested that its principal components are an overall higher pitch, a wider frequency and intensity range, and a slowed and markedly rhythmic structure. It is of no little interest that it is just these acoustic features which characterize the young child's speech (review by Kent, 1981), possibly indicating an early developmental coupling between perception and production.

Building on the earlier, more general hypotheses of Lewis (1936, pp. 112–123) on the importance of exaggerated intonation patterns for communication with prelinguistic infants in the first half-year of life, Stern, Spieker, and McKain (1982) have found that two types of pitch contours were used consistently by mothers of 2- to 6-month-old infants in specific contexts. When attempting to gain or regain eye contact, the mother usually used a high, rising pitch contour. When the infant was already looking and smiling at the mother, and she wished to maintain that posture, she typically used a bell-shaped or sinusoidal pitch contour. Such consistency of FM pattern in specific interactional contexts suggests that these intonation contours may be especially important for early prelinguistic communication with the infant, a hypothesis expanded in illuminating detail by Fernald (1983) and by Stern, Spieker, and Barnett (1983).

For the present purpose, it is most germane to describe the beginnings of an experimental approach to the perceptual side of the analysis, with the aim of determining whether exaggerated FM pattern is a critical feature for the infant's perception of "motherese." In contrast to question (a) concerning the perceptual basis of the newborn infant's recognition of its own mother's voice, question (b) concerns the perceptual basis of the older infant's response preference for *generalized* motherese, that is, the infant's responsiveness to speech directed to another infant by an unfamiliar mother. This is vaguely analogous to the research reviewed in the previous section, in which any maternal assembly call of the species can function as a basis for species identification in ducklings, in contrast to the problem of studying the perceptual basis of the duckling's recognition of its own mother's assembly call (a problem not dealt with in the preceding section). So we would not necessarily expect the perceptual dimensions to be the same, especially as we see (below) that the speech samples which permit newborns to identify their own mothers do not necessarily contain exaggerated FMs.

When analyzing samples of speech directed to infants and to adults, Anne Fernald (1982) noted that, among other differences, the infant-directed speech contained fundamental frequencies that ranged from 100 Hz to 800 Hz, whereas the adult-directed speech ranged from only 100 Hz to 300 Hz. Her first aim was to determine if she could get a behavioral measure of infants' preference between these speech samples. Thus, she tested 4-month-old infants in a choice situation where a $>30°$ right or left head-turn from midline produced one or the other speech sample. Most of the infants (33/48) turned on the infant-directed speech samples more than the adult-directed speech samples, so, in this sense, 4-month-old infants show a preference for infant-directed speech. To determine if the expanded FM range (a prominent feature of the BT intonation pattern) is one of the critical acoustic features mediating the infants' preference, Fernald altered the natural speech samples, with the assistance of a computer, so the pitch contours were synthesized as frequency-modulated sine waves with amplitude held constant. This alteration removed the lexical aspect and highlighted the differences in the sheerly acoustical components of FM and duration in the respective samples. Under these conditions, the infants (16/20) preferred the synthetic stimulus pattern derived from the infant-directed speech samples, thus implicating wide excursions in FM, and possibly (longer) duration, as critical acoustic aspects of the BT intonation pattern. Fernald reports that the pitch contours derived from adult-directed speech sounded like low, continuous murmers, whereas the BT contours sounded ". . . more like highly distinctive musical glissandi" (p. 40).

The next step in Fernald's analysis was to hold frequency constant and allow AM to vary. So, again with computer aid, she synthetized the AM features of the two samples, holding FM constant at the mean level of each sample. In this instance, the infants showed no preference between the infant- and adult-directed speech samples, thus indicating that AM variations are not as crucial as FM in mediating the infant's preference for BT intonations.

Finally, since the longer duration of the infant-directed speech was an uncontrolled variable in both of the previous experiments, Fernald's final manipulation was to present the different durational characteristics of the speech samples to infants holding FM and AM constant. As expected from the result of the previous experiment, in which both AM and duration differed, in the final experiment there was no difference between the synthetic infant- and adult-directed samples, thus confirming that longer duration, though omnipresent in BT, is not as influential as wide excursions in FM in mediating the infant's preference for BT. Neither the present author, nor Fernald herself, wish to argue that AM and duration are of no importance, but simply that FM is of greater relative importance in what is likely a hierarchy of acoustic features responsible for the infant's attraction to BT.

In an earlier experiment implicating the importance of intonation or tonal quality, Culp and Boyd (1974) used a dishabituation paradigm to see if 2-month-old infants could distinguish between the same female voice reading the same material either in a soft or a harsh tone. Based on the dishabituation evidence, these young infants could indeed distinguish between the intonation patterns, spectrograms of which are shown in Figure 14.

The results of Culp and Boyd and of Fernald provide clear experimental support for the widely mooted hypothesis that infants under one year of age are keenly responsive to the prosodic (nonsemantic) components of speech, especially the multifaceted variable of intonation pattern (Lewis, 1936, and a host of more recent authors).

Individual Auditory Recognition

We turn now to the even more remarkable ability of newborn infants to distinguish their own mother's voice from another mother's voice 2-3 days after birth. DeCasper and Fifer (1980) recorded mothers' voices as they read a standard children's story, and then the investigators used the recordings to reinforce a complicated operant suckling behavior: temporal modifications of

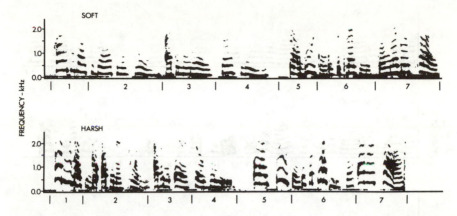

Figure 14. Narrow-band, scale-magnified spectrograms of a female voice reading the same verse of a nursery rhyme with a "soft" or "harsh" intonation. Note the prolongation of the phrases in the soft version. The numbers refer to the following components of the rhyme: 1, How would you like; 2, to go up in a swing; 3, up in the air; 4, so blue; 5, Oh, I do; 6, think it's the pleasantest thing; 7, ever a child... Space limitations prohibited a complete reproduction of the entire rhyme. (Recordings supplied by Raymond Culp.)

inter-burst suckling interval (IBI). The question was whether the infants would (could) modify their suckling IBIs in order to hear their own mother's voice vs. another mother's voice reading the same material, and the answer was positive.

Samples of some of the discriminations that infants actually made are presented in Figure 15. As can be seen, the mothers did not read the story with a BT intonation. Since the newborn babies had rather limited postnatal contact with their mothers, it is possible that the crucial exposure to their mothers' voice came before birth. It is known from a variety of studies that environmental sounds of 1000 Hz and below penetrate the uterus and the amniotic sac in which the fetus is enclosed (Armitage, Baldwin, & Vince, 1980; Grimwade, Walker, Bartlett, Gordon, & Wood, 1971; Querlew, Renard, & Crépin, 1981; Walker, Grimwade, & Wood, 1971). As can be seen in Figure 15, the dominant frequencies of speech occur well below 1000 Hz. (We know from comparative studies of early auditory development that the ability to respond to low frequency antedates high frequency in all species studied to date --see Gottlieb, 1971b; Rubel, 1978 and in this volume, and that the human fetus is capable of responding to sound --see Bernard & Sontag, 1947; Read & Miller, 1977; Sontag & Wallace 1935.) That there is something particularly attractive in maternal speech is shown by the fact that newborns, although they can discriminate between male voices, do not modify their IBI to hear their father's voice (DeCasper & Prescott, 1984), the dominant frequencies of which are also below 1000 Hz. As is well-known (e.g., Studdert-Kennedy, 1981), the fundamental frequency range of adult male voices is lower (about 90-250 Hz) than that of adult females (approximately 150-350 Hz), so that would be an obvious variable of interest when dissecting the critical acoustic features of maternal voices. Also,

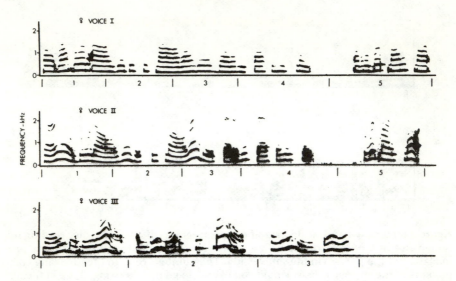

Figure 15. Narrow-band, scale-magnified spectrograms of three female voices reading the same story. Newborn infants in the DeCasper and Fifer study (1980) described in the text responded to their own mother's voice vs. another mother's voice. The above spectrograms were made of two of the actual discriminations: Voice I vs. Voice II and Voice II vs. Voice III. To the ear, none of these voices is in the baby talk mode; Voice III depicts a mother whose speech pattern is normally "slow." The components of part of a Dr. Seuss story are as follows: 1, No it won't do at all; 2, a zebra is too small; 3, a reindeer is better; 4, he's fast and he's fleet; 5, and he'd look mighty smart... (Recordings supplied by Anthony DeCasper.)

since harmonics are such a prominent feature of the human voice, that feature would obviously bear analysis. It also would be of great interest to utilize Fernald's computer technique to get at the importance of characteristic individual FM as a part of the maternal auditory "signature." Intonation pattern (tonal quality and tempo) is quite possibly the most important acoustic feature for individual auditory recognition (see Mehler, Bertoncini, Barrière, & Jassik-Gerschenfeld, 1978, for some support of this hypothesis with 4-to-6-week-old infants). With computer synthesis and abstraction, it should be quite feasible to "crack the codes" which (a) permit individual identification and (b) make maternal voices more attractive to newborn infants than paternal voices. Finally, the active investigation of the probable prenatal experiential basis of the infant's preference for its mother's voice is a most exciting prospect.

Thus, the stage is set in the human newborn for the kind of acoustic and experiential analysis that has proven so fruitful in ducklings. Such an analysis may also help us to understand the basis of the older infant's response to isolated fragments of synthetic speech (reviewed by Eisenberg, 1976, and, most recently, by Aslin, Pisoni, & Jusczyk, 1983).

SUMMARY AND CONCLUSIONS

Naturalistic observation (recording) of maternal vocal behavior in the origin and early development of the maternal-neonate social bond provides the most appropriate starting point for the functional analysis of audition in infants. The maternal voices so obtained can then be analyzed for similarities and differences on various known acoustic dimensions. Similarities provide the auditory basis for the very young infant's strong preference for female voices, whereas stable differences provide the basis for individual auditory recognition. The multifaceted variable of intonation pattern is a most important aspect for engaging and maintaining infants' attentiveness during at least the first six months or so of postnatal life. The experiential basis of individual auditory recognition probably begins in utero, and its acoustic basis is not yet known. Thus, the so-called prosodic (i.e., nonsemantic) features of the human voice provide a rich and analytically amenable source of information about the socially significant aspects of auditory function in the neonate and older infant.

In sum, further specification of the key acoustic aspects of the prosodic features of speech, a charting of their changes with time (age), and an analysis of the roles of experience in their maintenance and development would seem to be the currently most fruitful research tasks in the auditory realm with infants under one year of age.

ACKNOWLEDGMENTS

This review was written in connection with activities supported by Research Grant HD-17752 from the National Institute of Child Health and Human Development. I am grateful to Jo Ann Bell for her assistance in collecting and analyzing the previously unpublished data reported herein. I thank Rex E. Culp and Anthony DeCasper for supplying recordings of the voices used in their research so that I could analyze them. Richard Aslin, Michael Studdert-Kennedy, David B. Miller, and Anthony DeCasper provided useful comments on the first draft of the ms. Robert Wiard helped with the preparation of figures and tables.

REFERENCES

Armitage, S. E., Baldwin, B. A., & Vince, M. A. The fetal sound environment of sheep. *Science,* 1980, *208,* 1173–1174.

Aslin, R. N., Pisoni, D. B., & Jusczyk, P. W. Auditory development and speech perception in infancy. In M. M. Haith & J. J. Campos (eds.), *Handbook of child psychology.* Vol. 2. *Infancy and developmental psychobiology.* New York: Wiley, 1983.

Beecher, M. D. Development of parent-offspring recognition in birds. In R. N. Aslin, J. R. Alberts, & M. R. Petersen (eds.), *Development of perception.* Vol. 1. New York: Academic Press, 1981.

Bernard, J., & Sontag, L. W. Fetal reactivity to tonal stimulation: A preliminary report. *Journal of Genetic Psychology,* 1947, *70,* 205–210.

Culp, R. E., & Boyd, E. F. Visual fixation and the effect of voice quality and content differences in 2-month-old infants. In F. D. Horowitz (ed.), *Visual attention, auditory stimulation, and language discrimination in young infants. Monographs of the Society for Research in Child Development,* 1974, serial no. 158, *39,* nos. 5–6, 78–91.

DeCasper, A. J., & Fifer, W. P. Of human bonding: Newborns prefer their mothers' voices. *Science,* 1980, *208,* 1174–1176.

DeCasper, A. J., & Prescott, P. A. Human newborns' perception of male voices: Preference, discrimination, and reinforcing value. *Developmental Psychobiology,* 1984, *17,* 481–491.

Eisenberg, R. B. *Auditory competence in early life.* Baltimore: University Park Press, 1976.

Ferguson, C. A. Baby talk in six languages. *American Anthropologist,* 1964, *66,* 103–114.

Ferguson, C. A. Baby talk as a simplified register. In C. E. Snow & C. A. Ferguson (eds.), *Talking to children.* Cambridge: Cambridge University Press, 1978.

Fernald, A. Acoustic determinants of infant preference for "motherese". Unpublished Ph.D. thesis, University of Oregon, 1982.

Fernald, A. The perceptual and affective salience of mothers' speech to infants. In L. Fegans, C. Garvey, & R. Golinkoff (eds.), *The Origin and growth of communication.* Norwood, NJ: Ablex, 1983.

Fernald, A., & Simon, T. Expanded intonation contours in mothers' speech to newborns. *Developmental Psychology,* 1984, *20,* 104–113.

Gibson, J. J. *The senses considered as perceptual systems.* Boston: Houghton Mifflin, 1966.

Gottlieb, G. *Development of species identification in birds.* Chicago: University of Chicago Press, 1971. (a)

Gottlieb, G. Ontogenesis of sensory function in birds and mammals. In E. Tobach, L. R. Aronson, & E. Shaw (eds.), *The biopsychology of development.* New York: Academic Press, 1971. (b)

Gottlieb, G. On the acoustic basis of species identification in wood ducklings (*Aix sponsa*). *Journal of Comparative and Physiological Psychology,* 1974, *87,* 1038–1048.

Gottlieb, G. Development of species identification in ducklings: I. Nature of perceptual deficit caused by embryonic auditory deprivation. *Journal of Comparative and Physiological Psychology,* 1975, *89,* 387–399.

Gottlieb, G. Development of species identification in ducklings: IV. Change in species-specific perception caused by auditory deprivation. *Journal of Comparative and Physiological Psychology,* 1978, *92,* 375–387.

Gottlieb, G. Development of species identification in ducklings: VI. Specific embryonic experience required to maintain species-typical perception in Peking ducklings. *Journal of Comparative and Physiological Psychology,* 1980, *94,* 579–587.

Gottlieb, G. Roles of early experience in species-specific perceptual development. In R. N. Aslin, J. R. Alberts, & M. R. Petersen (eds.), *Development of perception.* Vol. 1. New York: Academic Press, 1981.

Grimwade, J. C., Walker, D. W., Bartlett, M., Gordon, S., & Wood, C. Human fetal heart rate change and movement in response to sound and vibration. *American Journal of Obstetrics and Gynecology,* 1971, *109,* 86–90.

Kent, R. D. Sensorimotor aspects of speech development. In R. N. Aslin, J. R. Alberts, & M. R. Petersen (eds.), *Development of perception.* Vol. 1. New York: Academic Press, 1981.

Lewis, M. M. *Infant speech.* New York: Harcourt Brace, 1936.

Mehler, J., Bertoncini, J., Barrière, M., & Jassik-Gerschenfeld, D. Infant recognition of mother's voice. *Perception,* 1978, *7,* 491–497.

Miller, D. B., & Gottlieb, G. Acoustic features of wood duck (*Aix sponsa*) maternal calls. *Behaviour,* 1976, *57,* 260–280.

Miller, D. B., & Gottlieb, G. Maternal vocalizations of mallard ducks (*Anas platyrhynchos*). *Animal Behaviour,* 1978, *26,* 1178–1194.

Miller, D. B. Maternal vocal control of behavioral inhibition in mallard ducklings (*Anas platyrhynchos*). *Journal of Comparative and Physiological Psychology,* 1980, *94,* 606–623.

Miller, D. B. Alarm call responsivity of mallard ducklings: I. The acoustical boundary between behavioral inhibition and excitation. *Developmental Psychobiology,* 1983, *16,* 185–194.

Querlew, D., Renard, X., & Crépin, G. Perception auditive et réactivité foetale aux stimulations sonores. *Journal de Gynecologie, Obstetrique, et Biologie de La Reproduction,* 1981, *10,* 307–314.

Read, J. A., & Miller, F. C. Fetal heart rate acceleration in response to acoustic stimulation as a measure of fetal well-being. *American Journal of Obstetrics and Gynecology,* 1977, *129,* 512–517.

Rubel, E. W. Ontogeny of structure and function in the vertebrate auditory system. In M. Jacobson (ed.), *Handbook of sensory physiology.* Vol. 9. *Development of sensory systems.* Berlin: Springer, 1978.

Sachs, J. The adaptive significance of linguistic input to prelinguistic infants. In C. E. Snow & C. A. Ferguson (eds.), *Talking to children.* Cambridge: Cambridge University Press, 1978.

Scoville, R. & Gottlieb, G. The calculation of repetition rate in avian vocalizations. *Animal Behaviour,* 1978, *26,* 962–963.

Sontag, L. W., & Wallace, R. F. The movement response of the human fetus to sound stimuli. *Child Development,* 1935, *6,* 253–258.

Stern, D. N., Spieker, S., & McKain, K. Intonation contours as signals in maternal speech to prelinguistic infants. *Developmental Psychology,* 1982, *18,* 727–735.

Stern, D. N., Spieker, S., & Barnett, R. K. The prosody of maternal speech: Infant age and context related changes. *Journal of Child Language,* 1983, *10,* 463–488.

Studdert-Kennedy, M. The beginnings of speech. In K. Immelmann, G. W. Barlow, L. Petrinovich, & M. Main (eds.), *Behavioral development.* Cambridge: Cambridge University Press, 1981.

Thomas, D. G., Campos, J. J., Shucard, D. W., Ramsay, D. S., & Shucard, J. Semantic comprehension in infancy: A signal detection analysis. *Child Development,* 1981, *52,* 798–803.

Walker, D. W., Grimwade, J. C., & Wood, C. Intrauterine noise: A component of the fetal environment. *American Journal of Obstetrics and Gynecology,* 1971, *109,* 91–95.

2

HOW SHOULD WE CHARACTERIZE VISUAL STIMULI?

Martin S. Banks

University of Texas at Austin

153.03

INTRODUCTION

Most of this volume concerns the responses one can use to measure visual and auditory capabilities in infants. Of equal importance, however, are the stimuli one uses. My task in this chapter is to consider the visual stimulus. Specifically, two related questions are discussed. How should developmental researchers characterize the visual stimuli infants are exposed to? And what sorts of stimuli should be used in infant vision research? These are not easy questions to answer when posed at this general level, for the simple reason that stimulus characterization and choice depend largely on the aspect of visual perception one chooses to study. Once a particular aspect is decided upon, stimulus choices are clearly based on what the experimenter thinks, based on intuition and previous work, is important about that aspect of perception. Consequently, good answers to these questions really require a good theory of scientific insight. In the absence of such a theory, my goals will be more modest. I will first describe three general principles that researchers should and often do use to guide stimulus characterization and choice. I will then illustrate these principles by describing two lines of infant research that followed the principles to different degrees.

THREE PRINCIPLES OF STIMULUS CHOICE

The Principle of Generality

The first principle, that of generality, is fairly obvious. It can be stated as follows: Once one has decided to study a particular aspect of perception, one

31

should use stimuli that can illuminate the properties of the system under investigation in the most general way possible. This is particularly important in a young field like infant vision. At the beginning of a search, one is far better off with a rough map containing most of the major landmarks, but no details, than with a detailed map of just one neighborhood. One should avoid idiosyncratic stimuli that cannot be related to other sorts of experimental stimuli or to everyday visual scenes. An example illustrates this. The use of just-detectable spots on a uniform background is too idiosyncratic for the study of pattern vision, because such stimuli are difficult to relate to other experimental stimuli, such as edges and gratings, and to real-world stimuli. In other words, results from experiments that used such stimuli would not be very generalizable. As I will describe below, other stimuli—sinusoidal gratings—have proven more useful in this regard because *any* complex pattern can be represented by a set of such gratings. Thus, one would expect results from grating experiments, rather than from spot experiments, to provide more useful information about pattern vision.

I should note, however, that things are not always so simple. As we will see, the generalizability of findings obtained with particular stimuli (spots and gratings, in this example) is dependent on the aspect of visual perception one wishes to describe. This leads to the second principle of stimulus choice.

The Principle of Appropriate Level

The second principle, that of appropriate level, is also obvious in some ways but subtle in others. It can be stated as follows: One should use stimuli that probe the aspect of vision under study as neatly as possible and thereby expose the important characteristics of that aspect. This usually entails deciding what level(s) of processing is (are) most significant for the aspect of perception under study, and choosing stimulus manipulations appropriate for that level(s). An example will illustrate this. Consider studying the development of light adaptation. There are good reasons to believe that the most important characteristics of light adaptation are mediated by the photoreceptors and retinal network mechanisms. We know that these adaptation mechanisms (in adults, at least) are strongly influenced by certain stimulus properties such as intensity, wavelength, retinal eccentricity, and spatial and temporal extent. Our experiments, then, should manipulate these variables. We also know that the important aspects of these mechanisms are not affected significantly by other properties such as viewing distance, stimulus shape, and uncertainty. Our experiments should control these variables to ensure that those aspects of perception do not intrude. If, on the other hand, one chose to study the development of shape recognition, the situation almost reverses. Since the interesting aspect of this phenomenon is the ability to recognize a given shape despite changes in intensity, wavelength, retinal eccentricity, and spatial and temporal extent, these stimulus properties are no longer of primary interest. Stimulus shape and uncertainty now become the important variables, so they are the ones that should be manipulated. These considerations would clearly influence the choice of stimuli for light adaptation experiments, on the one hand, and shape recognition experiments on the other.

Two more points about the principle of appropriate level should be made. One concerns the use of engineering approaches and their associated stimuli. A clear trend has emerged in visual science, infant vision included, to choose stimuli from an engineering standpoint rather than a psychological or physiological standpoint. One reason for this is that such stimuli allow one to use powerful mathematical tools for generalizing findings to a wide variety of stimuli. The journals, consequently, are now filled with patches of sinusoidal gratings, Bessel functions, delta functions, pseudorandom noise, and more. Some of these stimuli (grating patches, for example) have turned out to be quite useful (that is, they have revealed important properties and have allowed relatively general characterizations). Others (Bessel functions and delta functions, for example) have not. Why is this? I think it is because for stimuli to be useful they must in some sense match the properties of the system under investigation. To explain this requires a digression into the assumptions of the most common engineering approach: linear systems analysis.

The linear systems approach allows one to predict precisely the response of a linear optical or visual system to any two-dimensional, achromatic stimulus. The catch is the term "linear." A system is linear only if it possesses four properties. (a) Linearity: The output amplitude of the system must be a linear function of the input amplitude. (b) Homogeneity: The system must behave in a similar fashion to input stimuli in different positions in the stimulus field. (c) Isotropy: The system must behave in a similar fashion to input stimuli of any orientation. (d) State-invariance: The system must behave in a similar fashion despite changes in its adaptation level. If a system satisfied all of these requirements, any of a number of stimuli (sinusoidal gratings, delta functions, Bessel functions, etc.) could be used to characterize the system quite precisely. The problem is that mammalian visual systems do not satisfy any of the four requirements exactly. The human adult visual system, for example, does not exhibit linearity (its response generally grows as a decelerating function of stimulus strength), homogeneity (the quality of processing varies dramatically with retinal eccentricity), isotropy (sensitivity is greater to horizontal and vertical lines than to obliques), or state-invariance (the quality of processing changes with the overall illumination level or adaptation level). For these reasons, not just any stimulus adopted from linear systems analysis will do.

Now let us return to the question of why some stimuli, like gratings, have been useful, and others have not. Gratings have been useful because they at least approximate the shape of receptive fields at some levels of processing. For example, cortical neurons have elongated receptive fields of a particular width and orientation. They also possess adjacent excitatory and inhibitory sub-regions. Consequently, they respond quite favorably to gratings whose bars are oriented and spaced optimally (Albrecht, DeValois, & Thorell, 1980). As a result, gratings have revealed an important property of cortical neurons: their bandpass characteristic. Most cortical cells respond optimally to a narrow band of spatial frequencies; frequencies much lower or higher than optimum produce little, if any, response (Campbell, Cooper, & Enroth-Cugell, 1969; Albrecht et al., 1980). Gratings have also been useful in describing the properties of retinal ganglion cells (Enroth-Cugell & Robson, 1966) and lateral geniculate cells (Marrocco, McClurkin, & Young, 1982) as well as the response of the visual system as a whole (Schade, 1956). Thus, engineering techniques have and will continue to make an important contribution, but because visual systems are not linear, only in cases where they match to some extent the properties of the system under study. This point is meant to be a general one, not an argument for using gratings. Gratings, after all, match and thereby reveal only certain aspects of mechanisms. As I will note in the discussion of the third principle of stimulus choice, one should be open to other sorts of stimuli and manipulations that match other aspects.

The second point about the principle of appropriate level concerns the use of naturalistic or ecologically valid stimuli. Several researchers (e.g., Gibson, 1966, 1979) have argued forcefully that such stimuli must be used in order to assess perceptual capabilities. Those who subscribe to this view then choose visual stimuli from a psychological or even ecological standpoint rather than from an engineering standpoint. How valid is this argument? There is no simple answer, in part because the argument's validity depends heavily on the aspect of visual perception one wishes to characterize. (The chapters in this volume by Gottlieb and by Johnston argue for the use of naturalistic stimuli. Their arguments are persuasive because the questions they are investigating— e.g., determinants of responses to avian calls—are best answered from an ecological perspective. The chapter by Hecox and Deegan, on the other hand, argues implicitly for the use of simpler, less natural stimuli because he is most concerned with relatively "low-level" phenomena.)

Naturalistic stimuli are in general rather difficult to describe and to manipulate (see Harmon, 1973, for example). Thus, their use in experiments can render interpretation of the results difficult, too.[1] Numerous artificial stimuli are much easier to describe and manipulate, and they also allow one to use powerful mathematical tools for generalizing results. For this reason, researchers should, I believe, shy away from naturalistic stimuli unless a clear justification for their use can be made. (The chapters in this volume by Gottlieb and by Johnston present a number of possible justifications.) When examining low-

---

[1] For example, a recent paper by Harris, Fulton, and Hansen (1983) attempted to measure infants' visual acuity using naturalistic stimuli. The stimuli were composed of black and white line segments arranged on a gray background to look like a face. The acuity values they obtained were a bit higher than those obtained with less-natural grating stimuli. Unfortunately, the difference in results was impossible to interpret. The authors argued that the face-like stimuli yielded better thresholds because infants are more motivated to respond to naturalistic stimuli. However, another interpretation could not be ruled out. Parts of their stimuli actually presented spatial frequencies lower than the nominal frequency; this was necessary in order to make the stimuli look like faces. Thus, a skeptic could argue that higher acuities were not actually obtained with the face-like stimuli, because pattern information coarser than the nominal spatial frequency was presented.

level processes (e.g., light adaptation) that are probably not greatly influenced by how natural a stimulus is, the use of a naturalistic stimulus like a face would clearly be unwise. This point is obvious when we already know quite a lot about the process under study and have some confidence that the naturalness of a stimulus is irrelevant. The situation is often more complex, however, because we frequently do not know enough about the process under study to know whether it is "low-level" or "high-level" or, more importantly, whether the mechanisms involved are significantly affected by how natural a stimulus is. A strong case can be made in such situations for using both simple, non-naturalistic stimuli and more complex, naturalistic stimuli.

I will first develop the case for non-naturalistic stimuli. If one believed that the response of a particular visual process depended critically on how natural the stimuli is, there are several alternative explanations that would have to be ruled out. Consider, for example, infants' visual preferences. Some researchers have argued that early preferences reflect a strong bias to orient to, and engage with, social stimuli (Bowlby, 1969; Vine, 1973). Although this does not do complete justice to them, I will call these accounts social explanations. The fact that infants, when given a choice between a schematic face and a disk, preferentially fixate the face, is consistent with the social explanations. However, several alternative explanations, which do not require the additional assumptions concerning social meaningfulness, are also consistent with this observation. Fantz, Fagan, and Miranda (1975), for example, noted that a schematic face is more complex than a disk, so perhaps the preference simply reflects an attraction toward complexity. Other alternatives, none of which require extra assumptions about stimulus naturalness or social meaningfulness, have been offered (Banks & Salapatek, 1981; Karmel & Maisel, 1975; Haith, 1978). In the absence of a better term, I will refer to these simple accounts as sensory explanations. So how does one test the validity of the social explanations, given that sensory explanations are also consistent with the data? Obviously, experiments must be designed that control or render irrelevant the simple stimulus variables that the sensory theories claim influence preferences. This, unfortunately, is not as simple as it sounds, because the sensory explanations are still in the early stages of their development; considerable experimentation is still required to elucidate the sensory mechanisms of the developing system. In other words, a better understanding of sensory processes is needed before one would know how to control or render irrelevant sensory variables in a preference experiment. This argues then for continued use of simple, artificial stimuli that thus far have successfully revealed many basic properties of the developing visual system.

Now consider the case for naturalistic stimuli. Any investigation of the properties of a visual phenomenon should obviously attempt to address significant rather than trivial aspects of the phenomenon. However, significance is not easily determined. Many investigators of infant and adult visual perception have assumed implicitly that certain artificial manipulations must be significant simply because they produce large and reliable experimental effects. For example, considerable importance has been attached to infants' visual preference for bull's eyes over gratings, simply because it is a large preference. Two criticisms of this can be raised. First, the observation of large effects alone tells one nothing about *why* such effects exist. For example, what perceptual or developmental function is served by a greater fixation preference for bull's eyes than for gratings? Clues to answering this sort of question come from considering what the developing visual system is designed to do. Clearly, the visual system was designed through evolutionary adaptations to perform tasks in natural rather than artificial environments. This leads to the second criticism. The artificial manipulations and resulting effects may mislead one's attempt to understand the visual system as it is designed to operate, because it has not been investigated in its normal context of operation. For instance, most everyday visual scenes are composed of multiple, haphazardly distributed, partially occluded objects. Simple, segregated, high-contrast patterns like those in two-choice preference experiments may produce fixation behavior that is qualitatively different from that exhibited in natural settings. Data from such situations then might mislead our attempts to understand the development of fixation behavior. The solution to these problems involves careful consideration of the function the particular phenomenon one is studying in the laboratory might serve in natural settings. This is not to say everyone should at times use natural stimuli to test how well his or her findings with artificial stimuli generalize. The point is that researchers should at least consider how their findings *might* generalize, to assure themselves that significant rather than epiphenomenal properties are being studied.

I have argued that both natural and artificial stimuli are important for visual development research. Artificial stimuli have the advantages of ease of description and manipulation, so they greatly facilitate one's ability to probe particular processes. Furthermore, they allow one to use powerful mathematical tools for generalizing results. So, when one is studying processes that do not demand the use of more natural stimuli, artificial stimuli have clear advantages. Natural stimuli play two roles. First, their use is called for when one is investigating an aspect of perception that may be heavily dependent on how natural a stimulus is. In cases where it is unclear whether naturalness is important, one can find out by conducting the appropriate experiments. Second, even psychophysicists and physiologists examining simple, low-level mechanisms should consider carefully how their findings extend to everyday situations, to help clarify what the most biologically significant aspects of those mechanisms might be. (Marr, 1982, has illustrated how physiological and psychophysical findings can be related to real-world perceptual problems. Indeed, his efforts have cast a new light on the function of some basic mechanisms.)

The Principle of Nonperseveration

The third principle of stimulus choice, that of nonperseveration, can be stated as follows: Researchers should continually evaluate their current characterization and choice of visual stimuli and judge whether new characterizations and choices might be more fruitful. The importance of this principle is illustrated by the history of visual science. For example, most research during the middle of this century employed spatially and temporally punctate stimuli. Spots and bars were used in studies of spatial vision (e.g., Barlow, 1958; Hecht & Mintz, 1939; Hubel & Wiesel, 1962, 1968; Kuffler, 1953; Westheimer, 1967) and single and double flashes were used in studies of temporal vision (Barlow, 1958; Baumgardt & Segal, 1946; Crawford, 1947; Hartline & Ratliff, 1957). These stimuli revealed numerous properties of vision, including Ricco's and Bloch's laws of spatial and temporal summation, Weber's Law, and spatial and temporal interactions. Yet their utility was limited. They did not reveal several specific properties that were uncovered later, and they did not facilitate general statements about the spatial and temporal properties of the visual system. The introduction of spatial sinusoids (Schade, 1956) and temporal sinusoids (DeLange, 1958) led to the discovery of several new properties (e.g., Campbell & Robson, 1968; Campbell et al., 1969; Enroth-Cugell & Robson, 1966; Kelly, 1961). In other words, the partial replacement of punctate stimuli with periodic ones was quite healthy for visual science. (I will describe below how the introduction of periodic stimuli has been valuable to the study of infant vision as well.) Nonetheless, the time for new stimuli and characterizations will come, because periodic stimuli reveal only certain aspects of visual mechanisms, and the approach commonly used with such stimuli—linear systems analysis—does not address the important nonlinear aspects of visual perception. Indeed, the beginnings of change have already appeared in limited domains (e.g., Westheimer, 1979). This, of course, is not to say that once new stimuli and characterizations emerge, older ones should be discarded; their utility in some domains is likely to continue. The important point is that researchers should recognize the limitations of any approach and thus be open to the potential of new ones.

TWO EXAMPLES OF THE USE OF THESE PRINCIPLES

The remainder of this chapter is devoted to describing two lines of research in infant pattern vision, the area of infant work that has received the most attention. The first line did not follow the principle of generality well. It also did not follow the principle of appropriate level well, because the researchers misjudged the simplicity of the phenomenon they were studying. The second line followed both of these principles more closely, and by introducing a novel characterization of stimuli, followed the principle of nonperseveration. For these reasons, I believe it has been more productive.

The Fantz Approach

The first line began with the pattern preference studies of the late Robert Fantz. Fantz was originally interested in characterizing the pattern vision capabilities of very young infants and tracing how these capabilities changed with age. The first question he asked was: Can young infants demonstrate any ability to differentiate stimuli on the basis of differences in pattern? Quite reasonably, Fantz began his exploration of this question by presenting an arbitrarily chosen set of grossly different patterns: a patch of newsprint, a schematic face, a bull's eye, and disks of various colors (Fantz, 1961, 1963). Even newborns exhibited differential preferences, as indexed by differences in fixation times, among these stimuli. He concluded from this that some ability to detect and discriminate patterns was present at birth. This was very useful information which, as it turns out, spawned a enormous amount of research attempting to characterize these early visual capabilities. In the process, the experimental question changed somewhat. It became more often than not: What aspects of visual stimuli determine preferences? Unfortunately, the subsequent work has not been very fruitful. As mentioned above, I believe the major reason for this concerns the manner in which stimuli were characterized and chosen. I will use one example from this literature to illustrate this point, but it applies to the infant preference literature as a whole.

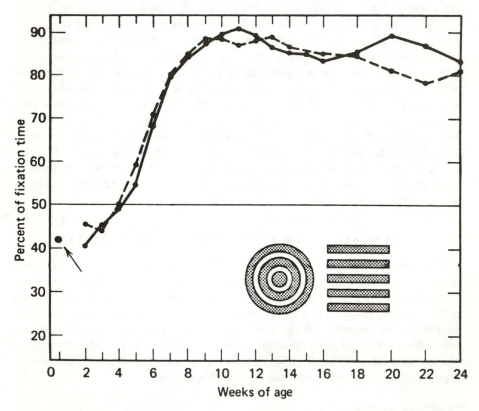

Figure 1. Relative preference for a bull's eye versus a grating at different ages. The inset displays the bull's eye and grating patterns used to collect these data. The graph plots the percentage of fixation time on the bull's eye (rather than the grating) as a function of age in weeks. The solid lines are data from infants reared at home. The broken lines are data from infants reared in an institution. The arrow indicates data from a newborn population. (From Fantz & Nevis, 1967).

In his early experiments Fantz found a developmental shift in the relative preference for bull's eyes versus gratings (Fantz, 1958; Fantz & Nevis, 1967). Figure 1 summarizes his observations. Neonates exhibited no differential preference, but by 2 months a strong preference (longer fixation times) for the bull's eye emerged, which persisted until 5 months, the oldest age tested. Fantz and several other researchers found this shift in preference interesting, and asked what aspects of these two stimuli determined it. They realized that bull's eyes and gratings differ in a number of ways. For example, the lines that create a bull's eye are curved, connected and concentric, and have many orientations. In contrast, the lines of a grating are straight, unconnected, and have only one orientation. Despite the fact that bull's eyes and gratings differ in so many different ways, Fantz and colleagues attempted to ascertain the stimulus determinants of the bull's eye/grating preference (Fantz et al., 1975; Fantz & Miranda, 1975; Fantz & Nevis, 1967; Karmel, 1969; Miranda, 1970; Ruff & Birch, 1974; Spears, 1964, 1966). Fortunately, a detailed review of the methodologies and results is not necessary here, so I will move on to the overall conclusions. An unambiguous picture of what determines the preference for bull's eyes over gratings never emerged. One reason was that it proved impossible to manipulate all of the potentially relevant dimensions independently of the others. For example, changing connectedness also changed contour density (Karmel & Maisel, 1975). This, however, is not the most significant problem.

More damaging problems become apparent when one asks: What has this approach told us about the development of pattern vision in general? Everyone who examined a particular preference, in this case bull's eyes versus gratings, seemed to note another, potentially relevant stimulus dimension. Unfortunately, empirical tests revealed that each new dimension affected preference at some age and hence could not be ignored. Where this has led is summarized by Table 1. The table lists only stimulus dimensions that may distinguish bull's eyes and gratings and have been shown to influence infants' visual preferences. For each dimension, qualitative weightings are given at different ages. Keep in mind that the table was created with only the bull's eye-versus-grating preference in mind. It would be longer if more types of stimuli were considered. This table illustrates a number of unsatisfying aspects of the current status of this research. First, the list seems to be expanding endlessly, which raises the possibility that it is part of a boundless search. Second, without a theory of how the items are related to one another, one cannot use the list to predict preferences for a new stimulus that has not previously been studied. In other words, it is unclear how general statements can be extracted from what has been learned. Third, the implicit description of development is unsatisfying. Development is represented by changes in the weightings of different, unconnected items in a list. Curvedness, for example, becomes more heavily weighted with age, while concentricity does not. This developmental description is unsatisfactory, because one cannot use it to gain any feeling for how an infant's pattern vision changes with age. We cannot use the list to answer even simple questions. For instance, one could not tell from the information given whether 3-month-olds see better than newborns.

Table 1. Stimulus Dimensions and Preferences

Age (Mos)	Curvilinearity	Concentricity	No. of Orientations	No. of Elements	Point Symmetry
0	0 (M1) + (F4) 0 (F1)		**0** (F1)	+ (M2)	**0** (F1)
1	0 (F1) 0 (G)		**0** (F1)	+ (F2)	**0** (F1)
2	+ (F3) + (F1)	+ + (F3)	***0*** (F1)	+ + (F2)	+ (F1)
3	+ (R) + (F1) + (F3) + + (G)	+ + (R) + + (F3)	+ (R) + (F1)	+ + (F2)	**0** (F1)
4	+ + (F3) + (F1)	+ + (F3)	**0** (F1)	+ + (F2)	**0** (F1)
5	+ (F3) + (F1)	+ + (F3)	**0** (F1)	+ + (F2)	**0** (F1)

R   = Ruff & Birch, 1974
M1 = Miranda, 1970
M2 = Miranda & Fantz, 1971
F1 = Fantz & Nevis, 1967
F2 = Fantz & Fagan, 1975
F3 = Fantz et al., 1975
F4 = Fantz & Miranda, 1975
G   = Greenberg & O'Donnell, 1972
0   = Preference for indicated dimension between 41% and 59% of total looking time
 + = Preference for indicated dimension between 60% and 69% of total looking time
+ + = Preference for indicated dimension between 70% and 79% of total looking time
Boldface symbols indicate those experiments in which indicated dimension was isolated reasonably well.

I will argue in the conclusion of this chapter that the Fantz approach to the study of early visual preferences reached a dead end because it did not follow the three principles of stimulus choice very well. Before presenting this argument, however, it is best to consider a more recent approach that has been more successful.

The Linear Systems Approach

The second line of research reviewed here is based on the contrast sensitivity function and linear systems analysis. This approach has been widely and successfully used to study adult pattern vision, but was only recently applied to infant vision.

The contrast sensitivity function (CSF) plots the contrast required to just detect a sinusoidal grating as a function of spatial frequency. Figure 2A shows a sinusoidal grating whose spatial frequency is increasing from left to right and whose contrast is increasing from top to bottom. Notice that one's ability to detect the grating varies with spatial frequency, medium frequencies being easier to detect than lows or highs. Figure 2B below shows a typical adult CSF. If the figure is held at a distance of about one-half meter, the visibility profile in Figure 2A and the CSF in 2B should match roughly. The primary reason for

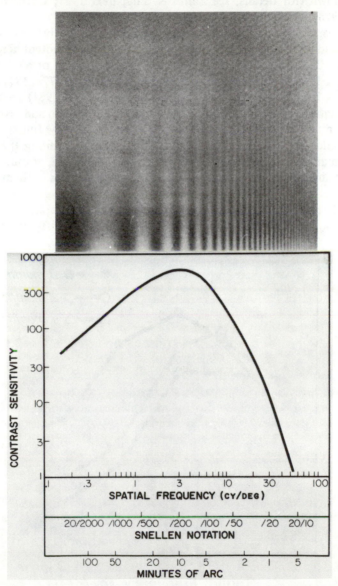

Figure 2. A sinusoidal grating varying in spatial frequency and contrast, and a typical adult contrast-sensitivity function. The upper half of the figure shows a grating whose spatial frequency increases from left to right and whose contrast increases from top to bottom. The lower half of the figure shows a typical adult contrast-sensitivity function. Contrast sensitivity (the reciprocal of contrast at threshold) is plotted as a function of spatial frequency (in cycles per degree—adapted from Cornsweet, 1970).

the usefulness of the CSF is its potential generality. Linear systems analysis capitalizes on Fourier's theorem. This theorem implies that any two-dimensional, achromatic pattern can be represented by its spatial frequency content. This allows in principle the prediction of sensitivity to any pattern once the CSF is known (for details, see Banks & Salapatek, 1981; Cornsweet, 1970; Gaskill, 1978).

Three research groups have measured CSFs in young infants. Atkinson, Braddick and colleagues have used behavioral and evoked-potential techniques to measure CSFs in infants from a few days to 6 months of age (Atkinson, Braddick, & French, 1979; Atkinson, Braddick, & Moar 1977a, 1977b; Harris, Atkinson, & Braddick, 1976). Banks and Salapatek (1978, 1981) used a behavioral technique to measure CSFs in 1- to 3-month-olds. Pirchio and his colleagues (Pirchio, Spinelli, Fiorentini, & Maffei, 1978) measured these functions in 2- to 10-month-olds using evoked potentials. The agreement among these sets of data is remarkable in light of the differences in technique, stimuli, etc. The agreement suggests that the functions and age-related shifts in them are fairly robust.

Figure 3 shows the group average data of Banks and Salapatek. Comparing these functions to the adults' in Figure 2 reveals striking differences. Infants'

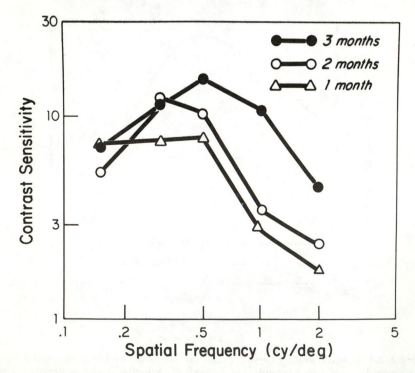

Figure 3. Contrast-sensitivity functions for 1-, 2-, and 3-month-olds as reported by Banks and Salapatek. The average contrast sensitivity for each age group is plotted as a function of spatial frequency. (From Banks & Salapatek, 1978).

CSFs are clearly shifted to lower spatial frequencies. Indeed, the highest detectable frequency, the acuity cut-off, is a factor of 10-20 below the adults'. Likewise, infant CSFs exhibit a large sensitivity deficit relative to adults. These deficits may in part reflect motivational differences between infants and adults, but the similarity of behavioral and evoked-potential results suggests that motivation is not the primary difference. The general qualitative picture that emerges from this line of research is that the young infant's visual system is able to detect only fairly large, high-contrast patterns in the environment. This ability improves gradually to 6 months, when infants are about a factor of 2 less sensitive than adults (Pirchio et al., 1978; Harris et al., 1976).

One should ask, however, how useful the linear-systems and CSF characterization of infant pattern vision is in a more general sense. The best way to answer this is to examine how well one can use the approach to predict performance in various situations. Accordingly, Banks and Stephens (1982) asked how well it can predict infants' sensitivity to gratings that vary in duty cycle rather than spatial frequency. This experiment was conceptually similar to one conducted in adults by Campbell and Robson (1968). Banks and Stephens measured 10-week-olds' contrast sensitivity for five different rectangular wave gratings. The spatial frequency of the gratings was always 1 c/deg, but they differed in duty cycle (the relative widths of light and dark stripes). The results, expressed as contrast sensitivity as a function of duty cycle, are shown in Figure 4. The adult data were obtained at 7 rather than 1 c/deg. The adult and infant results were very similar, except for a large difference in contrast sensitivity. In both cases, sensitivity varied systematically with duty cycle. The solid lines represent predictions of the linear systems model. The same function was fitted with suitable vertical shifts to both the adult and infant data. Clearly the linear systems predictions are quite accurate. Thus, these results illustrate the utility of linear systems analysis in predicting infants' sensitivity to different sorts of patterns.

Atkinson, Braddick, and Moar (1977c) also examined how well the CSF and linear-systems approach could be used to predict infants' performance in a novel situation. They tested 1- to 3-month-olds in a discrimination task in which two faces, one focused and one defocused to varying degrees, were presented on each trial. When the one face was severely defocused, infants preferentially fixated the focused version. Atkinson et al. varied the amount of defocus to find the point at which the focused face was preferred on 70% of the trials. This amount of just-detectable defocus was then converted to an estimate of the infants' high-frequency cut-off or visual acuity. The estimate was quite similar to one obtained in grating experiments. Thus, once again the CSF and linear-systems approach made accurate predictions of infants' sensitivity to another stimulus dimension.

The specific phenomenon considered earlier in this section is visual pattern preferences, so the next question is: Can the linear-systems approach be used to predict infants' pattern preferences? There are good reasons to believe that the approach would not make accurate predictions. For one thing, the assump-

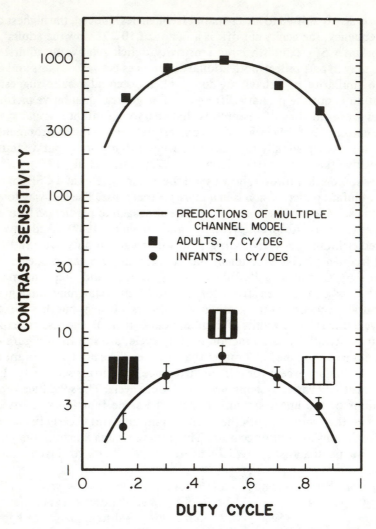

Figure 4. Average contrast sensitivity for rectangular-wave grating differing in duty cycle. Infant data are represented by filled circles. The sensitivity values are for 1 c/deg gratings. Adult data are represented by filled squares. Those sensitivity values are for 7 c/deg gratings. The two curves represent linear-systems predictions assuming multiple channel processing. They are identical in shape but have been shifted vertically for best fit. (Adapted from Banks & Stephens, 1982).

tions of linear-systems analysis are more likely to be violated when the approach is applied to suprathreshold rather than threshold stimuli (see Cornsweet, 1970). Nonetheless, two groups of investigators have employed the linear systems approach to predict preferences among suprathreshold patterns.

Banks and Salapatek (1981) and Banks and Ginsburg (in press) reanalyzed several pattern preference experiments in the infant literature. They computed predicted preference values for a variety of patterns and ages, and then compared those predictions to the observed preferences. To compute the predictions, they first assumed that the CSF was a good index of the filtering properties of the infants' visual system. Consequently, they used infant CSFs and linear-systems mathematics to filter various stimuli that have been used in the preference literature. They then applied two rules—the "largest-component rule" and the "square-root-of-sums rule"—to these filtered stimuli, in order to calculate predicted preference values for each stimulus.[2] A number of different preference experiments were reanalyzed, but only two examples will be presented here.

One set of experiments involved checkerboards. Several researchers have presented checkerboards of various check sizes in order to determine the most-preferred check size as a function of age. In general the most-preferred check size decreases with age. The solid symbols in Figure 5 illustrate this relationship. Banks and his colleagues used the average CSFs of 1-, 2-, and 3-month-olds, as reported by Banks and Salapatek (1978), to compute predictions of the most-preferred check size at each of those ages. The open squares represent the predictions of the largest-component rule, and the crosses the predictions of the square-root-of-sums rule. The agreement between the data and the predictions of both rules is quite good.

Banks and Ginsburg (in press) also reanalyzed the size and number experiment of Fantz and Fagan (1975). Fantz and Fagan wanted to determine how the size and number of pattern elements in a stimulus influenced preference, and how this changed with age. Figure 6 shows the stimuli they used. Note that size and number were manipulated orthogonally. Fantz and Fagan found quite different preferences among these stimuli. Furthermore, the relative preferences changed significantly with age. To reanalyze these results, Banks and Ginsburg used the average CSFs for 1- and 3-month-olds to predict Fantz and Fagan's 5- and 10-week data. As in the checkerboard studies, they filtered the various stimuli and then calculated predicted preference values for both the largest-component and square-root-of-sums rules. The correlation between the predictions of the square-root-of-sums rule and Fantz and Fagan's average looking times was .92 and .95 for 5-week-olds and 10-week-olds, respectively. The correlations were lower for the largest-component rule.

Gayl, Roberts and Werner (1983) used an approach quite similar to Banks and Salapatek's (1981) to reanalyze Karmel's (1969) experiment with regular and random checkerboards. They used the 3-month CSF of Banks and Salapatek to compute predictions for Karmel's 13-week data. Gayl et al. found

---

[2] The largest-component rule assumes that preference is determined by the single spatial-frequency component that is greatest in amplitude once filtered by the CSF. The square-root-of-sums rule is more complicated. It assumes that each stimulus is filtered by the CSF, and then channeled into one of several 2-octave-wide spatial-frequency filters (e.g., Campbell & Robson, 1968). The output of a filter is then squared and added to the squared output of the other filters. The square-root of this sum is then taken and is the assumed determinant of preference. This rule is similar to one used by Ginsburg (1978).

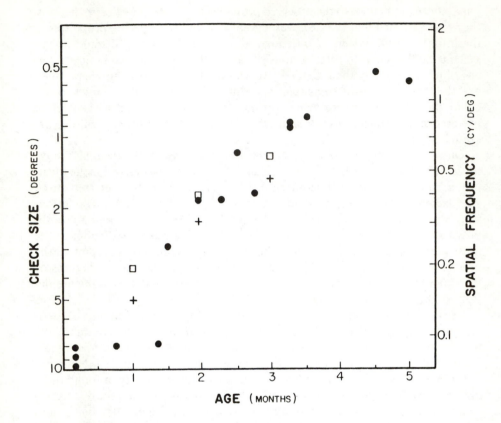

Figure 5. Preferences for checkerboards with different check sizes as a function of age. The most preferred check size is plotted on the left ordinate and the corresponding spatial frequency of the fundamental component on the right ordinate. The filled symbols represent the results of a number of different experiments as analyzed by Karmel and Maisel (1975). The open squares and the crosses represent the predictions of the linear-systems model of Banks and Ginsburg; the squares are predictions based on the largest-component rule and the crosses predictions based on the square-root-of-sums rule. (From Banks & Ginsburg, in preparation).

that a rule similar to Banks and Ginsburg's square-root-of-sums rule predicted looking times among Karmel's stimuli very well (r = .91).

In summary, the linear-systems approach has been very successful to date in predicting 1- to 3-month-olds' preferences for various sorts of patterns. Specifically, the approach predicted preferences among checkerboards and "size and number" stimuli quite accurately.

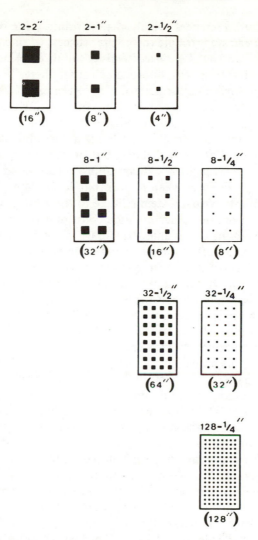

Figure 6. The stimuli used in the size-and-number experiment of Fantz and Fagan. The numbers to the right of each stimulus represent the number and size of pattern elements. (From Fantz & Fagan, 1975).

FINAL REMARKS

To date, the linear-systems and CSF approach has been more successful than the Fantz approach in characterizing early pattern detection capabilities and how they change with age. This is not surprising because the major focus of the linear-systems approach has been detection capabilities. The surprise is that the linear-systems approach has also been more successful in characterizing early pattern preferences, which was the primary focus of the Fantz approach. To what can we attribute the greater success of one approach relative to the other? The answer, I believe, involves the three principles of stimulus choice. First, the linear-systems approach clearly adheres better to the principle of generality. Any complex pattern can be represented by its spatial-frequency components, so the approach is useful in principle for any pattern. Moreover, the approach possesses explicit operations for generalizing results from one set of stimuli to another. The Fantz approach lacked guidelines for generalization, and, as mentioned above, this turned out to be a serious limitation. Second, I believe the linear-systems approach addresses the phenomenon of early pattern preferences at an appropriate level. The contrast sensitivity deficits of the infants' visual system relative to the adult's appear to be quite profound, and hence must place a major constraint on any visual behavior. Moreover, the high-order variables (familiarity, social significance, beauty, etc.) that are known to affect adults' visual preferences are much less likely to influence infants. Third, the linear-systems approach follows the principle of nonperseveration by adopting a new stimulus characterization.

This is not to say that the linear-systems approach is without weaknesses. As it has been employed to date, the approach has several shortcomings. I will mention three, two of which can probably be addressed within the linear-systems framework and one of which cannot.

CSF measurements alone only tell us how much perturbation in luminance must exist for a pattern to be detected, and perhaps how "salient" a pattern is once above threshold. They do not tell us much about the visual system's ability to encode spatial relations among features in a visual stimulus, clearly an important aspect of pattern recognition. This point is illustrated by an example from the amblyopia literature. (Amblyopia is defined as reduced acuity not correctable by glasses and not attributable to structural ocular anomalies.) Several researchers have noted that an adult amblyope's CSF often does not predict his or her Snellen letter acuity. Generally, the high-frequency cut-off of the CSF predicts a higher Snellen acuity than is actually observed. Pass and Levi (1982) may have discovered why. They presented two versions of sawtooth gratings to normal and amblyopic adults. The two versions were simply mirror-images of one another. These two stimuli have identical spatial-frequency components; they only differ in the relative phases of their components. Consequently, to discriminate them, one must encode relative phases. The subjects were given two tasks. In the detection task, they were asked simply to respond to the grating's presence or absence. In the discrimination task, they were asked to indicate which version of the grating was presented. For normal adults (and for the normal eye of the amblyopes), the contrast needed to reach discrimination threshold was about the same as that needed to reach detection threshold. For amblyopic eyes, however, the contrast threshold for discrimination was as much as 10 times higher than the detection threshold. In other words, the amblyopic eye has, in addition to a contrast sensitivity deficit, a large phase-encoding deficit. Since the spatial relations among letter features must be encoded accurately to identify letters, Pass and Levi argue that the phase deficit explains amblyopes' poor performance with Snellen letters. Such an experiment in infants might expand our understanding of visual development significantly.

Infant CSF work to date has also ignored spatial-temporal interactions. Two pieces of evidence suggest that such interactions may be important to investigate. First, spatial and temporal parameters affect adults' contrast sensitivity in fairly complex ways (Robson, 1966) and can lead to a different view of the CSF (Kelly, 1979). Second, Moskowitz and Sokol (1980) have shown in evoked-potential studies with checkerboards that spatial-temporal interactions are important in infants and, furthermore, that they vary with age.

The third shortcoming concerns stimulus meaningfulness. The linear-systems approach, as it stands, is completely insensitive to the meaningfulness or naturalness of a stimulus. This may not be a disadvantage for young infants, because much of their visual behavior seems to be mediated by fairly simple, low-level mechanisms. It is assuredly a disadvantage later on, however, because growth in the appreciation of meaningfulness or naturalness may be one of the most important aspects of later perceptual development. This is not to say that the linear-systems approach would not be useful at older ages. Clearly it could be, just as it has been in adult work. But as the complexity of visual perception grows with age, so too must the number of levels at which questions are posed. Consequently, as implied by the principle of appropriate level, useful ways to characterize stimuli may grow in number as well.

In summary, one cannot elucidate a good theory of stimulus characterization and choice without a good theory of what makes one person's experiment important and another's trivial; these two aspects of scientific investigation are, in an important sense, inseparable. Nonetheless, we can identify three principles that should be used: the principle of generality, the principle of appropriate level and the principle of nonperseveration. I think progress in our understanding of early visual development will depend on how well these principles are applied.

ACKNOWLEDGMENTS

Preparation of this chapter was supported by NIH Research Grant HD-12572 and by NIMH Research Scientist Development Award MH-00318. The author thanks Wilson Geisler and the reviewers for helpful comments.

REFERENCES

Albrecht, D. G., DeValois, R. L., & Thorell, L. G. Visual cortical neurons: Are bars or gratings the optimal stimuli? *Science,* 1980, *207,* 88–90.

Atkinson, J., Braddick, O., & French, J. Contrast sensitivity of the human neonate measured by the visual evoked potential. *Investigative Ophthalmology and Visual Science,* 1979, *18,* 210–213.

Atkinson, J., Braddick, O., & Moar, K. Contrast sensitivity of the human infant for moving and static patterns. *Vision Research,* 1977, *17,* 1045–1047. (a)

Atkinson, J., Braddick, O., & Moar, K. Development of contrast sensitivity over the first three months of life in the human infant. *Vision Research,* 1977, *17,* 1037–1044. (b)

Atkinson, J., Braddock, O., & Moar, K. Infants' detection of image defocus. *Vision Research,* 1977, *17,* 1125–1126. (c)

Banks, M. S. & Ginsburg, A. P. Early visual preferences: A review and new theoretical treatment. In H. W. Reese (ed.), *Advances in child development and behavior.* New York: Academic Press, in press.

Banks, M. S. & Salapatek, P. Acuity and contrast sensitivity in 1-, 2-, and 3-month-old human infants. *Investigative Ophthalmology and Visual Science,* 1978, *17,* 361–365.

Banks, M. S. & Salapatek, P. Infant pattern vision: A new approach based on the contrast sensitivity function. *Journal of Experimental Child Psychology,* 1981, *31,* 1–45.

Banks, M. S. & Stephens, B. R. The contrast sensitivity of human infants to gratings differing in duty cycle. *Vision Research,* 1982, *22,* 739–744.

Barlow, H. B. Temporal and spatial summation in human vision at different background intensities. *Journal of Physiology,* 1958, *141,* 337–350.

Baumgardt, E. & Segal, J. La fonction inhibitrice dans le processus visuel. *Comptes Rendus de Séances de la Société de Biologie,* 1946, *140,* 231–233.

Bowlby, J. *Attachment and loss.* Vol. 1. *Attachment.* New York: Basic Books, 1969.

Campbell, F. W., Cooper, G. F., & Enroth-Cugell, C. The spatial selectivity of the visual cells of the cat. *Journal of Physiology,* 1969, *203,* 223–235.

Campbell, F. W. & Robson, J. G. Application of Fourier analysis to the visibility of gratings. *Journal of Physiology,* 1968, *197,* 551–562.

Cornsweet, T. N. *Visual perception.* New York: Academic Press, 1970.

Crawford, B. H. Visual adaptation in relation to brief conditioning stimuli. *Proceeding of the Royal Society,* 1947, *134B,* 283–302.

DeLange, H. Research into the dynamic nature of the human fovea-cortex systems with intermittent and modulated light. I. Attenuation characteristics with white and colored light. *Journal of the Optical Society of America,* 1958, *48,* 777–784.

Enroth-Cugell, C. & Robson, J. G. The contrast sensitivity of retinal ganglion cells of the cat. *Journal of Physiology,* 1966, *187,* 517–552.

Fantz, R. L. Pattern vision in young infants. *Psychological Record,* 1958, *8,* 43–48.

Fantz, R. L. The origin of form perception. *Scientific American,* 1961, *204* (May), 66–72.

Fantz, R. L. Pattern vision in newborn infants. *Science,* 1963, *140,* 296–297.

Fantz, R. L. & Fagan, J. F. Visual attention to size and number of pattern details by term and preterm infants during the first six months. *Child Development,* 1975, *16,* 3–18.

Fantz, R. L., Fagan, J. F., & Miranda, S. B. Early visual selectivity. In L. B. Cohen & P. Salapatek (eds.), *Infant perception: From sensation to cognition.* New York: Academic Press, 1975.

Fantz, R. L. & Miranda, S. B. Newborn infant attention to form of contour. *Child Development,* 1975, *46,* 224–228.

Fantz, R. L. & Nevis, S. Perceptual preferences and perceptual-cognitive development in early infancy. *Merrill-Palmer Quarterly,* 1967, *13,* 77–108.

Gaskill, J. D. *Linear systems, Fourier transforms, and optics.* New York: Wiley, 1978.

Gayl, I. E., Roberts, J. O., & Werner, J. S. Linear systems analysis of infant visual-pattern preferences. *Journal of Experimental Child Psychology,* 1983, *35,* 30–45.

Gibson, J. J. *The senses considered as perceptual systems.* Boston: Houghton-Mifflin, 1966.

Gibson, J. J. *The ecological approach to visual perception.* Boston: Houghton-Mifflin, 1979.

Ginsburg, A. P. *Visual information processing based on spatial filters constrained by biological data.* Unpublished doctoral dissertation, University of Cambridge, 1978.

Greenberg, D. J. & O'Donnell, W. J. Infancy and the optimal level of stimulation. *Child Development,* 1972, *43,* 639–645.

Haith, M. M. Visual competence in early infancy. In R. Held, H. Leibowitz, & H. L. Teuber (eds.), *Handbook of sensory physiology.* Vol. 7. Berlin: Springer-Verlag, 1978.

Harmon, L. D. The recognition of faces. *Scientific American,* 1973, *229* (November), 70–82.

Harris, L., Atkinson, J., & Braddick, O. Visual contrast sensitivity to a 6-month-old infant measured by the evoked potential. *Nature,* 1976, *564,* 570–571.

Harris, S. J., Fulton, A. B., & Hansen, R. M. *"Face" acuity of 3-month-old human infants.* Paper presented at Association for Research in Vision and Ophthalmology, Sarasota, 1983.

Hartline, H. K. & Ratliff, F. Inhibitory interaction of receptor units in the eye of *Limulus. Journal of General Physiology,* 1957, *40,* 357–376.

Hecht, S. & Mintz, E. U. The visibility of single lines at various illuminations and the retinal basis of visual resolution. *Journal of General Physiology,* 1939, *22,* 593–612.

Hubel, D. H. & Wiesel, T. N. Receptive fields, binocular interaction and functional architecture in the cat's visual cortex. *Journal of Physiology,* 1962, *160,* 106–154.

Hubel, D. H. & Wiesel, T. N. Receptive fields and functional architecture of monkey striate cortex. *Journal of Physiology,* 1968, *195,* 215–243.

Karmel, B. Z. The effect of age, complexity, and amount of contour on pattern preferences in human infants. *Journal of Experimental Child Psychology,* 1969, *7,* 339–354.

Karmel, B. Z. & Maisel, E. B. A neuronal activity model for infant visual attention. In L. B. Cohen & P. Salapatek (eds.), *Infant perception: From sensation to cognition.* New York: Academic Press, 1975.

Kelly, D. H. Visual responses to time-dependent stimuli. I. Amplitude sensitivity measurements. *Journal of the Optical Society of America,* 1961, *51,* 422–429.

Kelly, D. H. Motion and vision. II. Stabilized spatiotemporal threshold surface. *Journal of the Optical Society of America,* 1979, *69,* 1340–1349.

Kuffler, S. W. Discharge patterns and functional organization of mammalian retina. *Journal of Neurophysiology,* 1953, *16,* 37–68.

Marr, D. *Vision: A computational investigation into the human representation and processing of visual information.* San Francisco: W. H. Freeman, 1982.

Marrocco, R. T., McClurkin, J. W., & Young, R. A. Spatial summation and conduction latency classification of cells of the lateral geniculate nucleus of macaques. *Journal of Neuroscience,* 1982, *2,* 1275–1291.

Miranda, S. B. Visual abilities and pattern preferences of premature infants and full-term neonates. *Journal of Experimental Child Psychology,* 1970, *10,* 189–205.

Miranda, S. B. & Fantz, R. L. Distribution of visual attention by newborn infants among patterns varying in size and number of details, *Proceedings of the Annual Convention of the American Psychological Association,* 1971, *6,* 181–182.

Moskowitz, A. & Sokol, S. Spatial and temporal interaction of pattern-evoked cortical potentials in human infants. *Vision Research,* 1980, *20,* 699–708.

Pass, A. F. & Levi, D. M. Spatial processing of complex stimuli in the amblyopic visual system. *Investigative Ophthalmology and Visual Science,* 1982, 23, 780–786.

Pirchio, M., Spinelli, D., Fiorentini, A., & Maffei, L. Infant contrast sensitivity evaluated by evoked potentials. *Brain Research,* 1978, *141,* 179–184.

Robson, J. G. Spatial and temporal contrast-sensitivity functions of the visual system. *Journal of the Optical Society of America,* 1966, *56,* 1141–1142.

Ruff, H. A., & Birch, H. G. Infant visual fixation: The effect of concentricity, curvilinearity, and number of directions. *Journal of Experimental Child Psychology,* 1974, *17,* 460–473.

Schade, O. H. Optical and photoelectric analog of the eye. *Journal of the Optical Society of America,* 1956, *46,* 721–739.

Spears, W. C. Assessment of visual preference and discrimination in the four-month-old infant. *Journal of Comparative and Physiological Psychology,* 1964, *57,* 381–386.

Spears, W. C. Visual preference in the four-month-old infant. *Psychonomic Science,* 1966, *4,* 237–238.

Vine, I. The role of facial-visual signaling in early social development. In M. Von Cranach & I. Vine (eds.), *Social communication and movement: Studies of interaction and expression in man and chimpanzee.* London: Academic Press, 1973.

Westheimer, G. Spatial interactions in cone vision. *Journal of Physiology,* 1967, *190,* 139–154.

Westheimer, G. Spatial sense of the eye. *Investigative Ophthalmology and Visual Science,* 1979, *18,* 893–912.

3

AUDITORY SYSTEM DEVELOPMENT

Edwin W Rubel

University of Virginia Medical Center, Charlottesville

INTRODUCTION

This chapter is divided into three parts. First, I briefly outline some of the major events and processes underlying the development of hearing in vertebrates. This part is mainly descriptive; I try to summarize the most salient and generalizable developmental events which occur during the development of the middle-ear conductive apparatus, the transductive machinery of the inner ear, the transmitting cells of the spiral ganglion, and the integrative machinery of the central nervous system. In addition, some of the general properties of functional development which are exemplified by physiological and behavioral responses to simple acoustic stimuli are discussed. There are several points I wish to emphasize in this section:

1. The major principles of auditory system development are general across a wide variety of species. Therefore, most of the principles derived from amphibian and avian embryos can be generalized to mammals including man.

2. The major central nervous system (CNS) pathways for the processing of auditory information are established, and probably become functional, independent of tonic peripheral influences. Following the onset of receptor function, normal CNS development requires an intact cochlea and auditory nerve.

3. The onset and maturation of peripheral auditory function does not appear to be activated by a single event, or trigger. Instead, there seems to be a highly regulated synchrony of the final stages of differentiation both at the cochlea and in the central nervous system.
4. There are temporal correlations between behavioral and physiological indices of sensory coding, and these correlate with anatomical and biochemical maturation along the auditory pathways. However, actual causative relationships between these developmental variables have not been established.

In the second part of this chapter, I summarize some of the evidence suggesting a systematic shift in the frequency organization of the cochlea during development. Two experiments which support this hypothesis are described, and its possible adaptive significance is considered.

Finally, in the last section I discuss recent findings on the responses of the developing auditory system to peripheral manipulations. Two points are stressed.

1. The response of the neonate to peripheral manipulations, be it an insult to the developing cochlea or to the central nervous system, is likely to be quite different from that of the adult.
2. Extrinsic events which are important for the regulation of subtle aspects of behavior may be quite different than those which influence gross aspects of nervous-system morphology. One example is presented in which a single manipulation may have had quite different effects on the environmental factors important for behavior development, and those important for the ontogeny of neurons.

EMBRYOLOGY OF THE AUDITORY SYSTEM

Peripheral Development

Several reviews on the embryology of the external, middle, and inner ear are available, including those of Anson (1973) and Anson and Donaldson (1981) on human developmental anatomy, that of Van de Water, Maderson, & Jaskoll (1980b) on the comparative embryology of the outer and middle ear structures, and the current account of Saunders, Kaltenbach, & Relkin (1983) regarding the functional development of these structures. Reviews of normal inner-ear development can be found in Yntema (1950), Van de Water & Ruben (1976), Rubel (1978) and Van de Water, Li, Ruben, & Shea (1980a). While there is not a comprehensive account of the ontogeny of the central auditory pathways or of the development of hearing, much of the work has been summarized by Pujol and Hilding (1973), Gottlieb (1971b), and Rubel (1978).

The earliest stages of auditory development in the vertebrate embryo are shown schematically in Figure 1. This figure points out several important principles. First, the inner ear of all vertebrates forms from a placodal thickening on the side of the head, which then invaginates and, in higher vertebrates, splits off from the overlying ectoderm to form the auditory vesicle, or otocyst. This vesicle then evaginates to form three primary ducts—the endolymphatic duct, the utricle and the saccule. All of the sensory structures of the inner ear, including both the auditory and vestibular end organs and their ganglion cells, are derived from this primitive otocyst. In man, otocyst formation and the beginnings of evagination into the three primary ducts are occurring during the third to sixth week of gestation.

The second important principle indicated in Figure 1 is that, during the early stages of hearing, man lives in an aquatic environment. In most birds and mammals, hearing develops postnatally. There is now ample evidence showing that the human fetus is quite capable of hearing during the last ten to twelve weeks of gestation. This aquatic environment has profound implications re-

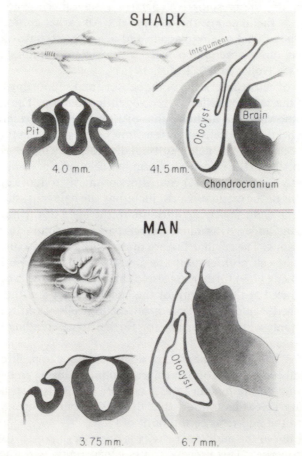

Figure 1. Shows placodal thickening and invagination of otic plate (left) and primary otic capsule (octocyst, right) in a primitive vertebrate (shark) and in man. Note similarities in embryogenesis and the environment (from Anson & Donaldson, 1981).

garding the relationship between human fetal hearing and the conductive properties of the middle ear. Since the middle ear of the fetus is filled with fluid, its
conductive properties will be quite different than during postnatal life. The
tympanic membrane will be largely transparent to sound, and the role of the
ossicles will be quite different. The aquatic human fetus probably utilizes
mechanisms similar to those used postnatally for bone conduction. Unfortunately, the mechanism of transmission for bone-conducted sounds is poorly
understood at this time (see Tonndorf, 1966). Most important is the fact that
the spectral content of sound energy transmitted to the inner ear may be very
different from that found in the uterus, because of the altered conductive properties of the fluid-filled external and middle ears.

The cochlear duct grows as an extension of the sacculus. By 10–12 weeks of
gestation, the cochlea has attained a full 2½ turns. During the early period of
otocyst formation, the presumptive cochlear ganglion cells bud off from the
marginal cells of the lumen of the otic vesicle. An earlier conjecture that this
ganglion may be of dual origin (placode and neural crest) has received no support from either direct observation or from experimental studies using chimera
preparations (see Noden, 1980; Rubel, 1978).

The pattern of cell proliferation of the sensory and supporting cells of the inner ear and of the ganglion cells has received little attention. The only thorough
investigation known to this author is that of Ruben (1967). Tritiated thymidine
was used to label dividing cells at various times of gestation in the mouse. The
first ganglion cells to go through their final division contribute primarily to the
basal region of the mature cochlea. Ganglion cells produced at progressively
later ages (up to gestation day 16) contribute primarily to more apical regions.
Most of the cells of the organ of Corti, including the hair cells, show the reverse
pattern; the cells maturing first contribute to the apex of the mature cochlea,
while those that undergo terminal mitosis later contribute to progressively
more basal regions. The cellular factors underlying these two distinctly different sequences of cell proliferation are unknown, and the result needs to be
replicated. Ruben (1969) further suggested that the earliest cells of the organ of
Corti are produced at the junction of the cochlear duct and the sacculus and
are then "pushed" apically by later proliferating cells. Confirmation of this
sequence of events will be important for further understanding the dynamics
of cochlear development.

Like neurons, hair cells of the cochlea do not continue to proliferate throughout life; the full complement of hair cells is produced during embryogenesis. In
fact, the 4½-month-old human fetus has more hair cells than it will have at
birth. Bredburg (1968) has shown that there is a continuous gradual loss of
hair cells from the mid-fetal period until old age.

The formation of the middle ear cavity is necessary in order to have normal
conductive properties. This process occurs concurrently with the final differentiation of the cochlea, and in some animals (for example the cat) it probably
severely restricts the transmission of energy to the cochlea at a time when the

cochlea itself is relatively well developed. Ossification of the ossicular chain will change both mass and stiffness components of the middle ear, and thereby its conductive properties. The precise functional ramifications of these changes in the middle ear are not entirely clear. Saunders et al. (1983) note that ossification of the middle ear bones will tend to limit high-frequency conduction, since the mass will be increased. At the same time, the degeneration of the mesenchyme around the ossicles will decrease their mass. Furthermore, there is some evidence that the ossicles may be changing position and overall size during this period. (Interestingly, during the last two months of fetal life, the stapes is actually being reduced in size.) What then will be the conductive changes as a function of age? The best studies done to date (e.g., Himelfarb, Popelka, & Shanon, 1979; Relkin & Saunders, 1980) suggest that the conductive properties of the middle ear improve markedly during the final stages of ossicular maturation. Interestingly, this improvement appears approximately flat across frequency.

A great deal more work on the development of the conductive properties of the middle ear is needed. While such work may not be considered in the realm of developmental psychology, these processes set the limit on what stimuli impinge on the receptor surface. Without knowing what stimuli are actually reaching the receptor, it will be impossible for us to realistically address the problems of perceptual development, especially those problems concerned with the identification of, and reactions toward, complex species-specific stimuli such as those addressed in the chapters by Johnston, Gottlieb, Kuhl, and others.

Figure 2, taken from Retzius' two volume tome on the structure of the vertebrate ear (Retzius, 1884), shows the late stages of organ of Corti differentiation in the cat. Some generalizable temporal sequences have been identified. For example, inner hair cells tend to differentiate prior to outer hair cells, and the establishment of efferent connections from the central nervous system follows synaptogenesis of the hair-cell-to-ganglion-cell connection. The major point which is emphasized by this figure, however, is that, during the final stages of differentiation, a large number of major structural and ultrastructural changes take place. Virtually every structural event has been assigned the role as "trigger" for the onset of cochlear function. It has now become clear that the development of cochlear function requires the simultaneous and synchronous maturation of many mechanical and neural properties (see Wada, 1923). Some of the important mechanical events are probably the thinning of the basilar membrane, degeneration of the pseudostratified epithelium of the inner spiral sulcus to form a single layer of cuboidal cells, maturation of the pilar cells, freeing of the inferior margin of the tectorial membrane from the organ of Corti, and development of tissue spaces of the tunnel of Corti and around the outer hair cells. Neural events which seem to occur at the same time include differentiation of the hair cells, establishment of mature cilia length, and the maturation of synaptic connection at the base of the hair cells.

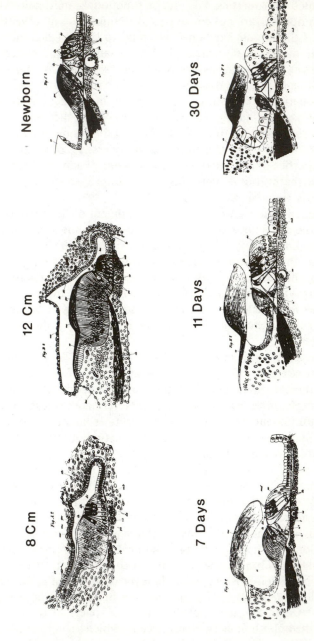

ORGAN OF CORTI DEVELOPMENT – CAT

(G. RETZIUS, 1884)

Newborn

30 Days

12 Cm

11 Days

8 Cm

7 Days

Figure 2. Successive stages of organ of Corti differentiation in the kitten (from Retzius, 1884).

Central Nervous System Development

Initial stages of development of the auditory centers in the CNS are independent of peripheral regulation. Thus, the proliferation and migration of neurons in the auditory system, like other neural systems (see Jacobson, 1978), do not depend on the cochlea. In addition, the commonly held opinion that receptor development precedes the development of CNS connectivity is probably wrong. While there are undoubtedly important changes in the detailed patterns of synaptic connectivity at each level of the auditory system, the major pathways are established prior to or simultaneously with the development of peripheral function. Marty (1962), for example, showed that in newborn kittens, cortical evoked responses can be elicited by electrical stimulation of the auditory nerve. The cochlea, however, is quite immature at this time, and it is not possible to reliably evoke cortical responses to sound.

Following the establishment of functional connections between the periphery and the central nervous system, the continued maturation of neurons is highly dependent on the functional integrity of their afferents. The best examples of this interrelationship come from studies on the avian auditory system. Rita Levi-Montalcini (1949) was the first to show that, when the otocyst is removed very early in development, there is no effect on the number of cells or size of the cochlear nuclei until the time when the nuclei are beginning to assume their adult characteristics. Continued investigation of this system by a number of laboratories, including my own (Saunders, Coles, & Gates, 1973; Rubel, Smith, & Miller, 1976; Parks, 1979; Jackson, Hackett, & Rubel, 1982; Jhavari & Morest, 1982) has revealed that, after the time at which functional connections normally are established between the eighth nerve and the cochlear nucleus cells (nucleus magnocellularis and n. angularis in avians), the absence of peripheral innervation causes rapid and severe degeneration of the neurons. Of considerable interest is the fact that the change in peripheral influence coincides with the period of functional development of the cochlea and with the establishment of functional connections between the eighth nerve and n. magnocellularis cells. The obvious implication is that the receptor-generated neural activity along this pathway may play a role in the maintenance of the postsynaptic neurons. Whether or not the important parameter is activity per se, it is apparent that, following the development of synaptic connections, CNS neurons *require* afferentation for survival. How the biology of the neurons has changed over this period is not known, but clearly worth pursuing.

Functional Development

It is now appropriate to begin discussing the initial stages of auditory function. Two fundamental properties of the adult auditory system are its sensitivity to sound and its ability to analyze the spectral properties of a sound. Considerable information is available on hearing sensitivity and frequency analysis in a variety of animals, and neuronal response properties thought to be important for hearing sensitivity and frequency selectivity have been extensively studied.

Therefore, it seems possible to analyze the *ontogeny* of these properties at both behavioral and neural levels, and to interrelate the findings. At this point, however, neither the data nor the principles for such integration are available. Thus, I can only report some of the phenomenology.

During the initial stages of functional development, auditory thresholds and latencies of responses to pure tones decrease. These relationships are exemplified in Figure 3, taken from a report on neuronal firing properties in the antero-ventral cochlear nucleus (AVCN) of cats (Brugge, Javel, & Kitzes, 1978). Temporally correlated with these physiological changes are, as expected, behavioral changes. For example, data from Ehret and Romand (1981) demonstrating ontogenetic changes in thresholds for evoking a pinna reflex or a conditioned response in cats is included in Figure 3. Similar relationships between the development of evoked-potential thresholds and behavioral sensitivity have been shown in a number of species, with a variety of methods. In humans, the physiological method of choice for studying the development of hearing sensitivity seems to be the brain stem evoked response (BSER). The chapter by Hecox in this volume presents data from neonates using this method.

In general, it is relatively easy to find physiological methods to study changes in auditory sensitivity; but, as this volume attests, the establishment of adequate behavioral tests for neonatal humans or animals is much more difficult. When considering this literature, it is important to note that behavioral studies on adult animals and man have yielded threshold estimates which are usually 15 to 20 decibels below those obtained by physiological measures. On the other hand, studies of neonatal animals have yielded the opposite relationship; physiological indices often provide lower threshold estimates than behavioral methods. In my opinion, this difference further emphasizes the need to establish more sensitive behavioral techniques for examining neonates.

Threshold and latency decreases thus appear to be general properties of auditory development. What are the biological mechanisms underlying these changes? Obviously, the periphery sets limits on what can be processed by the central nervous system. Therefore, we must first turn to the periphery for explanations. No single event during middle ear or inner ear development can be singled out as responsible for these functional changes. Saunders et al. (1983) have shown that tympanic-membrane admittance and compliance are temporally correlated with the development of evoked-potential thresholds in the hamster. These data, however, do not allow us to conclude that the development of middle-ear function is *responsible* for threshold development. There are a host of developmental events occurring concurrently in the cochlea and the central nervous system which may be equally important. Thus, we must conclude that the establishment of adult sensitivity is dependent on exquisitely timed developmental synchrony between conductive processes at the periphery, transductive properties of the cochlea and integrative centers in the central nervous system. Exemplifying this synchrony are the data shown in Figure 4, taken from several studies on the development of auditory function in the rabbit (Anggaard, 1965; Marty, 1962). The important principle to be noted

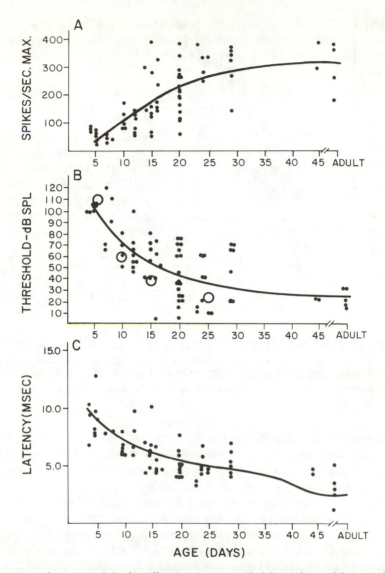

Figure 3. Development of single cell responses recorded from the cochlear nucleus of the cat. Postnatal changes in maximum spike rate (A, top), threshold (dB, SPL) to tone burst stimulation (B, middle), and latency to first spike (C, bottom). Points and axes from Brugge et al. (1978); lines fitted "by eye" by author. Open circles on threshold function (B) indicate the threshold for eliciting behavioral response to 2kHz tone as a function of age and frequency (taken from Ehret & Romand, 1981).

from Figure 4 is that all of the ontogenetic changes, including cochlear microphonic thresholds, endocochlear potential amplitudes, latency to a response at the trapezoid body, and cortical evoked-potential amplitudes, show a very similar developmental time-course. It is worth noting that the data from Ang-

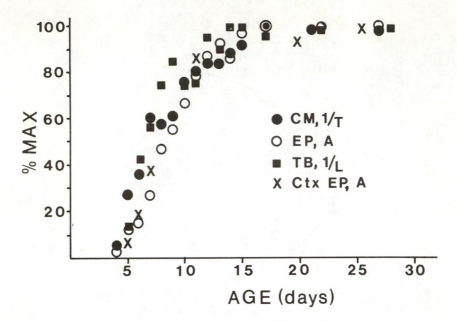

Figure 4. Synchrony of functional development is demonstrated by several measures taken from the postnatal rabbit auditory system. All measures have been normalized to percent of maximum response. O-inverse of cochlear microphonic threshold; •-endocochlear potential amplitude; ■-inverse of latency to record potential at the trapezoid body; X-cortical evoked-potential amplitude (data replotted from Anggaard, 1965, and Marty, 1962).

gaard's study are generated by direct stimulation of the round window, thereby bypassing middle ear properties. Similar examples of synchrony can be taken from physiological and anatomical studies on other species (Webster & Webster, 1980; Jackson et al., 1982; Smith, 1981).

Another general property of auditory development that has been studied by physiological means in a variety of species is the development of "tuning" or frequency selectivity. It is well known that cells at each level of the auditory system respond best (i.e., have lowest threshold) to a particular frequency, and at surrounding frequencies thresholds increase. The function generated by this property is called a *tuning curve*. Similarly, masking procedures can be used to derive tuning curves from evoked-potential responses by observing the frequency/intensity combinations that attenuate the evoked potential to a probe tone (Dallos & Cheatham, 1976; Harris & Dallos, 1979). The tuning curves recorded from cells in the cochlear nucleus or the inferior colliculus have been shown to become sharper during development in several species; evoked-potential tuning curves show similar changes (e.g., see Aitkin & Moore, 1975; Moore & Irvine, 1979; Brugge, Kitzes, & Javel, 1981; Carlier, Lenoir, & Pujol, 1979; Saunders, Dolgin, & Lowry, 1980).

Another neuronal response parameter which is related to the spectral properties of an acoustic stimulus is *phase locking*. This term relates the temporal properties of a spike train to the spectral properties of the stimulus. Brugge et al. (1978) have studied the ontogeny of phase locking in the kitten anteroventral cochlear nucleus, and found its development extends over a relatively long period, including at least the first postnatal month.

The biological principles underlying the development of spectral tuning properties and temporal response properties are even less well understood than those underlying the ontogeny of absolute sensitivity. Again, all levels of the auditory system may be involved. At the level of the middle ear, the spectral purity of transmission may change during development. At the level of the cochlea, the traveling wave may become increasingly sharply tuned, and changes in stereocilia length, number, or stiffness may be important (Tilney & Saunders, 1983). Furthermore, Pujol and his colleagues (Pujol, Carlier, & Devigne, 1978) have indicated that there is a remodeling of synaptic connections occurring at the base of the hair cells which also may change the tuning properties of axons in the auditory nerve. In the central nervous system, any number of processes may be involved. For example, it has been suggested that, in many systems, synaptic connections become "more specific" during ontogeny (Jacobson, 1978). An example in the auditory system is provided by Jackson and Parks (1982), who have shown that the degree of convergence onto single cochlear nucleus cells decreases during development. Processes such as these, which may occur at each level of the auditory system, could be responsible for increasing the frequency selectivity of neuronal responses.

At the behavioral level, we know relatively little about the development of frequency selectivity. The available data suggest that responses to pure tones also become more specific during development. For example, elsewhere in this volume (Gray & Rubel), we show that frequency discrimination improves and generalization functions sharpen during the first few postnatal days in chickens. Behavioral responses to complex stimuli seem to show similar properties. For example, Gottlieb (1971a) has shown that embryonic ducklings go through successive stages of increasing perceptual sharpening. Similarly, frequency discrimination and generalization functions in newborn human neonates also appear relatively nonselective, but reliable methodologies have not been discovered with which to trace the ontogeny of human frequency selectivity.

One general methodological point should be made at this time. It has been appreciated for some time that there are important changes in the temporal properties of neuronal responses during development (Rubel, 1971; Wiesel & Hubel, 1963; Jackson et al., 1982). An exquisite example of such changes is the development of phase locking by auditory neurons in the ventral cochlear nucleus (Brugge et al., 1978). A corollary of these findings is that the optimal rate for presentation of a sensory stimulus will change during ontogeny. Presentation rates used for neonatal animals must be considerably less, often by an order of magnitude, than those used to test adult animals. Since thresholds and tuning curves degrade with rapid stimulation, extreme care must be used when testing neonatal animals or humans so as to provide stimulation at a slow enough pace that maximum responsivity can be maintained. The time course for some of these events in the human fetus is provided in Table 1.

Table 1. Human Ear Development*

Fetal Week	Inner Ear	Middle Ear	External Ear
3rd	Auditory placode; auditory pit	Tubo-tympanic recess begins to develop	
4th	Auditory vesicle (otocyst); vestibular-cochlear division		Tissue thickenings begin to form
5th			Primary auditory meatus begins
6th	Utricle and saccule present; semicircular canals begin		6 hillocks evident; cartilage begins to form
7th	One cochlear coil present; sensory cells in utricle and saccule		Auricles move dorsolaterally
8th	Ductus reuniens present; sensory cells in semicircular canals	Incus and malleus present in cartilage; lower half of tympanic cavity formed	Outer cartilaginous third of external canal formed
9th		3 tissue layers at tympanic membrane are present	
11th	2½ cochlear coils present; VIII nerve attaches to cochlear duct		
12th	Sensory cells in cochlea; membranous labyrinth complete; otic capsule begins to ossify		
15th		Cartilaginous stapes formed	
16th		Ossification of malleus and incus begins	
18th		Stapes begins to ossify	
20th	Maturation of inner ear; inner ear adult size		Auricle is adult shape, but continues to grow until age 9
21st		Meatal plug disintegrates exposing tympanic membrane	
30th		Pneumatization of tympanum	External auditory canal continues to mature until age 7
32nd		Malleus and incus complete ossification	

Table 1. (continued)

Fetal Week	Inner Ear	Middle Ear	External Ear
34th		Mastoid air cells develop	
35th		Antrum is pneumatized	
37th		Epitympanum is pneumatized	
		Stapes continues to develop until adulthood; tympanic membrane changes relative position during first two years of life	

* From Northern and Downs (1974)

DEVELOPMENT OF THE PLACE PRINCIPLE

Most animals do not simultaneously begin hearing all of the frequencies which are included in their adult dynamic range. Table 2 summarizes most of the data available on the frequency range to which animals of a variety of species respond initially and as adults. Both behavioral and physiological data were used to construct this table. The important point to note is that, in each species, initial responses are elicited by low or middle frequencies for that species. As development proceeds, responsiveness to both lower and higher frequencies increases. Responsiveness to the highest frequencies develops last. This sequence appears to be remarkably universal across both avian and mammalian species (Gottlieb, 1971b; Rubel, 1978). Many other measures of auditory system functional ontogeny show this same general developmental sequence. For example, adult-like thresholds develop first for relatively low frequencies and later for high frequencies (Moore & Irvine, 1979), phase locking seems to mature first for low frequency units (Brugge et al., 1978), and the most sensitive frequency for a given species seems to shift toward progressively higher frequencies during development (e.g., see Rebillard & Rubel, 1981).

Since the pioneering work of von Békésy, the most fundamental principle of auditory science is the place principle. This principle states that there is a progression of positions along the basilar membrane which are most sensitive to (i.e., tuned to) successively higher frequencies. This relationship is thought to be due to the gradually changing mechanical properties of the basilar membrane, and consequently the amplitude of the traveling wave along the length of the cochlea. It is becoming increasingly evident that the place principle also involves changes in the characteristics of stereocilia (length, number, and stiffness) along the length of the cochlear partition (Weiss, Mulroy, Turner, &

Table 2. Initial Frequency Ranges

Species	Adult Frequency Range (kHz)*	Initial Frequency Range (kHz)	
Human	.03–20	.5–1.0	(hr, physiol, beh)
Cat	.06–75	.5–2.0	(physiol)
		.3– .75	(beh)
Dog	.04–50	.5– .75	(beh)
Mink	.1 –70	.5– .75	(beh)
Rabbit	.06–50	.5–3	(physiol)
		.3– .75	(beh)
Rat	.3 –76	.2–2	(physiol)
Mouse (mus)	1 –84	.6–2	(cm)
		1–3	(beh)
Bat (myotis)	10–120	7–12	(physiol)
Chicken	.1 –7	.1– .8	(physiol, beh)
Duck	.1 –8	.1– .5	(cn)

* Approximate range of audiogram at 70 dB (SPL); compiled with the help of Henry Hefner and William Stebbins.

Pike, 1976; Tilney & Saunders, 1983). The cochlea of birds and mammals is organized such that apical positions (distal in birds) are most sensitive to low frequencies, and progressively more basal regions are most sensitive to progressively higher frequencies.

Knowledge of the place principle and of the developmental data presented in Table 2 suggests that the apical or mid-apical (low-frequency) region of the cochlea is the first to mature, and the maturation of the cochlea must then spread primarily toward the high frequency, basal region. Paradoxically, just the opposite result has been consistently observed for the direction of maturation of the cochlea. As first shown by Retzius (1884) and repeated on a variety of animals using a large variety of measures (see Rubel, 1978, for review), cochlear differentiation seems to occur first in the basal or mid-basal high frequency region. Differentiation then spreads in both directions, and the *last* part of the cochlea to undergo differentiation is the apical, low frequency, region. In Figure 5, some of Retzius' elegant engravings of sections through the newborn-rabbit organ of Corti from the basal, middle, and apical turns are reproduced. Physiological studies indicate that the rabbit is just beginning to hear at about five days after birth. It is evident from this figure that the basal portion of the cochlea is the most mature, with the middle turn not far behind, and that the apical portion is very immature. As judged by a variety of indices such as the size and position of the tunnel of Corti, the establishment of a true inner spiral sulcus, the differentiation of hair cells, and tectorial membrane maturity, it has been repeatedly shown that a similar relationship holds at the ultrastructural level for chicks, rats, mice, and cats (Pujol & Hilding, 1973; Pujol & Marty, 1970; Shnerson, Devigne, & Pujol, 1982; Fermin & Cohen, 1983). A similar differentiation gradient appears to be occurring in the eighth nerve ganglion cells and cochlear nuclei; regions receiving input from the basal

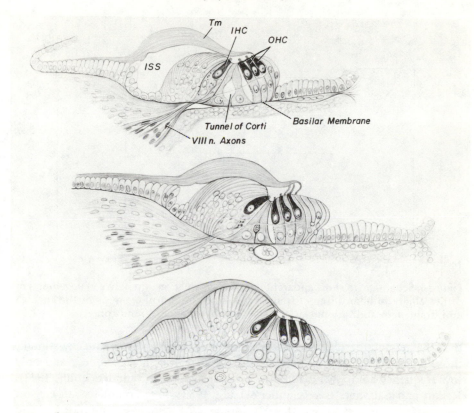

Figure 5. Organ of Corti in newborn rabbit. Note successive stages of maturity from apex (bottom) to middle turn (middle) and then to basal turn (top). (Redrawn from Retzius, 1884).

(high frequency) region of the cochlea mature prior to the apical projection areas (Romand & Romand, 1982; Rubel et al., 1976; Jackson et al., 1982; Schweitzer & Cant, 1984).

This paradoxical relationship between the ontogeny of responses to pure tones and the ontogeny of the cochlea and brain stem auditory nuclei is diagrammed in Figure 6. Simply stated, functional maturation of the auditory system seems to develop from low or mid-low frequencies to high frequencies (generally low-to-high). In contrast, the cochlea, the spiral ganglion, and the brain stem auditory areas show an opposite developmental gradient; the mid-basal regions (which in adults responds to high or mid-high frequencies) differentiate in advance of those regions responding to progressively lower frequencies (generally base-to-apex). Our studies, as well as those from other laboratories, indicate that these two gradients are occurring simultaneously (see Jackson et al., 1982).

One resolution of this apparent paradox is that the spectral properties of middle ear conduction are changing over development. That is, it is possible

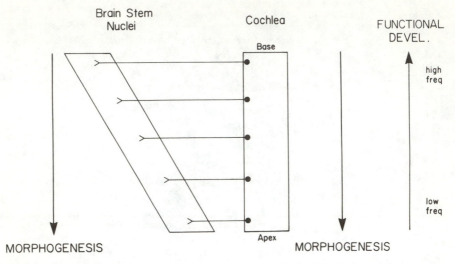

Figure 6. Schematic to show apparent paradoxical relationship between development of the ability to hear different frequencies, and the morphogenesis of the cochlea and brain stem auditory nuclei. Schematic shows general trends only.

that the neonatal middle ear acts as a low-pass filter; high-frequency stimuli, those which normally best activate the basal region, are excluded, and only low-frequency components impinge upon the cochlea (Saunders et al., 1973). Relkin and Saunders (see Saunders et al., 1983) have conducted an elegant series of studies examining the development of middle-ear admittance and compliance in both mammals and birds. Their findings do not support the above interpretation. While there is an obvious improvement in middle-ear transmission during the early stages of hearing, it appears to be relatively flat across frequency. Indirect data from our own laboratory also strongly suggest that the middle-ear transmission properties cannot account for the paradoxical relationship noted above or the results presented below.

Several years ago, on the basis of the developmental characteristics of the avian brain stem, we hypothesized that the place code along the cochlea might be changing during development (Rubel et al., 1976). This hypothesis, since expanded (Rubel, 1978), was recently tested (Rubel & Ryals, 1983; Lippe & Rubel, 1983). Our hypothesis and its implications are shown schematically in Figure 7. The upper diagram in each part schematically shows the cochlea, from base to apex, and the relative positions of the traveling wave produced by three different frequencies. In the adult (right-hand diagram), low frequencies cause a relatively broadly-tuned traveling wave which peaks near the apex. Progressively higher frequencies cause more sharply tuned traveling waves which peak at progressively more basal locations. (This is the relationship shown by von Békésy (see von Békésy, 1960) and is the basis of the place principle.) Figure 7 also shows the orderly representation of input from the cochlea to the central nervous system, which results in the neurons being selectively

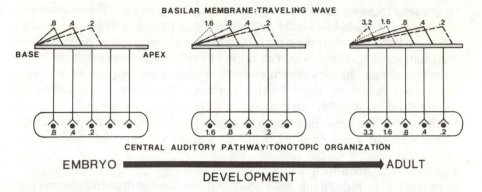

Figure 7. Model of inner-ear functional development. The sequence of development is shown from left to right. The basilar membrane, from base to apex, is depicted at the top of each section, and the positions of the traveling waves produced by pure tones of several frequencies (in kHz) are indicated. A region of the central auditory pathways which is tonotopically organized is shown connected to each basilar membrane. The numbers indicate the "best frequency" (in kHz) of neurons at each location. At the beginning of auditory function (left diagrams), the basal half of the cochlea is responsive to relatively low frequencies, and the central nervous system areas receiving projections from the base respond to low frequencies. With maturation (middle and right sections), the apex of the cochlea begins responding to low frequencies and the base is becoming more and more sensitive to high frequencies. The resulting shift in neuronal best frequencies is indicated at the bottom of each diagram.

tuned to the indicated frequencies (in kHz). This relationship in the central nervous system is usually referred to as *tonotopic organization*.

Our hypothesis and its predictions are shown in the left and middle diagrams of Figure 7. We propose that, during the early stages of hearing, the base or mid-basal region of the cochlea, and thereby the basal representation areas of the central nervous system, are most sensitive to relatively low frequencies, and not to high frequencies as in the adult. With maturation of both mechanical and neural processes, the place code (more correctly its numerical values) shifts toward the apex. That is, low frequencies first cause a maximal response in the basal or mid-basal region of the cochlea. As the organism matures, progressively more apical regions become most responsive to low frequencies. High frequencies, on the other hand, are initially ineffective, because of the mechanical or neural properties of the cochlea. As the basal region matures, it becomes selectively tuned to progressively higher frequencies.

This hypothesis makes two very specific predictions which we have recently tested. The first prediction is indicated in the upper parts of Figure 7. The frequency organization of the cochlea can be demonstrated by examining the area of damage produced by exposing an animal to high-intensity pure tones. That is, the position of damage and the spectral components of the hearing loss change as a function of the frequency to which the animal has been exposed. High frequencies cause hair cell damage near the base, and progressively lower frequencies cause maximum damage at more apical locations. This relationship is particularly reliable and stable in young chicks (Rubel & Ryals, 1982; Ryals & Rubel, 1982). The first prediction indicated by Figure 7 is that there will be a systematic ontogenetic shift in the position of hair cell damage produced by exposure to a high-intensity sound; damage produced by, say, low or midrange frequencies should be initially rather basal and then move toward the apex during development. This prediction can be tested by exposing animals at different ages to the same pure tone and observing the position of hair cell loss. The experiment was carried out using chickens of varying ages.[1]

Experiment 1: Acoustic Trauma

In our initial study (Ryals & Rubel, 1982), we showed that discrete and reliable lesions can be produced by exposure to high-intensity pure tones. A summary of these data is shown in Figure 8A. Ten days after hatching (P10), chicks were exposed to a high-intensity pure tone (123 dB SPL) for 12 hours. The shaded region in Figure 8 shows the mean number of hair cells (± 1 SE) at each level of the cochlea in normal control birds. The other three functions indicate average counts from animals exposed to each of the indicated frequencies. Obviously, there is a discrete region of hair cell loss which is dependent on the frequency of sound exposure (see Rebillard, Ryals, & Rubel, 1982, for physiological data). Furthermore, the region of hair cell loss is broad and positioned relatively toward the apex following low-frequency exposure. The lesion becomes increasingly narrow and positioned more toward the base when the animal is exposed to higher frequencies.

This experiment then was repeated on animals at two additional ages, just prior to hatching (E20) and one month after hatching (P30).[2] The mean hair cell counts from the three age groups exposed to a 1500 Hz tone are shown in Figure 8. The total amount of hair cell damage varied as a function of age, as did the spread of damage. More relevant to our hypothesis, the *position* of damage also shifted. In the youngest animals (E20), the position of damage produced by a 1500 Hz tone was located most toward the base; at the older ages, the position of damage shifted systematically toward the apex. In Figure 9, all of the data from this study are summarized. The position of maximum damage is plotted as a function of age for the chicks exposed to each frequency. Since the youngest animals had elevated thresholds to the 3000 Hz stimuli, and did not show any appreciable damage after exposure to this frequency, no data are available for this time point. Figure 9 shows that the position of maximum damage produced by each frequency shifted systematically toward the apex as a function of age, a result consistent with the hypothesis noted above.

---

[1] The advantages of the chick include the fact that the avian cochlea (basilar papilla) is not spiraled, which allows it to be dissected free, reproducibly oriented, and examined using conventional histological methods. The number of hair cells at 50-micron intervals along the cochlea, then, could be determined from serial sections of normal and sound-exposed cochleas.

[2] It is important to note that eighth-nerve evoked-potential thresholds to frequencies below 2 kHz have reached adult values by E20, and by P10 the chicks have adult thresholds to all frequencies (Saunders et al., 1973; Rebillard & Rubel, 1981).

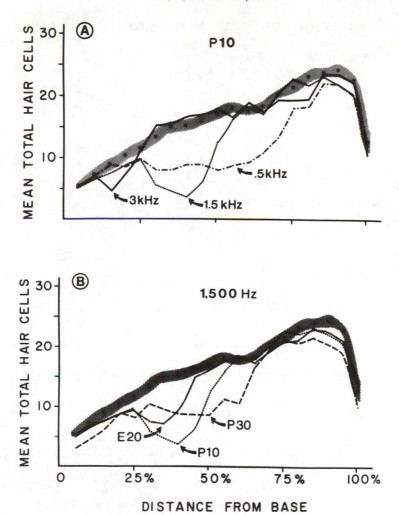

Figure 8. Total number of hair cells as a function of position along the chick basilar papilla (cochlea) from base to apex. The mean ± standard error for normal animals is shown by the dots and shading. Standard errors for the experimental groups are omitted for clarity, but were comparable to those for normal animals. (A) Mean number of hair cells of chicks exposed on postnatal day 10 to 500, 1500 or 3000 Hz high-intensity tones. (B) Mean number of hair cells from chicks exposed to 1500 Hz tone on embryonic day 20 (E20), postnatal day 10 (P10) or postnatal day 30 (P30). Arrows indicate positions of maximum damage (from Rubel & Ryals, 1983).

Experiment 2: Tonotopic Organization

A second prediction made by our hypothesis is shown in the bottom of Figure 7, and was tested by William Lippe (Lippe & Rubel, 1983). If the transduction properties of the cochlea are changing during development, and the orderly topography of projections from the cochlea to the central nervous system are remaining stable, then within each brain region, the position at which

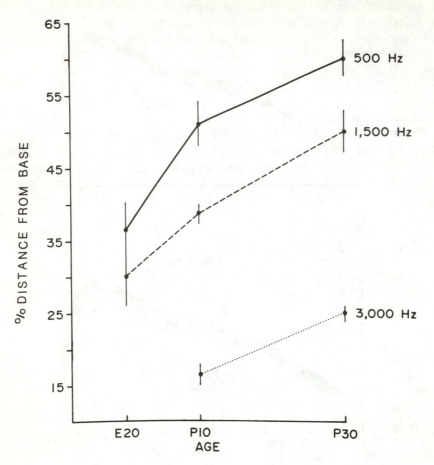

POSITION OF MAXIMUM HAIR CELL LOSS

Figure 9. Position of maximum hair-cell loss as a function of age. The ordinate represents the percentile position, from base to apex, at which maximum hair-cell loss occurred. Mean position is calculated for each group of chicks exposed to each frequency (from Rubel & Ryals, 1983).

neurons are responsive to a particular frequency will shift during development. Stated differently, the neurons at any given location within an auditory area of the central nervous system should respond to successively higher frequencies during development. This prediction was tested by "mapping" the location of neurons and the frequency to which they were most sensitive at two different ages.

Two separate nuclei of the chick brain were examined. Nucleus magnocellularis (NM) receives direct projections from the cochlea, and is tonotopically organized. It, in turn, sends axons bilaterally to nucleus laminaris (NL) which is also tonotopically organized (Rubel & Parks, 1975; Parks & Rubel, 1975). The tonotopic organization in normal chicks 15–20 days after hatching is shown by the solid lines and dashed lines in Figure 10. The solid lines show the regres-

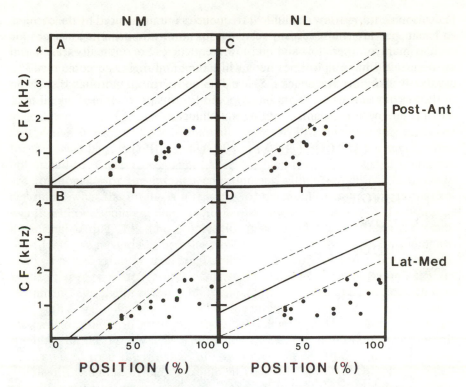

Figure 10. Best frequency as a function of percentile position along the posterior to anterior (A and C) and lateral to medial (B and D) dimensions of the magnocellular and laminar nuclei. The linear regressions that predict the best frequency of neurons in hatchlings are shown by the solid lines; the dashed lines represent ± standard error. The relation between position and best frequency actually observed in embryos is illustrated by the filled circles. Note that, for each response in embryos, the observed best frequency is markedly lower than that found in hatchlings.

sion of the best frequency of a neuron to its position in either brain region (the dashed lines are at one standard error of estimate). They show that there is an orderly progression toward higher frequencies at progressively more medial and anterior positions in both nuclei. The data points (dots) in Figure 10 show the positions and best frequencies of cells from 17-day-old embryos (hearing in the chick begins at around embryonic day 12). The characteristic frequency of each embryonic neuron is 1–1½ octaves below what would be predicted by the relationship between position and characteristic frequency derived from the older posthatch animals. Since neither the total number of neurons nor their relative positions in these nuclei change after embryonic day 17 (Rubel et al., 1976) these data support the prediction that the neurons at any given position in the nucleus respond to successively higher frequencies during development.

Conclusion and Interpretation

Taken together, these two experiments provide strong support for the model of cochlear development depicted in Figure 11. This model suggests that, early in development, only low or mid-low frequencies are transduced by the cochlea, and that they are transduced by relatively basal or mid-basal regions. As the cochlea matures, these low and mid-low frequencies are optimally transduced at successively more apical positions while the basal regions become tuned to progressively higher frequencies. Space does not permit a thorough discussion of the mechanisms which might be proposed for this process. In all likelihood, they include both mechanical and neural changes.

COCHLEAR DEVELOPMENT

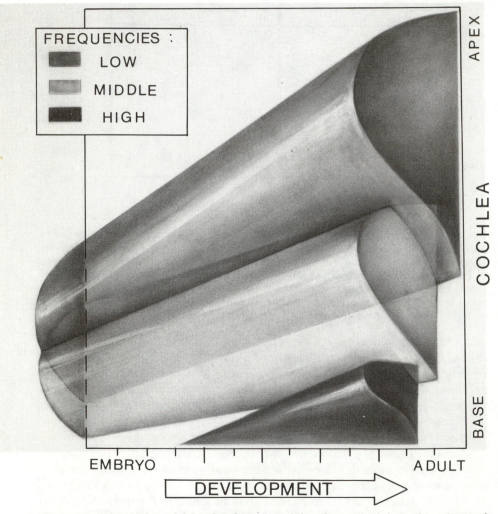

Figure 11. Proposed model for development of the place principle in the avian and mammalian inner ear. At the onset of hearing function, low and middle frequencies stimulate the basal and mid-basal region of the basilar membrane. As development proceeds, the basal region responds to progressively higher frequencies, while low and middle frequencies maximally stimulate progressively apical positions until the adult pattern (top) is attained.

In the present context, it is of greater interest to consider the generality of this process across species and its functional implications. While we have only tested the hypothesis using chickens, some support can be gained from data available on mammals. First, the paradoxical relationship between cochlea development and functional ontogeny is nearly universal across species. Second, Ryan and his colleagues (Ryan, Woolf, & Sharp, 1982) have shown that the position of neurons in the gerbil dorsal cochlear nucleus which increase glucose uptake in response to a 3 kHz tone shifts markedly during development; the direction of the shift is in correspondence with the prediction of this model. Third, Pujol and Marty (1968) present data suggestive of a similar change. While recording from the cerebral cortex of young kittens, Pujol noted that only relatively low-frequency tones produced recognizable evoked potentials. However, the potentials could only be recorded from relatively anterior regions of the suprasylvian gyrus, which in the adult receives input from the base of the cochlea and responds to relatively high frequencies (Woolsey & Walzl, 1942). Again, this finding is consistent with the interpretation noted above. Finally, Harris and Dallos (1983) and Charles Yancey and Peter Dallos (personal communication October, 1983) have found that the high frequency cut-off of cochlear microphonic potentials and summating potentials recorded from within the basal turn of the gerbil cochlea systematically increases over more than an octave during the second to fourth postnatal week.

The functional implications of this model are that, at some point during development, each part of the cochlea, and thereby each tonotopic region of the central nervous system, will be maximally responsive to relatively low frequency tones. With maturation, each area will be responsive to successively higher frequencies, until adult values are reached. In this context, it is intriguing to evaluate what sounds are present in the environment of young organisms.[3] The data currently available on the human in-utero sound environment are shown in Figure 12 (from Walker, Grimwade, & Wood, 1971). The ambient in-utero sound level as a function of frequency is indicated by the left curve as it relates to the left Y axis. The right function indicates the amount of sound attenuation by the body as a function of frequency. The difference between the intensity of sound recorded at the abdomen and that recorded in utero as a function of frequency is shown (right axis). The most important conclusion to be drawn from this figure is that both the transmission of external sounds into the uterus and internally generated sounds favor low frequencies, whereas high-frequency sounds are markedly attenuated. The match between a low-frequency-dominated environment and the sequence of hearing development which we have described may be coincidence. On the other hand, it is tempting to speculate that it represents an example of selection for a pattern of sensory-system development which makes use of the stimuli reliably available in the

---

[3] Acoustically, it is very difficult to block low frequency tones and very easy to block high frequency tones. Thus, whether an animal lives in a burrow, in an egg, or in utero, the acoustic environment will be dominated by low-frequency sounds. High frequencies may be available, but their availability is much more ephemeral and subject to environmental changes.

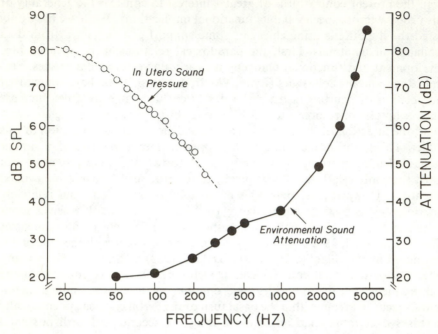

Figure 12. The mammalian intrauterine acoustic environment is determined by the sound level from fetal and maternal behavior as well as the attenuation of sound located from outside the mother. The data ("corrected for impedance of microphone") for the human fetus due to each of these sources has been replotted from Walker et al. (1971). These results emphasize the low-frequency domination of the fetal environment. Ambient sound levels (left line and left axes) are relatively loud at low frequency and quieter with increasing frequency. Attenuation (right line and right ordinate) of low-frequency external sounds is moderate but increases markedly above 2 kHz.

environment. If the development of normal function is dependent on external stimulation, then the developmental pattern we have proposed will provide a mechanism to insure that each neuronal region is likely, in turn, to receive maximal stimulation from the environment.

EXTRINSIC INFLUENCES ON AUDITORY SYSTEM DEVELOPMENT

One important class of extrinsic environmental influences is agents that are ototoxic. Some of these, such as environmental noise, are always present. Others, such as aminoglycoside antibiotics, are administered during the course of clinical treatment to people of all ages. The extent to which the infant is differentially susceptible to ototoxic agents is, therefore, of immediate clinical importance. Another example of extrinsic influences that may be of clinical and economic importance are those resulting from environmental sound deprivation. Conductive hearing losses, ranging from extreme in the case of atresias of external and middle ear structures, to episodic and relatively minor, such as from recurrent otitis media, are relatively common in babies and young children. Some of these are treatable in the infant, while others must await the approach of school age for surgical intervention. In most cases, however, it is possible to correct conductive hearing losses (Jharsdoefer, 1978). The question of how deprivation affects the development of the auditory system and whether such effects are permanent or transient should influence when and to what extent aggressive intervention, either by amplification or surgery, is indicated. At this time, it is a commonly held belief that all children with a moderate-to-severe conductive hearing loss should be stimulated by whatever means possible until the time at which surgical intervention is possible. The underlying assumption is that normal language development will be retarded or prevented due to continued deprivation (see Hanson & Ulvestad, 1979). On the other hand, programs to fit *every* handicapped child with amplification devices are both costly and possibly dangerous when considered in light of the possibility that young children or infants may be differentially susceptible to noise-induced sensorineural hearing loss. Thus, from a purely practical point of view, it is extremely important to determine the conditions under which conductive hearing losses result in abnormal neural structure or function, and those which influence the ontogeny of behavioral abilities.

Peripheral Susceptibility

Saunders and Bock (1978) have summarized the literature on the differential susceptibility to aminoglycosides and noise exposure in young animals. Studies by Saunders and by Pujol and his colleagues have shown that exposure of young rats, hamsters, or mice to these drugs or to noise at levels which would not produce damage in adult animals can cause severe hearing loss and histological damage of the cochlea (e.g., see Carlier & Pujol, 1980; Lenoir & Pujol, 1980). Pujol and his coworkers have gone on to show that the period of increased susceptibility corresponds to the final stages of anatomical and functional development of the cochlea. They suggest that during this period the cochlea is hypersensitive because of the lack of normal efferent input. Certainly, much more work needs to be done to determine the biological mechanisms underlying the differential susceptibility of young animals. In addition, we need to determine if and when hypersensitivity occurs in human infants and if it occurs during other periods of life—for example, during the aging process and/or during periods of heightened stress.

Peripheral Regulation of Central Nervous System

Turning now to the subject of extrinsic influences on central nervous system development, we will first consider how the presence of an auditory receptor, coupled with the neural activity emanating from it, influences the development of central nervous system auditory structures. In a series of studies since 1975, we have been examining how the integrity of the cochlea may influence the development of neurons in nucleus magnocellularis and nucleus laminaris of the chick brain stem auditory system. In the chick, it is possible to take out the cochlea at various ages ranging from the 2-day-old embryo (prior to formation of the cochlea or eighth nerve) to adulthood. The neural pathways in which we have studied the effects of these operations are schematically shown in Figure 13. It was noted above that otocyst removal does not noticeably effect the development of cells in the cochlear nucleus (nucleus magnocellularis in the chick) until after the time of normal innervation of these cells by the eighth nerve. The questions we will address now are: to what extent does the presence of an intact cochlea and eighth nerve effect the *final* number of cells in the nucleus magnocellularis, and to what extent are such effects age-dependent?

Figure 14 shows a typical result of cochlea removal from a 2-week posthatch chick which was then allowed to survive for 26 days. Cells from the control side (top) and the same area from the experimental side of the brain are shown. There is obviously a great deal of cell loss as well as considerable shrinkage of the remaining cells in the denervated region. In Figure 15, the relationship of cell loss to the age of animals at the time of the operation is shown (Born & Rubel, 1983). In all cases, the animals survived one to two months following surgical removal of one cochlea. It is quite clear from this figure that the effects of cochlea removal on cell loss in the central nervous system are quite age-dependent, and that the major change in susceptibiity occurs between six weeks after hatching and 66 weeks after hatching. While the conclusion that

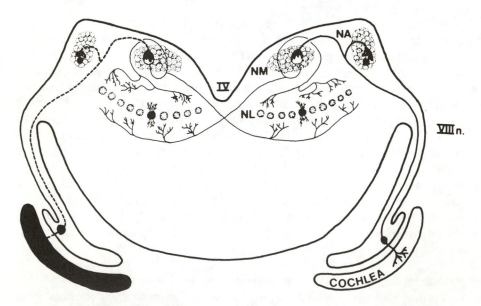

Figure 13. Schematic drawing of the chick brain stem auditory system showing 2nd order nuclei, n. magnocellularis (NM) and n. angullaris (NA), and 3rd order neurons in n. laminaris (NL). In the experiment described, one cochlea (blackened) was removed and the cells in NM on the two sides of the brain compared. IV = fourth ventricle, VIIIn = eighth nerve.

the brain of the young animals is more susceptible to denervation than that of older animals suggests some sort of "critical period," that term, in reality, only restates the findings. The biological reasons for such a finding are at this point a mystery. For example, has removal of the cochlea produced a quantitatively similar change in the innervation of the neurons at all the ages, and what are

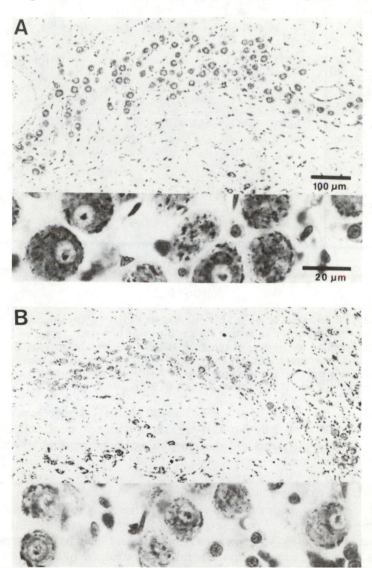

Figure 14. Low and high power photomicrographs showing (A) normal (contralateral) and (B) deafferented (ipsilateral) n. magnocellularis (NM) approximately one month following cochlea removal when the chick was 2 weeks posthatch. Note cell loss and cell shrinkage on the deafferented side of the brain (from Born & Rubel, 1983).

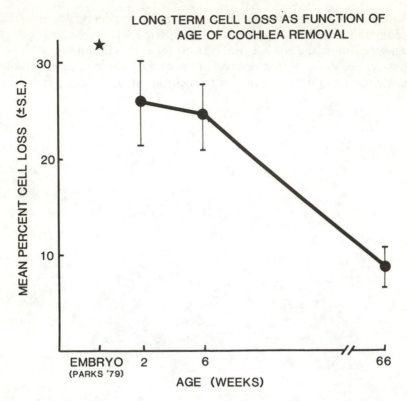

LONG TERM CELL LOSS AS FUNCTION OF AGE OF COCHLEA REMOVAL

Figure 15. Percent cell loss ($\pm$ 1 SE) in n. magnocellularis approximately one month following removal of the receptor. The cochlea was removed at various ages, from the young embryo to one year of age. Note that if receptor is removed in an embryo, at one week after hatching or at six weeks there is considerable transneuronal cell loss. The same operation in mature chickens resulted in little or no cell loss. Embryonic data from Parks (1979), other data from Born and Rubel (1983).

the differences between the neurons of an animal that is six weeks old and one that is 66 weeks of age? Both of these age groups can hear quite well, and there are no obvious differences in the morphology or physiology of either the cochlea or the central nervous system. Thus, the finding of a "critical period" is not an end in itself. Instead, it should be considered a crude beginning toward trying to understand the biological difference between the brain of the young animal and that of the adult. Similar differences between the effects of cochlear destruction on young versus adult rodents and cats have been shown by other investigators. For example, Trune (1982a, 1982b) has shown extensive effects of cochlear removal on the number and structure of cells in the mouse cochlear nucleus, whereas adult cochlear destruction seems to have little effect. Nordeen, Killackey, & Kitzes (1983) have replicated and extended these results in the gerbil.

The conclusion to be drawn from all of these studies is that an intact periphery is of critical importance for the normal development of the brain stem auditory areas. This suggests that activity and/or the integrity of presynaptic elements influences *normal* auditory-system ontogeny. An alternative explanation is that removal of the cochlea caused pathological conditions (i.e., degeneration, etc.) which, in fact, poisoned the central nervous system structures.

Deprivation Experiments

In an attempt to separate the variables related to synaptic activity and to further understand the effects of deprivation on behavioral development, several laboratories have begun investigating the effects of conductive hearing losses on the development of structural and functional properties in the central nervous system (see Clopton, 1980; Feng & Rogowski, 1980; Webster & Webster, 1979; Parks, 1979; Conlee & Parks, 1981; Gray, Smith, & Rubel, 1982; Coleman & O'Connor, 1979; Kerr, Ostapoff, & Rubel, 1979; Smith, Gray, & Rubel, 1983; Rubel, 1978). Changes in the size of neurons, relative size of neuronal elements, and changes in the binaural response characteristics of neurons following monaural auditory deprivation have been reported. Similar structural changes at the level of the cochlear nucleus seem to follow binaural conductive hearing losses.

Changes in perceptual behavior also seem to be produced by auditory deprivation. For example, we have previously demonstrated that stimulus generalization functions fail to show normal sharpening over the first few days after hatching when chicks are subjected to a 40-50 dB conductive hearing loss (Kerr et al., 1979). Using complex stimuli, Gottlieb (1971a, 1978) has provided an elegant series of studies showing the dependence of species-specific perceptual preferences on normal self-stimulation and sibling stimulation during development.

The implication that many psychologists and psychobiologists have drawn from the studies of extrinsic influences on sensory-system ontogeny and those on perceptual development is that the necessary and sufficient environmental conditions for "normal" development of these two aspects of the organism are the same. In fact, this may not be the case. When we consider "environment effects" they must be referred to an object. If that object is the whole animal or its behavior, the necessary and sufficient environmental conditions for "normal development" may be quite different than if the object is a cell in the brain. Neurons are affected by a very limited range of environmental conditions. Obviously, the environment of an organism does not impinge directly on neurons, but is transduced by receptor surfaces and sorted according to the rules of the presynaptic chain of neurons. We might consider the "environment" of a neuron as all factors which influence its metabolic conditions. Thus, the effective environment for a neuron, be it in the auditory system, the visual system, or some other system, is its history of extrinsic "events" at *its* cellular interface. One of these "events," for some neurons, following the development of receptors and neural pathways, is the presynaptic activity produced by the acoustic stimuli in the organism's environment. Furthermore, only certain components of the acoustic environment will change the life history of activity impinging upon neurons in the auditory system, and not all variables of this life history will be important. Thus, for the neuron, these later events which are related to afferent synaptic activity, and which alter development of that cell, are formally similar to what Gottlieb (this volume) identifies as the "usual supporting feature" necessary for ontogeny of perception of "critical acoustic features." These concepts, however, also have the same weakness; the relevant experiential parameters can only be defined circularly. It is important, nonetheless, to determine the extent to which the important parameters (e.g., possibly average rate of presynaptic activity in one case, and normal variations in repetition rate in the other) are general across ages, species, and neuronal systems.

While we can define spatially and chemically the environment of a neuron, that is not possible for a process such as "behavior." Thus, it is likely to be the integration of many aspects of an organism's acoustic history which influence its behavioral abilities. In other words, particular variations of an organism's acoustic environment may cause radical changes in the development of behavior, but may not produce a meaningful change in the activity impinging on a particular group of neurons within the auditory system. In this case, we might expect to affect behavioral abilities but not the ontogeny of the neuron of interest, even though that cell receives the acoustic information and is involved in neural encoding. For example, rearing an animal in white noise may cause little or no change in the total amount of activity of cells within some parts of the auditory system and, thereby, little change in the structure of these cells. On the other hand, it may severely disrupt the maturation of processing abilities, whose underlying biological principles are as yet undetecable.

One purpose of discussing what we mean by environmental deprivation versus extrinsic influences is to point out that a conductive hearing loss does not necessarily provide an interpretable change in the total amount of activity of neurons in the auditory system. The activity along the auditory nerve will be dependent on spontaneous activity generated at the level of the hair cells and the level of ganglion cells, and on evoked activity. Evoked activity may be due to the normal conductive mechanisms, including the tympanic membrane and ossicular chain, due to bone conduction, or due to internal mechanical factors. A conductive block such as an earplug or disruption of the ossicles may produce major definable changes in the reception of normal air-conducted sound, but at the same time produce unknown changes in the other processes. Therefore, it is not obvious how a conductive hearing loss will affect either the total amount or the pattern of activity within the auditory nerve. As pointed out by Rodieck and Smith (1966), a similar caveat is true regarding visual-deprivation studies, albeit for very different reasons. In order to relate changes in central nervous system development to the changes in the external environment of the organism, we eventually must be able to write the transfer function relating our various environmental manipulations to presynaptic activity impinging on the neurons in question. Until these transfer functions can be stated with some certainty, there is likely to be little advancement in our understanding of the biological principles underlying the role which stimulation plays in the developing nervous system. Because the same conductive loss may disrupt the reception of normal airborne sounds, deprivation may produce meaningful and consistent changes in behavior by disrupting "critical acoustic features." Ethologically oriented behaviorists often chastise sensory scientists and neurobiologists for using "artificial," non-evolutionarily relevant stimuli (see discussions by Johnston and by Gottlieb). Yet, it is my contention that these two groups are often asking the same general question, but with a different predicate for the preface, "environmental effects on...." The neurobiologist is attempting to change stimuli impinging on a known membrane surface in a definable way, and examine that membrane surface or some parameter related to it. The behaviorist's "membrane surface," on the other hand, is usually a meaningful skeletal response of the organism. Thus, a manipulation which involves the information which must be integrated into the production of the behavioral response is formally similar to manipulating one aspect of a neuron's environment, though operationally these two manipulations may be quite different.

An example of the importance of the above concerns is provided by recent studies performed in our laboratory in collaboration with Zaid Smith and Lincoln Gray. We reared chicks in very well-controlled acoustic environments, each chick with an earplug in one ear (Smith et al., 1983). Great pains were taken in this experiment to control all possible acoustic factors. The animals were stimulated with all frequencies of their dynamic range at 65 dB (SPL) (to the normal ear) throughout the first 25 days after hatching. The sound reaching the other cochlea was reduced by the earplug. The conductive loss provided by the earplug was carefully determined using evoked potentials recorded from the medulla; it is about 40 dB and is relatively flat across the dynamic range of the chicken (Kerr et al., 1979).

We then examined the size of dendrites in nucleus laminaris of the brain stem (see Figure 13). These cells usually have bipolar dendrites which are symmetrical. Each dendritic tree receives innervation from one ear. Thus, each cell had one set of dendrites which received input from the deprived ear, and another set which received input from the normal ear. As expected from our earlier investigations and those of Feng and Rogowski (1980), nucleus laminaris cells in the deprived animals were significantly less symmetrical than normal (Figure 16). However, to our surprise, the effects of deprivation were not uniform across the nucleus. Since this nucleus is tonotopically organized, we could determine how the deprivation affected cells in each frequency range. These data are presented in Figure 17 (from Smith et al., 1983). Cells in the high-frequency range had *smaller* dendrites on the deprived side of the cell than on the nondeprived side of the cell. On the other hand, cells in the low-frequency areas of the nucleus showed the opposite effects; the dendrites on the deprived side of the cell were *longer* than those on the nondeprived side of the cell.

There are several interpretations of this surprising result. The hypothesis that I currently favor is that whereas the conductive hearing loss was flat

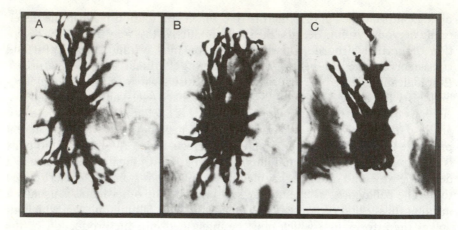

Figure 16. Normal and asymmetrical neurons from nucleus laminaris of 25 day post-hatch chicks. A: a normal cell from the middle of the nucleus. B and C: a representative neuron and an extremely asymmetrical neuron from n. laminaris, contralateral to the "deprived" ear of animals reared with an earplug in one ear. Cells were impregnated by a Golgi-Kopsch method; calibration bar equals 20 µm (from Gray et al., 1982).

across frequency, we did very different things to the *activity* impinging on cells responsive to low frequencies and those responsive to high frequencies. The ear plugs totally filled the external auditory meatus down to the tympanic membrane, which almost certainly had the additional effect of mass-loading the tympanum. It is well known that internal sounds and bone-conducted sounds are primarily of relatively low frequencies. Furthermore, occlusion of the external ear and mass loading of the tympanic membrane will enhance bone-conducted low-frequency sounds and attenuate high-frequency sounds (Tonndorf, 1966). For similar reasons, mass-loading of the tympanic membrane may also enhance internal sounds, which are primarily at low frequencies. Thus, by occluding one ear with the earplugs, we may have, in fact, *enhanced* the ongoing level of low-frequency activity in low-frequency regions of the cochlea while *decreasing* the overall level in high-frequency areas. While the effects on the neuronal dendrites were nonuniform, possibly because of non-uniform effects on activity, the conductive loss was quite stable at 40 dB, and may have eliminated most meaningful acoustic cues from the environment. Thereby, with isolated rearing, we would suggest that the earplugs will disrupt behavioral abilities in a more uniform way (Kerr et al., 1979).

   In summary, it is of obvious future importance to understand what aspects of an organism's environment are important for the development of perception, and what aspects influence the development of neurons within the auditory system. Each of these questions will require a systematic approach, which will be very different from experiments which merely try to vary the environment in undefined ways and examine the extent to which this or that neuron (or this or that behavior) is abnormal. To further understand environmental

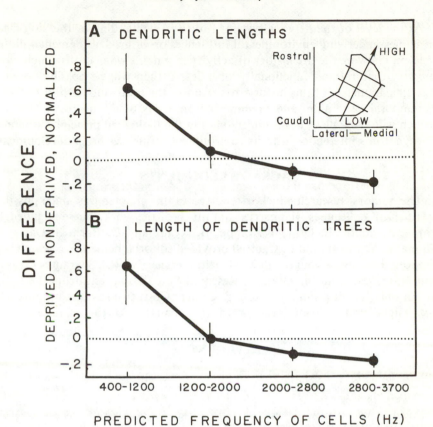

Figure 17. Mean difference ($\pm$ 1 SE) between deprived and non-deprived dendrites for four monaurally deprived chicks is shown as a function of the frequency region of the nucleus. The length differences for all the cells drawn for each animal were normalized (Z-scores). Averages for each frequency region were then computed and then the mean (and SE) across the four subjects was determined. In both graphs a positive number indicates that the length of the deprived dendrites was greater than the nondeprived dendrites. A negative number indicates the length of the deprived dendrites was *less* than the nondeprived dendrites. A: Mean differences in total dendritic lengths between the dorsal and the ventral dendrites are indicated. B: Mean differences in the length of the "dendritic trees" (total length/number of primary dendrites) between the deprived and nondeprived sides of the cells are shown. Note that the effect of a monaural ear plug differs markedly as a function of the tonotopic position of the cells, although the conductive hearing loss was relatively "flat" across frequency (from Smith et al., 1983).

influences on behavior development, we may first need reliable methods and a database in developmental psychoacoustics which will allow us to begin understanding how the coding of simple stimuli emerges in the organism. Without such understanding, we will not have the foundations necessary for understanding how perception of complex stimuli emerges, or for determining what aspects of the environment influence perceptual ontogeny.

At the level of the nervous system, future understanding of the biological principles underlying environmental influences on brain development will depend on knowing the life history of activity impinging on neurons which have known structural and functional properties. It then will be possible to vary specific parameters of this history, for example the total amount of activity or its temporal patterning, and examine the ontogeny of the neurons. This approach will allow us to begin understanding the biological principles whereby an organism's interaction with its environment influences brain development.

ACKNOWLEDGMENTS

The authors' research which is reported in this chapter was made possible by excellent colleagues who carried out much of the work. These included T. Parks, Z. Smith, L. Gray, W. Lippe, B. Ryals, and D. Born. S. Davis, S. Young, D. Durham, and E. Cantrell provided editorial help. The research was supported by funds from the Public Health Service (NINCDS Grants NS15478 and NS15395), from the Deafness Research Foundation, and from the Lions of Virginia Hearing Foundation. Dr. Gilbert Gottlieb provided insights and not-insignificant contributions toward the submission of the manuscript.

REFERENCES

Aitkin, L. M. & Moore, D. R. Inferior colliculus. II. Development of tuning characteristics and tonotopic organization in central nucleus of the neonatal cat. *Journal of Neurophysiology,* 1975, *38,* 1208–1216.

Anggaard, L. An electrophysiological study of the development of cochlear function in the rabbit. *Acta Otolaryngologica,* 1965, 203, 1–64.

Anson, B. J. Developmental anatomy of the ear. In M. M. Paparella & D. A. Shumrick (eds.), *Otolaryngology. Vol. I. Basic sciences and related disciplines,* Philadelphia: W. B. Saunders, 1973.

Anson, B. J. & Donaldson, J. A. *Surgical anatomy of the temporal bone.* Philadelphia: W. B. Saunders, 1981.

Born, D. E. & Rubel, E. W. Differential effects of age on transneuronal cell loss following cochlea removal in chickens. *Proceedings of the Midwinter Research Meeting of the Association for Research in Otolaryngology,* 1983. (Abstract)

Bredburg, G. Cellular pattern and nerve supply of the human organ of Corti. *Acta Otolaryngologica,* 1968, *236,* 1–135.

Brugge, J. F., Javel, E., & Kitzes, L. M. Signs of functional maturation of peripheral auditory system in discharge patterns of neurons in anteroventral cochlear nucleus of kittens. *Journal of Neurophysiology,* 1978, *41,* 1557–1579.

Brugge, J. F., Kitzes, L. M., & Javel, E. Postnatal development of frequency and intensity sensitivity of neurons in the anteroventral cochlear nucleus of kittens. *Hearing Research,* 1981, *5,* 217–229.

Carlier, E., Lenoir, M., & Pujol, R. Development of cochlear frequency selectivity tested by compound action potential tuning curves. *Hearing Research,* 1979, *1,* 197–201.

Carlier, E. & Pujol, R. Supra-normal sensitivity to ototoxic antibiotic of the developing rat cochlea. *Archives of Otorhinolaryngology,* 1980, *226,* 129–133.

Clopton, B. M. Neurophysiology of auditory deprivation. In R. J. Gorlin (ed.), *Morphogenesis and malformation of the ear.* New York: Alan R. Liss, 1980, pp. 271–288.

Coleman, J. R. & O'Connor, P. Effects of monaural and binaural sound deprivation on cell development in the anteroventral cochlear nucleus of rats. *Experimental Neurology*, 1979, *64*, 553–566.

Conlee, J. W. & Parks, T. N. Age- and position-dependent effects of monaural acoustic deprivation in nucleus magnocellularis of the chicken. *Journal of Comparative Neurology*, 1981, *202*, 373–384.

Dallos, P. & Cheatham, M. A. Compound action potential tuning curves. *Journal of Acoustical Society of America*, 1976, *59*, 591–597.

Ehret, G. & Romand, R. Postnatal development of absolute auditory thresholds in kittens. *Journal of Comparative and Physiological Psychology*, 1981, *95*, 304–311.

Feng, A. S. & Rogowski, B. A. Effects of monaural and binaural occlusion on the morphology of neurons in the medial superior olivary nucleus of the rat. *Brain Research*, 1980, *189*, 530–534.

Fermin, C. F. & Cohen, G. M. Developmental gradients in the embryonic chick's basilar papilla. *Proceedings of the Midwinter Meeting of the Association for Research in Otolaryngology.*, 1983. (Abstract)

Gottlieb, G. *Development of species identification in birds: an inquiry into the prenatal determinants of perception.* Chicago: University of Chicago Press, 1971. (a)

Gottlieb, G. Ontogenesis of sensory function in birds and mammals. In E. Tobach, L. A. Aronson, & E. Shaw (Eds.), *The biopsychology of development.* New York: Academic Press, 1971. (b)

Gottlieb, G. Development of species identification in ducklings: IV. Change in species-specific perception caused by auditory deprivation. *Journal of Comparative and Physiological Psychology*, 1978, *92*, 375–387.

Gray, L., Smith, Z. D. J., & Rubel, E. W. Developmental and experiential changes in dendritic symmetry. *Brain Research*, 1982, *244*, 360–364.

Hanson, D. G. & Ulvestad, R. F. (Eds.) Otitis media and child development: Speech language and education. *Annals of Otology, Rhinology and Laryngology* (Supp. 60), 1979, *88*, 1–111.

Harris, D. M. & Dallos, P. Action potential suppression, tuning curves and thresholds: comparison with single fiber data. *Hearing Research*, 1979, *1*, 133–154.

Harris, D. M. & Dallos, P. CM measurements of the place/frequency code in developing gerbils. *Proceedings of the Midwinter Meeting of the Association for Research in Otolaryngology*, 1983. (Abstract)

Himelfarb, M. Z., Popelka, G. R., & Shanon, E. Typanometry in normal neonates. *Journal of Speech and Hearing Research*, 1979, *22*, 179–191.

Jackson, H., Hackett, J. T., & Rubel, E. W. Organization and development of brain stem auditory nuclei in the chick: ontogeny of postsynaptic responses. *Journal of Comparative Neurology*, 1982, *210*, 80–86.

Jackson, H. & Parks, T. N. Functional synapse elimination in the developing avian cochlear nucleus with simultaneous reduction in cochlear-nerve axon branching. *Journal of Neuroscience*, 1982, *2*, 1736–1743.

Jacobson, M. *Developmental Neurobiology.* New York: Plenum Press, 1978.

Jharsdoefer, R. Congenital atresia of the ear. *Laryngoscope*, (Supp. 13), 1978, *88*, 1–48.

Jhaveri, S. & Morest, D. K. Sequential alterations of neuronal architecture in nucleus magnocellularis of the developing chicken: A Golgi study. *Neuroscience*, 1982, *7*, 837–853.

Kerr, L. M., Ostapoff, E. M., & Rubel, E. W. Influence of acoustic experience on the ontogeny of frequency generalization gradients in the chicken. *Journal of Experimental Psychology; Animal Behavior Processes*, 1979, *5*, 97–115.

Lenoir, M. & Pujol, R. Sensitive period to acoustic trauma in the rat pup cochlea: Histological findings. *Acta Otolaryngologica*, 1980, *89*, 317–322.

Levi-Montalcini, R. The development of the acousticovestibular centers in the chick embryo in the absence of the afferent root fibers and of descending fiber tracts. *Journal of Comparative Neurology*, 1949, *91*, 209–241.

Lippe, W. & Rubel, E. W. Development of the place principle: Tonotopic organization. *Science,* 1983, *219,* 514–516.

Marty, R. Développement postnatal des réponses sensorielles du cortex cérébral chez le chat et le lapin. *Archives d'Anatomie Microscopique et de Morphologie Expérimentale,* 1962, *51,* 129–264.

Moore, D. R. & Irvine, D. R. F. The development of some peripheral and central auditory responses in the neonatal cat. *Brain Research,* 1979, *163,* 49–59.

Noden, D. M. The migration and cytodifferentiation of cranial neural crest cells. In R. M. Pratt & R. L. Christiansen (Eds.) *Current research trends in prenatal craniofacial development.* New York: Elsevier, 1980, pp 3–25.

Nordeen, K. W., Killackey, H. P., & Kitzes, L. M. Reorganization of ascending projections to the inferior colliculus following unilateral cochlear ablations in the neonatal gerbil, meriones unguiculatus. *Journal of Comparative Neurology,* 1983, *214,* 144–153.

Northern, J. L. & Downs, M. P. *Hearing in children,* Baltimore, Maryland: Williams and Wilkins Co., 1974.

Parks, T. N. Afferent influences on the development of the brain stem auditory nuclei of the chicken: otocyst ablation. *Journal of Comparative Neurology,* 1979, *183,* 665–678.

Parks, T. N. & Rubel, E. W. Organization and development of brain stem auditory nuclei of the chicken: organization of projections from n. magnocellularis to n. laminaris. *Journal of Comparative Neurology,* 1975, *164,* 435–448.

Pujol, R., Carlier, E., & Devigne, C. Different patterns of cochlear innervation during the development of the kitten. *Journal of Comparative Neurology,* 1978, *177,* 529–535.

Pujol, R. & Hilding, D. Anatomy and physiology of the onset of auditory function. *Acta Otolaryngologica,* 1973, *76,* 1–10.

Pujol, R. & Marty, R. Structural and physiological relationships of the maturing auditory system. In L. Jilek & S. Trojan (Eds.) *Ontogenesis of the Brain,* Prague: Charles University Press, 1968.

Pujol, R. & Marty, R. Postnatal maturation of the cochlea of the cat. *Journal of Comparative Neurology,* 1970, *139,* 115–125.

Rebillard, G. & Rubel, E. W. Electrophysiological study of the maturation of auditory responses from the inner ear of the chick. *Brain Research,* 1981, *229,* 15–23.

Rebillard, G. Ryals, B. M., & Rubel, E. W. Relationship between hair cell loss on the chick basilar papilla and threshold shift after acoustic overstimulation. *Hearing Research,* 1982, *8,* 77–81.

Relkin, E. M. & Saunders, J. C. Displacement of the malleus in neonatal golden hamsters. *Acta Otolaryngologica,* 1980, *90,* 6–15.

Retzius, G. *Das Gehorogan der Wirbeltiere. II: Das Gehororgan der Reptilien, der Vogel and Saugetiere.* Stockholm: Samson and Wallin, 1884.

Rodieck, R. W. & Smith, P. S. Slow dark discharge rhythms of cat retinal ganglion cells. *Journal of Neurophysiology,* 1966, *29,* 933–942.

Romand, R. & Romand, M.-R. Myelination kinetics of spiral ganglion cells in kittens. *Journal of Comparative Neurology,* 1982, *204,* 1–5.

Rubel, E. W. A comparison of somatotopic organization in sensory neocortex in newborn kittens and adult cats. *Journal of Comparative Neurology,* 1971, *143,* 447–480.

Rubel, E. W. Ontogeny of structure and function in the vertebrate auditory system. In M. Jacobson (Ed.) *Handbook of Sensory Physiology, Development of Sensory Systems* (Vol. IX), New York: Springer-Verlag, 1978.

Rubel, E. W & Parks, T. N. Organization and development of brain stem auditory nuclei of the chicken: Tonotopic organization of n. magnocellularis and n. laminaris *Journal of Comparative Neurology,* 1975, *164,* 435–448.

Rubel, E. W & Ryals, B. M. Patterns of hair cell loss in chick basilar papilla after intense auditory stimulation: Exposure duration and survival time. *Acta Otolaryngologica,* 1982, *93,* 31–41.

Rubel, E. W & Ryals, B. M. Development of the place principle: Acoustic trauma. *Science,* 1983, *219,* 512–514.

Rubel, E. W, Smith, D. J., & Miller, L. C. Organization and development of brain stem auditory nuclei of the chicken: Ontogeny of n. magnocellularis and n. laminiaris. *Journal of Comparative Neurology,* 1976, *166,* 469–490.

Ruben, R. J. Development of the inner ear of the mouse: A radioautographic study of terminal mitoses. *Acta Otolaryngologica,* 1967, *220,* 1–44.

Ruben, R. J. The synthesis of DNA and RNA in the developing inner ear. *Laryngoscope,* 1969, *79,* 1546–1556.

Ryals, B. M. & Rubel, E. W. Patterns of hair cell loss in chick basilar papilla after intense auditory stimulation: Frequency organization. *Acta Otolaryngologica,* 1982, *93,* 205–210.

Ryan, A. F., Woolf, N. K., & Sharp, F. R. Functional ontogeny in the central auditory pathway of the mongolian gerbil: sequential development and supranormal responsiveness indicated by 2-deoxyglucose uptake. *Proceedings of the Midwinter Meeting of the Association for Research in Otolaryngology,* 1982. (Abstract)

Saunders, J. C. & Bock, G. R. Influences of early auditory trauma on auditory development. In G. Gottlieb (Ed.) *Studies on the development of behavior and the nervous system: early influences.* New York: Academic Press, 1978, *4,* 249–287.

Saunders, J.C., Coles, R. B., & Gates, G. R. The development of auditory evoked responses on the cochlea and cochlear nuclei of the chick. *Brain Research,* 1973, *63,* 59–74.

Saunders, J. C., Dolgin, K. G., & Lowry, L. D. The maturation of frequency selectivity in C57BL/6J mice studied with auditory evoked response tuning curves. *Brain Research,* 1980, *187,* 69–79.

Saunders, J. C., & Kaltenbach, J. A., & Relkin, E. M. The structural and functional development of the outer and middle ear. In R. Romand, & R. Marty (Eds.) *Development of Auditory and Vestibular System.* New York: Academic Press, 1983, In Press.

Schweitzer, L. & Cant, N. B. Development of the cochlear innervation of the dorsal cochlear nucleus of the hamster. *Journal of Comparative Neurology,* 1984, *225,* 228–243.

Shnerson, A., Devigne, C., & Pujol, R. Age-related changes in the C57BL/6J mouse cochlea. II. Ultrastructural findings. *Developmental Brain Research,* 1982, *2,* 77–88.

Smith, Z. D. J. Organization and development of brain stem auditory nuclei of the chicken: Dendritic development in n. laminaris. *Journal of Comparative Neurology,* 1981, *203,* 309–333.

Smith, Z. D. J., Gray, L., & Rubel, E. W. Afferent influences on brain stem auditory nuclei of the chicken: n. laminaris dendritic length following monaural acoustic deprivation. *Journal of Comparative Neurology,* 1983, *220,* 199–205.

Tilney, L. G. & Saunders, J. C. Actin filaments, stereocilia, and hair cells of the bird cochlea. 1. Length, number, width, and distribution of stereocilia of each hair cell are related to the position of the hair cell on the cochlea. *Journal of Cell Biology,* 1983, *96,* 807–821.

Tonndorf, J. Bone conduction: studies in experimental animals. *Acta Otolaryngologica,* 1966, (Supp. 213), 1–232.

Trune, D. R. Influence of neonatal cochlear removal on the development of mouse cochlear nucleus. I. Number, size, and density of its neurons. *Journal of Comparative Neurology,* 1982, *209,* 409–424. (a)

Trune, D. R. Influence of neonatal cochlear removal on the development of mouse cochlear nucleus. II. Dendritic morphology of its neurons. *Journal of Comparative Neurology,* 1982, *209:*425–434. (b)

Van de Water, T. R., Li, C. W., Ruben, R. J., & Shea, C. A., Ontogenetic aspects of mammalian inner ear development. In R. J. Gorlin (Ed.) *Morphogenesis and Malformation of the Ear.* New York: Alan R. Liss, 1980. (a)

Van de Water, T. R., Maderson, P. F. A., & Jaskoll, T. F. The morphogenesis of the middle and external ear. In R. J. Gorlin (Ed.) *Morphogenesis and Malformation of the Ear.* New York: Alan R. Liss, 1980. (b)

Van de Water, T. R., & Ruben, R. J. Organogenesis of the ear. In R. Hinchcliffe, & D. Harrison (Eds.) *Scientific Foundation of Otolaryngology,* London: W. Heineman Medical Book, Ltd., 1976.

von Békésky, G. *Experiments in Hearing.* New York: McGraw-Hill, 1960.

Wada, T. Anatomical and physiological studies on the growth of the inner ear of the albino rat. *American Anatomical Memoranda,* 1923, *10,* 1-74.

Walker, D., Grimwade, J. & Wood, C. Intrauterine noise: a component of the fetal environment. *American Journal of Obstetrics Gynecology,* 1971, *109,* 91-95.

Webster, D. B. & Webster, M. Effects of neonatal conductive hearing loss on brainstem auditory nuclei. *Annals of Otolaryngology, Rhinology, and Laryngology,* 1979, *88,* 684-688.

Webster, D. B. & Webster, M. Mouse brainstem auditory nuclei development. *Annals of Otolaryngology, Rhinology, and Laryngology,* 1980, *89,* (Supp. 68), 254-256.

Weiss, T. F., Mulroy, M. J., Turner, R. G., & Pike, C. L. Tuning of single fibers in the cochlear nerve of the alligator lizard: relation to receptor morphology. *Brain Research,* 1976, *115,* 71-90.

Wiesel, T. N. & Hubel, D. H. Effects of visual deprivation on morphology and physiology of cells in the cat's lateral geniculate body. *Journal of Neurophysiology,* 1963, *26,* 978-993.

Woolsey, C. N. & Walzl, E. M. Topical projection of nerve fibers from local regions of the cochlea in the cerebral cortex of the cat. *Bulletin Johns Hopkins Hospital,* 1942, *71,* 315-344.

Yntema, C. L. An analysis of induction of the ear from foreign ectoderm in the salamander embryo. *Journal of Experimental Zoology,* 1950, *113,* 211-244.

4

ENVIRONMENTAL CONSTRAINTS AND THE NATURAL CONTEXT OF BEHAVIOR: GROUNDS FOR AN ECOLOGICAL APPROACH TO THE STUDY OF INFANT PERCEPTION

Timothy D. Johnston

University of North Carolina at Greensboro

INTRODUCTION

199.6.

Organisms, especially the human organism, are exceedingly complex systems, and much of the success of the natural sciences in understanding how they function has come from a systematic application of reductionist methodology to their analysis. When a system is too complex to be understood in its entirety, the reductionist approach is to identify simpler subsystems and use experimental techniques to study their relatively simpler functioning, and the ways in which they interact, so as to determine the operation of the more complex system that they comprise. Thus, if we want to understand how a growing organism attains its mature form, for example, we can reduce the problem to a number of less complex (though still daunting) problems: How do morphogenetic fields interact to produce a hand with five digits? How do muscles and nerves form orderly connections in the arm? How do the various tissues differentiate? How do genes regulate the production of different proteins throughout development? and so forth. This procedure successively reduces the initial problem, posed at the level of the organism, to a series of problems at lower (more reduced) levels, in this example the levels of organs, tissues, and genes. Since organisms develop as the result of interactions with their environments, we can apply the reductionist program to ask a parallel series of questions about the environmental aspects of development. If we are interested in the developmental contribution of the infant's social environment, for example, we might ask: How do early mother-infant interactions contribute to the growing child's social competence? How do dialogues with the mother influence the child's acquisition of concepts that may underlie later social behavior? Do the words that the mother uses to communicate with her child affect the rate at which vocabulary is learned? How does auditory experience affect the perception of acoustic features in the speech stream? and so forth.

No one today needs convincing of the power of the reductionist method,[1] but we do often fail to appreciate that, like most powerful methodologies, it must be applied with care if it is to yield understanding as well as data. One of the most important requirements of the reductionist approach is that we recognize the importance of contextual constraints in analyzing the operation of a system. Briefly, this idea rests on the observation that no natural system exists in a vacuum; rather, each system is embedded in a context that plays an important part in determining its normal mode of operation. To understand the system, we must also understand the context that constrains its behavior. This principle holds at all levels of biological organization; the level of particular interest in this discussion is that at which the system under analysis is an organism (specifically a human infant), and the context is thus its external physical, biological, and social environment. The question I want to address is this: What methodological constraints must we impose on our analyses of the complex system that underlies an infant's perceptual capabilities? The position for which I shall argue is that these constraints must include, inter alia, ecological constraints on the kinds of stimuli that we use in the analysis.

The contrary position, and one that has, I think, been preeminent in studies of perception in the past, is that understanding the mechanisms of perception requires only an analysis of the organism that is doing the perceiving, not of the environment that is being perceived. That position has drawn criticism from psychologists such as Egon Brunswik (1952, 1956) and J. J. Gibson (1966, 1979), both of whom have argued, albeit from different philosophical positions, that the nature of environments is as crucial to an understanding of perception as is the nature of organisms. The basis for claims of this kind lies in a recognition of the unique relationship that exists between an organism and its environment by virtue of their joint evolutionary history. Evolution has

---

[1] The reductionist *method,* employed in one form or another by all scientists, is not to be confused with the reductionist *philosophy,* according to which phenomena at one level of description or analysis are claimed to be "nothing but" events occurring at some other, more reduced level (usually that at which the claimant's own professional expertise lies). The reductionist method is a heuristic; its power lies in the fact that it works, not in any presumption that it embodies some fundamental truth about the nature of the universe.

forged the organism and its environment into a single integrated system, the ecosystem, and it is the properties of the ecosystem, rather than those of the organism alone, that hold the key to a successful analysis of perception.

THE IMPORTANCE OF CONTEXT IN THE SIMPLEST OF SYSTEMS: A CAUTIONARY TALE

Before elaborating this general idea, and drawing from it some methodological principles for the study of infant perception, I would like to present some findings from a field very far removed from psychology. The methodological concerns of molecular biologists may seem of little direct relevance to the study of human development. However, molecular biology is perhaps the epitome of reductionism in the life sciences, and it certainly provides some of the greatest success stories of the reductionist methodology. Thus, caveats for the application of reductionism that emerge from the findings of molecular biology may serve as object lessons in caution for other fields (such as psychology) where the successes of reductionism are less dramatic, and its application more problematical.

The findings of interest come from studies of the role of the protein cytochrome c in the mechanisms of cellular respiration. Aerobic cellular respiration in eukaryotic (nucleated) organisms involves the oxidation of carbohydrate molecules to produce carbon dioxide and water. The energy that is released during this process is used to synthesize ATP, which can be transported to sites in the cell for release of the energy contained in its phosphate bonds. The synthesis of ATP involves, among many other steps, the oxidation of cytochrome c by the enzyme cytochrome oxidase. Cytochrome c is a relatively small protein, consisting of about 100 amino acid residues, and it is one of the most thoroughly studied of all biological macromolecules. The amino acid sequences of cytochromes c from about 80 different eukaryotic organisms (ranging from yeast to *Homo sapiens*) have been determined, revealing considerable diversity in their structures, despite their common role in the mechanisms of cellular respiration. Until quite recently, in vitro studies indicated that this structural diversity was of no functional significance: All cytochromes c, even those that differed in a goodly proportion of their amino acids, behaved identically in reactions with cytochrome oxidase and other enzymes involved in cellular respiration (Smith, Nava, & Margoliash, 1973). Because of this apparent identity of function, the structural diversity of cytochromes c was held to provide strong support for the neutral theory of molecular evolution (King & Jukes, 1969). This theory holds that many, if not most, of the transformations that are undergone by a taxonomically widely-distributed type of molecule (such as cytochrome c or hemoglobin) in the course of its evolution are not of any selective significance. They occur because of the random fixation in the population of amino acid substitutions by genetic drift and other nonselective factors.

However, as work on the function of cytochrome c and the details of its structural diversity among organisms progressed, a rather different story began to emerge, and it is this story that is germane to my discussion. The finding that cytochromes *c* are functionally indistinguishable came from experiments using conveniently available biochemical reagants, such as cytochrome oxidase purified from beef heart, *regardless of the species from which the cytochrome* c *under study had been obtained.* When the activity of several cytochromes *c* was reexamined using instead biochemical milieux characteristic of the species in question, a large amount of functional diversity appeared. From these studies, it rapidly became apparent that the structure of cytochrome *c* from a particular species is exquisitely adapted to the structure of other molecules with which it normally interacts in its species-typical cellular context (Margoliash, 1980). The nature of this adaptation is complex and can only be fully appreciated by reference to detailed studies of the reaction kinetics of cytochromes *c* under various experimental conditions (see Margoliash, 1980; Margoliash, Ferguson-Miller, Kang, & Brautigan, 1976). A general point of some interest, however, is that the difference in the behavior of a cytochrome *c* under species-typical and species-atypical conditions is not simply quantitative (more activity rather than less). Instead, there are important qualitative differences that have had substantial theoretical consequences for our understanding of the mechanisms of cellular respiration and their evolution (Margoliash, 1980).

The implications of this rather far-flung digression are, I hope, clear. In order to understand the operation of even so relatively simple a system as a single protein molecule, it is essential to base one's analyses on the context provided by the conditions under which the system has evolved and normally functions. If the existence and nature of these constraining conditions are not appreciated, both in theory and in empirical practice, even the best-designed experiments may produce data but little understanding.

TWO PROCEDURAL STANCES FOR INVESTIGATING NATURAL SYSTEMS

When we begin the analysis of a biological system, whether it be a cytochrome molecule or a human infant, we can adopt one of two different procedural stances. One, which is being advocated in this paper, may be called the "ecological stance." It holds that the system, as a natural biological entity, stands in a set of particular, unique relationships to the various other natural systems that comprise its environment. These external relationships, on the ecological view, are as much a part of the system as are the internal relationships among its various components. No scientist supposes that one could alter the internal relationships of a system at will, and claim to be analyzing the same system, because the nature of those relationships is essential to the very definition of the system under analysis. The ecological stance simply extends that point of view to include the external as well as the internal relationships of a system. On this view, understanding the system means explicating its behavior in terms of both sets of relationships: Just as we attempt to preserve the integrity of a system's internal relationships during the analysis, so we must try to preserve its external relationships as well, within the limits imposed by the questions we are asking. (This qualification is important, for nothing in these remarks should be construed to mean that the external relationships of a system are experimentally inviolable. The experimental neurophysiologist, for example, respects the functional integrity of the nervous system, even as he or she alters the relationships among its parts to understand how they interact. The experimental naturalist extends the same respect to the relationships between the organism and the outside world, while still recognizing the necessity of changing those relationships in search of understanding.)

The alternative to the ecological stance may be called the "system properties stance." It holds that the system is an isolable entity that possesses a set of properties intrinsic to it. That is, the properties are contained within the system's physical boundaries and determine the ways in which the system behaves with respect to its surroundings. On this view, understanding the system means explicating these intrinsic properties without reference to any particular set of external conditions. The properties are part of the system, and, when we move the system from one situation to another, we move the properties along with it. Some properties are revealed only by special (non-natural) conditions, and the more such conditions we employ in our analyses, the more of the system's properties we will discover.

To those who adopt the ecological stance, the constraints imposed by the system's natural context are essential to its understanding; indeed, in an important sense, those constraints are *part* of the system. To those who adopt the system properties stance, the constraints are simply a nuisance, obscuring the fundamental intrinsic properties of the system, and the aim of experimentation is to remove the constraints so as to uncover the full range of system properties. Those who adopt the system properties stance are sometimes described as being interested in how the system *can* behave, in explicating its full range of potentialities and capabilities under all conceivable circumstances. Those who adopt the ecological stance, on the other hand, are primarily interested in how the system *does* behave, in explicating its capabilities in relation only to those conditions under which the system actually exists, not in relation to those under which it might exist if things were different (e.g., McCall, 1977). If these two procedural stances led to the same understanding of how systems work, then the distinction between them would be of little or no practical significance. In fact, as we have seen in reviewing the case of the cytochrome *c* molecule, they can lead to quite different accounts of system function, and it therefore becomes of some importance to make a principled choice between the two. In the next section, I shall consider the grounds for choosing the ecological stance in the analysis of complex biological systems. *also p. 104.*

SYSTEMS AND THEIR CONTEXTS IN JOINT EVOLUTION

As the work of Margoliash and his colleagues demonstrates, the functional relationship between the cytochrome *c* molecule and its normal cellular context is a very intimate one, and that intimacy is of primary importance for an understanding of this molecular system. Such intimacy is not, of course, fortuitous;

it is the outcome of a long evolutionary history during which this molecular system has been selected on the basis of its behavior under the conditions provided by the context. Natural selection among structural variants of the cytochrome molecule takes place in reference to functional criteria specified by the context in which those variants exist, not in reference to some abstract criteria of "biochemical function" that might be specified independently of particular cellular milieux. In other words, the way in which a system such as the cytochrome molecule functions must be specified with reference to a context, namely that which has shaped its function in the course of evolution.

It is evident that a system can display functional properties other than those it exhibits in its normal context. Indeed, for suitably complex systems there must be an indefinitely large array of such properties, which can be revealed by subjecting the system to various kinds of (non-natural) experimental manipulations. Those properties represent degrees of freedom in the system's behavior that are normally "frozen out," or constrained, by the context in which the system functions. Defining the context automatically defines, by implication, a set of constraints on the system, and those constraints are part and parcel of its behavior under normal conditions. They are not something externally imposed on the "true" or "fundamental" properties of the system; indeed, if we are to define any set of properties as "fundamental," at least in a biological sense, it should be the set that has evolved jointly with the context provided by the system's normal environment.

The points that I have been making hold, by extension, for all natural systems of any degree of complexity, and the principle of contextual constraint is available to guide the analysis of organismic systems as well as their component molecules. At the organismic level of complexity, the context is provided by the organism's external environment, that set of physical, biological, and social factors with which it interacts in the course of its development and behavior (Mason & Langenheim, 1957). An understanding of an organism's behavior as an aspect of its biology can only be gained with reference to the set of constraints supplied by its environment.

If we adopt the ecological stance in our analyses of perception and behavior, and accept the evolutionary relationship between the animal and its environment as an important and relevant datum, then we shall be led to ask experimental questions that are quite different from those that might arise from the system properties stance described earlier. In particular, we will be led to consider carefully the *nature* of the animal's environment as an empirical problem for description and analysis, and to use the results of our descriptions to constrain the design of experiments on the various aspects of perception or behavior in which we are interested. This is a perspective that is lacking in a substantial proportion of the work on which our current understanding of perception and behavior is based, most of which has adopted the system properties stance, considering the animal (or infant) as an isolable system possessing certain properties that are to be described and explained.

ENVIRONMENTS AS OBJECTS FOR STUDY

199.6

The ecological stance for the study of natural systems is merely an expression of good intention unless some effort is made to investigate the nature of the external relationships that exist between the system under analysis and its natural context. When the system in question is an organism, that means that the external environment comes under scrutiny as an object of study. The general problems of environmental description are much more substantial than is commonly realized, and they have received rather little attention in the literature, even from those scientists (such as behavioral ecologists) who might be expected to take them most seriously. Within the scope of this paper, I cannot attempt to deal with them at any length, but I would like to mention briefly two problems of environmental description with which the ecological stance must come to terms, and that are particularly relevant for a comparative developmental approach to the study of perception and behavior.

Environments are Species-specific

There is no such thing as "the environment" whose description will serve for all organisms that might be studied. Members of each species interact with the physical and biological world in different ways that reflect their varying capabilities and requirements, and the sets of relationships that they maintain with the world are therefore different. The environments of a man and of a house fly are radically different, even though they often inhabit the same portions of the physical world, and any understanding of their perception and behavior must take these differences into account. Because the description of environments has traditionally not been seen as an empirical problem in the behavioral sciences, the tendency has been to consider "the environment" in a quite general sense, for example as made up of "stimuli" without any specification of the nature and organization of those stimuli in the environments of particular species.

The Environment Changes in Development

As an animal grows and develops, its relationship to the external world changes, so that its effective environment (the physical, biological, and social factors with which it interacts; Mason & Langenheim, 1957) also changes. These changes come about in a number of ways. During development, the animal may inhabit different kinds of habitats with radically different characteristics—consider, for example, the change from prenatal to postnatal life in a mammal, or from aquatic to terrestrial life in an amphibian. On the other hand, the animal may stay in the same kind of habitat but interact with it in different ways as it changes in size, strength, behavioral skills, and physiological requirements throughout development (Oppenheim, 1980, 1981). The ecologically salient characteristics of the world are quite different for a 2-day-old duckling and for its mother, and the same applies to the young and adults of most animal species. In the terminology of the early ethologist Jakob von Uexküll (1909, 1957), the *Umwelt* of an organism changes as the organism itself changes in development. One of the most formidable challenges for an ecological approach to the analysis of perceptual and behavioral development is to explicate the concept of environment in a way that incorporates an appropriately dynamic view of the changing relationship between the developing animal and the world in which it lives (Johnston, 1982).

THE ECOLOGICAL CONTEXT OF ANIMAL BEHAVIOR: TWO EXAMPLES

In my earlier discussion of the molecular biology of the cytochrome *c* molecule, I indicated the ways in which biochemists have been misled as a result of insufficient attention to the natural context of the system whose behavior they sought to understand. Let me now consider two similar examples from the behavioral literature to illustrate the importance of an ecological perspective at the organismic level. Both of these examples involve studies whose aim was to evaluate the behavioral and perceptual capabilities of an animal, and that permit a comparison of ecological and nonecological approaches to that problem. They complement each other, for while one example shows how an animal's capabilities may be *over*-estimated if the natural context of its behavior is not appreciated, the other shows how they may be *under*-estimated as a result of the same neglect.

Visual Species Identification in Neonatal Ducklings

If a young duckling is exposed to a visually conspicuous object shortly after hatching it will subsequently follow that object in preference to others that differ from it in appearance; this well-documented phenomenon is known as visual imprinting (Lorenz, 1935; Bateson, 1966). Because the first object that a duckling normally sees after hatching is its mother, and because adult ducks of different species differ in their visual characteristics, it has generally been assumed that imprinting is the developmental process by which ducklings come to recognize members of their own species under natural conditions. However, almost all studies of imprinting have employed highly artificial objects as "mother surrogates," rather than those objects (namely, adult waterfowl) that the duckling normally encounters and, by hypothesis, distinguishes among. Such artificial objects tend to be much simpler in form than do natural ones. For example, some recent investigators (e.g., Bateson & Jaeckel, 1976) have used flashing, rotating lights in studies of imprinting, stimuli that bear no resemblance to a mother duck, but whose physical appearance can be described in a few simple terms and whose presentation can readily be controlled under experimental conditions. To see whether the results obtained using such artificial imprinting objects could in fact be generalized to the natural situation (as the imprinting hypothesis of visual species identification requires), Johnston and Gottlieb (1981) examined the effects of using adult stuffed waterfowl as surrogates, in an experimental design that otherwise followed that of traditional imprinting studies.

Incubator-reared ducklings (*Anas platyrhynchos*) were given a single 20-minute exposure trial at about 24 hours posthatching, during which they followed one of five different models as the model moved around a circular arena 178 cm in diameter. Two of the models (a green ball and a red-and-white striped box) were of the artificial sort traditionally used in studies of imprinting; the other three were stuffed replicas of adult female waterfowl of different species: a mallard (*Anas platyrhynchos*), a pintail (*Anas acuta*), and a redhead (*Aythya americana*). During the exposure trial, the model emitted a recording of the mallard maternal call normally given by the mother duck in the context of the ducklings' first exposure to her. Subsequently, each subject was given two 10-minute test trials (at 48 and 60 hours posthatching) during which it was presented with a choice between the familiar imprinting object and a different, unfamiliar object. During the test trials, both models were silent, to permit an assessment of visual preferences formed as a result of the earlier exposure trial. Preferences were determined from the length of time the duckling spent following each of the models during the test trial: If it followed one model for more than twice as long as the other, then it was assigned a preference for that model. Other measures of preference are reported in the original publication and all of them support the conclusions presented here. The results of the choice tests are shown in Tables 1 and 2. When one of the test objects was of the highly artificial type normally used in imprinting experiments (Table 1), the ducklings showed a strong and persistent preference for the familiar object, as predicted by imprinting theory. However, when both models were the natural stuffed replicas, most of the groups did not show a preference for the familiar model (Table 2). Only that group trained with the mallard and tested for a preference between the mallard and the pintail models showed a preference for the familiar model (the mallard). None of the other groups showed such a preference, even when, in the case of one group, the length of the training trial was extended to 125 minutes, and then to 24 hours (Table 3).

The conclusion that visual imprinting is the developmental process by which young ducklings normally form an attachment to their mother is called in question by these results. It had been reached on the basis of experiments that overestimated the ducklings' abilities to discriminate among natural objects by using artificial objects to evaluate those abilities, and then generalizing to the natural case. By using a more naturalistic methodology, we were able to show that important questions remain to be answered about the role of imprinting in the overall process of social development in ducklings, which now seems to be a more complex phenomenon than it appeared to be on the basis of experiments that ignored the normal context of development.

Foraging Behavior in Hummingbirds

The study of foraging behavior in animals has always been of interest to behavioral ecologists, but of late it has come under scrutiny by psychologists

Table 1. Results of Imprinting Experiments Using Artificial Models

N	Age	n Responding	Prefer Familiar	Prefer Unfamiliar	No Preference
1. Trained with Mallard; tested with Mallard vs. Red Box:					
30	48 h	29	27***	1	1
	60 h	30	30***	0	0
2. Trained with Red Box; tested with Red Box vs. Mallard:					
30	48 h	30	26***	2	2
	60 h	30	24***	3	3
3. Trained with Red Box; tested with Red Box vs. Green Ball:					
19	48 h	18	14**	2	2
	60 h	19	18***	0	1
4. Trained with Green Ball; tested with Green Ball vs. Red Box:					
19	48 h	15	13**	2	0
	60 h	17	14***	0	3

Group preferences tested for significance by the binomial test.
*** $p < 0.001$; ** $p < 0.01$ (2-tailed)
Data from Johnston and Gottlieb (1981), reproduced by permission.

Table 2. Results of Imprinting Experiments Using Natural Models

N	Age	n Responding	Prefer Familiar	Prefer Unfamiliar	No Preference
1. Trained with Mallard; tested with Mallard vs. Redhead:					
29	48 h	29	13	14	2
	60 h	29	16	12	1
2. Trained with Redhead; tested with Redhead vs. Mallard:					
30	48 h	30	13	14	3
	60 h	30	18	10	2
3. Trained with Mallard; tested with Mallard vs. Pintail:					
33	48 h	33	21*	7	5
	60 h	33	20*	8	5
4. Trained with Pintail; tested with Pintail vs. Mallard:					
30	48 h	29	13	16	0
	60 h	29	12	16	1

Group preferences tested for significance by the binomial test.
* $p < 0.05$ (2-tailed)
Data from Johnston and Gottlieb (1981), reproduced by permission.

Table 3. Results of Imprinting Experiments Using Long Exposure To Natural Models (Mallard & Redhead)

N	Age	n Responding	Prefer Mallard	Prefer Redhead	No Preference
1. Two hours training with Mallard:					
14	48 h	14	5	8	1
	60 h	14	8	5	1
2. Twenty-four hours exposure to Mallard:					
15	48 h	14	5	8	1
	60 h	15	5	6	4

Data from Johnston and Gottlieb (1981); reproduced by permission.

as well (Kamil & Sargeant, 1981), for it seems to pose a number of psychologically interesting questions regarding the perceptual and cognitive abilities of animals. For example, the food of many animals is widely distributed in space and time, and its efficient utilization poses difficult problems for the organization of a foraging strategy, involving spatial orientation and memory, searching patterns, and the identification and utilization of food items. Nectar-feeding birds, such as hummingbirds, face particularly interesting problems of this kind. Their hovering mode of flight is energetically very expensive, and this expense must be offset by ensuring that their foraging strategy is correspondingly efficient. Each of the flowers on which they feed produces only a small amount of nectar, which takes some time to be replenished after it has been consumed. Thus, a hummingbird foraging on an inflorescence containing many flowers will be most efficient if it visits each flower only once during a foraging bout, rather than revisiting depleted flowers before they have had time to replenish their nectar supply. This requires that the bird remember which flowers it has just visited, a problem whose complexity is affected by both the number of flowers and their spatial distribution within the inflorescence. Pyke (1981) used artificial flowers arranged in a variety of ways to investigate the effect of spatial distribution within an inflorescence on the foraging efficiency of hummingbirds (*Selasphorus* spp.) foraging on the scarlet gilia (*Ipomopsis aggregata*). One arrangement was designed to mimic as closely as possible the natural arrangement of flowers in the *Ipomopsis* inflorescence, which form an irregular spiral around a vertical stalk. Two other artificial arrangements were simplified modifications of the natural one: a regular spiral of flowers, and a linear array. Individual hummingbirds were observed foraging on the three arrangements, and their relative efficiencies are compared in Figure 1, which plots the incidence of revisiting the same flower against the total number of visits in a foraging bout, for each of the three spatial arrangements. The 45° straight line indicates maximum efficiency (no flower revisited during a bout), with less efficient foraging appearing as points below the line. It can be seen that the birds' most efficient foraging was on the "natural" inflorescences (about 82% efficiency during the longest foraging bouts), whereas foraging on the simplest, linear arrangement was the least efficient of the three (about 45% efficiency).

This is an interesting and counterintuitive result. It might be expected that the simple and regular arrangement of the linear inflorescence would permit the most efficient foraging, since all the bird need do is to move in a straight line from one flower to the next. More complex arrangements, on this view, would make greater demands on the bird's limited cognitive abilities, and so produce less efficient foraging. In fact, what we see in these results is an increase in efficiency with increasing closeness to the natural arrangement, even though this arrangement is the most complex of the three.

We saw in the previous example of imprinting that an exclusive reliance on simple, artificial conditions has lead to an over-estimation of the perceptual abilities of ducklings vis-à-vis the natural context of filial behavior. In the present example, such reliance would have lead to an under-estimation of the

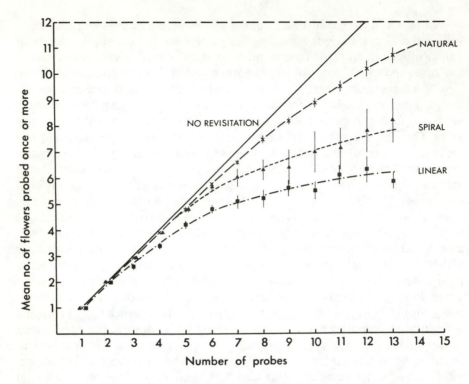

Figure 1. The relative efficiencies of hummingbirds foraging on differently arranged artificial inflorescences. From Pyke (1981); reproduced by permission.

spatial memory abilities of hummingbirds vis-à-vis the natural context of foraging. The lesson to be drawn from these examples is that, although artificially simplified experimental conditions can be more precisely described and more readily controlled, they can also mislead the investigator as to the capabilities of his or her subjects.

THE CONTEXT OF DEVELOPING SYSTEMS

The main aim of this volume to to consider methodological strategies for assessing the perceptual capacities of infants, rather than strategies for assessing their development. However, most workers in the field of infant perception must have at least a passing interest in problems of development, and so it seems appropriate to say a few words about the implications of the ecological stance for the analysis of developmental problems. The particular problem on which I shall focus is the question of determining how experience contributes to the development of some behavioral or perceptual capability of interest: the ability to reach for the closer of two visually presented objects, or the ability to perceive phonetic distinctions among speech stimuli, for instance. Since we

cannot control the experience of human infants in the way we can that of experimental animals, such problems are notoriously difficult to solve. By discussing a few results from research on the development of animal perception, I
hope the importance of taking ecological considerations seriously will be made
apparent to those investigators who are able to devise techniques for studying
related problems in the field of infant development.   *152.21*

The young of many species of precocial birds, such as the mallard (*Anas
platyrhynchos*) or wood duck (*Aix sponsa*), respond immediately after hatching
to a recording of the maternal assembly call of their species by approaching the
source of the call and remaining close to it (Gottlieb, 1971). The critical acoustic features of the call to which the young birds respond have been analyzed
and found to be different in the two species (see chapter by Gottlieb, this volume). In the case of the mallard, the critical feature is the repetition rate of the
notes in the call, normally about 4 notes/sec; a feature of secondary importance is the presence of a high frequency component in the spectrum of the
call. In the case of the wood duck, the critical feature is a pronounced descending frequency modulation (FM) of the individual notes in the call (Gottlieb,
1974).

The development of the ducklings' perceptual sensitivity to the species-
typical critical acoustic feature (repetition rate in the case of the mallard, and
FM in the case of the wood duck) depends in each case on prenatal (embryonic)
auditory experience (reviewed by Gottlieb, 1981). In the case of the mallard,
ducklings reared with normal prenatal auditory experience strongly prefer calls
with repetition rates of around 4 notes/sec (the normal rate) over calls with
either slower or faster rates. Ducklings that have been muted before the onset
of embryonic vocalization (about 3 days before hatching) show a much broader
range of repetition rate preferences. Development of the normal sharp preference for the species-typical rate can be assured, however, by exposing muted
embryos to a recording of the embryonic calls of siblings. What is of interest
for the present discussion is the extreme specificity of the prenatal experience
that is required for normal development of the postnatal preference. If muted
embryos are stimulated with recordings of the embryonic call at 4 notes/sec,
they develop the normal postnatal preference, but if they are stimulated with
the same call at slower or faster rates (2 or 6 notes/sec), their postnatal preference is the same as muted birds that received no auditory stimulation as embryos (Gottlieb, 1980a). The stimulation provided by a recording of the call at
4 notes/sec is much less variable than that normally available to the embryos,
which vocalize at a range of rates from 2 to 6 notes/sec (Scoville & Gottlieb,
1980; Scoville, 1982), and indeed embryos stimulated with this repetition rate
alone only show their normal preference if a 48 hr "consolidation period"
intervenes between exposure and testing (Gottlieb, 1980a). By stimulating embryos with embryonic calls that showed more normal variability (Gottlieb,
1982), this "consolidation period" could be eliminated, resulting in a more
normal schedule of development. In the same study, it was found that, al-

though embryonic stimulation with the species-typical repetition rate is necessary for normal development, repetition rate is not the only feature of the embryonic call that is important for normal development. Stimulating the embryos with white noise pulsed at the appropriate rate does not result in a normal postnatal repetition rate preference (Gottlieb, 1982). Apparently, other features of the embryonic call, such as the frequency modulation of the notes, are necessary for normal development.

A similar, though less exhaustive, set of results has been obtained in the case of the wood duck. The critical acoustic feature of the wood duck maternal call is the strongly descending FM of the notes (Gottlieb, 1974; Miller & Gottlieb, 1976). Wood ducklings produce a call that also has a strongly descending FM, and exposure to this call has been shown to be essential for development of the normal postnatal preference for the maternal call (Gottlieb, 1980b). Once again, wood ducklings that are exposed to calls whose notes have a different (ascending) FM show the same lack of postnatal preference as do birds that have had no auditory exposure to sibling stimulation: they do not prefer maternal calls with descending FM (the normal case), nor do they prefer calls having the same FM with which they were stimulated.

These results offer strong support for the importance of the ecological stance in analyzing the developing organism. They show clearly the intimate relation that exists between the developing organism and its normal developmental niche (Johnston, 1982). The developing embryo requires auditory stimulation for normal development, but the effective stimulation is precisely defined by that normally available in the course of development. Even quite small deviations from normal auditory experience (such as a reduction in the variability of repetition rates; Gottlieb, 1982) produce an atypical developmental outcome. It is clear that, without close attention to the context in which development normally occurs, and to the kinds of experience that are provided by that context, the analysis of development cannot proceed effectively. The examples discussed earlier in this chapter showed that an organism's perceptual capabilities may be very closely attuned to the requirements of its normal ecological context. The results discussed in this section show that the same close attunement may also be expected in the experiential requirements regulating the development of those capabilities.

CONCLUSION: ECOLOGICAL STRATEGIES FOR INVESTIGATING INFANT PERCEPTION

As is evident from the studies described in other contributions to this volume, most research on infant perception has adopted the system properties stance as its starting point. Indeed, that stance is fundamental to the psychophysical approach, with its emphasis on using physically simple stimuli in highly constrained experimental settings. There is thus rather little precedent for adopting a more ecological approach for the study of infant perception, although this would be at least a valuable complement to current nonecological approaches. In this concluding section, I will outline a strategy for an ecological approach to infant perception, applying the preceding general arguments to this specific case.

The most important requirement is that we come to grips with the question of what constitutes the environment in which the infant normally develops. That is, we need to be able to specify in some detail the various physical, biological, and social factors with which the infant interacts as it develops. The infant's environment will not include all aspects of its immediate surroundings, for there will be some of these that the infant either does not perceive or does not attend to. Clearly, we cannot specify which features of the surroundings are components of the infant's environment without empirical research to determine what the infant is attending to, but we also cannot begin that research without some guidance from naturalistic observations of the infant in its normal setting. To some people, this may sound like a "Catch 22" situation: Until we have described the environment, we can't begin an ecological analysis of the infant's perceptual abilities; but until we know those abilities, we can't specify what features of its surroundings constitute the infant's environment. But the problem is more apparent than real. What we can do is to start with a preliminary description of the infant's environment and use that as the basis of our experimental analyses, refining the description as our understanding of the infant's perception increases. The important point in this strategy is to treat the problem of environmental description as an *empirical* problem; the nature of the environment cannot be specified completely in advance—it must be *discovered*.

Suppose we begin with a specification of the infant's environment that includes only the mother's or other caretaker's face (in the visual modality) and voice (in the auditory modality). Certainly that is an incomplete description, but it is highly unlikely that any adequate description of the infant's environment could exclude those two features. We observe, in natural settings, how the infant responds to these features: by reaching towards the face, smiling at it, orienting towards the voice, and so on. This provides the baseline for designing experiments to determine what aspects of the mother's face and voice are responsible for the infant's natural responses; the reductionist analysis implied by such a procedure can then be carried as far as the experimenter's interests demand (see Gottlieb, this volume, for an example of the ecological strategy applied to maternal avian vocalizations). Traditional psychophysical methods may turn out to be important tools for this ecological analysis, but their use will be constrained by the description of the infant's environment on which the analysis is based. Only naturally occurring stimulus configurations, or configurations whose use in an experiment is designed to elucidate the infant's response to naturally occurring ones, are sanctioned by the ecological approach.

As the analysis progresses, it will be possible to further refine the initial description of the infant's environment. For example, it might be found that tactile or vestibular stimuli experienced by the infant during testing affect its sensitivity to stimuli in the visual or auditory modalities. That would encourage further study of the infant's tactile environment, so as to permit analysis of the ways in which intermodal influences may affect perception under normal circumstances. Or, it might be found that some features of the mother's face (the position of her ears, for example) do not affect the infant's behavior, no matter how they are manipulated. In that case, we might want to argue that those features do not constitute part of the infant's effective visual environment.

The ecological approach thus moves back and forth between observation and analysis: The results of experimental analysis define the need for new observational data, and those data, in turn, guide the next stage in the analysis. It certainly does not require that we eschew analysis and limit our understanding to just what can be gained by observation. But it does require that we pose questions and pursue analyses within the constraints provided by the environment in which the system we are trying to understand normally functions. By applying the ecological approach to the study of infant perception, we may be able to better identify and understand the nature of perception during the first year of life.

SUMMARY

All natural systems exist in a context provided by the other natural systems with which they interact in the course of their normal functioning. This context provides an important source of constraint on the operation of the system, which cannot be understood in isolation from its natural context. Contextual constraints are important in the analysis of all living systems, from the molecular to the organismic level. Where the system being studied is an organism, such as a human infant, the context that constrains its function is the external physical, biological, and social environment; recognizing the importance of this environmental context gives rise to an ecological approach to the study of infant behavior and perception.

ACKNOWLEDGMENTS

Preparation of this chapter, and of the author's research that is reported in it, was supported by Grant HD-00878 (now HD-17752) from the National Institute of Child Health and Human Development. I am grateful to Gilbert Gottlieb and an anonymous referee for helpful comments on an earlier draft of the manuscript.

REFERENCES

Bateson, P. P. G. The characteristics and context of imprinting. *Biological Reviews,* 1966, *41,* 177–220.
Bateson, P. P. G. & Jaeckel, J. B. Chicks' preferences for familiar and novel conspicuous objects after different periods of exposure. *Animal Behaviour,* 1976, *24,* 386–390.

Brunswik, E. *The conceptual framework of psychology.* Chicago: University of Chicago Press, 1952.

Brunswik, E. *Perception and the representative design of psychological experiments.* Berkeley: University of California Press, 1956.

Gibson, J. J. *The senses considered as perceptual systems.* Boston: Houghton-Mifflin, 1966.

Gibson, J. J. *The ecological approach to visual perception.* Boston: Houghton-Mifflin, 1979.

Gottlieb, G. *Development of species identification in birds.* Chicago: University of Chicago Press, 1971.

Gottlieb, G. On the acoustic basis of species identification in wood ducklings (*Aix sponsa*). *Journal of Comparative and Physiological Psychology,* 1974, *87,* 1038–1048.

Gottlieb, G. Development of species identification in ducklings: VI. Specific embryonic experience required to maintain species-typical perception in Peking ducklings. *Journal of Comparative and Physiological Psychology,* 1980, *94,* 579–587. (a)

Gottlieb, G. Development of species identification in ducklings: VII. Highly specific early experience fosters species-specific perception in wood ducklings. *Journal of Comparative and Physiological Psychology,* 1980, *94,* 1019–1027. (b)

Gottlieb, G. Roles of early experience in species-specific perceptual development. In R. N. Aslin, J. R. Alberts, & M. R. Petersen (eds.), *Development of perception.* Vol. 1, p. 5–44. New York: Academic Press, 1981.

Gottlieb, G. Development of species identification in ducklings: IX. The necessity of experiencing normal variation in embryonic auditory stimulation. *Developmental Psychobiology,* 1982, *15,* 507–517.

Johnston, T. D. Learning and the evolution of developmental systems. In H. C. Plotkin (ed.), *Learning, development, and culture: Essays in evolutionary epistemology,* pp. 411–442. London: Wiley, 1982.

Johnston, T. D. & Gottlieb, G. Development of visual species identification in ducklings: What is the role of imprinting? *Animal Behaviour,* 1981, *29,* 1082–1099.

Kamil, A. C. & Sargeant, T. D. (eds.) *Foraging behavior: Ecological, ethological, and psychological approaches.* New York: Garland STPM Press, 1981.

King, J. L. & Jukes, T. H. Non-Darwinian evolution. *Science,* 1969, *164,* 788–798.

Lorenz, K. Z. Der Kumpan in der Umwelt des Vogels. *Journal für Ornithologie,* 1935, *83,* 137–213.

McCall, R. B. Challenges to a science of developmental psychology. *Child Development,* 1977, *48,* 333–344.

Margoliash, E. Evolutionary adaptation of mitochondrial cytochrome *c* to its functional milieu. In D. S. Sigman & M. A. B. Brazier (eds.), *The evolution of protein structure and function,* pp. 299–321. New York: Academic Press, 1980.

Margoliash, E., Ferguson-Miller, S., Kang, C. H. & Brautigan, D. L. Do evolutionary changes in cytochrome *c* structure reflect functional adaptations? *Federation Proceedings,* 1976, *35,* 2124–2130.

Mason, H. L. & Langenheim, J. H. Language analysis and the concept *environment. Ecology,* 1957, *38,* 325–340.

Miller, D. B. & Gottlieb, G. Acoustic features of wood duck (*Aix sponsa*) maternal calls. *Behaviour,* 1976, *57,* 260–280.

Oppenheim, R. W. Metamorphosis and adaptation in the behavior of developing organisms. *Developmental Psychobiology,* 1980, *13,* 353–356.

Oppenheim, R. W. Ontogenetic adaptations and retrogressive processes in the development of the nervous system and behaviour: A neuroembryological perspective. In K. J. Connolly & H. F. R. Prechtl (eds.), *Maturation and development: Biological and psychological perspectives,* pp. 73–109. Philadelphia: Lippincott, 1981.

Pyke, G. H. Hummingbird foraging on artificial inflorescences. *Behaviour Analysis Letters,* 1981, *1,* 11–15.

Scoville, R. P. *Embryonic development of neonatal vocalizations in Peking ducklings.* Unpublished Ph.D. dissertation, University of North Carolina at Chapel Hill, 1982.

Scoville, R. & Gottlieb, G. Development of vocal behaviour in Peking ducklings. *Animal Behaviour,* 1980, *28,* 1095–1109.

Smith, L., Nava, M. E. & Margoliash, E. The relationship of the amino acid sequence and of substances bound to cytochrome *c* to its reaction with cytochrome *c* oxidase. In T. E. King, H. S. Mason, & M. Morrison (eds.), *Oxidases and related redox systems.* Vol. 2, pp. 629–647. Baltimore, Md.: University Park Press, 1973.

von Uexküll, J. *Umwelt und Innenwelt der Tiere.* Berlin: Springer, 1909.

von Uexküll, J. A stroll through the worlds of animals and men. In C. H. Schiller (ed.), *Instinctive behavior,* pp. 5–80. New York: International Universities Press, 1957.

INTRODUCTION TO SECTION 2

Psychophysical Approaches with Infants

In the three chapters in this section, Bruce Schneider and Sandra Trehub review auditory psychophysics in the human infant, Davida Teller reviews visual psychophysics of the human infant, and Lincoln Gray and Edwin Rubel review their approach to developmental psychophysics using animal infants.

Psychophysics is, of course, the oldest area of scientific study in psychology, having had its start with Gustav Fechner in the mid-1800s, long before the establishment of Wilhelm Wundt's "first" laboratory of experiment psychology in 1879. The application of psychophysical procedures to infants is rather recent and promises to tell us much about thresholds for basic auditory and visual functions such as intensity, frequency, wavelength, etc., the most fundamental parameters of perception, and how they change over the first year of life in the infant.

The relationship between behavioral and psychophysiological responses to auditory stimulation is vexing, often giving discrepant results. Schneider and Trehub argue for the value of behavioral, in contrast to neural, approaches to auditory psychophysics, and they describe the "rules" whereby behavioral and psychophysiological measures (e.g., heart rate) are most likely to give concordant results: Namely, when both measures are components of the infant's orienting response and when both are capable of conditioning.

One of the themes of the current volume is the value of animal models for an understanding of the prelinguistic human infant, and Schneider and Trehub point to several parallel lines of research in infant animal psychophysics and infant human psychophysics that mutually reinforce one another, and especially where the former offers leads for the latter. Schneider and Trehub conclude their chapter by reviewing in some detail their own procedure and findings on auditory development using the conditioned head-turning technique with infants 6 to 24 months of age. The inapplicability of conditioned head-turning to infants below 5 or 6 months of age indicates the need for other measures of auditory function at younger ages, such as a forced-choice preferential looking (FPL) technique analogous to that described by Davida Teller for the investigation of infant visual psychophysics in the next chapter.

Teller begins by offering four major defining features of an approach that would be considered consensually as "psychophysical": (a) When independent variables are basic stimulus parameters, and inter- and intra-subject reactions correlate reliably with changes in these parameters; (b) when "voluntary" responses are employed; (c) when intra-subject designs are used; (d) when results are interpretable within sensory or signal-detection theory. She then briefly describes her FPL technique, in which an adult observer is forced to say where the location of the stimulus is on each trial, using any and all information provided by the infant's looking behavior. She then turns to the question of whether there is a psychophysics of infant vision, given her definition of psychophysics and the description of, and data from, FPL and related techniques. She finds (a) and (b) defining features probably satisfied, (c) potentially so, but (d) presents a major problem: When an infant fails a discrimination or otherwise does not give a response, is the limitation sensory or not? She concludes that any estimate of infant sensitivity should be considered a lower boundary estimate and not an indication that the infant's sensory limit has been tapped. Teller thus argues for the use of multiple and various techniques (FPL, VEP, optokinetic nystagmus) in trying to arrive at the best estimate of infantile functioning at any given age. In the remainder of her chapter, Teller grapples with the problem of getting a best estimate for an infant's threshold when it is not possible to use 100 trials per point as it is with adults. Here she proposes a new "probit analysis," which is then compared with the more conventional "staircase" techniques and the method of constant stimuli.

Taken together, the reviews of Schneider and Trehub for audition and Teller for vision indicate that a psychophysical understanding of infant auditory and visual perception is at its beginning. Methods need yet to be worked out for the psychophysical investigation of infants' hearing under 5-6 months of age, and those for vision must be expanded and improved upon if better (truer) estimates of the young human infant's sensory competency are to be achieved.

A truly developmental approach to sensory psychophysics will involve not only the accurate charting of changes (improvements) with age and experience, but an experimental delineation of the maturational and experiential factors responsible for such improvements. Measurement problems aside, for ethical and moral reasons a truly developmental psychophysics is not likely to be realized with human infants, and thus we must turn to animals if our understanding is to be aided by the deprivation and substitution experiments that are necessary to the analysis of relevant maturational and experiential variables. An important first step in this direction has been taken by Lincoln Gray and Edwin Rubel, who review their work with chicks and that of others working with young animals, in the final chapter in this section. The behavioral response that Gray and Rubel use with the chick neonates is the cessation of vocalization (peep suppression) upon the introduction of a novel auditory stimulus. They show that the chick's peep suppressions are similar to perceived loudness functions in humans in that they increase with intensity. Gray and Rubel also find significant developmental trends, such as an increasing sensitivity to higher frequencies with age, as would be predicted from findings with other animals, including humans. They then show the value of the staircase method for determining thresholds of frequency discrimination in chicks. As would be expected, the chicks show an improvement (perceptual sharpening) in their frequency discrimination with age and experience. Thus, this animal model would appear to be a valuable one for determining the influence of maturational and experiential variables in a developmental approach to psychophysics, as well as for the determination of the neurophysiological and neuroanatomical correlates of such development.

As this book went to press, Lincoln Gray and Robert Jahrsdoerfer reported that using natural stimuli when doing auditory psychophysics with young animals (ducklings and chicks) results in lower absolute thresholds and steeper psychometric functions than pure tones (to appear in the *Journal of Comparative Psychology* in 1985). This is the first empirical report that would seem to call for a reexamination of the arbitrariness in the traditional approach to conventional psychophysics. The work of Gray and Jahrsdoerfer suggests that thresholds can be significantly underestimated when arbitrarily chosen stimuli are employed in psychological experiments.

5

INFANT AUDITORY PSYCHOPHYSICS: AN OVERVIEW

152.03

Bruce A. Schneider
Sandra E. Trehub

University of Toronto, Canada

Psychophysics is both an approach and a set of techniques designed to analyze the behavior of a sensory system. The essence of the approach is to describe the system in terms of a set of input-output functions, in such a way that these functions specify how information is encoded and processed by the system. For example, a classic problem in auditory psychophysics is to determine how the system encodes and responds to the intensity of an auditory stimulus. To address this question, a number of experimental procedures and paradigms have been developed in which some aspect of the behavior of a subject is related, for example, to the intensity of the auditory stimulus. For instance, the observer might be asked to give a numerical estimate of the perceived loudness of 1000-Hz tones of different intensities. Or he or she might be asked to respond as quickly as possible to the presentation of these tones. In the first case, we would expect the numerical estimates of the subject, at the very least, to increase uniformly with stimulus intensity, whereas in the second, we would expect the latency to decrease with increasing intensity. In both cases, we would have a functional relation between some aspect of behavior and some parameter of the physical stimulus; hence the name "psychophysics."

It should be noted that, when used appropriately, the methods of psychophysics do not simply serve to generate input-output relations, but to determine more generally the functional properties of the system. In the current example, these two techniques and others have been used to determine how the auditory system responds to the intensity of a stimulus. (For a theoretical review, see Marks, 1979). In sensory psychophysics, then, input-output functions are used to analyze the characteristic behavior of the sensory system in question.

RESPONSE-INTENSITY FUNCTIONS

In the auditory realm, response-intensity relations constitute one of the more important classes of input-output functions. They appear in absolute threshold studies, in which the probability of a response is related to stimulus intensity; in differential threshold studies, in which the probability of a response is related to the magnitude of stimulus change; and in estimation or reaction-time studies (such as the response-latency procedure described above), in which some parameter of a response changes systematically with stimulus intensity. Since response-intensity functions are often the major focus of a psychophysical investigation, it is not surprising that considerable effort has been expended to determine their precise nature. Hence, psychophysics may also be seen as a set of techniques designed to specify such input-output functions in their "purest" form, that is, uncontaminated by the biases and expectations of the subject making the judgment.

Behavioral, Autonomic, or Neural Responses?

Auditory psychophysics has traditionally concentrated on response-intensity functions in the behavioral realm. The reasons for this are historical, practical, and theoretical. Historically, the goal of psychophysics has been to show a one-to-one correspondence between mental and physical events. For human adults, the most direct way of assessing mental events is simply to ask the observer to report what is experienced when a stimulus is presented. Practically, it is considerably easier to ask an observer whether he or she hears a sound than to monitor a heart-rate response or evoked potential to this sound. Moreover, there are sound theoretical reasons for favoring behavioral or autonomic responses over their neural counterparts when the goal is to evaluate the sensory system of the intact adult.

The major function of any sensory system is to provide information that will allow the organism in question to behave appropriately and quickly with respect to the source of stimulation. Thus, in evaluating the entire system, it seems reasonable to look at the final product, which, in the case of a mature, intact, and alert organism is most likely to be an overt behavioral response or an orienting response in the autonomic nervous system. This does not mean that the analysis of neural response-intensity functions has little or no value for the understanding of sensory processes. It simply means that, without the framework provided by an output analysis of the entire system, it might be extremely difficult to pinpoint what aspect of the sensory system a particular neural response is monitoring. (For a similar argument in the visual realm, see Marr & Poggio, 1977.) Consequently, we will restrict our discussion to those measures that, in some real sense, reflect the output side of the sensory-processing system, namely behavioral and psychophysiological responses. In doing this we are by no means implying that neural measures are irrelevant to the input-output characteristics of the sensory system, only that the relation between neural mechanisms and input-output characteristics is, at best, uncertain.

Even when we restrict the domain of response-intensity functions to behavioral and peripheral psychophysiological responses, we often find a lack of correspondence between behavioral and autonomic measures. For example, Bernstein (1969) habituated electrodermal responses to a visual stimulus, then introduced a change in stimulus intensity. He found that many adult subjects who correctly reported the change showed no evidence of a change in electrodermal responding. In the auditory realm, Brown, Morse, Leavitt, and Graham (1976) had adult subjects listen to 60-sec strings of synthetic speech syllables containing a syllable change in the middle of a string. Although half of the subjects were specifically instructed to listen for the change, all reported hearing the change. However, cardiac responses occurred only in subjects instructed to listen for such a change. Thus, ironically, the cardiac system was only engaged when the subject was instructed to "listen," while the "listening" system was engaged with or without such instruction.

Bernstein, Taylor, and Weinstein (1975) explain this discrepancy between autonomic and behavioral measures of sensitivity by hypothesizing that central mediating processes evaluate all input, on a continuous basis, for "significance," and that all psychophysiological output reflects such internal judgments of stimulus significance. Accordingly, they predict no psychophysiological response in the peripheral nervous system when the specific input is judged to be without significance. Whether or not this particular theory is valid, these studies nevertheless show that psychophysiological and behavioral responses are often dissociated, and that the degree of dissociation depends, in part, on instructional set.

In general, if we look at a number of response-intensity functions, we find that the response threshold (the point at which the response magnitude or probability begins to change with intensity), as well as the form of the function above threshold, changes from one measure to the next. Thus, we are left with the problem of choosing the appropriate measure. Clearly, the measure of choice will depend on the aspect of the system that is of interest. For example, if we are interested in the "orienting" or attentional properties of signals, then it would be reasonable to study psychophysiological or behavioral components of the "orienting" response (e.g., heart rate) since they are directly linked to the "orienting" system (Sokolov, 1963). If we are interested, however, in the sensory system as a whole, then we need an analysis of the input-output characteristics of that system, and that is best obtained by behavioral measures.

It is also true that in adult (human) psychophysics, behavioral measures typically show the greatest sensitivity to stimulus change. For this reason alone, there is ample justification for using such methods to determine the basic sensitivity of the auditory system.

Response-Intensity Functions in Infant Psychophysics

An examination of the infancy literature shows that almost every conceivable response-intensity function has been used to explore hearing in human infants. Common response measures include the auropalpebral reflex, which involves blinking, or tightening of the eyelids (e.g., Froding, 1960), the acoustic reflex, which refers to a bilateral contraction of the stapedius muscle (Abahazi & Greenberg, 1977), the Moro or startle reflex (e.g., Hardy, Dougherty, & Hardy, 1959), eye movement (e.g., Turkewitz, Moreau, & Birch, 1966), non-nutritive sucking (e.g., Eimas, Siqueland, Jusczyk, & Vigorito, 1971), changes in general activity (e.g., Birns, Blank, Bridger, & Escalona, 1965); conditioned head turning (e.g., Suzuki & Ogiba, 1961), inhibition of startle blink responses (Berg, 1984), heart rate (Schulman, 1973), respiration (e.g., Steinschneider, 1968), skin resistance changes (e.g., Crowell, Davis, Chun, & Spellacy, 1965), and evoked responses from the cortex and brainstem (e.g., Hecox, 1975). When we examine the relevant studies, however, we find that only a few measures have proven relatively useful in the sense that they have helped us to understand the nature of the developing auditory system. These are non-nutritive sucking, heart rate, evoked brainstem responses, and conditioned head-turning. It is interesting to note that this opinion is also shared, at least implicitly, by the editors of this volume, since it is primarily these response measures that are addressed by the authors concerned with human infant hearing.

Others in this volume (e.g., Hecox, Deegan, Jusczyk, and Kuhl) discuss in detail these measures and the information concerning auditory development that they have provided. Given the psychophysicist's interest in specifying input-output relations for the auditory system as a whole, it might be profitable to search for some common properties that might underlie the success of the behavioral and psychophysiological measures. We contend that the successful behavioral and psychophysiological response systems share three characteristics. First, there is a high level of baseline responding, or the response is relatively easy to elicit. Second, some aspect of each response has been identified as a component of a general orienting response. Finally, each of these response systems is conditionable either classically or instrumentally.

Non-nutritive sucking has been used extensively in the infant speech discrimination literature (see Trehub, Bull, & Schneider, 1981a, for a recent review), and to a limited extent to determine auditory thresholds (e.g., Eisele, Berry, & Shriner, 1975). The measure is most useful from birth to approximately 4 months of age, since the response occurs with high frequency during this period. Aspects of non-nutritive sucking have also been identified as part of the infant's orienting system, insofar as sucking is suppressed by auditory and other stimulation and this suppression readily habituates to the repeated presentation of the stimulus (e.g., Bronshtein, Antonova, Kamenetskaya, Luppova, & Sytova, 1958). Finally, Trehub and Chang (1977) have shown that the rate of sucking is increased over baseline levels when sound is made contingent upon sucking.

Though not dealt with explicitly in the present volume, heart-rate deceleration is also considered to be part of the generalized orienting response to novel or "significant" stimuli (Graham & Clifton, 1966). The measure has been used extensively to index infant discrimination of speech stimuli (Lasky, Syrdal-

Lasky, & Klein, 1975; Miller, Morse, & Dorman, 1977; Leavitt, Brown, Morse, & Graham, 1976), but relatively infrequently to establish absolute thresholds (Schulman, 1973; Schulman & Wade, 1970). Although conditioned heart-rate measures have not been employed in infant psychophysics, it seems likely that they could be.

Head turning in the direction of a sound source is also part of the orienting response (Bronshtein et al., 1958). As Muir and Clifton (this volume) show, it is present at birth and disappears shortly after, only to reappear at about 3–4 months of age. After it reappears, it is readily elicited providing that a relatively intense or "significant" stimulus is used (Trehub, Schneider, & Bull, 1981). It is only at about 5 or 6 months of age, however, that it can be effectively conditioned (Moore, Thompson, & Thompson, 1975), and then it becomes particularly useful as a psychophysical technique (Trehub, Schneider, & Bull, 1981).

It would seem, then, that the most fruitful behavioral and psychophysiological response systems in infant auditory psychophysics are aspects of the infant's orienting response to sound. The fact that they are part of the orienting system means that they are easily elicited or modified by the presentation or change of auditory stimulation. Hence they can be employed even without reinforcement to evaluate the infant's responsivity to sound. The fact that they are also conditionable adds a potentially new dimension to their usefulness. We have already noted that different response-intensity functions have different thresholds for activation. Indeed, there is no reason to expect that different components of an orienting reflex would have identical thresholds to sounds. Thus, a particular sound might elicit a head turn and not a change in heart rate (or vice-versa). We might very well expect, however, that if infants were reinforced for turning toward a sound in one experimental situation, and if their heart rate were conditioned in a second, thresholds obtained from the two procedures would be comparable. As a result of conditioning, the salience of the sound signal would be increased, since it signals the availability of reinforcement in the case of instrumental conditioning, or the advent of the unconditioned stimulus in classical conditioning paradigms.

As far as we know, no one has attempted to use conditioned heart-rate responses in evaluating infant auditory sensitivity. That such a procedure might be fruitful and reduce the discrepancy often observed between behavioral and physiological measures (see Schneider, Trehub, & Bull, 1979) is indicated by some experiments by Berg (1984) that show that, under certain conditions, near-threshold stimulation can elicit components of an orienting response. In Berg's procedure, a brief puff of air is directed to the eye to elicit an eyeblink. Repeated presentations of a brief pure tone some 200 msec prior to the puff of air result in inhibition of the eyeblink reflex. Using this technique, Berg has demonstrated significant inhibition of the eyeblink response to sound intensities near behavioral thresholds. He suggests that this near-threshold enhancement may be due to the increased significance of near-threshold stimuli. It is not at all clear, however, why there is near-threshold enhancement in this procedure and not in others. For example, there is no evidence of near-threshold enhancement when head turning, a voluntary behavioral response, is used as a response measure (Trehub, Schneider, & Bull, 1981). Nevertheless, the near-threshold enhancement shown in the blink inhibition procedure suggests that other response measures might be feasible in determining absolute thresholds, providing some way can be found to make near-threshold stimuli "significant." Clearly, one possible way to make such stimuli significant is by means of a conditioning paradigm.

The advantages of conditioning techniques for nonlinguistic or linguistically immature organisms are seen in the animal psychophysical literature, where successful procedures with mature animals have involved either operant or classical conditioning (Blough & Blough, 1977). It is interesting to note that animal psychophysical studies with immature subjects also tend to employ orienting responses. For example, Gray and Rubel (this volume) used an orienting component of the peeping response to study auditory development in young chickens. According to Gray and Rubel, auditory stimuli interrupt or suppress peeping in much the same way that auditory stimuli supress human infant sucking. Thus, it appears that infant animal psychophysics and infant human psychophysics are following parallel courses in this respect.

Conditioned responses have frequently permitted training and testing to be conducted over periods of days, weeks, months, or even years. While ethical and practical considerations prohibit such extensive testing with human infants, we could, at the very least, expect to increase the number of trials per session with the use of conditioned orienting responses.

We have already noted that successful threshold techniques typically employ orienting responses that are conditionable, and that one advantage of such responses is their relative ease of elicitation or modifiability. Another advantage of orienting responses is their potential use without reinforcement in the initial months of life, when reinforcement may be ineffective. We have also noted that the discrepancies observed between behavioral and physiological measures of auditory sensitivity may stem from the failure of the same signal to engage the different response systems at the same stimulus value. That one sound, for example, might reliably elicit a heart-rate change, while another fails to do so, does not necessarily imply that the first sound is heard and the second is not. Thus, one could conceive of two different sounds, both equally perceptible to the infant, which differ in "significance" and, consequently, their ability to capture the attention of the infant. When a "significant" sound is presented, we would expect it to elicit an orienting response. On the other hand, the presentation of a sound that is well above the threshold of the sensory system might not elicit responses in an orienting or attentional system. This may explain the superiority of certain ecologically relevant auditory stimuli in eliciting responses (e.g., see the chapters by Gottlieb and by Johnston, this volume).

The use of a conditioning paradigm, however, confers "significance" upon the target stimulus by signalling the availability and/or imminent occurrence of the reinforcing stimulus. Thus, one possible way of reducing the discrepancies between different measures is to use conditioning paradigms. Trehub, Schneider, and Bull (1981) have shown that the percentage of correct responses was substantially increased when head turns in the direction of auditory stimulation were reinforced. Presumably, reinforcement, by conferring the test sounds with significance, generated responding at intensity levels that were below the attentional threshold. This study demonstrated increased sensitivity with reinforcement specifically for sound-localization responses, but it is likely that reinforcement would have similar effects for other responses, physiological and behavioral.

CONDITIONED HEAD-TURNING: A TECHNIQUE AND SOME RESULTS

Several psychophysical methods have been developed to determine response-intensity functions of human adults, but linguistic and cognitive constraints preclude their use before about 4 years of age. Similarly, motoric immaturity prevents the adaptation of well-developed animal psychophysical techniques to infants. Finally, ethical and practical limitations severely limit the number of judgments that can reasonably be obtained from an infant. Of these three limitations, the last may ultimately prove the most severe.

Standard psychophysical techniques often necessitate hundreds, if not thousands, of judgments from an observer. (For example, the accurate determination of thresholds in a signal-detection task may require thousands of trials.) In most cases, however, the payoff for the researcher is worth the effort. Because of the careful design of experiments and the large number of trials that are usually conducted, precise measurements of thresholds, loudness functions, etc. can be obtained from a single subject. Infants, however, seldom show such dedication to the pursuit of knowledge that they will sit still for thousands of trials, and few parents have the time and inclination to bring their children to the laboratory for multiple sessions. Accordingly, an upper limit on session length per subject is approximately 1 hour, with a half-hour session being more realistic for the majority of infants. Consequently, the number of training and testing trials per subject must be reduced below the "ideal" level. This means that the experimenter must select between the alternatives of reduced accuracy or data-pooling across subjects, the latter being especially galling to the classical psychophysicist and the former unacceptable to the experimental psychologist.

Despite these constraints, it is still possible to devise psychophysical procedures that are capable of elucidating the development of the human auditory system. Rather than specifying ways and means of devising such a procedure, we will simply describe one that we have developed in our own laboratory, one that, we believe, has provided some very useful information about the nature of the developing system.

By 6 months of age, infants turn quickly and reliably toward a novel sound. Without reinforcement, the response is likely to habituate, that is, to decline in frequency and vigor. Our practice, then, is to visually reinforce head turns toward the sound source. In this way, we can easily maintain the response during one or two 30-trial sessions.

During an experimental session, both the parent, seated on a test chair, and the infant, placed on his or her lap, face an experimenter seated in the opposite corner of a sound-attenuating booth. Both the parent and experimenter wear headphones over which masking noise is presented to prevent them from detecting the locus of a test signal. A trial is initiated only when the infant is quiet and is looking directly ahead, at which time the experimenter in the booth presses a button to initiate a trial. A signal is then presented on one of two speakers located 45° to the infant's left and right. The signal remains on until the infant makes a head turn of 45° or more toward either side, at which time the experimenter presses one of two buttons to indicate the direction of the turn. If the head turn is in the direction of the speaker producing the signal, a toy above that speaker is illuminated and activated for a period of 4 sec. If the head turn is in the other direction, there is a 4-sec silent interval.

To insure that all of the infants tested can perform the task of turning to the sound location, a training criterion is employed with sound intensity well above threshold. During the training period, the location of the signal is alternated between left and right speakers until the infant makes four successive correct responses. The intensity is then reduced 5 or 10 dB and the alternation continues until the infant again makes four successive correct responses. When this criterion is reached, the actual test series begins. Typically, more than 95% of the infants from 6 to 18 months satisfy this criterion, and usually 85-90% complete a session without fussing or crying. During a test session, five different levels of the signal are presented a total of five times each. The randomization of sound levels consists of five random permutations of the five levels presented sequentially. On any particular trial, the signal has a 0.5 chance of appearing at either speaker location, with the additional constraints that the signal appears on the same speaker no more than 3 times in a row and that it appears an approximately equal number of times on the left and right. These constraints on the random order are imposed to minimize the occurrence of a response bias.

At the conclusion of such a test session, we often run a second session in order to maximize the amount of information we obtain from any single infant. At the beginning of the second session, a training criterion is again introduced with only 2 correct responses required at each level.

To date, we have used this technique to determine absolute thresholds (Schneider, Trehub, & Bull, 1980; Trehub, Schneider, & Endman, 1980), masked thresholds (Bull, Schneider, & Trehub, 1981b; Trehub, Bull, & Schneider, 1981b), and intensity-increment thresholds (Schneider, Bull, & Trehub, in preparation; Schneider & Trehub, 1984) in infants from 6 to 24 months of age. To demonstrate that we can obtain reasonable psychometric functions using this behavioral technique, we will review the data from our first threshold

investigation. In this study (Trehub et al., 1980) thresholds were determined
for octave-band noises with center frequencies of 200, 400, 1,000, 2,000, 4,000,
and 10,000 Hz for infants 6, 12, and 18 months of age. The upper panel of
Figure 1 shows the percentage of correct head turns as a function of the decibel
level of the octave-band noises for the six different test frequencies, with each
point being based on a minimum of 85 trials. Note that, as the intensity level
increases, the percentage of correct responses also increases but never quite
reaches 100% even at the higher levels. The bottom panel of Figure 1 presents
psychometric functions for two adults who were tested in a similar manner at
frequencies of 400, 1,000, 4,000, and 10,000 Hz. Since each point of adult data
is based on only 40 trials, these functions are more variable than the infant
functions at the lower intensity levels.

Figure 2 plots the threshold values (defined as 65% correct) as a function of
of frequency for the three infant age groups. It can be seen that the threshold
function for the 12- and 18-month-old groups is similar across the frequency
range studied, but the 6-month-old group is approximately 5-8 dB less sensitive

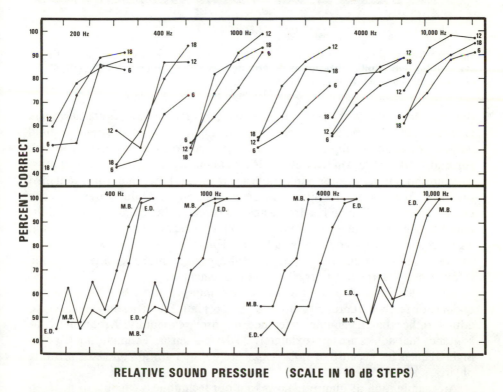

RELATIVE SOUND PRESSURE   (SCALE IN 10 dB STEPS)

Figure 1. Upper panel: percentage of correct head turns as a function of decibel level
of 6 test frequencies for infants 6, 12, and 18 months. Lower panel: percentage of
correct responses as a function of decibel level of 4 test frequencies for two adults.
Stimuli are octave band noises. From Trehub et al. (1980).

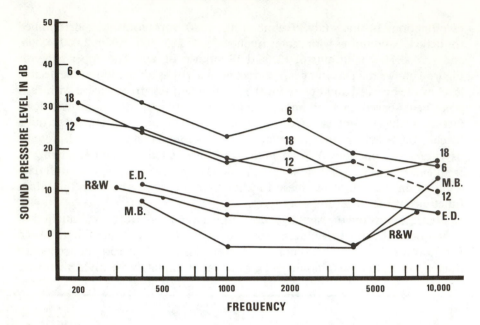

Figure 2. Threshold as a function of frequency for infants 6, 12, and 18 months of age and for two adults. Thresholds determined by Robinson and Whittle (1964) are also plotted. From Trehub et al. (1980).

than the older infants at the lower frequencies. At the higher frequencies, there is no substantial difference between groups. Figure 2 also indicates threshold values for two adult subjects, as well as adult thresholds determined by Robinson and Whittle (1964) in frontal-incidence conditions using a method of limits. The threshold functions for adult subjects are much flatter than for infants. At the lower frequencies, the difference between infant and adult thresholds can exceed 20-25 dB. For higher frequencies, however, thresholds for the adults and infants begin to converge. Indeed, in a later study (Schneider et al., 1980), we found that infants and adults had equivalent thresholds at 19,000 Hz. Thus, our results indicate that developmental changes in auditory sensitivity beyond infancy may be reflected largely in improvement at the lower frequencies. Green (1984) has advanced the alternative interpretation that this low-frequency difference represents infants' performance inefficiency relative to adults, rather than a genuine difference in sensory capability. Accordingly, he contends that adults are approximately 20 dB less sensitive than infants at very high frequencies because of noise exposure or the natural course of growing older.

An examination of Figure 1 shows that our technique is capable of generating good psychometric functions for group data. As noted, the functions never quite reach 100% correct responding even at the higher intensities, probably because of lapses of attention to the task. Occasionally, a child would make a head turn that, in the experimenter's opinion, was directed toward the parent, and unrelated to signal presentation. Similar lapses of attention have been described in animal psychophysics. (See Heinemann & Chase, 1975.) Fortunately, it can be shown that, unless the rate of inattention is quite large, it will not seriously affect the threshold estimate (Trehub et al., 1980). It is possible, then, to develop infant psychophysical procedures that generate good psychometric functions for group data. The restrictions on session duration, however, make it quite unlikely that we will be able to obtain *individual* psychometric functions for infants. Hence, one of the major advantages of adult and animal psychophysics, the ability to specify the operating characteristics of *individual* sensory systems, may never be fully realized in the infant realm.

This is not to say that individual infant psychophysics is totally out of reach. Wilson (1978) has used a staircase method of adjustment with a conditioned head-turn technique to measure individual thresholds in infants and young children. Unlike our technique, only a single loudspeaker, located to the infant's left, is used. On signal trials, the sound is presented over that loudspeaker, and if the infant turns within 4 seconds of sound onset, a toy is illuminated and activated above that loudspeaker. Catch trials, in which no sound is presented, are usually programmed to insure that the child is turning only when he or she "hears" the sound. Similar techniques have been employed by Berg and Smith (1983) and by Sinnott, Pisoni, and Aslin (1983) to determine thresholds for pulsed and pure tones in individual children. Since these studies differ from ours in terms of method (one versus two loudspeakers), psychophysical procedure (constant stimuli versus method of adjustment), signal duration (4 seconds versus unlimited), and stimuli (noise versus tones), it is difficult to make comparisons across studies. This is expecially true for those cases in which the techniques have not been fully evaluated. For example, we know that performance is better in the two-alternative forced choice procedure when an unlimited rather than limited trial duration is employed (Trehub, Schneider, & Bull, 1981). Furthermore, we know the extent to which inattention will affect the form of the psychometric function (Trehub et al., 1980). On the other hand, it is not known how trial duration and inattention affect threshold measures in the adjustment techniques used in the single loudspeaker situation. As is usual in infant psychophysics, more work needs to be done to evaluate how changes in various parameters will affect the precision of our psychophysical techniques.

In our own laboratory, we have adapted Taylor and Creelman's (1967) adjustive procedure (PEST) to determine individual thresholds (Trehub & Schneider, 1983). Simulation measures and test-retest measures indicate that the standard error of the threshold estimate is likely to be on the order of 5 or 6 dB (Bull, Schneider, & Trehub, 1981a). This would yield, for example, a 95% confidence interval of plus or minus 10-12 dB. Although this level of standard error is quite adequate for clinical testing, it is much higher than what we strive for in adult psychophysics.

Finally, as we pointed out in the Introduction, the goal of sensory psychophysics is to understand how a sensory system functions. Hence, the ultimate test of the adequacy of any methodological approach to the study of the developing auditory system is what it can tell us about auditory development. We would like to believe that our approach looks promising with respect to that criterion. From our studies of absolute and masked thresholds (see Schneider & Trehub, 1984), we have been able to demonstrate that the threshold differences between infants and adults are not due to conductive hearing losses or to a greater degree of "physiological noise" in the auditory system of infants. We will continue to map the course of development of these basic auditory abilities to add to and refine our understanding of auditory development.

One major limitation of our technique is its inapplicability prior to 5 or 6 months of age. Perhaps forced-choice techniques analogous to those used in infant visual psychophysics (Teller, this volume) can be developed for use in the initial months of life. Rather than call upon adult observers to judge the location of the signal, we will attempt to train them to judge the *presence* or *absence* of the signal based on cues (as yet unspecified) from the infant's behavior. If successful, this approach will permit the study of auditory development to begin at birth.

ACKNOWLEDGMENTS

The preparation of this chapter and the research reported herein were assisted by grants from The Medical Research Council of Canada and the University of Toronto.

REFERENCES

Abahazi, D. A. & Greenberg, H. J. Clinical acoustic reflex threshold measurements in infants. *Journal of Speech and Hearing Disorders,* 1977, *42,* 514–519.

Berg, W. K. Physiological measures of auditory sensitivity: Near-threshold intensity effects. In S. E. Trehub & B. A. Schneider (eds.), *Auditory development in infancy.* New York: Plenum Press, 1984.

Berg, K. M. & Smith, M. Behavioral thresholds for tones during infancy. *Journal of Experimental Child Psychology,* 1983, *35,* 409–425.

Bernstein, A. S. To what does the orienting response respond. *Psychophysiology,* 1969, *6,* 338–349.

Bernstein, A. S., Taylor, K. W., & Weinstein, E. The phasic electrodermal response as a differentiated complex reflecting stimulus significance. *Psychophysiology,* 1975, *12,* 158–169.

Birns, B., Blank, M., Bridger, W. H., & Escalona, S. K. Behavioral inhibition in neonates produced by auditory stimuli. *Child Development,* 1965, *36,* 639–645.

Blough, D. & Blough, P. Animal psychophysics. In W. K. Honig & J. E. R. Staddon (eds.), *Handbook of operant behavior.* Englewood Cliffs, New Jersey: Prentice-Hall, 1977.

Bronshtein, A. I., Antonova, T. G., Kamenetskaya, A. G., Luppova, N. N., & Sytova, V. A. On the early development of the functions of analyzers in infants and some animals at the early stage of ontogenesis. In *Problems of Evolution of Physiological Functions,* 1958, 106–116. Moscow Academy of Science, Moscow. (U.S. Office of Technical Services translation 60-51066.)

Brown, J. W., Morse, P. A., Leavitt, L. A., & Graham, F. K. Specific attentional effects reflected in the cardiac orienting response. *Bulletin of the Psychonomic Society,* 1976, *7,* 1–4.

Bull, D., Schneider, B. A., & Trehub, S. E. *PESTI: A procedure for infant psychophysical testing.* Paper presented at meeting of the Society for Research in Child Development, Boston, April, 1981. (a)

Bull, D., Schneider, B. A., & Trehub, S. E. The masking of octave-band noise by broad-spectrum noise: A comparison of infant and adult thresholds. *Perception & Psychophysics,* 1981, *30,* 101–106. (b)

Crowell, D. H., Davis, C. M., Chun, B. J., & Spellacy, F. J. Galvanic skin reflex in newborn humans. *Science,* 1965, *148,* 1108–1111.

Eimas, P. D., Siqueland, E. R., Jusczyk, P., & Vigorito, J. Speech perception in early infancy. *Science,* 1971, *171,* 303–306.

Eisele, W. A., Berry, R. C., & Shriner, T. H. Infant sucking response patterns as a conjugate function of changes in the sound pressure level of auditory stimuli. *Journal of Speech and Hearing Research,* 1975, *18,* 296–307.

Froding, C. A. Acoustic investigation of newborn infants. *Acta Oto-Laryngology,* 1960, *52,* 31–40.

Graham, F. K., & Clifton, R. K. Heart-rate change as a component of the orienting response. *Psychological Bulletin,* 1966, *65,* 305–320.

Green, D. M. Some comments on basic auditory processes in infancy. In S. E. Trehub & B. A. Schneider (eds.), *Auditory development in infancy.* New York: Plenum Press, 1984.

Hardy, J. B., Dougherty, A., & Hardy, W. G. Hearing responses and audiologic screening in infants. *Journal of Pediatrics,* 1959, *55,* 382–390.

Hecox, K. Electrophysiological correlates of human auditory development. In L. B. Cohen & P. Salapatek (eds.), *Infant perception: From sensation to cognition,* Vol. 2. New York: Academic press, 1975.

Heinemann, E., & Chase, S. Stimulus generalization. In W. K. Estes (ed.), *Handbook of learning and cognitive processes. Vol. 2: Conditioning and behavior theory.* Hillsdale, N.J.: Erlbaum, 1975.

Lasky, R. E., Syrdal-Lasky, A., & Klein, R. E. VOT discrimination by four to six and a half month old infants from Spanish environments. *Journal of Experimental Child Psychology,* 1975, *20,* 215–225.

Leavitt, L. A., Brown, J. W., Morse, P. A., & Graham, F. K. Cardiac orienting and auditory discrimination in 6-week-old infants. *Developmental Psychology,* 1976, *12,* 514–523.

Marks, L. E. A theory of loudness and loudness judgments. *Psychological Review,* 1979, *86,* 256–285.

Marr, D. & Poggio, T. From understanding computation to understanding neural circuitry, *Neurosciences Research Program Bulletin,* 1977, *15,* 470–488.

Miller, C. L., Morse, P. A., & Dorman, M. F. Cardiac indices of infant speech perception: Orienting and burst discrimination. *Quarterly Journal of Experimental Psychology,* 1977, *29,* 533–545.

Moore, J. M., Thompson, G., & Thompson, M. Auditory localization of infants as a function of reinforcement conditions. *Journal of Speech and Hearing Research,* 1975, *40,* 29–34.

Robinson, D. W. & Whittle, L. S. The loudness of octave-bands of noise. *Acustica,* 1964, *14,* 24–35.

Schneider, B. A., Bull, D., & Trehub, S. E. Intensity discrimination in infancy. In preparation.

Schneider, B. A., Trehub, S. E., & Bull, D. The development of basic auditory processes in infants. *Canadian Journal of Psychology,* 1979, *33,* 306–319.

Schneider, B. A., Trehub, S. E., & Bull, D. High-frequency sensitivity in infants, *Science,* 1980, *207,* 1003–1004.

Schneider, B. A. & Trehub, S. E. Basic auditory processes in infancy. In S. E. Trehub & B. A. Schneider (eds.), *Auditory development in infancy.* New York: Plenum Press, 1984.

Schulman, C. A. Heart rate audiometry. Part I. An evaluation of heart rate response to auditory stimuli in newborn hearing screening. *Neuropadiatrie,* 1973, *4,* 362–374.

Schulman, C. A. & Wade, G. The use of heart rate in the audiological evaluation of nonverbal children. Part II. Clinical tirals on an infant population. *Neuropadiatrie,* 1970, *2,* 197–205.

Sinnott, J., Pisoni, D., & Aslin, R. A comparison of pure tone auditory thresholds in human infants and adults. *Infant Behavior and Development,* 1983, *6,* 3–18.

Sokolov, E. N. *Perception and the conditioned reflex.* New York: Macmillan, 1963.

Steinschneider, A. Sound intensity and respiratory changes in the neonate. *Psychosomatic Medicine,* 1968, *30,* 534–541.

Suzuki, T. & Ogiba, Y. Conditioned orientation reflex audiometry. *Archives of Otolaryngology,* 1961, *74,* 192–198.

Taylor, M. M. & Creelman, C. D. PEST: Efficient estimates on probability functions. *Journal of the Acoustical Society of America,* 1967, *41,* 782–787.

Trehub, S. E., Bull, D., & Schneider, B. A. Infant speech and non-speech perception: A review and reevaluation. In R. L. Schiefelbusch & D. Bricker (eds.), *Early language: Acquisition and intervention.* Baltimore: University Park Press, 1981(a).

Trehub, S. E., Bull, D., & Schneider, B. A. Infants' detection of speech in noise. *Journal of Speech and Hearing Research,* 1981, *24,* 202–206 (b).

Trehub, S. E. & Chang, H. W. Speech as reinforcing stimulation for infants. *Developmental Psychology,* 1977, *13,* 170–171.

Trehub, S. E. & Schneider, B. A. Recent advances in the behavioral study of infant audition. In S. E. Gerber & G. T. Mencher (eds.), *Development of Auditory Behavior.* New York: Grune & Stratton, 1983.

Trehub, S. E., Schneider, B. A., & Bull, D. Effect of reinforcement on infants' performance in an auditory detection task. *Developmental Psychology,* 1981, *17,* 872–877.

Trehub, S. E., Schneider, B. A., & Endman, M. Developmental changes in infants' sensitivity to octave-band noises. *Journal of Experimental Child Psychology,* 1980, *29,* 282–293.

Turkewitz, G., Moreau, T., & Birch, H. G. Head position and receptor organization in the human neonate. *Journal of Experimental Child Psychology,* 1966, *4,* 169–177.

Wilson, W. R. Assessment of auditory abilities in infants. In F. D. Minifie & L. L. Lloyd (eds.), *Communicative and cognitive abilities: Early behavioral assessment.* Baltimore: University Park Press, 1978.

6

PSYCHOPHYSICS OF INFANT VISION: DEFINITIONS AND LIMITATIONS

153.931

Davida Y. Teller

University of Washington, Seattle

INTRODUCTION

Ten years ago, the field of infant sensory studies did not exist. If the average psychophysicist had been asked whether psychophysical studies could ever be carried out on infants, he or she would have said no, that infants are much too erratic and irresponsible to serve as subjects, and that no study of infants would be worthy of the name psychophysics. Yet today, we have at our disposal an accumulating, more or less internally consistent body of data, seeming to show the limitations of infant sensory capacities at birth, and their gradual or rapid development over the first months or years of postnatal life. This paper concerns the conceptualizations, and the theoretical and practical limitations, of this newly emerging discipline.

In the first part of this paper, I will address several conceptual and theoretical points. First I will try to develop a working definition of psychophysics that I hope would be acceptable to the practitioners in the field. Second, I will review briefly the technique developed in my laboratory—forced-choice preferential looking—which probably comes as close as anything yet developed to a psychophysical technique that can be used with infants, and describe a few of

its accomplishments. Third, I will ask in what sense this and similar infant testing techniques come close enough to fulfilling the definition of psychophysics
to warrant the extension of the term to include them. Fourth, I will address the
major theoretical limitations on the interpretation of psychophysical data obtained from infants—the problem of interpretation of negative results—and
ask in what ways we can strengthen the interpretations we place upon the data.

In the second part of the paper, I will address what I see as the major practical limitation on this and other behavioral techniques for the testing of infant
sensory capacities. This limitation concerns the fact that only a small amount
of data can be obtained from an infant of a given age before the flow of time
transforms him or her into a different entity—an older infant. Thus, we need
to explore the statistical characteristics, and the statistical power, of estimates
of thresholds based on small numbers of trials.

DEFINITIONS OF PSYCHOPHYSICS

Checklist

The term "psychophysics" has historically been used in two ways. Originally
it was used as a general descriptor for a body of techniques and data in which
behavioral measures were used to explore the properties of sensory systems.
More recently, it has also been used to refer to a specific branch of this discipline, mathematical psychophysics, which has its origins in the theory of signal
detection (Green & Swets, 1966).

The first usage—as a generic name for a large set of behavioral studies—
probably has no formal, uniformly agreed-upon definition. I attempt here to
capture its essence by means of a checklist. That is, in general, the more of the
following features an experiment has, the more comfortable most of us would
feel in calling it a psychophysical one.

Independent variables. The primary experimental variables in psychophysical
experiments are the simple physical parameters of stimuli: for example, the
size, duration, spatial and temporal pattern, wavelength, and location of a
visual stimulus. It is expected that the results of the experiment will show a
strong and regular dependence on these stimulus parameters, and hence that
careful stimulus control and specification are critical to the performance of
psychophysical experiments.

Dependent variables. The dependent variables measured are the verbal or nonverbal responses of a human (or animal) subject. The responses are collected in
such a way as to indicate whether or not the subject has detected a particular
stimulus, or discriminated between two stimuli; or in such a way as to indicate
properties of the subjective appearance of the stimulus, such as its perceived
brightness, color, or spatial or temporal pattern. The behaviors measured are
usually in some sense voluntary ones, including both verbal reports and other
motor responses. There is a belief that the responses are good indicators of

what the subject is actually seeing, and hence that essentially the same experimental results would be found across a wide choice of response systems. Studies of electrically recordable signals, such as the visually evoked potential (VEP), or involuntary responses, such as the pupillary response, form a closely allied field, but are not usually considered psychophysics.

Experimental design. In psychophysical studies, extensive data are typically gathered on individual subjects. Within-subject designs are usually used, and test-retest reliability is presumed to be high. In most instances, individual differences found between subjects are expected to be small. Consequently, only a few subjects are typically tested, and within-subject comparisons rather than group averages are usually the data of interest.

Theoretical context and interpretation. Typically, the experiments are motivated by interests in sensory processing. The data are usually interpreted in the context of theories of receptor processes and transduction, information processing properties of individual sensory neurons and neural networks, and the ways in which these physical and physiological processes leave their marks on our perceptual world. (It is of some interest to ask how and why we feel we can attribute the results of behavioral experiments to sensory processes. This point will be addressed further below.)

Contributions of Signal Detection Theory. The term psychophysics is also used in a slightly different way, to refer to the set of mathematical formalizations which stems from the theory of signal detection (TSD). Signal detection theorists and their successors have made the point that the subject's responses in psychophysical experiments can be influenced, or "biased", by nonsensory factors such as instructions, feedback, and payoffs. Both empirical data and mathematical models clearly establish these factors as important ones which must be taken into account in the design and interpretation of psychophysical experiments designed to investigate purely sensory factors. In general, mathematical and classical psychophysics have come together, and there is a consensus that forced-choiced paradigms with trial-by-trial feedback provide the most straightforward approach to maximizing estimated sensitivity, minimizing individual differences, and controlling the influence of bias parameters.

These factors form the core, then, of what we mean when we talk of psychophysical experiments. In the next section, I briefly describe the approach my group has developed, in analogy to adult psychophysics, as a means of beginning to carry out psychophysical experiments in infants. In the following section, I will return to the question: To what extent is "infant psychophysics" really psychophysics, and if it isn't, what then?

Forced-Choice Preferential Looking

The technique developed in my laboratory is called forced-choice preferential looking, or FPL (Teller, Morse, Borton, & Regal, 1974; Teller, 1979). It is based on earlier demonstrations (e.g., Chase, 1939; Fantz, 1958) that infants will visually track or stare at bold black-and-white or colored patterns.

In the current version of FPL testing, the infant is held in front of a stimulus display. The display contains a stimulus, such as a spot of light, in either a left or a right position. An adult, who is blind to the location of the stimulus, holds the infant in a more or less vertical position in front of the screen. One of the adult's hands supports the infant's chin, and the other hand supports the weight of the infant's body. A TV camera and monitor provide the adult with a view of the infant's face. The adult typically rotates his or her own hands or body during each trial of the experiment, as necessary, in order to try to point the infant's eyes at the two different stimulus locations. The attempt is to maximize the chance that the infant will notice the stimulus and respond to it by staring, by compensatory eye and head movements, or in any other detectable way.

Using any and all information provided by the infant, the observer must judge the location of the stimulus on each trial.[1] Thus, the *observer's* task is a forced-choice one, and hence the name: Forced-choice preferential looking. FPL works well on virtually all infants from near birth until about 4 or 5 months of age, at which time the infants tend to be willing to do fewer and fewer trials, as though they were bored with the procedure.

More recently, Mayer and Dobson (1980) have modified the FPL technique in an attempt to provide trial-by-trial feedback to the infant as well as the adult. Their technique has been called operant preferential looking (OPL). In OPL testing, a correct response on the part of the observer leads to a few seconds' exposure of an animated toy on the side of the apparatus corresponding to the correct location of the stimulus. This procedure keeps the infant's attention and/or reinforces the infant's looking behavior, and thus allows the testing of many older infants, from 5 months of age and up.

Experiments are carried out by using a series of carefully created and calibrated stimuli; for example, spots of light of various intensities. The observer's percent correct is determined for each intensity, generating a psychometric function. Points near 100% and 50% provide important controls: the former show that the infant can perform the task, while the latter reduce the likelihood that artifacts are causing the above-chance performance at other intensities. The data can be fit with an empirical or theoretical curve, and an estimate of the 75% point can be made from the fitted curve.

FPL, OPL, and related techniques have by now been used to explore many facets of infant vision in several different laboratories. Aspects of visual acuity (Dobson & Teller, 1978), contrast sensitivity functions (Banks & Salapatek,

---

[1] In earlier versions of the technique, one adult (the Holder) held the infant in front of the display, while another (the Observer) observed the infant's eye and head movements. The increase in the number of available sensory cues brought about by combining the Observer and Holder tasks can lead the adult holder to the curious sensation, sometimes discussed in robotics, of having a direct perception of the stimulus location, using the infant as a set of sensors.

1981), flicker perception (Regal, 1981), stereopsis (Fox, Aslin, Shea, & Dumais, 1980; Birch, Gwiazda, & Held, 1982), color vision (Teller & Bornstein, 1985), and light adaptation (Hansen & Fulton, 1981) have all been explored. In the best cases, test-retest reliability is acceptably high, individual differences are acceptably small, and similar answers can be found in different laboratories.

Infant Psychophysics?

We now apply the four criteria listed above—stimulus parameters, response parameters, experimental design, and theoretical orientation—to the FPL and OPL paradigms. To what extent do FPL and OPL data constitute a psychophysics of infant vision? The experiments and data clearly fulfill the first criterion—the independent variables are basic stimulus parameters, and the results show strong and regular dependence upon the values of those parameters. The second—the use of a voluntary response to indicate the detection or qualities of the stimulus—is a bit problematic, in that for ourselves the definition of a "voluntary" response is partly introspective, and we have no introspective reports available from infant subjects. However, we would probably achieve a rough intuitive consensus as to the relative degree of voluntariness we are willing to attribute to various responses the infant can make; for example, we would probably all agree that looking patterns are more voluntary than, say, pupillary constriction, optokinetic nystagmus, or the VEP.

The third criterion—within-subject design—has clear practical limitations which will be discussed in detail in the second part of this paper. However, if the experimental question is made small enough, there is no logical limitation on using a within-subject design.

The fourth criterion—convincing interpretation in the context of sensory theory—is the most difficult. We may take a subject's performance to chance by making the stimuli dim enough, but how do we arrive at the conviction that the major limits on the infant's performance are sensory ones? To address this question, we would need to step back and ask, how do we arrive at that conviction in psychophysical experiments on adults? The answer is not simple. But I would argue that, in adult psychophysics, a major justification for the use of sensory-based theory is that the data agree well with the perceptions of the experimenter, who is also often the subject. It seems to be a premise of the field that, loosely, what is prior to consciousness is "sensory." Without this premise, I would argue, psychophysicists would lose one of the main buttresses of psychophysical theory. But for infants, the introspective reports are missing, and the question, "How do you know the limitation is sensory?" must be dealt with in other ways.

Unfortunately, mathematical psychophysics can offer us only a limited amount of help. FPL is a forced-choice design with feedback for the adult observer, but not for the infant. OPL supplies feedback to the infant, but provides no guarantee that the infant can utilize that information. Neither technique provides any internal evidence that the optimum performance of the infant has been elicited.

I have argued elsewhere (Teller, 1979) that, contrary to the beliefs of scientists sold on the power of operant techniques, the question of the relative sensitivities of techniques for infant sensory testing is an *empirical* question. Even within signal detection theory, there is no guarantee that data collected with any given technique will force the subject to demonstrate his or her maximum sensitivity level. Scientists who study infant perception, even more than signal detection theorists, must live with this interpretative limitation.

Limitations and Strategies

In sum, it seems obvious that any single estimate of an infant's sensitivity to a stimulus will have to be treated as a lower bound estimate, rather than as an absolute estimate. That is, when the experiment is finished we have learned that the infant can see at least as well as is indicated by the data; but there is no evidence that the infant's sensory limit has been reached.

It seems to me that there are three strategies we can use in dealing with this fundamental limitation on the interpretation of our data. First, we can phrase our questions and our conclusions in such a way that they make this limitation clear. For example, we can ask, not What is the average acuity of 3-month-olds? or, At how early an age do infants have all three cone types? but rather, What is the best average acuity that has yet been demonstrated convincingly in 3-month-olds? or, What is the earliest age at which all three cone types have yet been shown to be present? In this way, we can make clear the lower-bound nature of the available information, and encourage the development of additional techniques designed to demonstrate a given capacity at ever younger ages.

Secondly, as in all of science, we can use the process of triangulation, by trying to get a set of consistent answers from the widest possibly variety of techniques. If several different techniques, such as preferential looking, optokinetic nystagmus, and VEPs, carried out with appropriate control of design parameters, all yielded the same absolute estimate of, say, an infant's stereoacuity, the most parsimonious interpretation would surely be that we had run into a sensory limitation which manifested itself through a variety of different response systems; and the burden of proof that the infant had better stereoacuity than yet demonstrated would shift to the critic.

For that reason, I would argue strongly that we should not ask which particular infant testing technique is "the best;" but rather, we should concentrate on developing several techniques, varying as widely as possible. Eventual convergence of the results from different techniques will provide the strongest possible evidence that we know what we are doing.

And thirdly, as in all branches of science, interpretations of data become more believable as they embed themselves more deeply in the nomological net —the body of definitions, measurement techniques, data, and theoretical structures provided by the gamut of neighboring sciences. Looking for a rhodopsin curve, and finding it (Powers, Schneck, & Teller, 1981), is like predicting the location of a new planet, pointing your telescope in the predicted direction, and finding one; it strengthens the entire network which includes the technique, the answer, and a range of general scientific theory. Our nearest neighbors in the nomological net are the disciplines related to adult psychophysics and sensory sciences. These ties must be closely maintained, and it is for this reason that I would emphasize the importance of testing adult as well as infant subjects in laboratory studies of infant visual capacities.

STATISTICAL PROPERTIES OF THRESHOLD ESTIMATORS

The Problem

I turn now to what I consider to be the major practical limitation of all discrete-trial measures of infant vision. This is the simple and obvious problem that the accuracy with which a threshold can be estimated depends heavily upon the number of trials available, and that the number of trials available is limited in the case of infant testing. In determining psychometric functions on adults using the Method of Constant Stimuli, it is feasible to use, say, 100 trials per point. A smooth curve can be fitted to the data by eye, and an estimate of the threshold—say, the 75% point in the 2AFC case—can be made by eye. Repetitions of the experiment would doubtless yield a tight distribution of estimated thresholds, and the standard error of estimation would be small. Usually, no elaborate curve-fitting or statistical analysis would be needed or used. Indeed, most psychophysicists depend for statistical analysis on the "interocular trauma test"—in a good experiment, given the data, the answer hits you between the eyes.

However, when infants are being tested, the number of trials is limited, and the more different conditions one wishes to test, the greater will be the limitation on the number of trials per point. The smaller the number of trials, the larger the binomial variability for each point on the psychometric functions, the more likely that there will be reversals and other disturbing irregularities in a significant fraction of data sets, and the less likely that the interocular trauma test will give one a reliable feel for the accuracy of the estimates found. Clearly, if one is to maximize the information obtained from minimum numbers of trials, one needs to make a serious analysis of the statistical aspects of the experiment.

There are actually two sets of questions. First, suppose one samples at several points on the psychometric function, fits a theoretical curve to the data, and thence estimates the threshold. If one were to repeat this experiment many times, what would be the distribution of estimates of the threshold? What would be the standard error, and what would be the fiducial interval? Would the standard error diminish as $\sqrt{N}$? Would the 95% fiducial interval be symmetrical about the mean, and would its width be ± 1.96 standard errors? Or would these intuitions, carried over from parametric statistics, give us misleading conceptualizations of the accuracy of our threshold estimates?

And second, if one knew approximately where the psychometric function were located along the stimulus dimension, and had a choice of which stimuli to present, which stimuli should one choose? How many different stimuli? How widely spaced? Should they be symmetrically placed around the estimated threshold value, or should the center of the range be displaced toward the right or left? To the extent that one has prior knowledge about the psychometric function, there must be an optimal deployment of the available trials in the experiment.

Several parameters are involved: n, the number of trials per stimulus; k, the number of stimuli used; $N=nk$, the total number of trials; R, the range of stimuli used, i.e. the distance on the abscissa between the highest and lowest stimulus; and X, the mean of the sampled stimulus array, or the distance between the center of the psychometric function and the center of the range of stimuli used. These parameters are illustrated diagrammatically in Figure 1.

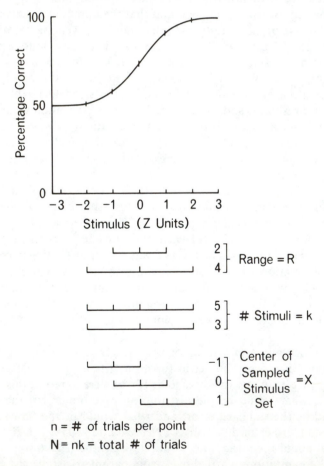

Figure 1. Possible stimulus sets, and illustration of the parameters *k* (the number of stimuli), *R* (the Range), and X (the displacement of the center of the Range from the mean of the cumulative normal distribution). The abscissa is scaled in units of the standard deviation of the cumulative normal curve ("Z" units).

Application of Probit Analysis

In the case where the underlying psychometric function is assumed to be the cumulative normal, the answers to these questions may be determined with the statistical technique of probit analysis (Finney, 1971). However, the equations for the standard errors and fiducial intervals (Finney, pp. 34, 79) are complex, and depend on many of the variables listed above. Furthermore, standard errors and fiducial intervals have not previously been tabulated in much detail, nor made intuitively real, particularly for the two-alternative forced-choice (2AFC) case.

Recently, McKee, Klein, and Teller (in preparation) have worked out a graphical analysis that provides an intuitive glimpse at some of the the statistical properties of 2AFC psychometric functions. Examples of Yes-No and 2AFC psychometric functions are shown in Figures 2A and 2B, respectively. In each case, the smooth curve is a cumulative normal function. The vertical bars show ± 1 standard error of the binomial distribution for samples taken at three different locations along the cumulative normal curve. The number of trials per point (n) is 100 in this example, for a total number of trials (N) of 300.

In the Yes-No case, the binomial error bar is largest at the 50% point (the threshold), and smaller toward the tails of the distribution. In the forced-choice case, the cumulative normal curve is scaled up to have its lower asymptote at 50%. But the size of the error bar is controlled not by the location of the sampled point along the rescaled cumulative normal curve (the right ordinate), but rather by the sample probability value (the left ordinate). Thus, in the 2AFC case, the binomial error bars are asymmetrical, being largest at the lower tail, near 50%, and smallest at the upper tail, near 100%.

There are two basic ways in which these error bars constrain the location of the best-fitting cumulative normal curve, and hence the estimate of the threshold. One is the length of the error bar itself, and the other is the steepness of the curve at the sampled point. Intuitively, when the curve is relatively steep, it cannot be moved left or right very much and still remain within an error bar of a given size. But, if an error bar of the same size is found near a tail of the distribution, where the curve is flat, the curve can slide left and right by long distances and still remain within the error bar.

In the 2AFC case, points near 50% suffer from two disadvantages. The error bars are relatively large, and in addition the curve is relatively flat. For this reason, data points near 50% in the 2AFC paradigm yield relatively little information that can constrain the location of the function along the abscissa; that is, little information concerning the threshold.

This point is made again more clearly in Figures 2C and 2D. In these figures, the ordinates of Figures 1A and 1B have been subjected to a probit transformation. In essence, the axes have been differentially stretched, with greater and greater stretching toward the tails of the distribution, to force the cumulative normal curve into a straight line. The error bars have likewise been transformed. In these figures, the slope of the curve is everywhere the same, so

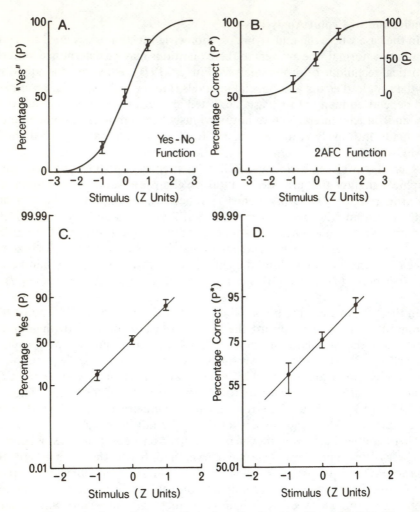

Figure 2. Theoretical psychometric functions for Yes-No (A) and 2AFC (B) experiments. The vertical bars are binomial standard errors for n = 100. C and D: Probit transformations of A and B, respectively.

the constraint that each data point puts on the location of the function due to both of the factors mentioned above is combined in the magnitude of the transformed error bar. The large error bar near 50%, and the asymmetry between the upper and lower parts of the curve in the 2AFC case, are shown more clearly in these linearized plots. This asymmetry is at the root of various pecularities and asymmetries which will be described below.

McKee et al. (in preparation) have also programmed the equations for standard errors and fiducial intervals derived from probit analysis, and tabulated the values obtained for a wide variety of values of experimental parameters. The question is also being pursued by means of computer simulations. The results from the use of probit analysis are presented here.

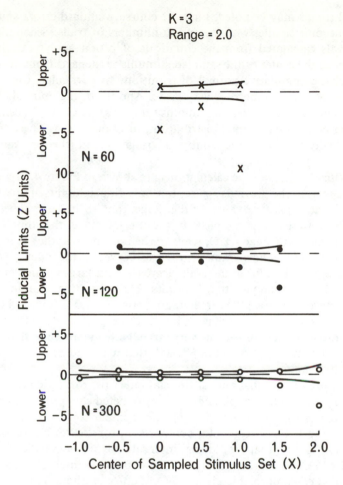

Figure 3. Estimates of fiducial limits. ± 1.96 standard errors (solid lines) and fiducial limits (points) calculated from probit analysis, for $k = 3$ and Range = 2. Top: $N = 60$. Middle: $N = 120$. Bottom: $N = 300$.

Results

For the 2AFC case, some typical results—standard errors and fiducial intervals for estimates of the threshold—are shown in Figure 3. In this case, we have sampled three points on the psychometric function ($k = 3$), and spaced them 1 Z-unit apart (Range = 2.0). The abscissa shows the mean of the sampled stimulus set (X), with zero indicating that the stimulus set was centered on the threshold value, and positive (negative) values showing displacements toward the upper (lower) asymptotes. The ordinates of each graph show two different estimates of upper and lower fiducial limits: the solid lines show ± 1.96 standard errors, while the points show upper and lower fiducial intervals calculated from Finney's equation. Results are shown for $n = 20$, 40, and 100 trials per point (N of 60, 120, and 300 respectively).

Several trends may be noted. First, of course, standard errors and fiducial intervals become smaller with increasing numbers of trials. Second, the fiducial intervals calculated from the equations of probit analysis deviate from ± 1.96 s.e. as the center of the sampled stimulus set departs from the center of the underlying cumulative normal distribution. In particular, the calculated lower fiducial limit can become very large. And third, the optimal placement of trials seems to be to center the stimulus range slightly above the center of the underlying cumulative normal distribution, at about $+0.5$. These trends are most markedly seen when the number of trials is small (the top graph, where $N = 60$).

Additional features of the calculations are shown in Figure 4. Here the axes are the same as in the previous figure, but only fiducial limits are plotted. The four panels show different values of the range, that is, the interval between the highest and lowest points sampled. In the top left panel the stimuli are relatively close together (range $= 1.5$), while in the bottom right they are spread far apart (range $= 3.0$). The parameter on the curves is the number of trials. Again, as expected, fiducial intervals decrease with larger numbers of trials. The optimal range is about 2 to 2.5 Z-units. The interesting point in this figure is that if the range is a little larger than optimal—3.0 Z-units—the fiducial limits are still relatively well behaved; but if the range is made too narrow—1.5 Z-units—fiducial intervals become very large. Note in particular that in the top left panel, there is no placement of 60 trials that will yield a lower fiducial limit less than 10 Z-units.

Figure 5 provides a final look at fiducial intervals, for a wide range of total numbers of trials (N). The solid lines show predicted changes if the fiducial interval decreases as $\sqrt{N}$. Figure 5A shows a comparison of the total fiducial interval for the 2AFC case, and for comparison, for the Yes-No case as well. It is interesting to note that the fiducial intervals are always smaller for Yes-No than for 2AFC techniques. Moreover, the fiducial intervals become well-behaved (decrease approximately as $\sqrt{N}$) at an N of about 30 for the Yes-No case, but only for an N of about 150 for the 2AFC case. Figure 5B shows that, as expected, most of the difficulty arises from the lower fiducial interval.

We do not yet know to what extent these very large fiducial intervals, calculated from the equations of probit analysis, really describe the properties of 2AFC data, and to what extent they result from violations of the assumptions of probit analysis as N becomes small. Our ongoing simulation study suggests that the latter may be at least partially the case, and that the true fiducial intervals may be smaller and more well-behaved than those indicated in Figures 3-5. Nonetheless, and even for near-optimal choices of stimuli, fiducial intervals still increase faster than would be expected from considerations of $\sqrt{N}$, for values of N less than about 60 trials.

Comparison to Staircase Techniques

So far, all of the results reported here deal with threshold estimators generated by the forced-choice method of constant stimuli. But we are now in a

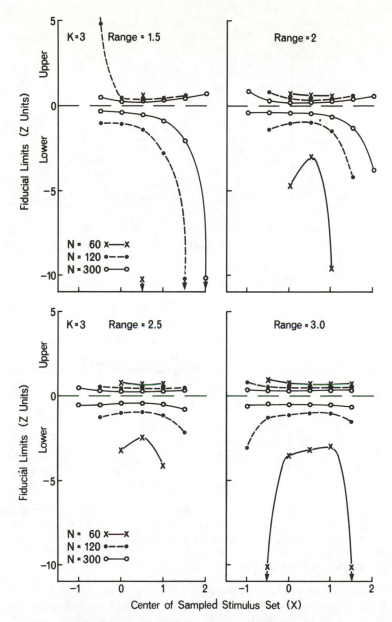

Figure 4. Influence of variations in the Range.

position to ask, How does the variability of such estimators compare with the variability of estimators resulting from the use of other psychophysical techniques? McKee et al. argue that the present calculations provide some limiting values for the variability of staircase estimators, as well as for the method of constant stimuli.

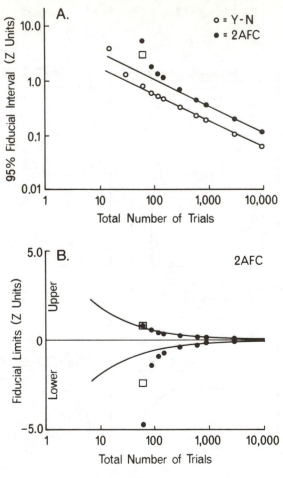

Figure 5. Effect of number of trials. The solid points show fiducial intervals (A) and fiducial limits (B) for a wide range of total number of trials, for parameter values $k = 3$, $X = 0$, Range = 2. The continuous lines show predicted changes if standard errors and fiducial intervals were to decrease linearly with $\sqrt{N}$. Squares show results from an optimal placement of 60 trials ($X = 0.5$).

In a staircase method, after the initial starting point, the outcomes on one or a few previous trials determine the stimulus to be presented on the next trial. In comparison to the method of constant stimuli, staircase techniques have the great advantage that one need not know much about the location of the psychometric function at the start. The intent is that the results on early trials will guide the sampling strategy to approximately the optimal stimulus locations on the later trials of the staircase. In fact, one can think of a staircase rule as an attempt to generate, from an arbitrary starting point, the optimum deployment of the available trials.

McKee et al. argue that, if a staircase could come close to accomplishing this objective, then the staircase would generate a set of trials placed at about the same locations as would be used by knowing the optimal placement of trials and using the method of constant stimuli, and the standard errors of the two procedures should be about the same. In the limit, if the staircase could achieve the ideal of producing exactly the optimum deployment of trials, then the standard error of threshold estimates resulting from the staircase procedure should be the same as that resulting if the optimal deployment of trials could be used with the method of constant stimuli. Thus, for each value of N, the *minimum* standard errors and confidence intervals found for the method of constant stimuli should also describe the limiting values of variability that can be achieved with staircase techniques, given an equal value of N and the same underlying psychometric function. Of course, this argument in no way denies the usefulness of staircase estimators, nor their potential superiority over the method of constant stimuli when no accurate initial estimate of the threshold is available. The point of the argument is simply to provide a means of estimating the limiting statistical properties of staircase techniques.

Although many variants of staircase rules have been proposed, the question of the standard errors and fiducial intervals of threshold estimates derived from staircases have rarely been explored. In the absence of the above argument, one might be tempted to entertain the hope that, in addition to the advantages of efficiency, staircase estimators could somehow have, statistically speaking, magical powers, and that binomial variability could somehow be circumvented by the use of an optimal staircase rule. McKee at al.'s argument, on the contrary, is simply that binomial variability limits the accuracy of staircase estimators, just as it does the accuracy of the method of constant stimuli, and that the limiting values for standard errors and fiducial intervals for the optimal placement of trials in the method of constant stimuli should also apply to staircases. Once stated, the argument seems obvious, but to our knowledge it has not been widely appreciated.

Application to Infant Psychophysics

What are the most relevant conclusions for infant psychophysics? First, in the forced-choice context, fewer than about 60 trials should be used with caution, on the grounds that the data may be unacceptably noisy. Second, with 60 to 100 trials, estimates of the threshold can be made with the method of constant stimuli, but only if the experimenter knows enough about the location and slope of the psychometric function at the start to place the stimuli close to the optimum locations on the psychometric function. Third, even then one should exercise caution in stating fiducial limits, and in assessing the statistical significance of differences in measured thresholds.

Finally, all of the above analysis has been presented scaled in Z-units, i.e., in units based on the standard deviation of an assumed underlying cumulative normal distribution. But the importance of the variability in one's estimate of the threshold will obviously depend upon its magnitude in *stimulus* units. If this standard deviation is small—if the psychometric function is steep in stimulus units—the variability in the threshold estimates will be correspondingly small. A translation to stimulus units is badly needed.

Unfortunately, we reach the limit of our knowledge here, because our understanding of the shapes and slopes of infant psychometric functions is not yet very extensive. If the true function is a cumulative normal, one might think that the standard deviations of best-fitting cumulative normal curves fit to real data (e.g., Allen, 1979; Mayer, 1980) could be used as estimators of the standard deviation of the underlying function. But these values may well not provide unbiased estimators, especially when the number of trials is small, individual differences appear to be non-negligible, and the upper asymptotes of the curves are not independently established. These problems remain for future empirical and statistical investigation. In the meantime, our understanding of the accuracy of estimates of infant thresholds can be said to be only moderate in statistical terms, and modest at best in stimulus terms.

SUMMARY AND CONCLUSIONS

In summary, in much of this paper I have emphasized the limitations of psychophysical techniques currently used to test visual functions in human infants. In logical terms, the most difficult problem we face—and it is common to all of science—is the interpretation of discrimination failures and other negative results. The best way to overcome this problem is to continue to expand our repertoire of techniques, so that we can triangulate to theories of the infant's sensory limits from more than one starting place. In practical terms, the most serious limitation facing us is the small number of trials that can be obtained from a single infant of a given age. Within the context of the presently available techniques, the only approach toward a solution to this problem is to increase our understanding of the variabiity of our estimators, and use this knowledge in generating our experimental designs and interpreting our results.

On the other hand, on a more positive note, we have come a long way in the last few years. Ten years ago, we knew virtually nothing about infants' vision. Today we have at least the outlines of a science. Every positive discrimination that an infant makes is a step forward. We can build a science on these positive outcomes, as long as we avoid the danger of overstating our case.

ACKNOWLEDGMENTS

This research has been supported in part by National Eye Institute Grant EY 02920. I thank Drs. Suzanne McKee and Stanley Klein for permission to report the results of our recent collaboration, Smith-Kettlewell Institute for the preparation of Figures 1-5, and Marjorie Zachow for secretarial assistance.

REFERENCES

Allen, J. *The development of visual acuity in human infants during the early postnatal weeks.* Unpublished doctoral dissertation, University of Washington, 1979.

Banks, M. S. & Salapatek, P. Infant pattern vision: A new approach based on the contrast sensitivity function. *Journal of Experimental Child Psychology,* 1981, *31,* 1–45.

Birch, E. E., Gwiazda, J., & Held, R. Stereoacuity development for crossed and uncrossed disparities in human infants. *Vision Research,* 1982, *22,* 507–513.

Chase, W. Color vision in infants. *Journal of Experimental Psychology,* 1939, *20,* 203–222.

Dobson, V. & Teller, D. Y. Visual acuity in human infants: A review and comparison of behavioral and electrophysiological studies. *Vision Research,* 1978, *18,*1469–1483.

Fantz, R. L. Pattern vision in young infants. *Psychological Record,* 1958, *8,* 43–47.

Finney, D. J. *Probit analysis.* 3rd ed. London: Cambridge University Press, 1971.

Fox, R., Aslin, R. N., Shea, S. L., & Dumais, S. T. Stereopsis in human infants. *Science,* 1980, *207,* 323–324.

Green, D. M. & Swets, J. A. *Signal Detection Theory and Psychophysics.* New York: John Wiley, 1966.

Hansen, R. & Fulton, A. Behavioral measures of background adaptation in infants. *Investigative Ophthalmology and Visual Science,* 1981, *21,* 625–629.

Mayer, D. L. *Operant preferential looking: A new technique provides estimates of visual acuity of infants and children.* Unpublished doctoral dissertation, University of Washington. 1980.

Mayer, D. L. & Dobson, V. Assessment of vision in young children: A new operant approach yields estimates of acuity. *Investigative Ophthalmology and Visual Science* 1980, *19,* 566–570.

McKee, S. P., Klein, S., & Teller, D. Y. Statistical properties of forced-choice psychometric functions: Implications of probit analysis. In preparation.

Powers, M., Schneck, M., & Teller, D. Y. Spectral sensitivity of human infants at absolute threshold. *Vision Research,* 1981, *21,* 1005–1016.

Regal, D. Development of critical flicker frequency in human infants. *Vision Research,* 1981, *21,* 549–555.

Teller, D., Morse, R., Borton, R., & Regal, D. Visual acuity for vertical and diagonal gratings in human infants. *Vision Research,* 1974, *14,* 1433–1439.

Teller, D. Y. The forced-choice preferential looking procedure: A psychophysical technique for use with human infants. *Infant Behavior and Development,* 1979, *2,* 135–153.

Teller, D. Y. & Bornstein, M. Infant color vision and color perception. In L. Cohen & P. Salapatek (eds.), *Handbook of Infant Perception.* New York: Academic Press, 1985.

7

DEVELOPMENT OF AUDITORY THRESHOLDS AND FREQUENCY DIFFERENCE LIMENS IN CHICKENS

Lincoln Gray

University of Texas Medical School, Houston

Edwin W Rubel

University of Virginia Medical School, Charlottesville

The field of human psychophysics is well established (Marks, 1974; Stevens, 1975; Trahiotis & Robinson, 1979; Robinson & Watson, 1972). It includes a set of elegant techniques allowing evaluation of sensory function through behavioral responses. Similar procedures have been successfully applied to well-trained animals (Stebbins, 1970). Only recently have behavioral tests been made useful for evaluating the auditory abilities of young animals and infants (Ehret, 1976, 1977; Ehret & Romand, 1981; Shnerson & Willott, 1980; Trehub, Schneider, & Endman, 1980). Few of these techniques, however, are suitable for newborn subjects.

Psychoacoustical studies in newborn animals may be important for two reasons. (a) There is little information in any species on how perceptual abilities develop over the first few postnatal days. This neonatal period may be interesting because this is when organisms first hear air-conducted sounds, and thus receive the same acoustic stimulation as adults. This early experience may play an important role in later perceptual development (Gibson, 1969; Gottlieb,

1976). (b) We have long sought to understand more fully the neural basis of perception (Hartline, 1940; Hubel & Wiesel, 1959; Lettvin, Maturana, McCulloch, & Pitts, 1959; Lippe, 1976). Comparisons between physiological and behavioral responses under similar conditions are required to correlate neural changes with perceptual development. To this end, an animal model for studying the development of basic auditory psychophysical abilities, such as absolute thresholds and frequency difference limens, is desirable for comparison with neurophysiological data.

We use the auditory system because the stimuli are easily varied along separate and independent dimensions. For example, the stimuli in these experiments are pure tones that differ in either frequency or intensity.

Although there are many advantages in using chickens for developmental studies, the primary reason that we use chickens in this research program is that they have a remarkable unconditioned response that is ideal for developmental psychophysics. Young chickens, when left alone in a room-temperature, well-lit chamber, peep almost incessantly. When the birds hear an acoustic stimulus, they orient to that sound and momentarily suppress their ongoing peeps (Kerr, Ostapoff, & Rubel, 1979).

For these reasons, our recent efforts have been two-fold: first, to find sensitive, powerful, and efficient psychophysical paradigms for neonatal chickens; and second, to establish baseline norms of perceptual development in these animals. This chapter will give an overview of some methods for making psychophysical estimates in these young animals, and will review some of the results.

The first study to be reviewed is a parametric analysis of the peep-suppression response to suprathreshold stimulation (Gray & Rubel, 1981). The data show that the duration of peep suppression varies systematically with both the intensity and the frequency of acoustic stimulation. This stimulation can include either the onset of a tone or a change in the frequency of that tone.

The second part of this review will describe several experiments that use peep suppressions to estimate auditory thresholds. Two kinds of thresholds are discussed: absolute thresholds and frequency difference limens.

RESPONSIVENESS TO SUPRATHRESHOLD STIMULI

An analogy with equal loudness contours in adult humans may help to explain this study. Figure 1 (from Robinson & Dadson, 1956) shows contours across a wide range of frequencies and intensities where perceived loudnesses are the same. All points along a given contour are perceived by an average person to be equally loud. This level of perceived loudness is expressed in phons, the intensity of a 1000 Hz tone perceived to be as loud as the test stimulus. Equal loudness contours for younger and older people are shown by solid and dashed lines, respectively; note that the data from young and old subjects are the same at low frequencies but different at high frequencies.

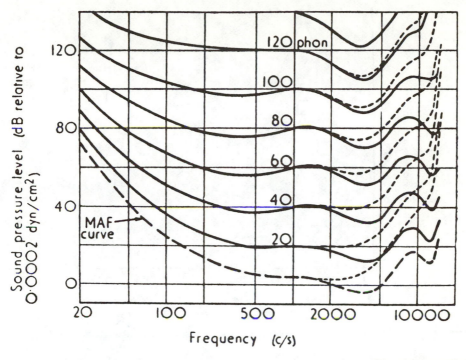

Figure 1. Equal Loudness Contours. The curves connect tones of various frequencies and intensities that are perceived to be equally loud. From Robinson & Dadson (1956), copyright of The Institute of Physics. Reprinted by permission. The solid lines are data from 20-year-old subjects; the dashed lines are from 60-year-old subjects. "MAF," for "minimal audible field," is a measure of absolute threshold.

Figure 2 shows selected data from Figure 1 redrawn in the form of the chickens' data. The data are the perceived loudness of 70 and 90 dB tones, expressed in phons, across four frequencies and two ages. The top and bottom panels are the same four curves rearranged to show the effects of intensity and age, respectively. Notice, in the top panel, that the responses to 90 dB tones are greater than the responses to the 70 dB tones. In the bottom panel, notice that the responses at high frequencies drop off more quickly in the older than the younger people.

Procedure

Young chickens cannot be asked to rank subjective loudness, but we can measure their responsiveness to sound by the length of time they suppress peeping when a sound is presented. To make our study manageable, we selected a small subset of possible stimuli —three different frequencies and two intensities—to present to two ages of chickens. The general procedure is described below. Chickens are acclimated to a small chamber for a few minutes, until they begin to peep regularly. Both "stimulus" and "control" trials can

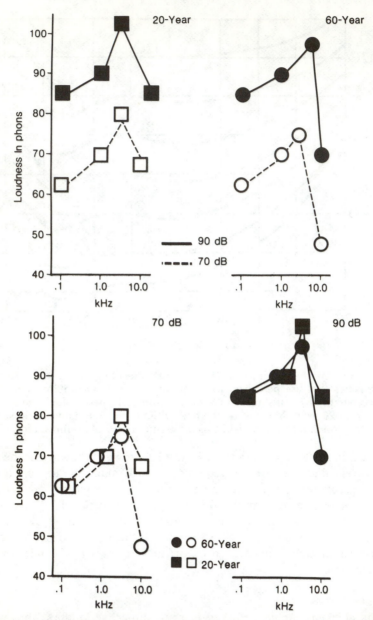

Figure 2. Human Responses to Suprathreshold Acoustic Stimulation. Some of the data from Figure 1 are rearranged in the form of the chickens' data to be shown in Figures 3 and 4 below. The loudness of tones at four frequencies and two intensities is graphed for two different ages. The response measure, phons, is the intensity of an equally loud 1000 Hz tone.

then be presented. Stimulus trials begin with the presentation of an acoustic stimulus, and the duration of peep suppression elicited by that stimulus is measured. This stimulus can be the onset of a tone. Alternately, the stimulus can be a change in an ongoing tone. After a tone is left on for a period of time, the birds habituate to this background noise and begin again to peep at their baseline rate. A change, in frequency for example, will reelicit an orientation and a suppression of peeping. Control trials are identical to stimulus trials, except there is no stimulus. These control trials provide measures of the baseline peep rate expected when the animals hear no stimulus.

More specifically, the paradigm used in this study involved an initial control trial and then two stimulus trials: one onset and one 6% change in frequency. After acclimation for 2 to 5 minutes in a silent, double-walled room, the suppression during a control trial, which is essentially an inter-peep interval, was measured, and then a tone was turned on. The bird oriented to that onset and momentarily suppressed its peeping. We measured the duration of peep suppression, the time from the onset of the tone until the next peep. The tone stayed on for at least 80 seconds, by which time the animals had habituated to the tone and their peep rate had returned to normal. The frequency of the tone was then changed by 6%. A reliable resuppression of peeping to this stimulus would be evidence that the young birds heard the 6% change in frequency.

There are several subtle but important points in the paradigm. First of all, the critical trials—that is, the baseline or control trials, the initial onset of the tone, and the subsequent change in the frequency of that tone—are started only when the birds are peeping. Two peeps in 2 seconds are required to start these trials, which greatly reduces variability in the response. That is, the computer waits until the animals are in a particular state with respect to the dependent variable before trials are started. A second point is that the tones are pulsing, and the computer changes the tone frequency only during the few milliseconds when the tones are off to eliminate any switching artifacts. Finally, the entire sequence of acclimation, baseline, onset, and change is repeated to provide an estimate of intrasubject consistency.

Two ages were studied, newly hatched and 4-day-old chicks. Stimuli were either 70 or 90 dB SPL, and in three frequency ranges: approximately 500, 900, or 2600 Hz. One quarter of the animals were controls, and at the end of the 80 seconds of habituation, the frequency of the tone was not changed but the duration of the peep suppression was measured, just as in the experimental animals. Three hundred eighty four birds were studied. In summary, this was a three-way, cross-classified design, with age, frequency, and intensity as independent variables.

Responses to the Onset of Tones

Figure 3 shows the responses to the onsets of the tones. Duration of suppression in seconds is plotted across three frequency ranges for two intensities and two ages. All of these responses were significantly greater than baseline suppression, which was so small it barely shows up on this graph ($.52 \pm .06$ seconds). Notice, in the top panel, that in every condition the responses to 90 dB were greater than responses to 70 dB, as expected. Thus, chicks' peep suppressions are like humans' perceived loudnesses in that they increase with intensity. Compare Figures 2 and 3.

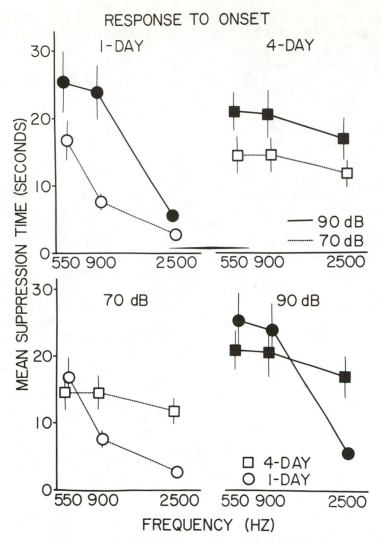

Figure 3. Responsiveness of Young Chickens to the Onset of a Tone. Shown are the durations of peep suppression elicited by the onset of pulsing tones. Tones are of two intensities and in three different frequency ranges. Data from two ages of chicks are shown. Means and standard errors are plotted. Sample sizes were 32 in each of the twelve groups. Pairs of points are horizontally separated slightly only to separate the error bars, and do not indicate a difference in frequency. As in Figure 2, the top and bottom panels are the same data, rearranged to show the effects of intensity and age, respectively. Note that responsiveness increases with intensity, and that there is an age-by-frequency interaction. From Gray & Rubel (1981). Copyright (1981) by the American Psychological Association. Reprinted with permission.

Most importantly, notice the developmental trend in these data. The young and old chicks responded similarly to low frequencies. The young chickens, however, responded less to high frequencies than birds which were a few days older, as seen most clearly in the bottom panel of Figure 3. This developmental trend, technically an age-by-frequency interaction, parallels known functional changes in the auditory system. As reviewed by Gottlieb (1971) and Rubel (1978), physiological data clearly indicate a developmental gradient across frequency and age; responses to low and middle frequencies develop before responses to high frequencies. We can now add these behavioral data to the list of responses that show this developmental gradient. We can also add chickens to the list of animals that show this gradient, which speaks to the generality of our animal model.

To summarize, an analysis of the duration of peep suppression to the onset of tones shows that responsiveness to low frequencies is the same at both of the ages. Responsiveness to high frequencies differs with age; neonates are less responsive than older birds to tones above 1000 Hz.

Responses to Frequency Changes

Figure 4 shows the duration of suppressions elicited by the six-percent change in frequency. Remember that the birds were habituated to a pulsing tone for at least 80 seconds, and then the frequency of that tone was changed. One quarter of the animals were controls, and the frequency of the tone they heard was not changed; the suppression measured during the control trials is shown by the "C" in Figure 4.

Notice, in the top panel, that once again the birds responded more when the stimuli were loud. This effect of intensity is similar to observations from human psychophysics indicating that frequency changes are easier to detect when the tones are loud (Geldard, 1972). Notice also that young birds responded no more to the 6% change at high frequencies than to the control trials. By 4 days of age, however, responses to these changes were relatively constant across frequencies. These flatter lines, on the right side of the top panel in Figure 4, indicate that Weber's law, a statement that constant percentage differences are perceived to be about equal, holds fairly well for peep suppressions in 4-day-old chickens across this range of frequencies. Furthermore, these responses to frequency changes show the same developmental gradient across frequencies with age as was seen in the onset data; responsiveness to low frequencies develops before responsiveness to high frequencies.

In addition, there is an overall difference between ages in their response to a 6% frequency change, as seen in the bottom part of Figure 4. The 4-day-old chicks responded more than the newborn chicks to the 6% change in frequency. This effect of age is consistent with psychological theories of perceptual development, indicating that responses to changes along a stimulus continuum improve with normal experience.

Discussion

To summarize what we have learned about methods for studying perceptual development, online computer technology is useful for reducing neonatal variability to manageable levels. Stimuli should be presented only when the subjects are in a particular state with respect to the dependent variable. Fur-

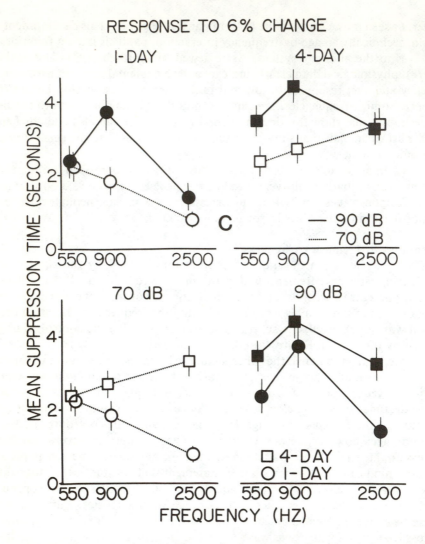

Figure 4. Responses to the 6% Change in Frequency. Durations of suppression elicited by a 6% change in the frequency of a pulsing tone are shown. As in Figure 3, the top and bottom panels are the same data, rearranged to show the effects of intensity and age, respectively. The "C" in the top panel shows ± 1 standard error of suppression times on control trials. From Gray & Rubel (1981). Copyright (1981) by the American Psychological Association. Reprinted with permission.

thermore, an unconditioned and continuously distributed response seems appropriate for psychophysical testing in developing neonates.

To summarize what we have learned about auditory perceptual development, peep suppressions are lawfully related to suprathreshold acoustic stimulation. Durations of suppressions to tone onsets change as a function of both frequency and age. Responsiveness develops to low frequencies before high.

That is, these data show a developmental gradient across frequencies and age in response to suprathreshold stimulation. Superimposed on this gradient is an effect of age, enhancing responses to changes along a stimulus continuum. Older animals respond more to a given percentage change in frequency than do newborn animals.

Since suppression times increase with both increasing intensity and amount of frequency change, then suppression times might decrease toward the average inter-peep interval as intensities and frequency changes decrease. Thus, peep suppressions might be useful in estimating both thresholds and difference limens in young chicks, as indicated in the next section.

THRESHOLDS

Although thresholds are probably the most basic psychophysical measures of perception, there have been few studies to present realistic estimates of these fundamental properties in newborns. We will present data on the development of two kinds of thresholds: the limits of detection and frequency discrimination. Absolute thresholds, the softest sounds of various frequencies to which chickens will respond, will be discussed first. Frequency difference limens, the smallest change in frequency that will elicit reliable suppression, will then be discussed.

From human psychophysics and signal detection theory (Green & Swets, 1966) we know the most efficient way to measure thresholds is with adaptive procedures, which include various modified up-down rules or staircase procedures (Wetherill & Levitt, 1965) discussed below. There are many versions of adaptive procedures, but they all vary the salience of a stimulus depending on the subject's responses to previous stimuli. The idea is to make the task harder whenever subjects successfully detect a stimulus, and to make the task easier when they behave randomly. "Up-runs" are sequences of trials where the subject's random responses cause the stimulus to become easier to detect. "Down-runs" are sequences of trials where more reliable responses cause the stimulus to become more difficult to detect. "Changes of direction" occur on trials when the subject's responses cause up runs to change to down runs or vice versa. A threshold is approached after several changes of direction.

Absolute Thresholds

Single-interval Procedure. Pilot data were collected with a single-interval staircase procedure, perhaps analogous to the Yes-No procedure of human psychophysics. Generally, the procedure was first to determine the expected duration of peep suppression if the animals did not hear a stimulus. This was done by presenting multiple control trials with no stimulus. Subsequent trials were stimulus trials in that they began with the onset of a pure tone. If the elicited suppression was greater than that expected when there was no tone, the animal was considered to have heard the tone, and the intensity of the tone was de-

creased on the next trial. Conversely, if the suppression was within the limits
of that observed during control trials, the animal was not considered to have
heard the tone and the intensity of that stimulus was increased on the next
trial. This procedure moved intensities up and down, depending on the
animal's responses, and converged on an estimate of threshold.

More specifically, after acclimation to a silent chamber for 2 to 5 minutes,
25 control trials were presented. From the distribution of these suppressions,
high and low cutoff values were calculated. The high cutoff was calculated as
three-quarters of a standard deviation above the mean suppression time on
control trials, selected to ensure that false positive responses were unlikely. A
low cutoff was calculated as one-fourth standard deviation above this mean,
selected to make false negative responses or "misses" unlikely. Consecutive
stimulus trials then followed. The intensity of the stimulus was decreased after
every suppression above the high cutoff. These "yes" trials formed part of a
down run. Conversely, the intensity of the stimulus was increased after every
suppression less than the low cut-off. These "no" trials formed part of an up
run. Threshold was arbitrarily calculated as the mean intensity (in dB SPL) on
all trials between the second and fourth change of direction in the staircase.

Figure 5 shows pilot data on absolute thresholds of 4-day-old chickens.
Thresholds were estimated with the single-interval procedure in about 10 birds
at each of 6 frequencies. These chicks show a standard audibility function
(Dooling, 1980). There is a best frequency around 2,000 Hz, expected from

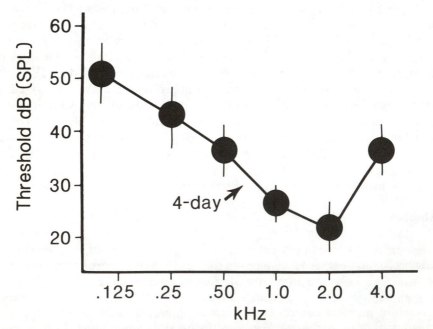

Figure 5. Pilot Data on Absolute Thresholds. This audiogram was collected with the
single-interval staircase procedure. Means and standard errors are shown for about
ten birds in each group.

physiologically recorded tuning curves (Rebillard & Rubel, 1981). There is a steep roll-off in sensitivity toward high frequencies, and a more gradual roll-off toward lower frequencies.

Figure 6 shows a comparison of these pilot data with other avian auditory thresholds obtained from the literature. The other data in this figure are all from mature birds, using operant conditioning techniques that take days and sometimes months to complete. It can be seen that the thresholds of 4-day-old chickens and other adult birds are similar, especially at low frequencies. Higher high-frequency thresholds in chickens than in other birds are predicted by physiological studies (Rebillard & Rubel, 1981; Rubel & Parks, 1975; Saunders, Coles, & Gates, 1973). Additionally, the relatively young age of these subjects is expected to elevate thresholds slightly at high frequencies. Most importantly, the close comparison of low-frequency thresholds derived from an unconditioned response with thresholds derived from more time-consuming conditioning procedures suggests that the peep-suppression procedure gives reasonable estimates of absolute thresholds. The speed of this procedure makes developmental studies possible.

This single-interval procedure is rapid, providing an estimated absolute threshold in about 10 minutes, but it may have two problems. First, since the control trials are measured at the beginning of the staircase, changing baseline peep rates from the beginning to the end of the staircase could affect the accuracy of the estimated thresholds. Second, the selection of a way to calculate the high and low cutoff values affects the estimate of threshold. Longer cutoffs cause higher thresholds, and vice versa. This is particularly troublesome for a developmental study, because the effect appears to be more noticeable in the younger animals, perhaps due to greater variability in the baseline response rates of the younger subjects. For these reasons, the major developmental analysis of absolute thresholds was done with a longer but more controlled procedure, described below.

Double-interval Procedure. In the "double-interval" staircase procedure (Gray & Rubel, in press) trials are presented in pairs: one stimulus trial and one control trial, given in random order within each pair. The stimulus is the onset of a series of tone pulses in tests for absolute thresholds. Control trials are the same as stimulus trials, except that the tones are not turned on. The bird's performance is evaluated after every pair of a stimulus and control trial. If the suppression on the stimulus trial is greater than that on the control trial, then the computer records a "correct" response. Conversely, if the suppression on the stimulus trial is less than or equal to the suppression on the control trial, then the computer records an "incorrect" response.

The intensity of the stimulus is decreased after two successive correct responses. Otherwise, the stimulus intensity is increased. That is, the task is made easier if there is no reliable suppression to the stimulus, and made harder when the animal demonstrates it heard the stimulus. This algorithm should allow a computer to converge rapidly on an animal's threshold.

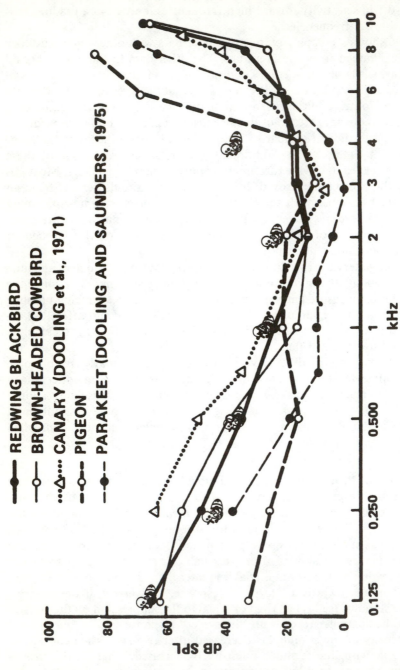

Figure 6. Comparison of Absolute Thresholds from 4-day-old Chickens with Thresholds of Mature Birds from the Literature. The pilot thresholds from Figure 5 are shown by the peeping chicks. The other data are from Hienz, Sinnott, & Sachs (1977). Copyright (1977) by the American Psychological Association. Reprinted with permission.

Figure 7 and Table 1 show the data from two absolute threshold tests at 2,000 Hz on a 0- and a 4-day-old chick. A correct response (graphed as a check) occurs when suppression on stimulus trials is greater than suppression on control trials of each pair. Otherwise, the response is considered incorrect and is graphed with an X. The intensity of the stimulus is varied according to the "2-down, 1-up" rule (Wetherill & Levitt, 1965) and is graphed in dB (SPL) along the "y" axis. The algorithm rapidly converges on an estimated threshold of about 30 dB SPL for the 4-day-old bird. The mean of the intensities where the staircase changed direction for the first four times (33, 27, 31 and 28 dB) is used as threshold (Levitt, 1971).

Figure 7 also shows a similar test on a newly hatched subject. Several incorrect responses at the beginning of the test drove the intensity upward. There was then some convergence around the estimated threshold of 65 dB SPL. Notice that the threshold of this young animal is much higher than the threshold of the older animal at this relatively high frequency.

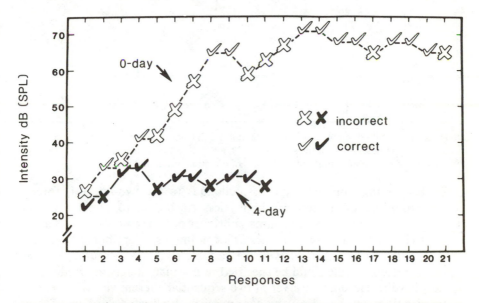

Figure 7. Examples of Absolute-Threshold Staircases from 0- and 4-day-old Chickens at 2000 Hz. Correct responses, graphed as a check, occur when suppressions on stimulus trials are greater than those on control trials. (See Table 1). Otherwise the response is considered incorrect and is graphed as X. The intensity of the stimulus is decreased after every two successive correct responses, and is increased after every incorrect response. The amount of change decreases as a function of the number of changes of direction because the procedure is supposedly converging on a more and more accurate estimate of threshold. The staircase is run for six changes of direction, but a mean of only the first four is used as an estimate of threshold. Note that the staircase converged on a much higher threshold for the younger subject, and that six changes of direction took many more trials than for the older bird.

Table 1. Data from the Double-interval Staircases Shown in Figure 7.

Response #	0-day-old			4-day-old		
	Stimulus	Control	dB	Stimulus	Control	dB
1	.3	.3	25	.3	.2	25
2	3.7	.1	33	.3	.3	25
3	.1	1.6	33	1.1	.2	33
4	.2	.1	41	.8	.3	33
5	.2	.2	41	.3	.4	27
6	.2	.2	49	1.0	.1	31
7	1.3	2.3	57	.3	.1	31
8	1.4	.2	65	.4	.4	28
9	.3	.2	65	.4	.3	31
10	.2	.8	59	4.9	.2	31
11	.2	.3	63	0	.3	28
12	.2	.2	67			
13	1.9	.3	71			
14	.4	.3	71			
15	.3	.2	68			
16	.3	.2	68			
17	.1	.1	65			
18	.5	.1	68			
19	.4	.1	68			
20	.2	.1	65			
21	.1	.2	65			

Note: Numbers under the columns labelled Stimulus and Control are the recorded durations of peep suppression in seconds for the stimulus and control trials, respectively. For each pair, dB is the intensity of the stimulus in dB SPL; changes of direction are underlined.

We believe that this procedure is analogous to the two-interval, forced-choice procedure of human psychophysics. According to signal detection theory (Green & Swets, 1966), a human observer of two sequential alternatives makes a choice based on two samples of a continuously distributed "evidence variable." If this hypothetical evidence variable could be measured, then an automated decision rule could be specified rather than merely inferred. Thus, we may have replaced an observer of two sequential alternatives with an automated decision rule based on the continuously distributed variable of peep suppression. In much the same way that Teller (1979) used the responses from trained observers of neonates' behaviors for psychophysical testing, we have used the "responses" of a programmed machine for psychophysical testing. The computer, and not the chicken, is forced to make a choice after every pair of the stimulus and control trials. This choice is either correct or incorrect, and the 2-down, 1-up rule is applied as normal.

Figure 8 shows the absolute thresholds obtained from 80 0- and 4-day-old chicks, using the two-interval procedure. The thresholds from 4-day-old chicks estimated with the single- and double-interval staircase procedures are very similar. A comparison of Figures 5 and 8 shows a replication of absolute thresholds.

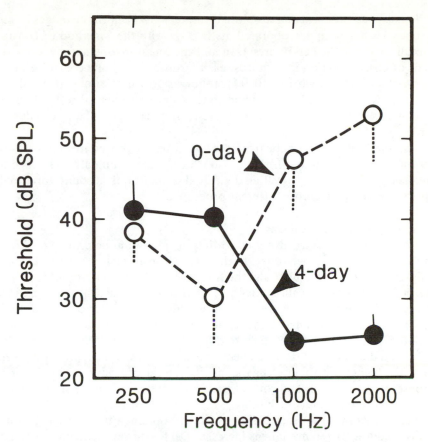

Figure 8. Absolute Thresholds in Two Ages of Chickens. Means and standard errors from the double-interval staircase procedure are shown for 10 birds in each group. Open circles indicate the estimated thresholds of 0-day-old chicks; filled circles the thresholds of 4-day-old chicks.

The developmental trends in absolute thresholds, shown in Figure 8, are of interest. There is roughly a 20 dB difference in thresholds between the age groups at high frequencies, but no reliable differences at low frequencies. Thus, there is in these threshold data the same age-by-frequency interaction that was seen in the responses to suprathreshold stimulation; responsiveness to low frequencies develops before responsiveness to high frequencies.

Other Procedures. This age-by-frequency interaction—maturing responsiveness to low frequencies before high frequencies—has also been replicated using a "modified method of limits" (Gray & Rubel, in press). In this test, each bird is tested at many frequencies, but for only two changes of direction at each frequency. The intensities increase by 10 dB until there are two correct responses, and then decrease by 5 dB until an incorrect response occurs. The results show that 0- and 4-day-old chicks have similar thresholds at low frequencies, but different thresholds at high frequencies.

Finally, the difference in absolute thresholds between the two ages at high frequencies has been corroborated at 1000 Hz with the "method of constant stimuli" (Gray & Rubel, in press). In an experiment involving only a few seconds of observation on many birds, each bird was given one control trial and then a stimulus trial, where a 1000 Hz tone was presented at one of five different intensities. Plots of suppression times from these near-threshold stimuli show that 4-day-old birds respond more to 1000 Hz tones than do 0-day-old birds.

The similarity of the data from several different procedures indicates the robustness of absolute thresholds in these young animals. The age-by-frequency interaction, as well as the actual estimates of absolute thresholds, are relatively stable across different procedures.

Frequency Difference Limens

Peep suppressions are also used to find the minimum detectable difference in frequency between two tones. In these tests, the animals are acclimated to a pulsing tone. On stimulus trials, the frequency of that background tone is increased by an amount called "delta-F." On control trials, the tone continues unchanged; that is, delta-F is zero. The size of delta-F is increased after incorrect responses; the change is made more noticeable after the subjects fail to suppress their peeping in response to a frequency change. Delta-F is decreased after an indication that the birds heard the change, after a suppression greater than the higher cutoff level in the single-interval procedure. That is, if responses to the stimulus and control trials are different, then the stimulus trials become more like control trials.

Figure 9 shows frequency difference limens obtained from the single-interval procedure. Difference limens increase with frequency, as in other animals. Furthermore, difference limens decrease with age, as discussed below.

The difference limens from 4-day-old chicks compare favorably with other estimates in the literature, as shown in Figure 10. Again, the other estimates were made on mature subjects, using conditioning procedures. The peep suppression technique seems to be as good as other techniques for estimating difference limens, and has the distinct advantage of allowing a developmental analysis.

Figure 11 shows these data replotted as delta-F/F, the ratio of the difference limen to the baseline frequency, expressed in percent. There is a consistent 1% improvement in difference limens at each frequency over the first 4 days of post-hatch life. This is consistent with psychological theories of perceptual sharpening (Gibson, 1969; Gottlieb, 1981; Rubel & Rosenthal, 1975), suggesting that normal development is accompanied by increasing abilities to detect changes along a sensory continuum. This same developmental trend, increasing sensitivity to frequency changes with age, was seen both in responsiveness to suprathreshold frequency changes, discussed earlier, as well as in difference limens.

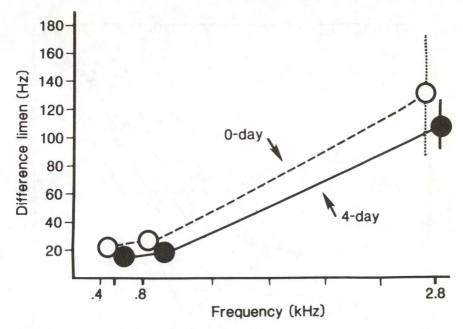

Figure 9. Frequency Difference Limens in Young Chickens. Shown are the minimum detectable changes in frequency, as estimated by the single-interval staircase procedure. Two ages of chickens were tested at three different frequencies; 500, 800, and 2813 Hz. Note that difference limens increase with frequency and decrease with age. Points are offset slightly to prevent overlap. Standard errors of the low-frequency means are just within the symbols.

Unfortunately, as indicated by the standard errors in Figure 9, the variability around these frequency difference limens is large. Clearly, however, after lumping over ages, a paired *t*-test of the points in Figure 11 would show a highly significant effect of age ($t\ (2) = 15.45$, $p < .005$). Although there appears to be a consistent 1% improvement in difference limens across frequencies, the variability is large enough to prevent a statistically significant effect of age at any one frequency. Thus, it may be premature to assess the extent of any age-by-frequency interaction in frequency difference limens.

The pattern of lower difference limens at the older age has been replicated in most but not all tests, with various modifications of the procedure. Data from the two-interval procedure were consistent with the single-interval procedure, though unexpectedly less sensitive; frequency difference limens at both 500 and 1000 Hz were estimated at 6% and 4% at 0 and 4 days of age respectively. A method of constant stimuli showed frequency difference limens at 1000 Hz were lower in 4-day-old than in 0-day-old birds, though the difference was not statistically significant. The modified method of limits has been used to test frequency difference limens at 12 different frequencies and intensities. Ten of these comparisons showed lower difference limens in older than in

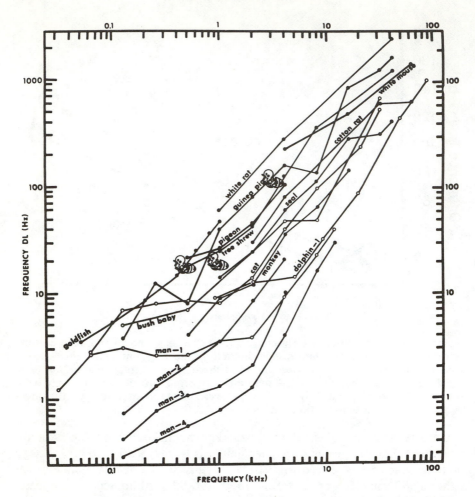

Figure 10. Comparison of the Frequency Difference Limens from 4-day-old Chickens with those of Mature Animals from the Literature. Difference limens from Figure 9 are plotted with data from Fay (1974). Copyright (1974) by the Acoustical Society of America. Reprinted with permission.

younger birds. Only at two low frequencies did this trend fail to replicate; and even then, the reversal was slight compared to the variability. Some failures to replicate the expected decrease between 0 and 4 days of age are expected, given the large amount of variability in the data. Nevertheless, the occasional similarity of limens at low frequencies, as well as the responses to suprathreshold frequency changes discussed earlier, make it hard to rule out an age-by-frequency interaction in frequency difference limens. This means that the available data are not consistent enough to indicate whether or not the trend of decreasing difference limens with age is stronger at higher than at lower frequencies.

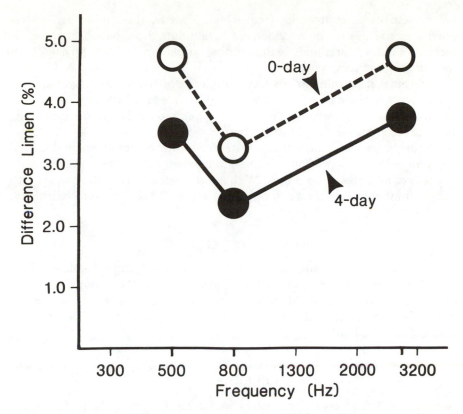

Figure 11. Frequency Difference Limens in Young Chickens. The data from Figure 9 are replotted as the "Weber Fraction." The minimum detectable change in frequency is divided by the frequency to which the birds were habituated and graphed in percent vs. frequency on a logarithmic scale.

In conclusion, the data taken all together strongly suggest that there is an overall trend of perceptual sharpening, that is, decreasing frequency difference limens with age. The variability in frequency difference limens was larger than the variability in absolute thresholds, perhaps because a change in frequency is not as salient a stimulus as the onset of a tone. Detecting a change in a tone may be more difficult for young animals than merely detecting the presence of that tone. This variability is consistent with data showing that humans are more prone to errors in discrimination tasks than in detection tasks (Jesteadt & Sims, 1975).

CONCLUSION

These studies provide estimates of absolute thresholds and frequency difference limens. These perceptual abilities change quickly over the first few days of postnatal life. The data show that responsiveness to low frequencies develops before responsiveness to high frequencies. That is, there is an age-by-frequency interaction in the development of absolute thresholds. The development of auditory thresholds is thus similar in pattern to other physiological measures of auditory function.

Perceptual sharpening brings increasing responsiveness to changes along a single sensory dimension (i.e. frequency) with age. Frequency difference limens appear to improve with age at all frequencies, although the trend may be stronger at higher than at lower frequencies.

In conclusion, we believe that a systematic study of developmental animal psychophysics is now possible. Unconditioned responses appear to be useful indicators of neonates' perceptions. With appropriate controls, the quickly estimated thresholds from these responses can approach adult levels of sensitivity.

ACKNOWLEDGMENTS

This research was conducted in the Department of Otolaryngology–Head and Neck Surgery, University of Virginia, and funded by the National Institutes of Health. Preparation of this review was aided by S. Stinson and supported by the Department of Otolaryngology–Head and Neck Surgery, University of Texas Medical School.

REFERENCES

Dooling, R. J. Behavior and psychophysics of hearing in birds. In A. N. Popper & R. R. Fay (eds.), *Comparative studies of hearing in vertebrates.* New York: Springer-Verlag, 1980.

Ehret, G. Development of absolute auditory thresholds in the house mouse (*Mus musculus*). *Journal of the American Audiology Society,* 1976, *1,* 179–184.

Ehret, G. Postnatal development in the acoustic system of the house mouse in the light of developing masked thresholds. *Journal of the Acoustical Society of America,* 1977, *62,* 143–148.

Ehret, G. & Romand, R. Postnatal development of absolute auditory thresholds in kittens. *Journal of Comparative and Physiological Psychology,* 1981, *95,* 304–311.

Fay, R. R. Auditory frequency discrimination in vertebrates. *Journal of the Acoustical Society of America,* 1974, *56,* 206–209.

Geldard, F. A. *The human senses.* 2nd ed. New York: John Wiley, 1972.

Gibson, E. J. *Principles of perceptual learning and development.* New York: Appleton-Century-Crofts, 1969.

Gottlieb, G. Ontogenesis of sensory function in birds and mammals. In E. Tobach, L. R. Aronson, & E. Shaw (eds.), *The biopsychology of development.* New York: Academic Press, 1971.

Gottlieb, G. The roles of experience in the development of behavior and the nervous system. In G. Gottlieb (ed.), *Studies on the development of behavior and the nervous system. Vol. 3. Neural and behavioral specificity.* New York: Academic Press, 1976.

Gottlieb, G. Roles of early experience in species-specific perceptual development. In R. N. Aslin, J. R. Alberts, & M. R. Petersen (eds.), *Development of perception.* Vol. 1. New York: Academic Press, 1981.

Gray, L., & Rubel, E. W. Development of responsiveness to suprathreshold acoustic stimulation in chickens. *Journal of Comparative and Physiological Psychology,* 1981, *95,* 188–198.

Gray, L. & Rubel, E. W. Development of absolute thresholds in chickens. *Journal of the Acoustical Society of America,* in press.

Green, D. M. & Swets, J. A. *Signal detection theory and psychophysics.* New York: John Wiley, 1966.

Hartline, H. K. The receptive fields of optic nerve fibers. *American Journal of Physiology,* 1940, *130,* 690–699.

Hienz, R. D., Sinnott, J. M., & Sachs, M. B. Auditory sensitivity of the redwing blackbird (*Agelaius phoeniceus*) and brown-headed cowbird (*Molothrus ater*). *Journal of Comparative and Physiological Psychology,* 1977, *91,* 1365–1376.

Hubel, D. H. & Wiesel, T. N. Receptive fields of single neurones in the cat's striate cortex. *Journal of Physiology,* 1959, *148,* 574–591.

Jesteadt, W. & Sims, S. L. Decision processes in frequency discrimination. *Journal of the Acoustical Society of America,* 1975, *57,* 1161–1168.

Kerr, L. M., Ostapoff, E. M., & Rubel, E. W. Influence of acoustic experience on the ontogeny of frequency generalization gradients in the chicken. *Journal of Experimental Psychology: Animal Behavior Processes,* 1979, *5,* 97–115.

Lettvin, J. Y., Maturana, H. R., McCulloch, W. S., & Pitts, W. H. What the frog's eye tells the frog's brain. *Proceedings of the Institute of Radio Engineers,* 1959, *47,* 1940–1951.

Lippe, W. Innate and experiential factors in the development of the visual system: Historical basis of current controversy. In G. Gottlieb (ed.), *Studies on the development of behavior and the nervous system. Vol. 3. Neural and behavioral specificity.* New York: Academic Press, 1976.

Levitt, H. Transformed up–down methods in psychoacoustics. *Journal of the Acoustical Society of America,* 1971, *49,* 467–477.

Marks, L. E. *Sensory processes: The new psychophysics.* New York: Academic Press, 1974.

Rebillard, G. & Rubel, E. W. Electrophysiological study of the maturation of auditory responses from the inner ear of the chick. *Brain Research,* 1981, *229,* 15–23.

Robinson, D. E. & Watson, C. S. Psychophysical methods in modern psychoacoustics. In J. V. Tobias (ed.), *Foundations of modern auditory theory.* Vol. 2. New York: Academic Press, 1972.

Robinson, D. W. & Dadson, R. S. A re-determination of equal-loudness relations for pure tones. *British Journal of Applied Physics,* 1956, *7,* 166–181.

Rubel, E. W. Ontogeny of structure and function in the vertebrate auditory system. In M. Jacobson (ed.), *Handbook of sensory physiology. Vol. 9. Development of sensory systems.* New York: Springer-Verlag, 1978.

Rubel, E. W & Parks, T. N. Organization and development of brain stem auditory nuclei of the chicken: Tonotopic organization of N. magnocellularis and N. laminaris. *Journal of Comparative Neurology,* 1975, *164,* 411–433.

Rubel, E. W & Rosenthal, M. H. The ontogeny of auditory frequency generalization in the chicken. *Journal of Experimental Psychology: Animal Behavior Processes,* 1975, *1,* 287–297.

Saunders, J. C., Coles, R. B., & Gates, G. R. The development of auditory evoked responses in the cochlea and cochlear nuclei of the chick. *Brain Research,* 1973, *63,* 59–74.

Shnerson, A. & Willott, J. F. Ontogeny of the acoustic startle response in C57BL/6J mouse pups. *Journal of Comparative and Physiological Psychology,* 1980, *94,* 36–40.

Stebbins, W. C. (ed.). *Animal psychophysics: The design and conduct of sensory experiments.* New York: Appleton-Century-Crofts, 1970.

Stevens, S. S. *Psychophysics: Introduction to its perceptual, neural, and social prospects.* New York: John Wiley, 1975.

Teller, D. Y. The forced-choice preferential looking procedure: A psychophysical technique for use with human infants. *Infant Behavior Development,* 1979, *2,* 135–153.

Trahiotis, C. & Robinson, D. E. Auditory psychophysics. *Annual Review of Psychology,* 1979, *30,* 31–61.

Trehub, S. E., Schneider, B. A., & Endman, M. Developmental changes in infants' sensitivity to octave-band noises. *Journal of Experimental Child Psychology,* 1980, *29,* 282–293.

Wetherill, G. B. & Levitt, H. Sequential estimation of points on a psychometric function. *British Journal of Mathematical and Statistical Psychology,* 1965, *18,* 1–10.

INTRODUCTION TO SECTION 3

Behavioral Measures of Higher Psychological Processes

In this section, we begin to deal with higher-order psychological processes than those which engaged the psychophysicists in the previous section. In Chapter 8, Darwin Muir and Rachel Clifton review the onset and course of the human infant's head-turning response to sound or, more generally speaking, the auditory spatial localization abilities of the developing infant. The infant's head-turning response to sound is readily elicited during the first 2 months or so of postnatal life; then it wanes for several months (at least to nonvocal stimuli), only to reappear around 4 or 5 months of age. The neonatal head-turn response to sound is a very basic and robust behavioral response, which is not only present in the newborn but rather impervious to perinatal trauma and congenital malformations associated with mild to severe hearing loss. The authors hypothesize that around 5 to 6 months of age the function of the head-turn response may be more in the service of visual search than it is earlier on.

In the next chapter, Peter Jusczyk describes the history and present use of the high-amplitude sucking (HAS) technique in studies of speech perception. Infants appear to readily change their level of sucking when such changes are made contingent upon auditory stimulation, thus making the HAS a useful method for studying speech and hearing in prelinguistic infants. Considerable controversy surrounds the very young infant's ability to distinguish speech sounds: Is this ability a general property of many mammalian auditory systems, or is it specialized for speech sounds as such? Jusczyk discusses the manifold of variables that must be considered when using the HAS procedure for inferring auditory perceptual discrimination in the infant, as well as attempts to increase the reliability and sensitivity of the procedure. Of special relevance to studies of speech perception, HAS is not well suited to making comparisons of the relative discriminability of phonetic constrasts. Efforts to improve this aspect of the procedure have not been particularly successful. In addition to its use as a measure of discrimination, the HAS procedure has been extended to the study of perceptual categories (similarity). It is clear that further refinements are in order if the procedure is to continue to be useful in the study of the infant's auditory capacities, especially the measurement of the capacity of individual infants, which is now not possible. More on this problem below.

Patricia Kuhl continues the review of methods of studying infant speech perception by describing the head-turn, auditory preference, and auditory-visual speech perception techniques. In an interesting corollary to Muir and Clifton's review, Kuhl finds the head-turn technique particularly well suited to the study of speech perception in infants from about 6 to 10 months of age. It has the advantage over the HAS technique of being able to provide data on individuals, for example. The auditory-preference technique is especially useful in determining the preferential attention-getting value of acoustic stimuli, and can be used to chart aspects of the infant's social as well as linguistic development. The recently developed auditory-visual speech perception technique involves cross-modal interactions, and so may prove valuable in studying the more cognitive aspects of speech in infancy.

In the most ambitious and wide-ranging review in the book, Marc Bornstein synthesizes the vast literature bearing on the habituation of attention as a measure of visual information processing in human infants. Specifically, he covers the use of habituation to study the infant's sensation, perception, and cognition in the form of experiments concerning detection and discrimination, categorization, memory, concept formation, and individual differences in cognition. He concludes that habituation is a powerful, mutually understandable (although situationally-specific) experimental language that can be established readily between developmental investigators and human infants. Thus, habituation has proven a very powerful procedure for understanding the psychology of infancy, and Bornstein's chapter attests to the versatility and success of this otherwise "lowly" behavioral phenomenon which is found throughout the animal kingdom.

Among the principal things that the infant does naturally or spontaneously are *looking* and *reaching*. While we have so far covered "looking" as a measure of one or another aspect of infant perception, we now turn to the use of reaching as a measure of tri-dimensional or visual depth perception. In their chapter, Albert Yonas and Carl Granrud outline the problems and limits of inference, using reaching as evidence for depth perception in the human infant and other primate infants as well. They want to know that the infant is responding to "spatial information," and that kind of information, according to Yonas and Granrud, is available in three forms: binocular, static-monocular, and kinetic. A recurrent problem in infant research is making statements about their abilities from negative instances. For example, when an infant under 5 months of age fails to reach appropriately for a graspable object, does that signify the absence of depth perception? The matter is much clearer, of course, when the infant *does* reach appropriately for a graspable object. In any event, these are the common problems faced by all students of infant behavior—it is just made more obvious in the chapter at hand. In general, infants of 5 months or more of age tend to reach for the nearer of two objects that have been matched for retinal size, and they do so when binocular cues are available but not when restricted to monocular viewing. The so-called "pre-reaching" stage (0-5 months) remains to be further analyzed by innovative approaches, some of which are already available. Reaching does show promise as a measure of depth perception.

In the final chapter in this section on behavioral measures of higher-order psychological processes, Elizabeth Spelke reviews preferential looking methods as tools for the study of cognition in infancy, examining in detail the infant's looking at (a) novel visual displays, (b) sounding objects (audiovisual objects), and (c) novel events (the causes of object movement and the persistence of material bodies). Spelke compares reaching and looking and what they may, respectively, be measuring, and she explores the potentials of preferential looking not only as a measure of perception but as an indication of the infant's conception of objects and events; to wit, the origins and development of human knowledge. For the young infant of 4 to 5 months, objects in motion bring out object perception much more readily than static two-dimensional surfaces, or even tri-dimensional patterns. Human faces are of special interest to infants, and such faces are usually mobile, thus possibly laying the experiential basis for the maturational emergence of the perception of a partly occluded face as a unitary, connected object between 4 and 5 months of age. Spelke next moves to a consideration of the infant's perception of intermodal (audiovisual) unity. Since there is a close tie between intermodal unity and knowledge, the infant's perception of intermodal relations is of special relevance to the question of the development of cognition. Obviously, now the infant is not only looking but listening! By at least 4½ months, infants look longer at objects with a corresponding sound; for example, a stuffed animal bouncing in concert with a percussive sound. Infants differ from adults in that they relate sound to pattern (not necessarily impact) of movement, whereas adults relate sound to moments of impact. Again, their early experience with faces talking may facilitate the perception of *synchrony* between movement and sound: Young infants look longer at a face that is moving in synchrony with a voice than at one that is not. Six- to 8-month-old infants are sensitive to abstract properties of sound and sight as well: They look longer at the objects in a visual display when the number corresponds to the number (two or three) of drumbeats they were previously exposed to. Preferential looking can thus be used to assess infants' knowledge of at least one abstract property of the world. Spelke explores these and other issues, including the limitations of preferential looking, in considerable and critical detail in her review of this literature, to which she herself has made such a significant contribution.

8

INFANTS' ORIENTATION TO THE LOCATION OF SOUND SOURCES

Darwin Muir

Queen's University
Kingston, Ontario, Canada

Rachel Keen Clifton

University of Massachusetts,
Amherst

161.12

Historically, two conflicting views exist concerning the development of infants' spatial responses to sounds. Piaget (1952), who represents a gradual emergence position, theorized that little perceptual organization exists in neonates, and that the few reflexes that can be elicited by auditory, visual, and tactile stimulation are not perceptually unified. In terms of sound localization, he noted that his own infants responded crudely to moving visual targets during their first month of life, but did not respond to laterally presented sounds. The infants began to turn in search of a sound source during their second month, responding more accurately as they explored the natural correlations between sights, sounds, and touches, enabling them to begin construction of a multimodal representation of space. Thus, the ability to orient to sounds is seen to be accomplished gradually through interaction with the environment.

A contrasting point of view has been expressed by Bower (1979, 1982), who argued that infants are born with a crude perceptual organization. He stated that newborns respond immediately to certain "amodal" properties of a stimulus, such as intensity, tempo, and location in space. Their initial deficit is the inability to distinguish the modality of inputs, whether they are visual, auditory, or tactile. In support of his theory, Bower noted that newborns will flick

171

their eyes toward laterally positioned sounds of moderate intensities (e.g., Crassini & Broerse, 1980; Turkewitz, Birch, Moreau, Levy, & Cornwell, 1966; Wertheimer, 1961). More to the point, Mendelson and Haith (1976) reported that newborns scanned initially toward, and then away from, the location of a voice reading poetry, suggesting that location of sound will influence scanning patterns as well as initial eye movements.

In the eye movement experiments, investigators attenuated or eliminated infants' head movements to achieve clean oculomotor records. However, we normally react to off-centered sounds by turning our heads as well as our eyes in their direction. One might expect even more dramatic auditory localization responses if infants were free to move their heads during testing. Indeed, evidence for the ability to orient toward sound has existed for many years in clinical reports (Brazelton, 1973; Hammond, 1970; Wolff, 1959), but only recently has it been demonstrated in controlled laboratory conditions. Using specific procedures that will be described later in this chapter, we have demonstrated unequivocally that newborns will turn their heads in the direction of sounds on the majority of trials (Muir & Field, 1979; Clifton, Morrongiello, Kulig, & Dowd, 1981a).

To summarize, the behavioral data from numerous studies are consistent. Newborns show head and eye movements, including scanning, that are spatially coordinated with sound. The theoretical difficulty is to resolve the meaning of these directional responses. What inferences, if any, may we draw concerning the infant's construction of auditory and visual space? In exploring this question, two points are relevant. First, spatially oriented head and eye movements can be elicited subcortically; thus, their mere presence does not imply a sophisticated representation of space. Second, the performance of the oculomotor system should not be confused with visual space perception. Since eye movements are intimately involved with vision, one is tempted to infer that vision itself is coordinated with sound rather than the oculomotor system. This inference is seductive, because eye movements can be spatially oriented, just as sound is. In contrast, no one would argue that the auralpalpebral reflex (eyeblink to a loud sound) provides evidence for auditory/visual coordination, because this oculomotor response has no obvious spatial direction. Although a conservative view would prohibit the inference of innate intersensory coordination based on eye movements to sound, this view does not rule out a special role for this response in later development. Butterworth (1981) pointed out that a functional connection between sensory systems at birth would predispose the organism for later learned associations. In the natural world, sights often accompany sounds. A sensory-motor program that directed the eyes toward a sound would have adaptive value for the organism, laying the basis for acquiring knowledge of cross-modal properties of objects.

In this chapter, we will review research from our laboratories on the development of sound localization in infants. First, the characteristics of the newborn localization response, and variables affecting its occurrence, will be discussed. Next, the developmental course of head turning to sounds will be described to point out a dramatic decline in localization behavior between 2 and 4 months, followed by reappearance after 4 months of age. Finally, developmental changes between newborns and 4- to 6-month-olds will be described, in an attempt to evaluate the notion that neonatal head turning is a subcortically mediated reflex, while older infants' turning is a higher-level response to sound, incorporating a representation of auditory space.

AUDITORY LOCALIZATION RESPONSES IN NEWBORNS

General Methodology

Newborn infants have been tested under controlled laboratory conditions using a procedure adapted from Brazelton's Neonatal Assessment Scale (Brazelton, 1973). The stimulus, the baby's posture during sound presentation, and an alert state are all considered important components of the procedure. The auditory stimulus is a rattle sound produced by a plastic bottle partially filled with popcorn kernels, shaken rhythmically at a rate of approximately two shakes per sec. The rattle sound may be produced "live" during the session, or may be pre-recorded and presented through stationary loudspeakers. A spectrum analysis shows that this sound is a broadband stimulus with a relatively flat energy distribution between 10 and 13,000 Hz, with a peak around 2900 Hz. The average peak sound pressure level varies across studies from 75 to 85 dB (SPL), against background levels from 48 to 58 dB; sound pressure level differences within these values do not appear to affect localization responses.

In most experimental studies, newborn subjects have generally been 2-3 days of age, and are chosen on the basis of a normal, complication-free pregnancy, delivery, and early neonatal medical course. They are tested approximately 1½ hrs after a feeding and, to remain in the sample, they must maintain an alert state throughout testing. Subject loss varies from 10 to 50% across studies.

During testing, one experimenter holds the baby in a semi-supine position facing the ceiling with the baby's head and back supported in such a way that head movements are unrestrained. The baby's head is placed in the midline at the beginning of each trial, and a second experimenter presents the sound approximately 20 cm from one side of the baby's head for 10-20 sec, or until the baby makes a large head rotation, usually greater than 30° off midline. When a rattle is used, a "silent" rattle, consisting of an empty plastic bottle, is shaken opposite the other ear to balance tactile and visual cues. Between trials, the experimenter attempts to maintain alertness by bringing the baby to his or her shoulder, patting and crooning to the baby, then placing it in position for the next trial. Experimenter bias by the person holding the infant is controlled by presenting the rattle sound simultaneously to both of that person's ears over earphones, resulting in a sensation of midline sound on every trial. Observer bias in scoring the response is controlled by videotaping the baby's performance for later analysis by observers naive to the actual location of the sound.

Response measures include the direction and latencies of the first head movement (greater than 10°) and that of the first large head rotation (usually greater than 30°)—generally they are the same. Interobserver reliabilities on all response measures are greater than 88%, and most are above 94%.

The performance of infants in four studies, two from Clifton's and two from Muir's laboratories, are summarized in Figure 1. The percentage of major head turns toward and away from the sound source and the number of trials

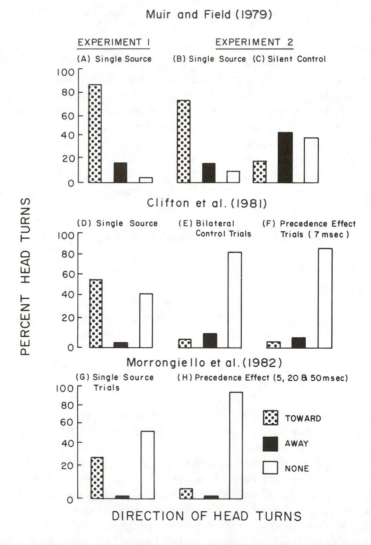

Figure 1. A comparison of three neonatal auditory-localization studies from Muir's and Clifton's laboratories. Note the higher percentage of head turning toward sound on single-source trials (A, B, D, and G) compared to the lack of such responses on various types of control conditions (C, E, F, and H). See text for details.

on which no large head turn occurred are shown in Figures 1-A, B, D, and G. Obviously, when newborns turn their heads, it is in the direction of sound source on the vast majority of trials (between 80% and 100% of head turning trials). On control trials, either silent (Figure 1-C) or with midline sound (Figure 1-E), infants show less head turning and have a tendency to turn to the right when they do turn. Also, they turn farther on lateral sound than on silent-control trials, usually rotating their heads to face the stimulus. Finally, the response is very slow; following sound onset, latency to begin a turn is an average of 2½ to 4 sec, with 3½ to 5½ sec required to complete a turn (Muir & Field, 1979; Clifton et al., 1981a). The long latency of the response, coupled with its slow movement and the need to manipulate the infant during intertrial intervals to maintain alertness, result in trial periods lasting as long as 20 sec. Usually, 16 to 18 trials are the maximum possible in a session, because, for many newborns, a state of calm alertness will not last beyond 5 or 6 minutes. Longer sessions can be expected to produce greater subject loss from the sample, because state changes toward drowsiness or fussiness will inevitably occur. We find that attempting to maintain an alert state in the face of an endogenous state change is useless. One of the greatest difficulties of this procedure is the necessity for the baby to be in a calm, alert state—a state occupying a very small proportion of the newborn's day.

Perhaps the most striking disparity between the results of Muir and Field and those of Clifton and colleagues is the frequency of lateral sound trials on which no head turn occurs (comparing Figures 1-A and B with Figures 1-D and G). Although attempts were made to test under identical conditions, Clifton's subjects only turned on 50% or less of the trials, while Muir's subjects consistently turned on 75-85% of total trials. Several procedural differences may account for this discrepancy. One factor is the number of trials on which a sound was presented from the side. Clarkson, Morrongiello, and Clifton (1982) found that the likelihood of a turn toward the sound source on lateral sound trials increased as the probability of lateral sounds increased from .25 to .75 relative to trails where sound was presented at the midline. In Clifton's work, lateral trials were presented on 33% of trials for Figures 1-D, E, and F, and 25% of trials for G and H panels. In contrast, Muir and Field had 100% for panel A and 67% for panels B and C, respectively.

Muir's infants also turned more frequently on control trials. In Clifton's studies, the lower incidence of correct head turning toward sound was matched by less turning on midline control trials. (Response on control trials was 65% vs. 20% for Muir and Clifton, respectively.) Clifton's procedures tended to keep infants in the midline. For establishment of statistically reliable head turning, this procedure appears adequate, since the false alarm rate is lowered along with correct head turning toward sound. Clarkson, Morrongiello, and Clifton (1982) suggested that lateral sound trials occupy at least 50% of total trials, to ensure that reliable head turning is elicited. With proportions less than 50%, one risks having the incidence of correct responding drop to chance levels.

In conclusion, the alert newborn will turn its head toward sound presentation from the left or right side, with a slow but reliable movement. Very few contralateral turns are observed. The rhythmically shaken rattle stimulus may be critical, but a careful comparison of different stimuli has not been made. Having the baby held by an experimenter during the test, rather than lying supine in a crib, is considered important. Generally, short sessions are advisable, because fatigue and state changes can produce response decrements that could be mistaken for habituation. In our labs, reliable habituation of the response has not been observed in 12 to 15 trials (Clifton, Morrongielo, Kulig, & Dowd, 1981b) but appears to occur in longer sessions (Brody, Zelazo, & Chaika, 1984).

Individual Differences: Responses of High-Risk Infants

Because the vast majority of "normal" newborns turn toward sound at birth, we assumed that spontaneous head orienting toward sounds had potential as a clinical tool to assess the hearing of newborns. Its advantages over other methods, such as cribograms, cardiac responses, and brainstem evoked potentials, include: (a) simple procedures, easily taught to pediatric nurses; (b) short test duration of a few minutes; (c) inexpensive equipment—a homemade rattle; and (d) the simple scoring and recording of the data.

Many infants who are suspected of hearing problems have other problems as well. The use of head orienting to sound as an assessment would be greatly enhanced if this behavior were unaffected by neonatal trauma unrelated to hearing problems. That is, if neonatal head turning proved sensitive to a broad range of neonatal problems, its utility for assessing hearing would be reduced. In the early experimental work, only normal infants were tested; indeed, subject criteria for many studies demanded optimal obstetric, delivery, and postnatal medical histories. The actual contribution of various risk factors is unknown, although clinical reports by Als, Tronick, Lester and Brazelton (1977), and Kurtzberg, Vaughan, Daum, Grellong, Albin, and Rotkin (1979), suggest that infants with low birth weights due to prematurity or fetal malnourishment perform poorly on various localization tasks. Muir and colleagues (Low, Galbraith, Muir, Killen, Pater, & Karchmar, 1983) conducted a study to screen for early identification of handicaps among survivors of neonatal intensive care at the regional hospital. As part of their newborn assessment, auditory localization tests were conducted. An examiner, naive with respect to stimulus location, held the baby while a second examiner presented rattle sounds for 30 sec, or until the baby turned his or her head greater than 45° from the midline. Each baby received eight trials; at the end of each trial, the second examiner recorded the direction and latency of the response. All infants were tested within 2 weeks of their estimated due date (i.e., their conceptual age = 40 weeks); any medically unstable babies were excluded.

Preliminary results, presented in Table 1, show that infants classified into certain high-risk categories perform as well as normal infants, but there were notable exceptions. Preterm infants and infants of diabetic mothers (groups 1,

Table 1. High-Risk Infants
Influence of Biological Risk Factors on Performance of Infants Tested
at 40 Weeks Conceptional Age
(Percentage = turns toward sound/total turns)

High-Risk Category	N	Percent	Standard Deviation
1. Premature (GA < 34 weeks) B.Wt. < 1500 g	53	77	19
2. Premature B.Wt. > 1500 g	52	85	14
3. Infants of Diabetic Mothers	18	77	24
4. Neurologically Suspect (e.g. seizures)	16	70	23
5. Growth Retarded (< 3rd percentile)	66	70	21
6. Asphyxiated (Blood gas analysis)	16	72	19

($F = 3.91$, $p < .002$, $df = 5$, 215)

2, and 3) turned to sound significantly more often than full-term infants (groups 4-6) who exhibited signs of neurological damage (such as seizures), or those who experienced intrauterine growth retardation or asphyxia (according to blood-gas analysis). Furthermore, 43 preterm infants who were healthy enough to be tested during their preterm period (average conceptional age = 35 weeks) performed almost as well as when they were retested near their expected due date. These infants turned toward sound on 75% and 88% of the trials, respectively (Muir, in press). However, on preterm tests, infants exhibited poor tone and less spontaneous activity, took significantly longer to complete a response (median latency = 12 sec, compared with 7 sec at term), and failed to respond on more trials (16% compared to 2% at term).

The performance of these preterm infants is much better than those of Kurtzberg, et al. (1979), but procedural differences may account for the discrepancy. Kurtzberg's auditory stimulus lasted 5 sec, while Muir's 30-sec stimulus may have allowed preterms time to complete the response. The results on growth retarded infants agree with Als, et al. (1977). Muir (1982) has speculated that, given their state of malnourishment, once these infants have been manipulated into an alert state prior to testing, they immediately become aware of nutritional needs and seek food rather than remaining quietly attentive to sound localization cues.

Our tentative conclusion is that, although some infants who suffer severe perinatal insults respond poorly, many are quite capable of orienting toward sounds. In particular, preterm infants perform this response with surprising competence when tested properly. Thus, the auditory localization task may be relatively independent of neonatal problems unrelated to hearing disorders. Unfortunately, Muir (in press) also found that this task may not be helpful in detecting certain types of hearing loss. Two babies suffering unilateral aural atresia and microtia on their right side (a blocked ear canal and absent pinna) were tested as newborns. This extreme congenital malformation is associated with mild to severe hearing loss on the abnormal side (see Jaffe, 1977). These babies were expected either to perform at chance levels or to turn toward the side on which sound was louder, i.e. their left or normal side. In fact, both infants turned toward the sound on the vast majority of trials, irrespective of its direction, on repeated test sessions which were conducted using the "blind" handler and scoring methods described above in "General Methodology."

We do not rule out the use of auditory localization tests as a neonatal hearing assessment. Indeed, we have tested several newborns, later determined to have severe bilateral deafness, who failed to turn toward off-centered sound, even at intensities between 90-110 dB SPL. However, to be useful as a clinical instrument to screen for less-severe hearing loss, stimuli near threshold should be capable of eliciting head turning. The research manipulating sound pressure level remains to be done before we can determine how sensitive this procedure is.

Contextual Problems in Localization Testing

A final methodological issue concerns the background, nonauditory aspects of the testing environment. As discussed in "General Methodology," Muir's infants may have turned more often on lateral sound trials than Clifton's because he used a higher density of lateral, as opposed to central, or control, trials. However, another factor may have contributed to their performance differences. Muir's infants faced a uniform, dimly lit, white ceiling with a video-camera positioned at an angle below their line of sight at a distance of 1.5 m, while Clifton's infants directly faced a camera approximately .45 m away. Perhaps the view of the circular camera lens, highly contrasted against the white ceiling, provided the babies with an attractive visual target which held their attention throughout some trials. Also, Clifton's babies were tightly swaddled, which might have produced symmetrical tactile stimulation near their faces and possibly inhibited general arousal levels. Muir's babies were usually loosely swaddled or unwrapped. The issue of competing auditory, visual and tactile cues has been investigated by Muir and co-workers using an intermodal conflict paradigm.

The theoretical rationale behind these studies (also see Butterworth, 1981) has to do with whether infants have intersensory spatial coordination at birth (Bower's position) or develop it later through maturation and experience (Piaget's position). In the typical intermodal spatial-conflict study, infants' responses are recorded when they are presented with, for example, a salient visual target on one side and an auditory event on the other side. If there is no common spatial framework but some localization ability in all modalities, newborns should respond to stimuli in either one modality or the other (dominance) or distribute responses equally between modalities (nondominance), but not show conflict. In Bower's view, newborns have a primitive intermodal spatial unity and either do or do not differentiate among modalities. If they differentiate, they should show signs of conflict when stimuli are in discordant locations, perhaps becoming upset. Alternatively, if they have a primitive unity but cannot differentiate among modalities, (a view Bower favors), they would be faced with relatively "equivalent" stimuli emanating from two directions, and should compromise. Given the symmetrical nature of this "equivalent" bilateral input, they might be expected to keep their heads centered, rather than turn to face one or the other stimulus.

The conflict paradigm has been used to investigate auditory-visual coordination in newborns by McGurk, Turnure, and Creighton (1977), Butterworth and Castillo (1976), and Castillo and Butterworth (1981). They measured the direction of neonates' eye movements when auditory and visual stimuli were presented off the midline in the same or opposite directions, and found that the presence of sound had no effect; infants appeared to be captured by the visual stimulus, supporting Piaget's (1952) nonintegration view. However, the results are not surprising, given that the newborns also failed to orient their eyes toward the auditory target when it was presented alone, indicating that they may not have appreciated the direction of the sound and thus experienced no conflict. As a prerequisite condition for testing auditory-visual conflict, reliable orientation responses must be established in both auditory and visual modalities.

Three studies have demonstrated that salient, competing visual and tactile stimuli can interfere with an infant's localization responses to sounds. Fischer-Fay (1981) tested 20 infants in total darkness with rattle sounds presented from a speaker $90°$ from an infant's midline and a stationary circular pattern of light-emitting diodes, placed $30°$ to one side of midline. Four stimulus conditions comprised a 4-trial block; visual alone (V), auditory alone (A), visual and auditory stimuli on the same side (A + V) or visual and auditory stimuli on opposite sides (A vs. V). Each infant received four 4-trial blocks. The babies' head movements were recorded throughout each 20-sec trial by videotaping the crowns of their heads with an infrared-sensitive camera and light source. A thin line was placed on top of their heads along the midsagittal suture to provide more precise scoring of head rotations. The results for the direction of the first head turn greater than $10°$ are summarized in Table 2 (Exp. I). The A and

Table 2. Conflict Studies
Percentage of Head Turning Directed Toward Different Stimuli
(A = rattle, V = red circles; T = air puffs)

Experiment		Stimuli on One Side				Stimuli on Opposite Sides		
		A	V	A+V	T	V vs. A	V vs. T	A vs. T
Exp. I.	Fischer-Fay (1981) (turn > 10°) N = 20	78	76	85		65 vs. 34		
Exp. II	Muir (unpub) (turn > 30°) N = 12	67	88	83		44 vs. 54		
Exp. III	Muir, Whalley, and Pilon (unpub) (turn > 30°)	(Study 1—N = 18)				(Study 2—N = 12)		
		100	93		75	57 vs. 43	55 vs. 45	56 vs. 44

V stimuli were equally effective in eliciting a head turn when they were presented alone, and together on the same side. Furthermore, presenting stimuli on opposite sides of the midline significantly disrupted the reliable localization responses to either stimulus presented alone or together, although the red circle attracted significantly more head movements than the sound in this condition.

Muir (unpublished) replicated Fischer-Fay's finding using a different set of stimuli matched for movement properties. Twelve 3-day-olds received 16 10-sec trials in four 4-trial blocks (A, V, A + V, and A vs. V), using the same design and procedure as Fischer-Fay's, with the following exceptions. The auditory stimulus was a popcorn rattle and the visual stimulus was a red circle of light 4 cm in diameter, constructed by placing filters on the lens of a manually operated flash light. Both stimuli were held by the experimenter 20 cm away from the infant's head and moved in the same rhythm (2 beats per sec). The rattle was shaken approximately 60° from the infant's midline, while the light was rotated in a small circular arc centered approximately 45° from the infant's midline; on compound trials, the stimuli were presented simultaneously. As before, the room was completely dark except for a TV monitor which displayed a very dim, outline frontal view image of the baby's upper trunk and head (the monitor was adjusted to low "brightness" and high "contrast"). The monitor could be seen by the experimenter holding the baby, which allowed her to keep the baby in the proper position throughout the trial. On each trial the direction of the first head turn greater than 30° was scored by a naive observer from the video record. The results, presented in Table 2 (Exp. II), suggest that in certain A vs. V conditions, no visual capture will occur. In this case, when the auditory and visual events were placed on opposite sides, the babies failed to turn significantly more often towards one or the other stimulus (averaging 1.8 out of 4 trials to the visual and 2.2 out of 4 trials to the auditory stimuli). This occurred in spite of the fact that the babies turned significantly less often toward the A condition compared with the V condition. The poorer auditory localization performance may have been due to the fact that the sound source was closer to the midline than in earlier studies, making its direction harder for the newborns to detect.

Finally, two studies were conducted to evaluate the extent of localization to off-centered touch and its potential for disrupting auditory and visual localization. In Exp. III, Studies 1 and 2, the stimuli consisted of the rattle, the red circle, and an air puff which was produced by an experimenter squeezing a nasal aspirator with its nozzle pointed 1.5 cm from the corner of the infant's mouth, toward the cheek. Stimuli were presented as in Exp. II, with a rhythm of 2 rattle shakes, visual rotations, or air puffs per sec.

In Exp. III, Study 1, 18 infants were randomly assigned to receive either the sound, light, or air puff on 8 stimulus trials, 4 per side, along with 4 silent control trials. Video recordings were analyzed as before, to determine the degree to which the different stimuli elicited head turns. The percentage of turns toward each stimulus is given in Table 2, Exp. III, Study 1; the auditory and visual stimuli were equally effective, while the tactile stimulus (T) elicited significantly fewer major head turns in its direction.

Next, in Exp. III, Study 2, the same stimuli were presented to 12 subjects for 18 trials. However, this time a trial lasted 10 sec, and each infant received six 3-trial blocks where the auditory and visual stimuli were presented on opposite sides on one trial, the auditory and tactile stimuli conflicted on the next, and the visual and tactile stimuli conflicted on a third trial. Each stimulus appeared on a side equally often, and the 6 possible orders of presentation of the 3 trial types were arranged in a balanced Latin square design using the sequence given in Cochran and Cox (1957, p. 134). Two subjects were assigned to each of the 6 sequences. There were no order effects or changes in performance with respect to trials. The percentage of trials on which the first head turn was directed toward each of the components in the three conflict conditions are shown in Table 2 (Exp. III, Study 2). Clearly, the results of these two studies are in line with the first two experiments, showing that conflict between stimuli in two modalities always reduces the probability of a head-turn response to either one, relative to those when the stimuli are presented alone. Furthermore, in Study 2 no evidence of dominance in any modality emerged.

Two methodological conclusions can be drawn from the results of these intermodal spatial-conflict studies. First, precautions should be taken to insure the absence of potentially interfering visual or tactile stimuli in auditory localization experiments. Second, in contrast with the results of McGurk et al. (1977) and Butterworth and Castillo (1976), when appropriate stimulus conditions and the head-turning responses are used, sound in one location can lead an infant away from a visual target in a different location. Although there is a trend for vision to dominate audition, it does not always appear.

Finally, a theoretical conclusion regarding Bower's intermodal unity versus Piaget's intermodal independence positions cannot be drawn from the above research. No support was found for Bower's contention that babies would cry or fail to respond more often under spatial conflict than nonconflict conditions. Instead, they appeared to distribute their attention almost equally between the locations when presented with two spatially discrete, salient events, a result which may be expected if infants perceived the two stimuli to be the same or different. Additional control conditions are needed. For example, one might infer intermodal discrimination if infants adopt a side bias when identical stimuli are presented on either side of midline. Alternatively, if they distribute attention equally among redundant elements positioned along the horizontal plane, infants might focus on an odd stimulus from one modality surrounded by several equally salient identical stimuli from a second modality.

AUDITORY LOCALIZATION RESPONSES OF OLDER INFANTS

Early Developmental Changes in Auditory Localization

Studies conducted independently in our laboratories (Clifton et al., 1981b; Clifton, Morrongiello, & Dowd, 1984; Field, Muir, Pilon, Sinclair, & Dodwell, 1980; Muir, Abraham, Forbes, & Harris, 1979; Muir, in press) have established that, while infants locate off-centered sound sources with high frequency during their first and fourth months of life, they pass through a period between 2 and 4 months of age when head turning drops to chance levels. Both cross-sectional and longitudinal studies have shown that, around 40 to 60 days of age, head turning toward sound decreases and turning away from sound increases, compared to performances at earlier ages. Thus accuracy of direction as well as overall frequency is reduced in this age range. Muir et al. (1979) tried to reinstate responding during the period of decline by presenting novel sounds and familiar voices to the infants in case they were bored, and by testing them in complete darkness in case they were "captured" by competing visual stimuli. None of these procedural modifications succeeded in increasing the response. The sound stimulus did prove crucial in Clifton's studies with 6- to 8-week-olds (Clifton, Morrongiello, & Dowd, 1984). An initial effort used a train of 3 msec clicks and resulted in ipsilateral head turning on 17.5% of trials, which was not significantly different from contralateral turns. A tape-recorded voice that greeted the infant ("Hello, baby! How are you?") elicited correct responding on 42.5% of trials. Accuracy also improved as contralateral turns remained at 8% of total trials under both stimulus conditions, resulting in an increased proportion of ipsilateral turns (82% of turning trials for the voice stimulus). Field, DiFranco, Dodwell, and Muir (1979) also found that 2½-month-olds turned their heads and eyes toward a tape-recorded female voice on 75% of trials in two studies.

We can conclude that some stimuli will elicit accurate turning in the 6- to 8-week-old infant, but the behavior has become much more fragile than during the first month of life. At the same time, latency to respond and complete a turn is still slow (4 to 8 sec) and is comparable to that of the very young babies (Muir et al., 1979). Latency, accuracy, and frequency improve together when the infant reaches the ascending arm of this behavior's U-shaped function. Although the precise timing varies with the individual infant, between 4½ and 5½ months of age the infant's head turning toward sound returns to its previous high level of performance, with latency sharply decreased to 1-2 sec. At this stage, the head-orienting response appears to change qualitatively. Not only has the expected improvement in motor control taken place, but the function of the head turn for the infant seems to shift. Whereas the newborn response was slow, not well-coordinated with eye movements, and habituated slowly if at all, the 6-month-old's response appears to be in the service of visual search for the source of sound. In fact, if 5- to 6-month-olds fail to see anything interesting when they turn toward lateral sound, they habituate within 3 to 4 trials (Clifton et al., 1984; Moore, Thompson, & Thompson, 1975). Finally, one source of variance determining the timing of the U-shaped function is biological maturity. Muir (in press) found that 45 preterm infants (discussed in the section on "Individual Differences"), who were born less than 34 weeks after conception and tested at approximately 2 mo (within one week of their expected birth date at term), and again at 5 and 7 mo of age, turned toward the sound of 76%, 40%, and 91% of the trials, respectively. This apparent developmental delay disappears when their maturational age (subtracting approximately 2 mo) is used rather than chronological age.

In summary, the head-orienting response to sound undergoes two transformations between birth and 5 months: the decline in frequency and accuracy around 6 weeks and the reappearance around 5 months of a more sophisticated response. In previous publications (Clifton et al., 1981a, 1981b; Field et al., 1980; Muir et al., 1979) we attempted to explain these transitions by speculating that the newborn's auditory localization response belongs to the same class of behaviors as a number of other neonatal responses such as the Moro, stepping, and palmar grasp reflexes. McGraw (1943), Lipsitt (1976), and Gibson (1981) all have emphasized that the diminishing strength of these early reflexes around 2 to 4 mo of age reflects maturation of the nervous system, marking a major transition between subcortical control of primitive reflexes and the onset of voluntary, cortically mediated behavior. This transition has been characterized by "cortical suppression" and "response confusion" (e.g., Lipsitt, 1982). We argued that the newborn response to sound may not reflect the existence of a true spatial representation, but rather a reflexive movement in response to binaural intensity and time cues. At 5 mo, the infant may perceive a sound source as having a particular set of coordinates in auditory space, and then turn toward it. Although no direct test of this notion exists, it generated much of the work reviewed in the next four sections dealing with age changes in accuracy of orientation to sound, neonatal responses to brief stimuli, and response to an auditory illusion, called the precedence effect.

Ability to Orient Toward Sounds at Different Positions on Either Side of the Midline

All work reported in this chapter so far used only two stimuli, one positioned to the right of midline and one to the left. Moreover, responses were considered "correct" if they were directed toward the hemifield containing the sound. In order to determine if newborns respond simply to the right or left side rather than to the specific sound locus, Forbes, Abraham, and Muir (1979, described in Muir, 1982) tested 3-day-old babies using the standard procedure, except that on each trial the rattle sound was presented through 1 of 5 loudspeakers arranged along a perimeter approximately 25 cm from the infant's head. The loudspeakers were positioned at the baby's midline and at ±45° and ±90° from the midline. Visual interference was eliminated by testing in the dark. A black line was placed along the midsaggittal suture on the crown of the baby's head, and the degree of head rotation was estimated from videorecords of the crown view by placing a protractor on the screen of the TV monitor. In Figure 2, the percentage of major head turns toward and away from the side of the sound is given as a function of the position of the loudspeakers. Newborns turned 90% of the time toward the sound 90° from midline, but performance at 45° was equivalent to that on center-loudspeaker and control trials. This result suggests that newborns are responding to the

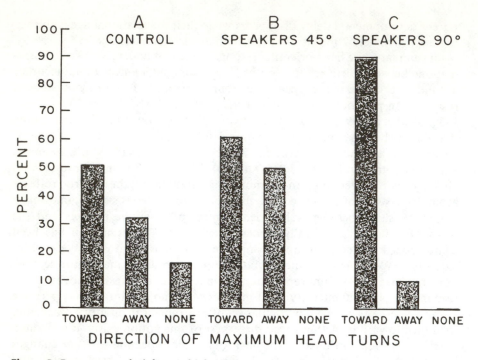

Figure 2. Percentage of trials on which newborns turned toward or away from sounds presented 45° (B) or 90° (C) from their line of sight. The control condition (A) consisted of both centered sounds and silent trials; the "sound side" was randomly assigned (from Muir, 1982).

general direction of sounds far off the midline. However, a closer inspection of the videotape records revealed that, on trials where head turns were toward the sounds, the babies rotated their heads significantly farther toward 45° loudspeakers than the 0° loudspeaker, and even farther when the source was 90° from midline (see Table 3).

In another study, Forbes (1981; for details, see Muir, in press) tested 4½-month-olds using a more elaborate procedure. Babies were videorecorded while they sat on their mothers' laps in the dark, facing a perimeter on which loudspeakers were placed at the midline and ±30° and ±60° on either side. On each trial, the recorded rattle sounds were played for 10 sec to the babies through one of the loudspeakers and to the mother, via earphones, simultaneously to both ears, thereby preventing her from knowing the sound's location. These infants turned toward the sound source on almost every trial, irrespective of its distance from midline. Thus, any difference between 30° and 60° sound sources may have been obscured by the ceiling effect.

Forbes also derived an estimate of the position of an infant's head at the end of the first head turn following the onset of sound. He assumed that the baby's nose projected from a flat plane (the face) and measured the distance of a point on the infant's nose from vertical and horizontal axes drawn between

Table 3. Localization Accuracy
Average Degree of Maximum Head Turn on Trials Where the Turn Was Toward
the Sound Source at Locations of 0, 45, and 90°
Loudspeaker Location

Subject	0°	45°	90°
1	5	70	82
2	19	68	78
3	83	51	76
4	14	38	69
5	27	35	65
6	50	70	62
7	0	40	46
8	12	55	73
9	40	60	68
10	12	43	57
Average	26	53	68

fiducial points on the chin and forehead and the two cheeks, respectively. These values were converted to degrees of rotation from the midline using vector geometry. He found that the average extent of the first head turn was 30° toward the loudspeaker at that position, and 48° toward the 60° loudspeaker. This performance was comparable to adults who were tested under identical conditions and asked to point their noses at the sound source. Their average head rotation was 25° and 49°, to the 30° and 60° loudspeakers, respectively.

Several conclusions can be drawn from these results. First, anyone wishing to elicit maximal head turning toward sounds from neonates should position the source 90° from the interaural midline. Second, our hypothesis, that initial responses to sounds at different positions within a hemifield would be equivalent, was not supported. Perhaps newborns simply respond to the "directional intensity" of the cue; the further from the midposition, the more compelling the stimulus. Third, the accuracy of the newborns' final head position, relative to the sound source, was much poorer than that of the 4½-month-olds', as expected. But neonates did demonstrate a crude ability to position their heads in relation to the source. We have previously hypothesized that a continuously available sound during head movements may be necessary for achieving this differential orientation response (Clifton et al., 1981b; Muir et al., 1979). However, this hypothesis now seems unlikely in light of data to be presented in the section on "Response Latency" below.

Directional Responses to Sounds on the Vertical Median Plane

Auditory space consists of both a horizontal and a vertical axis. While human adults, and possibly neonates, depend upon interaural time/intensity differences to identify a sound's position along the horizontal plane, another set of cues are needed to specify a sound's position on the vertical median plane. On this plane, spectral differences, generated in part by sound diffraction of high frequencies by the pinna, provide directional information, and it is assumed that experience is required to associate these spectral properties with a sound's elevation (see Kuhn, 1982 and Searle, Braida, Davis, & Colburn, 1976, for discussions of auditory localization cues). Thus, we might expect an infant to begin locating a sound's horizontal position before being able to locate its vertical position. This is exactly what clinical investigators have reported (e.g., Northern & Downs, 1978; Watrous, McConnell, Sitton, & Fleet, 1975); that is, infants begin to turn toward a sound's position on the horizontal plane around 5-7 months of age, and to its elevation around 9-12 months. Unfortunately, these investigators did not test very young infants, and thus may have missed the full development of these abilities. Because no one has tested infants using experimental procedures, a careful investigation might reveal that very young babies make reflexive directional responses to sounds above and below the horizon as well as to the left and right.

Muir (unpublished; in press) conducted several studies on vertical plane localization by newborns and 4½-month-olds. In the newborn experiment, 16 infants were tested in the dark, using the standard procedure, except that they were given at least three 5-trial blocks. Within each block, sound was presented for 20 sec, approximately 60° above and below the line of sight along the vertical median plane, 60° left and right of the midline along the horizontal plane, and directly behind the baby's head. The directions of the infants' head turns were judged from frontal-view videotape recordings by naive observers. We were aware from pilot work that newborns rarely, if ever, move their heads directly up or down. In an attempt to provide a description of any vertical rotations, the first major head turn greater than 10° was classified as either "left" or "right" if it was within a 30° sector surrounding the horizontal plane, and "up" or "down" if it was outside the sector.

The results are shown in Figure 3B and, as usual, our newborns turned correctly when sounds were to the left or right side. Furthermore, they also made clearly identifiable vertical head movements when sound was above the horizon, although compared with horizontal localization, these responses were never as far or well directed. Finally, "down" responses were rare and the distribution of responses to sound sources below the horizon and behind the infant's head were similar.

For developmental comparisons, ten 4½-month-olds were tested in the dark using the newborn procedure, except that they sat on their mothers' laps. Between trials, a mechanical toy in front of the baby lit up, serving as a centering stimulus and a distractor, which allowed the experimenter to position the rattles for the next trial. Trials lasted 10 sec or until a head turn was completed. The first major head turn was classified this time into one of the four 90° sectors surrounding the vertical and horizontal planes. These infants turned toward the sound source on almost all trials when it was along the horizontal plane, and turned in the correct direction 70% of the time when it was along the vertical median plane (see Figure 3A). Performance on all planes is better than chance, using either a 25% estimate or the distribution in the midline

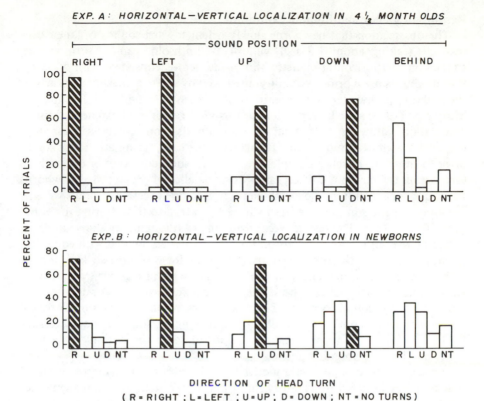

Figure 3. Percentage of trials on which 4½-month-olds (A) and newborns (B) turned in one of four directions, or not at all, when sounds were presented in different directions away from their line of sight.

"control" condition where sound was behind the infant's head. Finally, 9 of 10 subjects had longer response latencies for sounds in the vertical plane (averaging 4.3 sec), compared with those (averging 1.7 sec) in the horizontal plane. A similar result was obtained by Forbes (1981), using the procedure described earlier.

In summary, some rudimentary appreciation of the elevation of sound sources above the horizontal plane may exist at birth, and by 4 months of age infants will turn on some trials to sounds above and below their midlines. At the same time, compared with horizontal plane performance, vertical localization is very immature, being much slower and less accurate. It should be noted that this poorer performance by the 4½-month-olds was not due to a simple anisotropy of muscle control, because the same infants readily and accurately pointed their noses at small lights in the speaker positions during calibration tests. Thus, the planar differences may indicate that a lengthy process of learning, combined with cortical maturation, is required before infants construct a complete representation of auditory space.

Response Latency and Stimulus Duration

The observation that newborns slowly orient toward sounds off their central axis (taking about 7-8 sec) while 4½-month-olds rapidly turn to face sounds on the horizontal plane (within a few sec) is consistent with our view that newborns use a primitive ability, mediated by a neural mechanism early in the auditory pathway, to scan continuously presented sounds. As Jenkins and Masterton (1979) stated, responding at this level requires an extended train of stimulation, allowing the animal to scan sounds from changes in binaural disparities with head movement. If this were the case, termination of a sound prior to either the onset or completion of a turn should prevent or discontinue the response. Clarkson, Clifton, and Morrongiello (in press) tested newborns for sound localization in the usual manner, with one exception. Trials were 20 sec long, but the stimulus duration varied from trial to trial, lasting for either 1, 5, 10, or 20 sec. The results were surprising. Although they showed less responding overall (about 40% of total trials), babies responded with equal frequency to all four stimulus durations. The behavior was most striking for the 1-sec sound: on approximately 80% of the trials where turns occurred, infants slowly rotated their heads toward the loudspeaker several seconds after termination of the sound. Amplitude and latency of response were similar for all durations. Thus, continuous feedback from ongoing sound is not necessary for the neonatal head-turning response as postulated in the section on "Ability to Orient Toward Sounds" above.

Perhaps a more appropriate model for this response is a motor program that becomes initiated by auditory input and is executed in a similar manner regardless of further input. The movement plan would be executed in a ballistic fashion rather than as a search dependent on continuous cues. This model fits with the findings of Whittington, Hepp-Reymond, and Flood (1981) on intact monkeys who showed no difference in latency and accuracy of head and eye movements directed toward a single click vs. a train of clicks available throughout the response. They concluded that the "eye-movement strategy is ...a triggered movement program," independent of auditory feedback. Further experimentation is necessary before we can fully describe the newborn's head movement to sound, but we can rule out a search model based on changing binaural disparities as the head moves.

The Precedence Effect

One strategy for assessing developmental differences in sound localization is to present a perceptual task having two levels of stimulus difficulty, only one of which is thought to be dependent on cortical functioning. All sound stimuli described thus far in this chapter originated from one source in space, either a loudspeaker or a sounding object. A phenomenon known as the precedence effect is produced when the same sound is fed at equal intensity to two loudspeakers, with the input to one loudspeaker delayed by several milliseconds (msec) relative to the other (Wallach, Newman, & Rosenzweig, 1949). The resulting percept is of a single sound image located at the position of the leading loudspeaker; no sound is localized at the lagging loudspeaker. Traditionally, the precedence effect has been described as an echo suppression mechanism that enhances the perception of the true location of a sound's source (Green, 1976, pp. 215-218; Mills, 1972). Ordinary rooms provide numerous reflecting surfaces that bounce sound back to the listener in a complex array of echoes. These reflected sounds, if localized, would make the true source of the sound very difficult to localize. Being able to localize the spatial origin of a sound has obvious adaptive value for most organisms (Erulkar, 1972). As would be expected, many mammals tested with the precedence effect, such as cats (Whitfield, Cranford, Ravizza, & Diamond, 1972), rats (Kelly, 1974), and monkeys (Heffner, 1973), appear to localize sounds at the leading source, and at the same temporal delays effective for human adults.

The impetus for pursuing developmental studies of the precedence effect came from research that implicated the auditory cortex in the perception of this phenomenon. Cats with lesions in the auditory cortex were impaired in their localization of precedence effect sounds, but retained the ability to localize sounds from a single source (Cranford & Oberholtzer, 1976; Whitfield et al. (1972). Children with epileptic foci in the temporal region showed impaired localization of precedence effect stimuli, whereas they localized single source stimuli with virtually no errors (Hochster & Kelly, 1981). Normal children and adults localize both types of stimuli identically, as do intact animals, apparently. Clifton predicted that, early in development, infants would turn toward single source stimuli but would fail to respond to precedence effect stimuli. The comparison of these two stimuli was especially appealing, because the same motor behavior (head turning toward sound) would be elicited but the perceptual processing should be more difficult under precedence-effect conditions.

In a series of studies, Clifton and colleagues determined that the same newborn fails to turn to precedence-effect stimuli (two loudspeakers with one input delayed 7 msec relative to the other), while reliably turning to the same sound presented from one loudspeaker (Clifton et al., 1981a). On the other hand, 5-month-olds turned readily to both types of sound (Clifton et al., 1981b). To ensure that the newborns' response was not due to the particular delay used (7 msec), a subsequent study varied delays between signal onsets from 5 to 20 msec (see Figures 1-F and 1-H). No reliable head turning was elicited at any of these delays, but turning to single source stimuli was replicated (Morrongiello, Clifton, & Kulig, 1982).

In testing at interim ages of 6 to 9 weeks, Clifton et al. (1984) found a response to single source stimuli but no head turning to precedence-effect stimuli. As noted above, infants in this age range have a depressed rate of head turning to sound, but voice stimuli elicited ipsilateral turning above chance in the single source condition, while the same stimuli in a precedence-effect presentation did not. Clifton tentatively related brain growth in the auditory cortex to both the reappearance of head turning to single source at 4 to 5 months, and the appearance of responding to the precedence effect at about the same age.

Through repeated testing of the same infants, we may be able to establish that these two perceptual behaviors are related if they appear around the same time in the individual infant. Their co-occurrence may mark the beginning of the infant's sense of auditory surround, where audible objects are located in space separate from the infant's own body. No direct attribution of cause can be made between any specific anatomical change and a particular behavioral development during infancy, because of the multidetermined nature of all motor acts. However, knowledge of the developmental sequence and growth rates of the central nervous system allows specific predictions about behavioral sequences and can aid selection of appropriate stimuli and responses to be studied. Only in this way can we gain understanding of brain-behavior relations during this period of rapid auditory development.

SUMMARY AND FUTURE DIRECTIONS

The developmental course of the infant's orientation to off-centered sound may be summarized as follows. Newborns will turn reliably toward laterally located sounds under specified stimulus and state conditions. Latency to respond is long, but accuracy to the correct hemifield is high, reflected in very little contralateral turning. Contrary to our expectations, continuous sound is not necessary to drive responding in the newborn, indicating a "triggered" motor pattern rather than one based on search. Between 1 and 4 months of age, this behavior declines, so that visual alerting to sounds is often unaccompanied by turning toward it. When turning is observed in this age range, response latency remains similar to that of neonates. Between 4 and 5 months of age, head orientation to sound reemerges as a short latency response, with greater accuracy for positions within the hemifield. By 6 months, this response habituates rapidly if not reinforced, but is easily conditioned, a fact that has been exploited in research on speech sound discrimination and infant psychophysics (see Schneider & Trehub, this volume). Although crude vertical-localization responses are present in both newborns and 4-month-olds, speed and accuracy at both ages are similar to newborn horizontal-localization responses. Newborns fail to respond to the precedence effect which may be cortically mediated, whereas 6-month-olds do respond. The developmental progression described above may reflect a maturational shift in locus of control from lower to higher neural structures (see Clifton et al., 1981a, 1981b; Field et al., 1980; Muir et al., 1979).

Based on the methodological considerations presented in this chapter, we make the following recommendations to investigators employing the neonatal head turning response as a dependent measure:

1. Infants should be tested in a quiet alert state, rocking and manipulating them between trials if necessary to maintain alertness.
2. A background free of distracting tactile and visual cues should be provided; testing in total darkness may be optimal for some studies.

3. Control trials, either silent or midline sound, should not be presented on more than 30% of total trials, to insure high levels of performance.
4. Sound sources should be located at 60° or greater off the interaural midline.
5. Trials should last at least 15 sec, and be terminated when the baby responds.

These procedures will elicit the highest probability of response in neonates. Many of these variables, such as spatial location of sound and stimulus duration, are interesting in their own right and can be manipulated accordingly. Our recommendations simply summarize the optimal testing conditions.

A number of directions for future research follow from the methodological considerations reviewed in this chapter:

(a) Extensive testing of different neonatal high-risk populations should be undertaken to determine the clinical significance of atypical auditory localization responses. Infants with cerebral damage might turn reliably in the direction of sounds at birth but show an unusual developmental course, i.e., a delay in either onset or end of the "dip" in the U-shaped function. An auditory battery might be developed using conditions known to have a distinct developmental course, such as localization of precedence-effect sounds. Our caveat for testing high risk populations remains: one cannot infer a hearing loss when infants fail to orient, nor can normal hearing be inferred from correct responding. (b) Stimuli varying in spectrum, bandwidth, duration, and rise time should be examined to determine their effectiveness, analogous to preferential-looking tasks (Fantz, Fagen, & Miranda, 1975) which revealed that some visual stimuli have superior eliciting properties right from birth. (c) Infants should be tested on accuracy of localization to sources at several positions within a hemifield, to provide a more comprehensive description of their overall spatial sensitivity at different ages. Planar differences, as well as sensitivity to objects moving in depth (analogous to looming visual objects), should be studied. (d) Using a longitudinal approach, investigators could determine the degree of coincidence between the upswing in the U-shaped function and the initial appearance of appropriate head orienting to precedence-effect stimuli. The onset of reaching responses to visual targets appears around 4 to 5 months of age, signifying the coordination of motor schemes across modalities. If different localization behaviors appeared in a certain sequence or coincided, we might infer a 3-dimensional auditory space for infants this age. (e) Finally, we would stress the value of multiple responses, although we have not presented such data in this chapter. To interpret head orienting in the full context of the infant's behavior, other responses, such as heart rate change, eyeblink, preliminary arm movements, and reaching, are needed. Each of these responses carries its own special methodological problems, many of which are considered in other parts of this book. Head orienting to sound is only one aspect of the infant's ability to localize sound in space. Its advantages are its early occurrence soon after birth and easy availability for observation. However, we must not mistake it for the "whole story," which requires looking at the full gamut of behavior to sound.

ACKNOWLEDGMENTS

Research from Muir's laboratory described in this chapter was supported by an Ontario Mental Health Foundation Grant to D. Muir and a Natural Sciences and Engineering Research Council of Canada Grant to D. Muir and P. C. Dodwell. Research from Clifton's laboratory was supported by grants from the National Science Foundation (BNS 810354), the National Institute of Mental Health (MH-00332), and a Biomedical Research Support Grant (RR0 7048) from the University of Massachusetts.

Study 1, in Table 2, is part of an unpublished honors thesis entitled"Responses of newborns to stimuli in different modalities" conducted in 1982 at Queen's University, Kingston, Ontario by F. Whalley.

REFERENCES

Als, H., Tronick, E., Lester, B. M., & Brazelton, T. B. The Brazelton neonatal behavioral assessment scale (BNBAS). *Journal of Abnormal Child Psychology,* 1977, *5,* 215–231.

Bower, T. G. R. The origins of meaning in perceptual development. In A. D. Pick (ed.), *Perception and its development: A tribute to Eleanor J. Gibson.* Hillsdale, N.J.: Erlbaum, 1979.

Bower, T. G. R. *Development in infancy.* 2nd ed. San Francisco: Freeman, 1982.

Brazelton, T. B. *Neonatal behavioral assessment scale.* London: Spastics International Medical Publicatons, 1973.

Brody, L. R., Zelazo, P. R., & Chaika, H. Habituation-dishabituation to speech in the neonate. *Developmental Psychology,* 1984, *20,* 114–119.

Butterworth, G. & Castillo, M. Coordination of auditory and visual space in newborn human infants. *Perception,* 1976, *5,* 155–160.

Butterworth, G. Auditory-visual perception and visual proprioception. In R. D. Walk & H. L. Pick (eds.), *Intersensory perception and sensory integation.* New York: Plenum Press, 1981.

Castillo, M. & Butterworth, G. Neonatal localization of a sound in visual space. *Perception,* 1981, *10,* 331–338.

Clarkson, M. G., Clifton, R. K., & Morrongiello, B. A. The effects of sound duration on newborns' head orientation. *Journal of Experimental Child Psychology,* in press.

Clarkson, M. G., Morrongiello, B. A., & Clifton, R. K. Stimulus-presentation probability influences newborns' head orientation to sound. *Perceptual and Motor Skills,* 1982, *55,* 1239–1246.

Clifton, R., Morrongiello, B., Kulig, J., & Dowd, J. Newborns' orientation toward sound: Possible implications for cortical development. *Child Development,* 1981, *52,* 833–838. (a)

Clifton, R. K., Morrongiello, B. A., Kulig, J. W., & Dowd, J. M. Developmental changes in auditory localization in infancy. In R. Aslin, J. Alberts, & M. Petersen (eds.), *The development of perception: Psychobiological perceptives (Vol. 1). Audition, somatic perception, and the chemical senses.* New York: Academic Press, 1981. (b)

Clifton, R., Morrongiello, B., & Dowd, J. A developmental look at an auditory illusion: The precedence effect. *Developmental Psychobiology,* 1984, *17,* 519–536.

Cochran, W. C. & Cox, G. M. *Experimental designs.* 2nd ed. New York: John Wiley and Sons, 1957.

Cranford, J. & Oberholtzer, M. Role of neocortex in binaural hearing in the cat, II: The "precedence effect" in sound localization. *Brain Research,* 1976, *111,* 225–239.

Crassini, B. & Broerse, J. Auditory-visual integration in neonates: A signal detection analysis. *Journal of Experimental Child Psychology*, 1980, *29*, 144–155.

Erulkar, S. Comparative aspects of spatial localization of sound. *Physiological Review*, 1972, *52*, 237–337.

Fantz, R. L., Fagan, J. F., & Miranda, S. B. Early visual selectivity. In L. B. Cohen & P. Salapatak (eds.), *Infant perception: From sensation to cognition*. Vol. 1. New York: Academic Press, 1975.

Field, J., DiFranco, D., Dodwell, P., & Muir, D. Auditory-visual coordination in 2½-month old infants. *Infant Behavior & Development*, 1979, *2*, 113–122.

Field, J., Muir, D., Pilon, R., Sinclair, M., & Dodwell, P. Infants' orientation to lateral sounds from birth to three months. *Child Development*, 1980, *51*, 295–298.

Fischer-Fay, A. *The effect of a visual stimulus on auditory localization in the newborn infant.* Unpublished honors thesis, Queens University, 1981.

Forbes, B., Abraham, W., & Muir, D. W. *The accuracy of newborn auditory localization.* Paper presented at the Canadian Psychological Association, Quebec, P.Q., 1979.

Forbes, B. *Orientation differences in sound localization abilities of 4 to 5 month old infants.* Unpublished master's thesis, Queen's University, 1981.

Gibson, K. R. Comparative neuro-ontogeny: Its implications for the development of human intelligence. In G. Butterworth (ed.), *Infancy and epistemology*. Brighton, England: Harvester Press Ltd., 1981.

Green, D. *An introduction to hearing*. Hillsdale, N.J.: Lawrence Erlbaum, 1976.

Hammond, J. Hearing and response in the newborn. *Developmental Medicine and Child Neurology*, 1970, *13*, 3–5.

Heffner, H. E. *The effects of auditory cortex ablation on sound localizations in the monkey (Macaca mulatta).* Unpublished doctoral dissertation, Florida State University, 1973.

Hochster, M., & Kelly, J. B. The precedence effect and sound localization by children with temporal lobe epilepsy. *Neuropsychologia*, 1981, *19*, 49–55.

Jaffe, B. F. Atresia: Isolated and associated anomalies. In B. F. Jaffe (ed.), *Hearing loss in children*. London: University Park Press, 1977.

Jenkins, W. M. & Masterton, R. B. Sound localization in pigeons (*Columba livia*). *Journal of Comparative and Physiological Psychology*, 1979, *93*, 403–413.

Kelly, J. B. Localization of paired sound sources in the rat: Small time differences. *Journal of the Acoustical Society of America*, 1974, *55*, 1277–1284.

Kuhn, G. F. Towards a model for sound localization. In R. W. Gatehouse (ed.), *Localization of sound: Theory and applications*. Groton, Ct.: Amphora Press, 1982.

Kurtzberg, D., Vaughan, H. E., Daum, C., Grellong, B. A., Albin, S., & Rotkin, L. Neurobehavioral performance in low-birthweight infants at 40 weeks conceptual age: Comparison with full-term infants. *Developmental Medicine and Child Neurology*, 1979, *21*, 590–607.

Lipsitt, L. P. Developmental psychobiology comes of age: A discussion. In L. P. Lipsitt (ed.), *Developmental psychobiology: The significance of infancy*. Hillsdale, N.J.: Erlbaum, 1976.

Lipsitt, L. P. Infant learning. In T. M. Field, A. Huston, H. C. Quay, L. Troll, & G. E. Finley (eds.), *Review of human development*. New York: Wiley and Sons, 1982.

Low, J. A., Galbraith, R. S., Muir, D. W., Killen, H. L., Pater, E. A., & Karchmar, J. E. The predictive significance of biological risk factors for deficits in children of a high risk population *American Journal of Obstetrics and Gynecology*, 1983, *145*, 1059–1068.

McGraw, M. B. *The neuromuscular maturation of the human infant*. New York: Columbia University Press, 1943.

McGurk, H., Turnure, C., & Creighton, S. Auditory visual coordination in neonates. *Child Development*, 1977, *48*, 138–143.

Mendelson, M. & Haith, M. The relation between audition and vision in the human newborn. *Monographs of the Society for Research in Child Development*, 1976, *41*, No. 167.

Mills, A. W. Auditory localization. In J. V. Tobias (ed.), *Foundations of modern auditory theory*. Vol. 2. New York: Academic Press, 1972.

Moore, J. M., Thompson, G., & Thompson, M. Auditory localization of infants as a function of reinforcement conditions. *Journal of Speech and Hearing Disorders,* 1975, *40,* 29–34.

Morrongiello, B., Clifton, R., & Kulig, J. Newborn cardiac and behavioral orienting responses to sound under varying precedence effect conditions. *Infant Behavior & Development,* 1982, *5,* 249–259.

Muir, D. The development of human auditory localization in infancy. In R. W. Gatehouse (ed.), *Localization of sound: Theory and applications.* Groton, Ct.: Amphora Press, 1982.

Muir, D. W. The development of infants' auditory spatial sensitivity. In S. E. Trehub, & B. A. Schneider (eds.), *Auditory development in infancy.* New York: Plenum Press, in press.

Muir, D., Abraham, W., Forbes, B., & Harris, L. The ontogenesis of an auditory localization response from birth to four months of age. *Canadian Journal of Psychology,* 1979, *33,* 320–333.

Muir, D. & Field, J. Newborn infants orient to sounds. *Child Development,* 1979, *50,* 431–436.

Northern, J. L. & Downs, M. P. *Hearing in children.* Baltimore: Waverly Press, 1978.

Piaget, J. *The origins of intelligence in children.* New York: Norton, 1952.

Searle, C. L., Braida, L. D., Davis, M. F., & Colburn, H. S. Model for auditory localization. *The Journal of the Acoustical Society of America,* 1976, *60,* 1164–1175.

Turkewitz, G., Birch, H. G., Moreau, T., Levy, L., & Cornwell, A. C. Effect of intensity of auditory stimulation on directional eye movements in the human neonate. *Animal Behaviour,* 1966, *14,* 93–101.

Wallach, H., Newman, E., & Rosenzweig, J. The precedence effect in sound localization. *American Journal of Psychology,* 1949, *62,* 315–336.

Watrous, B. S., McConnell, F., Sitton, A. B., & Fleet, W. F. Auditory response of infants. *Journal of Speech and Hearing Disorders,* 1975, *40,* 357–366.

Wertheimer, H. Psychomotor coordination of auditory and visual space at birth. *Science,* 1961, *134,* 1692.

Whitfield, I. C., Cranford, J., Ravizza, R., & Diamond, I. Effects of unilateral ablation of auditory cortex in cat on complex sound localization. *Journal of Neurophysiology,* 1972, *35,* 718–731.

Whittington, D. A., Hepp-Reymond, M., & Flood, W. Eye and head movements to auditory targets. *Experimental Brain Research,* 1981, *41,* 358–363.

Wolff, P. Observations on newborn infants. *Psychosomatic Medicine,* 1959, *21,* 110–118.

9

THE HIGH-AMPLITUDE SUCKING TECHNIQUE AS A METHODOLOGICAL TOOL IN SPEECH PERCEPTION RESEARCH

Peter W. Jusczyk

University of Oregon, Eugene

GENERAL BACKGROUND

Those of us who study perceptual processes in human infants owe a great debt of gratitude to the researchers of the 1960s. It was during this period of time that the first breakthroughs occurred in the development of methodology appropriate for studying perceptual processes in the infant. As a direct result of the progress in this area, our view of the infant has changed from one of a relatively passive creature with few innate abilities to one that acknowledges the competence that the infant has for dealing with events in the real world within the first few hours of life.

One of the great problems associated with any attempt to develop a behavioral measure for use in testing infants is the selection of an appropriate behavioral response. Obviously, it is most desirable to try to tap into a system that the infant has a good deal of control over, rather than one that might add the difficulties of motor coordination to any other difficulties in adapting the response to the test situation. For this reason, the choice of the infant's sucking response as a behavioral measure was a very reasonable place to begin. Since, under normal circumstances, the infant's very survival depends upon the ability to suck, it is one response that we might expect all infants to show some mastery of. Of course, in the real world, sucking is closely tied to acquiring food. However, as any simple observation will reveal, it also seems to be a source of pleasure and comfort in and of itself for the infant.

The first question that early researchers in the area faced was whether there was some way of adapting the response as a perceptual measure. How could one use the response as an index of what the infant is perceiving? There were some attempts to use the sucking response in the same way that physiological response measures such as GSR and heart-rate were used, i.e., to look for a change in ongoing activity with the presentation of certain kinds of stimuli. This is essentially the way in which Bronshtein and Petrova (1967) employed the response. However, this measure proved not to be very sensitive and, consequently, never did gain widespread use.

The real advance in the use of the sucking response came when researchers began to explore the possibility of modifying the response through operant conditioning techniques. Hence, Siqueland and DeLucia (1969) explored the possibility that one could condition the sucking response by providing the infant with visual reinforcement. The procedure that they adopted was essentially one of "conjugate reinforcement." With this procedure, the infant is reinforced in proportion to the magnitude of his or her response. In the task that Siqueland and DeLucia used, the reinforcement was being able to see a visual display. The infant sat in an infant seat facing a dimly lit screen. Sucking responses that exceeded a predetermined criterion amplitude increased the intensity of the light source, making the picture on the screen more visible. The harder the infant sucked, the brighter the picture became.

Using this type of procedure, Siqueland and DeLucia demonstrated that the infants systematically changed their sucking responses as a result of the reinforcement contingencies. In particular, by comparing subjects who received such conjugate reinforcement to a control group whose spontaneous sucking rate was monitored for the same period, they discovered marked increases in sucking for the experimental group when reinforcement was available. They also explored the consequences of introducing an extinction period for the experimental group, in order to determine how the sucking response would change if reinforcement were no longer available. In part, this portion of the experiment also served as a check to see if the increases in sucking really were occurring in response to the availability of visual reinforcement. Siqueland and DeLucia found significant drops in sucking during such periods, thus supporting the notion that the increases in sucking were associated with the presence of the reinforcer. The data from their experiment are displayed in Figure 1. They also tested a third group of subjects in what they termed a stimulus-withdrawal condition. For subjects in this last condition, sucking actually resulted in the disappearance of the visual stimulus (which was otherwise present) for a 5-second period. In effect, performance by subjects in this group did not differ from that of the controls.

Siqueland and DeLucia demonstrated the feasibility of using the high-amplitude sucking procedure with infants as young as 4 months of age. The procedure that they used demonstrated that infants would increase their sucking rates in response to conjugate visual reinforcement. However, the technique as used in this first experiment was not a measure of discrimination. It

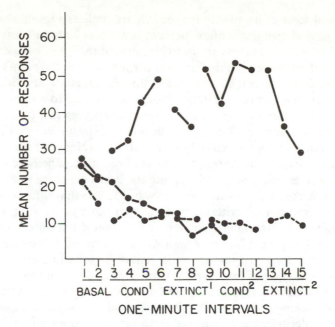

Figure 1. Mean response rates for the three groups of 4-month-old infants over conditioning and extinction phases. Solid circles, sucking-reinforcement group; open circles, stimulus-withdrawal group; open triangles, base-line group.

was subsequent research by Siqueland (1969) that demonstrated that the technique could be adopted for this purpose. In particular, Siqueland modified the procedure slightly by eliminating extinction periods and changing the way that the stimuli were presented. In the original study, the stimuli were changed every 30 seconds. In place of this, Siqueland (1969) adopted the tactic of presenting the same stimulus for a fixed period (e.g., 7 minutes) and then switching to another stimulus for a fixed period thereafter. In this way, he could compare the sucking rates in the periods before and after the change in stimulation. Reasoning that infants often show increased interest to novel stimuli, he hypothesized that an increase in sucking might accompany the presence of a discriminably different stimulus. Using the procedure in this manner, Siqueland was able to demonstrate that it could be used as a measure of pattern discrimination for infants.

The next major evolution in the procedure came when the high-amplitude sucking procedure was applied to the study of speech discrimination. In place of the fixed periods of stimulus presentation, Eimas, Siqueland, Jusczyk, and Vigorito (1971) adopted a procedure that was geared to the performance of individual infants. One difficulty with using fixed periods of stimulus presentations had been the fact that infants often received considerably different amounts of experience with the first stimulus prior to the stimulus change simply because of individual differences in sucking rates. For infants who did not do a great deal of sucking during the initial period, the first stimulus may have retained some of its novelty for the infants, and, as a result, these infants might not have shown much of an increase in sucking with the presentation of the second stimulus. One way to try to circumvent this problem was to ensure that all the infants were suitably familiar, perhaps even to the point of disinterest, with the first stimulus. To accomplish this, Eimas et al. established a criterion for satiation to the first stimulus prior to any change to a second stimulus. Specifically, the infants had to show a decline in sucking rate of 20% or more for 2 consecutive minutes. The one additional constraint was that the decline in sucking was to be measured only from the third minute of stimulation onwards. This latter constraint was adopted in order to compensate for the fact that sucking rates fluctuate greatly during the initial exposure to the stimulus. Without some constraint of this sort, it was possible that infants might accidentally achieve the shift criterion without ever having picked up the contingency between their sucking behavior and the presentation of the auditory reinforcer. While even a 3-minute waiting period would not entirely rule out this possibility, it was felt that it would reduce its consequences somewhat.

Another change that Eimas et al. instituted was to attempt to set a criterion sucking level that took into account the individual differences in the type and intensity of sucking responses. In the initial study by Siqueland and DeLucia (1969), a fixed criterion level was set at 18 mm-Hg for all infants. However, there are large individual differences in the intensity with which infants suck, and thus, for some infants, this meant that practically every suck exceeded the criterion, while for others very few sucks were acceptable. To remedy this, Eimas et al. set the criterion sucking amplitude level so as to include only the top 33% of the infant's sucking responses. The criterion level was set during the first minute or two of the experiment, prior to obtaining a baseline rate of sucking for the infant.

Since the procedure that Eimas et al. used is the forerunner of the ones employed at the present time, it is worth describing the procedure in some detail. The infant is placed in a slightly reclining infant seat and faces a projection screen, situated directly above a loudspeaker, in an otherwise darkened room. There is a brightly colored picture on the screen so as to attract the infant's attention and thus lessen the possibility that the infant will be distracted in looking around the room. An experimenter wearing headphones and listening to recorded music (to mask the speech sounds, so that he or she does not inadvertently cue the infant to the stimulus change) sits to one side of the infant. The experimenter's task is to hold a pacifier gently in the infant's mouth during the procedure. The pacifier is a blind nipple (i.e., one without a hole) that is connected by means of a rubber tube to a pressure transducer. This transducer sends a weak electrical charge to a polygraph machine where it is amplified and displayed as changes on a chart recorder. A Schmitt trigger or some comparable device provides a digital output of the criterion sucking responses. Various relays activate counters and the auditory reinforcers. In the Eimas et al. experiment, a tape loop played continuously in the background, and the audio portion of the signal was increased in intensity depending on the frequency of the criterion level sucks. Although the sounds increased in intensity as the frequency of the criterion sucks increased, a maximum intensity level was set at about 15 dB above the background noise level, so as not to frighten the infants. In effect, each criterial response activated the auditory signal for a 1-second interval. However, when responses were closely clustered, the signal was shut off approximately one second after the last response.

As the procedure begins, the first step is to establish the suitable criterion level for each infant. This must be accomplished as rapidly as possible, because infants soon become fussy if left for long periods in the test situation without any auditory reinforcers. Next, a 1-minute baseline rate of the infant's criterion level sucking responses is measured in the absence of any auditory reinforcement. After this is done, the test period begins and the infant's criterial level responses activate the auditory signal. During the first few minutes of the procedure, the infant's sucking rate may hover around the baseline level, but then, in most cases, sucking rates increase considerably. This high rate of criterial sucking may last for some time (in some instances, as much as 30 minutes!) At some point, however, a decline in sucking occurs. When a decrement of 20% occurs with respect to the immediately preceding minute and this decline continues at or below this level for a second minute, the criterion for habituation to the first stimulus has been met. For subjects in experimental groups, the auditory stimulus is changed, and sucking is measured for the next 4 minutes. For subjects in the control condition, no stimulus change occurs but sucking is measured over the same 4-minute period. This latter group serves as a standard for determining whether the sucking rate to the second stimulus is reliably different from what would be expected from spontaneous changes in sucking rate.

Discrimination of a given stimulus contrast is inferred from net changes in sucking rate between the 2-minute period prior to the shift to the second stimulus and the minutes following the shift. If the net changes in sucking rate are reliably different from any spontaneous changes that occur for the control group, then the infants are assumed to have discriminated the contrast in question.

In their experiment, Eimas et al. used the high-amplitude sucking (HAS) procedure to investigate the infant's discrimination of synthetic speech sounds corresponding to /ba/ and /pa/. In English, these two sounds are said to differ phonetically in terms of their voicing characteristics. Sounds like /ba/ are produced by vibrating the vocal cords at or before the time that the lips are opened, and hence are said to be voiced. By contrast, for sounds like /pa/ the vocal cords do not begin to vibrate until some time after the lips are released, and thus are designated as voiceless. It is a well-established fact that adult listeners perceive these sounds categorically, in the sense that, while they can easily discriminate tokens of /ba/ and /pa/ from one another, their discrimination of two tokens of /ba/ from one another tends to be at about chance level (Lisker

& Abramson, 1970). By using synthetic speech tokens, one can gain precise control over the voicing factor and vary it systematically to produce a series of sounds ranging from /ba/ to /pa/. It is under such circumstances that adults will show the characteristic pattern of categorical perception despite the fact that the contrasts involving sounds chosen from within the same category differ by the same amounts of voicing as do the ones chosen from between the two categories.

When Eimas et al. undertook their study, they endeavored to determine not only if infants could discriminate speech contrasts involving voicing, but also if they did so in a categorical manner like adults. For this reason, they employed two types of shift conditions for their subjects—a between-category shift (i.e., /ba/ vs. /pa/) and a within-category shift (e.g., /ba/ vs. /ba/). Their results, which are displayed in Figure 2, indicated that, like adults, infants discriminated the between-category contrasts, but not the within-category ones.

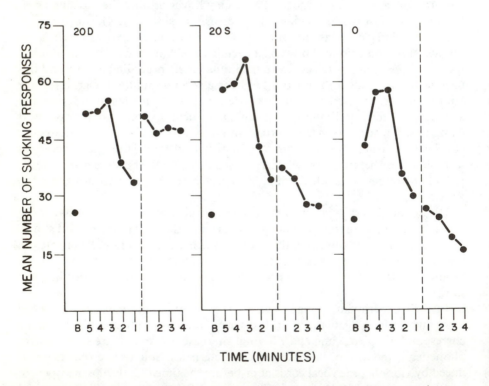

TIME (MINUTES)

Figure 2. Mean number of sucking responses for the 4-month-old infants, as a function of time and experimental condition. The dashed line indicates the occurrence of the stimulus shift, or, in the case of the control group, the time at which the shift would have occurred. The letter "B" stands for the baseline rate. Time is measured with reference to the moment of stimulus shift and indicates the 5 minutes prior to and the 4 minutes after shift.

Following the success that Eimas et al. had with the HAS procedure, the methodology has been used extensively in further studies of the perception of speech contrasts by infants (e.g., Bertoncini & Mehler, 1981; Eilers, 1977; Eimas, 1974, 1975; Eimas & Miller, 1980a, b; Jusczyk, 1977; Jusczyk, Copan, & Thompson, 1978; Jusczyk & Thompson, 1978; Morse, 1972; Trehub, 1973; 1976a, b; Trehub & Rabinovitch, 1972) and nonspeech (e.g., Jusczyk, Pisoni, Reed, Fernald, & Myers, 1983; Jusczyk, Pisoni, Walley, & Murray, 1981). Thus, while the technique has a number of limitations (discussed in what follows), it is fair to say that it has provided some very important information regarding the perceptual capacities that infants have for dealing with contrasts between speech sounds.

SOME QUESTIONS ABOUT THE WAY IN WHICH HAS WORKS

After the initial success with the HAS procedure, a number of questions were raised about the validity of the procedure as a means of assessing infant discriminative capacities. Thus, Trehub (1973) pointed out that the lack of a difference between control and experimental groups need not imply a lack of discriminative capacity. It is also plausible that the infants might discriminate the difference between the stimuli, but not be motivated to increase their sucking rates. Certainly, this is a point that must be taken very seriously. Nevertheless, over the years a consideration of the types of contrasts that are and are not discriminated reveals a relatively systematic and intelligible pattern that conforms well to expectations based on studies with adults, where more powerful procedures are available. While it is possible that some within-category contrasts are discriminable for infants (e.g., Eimas & Miller, 1980), at the very least these differences are not as salient (or perceptually different enough) to motivate infants to respond in the way that they do for between-category contrasts. Still, Trehub's point should be borne in mind whenever interpreting these kinds of results.

A number of objections to the HAS procedure were raised by Butterfield and Cairns (1974). In particular, they questioned a number of underlying assumptions, such as whether the infants were really mastering a contingency between their sucking responses and the presentation of the auditory stimulus, whether infants could be said to habituate to the presentation of the first stimulus, and whether increased responding after shift might not reflect the removal of an aversive stimulus rather than true discrimination. With respect to the latter issue, Butterfield and Cairns presented data of their own that indicated that the increase in sucking after shift reflects the discrimination of the stimulus change rather than a reaction to the removal of an aversive stimulus.

A number of investigations were conducted subsequently to determine whether or not the infant responds to contingent reinforcement. For example, Kuhl (1976) included a control group in which no sound was presented in her study. She noted the absence of a significant increase in sucking for these subjects, in contrast to the groups who received contingent reinforcement. However, the essence of the critique by Butterfield and Cairns lay in the possibility that the auditory stimuli might be a source of arousal for infants, and that increases in sucking might reflect changes in state of arousal rather than any attempt on the infant's part to control the presentation of the stimuli. Hence, the most appropriate control is one in which auditory stimulation was available to the infant but not in a way that was contingently linked to sucking. Studies by Trehub and Chang (1977) and by Williams and Golenski (1978) were designed to meet this prerequisite.

Trehub and Chang (1977) sought to clarify the role of reinforcement and contingency in the application of the HAS technique. They actually modeled their procedure more closely after that of Siqueland and DeLucia (1969) than that of Eimas et al. Thus, the procedure included a fixed period of reinforcement, followed by an extinction period and then a fixed reconditioning period. In order to assess the importance of contingency and reinforcement, they tested four groups of infants. For the first group, criterion-level sucking initiated an auditory reinforcer. For the second group, criterion-level sucking resulted in a 2-second termination of the sounds which were otherwise played continuously. Hence, for the first two groups of subjects, there was a contingency established between sucking and the occurrence of the sounds. Such was not the case for the third group of subjects, who received noncontingent presentations of the auditory reinforcer. This group was a yoked-control in which subjects received auditory presentations matched to those for subjects in either the first or second groups. The final group was a no-sound control which received no auditory presentations for the entire test period. The results of the study, displayed in Figure 3, indicated that the first group of subjects exhibited consistently higher rates of responding than the other three groups. None of the other comparisons between groups was significant. Trehub and Chang interpreted these results as offering some support for the notion that infants acquire a conditioned response under conditions of contingent auditory reinforcement with the HAS procedure, in that the contingent sound-initiation group attained higher rates of sucking than the other groups. However, Trehub and Chang pointed out that the absence of extinction and reconditioning trends tended to undercut this interpretation. Moreover, one might have expected to observe a decrease in sucking responses relative to the controls for infants in the group in which sucking removed the auditory signal, if the latter had reinforcing properties. One possible explanation for their failure to find evidence of the latter—viz., that the infants may have been close to floor level responding—seems unlikely, given that infants have been observed to display below-baseline levels of sucking in other studies (e.g., see Figure 2). Instead, other factors may also have been at work here as well, such as the possibility that the infants may have been interested in disrupting the auditory signal occasionally. Nevertheless, the fact that the infants in the contingent sound-initiation group displayed reliably higher rates of responding than the yoked-control group is an indication that contingent reinforcement is an important component of the procedure.

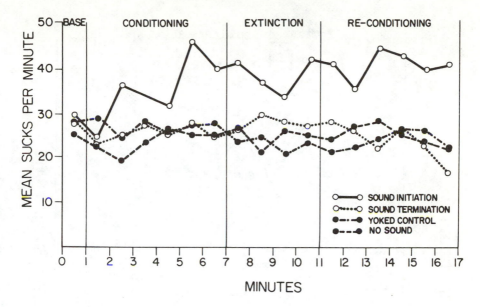

Figure 3. Mean number of sucks per minute as a function of experimental condition.

The issue of whether contingency learning is an important component of the HAS procedure has also been considered by Williams and Golenski (1978). In contrast to Trehub and Chang (1977), they modeled their procedure directly after that of Eimas et al. (1971). One interesting facet of their study was the fact that they looked at comparisons of stimulus-change and no-shift control groups under conditions of contingent and noncontingent reinforcement. They also included two types of noncontingent auditory presentations: a *periodic* condition in which the sounds were presented at constant intervals, and a *random* condition in which the interstimulus interval fluctuated randomly. Their results, shown in Figure 4, indicated that the contingent reinforcement group differed from the noncontingent groups in the important respect that it was the only group in which there was a reliable difference in the performance of the group relative to the no-shift control group. On the basis of these results, they concluded that contingent reinforcement is indeed an important component of the HAS procedure and that infants do seem to acquire the contingency between auditory reinforcement and their sucking behavior. They also noted that infants in the noncontingent reinforcement group showed a much higher incidence of crying than those in the contingent reinforcement group. They hypothesized that the likelihood that an infant will stay in an experiment of this sort may be directly related to the degree to which he or she is able to predict and control the presentation of the sound.

In summary, there is evidence from these experiments that infants in the HAS procedure do learn the contingency between criterion-level sucking and the presentation of the auditory reinforcer. Moreover, there is some indication that the acquisition of this contingency is important to the success of the procedure as a methodological tool for measuring discrimination.

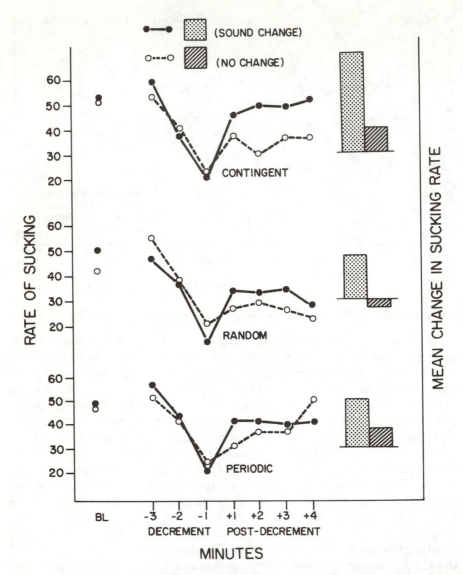

Figure 4. Average sucking rates for the last baseline minute, the last 3 min prior to decrement criterion, and 4 post-decrement min, by sound presentation condition (N = 12 per treatment group). Histograms show the difference between the mean of the first 2 post-decrement min and mean of the last 2 decrement min.

Given that the acquisition of the contingency is an apparently crucial element in the success of the procedure, it is of some interest to know how state variables affect the infant's performance. For example, one might suppose that the procedure might depend in some measure on the way that the infant attends to the task. Hence, infants who are distracted because they are sleepy or uncomfortable and crying might be expected to perform less successfully than those who are wide awake and seemingly interested in the task. Indeed, the degree to which the infant's state affects performance on the task is of considerable importance, because decisions regarding whether or not to include a given infant's data in an analysis of test results are often made on the basis of considerations of state. A number of researchers have voiced concern over the fact that the high dropout rates present in some studies may work in favor of finding evidence for discrimination (e.g., Mehler & Bertoncini, 1978; Trehub, 1975).

Williams and Golenski (1979) undertook a direct investigation of the effects of state on speech-sound discrimination. They were particularly concerned with the possibility that state might directly interact with speech-sound discrimination results. They reanalyzed data from three prior studies (Williams & Bush, 1978; Williams & Golenski, 1978; Williams, 1977a) with respect to the influence of state variables. Their investigation provided some indication that state does interact with sensitivity to sound change, in that infants who were in more alert states demonstrated evidence of significantly higher rates of sucking following the sound change than did infants in less alert states. But, most importantly, there was no indication of differential effects of state on subjects in stimulus-change versus no-shift control groups. An interaction of this sort would have meant that one could not attribute increases in sucking after shift to the discrimination of sound change. In effect, then, these results provide some justification for the practice of excluding subjects on the basis of state variables, especially those subjects who fall asleep during the course of the experiment. On the other hand, Williams and Golenski noted that the best results were actually obtained with infants who were actively moving and alert, rather than those who were defined as being in a quiet alert state.

In summary, the attempts to investigate the way in which the HAS procedure works provide some evidence for the view that the infant learns a contingency between criterion-level sucking and the occurrence of the auditory reinforcer. Moreover, it seems as though the presence of contingent reinforcement is important to the success of the HAS procedure as a measure of discrimination. Hence, factors that might be expected to affect the infant's ability to master the contingency (e.g., state variables) should be carefully considered in employing this technique as a measure of discrimination.

VARIATIONS IN THE WAY THAT HAS IS USED

Over the years, there have been a number of variations in the way that the HAS procedure has been employed. At times, it seems as though no two laboratories ever employ the procedure in exactly the same way. Moreover, given the fact that the consequences of varying the different aspects of the procedure have not been well studied, it is often difficult to make sensible comparisons of results obtained in different laboratories. There are a number of areas of the procedure in which slight variations have been made, such as the baseline level of sucking, the criterion for shift to the second stimulus, and even the criterion for inferring discrimination. We briefly consider the sorts of variations that have occurred and the possible implications that they might have for research findings.

Selection of the Criterion Level of High-Amplitude Sucking

As noted earlier, in the original version of the procedure as employed by Siqueland and DeLucia (1969), the criterion level for what constituted a high-amplitude suck was set at a fixed value (18 mm-Hg) for all infants. Subsequent versions of the procedure have tried to adjust the criterion sucking level in such a way to compensate for individual differences in sucking amplitude. The manner in which this has been implemented has varied from study to study. Hence, in the Eimas et al. (1971) study, a criterion was set so as to include only the top 33% of each infant's responses. Other studies have employed criterion levels that include the top 50%, and Eilers (1977) designated up to 80% of the infant's responses as criterion ones. Still another way of setting the criterion level is to fix a range of acceptable responses rather than basing a value on some percentage of the infant's responses. Hence, Trehub and Chang (1977) employed a range of between 15 and 40 responses per minute to set the criterion level, and Jusczyk has used a range of 15 to 35 responses per minute (e.g., Jusczyk, 1977; Jusczyk & Thompson, 1978; Jusczyk et al., 1978).

Ideally, the criterion level should be chosen in such a way so that the infant is able to demonstrate an increase in criterion-level sucking as a result of having learned the contingency between high-amplitude sucking and the presentation of the auditory signals. If the level is set too high or too low, various kinds of difficulties can ensue. In the case of a criterion that is set too high, one potential problem is that some infants may only emit very few sucks that actually exceed the criterion level in the course of a given minute during the test period. Indeed, if a great deal of effort is required to maintain sucking at this level, one consequence might be that the infant would show a decline in sucking not because of lack of interest in the auditory reinforcer but because of fatigue. Accordingly, if the rate drops off to satisfy the criterion for shifting to the second stimulus, it could be the case that an infant might not display an increase in sucking at that time, not because he or she is unable to perceive a difference in the stimuli, but because he or she is unable to muster enough effort to continually exceed the criterion level. Another problem that might also arise with too high a baseline level is the possibility that the infant might not acquire the contingency between sucking and the reinforcer in the first place. This latter situation could arise as a result of the fact that the infant might not produce criterion-level responses in a consistent enough manner to detect the contingency. It is for this reason that some investigators have adopted the tactic of setting a lower limit of responses per minute in determining the criterion level (e.g., Jusczyk, 1977; Miller & Eimas, 1983, Trehub & Chang, 1977). On the other hand, if too lax a criterion is set, then almost all of the infant's responses will be designated as high-amplitude sucks. The problem with this situation is that the infant may rapidly achieve a ceiling level of responses such that further criterion-level responses have no effect with respect to the presentation of the stimulus. Such would be the case if the sucking rate exceeded the maximum number of reinforcers that could be presented within a given minute (e.g., if the stimuli are 500 ms in duration and there is a 500 ms interstimulus interval, the maximum number of reinforcers per minute is 60). One potentially disastrous consequence in this situation would arise if the infant shows large fluctuations in sucking rates without really affecting the presentation rate of the auditory stimuli. Under these circumstances, large decreases in criterion-level sucking (which might be taken as evidence for satiation to the first stimulus) or large increases in sucking after the shift (which would be viewed as evidence for discrimination) could arise for purely artifactual reasons. Also, in the sense that the use of such a low criterion level might increase the overall variability in response rates, the sensitivity of the procedure as a measure of discrimination would be lessened.

Choosing a Criterion for Shifting to a Second Stimulus

There have been several approaches used in determining a criterion for the shift to the second stimulus. In the Eimas et al. (1971) study, the criterion was defined as a decrement in responding of 20% or more from the immediately preceding minute such that this decreased level of responding is maintained for 2 consecutive minutes. In principle, this means that the response rate during the second minute of the 2-minute period could be at or even above the level of the first minute, provided that it is still a 20% decrement from the minute preceding this period. Note, too, that the decline need not occur with respect to the minute in which the infant attained his or her highest level of responding. If there were some fluctuation in responding, then a minute that occurred at some later point during the course of reinforcement with the first auditory stimulus might serve instead as the minute from which the decline is measured. While a 20% decline was used in the Eimas et al. study, other investigators have employed slightly different values, e.g., 25% (Jusczyk, 1977) or 33% (Trehub, 1976a, b). It is difficult to say whether there are any direct consequences on discrimination results that follow from using these different criterion values, because the necessary empirical studies have not been undertaken. Although it is unlikely that the range of values considered here would result in marked differences in performance, it is possible that some slight differences in the sensitivity of the procedure for certain subtle contrasts might ensue. On the other hand, direct comparison of results using this type of criterion against those that employ a decrement criterion of 80% (e.g., Eilers, 1977) would seem to be especially problematic.

Not only has the degree of decrement in sucking employed for the shift criterion differed from laboratory to laboratory, but the manner in which the decrement is defined has differed as well. For example, in contrast to the procedure outlined above, some investigators have defined the 2-minute decrement with respect to the highest minute of sucking that is obtained during the preshift period, so long as it occurs at or after the third minute (e.g., Bertoncini & Mehler, 1981; Trehub, 1976a, b). Again, formal observations have not been carried out on the possible consequences that this variation might have for discrimination results. However, in our own laboratory we have carried out some informal comparisons of the two types of criteria. Specifically, we looked at the data of individual subjects to determine how often the use of the highest minute criterion would have resulted in an earlier shift to the second stimulus. (Given the way the criterion is defined, the use of the highest minute measure could only result in a shift either prior to or at the same moment as the measure used in Eimas et al., 1971). We found that, in over 90% of the cases, the shift point would have remained the same. Thus, once again it seems likely that the two types of criteria are not apt to lead to large differences in results, although whether more subtle sorts of differences are present is not known.

The final variant of the shift criterion is actually a return to the fixed interval criterion as originally employed by Siqueland and DeLucia (1969). This criterion has recently been employed in studies by Eimas and Miller (1980a) and Miller and Eimas (1983). They argue that the use of the fixed interval procedure helps to reduce the number of infants who drop out due to sleeping or crying, and they suggest from informal observation in their laboratory that the overall sensitivity of the procedure is not adversely affected.

Methods of Inferring Discrimination

In evaluating whether or not discrimination of a given contrast has occurred, investigators have typically used measures which compare post-shift performance against that during the period immediately preceding the shift. However, once again there are differences of definition with respect to the periods involved. In the Eimas et al. (1971) study and the ones immediately following by Eimas (1974, 1975a), the entire 4-minute postshift period was compared to that of the 2 minutes preceeding shift. The performance of experimental groups was always referenced with respect to that of the control group. Discrimination was inferred if performance differed significantly from that of the controls.

One of the first variations on this measure was to base the comparison primarily on performance during the 2 minutes immediately preceding and the 2 minutes immediately following shift (e.g., Jusczyk, 1977). The rationale behind this change was that, since it is apparently the novelty of the second stimulus that prompts the increase in criterion rate after the shift, such novelty effects are likely to be greatest soon after the change in stimuli. As the infant becomes more and more familiar with the second stimulus, one might expect that performance would begin to drop off. The first 2 minutes after shirt were used rather than just the first postshift minute because there tends to be a great deal of variability in performance during the first minute, due to a variety of factors. For example, given the way that the HAS procedure is typically employed, the infant will not have a chance to hear the new stimulus until he or she emits a criterion-level suck. Given that, in the preshift period, sucking has declined considerably, such a response may not occur until 10-20 seconds into the first postshift minute. In effect, this means that the infant would have somewhat less time than a full minute to increase sucking rate in the event that a new stimulus is discriminated (for a possible solution to this problem, see the discussion below of the experiment by Jusczyk, Mehler, Bijeljac-Babic, & Bertoncini, in preparation). Indeed, it is not unusual to find that sucking rates in the second minute frequently exceed that of the first minute after the shift. Thus, the use of the 2-minute postshift data insures that all of the infants have had an opportunity to listen to the new stimulus for at least one full-minute period.

Several other periods for comparing preshift and postshift performance have also been utilized. Bertoncini and Mehler (1981) based their comparisons on performance in the minute before and the minute after shift. Given the problems of variability in the first minute of postshift responding, this measure is probably less sensitive with respect to measuring discrimination than is the 2-minute measure. On the other hand, Eilers (1977) employed a measure involving the 4-minute period before shift and a comparable 4-minute period after shift. This measure also seems to be less than satisfactory, since increasing the length of the preshift period in this way introduces considerable variability into the data, as it includes several minutes of high level responding into the preshift period along with the 2-minute decrement period prior to shift. The likely consequence of this increased variability is to render the HAS procedure a less-sensitive instrument for measuring discriminability.

Another question that arises in conjunction with inferring discrimination concerns the role of the control group in analyzing the data. Specifically, can the control group data be dispensed with in favor of a measure that simply checked whether a reliable increase in sucking occurred in the postshift period with respect to the 2-minute decrement period? Certainly, while a significant increase in sucking after the shift could be a reliable index of discrimination, it could also be artifactual for a number of reasons that might go undetected by the investigator (e.g., one could envision a systematic artifact introduced by the equipment when the stimuli are changed). By basing a comparison on performance relative to that of control subjects, whatever systematic artifacts there might be in the experimental setting itself would be dispersed across groups. Thus, one could have a good deal more confidence in the fact that any remaining differences would reflect facts about the infant's discriminative capacities.

The HAS procedure has usually been used only to provide data regarding group performance. Owing to the variability in the performance of individual subjects, which undoubtedly stems from a variety of factors including changes in the behavioral state of the infant, it is very difficult to draw any conclusions about individual performances. Although one might think that an 80% increase in criterion sucking for an infant in an experimental group might provide an indication that a particular phonetic contrast was discriminated, one must balance such findings against the fact that subjects in control groups sometimes show similar increases. Still, it is worth considering whether one might be able to provide some measure that is an index to individual performance. Bertoncini and Mehler (1981) proposed a "dishabituation ratio" to insure that infants were responding only to the stimulus change. The ratio is expressed as:

$$\frac{\text{Rate after change} - \text{Rate before change}}{\text{Rate before change}}$$

They then suggested that, if the dishabituation ratio exceeded 15%, this would be an indication that infants were responding solely on the basis of the stimulus change. In their study, they found that the proportion of subjects in two of their experimental groups who had dishabituation ratios greater than 15% was reliably higher than that of the control group. Thus, the measure provided some indication of group differences in performance. However, the utility of the measure with respect to individual subject performance is less clear. In particular, it is not clear that one can accept the 15% criterion as an indication that the infants were responding solely on the basis of the stimulus change, because four of the 10 control subjects had scores in this range. One possible alternative might be to set the cutoff value for the dishabituation ratio such that it falls at a level that is 1.96 standard deviations above the mean value obtained by the control subjects (i.e., that the probability of obtaining such a score by chance would be less than 5%). In this instance, one might be able to say with a bit more confidence that it was likely that individuals with scores above this value were responding solely on the basis of the stimulus change. The likely problem with such a solution is that, owing to the large amounts of variability in the performance of subjects in the control condition, the cutoff value is apt to be set at so high a level that only a few subjects in the experimental groups would attain it.

ATTEMPTS TO INCREASE THE SENSITIVITY OF THE PROCEDURE

While the HAS procedure has served investigators well as an overall index of discriminability, it is not particularly well suited for making comparisons of the relative discriminability of phonetic contrasts to one another. There have been a number of attempts to improve on this aspect of the procedure.

Spring and Dale (1977) introduced a variation on the procedure whereby, after the shift period, the infant is presented with an alternating series of stimuli consisting of the familiar preshift stimulus and the novel postshift stimulus. The rationale behind this change was that it would juxtapose the contrasting stimuli continually, thus presumably increasing the possibility that the infant might detect the difference between them. Such a procedure might prove advantageous in situations where, because of inattention or failure to remember the preshift stimulus, the infant fails to detect a particular contrast. The notion that such factors might affect the infant's performance receives some support from work by Morse and his colleagues. Specifically, Swoboda, Kass, Morse, and Leavitt (1978) found that, over the range of 0-30 seconds, the longer the silent interval between the last token in the preshift period and the first one in the postshift period, the worse the infant's ability to discriminate the sound change. In principle, then, Spring and Dale's idea was a good one. In practice, the results to date have not indicated any significant gain in sensitivity with this procedure. There are a couple of possible reasons for this state of affairs. The first is that the original procedure might already be quite effective in presenting the infant with the distinctions in question. Hence, the infants may be performing at close to ceiling level and, thus, the additional reduction in memory demands may be of no consequence. Second, the reduction in memory demands could have conceivably been offset by a reduction in the novelty effect after the shift, due to the fact that the preshift stimulus is once again presented.

A different sort of attempt to increase the sensitivity of the HAS procedure was undertaken by Jusczyk (1977; see also Jusczyk, Rosner, Cutting, Foard, & Smith, 1977; Jusczyk & Thompson, 1978). He endeavored to collect within-subject data in hopes of compensating for the large amounts of between-subject variability. It was hoped that, by testing the same group of subjects on several contrasts, one might be able to gain a better indication of the relative discriminability of certain contrasts. Unfortunately, this attempt proved no more successful than that of Spring and Dale (1977). There was a considerable amount of within-subject variability, and the gain, if any, in sensitivity was more than offset by the problems in getting the infants to sit through the procedure on more than one occasion.

Most recently, Jusczyk et al. (in preparation) have modified the HAS procedure in another way so as to improve its sensitivity. In an effort to cope with the problems that arise from the fact that infants may not produce a criterion suck until well within the first postshift minute (i.e., that performance in the first postshift minute may not reflect the first full minute of exposure to the novel stimulus), they commenced the timing of the first postshift minute not from the point at which the soundtrack on the tape recorder is changed, but from the moment at which the infant emits the first criterion suck. The same procedure is followed with subjects in the control group as well (i.e., after the shift point is reached, timing for the postshift period commences only after the first criterion suck is achieved). Although it is too early to tell at this point whether the procedure might prove more powerful in providing information about the relative discriminability of contrasts, it does seem to be a more realistic way to measure postshift performance. The first postshift minute is now one in which the infant has an opportunity to listen to the novel stimulus for an entire minute. This change renders performance during the first postshift minute more informative than before.

EXTENSIONS OF THE HAS PROCEDURE

The basic use for the HAS procedure has been as a measure of discrimination for a single stimulus contrast. However, there have been attempts to extend the applicability of the procedure in several other directions as well. In this section, we consider some of the ways in which the procedure has been extended.

Typically, the HAS procedure has been used to provide information about a single stimulus contrast in a given experimental session. In large part, this limitation has been imposed because of the amount of time that it takes to complete a single session. While, on the average, a typical session might last approximately 15 minutes, some infants take much longer, due to the fact that they do not achieve the preshift criterion as rapidly. As the sessions get longer, one often encounters more problems in maintaining the infant's attention. Fatigue, sleepiness, and sheer boredom may force the termination of a given session before critical data regarding discrimination can be obtained. For this reason, most studies have not tried to gather data about more than a single contrast per session.

A notable exception to the tendency to look at only a single contrast per session occurs in those studies that have looked at laterality effects in infants (e.g., Bertoncini, 1982; Entus, 1977; Vargha-Khadem & Corballis, 1979). In these studies which have employed the dichotic listening paradigm, researchers have adopted a policy of testing infants on two contrasts per session. As illustrated in Figure 5, during the first portion of the experimental session, testing proceeds in much the same manner as in the standard procedure, with the exception that the stimulus change occurs only for one ear. The other ear is presented with the same stimulus both before and after shift. Data are collected for a 5-minute period after the shift, then there is a 1-minute pause and the entire procedure commences again. During this second test period, the stimulus change after the shift is presented to the other ear. In order to determine whether there is evidence of an ear-superiority effect, comparisons are made of the postshift performance by each infant on the two contrasts. While the issue of whether infants give evidence of an ear-superiority effect remains controversial, there seems to be no doubt that useful data can be obtained regarding infants' abilities to discriminate the second contrast, even for infants as young as 4 days (e.g., Bertoncini, 1982). Of course, the question remains as to whether there is any significant gain that accrues from testing the same infant on different contrasts. As noted above, there is often almost as great an amount of within-subject variability as there is between-subject variability. This fact, plus the difficulty of concluding much about the performance of individual subjects, tends to make the notion of multiple tests per session seem less attractive, given the additional difficulties posed by maintaining the infant in a ready state for testing for so long a period.

Thus far, all of the experiments described have employed the HAS procedure as a measure of the infant's discriminative capacities. However, there have also been some attempts to adapt the procedure in ways that might provide information about the way in which the infant categorizes information. In

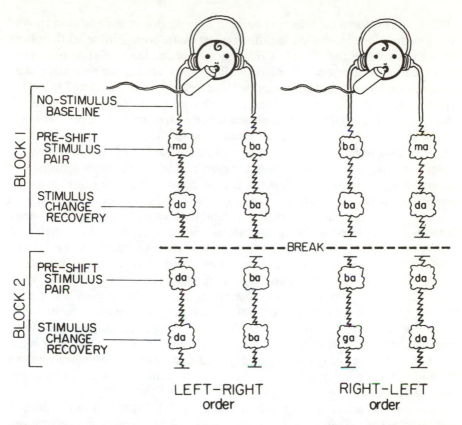

NO-STIMULUS BASELINE

BLOCK 1

PRE-SHIFT STIMULUS PAIR — ma / ba / ba / ma

STIMULUS CHANGE RECOVERY — da / ba / ba / da

—————————————— BREAK ——————————————

BLOCK 2

PRE-SHIFT STIMULUS PAIR — da / ba / ba / da

STIMULUS CHANGE RECOVERY — da / ba / ga / da

LEFT–RIGHT order   RIGHT–LEFT order

Figure 5. Schematic representation of the experimental procedure, showing stimulus sequence and ear order.

general, the HAS procedure can only provide indirect information about possible perceptual categories. For example, one might assume that differences that are not discriminable for infants are assigned to the same category. On the other hand, one cannot assume the converse—i.e., that two stimuli that are discriminable are *not* assigned to the same category—for it is perfectly plausible that the infant might, for all intents and purposes, treat them as two different members of the same category. Hence, in order to make inferences about what the infant does categorize, one must try to find a way of determining what stimuli are treated as being the same in some way.

One way of approaching the issue of categorization is to examine the consequences of introducing multiple tokens of a given stimulus. In particular, in the face of considerable variation between tokens, will the infant give evidence of making the same kinds of discriminations as before, or will the intertoken variability confuse the infant in some way? An indication that discrimination performance is relatively unaffected by such intertoken variability might be taken as a sign that the infant detects some underlying similarity between the preshift tokens. One of the first attempts in this direction was reported by Kuhl

(1976). She explored the effects of varying both pitch contour and vowel color. In one condition, infants during the preshift phase were reinforced by tokens of the same vowel (either /a/ or /i/) that varied randomly in their pitch contours (either a flat monotone or a rise-fall pattern). During the postshift phase, criterion responses were reinforced with presentations of tokens of the other vowel which also varied with respect to pitch contour. For a different group of infants, the critical stimulus change was made with respect to the pitch contour of the tokens. That is, during the preshift phase, subjects heard one type of pitch contour (e.g., monotone) in a set of stimuli that varied randomly in vowel color between /a/ and /i/. During the postshift phase the pitch contour was changed (e.g., to rise-fall) while the tokens continued to vary in their vowel color. The results indicated that the infants were able to detect a change in vowel color when pitch was varied irrelevantly. However, there was no evidence that the infants detected the pitch contour change in the face of the irrelevant vowel variations. Therefore, these results provide some indication that infants are capable of ignoring irrelevant variations along certain speech dimensions (e.g., pitch contour), but perhaps not along others (e.g., vowel color). While these results do not prove that infants perceive the different versions of each vowel to be the same in some essential respect, they do indicate that the variations that do occur in pitch contour are not sufficient to distract them from making the critical distinction between the different vowels. At the very least, this tendency is consistent with what one would expect if the infants recognized an important similarity between members of the same vowel class, and therefore categorized them in the same way.

A somewhat different approach to obtaining data regarding categorization has been taken in our own laboratory (Jusczyk & Derrah, in preparation; Jusczyk et al., in preparation). We have attempted to determine whether one might obtain information about the structure of the infant's perceptual categories by trying to habituate the infant to a particular category. The basic notion behind the procedure is borrowed from studies of categorization using the visual habituation procedure (e.g., Bornstein, Kessen, & Weiskopf, 1976; Cohen, 1977). In essence, one tries to habituate the infant to the category as a whole by repeatedly exposing the infant to a number of different instances from the category. Presumably, such exposure to diverse members from the same category might serve to reduce the level of responding not only to the category members that have already been presented but to the category itself, and hence, even to new instances of the familiar category. In the habituation procedures employing visual looking measures, different instances from a given category are presented to the infant repeatedly, either for a fixed number of trials or until looking drops off to some criterion level, at which point test trials occur consisting of new instances from the familiar category or instances from a new category. In such a case, the measure of categorization is an indirect one. It relies on the following sorts of assumptions: (a) that infants perceive the similarity between category members, (b) that they become habituated to the category as a whole, and (c) that the effects of satiation to the category are enough to offset any effects of novelty that might accrue to the new category instance.

In attempting to examine categorization with the HAS procedure, we have followed a similar approach to that outlined above. For example, in the Jusczyk and Derrah study, the preshift phase of the experiment employed a set of auditory reinforcers that were instances from a particular phonetic category. Thus, the infants were presented with a randomly varying series of the syllables /bi/, /bə/, /bo/, /ba/, all of which are instances of the phonetic category /b/. During the postshift phase of the experiment, a new stimulus was added to the members of the original stimulus set. The new stimulus was either a new member from the original category (e.g., /bu/) or a member of a different phonetic category (e.g., /du/). In order to insure that the infants would have an ample opportunity to detect the fact that a new item was included in the set of auditory reinforcers, the frequency with which the new token occurred was set so that it occurred as often as the other tokens combined (i.e., if there are four other tokens, the novel token occurred four times as frequently as any given one of them). The decision to present the original category members along with the new stimulus during the postshift period was motivated by the concern that switching from a varied set of stimuli to a single repetition stimulus might be sufficient in itself to produce increases in criterion sucking. Indeed, there is some evidence that infants are sensitive to shifts from multiple tokens to a single token (e.g., Eilers, 1977). Moreover, such a procedure might be more apt to lead the infant to focus on the difference in the vowels rather than on the similarity of the consonants, if the postshift stimulus were to occur in isolation.

As a precaution that the increased frequency of one of the tokens with respect to the others was not in itself a sufficient cause for increased responding, Jusczyk and Derrah ran an additional control condition. In this additional condition, the original stimulus set was played both before and after shift, but after the shift the frequency of one of the set members, /ba/, was increased so as to occur as often as the other members of the set combined. Hence, if the change in the frequency of the tokens was sufficient to produce an increased level of responding, then infants in this group should have shown a reliable in increase in responding relative to that of no-shift controls.

As is illustrated in Figure 6, the results that Jusczyk and Derrah obtained did not support the notion that the infants were habituated to a phonetic category corresponding to /b/. Specifically, the infants who heard instances of a new token (i.e., /bu/) from the familiar category did not differ from infants who received a new token (i.e., /du/) from a different category. Both groups showed significant increases in sucking after the shift relative to that of the control groups. With respect to the latter, it is worth noting that there was also no difference between the no-shift controls and those subjects for whom one of the members of the preshift stimulus set was increased in frequency after the shift. Evidently, then, the increase in sucking after shift is due to the addition of a new token (from either the same or a different phonetic category), rather

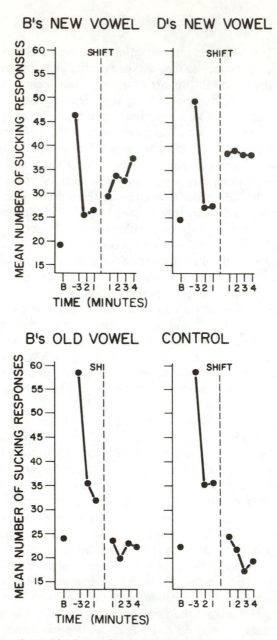

Figure 6. Mean number of high-amplitude sucking responses as a function of time and experimental group. Time is measured with reference to the moment of the stimulus shift, marked by the vertical dashed line. The baseline rate of sucking is indicated by the letter "B".

than to the detection of a change in the relative frequency of occurrence of members of the preshift stimulus set.

Given the results of this experiment, one cannot say for certain whether the HAS procedure can be adapted in this fashion as a measure of categorization, because the failure to find evidence for categorization for /b/ might be the result of the insensitivity of the procedure, or due to the fact that infants at this age do not have categories corresponding to phonetic segments like /b/. In order to establish which factor is at work here, it is necessary to test for other sorts of categories that infants might have. If the procedure is applicable to the study of categories, then one should eventually find evidence that new instances from the familiar category are responded to less strongly than instances from new categories.

Evidence that the HAS procedure can be used to provide information about categorization appears to be forthcoming in a more recent experiment that we have conducted (Jusczyk et al., in preparation). In order to determine whether there might be some classes of speech sounds that infants might show evidence of categorization for, we chose ones that we thought might be more salient for infants, viz. vowel categories. There were a number of reasons for thinking that categorization might be more likely to occur with vowels than with stop consonants. First, in terms of their acoustic characteristics, stop consonants are characterized by rapidly changing spectral characteristics and are of short duration, whereas, by comparison, vowels are relatively unchanging and are of longer duration (Pisoni, 1973). Second, in previous attempts to train 6-month-old infants to respond to phonetic categories, it has been observed that it is considerably easier to train infants to respond to vowel classes as opposed to consonant classes (e.g., Holmberg, Morgan, & Kuhl, 1977; Katz & Jusczyk, 1980; Kuhl, 1983).

Jusczyk et al. also made two slight modifications in the HAS procedure in an effort to improve its sensitivity. The first of these was to modify the procedure so as to start the timing of the first postshift minute only after the first criterion-level suck is emitted after the shift. The second modification was one which resulted in an additional measure that might serve to index the degree to which the infants might categorize the speech. The length of the postshift period was increased to include a second period of habituation. In other words, rather than terminate the session 4 minutes after the change in stimulus set, testing continued until the decrement criterion was met with the postshift stimulus set. The underlying rationale for this change was that a measure of the time that it takes to show a decrement to the postshift stimulus set might prove to be a more reliable index of the infant's underlying categories than the standard measure of the amount of dishabituation that infants show after the shift. For example, if infants greet any detectable change in stimulation with roughly the same level of postshift responding, then the standard measure of the amount of dishabituation would be unsuitable. However, under these circumstances it is possible that, if the infants did perceive more intrinsic similarity between a new member of the old category and the other members of the category, the novelty of the new category member might abate sooner than would that for a member of a different category that contrasts with the other members of the stimulus set. If so, then one might find that the time to habituate to the post-shift stimulus set is shorter when new instances of the familiar category are introduced than when members of a different category are introduced.

In their study, Jusczyk et al. used stimulus sets that paralleled those of the Jusczyk and Derrah study. Specifically, during the preshift period the stimulus set consisted of randomly varying presentations of the syllables /bi/, /si/, /li/, /mi/—all of which are instances of the vowel category /i/. During the post-shift period, the stimulus set was changed in one of a number of ways. For one group, a new instance (i.e., /di/) from the familiar category was added to the stimulus set (as before, the frequency of appearance of a new token was set at a level equal to that of all the other tokens). In two other groups, "near vowel category" and "far vowel category," a token from another vowel category was added to the stimulus set. In the case of the near vowel category set, the token, /dI/, was one in which the vowel was rated as highly similar to that in the original stimulus set (e.g., Shepard, 1972), whereas the token in the far vowel category, /da/, was chosen to be dissimilar to that of the stimulus set. In addition to these groups, there was also a control condition in which only the frequency of occurrence of one of the members of the stimulus set (i.e., /mi/) was increased after the shift. The results indicated that reliable increases in sucking after the shift, relative to that of the control subjects, occurred only for groups that received instances from a new vowel category—i.e., the near and far vowel category groups. By contrast, the performance of subjects who heard a new member /di/ from the old category gave no evidence of a reliable increase in sucking relative to the controls. Hence, the standard measure of habituation appears to be useful as a measure of categorization, at least under some circumstances. By contrast, it must be noted that the measure based on the amount of time to rehabituate to the second stimulus proved to be con-siderably less successful. Although there was a tendency towards more rapid habituation to a new member from the familiar category, there were no reliable differences among any of the groups. One possible mitigating factor here is that infants in the present study were but 4 days old. It is possible that the over-all effects of fatigue may have offset any tendency that there might have been for any differential similarity between the stimuli. Such fatigue effects might be greater for infants at this age than they might be for older infants. Hence, it may be useful to try the procedure with 2-month-olds.

While a final verdict on the utility of this version of the HAS procedure as a way of indexing the infant's perceptual categories awaits further testing, the present results have to be seen as encouraging. Though the measure of categori-zation is an indirect one, it may serve to provide some indication of what form perceptual categorization takes in infants of this age.

Another encouraging development in employing some form of the HAS procedure to explore the nature of the infant's perceptual categories is the recent work reported by DeCasper and Fifer (1980). Although they were not interested in the issue of perceptual categorization per se, the variation on the HAS procedure that they developed may prove useful in this regard. In particular, DeCasper and Fifer describe a way of developing a differential response with the sucking procedure. Differential feedback was presented to infants depending on whether the interval between successive sucking bursts was greater or less than the median interval measured during a 5-minute baseline period with no reinforcement. A burst was defined as a series of individual sucks that were separated from one another by less than 2 seconds. In their experiment, the differential reinforcement consisted of presentation of the infant's own mother's voice or that of another infant mother's voice. DeCasper and Fifer reported evidence that infants adjust their interburst interval so as to hear the voice of their own mother. Moreover, a number of infants were brought back for a second day of testing in which the response requirements were reversed. Thus, infants who previously had to produce interburst intervals greater than the median in order to hear their own mother's voice now had to produce interburst intervals less than the median to hear it. Once again, the infants showed the capability of adjusting their sucking burst intervals so as to produce their own mother's voice. This result suggests the feasibility of using a categorization procedure based upon differential sucking responses. Some steps were taken in this direction by DeCasper and Fifer in another experiment. The procedure was varied so as to eliminate the interburst interval measure. In its place, differential auditory cues were provided in the form of an alternating sequence of 4-second periods of tones and silence. The sequence was played during the interburst intervals. If a sucking burst occurred while the tone was being played, then the infant was reinforced with a presentation of the mother's voice. By contrast, if the sucking burst was initiated during the silent period, presentations of a stranger's voice were played. The testing period lasted for twenty minutes. The results indicated that, although infants were as likely to suck during a silent period as during a tone period during the first third of the test period, there was significantly more sucking during the tone periods for the final third of the experiment.

It is the second version of the procedure that DeCasper and Fifer developed that would seem to have the most potential for application to the study of perceptual categorization. Specifically, one could envision a test procedure of the following sort. The infants would be trained to respond differentially to two endpoints of a synthetic speech continuum (e.g., /ba/—/pa/) such that alternating 4-second periods of each stimulus would be played, and responses during one of the intervals would produce reinforcement (e.g., the mother's voice or perhaps music), whereas responses during the other interval would produce some less desirable outcome (e.g., a stranger's voice or silence). After obtaining an indication of differential responding to the two endpoints, one might then begin to introduce other tokens from the stimulus continuum in a systematic manner, and observe what sorts of responses are made to them.[1] One might expect that, as the category boundary is approached, the ability to produce differential responding would break down. Whether such a procedure or some variant of it can be implemented successfully remains to be seen, but it does have the potential of providing additional information about the nature of perceptual categories in infancy.

CONCLUSIONS

Despite its many limitations, particularly with respect to providing information about individual infants, the HAS procedure has proved to be an important tool for providing information about the discriminative capacities of young infants. One problem which has arisen in past uses of the procedure is the variations which have occurred from laboratory to laboratory in the way that various aspects of the procedure are defined. Some comparative studies of the consequences of these different variations would be very helpful, as would some general agreement towards standardizing the procedure.

Undoubtedly, the HAS procedure will continue to be useful as a general measure of discriminative capacity. However, as investigators seek to explore questions regarding more subtle perceptual issues, greater precision is necessary. Hence, the future success of attempts to modify the procedure to provide information about these issues will determine whether it will continue to occupy an important place among the methods employed in infant perceptual research.

ACKNOWLEDGMENTS

I wish to thank Josiane Bertoncini for her helpful comments on an earlier version of the present manuscript. In addition, I am grateful for the hospitality and support extended to me by the Laboratoire de Psychologie, C.N.R.S., 54 Boulevard Raspail, Paris, France, during the preparation of this manuscript. I also received support from NICHD Grant #15795 during this period.

---

[1] One obviously encounters the problem here of what to do about reinforcing responses on test trials. Essentially, there are several possibilities; none of them is completely satisfactory. One could elect to provide no reinforcement whatsoever on these test trials, but to intersperse them with endpoint trials. Provided that the proportion of endpoint to test trials was relatively great, the occasional appearance of these test trials might not disrupt performance on the endpoint trials. Of course, with this procedure one could only obtain one or two estimates per data point for each subject. Alternatively, one could reinforce all responses on test trials, as before. The problem with this latter approach is that one could argue that, because of the reinforcement, the infants are being trained to respond to the phonetic categories. There are a couple of ways that one could try to counter this objection: either score only the first observation of each data part, or test some infants using an arbitrary pattern of reinforcement for the test trials (i.e., one that mixes up tokens of different adult phonetic classes). Once again, neither of these solutions is perfect, but the only way to evaluate their utility effectively is to try them out and hope that one or the other yields an intelligible pattern of results.

REFERENCES

Bertoncini, J. *Quelques aspects de la perception de la parole chez l'enfant de 0 à 2 mois.* Doctoral dissertation, Ecole des hautes études en sciences sociales, Paris, France, 1982.

Bertoncini, J. & Mehler, J. Syllables as units in infant speech perception. *Infant Behavior & Development,* 1981, *4,* 247–260.

Bornstein, M. H., Kessen, W., & Weiskopf, S. The categories of hue in infancy. *Science,* 1976, *191,* 201–202.

Bronshtein, A. I. & Petrova, E. P. An investigation of the auditory analyzer in neonates and young infants. In Y. Brackbill & G. G. Thompson (eds.), *Behavior in infancy and early childhood: A book of readings,* New York: Free Press, 1967.

Butterfield, E. C. & Cairns, G. F. Discussion summary—infant reception research. In R. L. Schiefelbusch & L. L. Lloyd (eds.), *Language perspectives: Acquisition, retardation and intervention,* Baltimore: University Park Press, 1974.

Cohen, L. B. *Concept acquisition in the human infant.* Paper presented at the Society for Research in Child Development Meeting, New Orleans, March 1977.

DeCasper, A. J. & Fifer, W. P. Of human bonding: Newborns prefer their mothers' voices. *Science,* 1980, *208,* 1174–1176.

Eilers, R. E. Context sensitive perception of naturally produced stop and fricative consonants by infants. *Journal of the Acoustical Society of America,* 1977, *61,* 1321–1336.

Eimas, P. D. Auditory and linguistic processing of cues for place of articulation by infants. *Perception & Psychophysics,* 1974, *16,* 513–521.

Eimas, P. D. Auditory and phonetic coding of the cues for speech: Discrimination of the [r-1] distinction by young infants. *Perception & Psychophysics,* 1975, *18,* 341–347. (a)

Eimas, P. D. Speech perception in early infancy. In L. B. Cohen & P. Salapatek (eds.), *Infant perception: From sensation to cognition* Vol. 2. New York: Academic Press, 1975. (b)

Eimas, P. D. & Miller, J. L. Contextual effects in infant speech perception. *Science,* 1980, *209,* 1140–1141. (a)

Eimas, P. D. & Miller, J. L. Discrimiantion of the information for manner of articulation by young infants. *Infant Behavior and Development,* 1980, *3,* 367–375. (b)

Eimas, P. D., Siqueland, E. R., Jusczyk, P., & Vigorito, J. Speech perception in infants. *Science,* 1971, *171,* 303–306.

Entus, A. K. Hemispheric asymmetry in processing of dichotically presented speech and non-speech stimuli by infants. In S. J. Segalowitz & F. A. Gruber (eds.), *Language development and neurological theory.* New York: Academic Press, 1977.

Holmberg, T. L., Morgan, K. A., & Kuhl, P. K. *Speech perception in early infancy: Discrimination of fricative consonants.* Paper presented at the 94th meeting of the Acoustical Society of America, Miami Beach, Florida, December 16, 1977.

Jusczyk, P. W. Perception of syllable-final stop consonants by two-month-old infants. *Perception and Psychophysics,* 1977, *21,* 450–454.

Jusczyk, P. W., Copan, H. C., & Thompson, E. J. Perception by two-month-olds of glide contrasts in multisyllabic utterances. *Perception & Psychophysics,* 1978, *24,* 515–520.

Jusczyk, P. W. & Derrah, C. Are stop consonants categorized by two-month-old infants? (In preparation).

Jusczyk, P. W., Mehler, J., Bijeljac-Babic, R., & Bertoncini, J. Studies of categorizations of speech sounds by young infants. In preparation.

Jusczyk, P. W., Pisoni, D. B., Reed, M., Fernald, A., & Myers, M. Durational context effects in the processing of nonspeech sounds by infants. *Science,* 1983, *222,* 175–177.

Jusczyk, P. W., Pisoni, D. B., Walley, A., & Murray, J. Discrimination of relative onset time of two-component tones by infants. *Journal of the Acoustical Society of America,* 1980, *67,* 262–270.

Jusczyk, P. W., Rosner, B. S., Cutting, J. E., Foard, C. F., & Smith, L. B. Categorical perception of nonspeech sounds by two-month-old infants. *Perception and Psychophysics,* 1977, *21,* 50–54.

Jusczyk, P. W. & Thompson, E. Perception of a phonetic contrast in multisyllabic utterances by two-month-old infants. *Perception and Psychophysics,* 1978, *23,* 105–109.

Katz, J. & Jusczyk, P. W. *Do six-month-olds have perceptual constancy for phonetic segments?* Paper presented at the International Conference on Infant Studies, New Haven, April, 1980.

Kuhl, P. K. Speech perception in early infancy: The acquisition of speech-sound categories. In S. K. Hirsh, D. H. Eldridge, I. J. Hirsh, & S. R. Silverman (eds.), *Hearing and Davis: Essays honoring Hallowell Davis.* St. Louis, Mo.: Washington University Press, 1976.

Kuhl, P. K. Perception of auditory equivalence classes for speech by infants. *Infant Behavior & Development,* 1983, *6,* 263–285.

Lisker, L. & Abramson, A. S. The voicing dimension: Some experiments in comparative phonetics. In *Proceedings of the Sixth International Congress of Phonetic Sciences, Prague, 1967.* Prague: Academia, 1970.

Mehler, J. & Bertoncini, J. Infants' perception of speech and other acoustic stimuli. In J. Morton & J. Marshall (eds.), *Psycholinguistic Series II.* London: Elek Science Books, 1978.

Miller, J. L. & Eimas, P. D. Studies on the categorization of speech by infants. *Cognition,* 1983, *13,* 135–165.

Morse, P. A. The discrimination of speech and nonspeech stimuli in early infancy. *Journal of Experimental Child Psychology,* 1972, *14,* 477–492.

Pisoni, D. B. Auditory and phonetic memory codes in the discrimination of consonants and vowels. *Perception and psychophysics,* 1973, *13,* 253–260.

Shepard, R. N. The psychological representations of speech sounds. In E. E. David & P. B. Denes (eds.), *Human communication: A unified view.* New York: McGraw-Hill, 1972.

Siqueland, E. R. *The development of instrumental exploratory behavior during the first year of human life.* Paper presented at meeting of the Society for Research in Child Development, Santa Monica, Ca., March 1969.

Siqueland, E. R. & DeLucia, C. A. Visual reinforcement of non-nutritive sucking in human infants. *Science,* 1969, *165,* 1144–1146.

Spring, D. R. & Dale, P. S. Discrimination of linguistic stress in early infancy. *Journal of Speech and Hearing Research,* 1977, *20,* 224–232.

Swoboda, P., Kass, J., Morse, P., & Leavitt, L. Memory factors in infant vowel discrimination of normal and at-risk infants. *Child Development,* 1978, *49,* 332–339.

Trehub, S. E. Infant's sensitivity to vowel and tonal contrasts. *Developmental Psychology,* 1973, *9,* 91–96.

Trehub, S. E. The problem of state in infant speech discrimination studies. *Developmental Psychology,* 1975, *11,* 116.

Trehub, S. E. The discrimination of foreign speech contrasts by infants and adults. *Child Development,* 1976, *47,* 466–472. (a)

Trehub, S. E. *Infants discrimination of multisyllabic stimuli: The role of temporal factors.* Paper presented at the annual convention of the American Speech and Hearing Association, Houston, Texas, November 21, 1976. (b)

Trehub, S. E. & Chang, H. Speech as reinforcing stimulation for infants. *Developmental Psychology,* 1977, *13,* 170–171.

Trehub, S. E. & Rabinovitch, M. S. Auditory-linguistic sensitivity in early infancy. *Developmental Psychology,* 1972, *6,* 74–77.

Vargha-Khadem, F. & Corballis, M. C. Cerebral asymmetry in infants. *Brain and Language,* 1979, *8,* 1–9.

Williams L. *The effects of phonetic environment and stress placement on infant discrimination of place of stop consonant articulation.* Paper presented at the Second Annual Boston University Conference on Language Development, Boston, October 1, 1977. (a)

Williams, L. The perception of stop consonant by Spanish-English bilinguals. *Perception & Psychophysics,* 1977, *21,* 289–297. (b)

Williams, L. & Bush, M. The discrimination by young infants of voiced stop consonants with and without release bursts. *Journal of the Acoustical Society of America,* 1978, *63,* 1223–1225.

Williams, L. & Golenski, J. Infant speech sound discrimination: The effects of contingent versus noncontingent stimulus presentation. *Child Development,* 1978, *49,* 213–217.

Williams, L. & Golenski, J. Infant behavioral state and speech sound discrimination. *Child Development,* 1979, *50,* 1243–1246.

10

METHODS IN THE STUDY OF INFANT SPEECH PERCEPTION

161.68

Patricia K. Kuhl

University of Washington, Seattle

INTRODUCTION

This chapter describes two techniques used in the study of speech perception in early infancy—the Head-Turn and the Auditory-Visual Speech Perception techniques. Both are relatively new. The first study applying the Head-Turn technique to the study of infant speech perception was published just seven years ago (Eilers, Wilson, & Moore, 1977). It has been widely applied since that time (Eilers, Gavin, & Wilson, 1979; Eilers, Wilson, & Moore, 1979; Kuhl, 1979a, 1980, 1983; Aslin, Pisoni, Hennessey, & Perey, 1981; Hillenbrand, 1983, 1984).

The latter technique has been developed even more recently. In a study published two years ago, Kuhl and Meltzoff (1982) described the Auditory-Visual Speech Perception technique to study infants' cross-modal perception of

223

speech. Since that time, it has been used in a variety of studies by the original research team (Kuhl and Meltzoff, 1984a, b) and others (e.g., MacKain, Studdert-Kennedy, Spieker, & Stern, 1983).

For each of the techniques, we will discuss (a) the motivation for its development, (b) the history of its development, (c) the refinement of the technique, and (d) some of the questions posed and the data yielded by its current application to the study of infant speech perception. The discussion will focus on the advantages and disadvantages of each technique. This will be possible particularly in instances in which studies have been aimed specifically at revealing the factors that limit its application.

THE HEAD-TURN TECHNIQUE (HT)

Motivation for Its Development

The study of the perception of speech by infants is just over a decade old. In the first half of the decade, the only behavioral technique available to study infants' responses to speech was the high-amplitude sucking (HAS) technique (Jusczyk, this volume). The HAS technique has produced many valuable findings, but it has serious limitations. They include (a) a restricted age range over which the technique is applicable, (b) the inability to provide data on individual subjects, and (c) particular difficulty in interpreting negative results.

The age range over which HAS has been applied extends from about 1 month to 4 months, though very young infants have been tested (see Jusczyk, this volume, for discussion). Infants younger than a month are difficult to test because they fall asleep; infants older than 4 months are not content to suck on a non-nutritive nipple and do not like sitting in the infant seat (Kuhl, 1979b). Perhaps changes in the technique could be made to extend the age range over which it is applicable, but the technique as it is now used imposes limits on the age range over which it can be applied.

HAS's second limitation is its inability to provide individual data. The design of the experiment depends upon group data—infants in the experimental group receive a sound change and infants in the control group do not. Evidence of discrimination is derived by comparing the sucking rates of the two groups at the point in time at which the experimental group is presented with a change in the sound. Comparisons of the two groups thus demonstrate that rate changes cannot be attributed to cyclic changes in sucking. A different design might allow individual data to be obtained (for example, one in which the sound is changed twice for each infant), but as HAS is designed and used, individual data are not provided.

Finally, and most difficult to contend with, the design of the experiment makes negative results particularly difficult to interpret. This is due to the fact that the reinforcing stimuli in the HAS technique are the stimuli under test. Presumably, infants produce sucking responses because they find the auditory stimuli reinforcing. If the sound presented in the postshift period is not reinforcing, infants might fail to produce sucking responses—not because they cannot discriminate it from the preshift stimulus, but because they fail to find it reinforcing. Thus, if infants provide evidence of discriminating one contrast but not another, it can be due either to the differential discriminability of the sound pairs or to their differential reinforcing properties. This problem is inherent to the technique.

The operant head-turn (HT) technique provides partial solutions to these problems. It involves conditioning an infant to produce a head-turn response when a repetitive sound is changed to another sound. Correct head-turn responses are reinforced with the presentation of a visual stimulus known to be interesting to infants (i.e., an animated toy). Regarding the three points raised concerning HAS, the initial data suggest that the HT technique can be applied over a large age range—from 6 to about 18 months. Second, individual data can be obtained. Third, since the reinforcer is independent of the stimuli under test, failures to obtain significant results are not attributable to any differential reinforcing properties of the stimuli themselves.

The head-turn technique thus holds promise as a powerful tool in infant speech-perception research. As with the development of most techniques, however, its evolution towards a valid, routinely usable technique has taken many years. A considerable number of refinements have been made since its first use as a technique to obtain sensory thresholds for auditory stimuli (Moore, Thompson, & Thompson, 1975). The gradual tightening up of a procedure over a long period should not be considered a criticism, but rather it should be considered the natural course of events in the development of research techniques. From this point of view, an examination of the steps in the process becomes an instructive exercise. The following sections detail the historical development of the HT technique as a tool used in clinical audiology, its adaptation to speech perception, and its refinement toward a valid and routinely usable measure of infants' speech perception abilities.

History of Its Development

Initial Application to Clinical Audiology. The behavioral assessment of auditory function in infants has commonly relied on the infant's natural tendency to turn toward a sound source. For example, audiologists testing infants under 12 months of age typically use "Behavioral Observation Audiometry" (BOA) to examine the infant's responsiveness to the presentation of precisely controlled auditory signals. While eye-blinks and other behaviors are used in BOA to judge whether the infant has heard the sound, a head-turn response in the direction of the source of the stimulus (i.e., a localization response) is one of the most common components used to judge infant responsiveness.

While BOA has served to provide the clinician with some idea of the range of sound intensity an infant is responsive to, its ability to provide a valid estimate of the infant's "threshold" has been questioned (Weber, 1969; Ling, Ling, & Doehring, 1970; Moore et al., 1975; Thompson & Weber, 1974). Wilson (1979) cited three factors which limit BOA's application severely. First, as used clinically, BOA does not control for examiner bias. Second, it has been demonstrated that, in the absence of reinforcement, infants quickly habituate their head-turn responses, thereby making it difficult to use the technique for any extended period of time. Third, thresholds obtained from infants presumed to have normal hearing vary extensively when this technique is used to assess thresholds.

These shortcomings led a variety of clinical audiologists to examine the use of a head-turn response in an operant-conditioning format with a visual stimulus as the reinforcer (Haug, Baccaro, & Guilford, 1967; Liden & Kankkunen, 1969; Motta, Facchini, & D'Auria, 1970; Suzuki, Ogiba, & Takei, 1972; Tyberghein & Forrez, 1971; Warren, 1972). These authors generally examined infants no younger than 12 months, although Haug et al. (1967) reported some success with infants as young as 5 months of age.

Adaptation of the HT technique for use with infants in the 5- to 12-month age range is attributable to a team of clinical audiologists from the University of Washington in Seattle. Their basic procedure involved training the infant to produce a head-turn response toward a loudspeaker when an auditory signal was presented. Correct head turns were reinforced. In the first in a series of parametric studies on the procedure, Moore et al. (1975) examined the effects of the type of reinforcer on head-turn responses to sound in infants between 12 and 18 months of age. Four types of reinforcement were examined: (a) no reinforcement; (b) social reinforcement (a smile, verbal praise and/or a pat on the shoulder); (c) simple visual reinforcement (a blinking light); and (d) complex visual reinforcement (an animated toy).

Forty-eight infants between 12 and 18 months of age were tested. The stimulus was a complex noise presented at a level well above threshold (70 dB SPL). Each infant was given 40 trials; each trial consisted of a 4-second observation interval during which head-turn responses were judged by both an assistant and an experimenter. During 30 of the 40 trials, the test signal was presented (experimental trials) and infants were reinforced for making the head-turn response. During the remaining ten of the 40 trials, no signal was presented (control trials), but head-turn responses were still monitored. Reinforcement was never presented during control trials.

The test room (Figure 1) consisted of a commercially available sound-treated suite. An examiner in the control room had full view of the testing situation through a one-way mirror. The test room was arranged with the infant seated on the parent's lap at a table in the center of the room. A loudspeaker was located at eye level approximately 1.3 meters from the infant and at a 45° angle to the left of the infant's midline of vision. The visual reinforcer was located approximately 1 meter from the infant in front of the loudspeaker and at the infant's eye level. The complex visual reinforcer consisted of a commercially available, battery-operated animal that could be animated (a monkey that clapped cymbals, a bear that pounded a drum, etc.). It was mounted in a clear plexiglass box in the initial studies; later, it was placed in a smoked plexi-

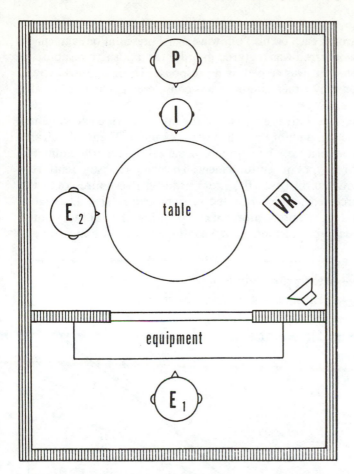

E₁-Experimenter 1
E₂-Experimenter 2
P-Parent
I-Infant
VR-Visual Reinforcer

Figure 1. The experimental/control suite used in the Head-Turn Technique. (Reprinted from Eilers, WIlson, & Moore, 1977.)

glass box (Wilson, 1979). This reduced its visibility during any time other than the reinforcement period, when the lights, located in the four corners of the box, were lit. An assistant was seated to the infant's right side. This person manipulated quiet toys in order to maintain the infant's head in a rightward or midline position.[1]

Auditory stimuli were not presented if the infant was crying or vocalizing, gazing directly at the assistant or at the loudspeaker, was excessively preoccupied with his or her hands or feet, or was moving excessively. The authors reported that only a clear head turn in the direction of the speaker was counted

---

[1] In the earliest experiments, the visual reinforcer and loudspeaker were located to the infant's right, and the assistant to the infant's left. In later experiments, this right-left orientation was reversed so that the reinforcer and loudspeaker were located to the infant's left and the assistant to the infant's right. This was done to minimize head-turn responses in the absence of a stimulus (false-positives).

as a response; eye movement alone was considered as no response. Two examiners independently scored each event. Following signal presentation, agreement that a head turn had occurred was required in order for a positive response to be recorded—disagreement was scored as no response. During control trials, indication of a response by either examiner was considered evidence of a false positive.

Figure 2 shows the cumulative responses of the infants during experimental intervals (trials in which an auditory stimulus was presented). The results clearly demonstrated the superiority of the complex visual reinforcer (the animated toy) over the other three types of reinforcement. The complex visual reinforcement resulted in significantly ($p < 0.01$) more head-turn responses than the simple visual reinforcement, which resulted in significantly ($p < 0.05$) more head-turn responses than the no-reinforcement condition. The authors noted that the complex visual reinforcement group continued to show a high rate of

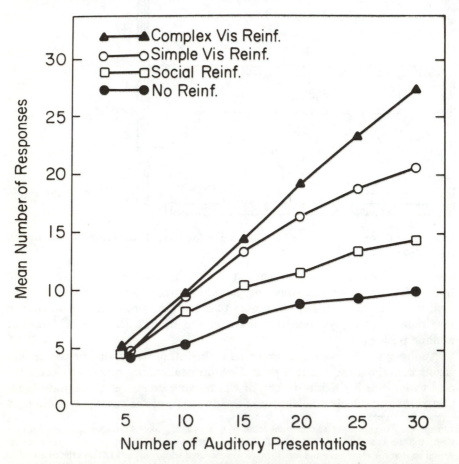

Figure 2. Cumulative mean head-turn responses in blocks of stimulus trials as a function of reinforcement type. (Reprinted from Moore, Thompson, & Thompson, 1975.)

response over the 30 trials, averaging eight responses during the last ten stimulus presentations. The social-reinforcement group continued to respond over the full 30 stimulus presentations, but averaged only three to four responses during the last ten presentations. In contrast, the no-reinforcement group failed to respond after the twelfth stimulus presentation. They averaged less than one positive response over the final ten stimulus presentations.

The authors reported that the subjects randomly looked toward the sound source only 4.8% of the time during the control periods, when no auditory stimulus was presented. They therefore ruled out random head-turning as a major factor accounting for the number of correct responses that were obtained using the various reinforcement conditions. In addition, inter-judge agreement was reported to be very high. The examiners purportedly recorded the same response independently 98.6% of the time immediately following an auditory presentation, and 98.9% of the time during the control periods.

In the second study in this series, Moore, Wilson, and Thompson (1977) examined the technique's effectiveness with younger infants. They were particularly interested in whether or not infants under 12 months of age could be reliably tested. They tested 20 infants in each of three age groups: 3-4 months, 5-6 months, and 7-11 months. In each age group, infants were divided into two groups of ten infants each. One group was reinforced with the complex visual reinforcer, and the other group was not given reinforcement.

Figure 3 illustrates the mean number of head-turn responses as a function of the number of trials for the three age groups. The data illustrate two points: First, an age effect was obtained. While 5- to 6-month-olds and 7- to 11-month-olds responded significantly more often ($p < 0.01$) when the complex visual reinforcer was presented, as opposed to no reinforcer, 3- to 4-month-olds showed no significant difference in the two conditions. This suggests that the head-turn response, when reinforced with an animated toy, may be reliably used with infants as young as 5 months of age. Second, within the design used here, that is, using the 40-trial test period, no habituation of the response was seen for the two older age groups. The authors again reported a low false-positive rate (6.2% of the control trials), suggesting that random head-turning did not account for the high rate of responding during Experimental intervals. Moreover, inter-judge reliability was reportedly high—98.6% during experimental intervals and 96.0% during control intervals.

Further evidence that the infants' continued responding was dependent on the visual reinforcer was obtained by Wilson, Moore, and Thompson (1976). They tested two infants in a single-subject design. The experiment used an ABA reversal design. Reinforcement for head turns on experimental (signal) trials was available during the A phases, while reinforcement was withheld (extinction) during the B phase. Control (no signal) trials were randomly interspersed on 25% of the trials. Each infant was given five trials at the outset of the experiment, in which the complex visual reinforcer was available for correct head turns during the presentation of the signal (A phase). Then the reinforcer was removed for 15 trials (B phase). The twenty-first trial was a training trial

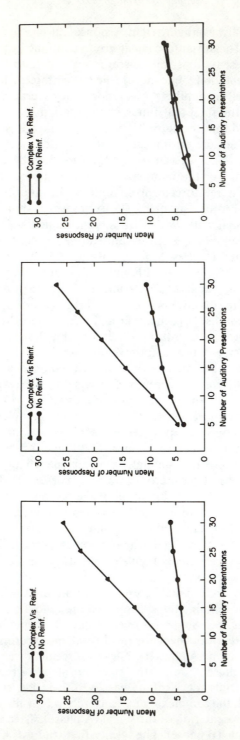

Figure 3. Cumulative mean head-turn responses in blocks of stimulus trials as a function of reinforcement and age: Panel A, 7- to-11-month-olds; Panel B, 5- to-6-month-olds; Panel C, 3- to-4-month-olds. (Reprinted from Moore, Wilson, & Thompson, 1977.)

in which the visual reinforcer was automatically paired with the signal. For the remaining nine trials, each correct head-turn response was followed by reinforcement (A phase).

The data for the two 6-month-old infants are shown in Figure 4. As is readily apparent, the head-turn responses of both infants extinguished during the B phase when reinforcement was withheld, but were reinstated when reinforcement was again available. The data also illustrate that false-positive responses did not occur for either infant during the ten randomly interspersed control intervals.

Collectively, these three studies demonstrated that a complex visual reinforcer significantly increased the number of head-turn responses to auditory signals by infants 5 months of age and older. Furthermore, the data showed that infants' correct responses were not due to random head-turning, since the number of false-positive responses occurring during control intervals was small. Parametric investigations demonstrated two important effects—the effect of type of reinforcer and the effect of age. Studies showed that when a complex visual reinforcer was used infants as young as 5 months of age would respond to the presentation of a sound without habituating over a 40-trial test period. Thus, the basic procedure had been defined—it involved conditioning the infant to make a head-turn response toward a sound source when an auditory

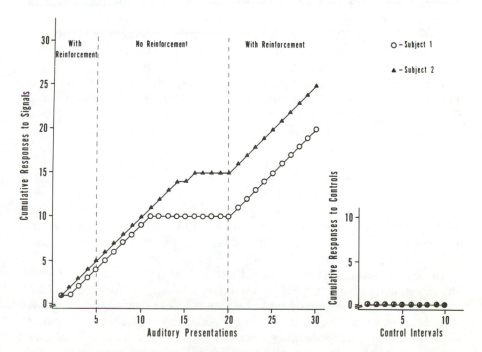

Figure 4. Cumulative head-turn responses during experimental trials as a function of reinforcement for two individual subjects. Responses on control trials are shown on the right. (Reprinted from Wilson, Moore, & Thompson, 1976.)

signal was presented. Correct head-turn responses were reinforced by a complex visual stimulus. An assistant occupied the infant's attention throughout testing by manipulating silent toys.

Refinement of the technique: Early controls for bias. There are many potential sources of bias in the head-turn technique. First, and most obvious, the two judges (experimenter and assistant) can bias the outcome by recording head-turns only on experimental (signal) trials, and not on control (no-signal trials). Obviously, the judges must be "blind" to the type of trial occurring. In addition, the parent could bias the infant's behavior by providing some cue that correlates with the presentation of the signal. A parent could, for example, move differently on experimental as opposed to control trials, and an infant could learn that the presentation of the visual reinforcer co-occurred with such movement. In this situation, the infant's head-turn would be precipitated by the parent's movement rather than by the detection of the acoustic signal.

Kuhl (1980) pointed out an even more subtle problem. The person who initiates the trials can bias the outcome by knowing the type of trial that will occur, prior to its initiation. This can happen by initiating experimental trials when infants are not visually engaged with the toys, or are generally inattentive. At such times, infants show a greater probability of orienting toward the visual reinforcer, whether or not a sound is presented. Similarly, control trials can be initiated when the infant is very engaged with the toys, and thus unlikely to turn towards the reinforcer. This kind of "optimum placement" of trials could lead to good performance by the infant but would not necessarily produce a valid estimate of the infant's sensory or perceptual abilities.

Moreover, the assistant can produce similarly spurious performance by differentially manipulating the infant's attention during the two kinds of trials. Those of us who have served as the assistant in these experiments are well aware of the extent to which the kind of toy that is manipulated, the speed and style with which the toy is moved, and even its distance from the infant, can influence the infant's attention to it. These effects are sufficiently powerful that an assistant can virtually assure the presence or absence of a head-turn response by manipulating these factors. Thus, if the assistant knows the type of trial, experimental or control, that is being run, the assistant can determine the infant's performance. Therefore, the assistant must be kept blind to the trial type, not only to avoid voting in a biased fashion, but also to avoid producing the appropriate behavior artifactually.

The initial studies just reviewed did not control for these sources of bias. The experiments were controlled by a standard audiometer (Allison, Model 22) and the experimenter and assistant knew both before and during a trial the type of trial that was run. The assistant simply nodded to indicate the judgment of a head-turn, and the experimenter, located in the adjacent control suite and watching through a one-way mirror, decided whether or not to activate the reinforcer using a simple switch. Interjudge reliability was recorded by having the experimenter write down the assistant's head nods and his or her own vote; no automatic recording system was involved. In addition, the absence of an automatically timed response interval made it difficult to judge head turns that occurred at or near the end of the response interval. Moreover, potential bias on the part of the parent was not eliminated. The parent was instructed not to influence the infant's head turns by moving differentially, but there was no system which prevented the parent from doing so.

In a first step toward providing controls over bias, Wilson, Lee, Owen, and Moore (1976) developed a simple logic circuit which consisted of an AND-gate and two timers. The presentation of the signal started one of the timers, and if, during that interval, the two judges both "voted," the reinforcer was activated for the duration of the second timer. This served two purposes. First, the two judges could vote completely independently of one another by pressing a switch, rather than having the experimenter watch for a head-nod and then decide whether or not to activate the reinforcer. Also, the reinforcer was activated only if both judges voted; if a single one did, it was not activated. Secondly, the interval was precisely timed, so that votes occurring outside the interval were not counted.

In addition to the use of this simple logic circuit, some controls over bias on the part of the assistant were instituted. The assistant wore headphones and listened to a tone during both experimental and control trials. Wilson (1979) stated that this tone masked the test stimulus, thereby removing this person's ability to bias the outcome either by voting in a biased way or by differentially attempting to manipulate the infant's attention to the toys. The assistant now indicated by a head nod when the infant was "ready" for a trial. The experimenter initiated the trials using a randomly-predetermined sequence of experimental and control trials.

But problems still remained. The experimenter knew, prior to the initiation of the trial, the type of trial that would occur. Also, there was no way the experimenter could vote during control trials. If the person did vote to indicate a false-positive response, and the assistant voted as well, the reinforcer would incorrectly be activated because the logic did not differentiate between experimental and control trials. Finally, there was no formal way of assessing interjudge reliability.

Modification of the technique to study speech perception. The technique was modified by Eilers et al. (1977) to study speech-sound discrimination with infants 6 to 8 months old and infants 12 to 14 months old. The modification involved presenting a speech sound constantly as a "background" stimulus. During an equal number of "control" trials, no change in the stimulus occurred, but head-turn responses were similarly monitored (illustrated in Figure 5).

The procedure used to test the infants is basically similar to that described in the previous section. Infants are trained to produce head-turn responses in the presence of a sound change. This is fairly straightforward; some infants spon-

TRIAL STRUCTURE

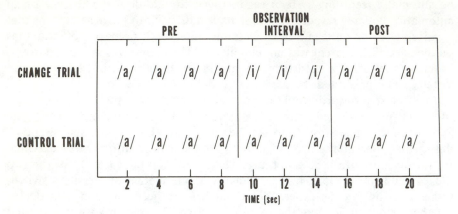

Figure 5. Trial structure during change and control trials during speech discrimination testing. (Reprinted from Kuhl, 1979a.)

taneously orient towards the loudspeaker when the stimulus changes from one sound to another. For those who do not automatically orient when the sound is changed, the reinforcer is turned on. Since activating the reinforcer results in both a visually and auditorially prominent event, infants readily turn away from the assistant to look at it. Eventually, the infant anticipates the occurrence of the reinforcer when the sound is changed. Once the infant is reliability producing head turns on change trials, control trials are introduced, typically with equal probability.

The refinements in the procedure discussed by Wilson (1979) and described in the preceding section were included. Figure 6, taken from Eilers et al. (1977), displays the simple logic system used. It consisted of two timers, two vote switches, and an AND-gate. When both votes occurred during the interval specified by Timer 1, the visual reinforcer was activated for the duration specified by Timer 2. If only a single vote occurred, the reinforcer was not activated. The only other equipment used in the Eilers et al. study was a four-channel tape deck and a standard audiometer. The tape deck contained the speech syllables on separate channels, and the audiometer allowed the experimenter to switch manually from one channel of the tape recorder to another without introducing a noise.

The audiometer also generated a tone signal that coincided with trial intervals. This served to mark the duration of the voting interval. Both the assistant and the experimenter could hear this tone. The experimenter listened to it free-field in the control room, and the assistant wore headphones which allowed him or her to monitor the control room. This also allowed the experimenter to talk to the assistant. Unfortunately, it is unlikely that the intensity of the tone was sufficiently loud to mask the change from one stimulus to another, thereby removing any potential source of bias on the part of the assistant. The authors did not, in fact, state that the assistant was blind. The experimenter was defi-

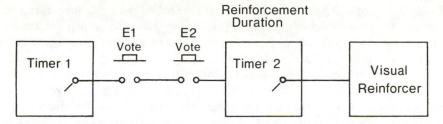

Figure 6. Diagram of the logic circuit used in the initial speech-discrimination studies using the Head-Turn Technique. (Reprinted from Eilers, Wilson, & Moore, 1977.)

nitely not blind, because this person was responsible for manually switching from one channel to another on change trials. This person determined directly whether a change or control trial was presented.

Moreover, because a simple AND-gate controlled the presentation of the reinforcer, the experimenter could not vote on control trials. If the experimenter did vote to record an infant's false-positive response, and the assistant happened to have voted as well, the reinforcer would be presented. This is the case because the simple AND-gate logic used could not distinguish between change and control trials. This meant that the experimenter simply had to refrain from voting on control trials, regardless of the infant's performance. Any record that was to be kept on the infant's overall performance, or on interjudge reliability, had to be obtained by the experimenter writing the information down after each trial. In fact, no interjudge reliability figures were reported. The parent was also not protected from potential sources of bias.

In a later study, Eilers, Gavin, and Wilson (1979) made modifications in the procedure to ensure that the assistant and the parent were not biased. In this study, the assistant and the parent listened to music over headphones. This masked the change from one stimulus to another, thus removing that potential source of bias. The same simple logic circuit controlled the presentation of the reinforcer, and the experimenter controlled the presentation and switching of the stimuli and therefore was not blind. Interjudge reliability was reported to be very high (96%), but the method used to obtain the data was not described. It undoubtedly involved the experimenter's written record of the agreement between the two judges. No other changes in the procedure were reported.

In a critique of the procedures employed by Eilers, Gavin, and Wilson (1979), Aslin and Pisoni (1980) commented on the lack of controls over bias on the part of the experimenter. In a reply to this criticism, Eilers et al. (1980) admitted that the potential for examiner bias was not fully controlled for in the experiment, but argued that the reliability between the assistant (who was blind) and the experimenter (who was not) was high. No details were provided on how these data were collected.

Further refinements in the technique. In subsequent studies, further improvements in the controls over bias on the part of the parent, assistant, and experimenter were instituted. Kuhl (1979a) designed a more complex logic device (see

Kuhl, 1980, for complete description) that controlled the experimental contingencies. Its main features included a probability generator which determined the presentation of change and control trials as well as automatically effecting the change from the "background" stimulus to the "comparison" stimulus. The experimenter began trails when the infant was in a "ready" state, but had no control over the type of trial that was run, and did not know prior to its initiation what kind of trial was to be run. This ensured that the experimenter could not affect performance on change vs. control trials by beginning them when the infant was either very attentive or excessively restless.

Controls for bias on the part of the assistant and parent were also tightened. They both wore headphones and listened to music, as was reported in earlier studies, but Kuhl (1979a) used a small vibrating pin, located on the assistant's hand-held vote button, to inform the assistant when trials were occurring. It is unclear in previous studies how the assistant knew when a trial was occurring (and thus when to vote) if the music delivered through the headphones was really sufficiently loud to mask the stimulus. Parents were not informed when trials occurred. Thus in these studies neither the assistant nor the parent could inadvertently cue the infant.

This logic circuit also incorporated, for the first time, contingencies for both kinds of trials, change and control. In all previous experiments, the logic automatically activated the reinforcer when both votes occurred. This produced the appropriate reinforcement on change trials, but inappropriate reinforcement when infants produced head-turn responses (false positives) on control trials. Since the logic circuit could not differentiate "hits" (head turns on change trials) from "false positives" (head turns on control trials), the experimenter had to refrain from voting on control trials. Using Kuhl's (1979a) logic device, the four outcomes that were possible on each trial ("hits," "misses," "false positives," and "correct rejections") were each recorded, and the contingencies appropriate to each were delivered.

The logic device timed the trial interval, recorded both the experimenter's and the assistant's votes, scored the trial as correct or incorrect, activated the reinforcer appropriately, recorded the infant's latency of response, and printed all of the data on each trial. This last point is an important one, because it provided the first formal measure of interjudge reliability for experiments of this kind. As Kuhl (1980) pointed out, the remaining source of bias using this procedure was that the experimenter could still hear the stimuli during the trial and could therefore judge head-turn responses differentially on change and control trials. However, the automatic recording of both votes allowed this source of bias to be objectively assessed. Interjudge agreement on the presence or absence of a head turn occurred on 98.3% of the trials (Kuhl, 1979a).

Later studies in Kuhl's laboratory (Kuhl, 1980, 1983; Hillenbrand, 1983, 1984) utilized this same technique. In recent studies (Aslin et al., 1981), as well as in work underway in our own laboratory and in Eilers' laboratory (see Eilers & Gavin, 1981), the experiment is under the control of a computer which presents the stimuli, records the judges' responses, and controls the delivery of the contingencies. In all instances, only one judge now votes (the experimenter), since agreement between this person and the assistant has been uniformly high. The experimenter does not know ahead of time what kind of trial will be presented, and cannot hear the stimuli during trials. The assistant (who now does not vote) still listens to music, which masks the change in the stimulus and prevents differential manipulation of the toys. The parent also listens to music. Thus, the current applications achieve a situation in which all potential sources of bias are removed.

Current Application of the HT Technique

Age range. The technique has been successfully employed with infants as young as 5.5 months (Wilson et al., 1976) and as old as 18 months of age (Eilers et al., 1977). It is ideally suited to infants in the 6- to 10-month age range. Beyond this age, infants tend to become increasingly restless when sitting on the parent's lap. The 12-month-old appears to realize that the monkey is still in the box, even if the lights are out and it can no longer be seen; this causes the infant to want to peer into the darkened box between trials. For the 6- to 10-month-old, this is not a problem. When the lights in the box go out and the stimulus can no longer be seen, the infant acts as though he or she thinks it is gone.

Infants in this age range are readily trained to respond to a change from one sound to another. Using an easily discriminable vowel contrast, such as /a/ vs. /i/, Kuhl (1979a) reported a 90% success rate in conditioning infants in the 5.5- to 6.5-month age range within one session (about 30 trials). However, using a more difficult computer-synthesized voice-voiceless contrast, Aslin et al. (1981) reported that only 55% of the infants showed evidence of acquiring the head-turn response after two sessions. Further studies will have to be completed before a general success ratio in conditioning infants can be predicted.

Measures used. The head-turn task is similar to a "yes-no" task in classic psychophysics. On each trial, a sound change is either present or absent, and the infant's head-turn response is either present or absent. In standard terminology, this produces four possible outcomes (Table 1): (a) the sound is changed (change trial) and the infant produced a head turn ("hit"); (b) the sound is changed and the infant fails to produce a head turn ("miss"); (c) the sound is not changed (control trial) and the infant does not produce a head turn ("correct rejection"); and (d) the sound is not changed and the infant produces a head turn ("false positive").

The data can either be (a) a comparison of the number of head-turn responses that occur during change as opposed to control trials, or (b) the number of "correct" responses regardless of the trial type. In the first case, significance can be obtained by demonstrating a significantly higher number of head-turn responses on change as opposed to control trials. In the second, significance

Table 1. Four Possible Outcomes in the Head-Turn Procedure

		Trial Type	
		Change	Control
	Head Turn	"Hit" P(D/D)	"False Positive" P(D/S)
RESPONSE			
	No Head Turn	"Miss" P(S/D)	"Correct Rejection" P(S/S)

can be obtained by demonstrating that performance differs significantly from the 50% chance level. Even though the probability of a head turn cannot be predicted for a given trial, the chance probability of being correct on each trial is always 0.5 (see Eilers & Gavin, 1981, for statistical derivation).

Since the data can be scored dichotomously as "correct" or "incorrect," the data can be expected to conform to a binomial distribution (Siegel, 1956). Most published experiments have therefore used the binomial test to examine significance. For example, Eilers et al. (1977, 1979) and Eilers, Gavin, and Wilson (1979) used six trials and considered five out of six correct responses to meet the criterion for significance. Hillenbrand, Minifie, and Edwards (1979) used six to eight trials and considered five out of six correct, or six out of eight correct, to meet the criterion for significance. Unfortunately, neither of these two criteria met significance by the binomial distribution. The five-out-of-six rule barely misses criterion ($p < 0.051$), as does the six-out-of-eight rule ($p < 0.08$). Using these two criteria in tandem (e.g., using the six-out-of-eight criterion after infants fail the five-out-of-six criterion) inflates estimates of discriminability even further. In some of these studies (Eilers, Gavin, & Wilson, 1979; Hillenbrand et al., 1979), only group data were reported, and parametric statistics were used to contrast the number of head-turn responses occurring during change and control intervals, so this was not a problem.

Other studies designed to test the infant's ability to perceive speech-sound categories (Kuhl, 1979a, 1980, 1983) have used a combination of measures. The issue in these studies is not the discriminability of the sounds, but the infant's ability to recognize the similarity among discriminably different instances of the same phonetic category—that is, the ability to categorize sounds. Kuhl (1979a) introduced a new design to test infants' categorization of speech. This technique was aimed at examining infants' "transfer-of-learning" from discrimination of a pair of training stimuli (e.g., the vowel sounds /a/ vs. /i/) to novel instances representing the two vowel categories. The initial studies (Kuhl, 1979a, 1983) addressed infants' abilities to recognize similarity among vowel sounds produced by different talkers. Later studies examined equivalence classification for consonants (Kuhl, 1980) and for the featural components of consonants (Hillenbrand, 1983, 1984; see Kuhl, 1983, 1985, for discussion), as well as to categories based on suprasegmental dimensions such as pitch (Kuhl & Hillenbrand, 1979) and the sex of the talker (Miller, Younger, & Morse, 1982).

Kuhl (1979a) modified the HT technique so that infants were initially trained on a speech-sound contrast until they met a criterion (nine out of ten correct). Then, novel instances representing both the "background" and the "comparison" categories were introduced. The introduction of new stimuli was done in one of two ways: progressive transfer-of-learning, and immediate transfer-of-learning. In progressive transfer-of-learning, novel stimuli are introduced in a series of stages, typically five (Kuhl, 1979a, Experiment 1; Kuhl, 1983, Experiment 1). Progression from stage to stage occurs when the infant reaches a preset criterion (nine out of ten consecutive trials correct). Change and control trials are run as before, but now the infant has to monitor the stimuli for a change in the *category* rather than simply in the sound. Head-turn responses to all variants in the comparison category are reinforced, but head-turn responses to any of the variants in the "background" category are not reinforced. This is not a trivially easy task, because the sounds representing each category are discriminably different—the infant has to ignore these prominent differences and recognize their similarity, their membership in a category, to succeed in the task (see Kuhl, 1985, for further discussion). A trials-to-criterion measure is used to assess the infant's ease of transfer. If the infant readily perceives the similarity between members of the same category, the trials-to-criterion measure should not increase significantly as novel members are introduced. Parametric statistics are used to make these comparisons (e.g., Kuhl, 1983).

The immediate transfer-of-learning design is similar, but provides a more sensitive measure of the infant's ability to generalize to novel members of a phonetic category. The initial stage again consists of training the infant to produce a head-turn response for discriminating between single exemplars representing two different phonetic categories. Following this training, infants are presented with all of the novel stimuli presented in the final stage of the progressive transfer-of-learning design, without the intermediate stages. A fixed number of trials is presented, and percent correct is measured for each novel stimulus. Analysis of first-trial data can be used to measure whether the infants detect similarity between the training stimulus and a novel stimulus from the same category before they are reinforced for doing so. This has been done by comparing the proportion of correct responses to the training and the novel stimuli, using the binomial test (Kuhl, 1979a, 1983). In addition, parametric statistics have been used to compare percent correct performance for the training stimulus and the novel stimuli (Kuhl, 1979a; 1983).

In other studies on categorization (Hillenbrand, 1983, 1984; Miller et al., 1982) parametric comparisons were made between the performances of two groups of infants. One group was tested as they had been in previous experiments. For these infants, the reinforcement contingency was determined by the assignment of speech sounds to phonetic categories. For another group, the assignment of sounds to the reinforced vs. the unreinforced categories was random. These experiments demonstrated far superior performance by infants tested in conditions in which the reinforcement contingencies were dictated by a specifiable dimension, as opposed to infants tested in conditions in which reinforcement was determined by the random assignment of stimuli to categories

(Hillenbrand, 1983). Such comparisons show that infants do not succeed in these category-formation experiments by simply memorizing the stimuli in the reinforced category. Rather, the data suggest that infants succeed in the task because they perceive category membership (see Kuhl, 1985, for further discussion).

Questions addressed using the head-turn technique. Since its development in the early 1970s, the HT technique has been widely applied, not only to the study of speech perception but to the study of other complex auditory phenemona. Wilson et al. (1976) used the technique to obtain auditory thresholds for 6-month-olds. Olsho, Schoon, Sakai, Turpin, and Sperduto (1982) obtained limited data on difference limens for frequency.

Regarding speech perception, many studies have examined the extent to which certain speech-sound contrasts are discriminable (Eilers et al., 1977; Eilers, Gavin, & Wilson, 1979; Eilers, Wilson, & Moore, 1979). These studies have addressed age differences in discriminative capacities (Eilers et al., 1977) and cross-language differences (Eilers, Wilson, & Moore, 1979; Eilers, Gavin, & Wilson, 1979; Werker, Gilbert, Humphrey, & Tees, 1981), as well as more complex perceptual phenomena such as cue-trading effects in speech (Morse, Eilers, & Gavin, 1982).

Aslin et al. (1981) combined the technique with an up-down staircase procedure to determine the minimum change in VOT that infants could detect at various VOT values along the continuum. They were attempting to show that infants could detect intra-category variants for the Spanish prevoiced category, an important point for theoretical discussions of categorical perception. In this application, the VOT value of the "comparison" stimulus was altered on each change trial, depending upon the infant's behavior. Successful discrimination of the comparison stimulus from the background stimulus resulted in a change in the VOT value of the comparison stimulus to make it more similar to the VOT value of the background stimulus. An algorithm was used to estimate the smallest VOT difference that the infant could reliably detect. This up-down staircase procedure is similar to that used in threshold-tracking and in frequency-discrimination tasks.

As previously described, Kuhl (1979a, 1980, 1983) adapted the technique to study infants' abilities to categorize speech sounds. The modifications involved training infants to respond differently to two speech stimuli, one representing each of two categories, and then testing generalization of the response to novel stimuli from the two categories.

Table 2 describes the stimuli in the background category and in the comparison category for each of five stages in the first experiment of this type, one involving the vowel categories /a/ and /i/ (Kuhl, 1979a). In each category, the number of vowels was increased until the two categories contained six stimuli spoken by three different talkers (male, female, and child), each with two different pitch contours (rise and fall). In the initial training stage of the experi-

Table 2. The stimuli in the background and comparison categories for all stages in the /a/ vs. /i/ experiment. The talker and pitch contour values for each stimulus are given in parentheses. (From Kuhl, 1979a.)

| | Experimental Stages | |
	Background	Comparison
Conditioning	/a/ (Male, fall)	/i/ (Male, fall)
Initial training	/a/ (Male, fall)	/i/ (Male, fall)
Pitch variation	/a/ (Male, fall)	/i/ (Male, fall)
	/a/ (Male, rise)	/i/ (Male, rise)
Talker variation	/a/ (Male, fall)	/i/ (Male, fall)
	/a/ (Female, fall)	/i/ (Female, fall)
Talker × pitch variation	/a/ (Male, fall)	/i/ (Male, fall)
	/a/ (Male, rise)	/i/ (Male, rise)
	/a/ (Female, fall)	/i/ (Female, fall)
	/a/ (Female, rise)	/i/ (Female, rise)
Entire ensemble	/a/ (Male, fall)	/i/ (Male, fall)
	/a/ (Male, rise)	/i/ (Male, rise)
	/a/ (Female, fall)	/i/ (Female, fall)
	/a/ (Female, rise)	/i/ (Female, rise)
	/a/ (Child, fall)	/i/ (Child, fall)
	/a/ (Child, rise)	/i/ (Child, rise)

ment, each of the two categories was represented by a single stimulus matched in every detail except for the critical cues which differentiate the two categories. In stage two, the pitch contour of the vowels in both categories was randomly changed from rise to fall. In stage three, the talker producing the vowels was randomly varied between the male voice and the female voice. In stage four, both talkers produced the vowels with a randomly changing pitch contour. In the final stage, the child's voice, also with pitch contour variations, was added to the categories, bringing the total number of stimuli in each category to six (three talkers × two pitch contours).

The results of the progressive transfer-of-learning experiment on the /a-i/ contrast showed that infants demonstrated excellent transfer to the novel stimuli. Most infants met the performance criterion in the minimum number of trials necessary. More convincingly, however, in the immediate transfer-of-learning experiment, performance was significantly above chance on each of the novel stimuli on the first trial during which it was presented. Thus, the infant's responses could not be attributed to training.

Data for individual infants are shown in Figure 7. The percentage of head-turn responses to each of the stimuli during the transfer-of-learning phase is shown. Performance was typically above 70% correct. For nearly half of the infants, performance was near perfect.

These results have been extended to other more spectrally similar vowel categories, such as /a/ vs. /ɔ/ (Kuhl, 1983), to a variety of consonant categories (Kuhl, 1980; Hillenbrand, 1983, 1984), and to categories based on

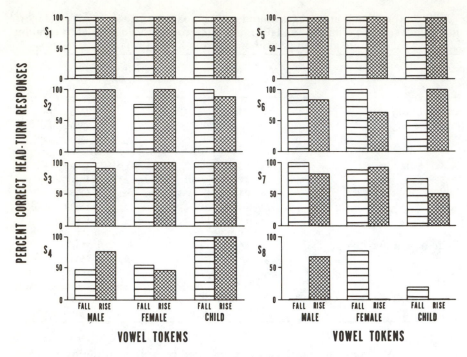

Figure 7. Individual-subject data showing the generalization of head-turn responses from the training stimulus (male-fall) to novel instances of vowels spoken by female and child talkers, with varying intonation contours. (Reprinted from Kuhl, 1979a.)

suprasegmental cues (Kuhl & Hillenbrand, 1979; Miller et al., 1982). In each case, the data provide strong evidence in support of the notion that 6-month-old infants recognize auditory equivalence classes that conform to adults' perceptual categories (see Kuhl, 1985, for further discussion).

Summary

The head-turn procedure was developed for use in clinical settings and then applied to more basic research questions. The application of the technique to infant speech perception has resulted in a substantial number of published research reports on infants' abilities to discriminate and categorize speech sounds.

The technique is ideally suited to infants ranging in age from 6 months to 10 months, though it has been applied to infants as old as 18 months of age. It is possible that, with modifications of the technique, younger infants could be tested, but to date no one has succeeded in applying this particular form of the procedure to infants under 5.5 months of age. As used in all laboratories today, controls for bias have been instituted which ensure that neither the parent, the assistant, nor the experimenter can influence the outcome of the experiment. These controls for bias were developed gradually as the technique was more widely applied. A variety of statistical measures, both parametric and nonparametric, have been used to analyze the data.

The data provided by these experiments have two advantages over previous techniques such as HAS: (a) individual data can be obtained, and (b) since the reinforcer is independent of the stimulus contrasts under test, negative results cannot be attributed to the differential reinforcing properties of particular acoustic stimuli. The technique is in fairly wide use in a number of laboratories. It holds promise as a routinely applicable behavioral measure of speech perception in infants.

AUDITORY-VISUAL SPEECH PERCEPTION TECHNIQUE (AVSP)

Motivation for Its Development

The head-turn technique, and others such as the high-amplitude sucking technique (Jusczyk, this volume), examine speech perception as an exclusively auditory phenomenon. The technique described next is not limited to the auditory assessment of speech perception. Rather, it examines the corepresentation of auditory and visual information in speech perception. This is important because the impact of visual information on speech perception has been well established in experiments on hearing-impaired and normal adult populations (Erber, 1972; Summerfield, 1979). Classic studies in the field (see Erber, 1975, for review) have shown that when auditory information is restricted—either naturally, as it is for hearing-impaired listeners, or artificially, as in laboratory experiments on lip-reading—the visual information provided by watching a talker's mouth movements significantly improves the perception of speech.

More importantly, recent data on normal-hearing adults has revealed another phenomenon. This research shows that when auditory information is not degraded in any way but is presented simultaneously with visual information that does not agree with that presented auditorially, illusory percepts can result (McGurk & MacDonald, 1976; Summerfield, 1979). That is, the perceiver reports a syllable that was presented neither to the visual modality nor to the auditory modality. Interestingly, even though this information is discrepant and picked up by two different modalities, the perceiver experiences a phenomenally unified and coherent percept of a single talker and a single message. Theoretical accounts of this phenomenon recognize that information about speech entering the two modalities must be coregistered in a common "metric" in order for the optic and acoustic streams to mix. Thus, speech information in adults must, at some level, be represented bimodally (Kuhl and Meltzoff, 1984a).

Classic lip-reading phenomena imply that perceivers (adults in this case) relate specific articulatory postures that they see another produce to their auditory concomitants. Thus, the ability to lip-read signifies the recognition of equivalences between a sound heard and the sight of someone producing that sound. Knowledge of the relationship between audition and articulation is not surprising in adults, because they are practiced both at speaking and at watching others speak. In other words, knowledge of the relationship between audition and articulation (as represented visually) may derive from experience in producing speech oneself and in watching others produce it (see Kuhl & Meltzoff, 1984, for discussion). However, the infant has not had extensive experience in either task. Thus, an examination of infants' recognition of the visual correlates of auditorially presented speech sounds contributes to our understanding of the development of these auditory-visual phenomena.

Kuhl and Meltzoff (1982) developed a technique which posed the auditory-visual mapping problem to infants. The technique examined the degree to which the infant recognized the correspondence between a particular articulatory gesture, presented visually, and a particular sound, presented auditorially. The basic Auditory-Visual Speech Perception (AVSP) technique involved showing the infant two filmed facial images producing, in synchrony, two different vowel sounds. A single sound that matched only one of the two faces was auditorially presented through a loudspeaker located midway between the two faces. The hypothesis was that if infants were capable of detecting the correspondence between the auditorially and visually presented speech information, they would look significantly longer at the face that "matched" the sound, rather than at the "mismatched" face; if they did not, they would devote an equal amount of time looking at each face. While the technique has been applied in a limited number of experiments to date, it opens up new possibilities for investigating cross-modal speech perception. Such studies may eventually lead to an understanding of infants' cognitive representation of speech.

History of Its Development

The visual preference technique has been used extensively in studies of visual perception (Fantz, Fagan, & Miranda, 1975). It was adapted by a number of authors to study cross-modal perception (Spelke, 1979; Meltzoff & Borton, 1979).

In the visual preference procedure, two visual stimuli are shown side by side, and the amount of time the infant fixates each one is assessed. If infants show a differential fixation response to one of the two stimuli, discrimination is evidenced, and a behavioral choice, operationally termed a "visual preference," has been demonstrated.

The adaptation for purposes of assessing cross-modal perception involved a similar presentation of two visual stimuli side by side. However, a single stimulus, one that "matched" one of the two visual stimuli, was presented to another modality. For example, Meltzoff and Borton (1979) presented infants with two visual shapes side by side. One was a smooth sphere; the other was a sphere with bumps on it. Prior to the presentation of the visual stimuli, infants were familiarized with a tactual shape. The tactual shape, a modified pacifier, was either a smooth sphere or a sphere with bumps. The measure of cross-modal perception was visual-fixation time; that is, the percentage of total fixation time the infant spent looking at the "matched" vs. the "mismatched" shape. The results showed that infants demonstrated a visual preference for the "matched" shape.

The Auditory-Visual Speech Perception (AVSP) technique developed by Kuhl and Meltzoff (1982) examined infants' cross-modal perception of speech. Infants were shown two filmed images, side by side, of a talker articulating, in synchrony, two different vowel sounds (Figure 8). The vowel sounds were /a/, as in "pop," and /i/, as in "peep." The sound track corresponding to one of the two faces (either /a/ or /i/) was presented through a loudspeaker directly behind the screen and midway between the visual images. This placement of the loudspeaker eliminated all spatial cues.

The visual and auditory stimuli were recorded on 16 mm film (see Kuhl and Meltzoff, 1984a, for full details). Multiple instances of each of the vowels were selected and used to create a two-image 16 mm visual loop. Two auditory loops, one containing multiple instances of /a/, the other of /i/, were also

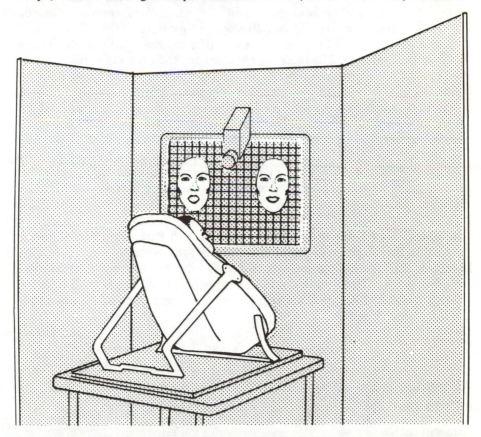

Figure 8. The experimental apparatus used in the Auditory-Visual Speech Perception Technique. The infants were shown two facial displays of the same female talker, one articulating the vowel /a/ and the other articulating the vowel /i/. The soundtrack corresponding to one of the two faces was presented through a loudspeaker placed behind the screen midway between the two faces. (Reprinted from Kuhl & Meltzoff, 1982.)

created. The auditory stimuli used were not those actually produced by the faces used in the experiment. The auditory and visual stimuli were carefully selected so that their durations fell within a narrowly constrained range. Professional film studio equipment was used to align the sound and film tracks. This ensured that the auditory stimuli were temporally synchronized equally well with both the "matched" and the "mismatched" facial images.

The experimental procedure involved a familiarization phase and a test phase (Figure 9). During the familiarization phase, an infant was shown each face separately for 10 sec without sound. Following this 20-sec period, the faces were briefly covered until the infant's gaze returned to midline. Then the sound was turned on and both faces were presented for the 2-min test phase. The sound presented to the infants, the left-right positioning of the two faces, the order of familiarization, and the sex of the infant were counterbalanced. Thirty-two infants between 18 and 20 weeks of age were tested.

Infants were placed in an infant seat within a three-sided cubicle, 46 cm the two facial displays. The faces were life-size and their centers were separated by 38 cm. The only source of visible light in the room was that provided by the films. An infrared camera positioned between the two faces provided a recording of the infant's face. All the experimental sessions were videotaped, and the observer scored the videotape. This person recorded the amount of time spent fixating the left and right facial images, and could neither hear the sounds nor see the faces presented to the infants. Reliability was assessed by having an independent observer rescore the videotapes. Inter- and intra-judge reliability was very high; the mean percent agreement between observers was greater than 96%.

Questions Posed Using the Auditory-Visual Speech Perception Technique

In this first experiment on the auditory-visual perception of speech by 4-month-old infants, Kuhl and Meltzoff (1982) chose to use simple vowel stimuli, /a/ and /i/. These vowels have been shown to be auditorily distinct for infants (Kuhl & Miller, 1982), and are easily distinguished by adults when they are presented visually.

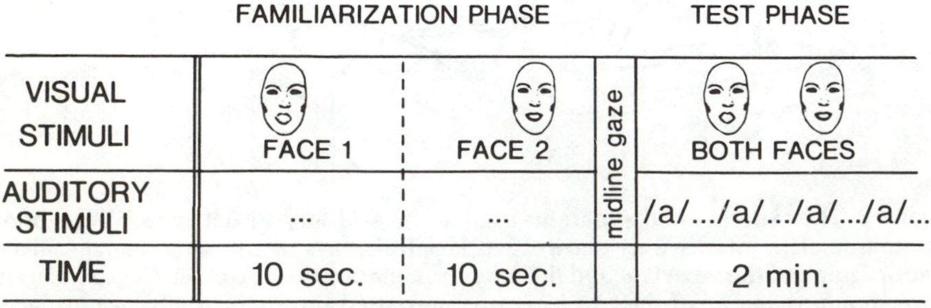

	FAMILIARIZATION PHASE			TEST PHASE
VISUAL STIMULI	FACE 1	FACE 2	midline gaze	BOTH FACES
AUDITORY STIMULI	...	...		/a/.../a/.../a/.../a/...
TIME	10 sec.	10 sec.		2 min.

Figure 9. Experimental procedure used in the Auditory-Visual Speech Perception Technique. (Reprinted from Kuhl & Meltzoff, 1982)

Kuhl and Meltzoff hypothesized that the vowel presented auditorially would systematically influence infants' visual preferences. They specifically argued that infants would look longer at the face that "matched" the sound rather than at the "mismatched" face. Thus, the test involved an examination of infants' abilities to detect that /a/ lips go with /a/ sounds, and /i/ lips with /i/ sounds. The results of the experiment illustrated infants' abilities to detect such matches. The percentage of total fixation time devoted to the matched vs. mismatched faces was calculated for each infant. Twenty-four of the 32 infants looked longer at the face matching the sound than at the mismatched face ($p <$ 0.01, binomial test). The mean percentage fixation time devoted to the matching face across all infants was 73.63%, which is significantly different from the 50% chance level ($t = 4.67, p < 0.001$). There were no significant left-right preferences, face preferences, or familiarization order effects.

In a second experiment, Kuhl and Meltzoff (1982) made an initial attempt to specify the nature of the auditory information that was critical to the detection of these auditory-visual correspondences. If infants' detection of correspondence was based on knowledge of the relationship between a particular articulatory movement (such as /a/) and its concomitant speech sound, then the auditory information provided the infant might have to be sufficient to identify the speech sound. As a first step toward answering this question, they altered the original auditory stimuli (the sets of /a/ and /i/ vowels) so as to remove the spectral information necessary to identify the vowels (formant frequencies), while preserving their temporal characteristics (amplitude and duration). The stimuli were computer-generated pure-tone signals centered at the average fundamental frequency of the female talker (200 Hz). The onset and offset characteristics and overall amplitude envelopes were synthesized to duplicate those of the original vowels. Thus, these pure-tone signals did not contain the appropriate spectral information to identify the vowels, and Kuhl and Meltzoff predicted that the auditory-visual matching effect would not obtain under this circumstance.

In effect, this second experiment also served as a test of an alternative hypothesis, namely that infants in the first experiment were not relying on spectral information, but on temporal information, to link particular face-voice pairs. Other experiments on infants suggest that they can detect gross temporal misalignment between mouth movements and sound in speech (Dodd, 1979) and temporal correspondences between auditory and visual nonspeech events (Spelke, 1979). While Kuhl and Meltzoff argued that the technique they employed to align the sound and film tracks made such a temporal hypothesis an unlikely explanation for the outcome of their first experiment, the second experiment addressed the issue directly. If infants in the first experiment were relying on temporal information to link particular face-voice pairs, then they should still look longer at the "matched" face, even though it was represented only by its sine-wave amplitude envelope. Alternatively, if the spectral information contained in the vowels was necessary for the detection of these auditory-visual correspondences, performance should drop to chance.

A new group of 32 infants between 18 and 20 weeks were tested using exactly the same procedure and the new stimuli. The results showed that the mean percent fixation time to the "matched" face dropped to chance (54.6%, $p < 0.40$). In this case, only 17 of the 32 infants preferred the matched face. Thus, the data suggest that some aspect of the spectral information is critical. Further experiments will be necessary to determine whether the detection of these correspondences requires spectral information that allows the vowel to be identified, or whether a signal that matches the vowel's spectral pattern, without specifying its identity, is sufficient.

These findings show that infants relate particular speech sounds to mouths moving in particular ways. Detection of these auditory-visual correspondences for speech suggests that, by 18 weeks of age, the infant may possess some rather specific knowledge of the relationship between the auditory and articulatory correlates of speech. This ability could simply reflect specific associations that were learned by watching caretakers speak. On the other hand, this demonstration may reflect a more general intermodal representation of speech, one not limited to specific associative pairings between speech information presented auditorily and visually, but one that encompasses its sensorimotor equivalents as well.

Kuhl and Meltzoff (1982) advocate consideration of the broader interpretation. They cite the fact that about a third of the infants tested in their first experiment (who listened to the vowels), but only one of those tested in their second experiment (who listened to the nonspeech signals), produced utterances typical of "babbling." These infants appeared to be imitating the female talker, mimicking the spectrum, duration, and fundamental frequency contours of her vowels (see Kuhl & Meltzoff, 1982, for examples). This suggests that infants are aware of auditory-motor equivalents for speech, and that they are capable of directing their articulators to produce an auditorily specified target.

Observations of the infant's tendency to imitate in this situation, in combination with the demonstration of the infant's ability to detect auditory-visual correspondences in speech, suggest that a broader knowledge of auditory-articulatory relations, rather than specific associative pairings learned by watching caretakers speak, may underlie infants' cross-modal speech-perception abilities. Future studies will aim to specify the nature of the relationship between these auditory-visual mappings and vocal imitation, and the extent to which either or both depend on "babbling" or any other specific kind of experience (see Kuhl and Meltzoff, 1984a, for further discussion).

Summary

The application of the Auditory-Visual Speech Perception (AVSP) technique to the study of speech perception in infancy is very recent. Systematic studies examining the age limitations imposed by the technique have yet to be done. Moreover, modifications will undoubtedly be required in order to test the age limitations. The presentation of the visual stimuli to younger and older infants may require adaptation to ensure their optimum distance from the infant and optimum spacing. Adaptations will also be required in the length of the familiarization and test phases of the experiment, as well as in minor details such as in the seating arrangement. Nonetheless, the data obtained in these first experiments suggest that the bimodal perception of speech will be a fruitful area in which to pursue the cross-modal representation of speech in infancy.

SUMMARY AND CONCLUSIONS

This chapter reviewed two techniques used in the study of infant speech perception. The first, the Head-Turn Technique, is currently in wide use among investigators. As currently designed, it is ideally suited to infants and toddlers between the ages of 6 and 18 months. It is being used primarily to examine the discrimination and categorization of speech sounds. It is also being used to study auditory psychophysics, as in studies of frequency and intensity resolution. It stands alongside the High-Amplitude Sucking procedure as one of the major techniques used by investigators studying the perception of speech by young infants.

A newer procedure, the Auditory-Visual Speech-Perception Technique, was also described. This technique was designed to go beyond the infant's auditory perception of speech and examine its cross-modal representation in infants. It has been applied in only a limited set of studies to date, but those studies suggest that the technique will be extremely useful in mapping out the infant's understanding of the relationship between the optic and acoustic concomitants of speech sounds. These studies should eventually lead to a specification of infants' cross-modal representation of speech.

Taken together, the techniques provide vehicles for assessing a broad range of questions about infants' abilities to perceive speech. The next decade will demonstrate whether or not this extension of our measurement techniques will result in a greater understanding of the role that the perception of speech plays in the acquisition of linguistic and cognitive abilities by infants.

ACKNOWLEDGMENTS

The preparation of this manuscript was supported by a grant to the author from the National Science Foundation (BNS 8103581).

REFERENCES

Aslin, R. N. & Pisoni, D. B. Effects of early linguistic experience on speech discrimination by infants: A critique of Eilers, Gavin, & Wilson (1979). *Child Development*, 1980, *51*, 107–112.

Aslin, R. N., Pisoni, D. B., Hennessey, B. L., & Perey, A. J. Discrimination of voice onset time by human infants: New findings and implications for the effects of early experience. *Child Development*, 1981, *52*, 1135–1145.

Dodd, B. Lip reading in infants: Attention to speech presented in- and out-of-synchrony. *Cognitive Psychology*, 1979, *11*, 478–484.

Eilers, R. E. & Gavin, W. J. The evaluation of infant speech perception skills: Statistical techniques and theory development. In R. E. Stark (ed.), *Language behavior in infancy and early childhood.* New York: Elsevier, 1981.

Eilers, R. E., Gavin, W., & Wilson, W. R. Linguistic experience and phonemic perception in infancy: A cross-linguistic study. *Child Development,* 1979, *50,* 14–18.

Eilers, R. E., Gavin, W. J., & Wilson, W. R. Effects of early linguistic experience on speech discrimination by infants: A reply. *Child Development,* 1980, *51,* 113–117.

Eilers, R. E., Wilson, W. R., & Moore, J. M. Developmental changes in speech discrimination in infants. *Journal of Speech and Hearing Research,* 1977, *20,* 766–780.

Eilers, R. E., Wilson, W. R., & Moore, J. M. Speech discrimination in the language-innocent and the language-wise: A study in the perception of voice onset time. *Journal of Child Language,* 1979, *6,* 1–18.

Erber, N. Auditory, visual, and auditory-visual recognition of consonants by children with normal and impaired hearing. *Journal of Speech and Hearing Research,* 1972, *2,* 413–422.

Erber, N. Auditory-visual perception of speech. *Journal of Speech and Hearing Disorders,* 1975, *40,* 481–492.

Fantz, R. L., Fagen, J. F., & Miranda, S. B. Early visual selectivity. In L. Cohen & P. Salapatek (eds.), *Infant perception: From sensation to cognition.* New York: Academic, 1975, pp. 249–345.

Haug, O., Baccaro, P., & Guilford, F. R. A pure-tone audiogram on the infant: The PIWI technique. *Archives of Otolaryngology,* 1967, *86,* 435–440.

Hillenbrand, J. Perceptual organization of speech sounds by infants. *Journal of Speech and Hearing Research,* 1983, *26,* 268–282.

Hillenbrand, J. Speech perception by infants: Categorization based on nasal consonant place of articulation. *Journal of the Acoustical Society of America,* 1984, *75,* 1613–1622.

Hillenbrand, J. H., Minifie, F. D., & Edwards, T. J. Tempo of frequency change as a cue in speech-sound discrimination by infants. *Journal of Speech and Hearing Research,* 1979, *22,* 147–165.

Kuhl, P. K. Speech perception in early infancy: Perceptual constancy for spectrally dissimilar vowel categories. *Journal of the Acoustical Society of America,* 1979, *66,* 1668–1679 (a).

Kuhl, P. K. The perception of speech in early infancy. In N. J. Lass (ed.), *Speech and language: Advances in basic research and practice.* New York: Academic Press, 1979, pp. 1–47 (b).

Kuhl, P. K. Perceptual constancy for speech-sound categories in early infancy. In G. Yeni-Komshian, J. Kavanagh, & C. Ferguson (eds.), *Child phonology: Vol. 2, Perception.* New York: Academic Press, 1980, pp. 41–66.

Kuhl, P. K. Perception of auditory equivalence classes for speech in early infancy. *Infant Behavior and Development,* 1983, *6,* 263–285.

Kuhl, P. K. Categorization of speech by infants. In J. Mehler & R. Fox (eds.), *Neonate cognition: Beyond the blooming, buzzing confusion.* New York: Erlbaum, 1985, pp. 231–262.

Kuhl, P. K. & Hillenbrand, J. H. *The perception of categories based on pitch.* Paper presented at the meeting of the Society for Research in Child Development. 1979.

Kuhl, P. K. & Meltzoff, A. N. The bimodal perception of speech in infancy. *Science,* 1982, *218,* 1138–1141.

Kuhl, P. K. & Meltzoff, A. N. The intermodal representation of speech in infants. *Infant Behavior and Development,* 1984, *7,* 361–381 (a).

Kuhl, P. K. & Meltzoff, A. N. Infants' recognition of cross-modal correspondences for speech: Is it based on physics or phonetics? *Journal of the Acoustical Society of America,* 1984, *76,* 580 (b).

Kuhl, P. K. & Miller, J. D. Discrimination of auditory target dimensions in the presence or absence of variation in a second dimension by infants. *Perception and Psychophysics,* 1982, *31,* 279–292.

Liden, G. & Kankkunen, A. Visual reinforcement audiometry. *Acta Otolaryngologia,* 1969, *67,* 281–292.

Ling, D., Ling, H., & Doehring, D. G. Stimulus response and observer variables in the auditory screening of newborn infants. *Journal of Speech and Hearing Research,* 1970, *13,* 9–18.

MacKain, K., Studdert-Kennedy, M., Spieker, S., & Stern, D. Infant intermodal speech perception is a left-hemisphere function. *Science,* 1983, *219,* 1347–1349.

McGurk, H. & MacDonald, J. Hearing lips and seeing voices. *Nature,* 1976, *264,* 746–748.

Meltzoff, A. N. & Borton, R. Intermodal matching by human neonates, *Nature,* 1979, *282,* 403–404.

Miller, C., Younger, A., & Morse, P. Categorization of male and female voices in infancy. *Infant Behavior and Development,* 1982, *5,* 143–159.

Moore, J. M., Thompson, G., & Thompson, M. Auditory localization of infants as a function of reinforcement conditions. *Journal of Speech and Hearing Disorders,* 1975, *40,* 29–34.

Moore, J. M., Wilson, W. R., & Thompson, G. Visual reinforcement of head-turn responses in infants under 12 months of age. *Journal of Speech and Hearing Disorders,* 1977, *42,* 328–334.

Morse, P. A., Eilers, R. E., & Gavin, W. J. The perception of the sound of silence in early infancy. *Child Development,* 1982, *53,* 189–195.

Motta, G., Facchini, G. M., & D'Auria, E. Objective conditioned-reflex audiometry in children. *Acta Otolaryngologia,* Suppl., 1970, *273,* 1–49.

Olsho, L. W., Schoon, C., Sakai, R., Turpin, R., & Sperduto, V. Preliminary data on frequency discrimination in infancy. *Journal of the Acoustical Society of America,* 1982, *71,* 509–511.

Siegel, S. *Non-parametric statistics.* New York: McGraw-Hill, 1956.

Spelke, E. S. Perceiving bimodally specified events in infancy. *Developmental Psychology,* 1979, *15,* 626–636.

Summerfield, Q. Use of visual information for phonetic perception. *Phonetica,* 1979, *36,* 314–331.

Suzuki, T., Ogiba, Y., & Takei, T. Basic properties of conditioned orientation reflex and audiometry. *Minerva Otorinolaringology,* 1972, *22,* 181–186.

Thompson, G. & Weber, B. A. Responses of infants and young children to behavior observation audiometry (BOA). *Journal of Speech and Hearing Disorders,* 1974, *39,* 140–147.

Tyberghein, J. & Forrez, G. Objective (E.R.A.) and subjective (C.O.R.) audiometry in the infant. *Acta Otolaryngolgia,* 1971, *71,* 249–252.

Warren, V. C. *A comparative study of the auditory responses of normal and "at-risk" infants from twelve to twenty-four months of age using COR audiometry.* Unpublished dissertation, University of Southern California, Los Angeles, 1972.

Weber, B. A. Validation of observer judgments in behavioral observation audiometry. *Journal of Speech and Hearing Disorders,* 1969, *34,* 350–355.

Werker, J. F., Gilbert, J. H. V., Humphrey, K., & Tees, R. C. Developmental aspects of cross-language speech perception. *Child Development,* 1981, *52,* 349–355.

Wilson, W. R. *Auditory sensitivity.* Final report of Research Contract (NIH-NICHD-N01-HD-3-2793) entitled "Language acquisition in normal, hard-of-hearing, and Down's Syndrome children," 1979.

Wilson, W. R., Lee, K. H., Owen, G., & Moore, J. M. *Instrumentation for operant infant auditory assessment.* Seattle: Child Development and Mental Retardation Center, 1976.

Wilson, W. R., Moore, J. M., & Thompson, G. *Soundfield auditory thresholds of infants utilizing visual reinforcement audiometry (VRA).* Paper presented at American Speech and Hearing Association Convention, Houston, 1976.

11

HABITUATION OF ATTENTION AS A MEASURE OF VISUAL INFORMATION PROCESSING IN HUMAN INFANTS: SUMMARY, SYSTEMATIZATION, AND SYNTHESIS

135.50

Marc H. Bornstein

New York University

The absence of language responses in the newborn infant has restricted the investigation of just those problems which are the basis of adult behavior. If some substitute for such responses could be secured, a new field of inquiry would be opened and light shed on many problems which had not even been formulated.

—K. Jensen (1932, p. 367)

Few behavioral phenomena rival habituation in usefulness as a measure of the infant's sensitivity and few have as many implications for theories of psychological development.

—W. Kessen, M. M. Haith, and P. Salapatek (1970, p. 346)

INTRODUCTION

If an infant is placed in an otherwise homogeneous environment and a stimulus is then switched on, typically the infant will visually orient and attend to that stimulus. If, however, the stimulus is made available continuously or is presented repeatedly, the infant's visual attending to it will wane. This decrement in observed behavior is inferred to comprise, at least in part, joint underlying cognitive processes that reflect the infant's increasing knowledge of the stimulus: They are the infant's passive or active construction of an internal (and perhaps mental) representation or memory of the stimulus, and the infant's ongoing comparison of new stimulation with that representation. These processes have been termed, in the literature of infancy, *habituation*.[1]

Robert Fantz was among the first to bring the phenomenon of habituation to the attention of researchers in infancy.[2] In a seminal study, Fantz (1964) showed 10 pairs of stimuli serially to infants in four age groups; one member of each pair remained the same and one member varied from trial to trial. The groups included babies 1-2, 2-3, 3-4, and 4-6 months of age; the stimuli included magazine advertisements and photographs; and the presentation schedule included one stimulus pair per minute over 10 consecutive minutes. Fantz found that only older infants showed declining interest in the repeated stimulus (Figure 1): Babies younger than 2 months looked equally between the constant and novel patterns, while babies older than 4 months clearly habituated to the constant pattern.[3] Fantz's simple experiment served several purposes. First, it pro-

---

[1] Construed broadly, habituation has a long and complex history that dates back at least to the eighteenth century. For example, Etienne Bonnot de Condillac (1715-1780) intuitively described his sensationalist epistemology (1780) in a way that reminds us of habituation. Condillac invited his reader to imagine arriving at a chateau at night. In the morning, the shutters are opened for just an instant, permitting the visitor a glimpse at a magnificent landscape. A second glimpse, or a third, each time would yield exactly the same sense impressions as the first, the impression that the landscape would yield if the shutters were left open. Just one glimpse is insufficient, Condillac argued, for the visitor to become familiar with the countryside; he could hardly recount what he had seen. But more time for inspection allows the visitor to sort out the major features of the view, then to distinguish and relate more and more minor features to these, and finally to embrace the landscape.

As a psychological construct and method, habituation has in modern times recruited the attention of learning theorists, psychophysiologists, and the like (e.g., Groves & Thompson, 1970; Harris, 1943; Horn, 1967; Kandel, 1976; Mackworth, 1968; Razran, 1971; Sokolov, 1958/1963, 1969; Stein, 1966; Thompson & Spencer, 1966). For general treatments, see Peeke & Herz (1973), Tighe & Leaton (1976), and Siddle (1983); for a discussion of terminology, see Jeffrey (1976); for a comparison of developmental versus animal-neurophysiological perspectives, see Leaton & Tighe (1976). Some prominent references to habituation in preschool and school-age children might include Dodd & Lewis (1969), Freedle (1971), Kulig & Tighe (1981), and Lewis & Goldberg (1969a).

[2] Habituation with newborns and young infants was used earlier in the Soviet Union (e.g., Bronshtein, Antonova, Kamenetskaya, Luppova, & Sytova, 1958) and in the United States (e.g., Bridger, 1961), though these investigations seem not to have had the impact of Fantz's work.

[3] Caveat: The claim for Fantz (1964) to the contrary notwithstanding, only a decline dependent on stimulus repetition and independent of the influence of the competing novel pattern technically qualifies as habituation.

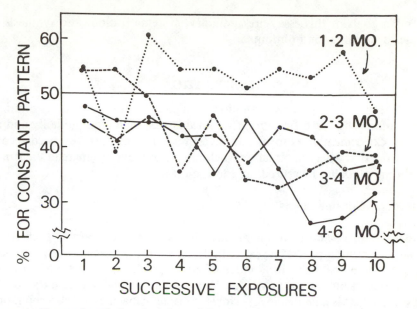

Figure 1. Change in relative duration of fixation of a repeatedly exposed (constant) pattern relative to a novel (variable) pattern (the position of each being controlled) during a series of exposure periods. Each curve is the mean for six to eight infants. (Figure is redrawn and legend quoted after R. Fantz in *Science,* 1964, *146,* 668–670. Copyright 1964 by the Amerian Association for the Advancement of Science.)

vided some basic information about visual perception and cognition in infants in the first half-year of life. Second, it raised a set of provocative questions related to age differences in infant information processing. Third, and most importantly, his experiment introduced a new and versatile paradigm to studies of infancy.

The chief aims of this essay are to review and evaluate the habituation method and to provide a functional taxonomy of the diverse uses to which habituation has been put with infants in the 20 years since its introduction. The essay is divided into three main parts. The first part discusses methodological issues associated with the experimental use of habituation. The second part advances the taxonomy. Specifically, this part focuses on the application of habituation in studies of *detection* and *discrimination, categorization, memory,* and *concept formation* in infants, and on the use of habituation toward identifying *individual differences in cognition.* (This list is not exhaustive of mental functions, nor, as we shall see, are the functions on this list mutually exclusive.) The third part of the essay overviews theories of habituation, raises some questions about habituation, and discusses future directions of habituation studies in infancy. This essay is not intended to constitute a comprehensive review of the literature—several additional treatments of the subject are available elsewhere (e.g., Cohen & Gelber, 1975; Friedman, 1975; Jeffrey & Cohen, 1971; Kessen, Haith, & Salapatek, 1970; Lewis & Baldini, 1979; Olson, 1976); rather, the main goals of this essay are summary, systematization, and synthesis of studies of habituation in infants.

HABITUATION

This section briefly treats methodological considerations in studies of infant habituation. Discussed first are procedural issues, including modality and response, experimental regimens and measures, and controls; reviewed second are factors that affect habituation, including those that originate in the stimulus, in the modality measured, and in the infant.

Procedural Considerations

Modality and response. Infant habituation studies have largely focused on visual information processing, and, in doing so, most have taken infant looking as the principal behavioral index of attention. In infancy studies, it is advantageous to build on a system or behavior that is under voluntary control early in life, as visual attending is. However, other capacities are also commonly tapped for habituation: Many investigators have capitalized on infants' nonnutritive sucking (see Jusczyk, this volume; Siqueland & DeLucia, 1969) and heart rate (see Berg & Berg, 1979; Clifton & Nelson, 1976). Procedures that use these two indexes are more difficult to implement and harder to assess in babies than is visual attending, but both can be used earlier in infancy and can be applied to more modalities than can the visual paradigm. A smaller number of studies have evaluated habituation of eye movements, respiration, and GSR, or inhibition of sucking, body movement, vocalization, or other activity (see Kessen et al., 1970); and a few have measured habituation of cortical evoked potentials (see Salapatek, this volume).

If one considers modality of investigation and response measure jointly, the most common pairing is visual stimulus–visual response; auditory-sucking (originally based on the visual-sucking paradigm developed by Siqueland & DeLucia, 1969) is probably the next most common combination (see Jusczyk, this volume); other paradigms, though feasible, are even less common, as for example an auditory-visual combination (e.g., Demany, McKenzie, & Vurpillot, 1977). Representatively, this essay concentrates on habituation of visual attending and its implications, though from time to time other paradigms are invoked by way of example or comparison.

Experimental regimens and dependent measures. Four main habituation regimens have been developed; each has different and significant consequences. (a) In a *fixed-trials procedure* (e.g., Fantz, 1964), a stimulus is presented to the infant for a set number of discrete predetermined exposure periods of predetermined duration, with or without interstimulus intervals. (b) In a *fixed-level procedure* (e.g., McCall, Hogarty, Hamilton, & Vincent, 1973), a stimulus is presented for periods of predetermined duration until the infant reaches a fixed, low absolute level of looking (say, 3 seconds per stimulus). (c) In an *infant-control procedure* (e.g., Horowitz, 1974; Horowitz, Paden, Bhana, & Self, 1972), a stimulus is presented to the infant for as long as the infant looks, and presentations continue until the infant reaches a predetermined habituation criterion (commonly 2 or 3 consecutive looks less than 50% of the mean of the infant's initial 2 or 3 looks). (d) In a *free-looking procedure* (e.g., Bornstein, Ferdinandsen, & Gross, 1981), a stimulus is presented to the infant for one, usually lengthy, predetermined duration, and infant looking is afterward assessed in terms of fixed intervals or individual looks.

The fixed-trials procedure was the first to be introduced and has maintained wide popularity, although it is subject to compelling criticisms. For example, if presentations are experimentally fixed, infants not looking at the location of the stimulus at its onset have their inspection time artificially truncated, just as they do if they are still looking at the stimulus at its offset. Thus, looking in the fixed-trials procedure is influenced by experimental parameters (e.g., trial length, number of trials, intertrial interval length, etc.), rather than by infant interest or volition. The fixed-level procedure is also problematic, since some infants, so-called "short-lookers," may not start out inspecting the stimulus sufficiently much to show a decrement to the required asymptote (whose value is arbitrarily determined anyway). The infant-control and free-looking procedures, which are of more recent vintage, give over stimulus control to the infant and so attempt to meet these criticisms; moreover, these procedures are increasingly popular, since they permit experimenters to track individual patterns of habituation and to equate infants for eventual level of habituation. When stimulus presentation is under infant control, however, the habituation paradigm is necessarily more complex and requires online estimation of infant regard, instantaneous linkage to stimulus presentation, simultaneous calculation of habituation criterion, etc.; additionally, false determination of the termination of individual looks and the possibility that infants may meet a habituation criterion by chance (Type I error) must be guarded against. The fixed-trials and infant-control procedures (which are the most common) have not yet been adequately compared experimentally. (In a simple preference task, however, Haaf, Smith, & Smitley, 1983, have recently determined that fixed-trials and infant-control regimens do not result in different average looking times—per trial or per look; not unexpectedly, however, the infant-control procedure produced greater variation—yielding more very long and very short looks—relative to the fixed-trials procedure.)

Fixed-trials procedures permit the determination of first or total look length per trial, mean look length per trial, total looking time, longest look, number of looks, etc.; by far the most popular summary statistic of such procedures has been relative *amount of habituation*. Calculation of this value derives from McCall and Kagan (1970, p. 94):[4]

---

[4] This formulation actually provides an inverse measure of habituation; in the authors' words, "positive or low-negative ratios indicated slow habituation and high-negative ratios reflected rapid habituation" (McCall & Kagan, 1970, p. 94).

$$\frac{\text{(total duration of last two looks)} - \text{(total duration of first two looks)}}{\text{(total duration of first two looks)}}. \quad (1)$$

Infant-control procedures permit determination of duration of longest look, trial of longest look, total accumulated time to criterion, and trials to criterion; these procedures tend to emphasize *rate of habituation*. Independent of paradigm, of general interest are how quickly, efficiently, and completely infants habituate. How *quickly* an infant habituates might be indicated by the number of trials or exposures to a stimulus an infant requires to reach a preset habituation criterion. How *efficiently* an infant habituates might be indicated by how much exposure time to a stimulus an infant requires to reach criterion. How *completely* an infant habituates might be indicated by how much an infant descends from an initial level of looking to a final level in the time or number of exposures allotted to stimulus presentation. Measures of amount and rate of habituation may be quantitative or qualitative. The course of habituation may be characterized qualitatively, as by the nature or pattern of the habituation function (see below). Amount can be indexed quantitatively by a single decrement score considering the infant's initial and final levels of looking, and rate can be indexed by a trials-to-criterion score. Amount and rate measure different aspects of habituation and are conceptually different values. For example, one infant might descend over nine trials from 10- to 4-second average looks, whereas another infant might descend over five trials from 10- to 2-second average looks—both meet a minimum 50% criterion drop, but the two differ on amount and rate of habituation. In practice, however, the two measures are related: Among 20 4-month-olds habituated over 15 trials to a single simple geometric pattern, Ruddy and Bornstein (1982) found that amount and rate correlated at $-.78$.

Three additional observations about habituation data and their analysis warrant mention. First, some investigators have argued that response decrement in habituation is a *gradual function,* characterizing it as negatively linear (e.g., Lewis, Goldberg, & Campbell, 1969) or negatively exponential (e.g., Dodd & Lewis, 1969; Freedle, 1971; Thompson & Spencer, 1966); other investigators have argued that response decrement follows a *step function* (e.g., Cohen & Gelber, 1975). Clearly, individual habituation functions might adhere to any one of these or to other, idiosyncratic patterns, and, even with clear criteria, the true shape of habituation curves may be difficult to assess. More importantly, group mean functions are not necessarily representative of individual habituation (Cohen & Menten, 1981). To tell the same story from another perspective, individual habituation need not necessarily predict or adhere to a group mean. Second, whether individual functions follow a genuinely monotonic decline or a nonmonotonic pattern, habituation may be perturbed by several factors, including "noise" arising from distractions that are internal or external to the infant (Freedle, 1971) as well as observer error in judging infant looking (Ames, Hunter, Black, Lithgow, & Newman, 1978). Observed habituation therefore consists of true attention plus noise. (Noise also raises the potential of false alarms in infants' reaching a habituation criterion.) Third, in the repeated-measures analysis of habituation data, assumptions of homogeneity of covariance are not usually met; McCall and Appelbaum (1973) have therefore recommended a conservative multivariate approach to this analysis.

Control conditions. A decrement in fixation duration may reflect genuine habituation of underlying attention, that is, acquisition of information about a repeated stimulus and consequent loss of interest in it. However, response decrement per se could alternatively reflect (a) *sensory adaptation,* (b) *effector fatigue,* or (c) *change in behavioral state.* To defend against these alternative interpretations, investigators of infant habituation have adopted diverse strategies of control. If a baby is assessed to look (or suck, etc.) at a given level to a pretest stimulus (different from the habituation stimulus), and that pretest stimulus is presented again as a posttest following habituation and the infant's level of looking (etc.) at it is not changed, habituation can be inferred, as opposed to effector fatigue or change in state of arousal. (Since the child's initial level of responding is so important in habituation, a pretest is additionally valuable as a warm-up to obviate startle effects.) Likewise, if, following habituation of looking, an infant is tested with a novel stimulus and shows recovery of looking relative to the infant's level of looking at the end of habituation, effector fatigue and state changes can be eliminated as alternative interpretations of response decrement; if the infant displays habituation and recovery between both members of a counterbalanced stimulus pair, sensory adaptation can also be eliminated as an explanation of response decrement. Of course, habituation and test stimuli must be preselected so as to be equally preferable, intense, etc.; otherwise, response recovery in the test may merely reflect preference or startle. Proper pretests, as well as counterbalancing assignment of stimuli, can be used to address these possibilities. In addition, serial learning paradigms, like habituation, risk a criterion artifact (Bogartz, 1965) or spontaneous regression (Bertenthal, Haith, & Campos, 1983) if subjects reach criterion through chance. To offset such eventualities, some investigators have counseled the use of highly conservative habituation criteria, some have extended the habituation sequence with "suppression" or "overlearning" trials with the familiar stimulus after the infant has reached criterion, some have added a no-change control group whose performance after habituation is compared with that of the test group, and, finally, some investigators have advocated alternative design cum statistical procedures to assess regression versus recovery simultaneously. Unfortunately, none of these approaches is entirely satisfactory or efficient (suffering severally from questionable assumptions, problems of subject maintenance or recruitment, cyclicity of attention, etc.). Finally, if it can be shown that varying the interstimulus interval over a reasonable range does not affect the course of habituation to a stimulus, or if the delay between habituation and test can be reasonably prolonged without adverse effect on discrimination, general organism fatigue and sensory adaptation can be eliminated as explanation of response decrement.

It may be considered a shortcoming of research in this area, however, that signal detection theory has not been more widely applied to disambiguate habituation, differences in sensitivity, and changes in behavioral state. In general, the significance of behavioral state in a procedure that is deliberately manipulating attentiveness in an uncommonly volatile organism such as the human infant has been underestimated.

Factors that Influence Habituation

Factors "in the stimulus." Habituation is sensitive to stimulus control (logically through the infant's perception of the stimulus). Two kinds of stimulus heterogeneity especially affect habituation: degree of stimulus complexity, and degree of interstimulus variation over a presentation series. Heterogeneity of either kind maintains looking behavior in infants. Caron and Caron (1969), for example, showed three groups of 32 3.5-month-olds four different multicolored geometric designs serially followed by five repetitions of 2×2, 12×12, or 24×24 checkerboards. As shown in Figure 2, all three groups maintained a high level of looking on the initial trials, during which stimuli varied (like those in Fantz, 1964), and all three groups declined on the stimulus repetition trials, but the groups declined differentially quickly, reflecting the complexity of their repeated stimulus. Trend analysis of the repetition trials revealed that linear slopes among the three groups were significantly different and transitively ordered. (For other examples, see Cohen, DeLoache, & Rissman, 1975; Martin, 1975.)

Cohen and Strauss (1979) have contributed complementary data that show the effects of interstimulus heterogeneity on habituation of infant looking. Three age groups of babies between 4.5 and 7.5 months were seen. At each age, babies who habituated to repeated presentations of a single face in a single orientation (position and expression) cumulated the least total looking time in achieving a criterion of 50% of their initial level of looking, babies who habituated to presentations of a single face in different orientations cumulated more, and babies who habituated to presentations of different faces in different orientations cumulated the most time. (For a similar example, see Cohen, 1969, and, for an interesting adult comparison, see Berlyne, 1970.)

Other stimulus factors seem also to influence habituation significantly. Babies are reported to habituate more quickly, more efficiently, or more completely to salient vs. less conspicuous features of complex patterns (Jeffrey, 1968; Miller, 1972; cf. Lasky, 1979), happy faces vs. other expressions (Cornell, 1974; Nelson, Morse, & Leavitt, 1979; see also Field, Woodson, Greenberg, & Cohen, 1982), preferred vs. nonpreferred stimuli (Bornstein, 1981a), mirror-image vs. orthogonal rotations of patterns (Bornstein, Gross, & Wolf, 1978), structured vs. unstructured percepts (Bornstein et al., 1981), looming vs. rotational movement of objects (Gibson, Owsley, & Johnston, 1978), three-dimensional vs. two-dimensional representations of objects (Ruff, Kohler, & Haupt,

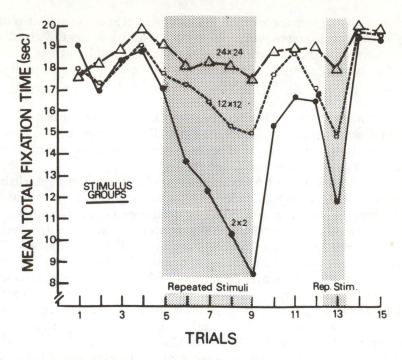

Figure 2. Mean total fixation during varied (1-4, 10-12, 14-15) and repeated (5-9, 13) 20-sec trials for three stimulus groups. (Figure redrawn and legend quoted after A. J. Caron & R. F. Caron, 1969. Copyright Psychonomic Society.)

1976), and category prototypes vs. nonexemplars (Bornstein, 1981b). The effects of stimulus duration, interstimulus interval, stimulus intensity, etc., and their interaction with age are underresearched.

Factors "in the modality." Different modalities are commonly studied in habituation, but different modalities may yield different habituation functions even to the same stimulus (see Leaton & Tighe, 1976). Thus, habituation of visual fixation and heart rate (e.g., Clifton & Nelson, 1976; McCall, 1979a) or habituation of eye movement and heart rate (e.g., Moreau, Birch, & Turkewitz, 1970) to a given stimulus on a given regimen may take place at different rates, in different amounts, or with differential stability. McCall (1979a), for example, found different patterns of habituation of visual attending and heart-rate deceleration measured simultaneously in the same 5-month-olds shown the same visual stimuli.

Relationships among such multiple assessments of habituation are unfortunately not yet well worked out; if they could be, they might further illuminate sensory and perceptual function in infants. For example, Kulig and Tighe (1981) measured habituation of skin conductance and suppression of behavioral response simultaneously in 7- and 11-year-old children. The two measures interacted with age and with the test regimen, and therefore permitted a differential analysis. Skin conductance proved to be more sensitive to specific stimuli and hence to detection and storage of perceptual information; behavioral response proved to be more sensitive to the utilization of perceptual information after encoding.

Factors "in the infant." Diverse characteristics of infants themselves seem also to influence habituation. Three are especially significant, though none has yet attracted adequate attention: They are (a) *habituation reliability,* (b) *individual differences in habituation,* and (c) *age.*

Remarkably few studies have examined empirically the short-term reliability or long-term stability of habituation in infants. Clearly, if a style of habituation is characteristic of an individual, or if differences in habituation are to find value as concurrent or predictive correlates of other cognitive or social behaviors, habituation ought to be reliably attached to the individual. Three experiments have investigated short-term reliability of habituation. In one experiment, Pêcheux and Lécuyer (1983) studied 24 4-month-olds in two experimental sessions separated by 2 weeks. Each session consisted of two infant-control habituation tasks; in one session, the stimuli were geometric patterns (a bull's-eye and a square), and in the other, the stimuli were social patterns (a baby's face and a woman's face). Babies showed reliable habituation within and between assessments in terms of accumulated looking times: The average Pearson product-moment correlation (*r*) within a session—i.e., immediate reliability between two different geometric or between two different social stimuli—was .61. The average *r* between sessions—i.e., 2-week reliability between different social and geometric stimuli—was .56. Trials to criterion was never reliable, though the average correlation between accumulated looking times and trials to criterion was .41. In this study, the assessment of 2-week reliability is confounded with a change in stimulus category; hence, it may underestimate true reliability. (On the other hand, these data suggest that, beyond immediate reliability of habituation, infants may possess characteristic styles of habituation that transcend variations in stimulation.) In a second experiment, Bornstein and Benasich (1983) studied 30 5-month-olds in two similar infant-control habituation sessions separated by 10 days. Infants were habituated either to a single female face wearing a single expression, or to a single female face wearing different expressions; different faces were used in the two sessions. This study included a visit to the laboratory approximately 1 month before the reliability assessments to inoculate babies psychologically to the assessment situation, different but equivalently attractive habituation stimuli, controls for infant behavioral state, and an assessment of intensity of infant involvement with the stimulus. Infants in this study showed reliable habituation between the two assessments in quantitative terms, for example, trials to criterion (.46) —and accumulated looking times and amount of decrement, which were interrelated, followed the same pattern; they also showed reliability in the qualitative patterns of habituation they produced in the two sessions (.39; see below).

A general problem with using some quantitative dependent measures in conjunction with certain simple habituation stimuli in the assessment of reliability is that restriction of variance may artifactually limit the magnitude of the correlation. In the third experiment, Fenson, Sapper, and Minner (1974) found a nonreliable test-retest correlation (.31) over 3 weeks for fixed-trials habituation of total amount of looking (Equation 1) at a face; their sample included 18 1-year-olds.

Three studies have examined longer-term stability of habituation. In one, Riksen-Walraven (1978) showed 25 babies colored slides of a "nonsense figure" over five consecutive 20-second trials when the babies were 9 months and again when they were 12 months of age. She then fit linear regression functions to each child's habituation data: The 3-month test-retest correlation of regression coefficients proved reliable (.60). In a second study, McCall (1979a) saw 77 babies at 5 months and again when they reached 10 months of age. Similar procedures and analysis at the two age periods (elaborated below) showed "habituation patterns...not as straightforward, consistent, or as interesting [at 10 months] as at 5 months" (p. 566). Finally, summarizing over longitudinal measurements made between 2-4 and 39 months in 35 infants, Miller, Ryan, Aberger, McGuire, Short, and Kenny (1979) reported a reliable correlation (.28) of habituation of total amounts of fixation (Equation 1). One important difference between the latter studies is that McCall used the same stimulus in both sessions (thereby confounding reliability measurement with memory or with stimulus difficulty), whereas Miller consistently adjusted stimulus difficulty for age. Future reliability studies ought to control state of arousal, assess converging dependent measures, use different (but matched) stimuli to avoid memory effects associated with repeated testing, utilize infant-control procedures, and attempt to circumvent confounding reliability assessments with age changes in mental capacity.

Probably every investigator of infant habituation has observed that babies differ widely in whether and when they habituate. Since the adoption of the infant-control procedure, with discrete trials equated to individual looks and common baselines and a common criterion for all babies, it has been possible to specify individual differences in habituation according to neat indexes, such as trials to criterion. In one study, DeLoache (1976) observed that 4-month-olds took between 4 and 24 trials to habituate to a pattern of geometric shapes, and she suggested that the distribution of babies on trials to criterion was bimodal. In a second study, Pêcheux and Lécuyer (1983) observed that 4-month-olds took between 4 and 19 trials to habituate to simple social and geometric patterns, but they found that trials to criterion was normally distributed. In a third study, Bornstein and Ruddy (1984) observed habituation to a simple geometric pattern in 4-month-old singletons and twins. Infants in both groups habituated in 2 to 15 trials, and, although the distribution tended toward bimodal, it did not differ statistically from normal (see Figure 3).

Remarkably few studies have examined individual differences in patterns of infant habituation. In one, McCall and Kagan (1970) showed 72 4-month-olds

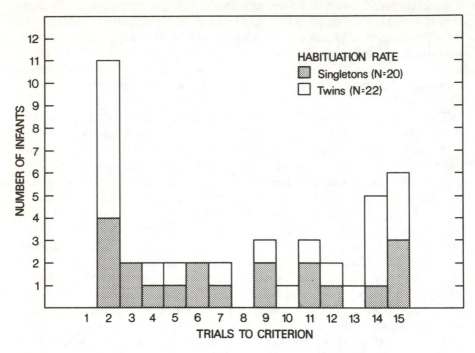

Figure 3. Distribution of trials to criterion among 42 4-month-olds habituated to a simple geometric pattern. (Data from Bornstein & Ruddy, 1984.)

a standard set of three heterogeneous toys four times in a fixed-trials procedure (30-second trials with 15-second interstimulus intervals). They first segregated out "short lookers" (36% of the sample), that is, babies who fell in the bottom third of a distribution based on first-look times. McCall and Kagan then determined amount of habituation for each baby in the remainder of the sample using the formula given in Equation 1. Based on this analysis, they designated half the remaining babies "slow habituators" (25% of the original sample); these were babies who, in fact, increased looking over trials. And they designated half "rapid habituators" (22%); these were babies who actually declined. The remaining infants in the sample (17%) produced too heterogeneous, irregular, and idiosyncratic looking patterns to be assigned meaningfully to these habituation groups. Figure 4 shows average habituation functions for McCall and Kagan's three identifiable groups. Later, McCall (1979a) adopted a substantially sophisticated statistical strategy to assess individual differences in habituation pattern; the aim again was to describe "clusters" of babies who were homogeneous within clusters but heterogeneous between clusters. Briefly, 86 5-month-olds experienced six trials of repeated visual (infant-control) or auditory (fixed-trial) stimulation, and their looking times and heart rates in each condition were cast into separate Subjects × Trials matrices; each of the four matrices was then decomposed into generalized patterns of change over

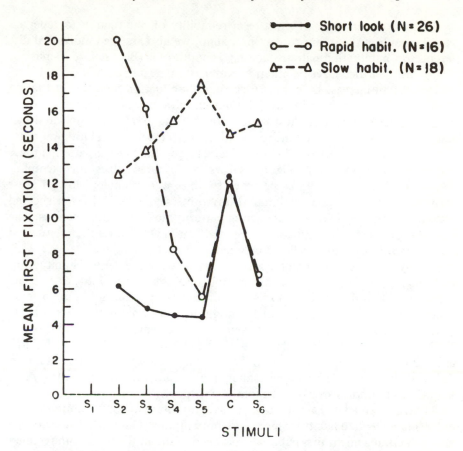

Figure 4. Mean first fixation times for the three groups of infants. S_1-S_6 are stimulus repetitions; C is the dishabituation stimulus. (Figure adapted and legend quoted after McCall & Kagan, 1970. Copyright 1970 by the American Psychological Association. Adapted by permission of the author.)

trials and into indexes of direction and extent of individual subject variation; finally, derived composite scores for individual infants were submitted to direct cluster rotation to yield homogeneous but differentiated groups (see McCall, 1979a, for details). For McCall's 5-month-olds, these procedures yielded distinct clusters for different modality-by-response measures: For example, for habituation of looking at the visual stimulus, Cluster 1 (44% of the sample) showed a smooth monotonically decreasing function, while Clusters 2 (19%) and 3 (25%) increased looking to the fourth and fifth trials, respectively, before decreasing on trial six. The balance of infants in the sample displayed idiosyncratic patterns of habituation. Habituation to visual stimuli measured by cardiac deceleration clustered differently, and although habituation clusters to auditory stimuli measured by cardiac deceleration were similar, infants showed little agreement with themselves across measures.

As part of our study of short-term reliability of habituation to repeated visual stimuli in the infant-control paradigm, we also assessed individual differences in habituation patterns among 5-month-olds (Bornstein & Benasich, 1983). We identified three habituation patterns: (a) negative exponential habituation, (b) an increase in looking then rapid habituation, and (c) fluctuating looking-time functions prior to habituation. Infants who gave negative exponential patterns required just more than half the number of trials and just less than half the exposure time to the stimulus to reach the habituation criterion as did infants who gave increase-decrease and fluctuating patterns; these groups performed similarly. Figure 5 shows data of three babies who exemplify the three patterns. Sixty-three percent of babies were reliable: Most of these showed a negative exponential pattern in both sessions (63%); fewer showed increase-decrease (11%) and fluctuating patterns (26%) between sessions. The remaining babies were unreliable between sessions (37%). Overall, habituation pattern in infants proved reliable between sessions (.39).

Clearly, there is more than gross similarity between the derived habituation patterns McCall reported using fixed-trials and hybrid first-look fixed-trials procedures, and the patterns Bornstein and Benasich found using the infant-control procedure. To date, most investigators have adopted the fixed-trials procedure and McCall and Kagan's amount-of-decrement formula (Equation 1); however, the infant-control procedure and its attendant measures of habituation are increasing in popularity. Either way, it would appear that habituation of visual attention in infants is reasonably reliable and exhibits three clearly differentiated patterns as early as 5 months postnatal.

As first observed by Fantz (1964), younger infants tend not to habituate, and older infants tend to habituate more and more rapidly (Figure 1). The exact age at which infants might first habituate has been found to fluctuate with regimen and with stimulus. Although, in general, habituation in infants younger than 2 months is acknowledged to be controversial, Friedman (1975), using an infant-control procedure, demonstrated habituation in newborns (see, too, Siqueland, 1981). Apparently, simple exposure to a stimulus is insufficient to habituate very young infants, whereas habituation is more sensitively extracted when stimulus exposure depends on particular responses, or when contingent procedures are employed in stimulus presentation.

Figure 5. Results of two infant-control habituation sessions for three infants who were shown a female face wearing an affectively neutral expression. These babies illustrate three main patterns of habituation and the short-term reliability of habituation patterns. "Sam" (at the top) showed a negatively exponential decrease from his baseline to a 50% habituation criterion in both his sessions; "William" (in the middle) first looked more then rapidly habituated to criterion both times; and "Lewis" (at the bottom) showed a fluctuating looking-time function in each session before reaching the habituation criterion. (Data from Bornstein & Benasich, 1983.)

SESSION 1   SESSION 2

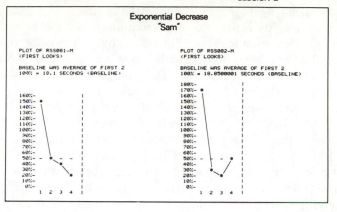

Exponential Decrease
"Sam"

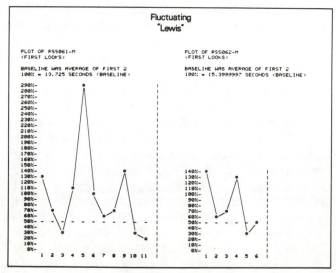

LOOKING TIME (percent of baseline)

TRIALS (first looks)

267

Habituation studies with older infants show consistent age effects. Wetherford and Cohen (1973) compared habituation in 1.5-, 2-, 2.5-, and 3-month-old infants both longitudinally and cross-sectionally, using a fixed-duration discrete-trials presentation schedule. The results of their cross-sectional comparison were clear and help to establish a lower age bound for infants observed under these very general conditions: The younger two groups of babies looked continuously, while the older two groups habituated. (Repeated measurements reportedly confounded the longitudinal comparison in this study, though Miller, Ryan, Sinnott, & Wilson, 1976, found clearer habituation patterns in longitudinal comparisons than in cross-sectional comparisons in similar age groups.) Martin (1975), who tested 2-, 3.5-, and 5-month-olds with six trials each, also found that age interacted with trials, such that the two older groups habituated quickly while the youngest group did not habituate. Applying habituation categories of Bornstein and Benasich (1983), Pêcheux (personal communication, 15 Sept. 1983) found that "fluctuating curves are most common in 2-mo-olds, and increase-decrease may be found only after 2 mo." When 5-month-olds in the reliability experiment of Bornstein and Benasich (1983) participated in the same experiment again at 6 months (that is, with stimulus held constant), almost all showed negative exponential habituation functions, as though they had developed to the most efficient form. In a cross-sectional study that reached beyond the period of infancy, Lewis et al. (1969) failed to find habituation at 3 months but calculated that response decrement was positively related to age between 3 months and 18 months. Finally, Schaffer, Greenwood, and Parry (1972) studied habituation of first looks over seven fixed trials at monthly intervals between 6 and 12 months in 20 infants. The best-fitting function for their group habituation data changed with age from negative exponential to negative linear. This development is paradoxical, since one might have expected steeper curves from older babies. Though consistent, age comparisons are plagued by problems: Baseline levels of looking vary with age, and, consequently, habituation criteria may not be comparable across ages, or they may lead to false conclusions about the relationship between age and rate of habituation.

The following have been identified as other more or less significant individual difference factors that influence habituation negatively: *low parental education* (Lewis et al., 1969; McCall, 1972, cited in McCall et al., 1973; but see McCall, 1979a), *perinatal risk* (Eisenberg, Coursin, & Rupp, 1966; Friedman, 1975; Lewis et al., 1969; Sigman, Kopp, Parmelee, & Jeffrey, 1973), *obstetrical medication* (Brackbill, 1979), *later parity* (Friedman, 1975), *illness* (Haskins, Collier, Ramey, & Hirschbiel, 1978), *poor nutrition* (Lester, 1975), *physical anomaly* (Schexnider, Bell, Shebilske, & Quinn, 1981), *trisomy-21* (Barnet, Ohlrich, & Shanks, 1971; Cohen, 1981), and *negative behavioral state* (Barnet & Goodwin, 1965; Berg & Berg, 1979; Clifton & Nelson, 1976; Friedman, 1975; Hutt, von Bernuth, Lenard, Hutt, & Prechtl, 1968; Kessen et al., 1970). Each of these factors has associated with it only a small literature from which contemporary investigators may draw conclusions. Some conclusions may be more certain (e.g., about age). Other data sets (e.g., about gender; see Cohen, Gelber, & Lazar, 1971; Cornell & Strauss, 1973; Johnson & Brody, 1977; Pancratz & Cohen, 1970) provoke less certain conclusions: Kessen et al. (1970, p. 344) called gender differences "perplexing," but, reviewing a burgeoning literature years later, Tighe and Powlison (1978, p. 337) deduced "faster stimulus processing by male infants and/or more complete or detailed processing by females." (In the section on Individual Differences in Cognition, the significance of variation among infants is explored in greater detail.)

It seems safe to summarize thus: Infant habituation reflects many factors—in the stimulus, in the procedure, and in the infant—and appears to depend as much on measure as on mind. This said, I turn to introduce a taxonomy of habituation studies of infancy.

150.03

A TAXONOMY: DETECTION AND DISCRIMINATION

Among the first questions developmental investigators might ask of infants are which stimuli they detect and which stimulus differences they see, hear, taste, smell, or feel. Describing and delineating infants' capacities to detect (absolute threshold) and to discriminate (difference threshold) are invaluable in infancy research, since they constitute first steps toward a basic psychological description of the developing organism.

Two habituation methods have been applied to assess infants' capacities to detect and to discriminate environmental stimulation. In the first, habituation to one stimulus is followed by a test with a second (third, etc.) stimulus; recovery or dishabituation to the change stimulus (assessed either from the end of habituation or relative to the re-presentation of the habituation stimulus in the test) indicates detection or discrimination. In the second method, habituation to randomization of a pair (or triad, etc.) of to-be-discriminated stimuli is compared with habituation to repetition of a single stimulus; slower, less efficient, or less complete habituation in the heterogeneous condition relative to the homogeneous condition indicates detection or discrimination of stimuli. Using either technique, simultaneous or successive comparisons may be investigated. In general, successive discrimination in habituation-test studies of visual perception has proven to be the paradigm of choice among investigators of infant perception. There are probably several reasons for this: Among them are the fact that few infant investigators are psychophysicists interested in issues of sensory threshold, and the fact that this paradigm is relatively easy to implement.

Habituated to one stimulus and then tested with other stimuli that are similar or dissimilar to the original, infants could show a variety of patterns of discriminative behavior. Below, four logical (though not exhaustive) possibilities

are examined. Different patterns indicate differences in infant capacity or proclivity to discriminate. These patterns are significant also because inferences
about habituation itself are frequently made on the basis of posthabituation
behavior. The four patterns are shown graphically in Figure 6; this figure omits
the null result, and reciprocal patterns of suppression of looking that also indicate discrimination.

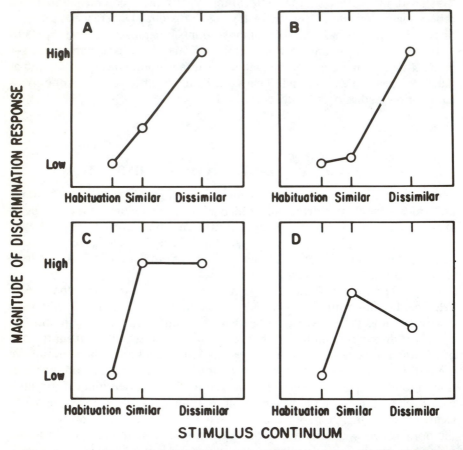

Figure 6. Four patterns of discriminative response to novel stimuli differing in psychological similarity from a habituation stimulus. A: Response magnitude is a monotonic (and perhaps linear) function of the degrees of difference among test and
habituation stimuli. B: Response magnitude is related to the degrees of difference
among test and habituation stimuli; habituation generalizes to similar stimuli but not
to dissimilar ones. C: Response magnitude reflects any difference among test and
habituation stimuli; all discriminable stimuli elicit equivalent amounts of dishabituation. D: Response magnitude is a nonmonotonic function of the "discrepancy" of
test stimuli from the habituation stimulus; similar stimuli elicit more dishabituation
than do dissimilar stimuli. Positions of similar and dissimilar stimuli in this figure
have been scaled arbitrarily; the dissimilar stimulus is displaced three times the distance from the habituation stimulus as the similar stimulus. This is a general set of
relations meant to be independent of any particular stimulus dimension. (After Bornstein, 1981b. Copyright Ablex Publishing Corporation. Reprinted by permission.)

In one type of dishabituation pattern, stimulus change following habituation provokes discrimination in the degree that test stimuli differ from the habituation stimulus; this pattern is shown graphically in Figure 6A. Many studies of infants' visual perception of colors (e.g., Bornstein, 1981b), of forms (e.g., Cornell, 1975; Saayman, Ames, & Moffett, 1964; Welch, 1974), and of faces or facial expressions (Barrera & Maurer, 1981a, b; Field et al., 1982; LaBarbera, Izard, Vietze, & Parisi, 1976; Nelson et al., 1979; Young-Browne, Rosenfeld, & Horowitz, 1977) as well as studies of auditory (e.g., Bartoshuk, 1962; Bridger, 1961) and olfactory perception (e.g., Engen & Lipsitt, 1965) give evidence that discrimination follows this pattern. A strong form of this general association is that the greater the physical discrepancy between a new stimulus and the habituation stimulus, the greater the infant's discriminative response to the new stimulus. Such a relationship suggests a monotonic, and perhaps linear, pattern of responsivity; clearly, however, discrimination responses may be monotonically related, but need not be linearly ordered. Where monotonic recovery indicates discrimination, linear monotonicity indicates a direct relationship between discrimination sensitivity and magnitude of stimulus change. In practice, unfortunately, it is difficult to distinguish between linear-monotonic and simply monotonic patterns. (Additionally, spacing of stimuli on the abscissa, and the units in which attention is measured on the ordinate, will influence the final form of the functional relationship between dependent and independent variable.) Pattern A is explicitly or implicitly predicted by many investigators of infant perception (e.g., Caron, Caron, Caldwell, & Weiss, 1973; Cohen & Gelber, 1975; Jeffrey & Cohen, 1971; Kessen et al., 1970; Rose, 1977; Weiffenbach, 1977; Welch, 1974). For example, Cohen et al. (1971) habituated 64 4-month-olds over 12 successive 15-second presentations of a geometric stimulus; babies were then tested with the original habituation stimulus, with the same stimulus in a novel color, with the same stimulus in a novel form, and with a stimulus novel in both color and form. Infants dishabituated equally to the two changes in a single dimension, and they dishabituated in a nearly additive way to the change in two dimensions. Welch (1974) found a similarly linear recovery among 4-month-olds to novelty changes in one dimension, two dimensions, and three dimensions.

A second possible pattern of posthabituation behavior arises when stimulus change fails to provoke a psychological discrimination. The result is a generalization of habituation as shown in Figure 6B. This generalization could, in turn, reflect an actual failure to discriminate or a perceptual proclivity to treat discriminable stimuli similarly. Failures of discrimination could arise for legitimate or for artifactual reasons. If habituation had not actually occurred, or if infant encoding in habituation were insufficient, generalization of habituation would constitute a false index of infant discrimination capacity. However, generalization of habituation could eventuate legitimately if the similar test stimulus were indiscriminable from the habituation stimulus (i.e., were less than a JND), or, alternatively, if a test stimulus closely resembled the habituation stimulus psychologically (i.e., if infants coclassified the stimuli; see the section on Categorization). To disambiguate these interpretations, it must be demonstrated that, under some circumstances, infants can discriminate between habituation and similar targets. To show that infants are responding at all in an experiment at risk for generalization of habituation, investigators often include a highly dissimilar stimulus to which they believe infants will certainly dishabituate.

The third general pattern of posthabituation performance might be called "all-or-none" discrimination. Here, discriminable changes, regardless of their physical or psychological distance from the habituation stimulus, elicit from the infant roughly equivalent degrees of interest, as shown in Figure 6C. This result has been most powerfully demonstrated where stimulus change (regardless of its physical magnitude) crosses boundaries among psychological categories. For example, Eimas (1975) reported that infants discriminate among different phonemes equivalently, and Bornstein (1981b) reported that infants discriminate among different hues equivalently. In these studies, following habituation to one token (/*b*/, blue), infants dishabituated equivalently to a second token (/*d*/, green) and a third token (/*g*/, red) that were equally different from the habituation stimulus qualitatively (in phoneme, hue) but unequally different quantitatively (in voice-onset time, wavelength). Experiments that claim this pattern of results need to demonstrate, usually through the introduction of a third very different stimulus that provokes even greater dishabituation, that infants have not merely hit a "ceiling" of responding that results in their artifactually treating the similar and dissimilar stimuli in the same way.

A fourth pattern of posthabituation behavior is possible where infant responsiveness is a nonmonotonic function of degree of dissimilarity between the test and habituation stimuli, as shown in Figure 6D. Here, attending to test stimuli after habituation is an inverted-U function if discrepancy between novel and familiar stimuli. Presumably, in this case, a moderate difference between the test stimulus and the internal or mental representation of the habituation stimulus excites further exploration, whereas a too-novel stimulus that cannot be related to the infant's representation does not motivate the infant sufficiently to explore the stimulus further (e.g., Berlyne, 1960; Dember & Earl, 1957; Kagan, 1971; McCall, 1971; McCall, Kennedy, & Appelbaum, 1977; McCall & McGhee, 1977; McCall & Melson, 1969; Zelazo, Hopkins, Jacobson, & Kagan, 1973). This fourth view is an expression of the "discrepancy hypothesis." For example, McCall et al. (1977) habituated groups of 2.5-month-olds to arrowlike stimuli that pointed toward 12, 1, 2, or 3 o'clock, and for different groups these stimuli also served in a posthabituation test. The results showed a quadratic trend (like Figure 6D) relating discrepancy effect to magnitude of discrepancy. Interestingly, among the four main possible outcome patterns, the discrepancy view is the only one for which it is necessary to invoke an implicit theory of motivation, overlaid on perceptuocognitive performance.

The pattern and validity of test results following habituation reflect several premises and assumptions in addition to those already implied or explicitly stated. (a) Fair assessments using this technique require habituation and test stimuli of equivalent attractiveness, potency, etc. If one stimulus naturally provokes more looking than another, greater responsiveness to it in the test may bear little or no relation to habituation. Similarly, a presumption of the method is that a baby habituated with one stimulus, and tested with a second, is responding to the second relative to the first, and not responding to any third stimulus that happens to be in the visual field (or in the baby's mind). A further related presumption of the technique is "symmetry" between stimuli in habituation and test; that is, the pattern of results obtained from habituation to one stimulus, followed by a test with a second, ought to parallel the pattern of results obtained from habituation to the second stimulus followed by a test with the first. (b) Dishabituation may require a minimal amount of habituation initially (Lasky, 1980), or it may depend on the terminal level of habituation performance infants reach (Caron, Caron, Minichiello, Weiss, & Friedman, 1977). If an infant meets the habituation criterion by chance, the infant's true level of looking is actually higher than the criterion, and so, on account of regression to the mean, the baby's dishabituation looking on postcriterion trials would be artifactually high. To guard against such an eventuality, trials that continue presentation of the habituation stimulus can be run after criterion is reached, and they may be statistically compared with change trials (see the above discussion and Bertenthal et al., 1983). (c) The pattern of discrimination infants show may be related to their prior pattern of habituation. McCall et al. (1973) suggested that "nonhabituators" give pattern 6A to equivalent stimulus changes, whereas "habituators" give pattern 6D. DeLoache (1976) found that babies who habituate to a common level, independent of whether they do so quickly or slowly (in terms of trials to criterion), recover looking to a novel stimulus equivalently, and data from Bornstein and Benasich (1983) confirm this. McCall (1979b) further argued that, even if babies habituate to a common level, those who spend a longer time studying the standard should dishabituate more to a novel stimulus than those who study the standard less. Data from Bornstein and Benasich (1983) show that amount of dishabituation to a novel stimulus is unrelated to accumulated study time—all babies who habituate to a criterion, no matter how long they take, recover essentially equally. (Interestingly, however, babies who habituate reliably—that is produce the same habituation pattern between two sessions—recover more than babies who are unreliable.) However infants form internal or mental representations based on habituation, it seems that, once a representation is formed, it is useful in decision making and determinative of subsequent exploratory behavior. (d) It could be that recovery assessed immediately after habituation conforms to the montonic pattern, but that recovery assessed after some retention interval is curvilinear (Zelazo et al., 1973).

Overall, the distinctiveness of these several discrimination patterns is itself manifestly precarious, often turning on the relative position of a single datum in the test series. As a consequence, stable, low-variance data are requisite (though an unhappy requirement) of babies who participate. Beyond these several considerations, special design factors must also be taken in account in divining among different patterns of results: Suppose, for example, that 3-

month-olds failed to dishabituate to a stimulus similar to the habituation stimulus (showing pattern 6B), while 6-month-olds dishabituated (6C). The difference between groups may reside in a genuine growth of discrimination capacity; alternatively, babies in the two age groups may discriminate equally but differ in average response level. To obviate this alternative requires that the habituation criterion be set above a "floor" in infant responsivity (see Rubel & Rosenthal, 1975).

Finally, the conservative Type II error, concluding that no discrimination exists where it may, is a danger in infant studies that use the habituation-test design. After all, in this paradigm a recovery in attention is sought to a novel stimulus only after a period of purposeful suppression of the infant's general attention.

Clearly, these divergent patterns of results can divulge a great deal about the infant's eye (and mind): They index sensory capacity as well as reveal what there is to know about infants' internal representations of information in the world. For example, results of Cohen et al. (1971), cited above, indicate that, during inspection of a color-form, infants must be storing information about both color *and* form separately. By probing with different stimuli in the test, investigators may define the exactness of infants' mental models and the latitude of those models. The second application of habituation sheds more light on this specific issue.

CATEGORIZATION

Human beings frequently treat discriminably different properties, objects, or events in the environment as effectively similar; that is, we "categorize" (e.g., Smith & Medin, 1981). Many kinds of categories have been defined and distinguished; at least two kinds have been identified and studied in infants using habituation. They are *referent equivalence* and *perceptual equivalence* categories (Bornstein, 1984). Referent categories reflect our treating as similar different manifestations of one original stimulus, as when we perceive an object as the same despite variations in its apparent shape or size, in whether it is presented in two or three dimensions, or in the modality in which it is presented. Perceptual equivalence categories reflect our similar treatment of different physical stimuli that give rise to different perceptual appearances, as when we generalize over distinct wavelengths to categorize hues, and over different voice-onset times to categorize phonemes. Both kinds of categorization reflect a many-to-one reduction characteristic in perception.

Students of infancy have used two kinds of habituation paradigms to assess the early emergence of these categorization abilities; using each, the experimenter tests an a priori hypothesis of category structure, one that is usually founded in adult perception. In the habituation-test approach, infants are first habituated with one stimulus, and in within-subjects designs they are subsequently tested with the same stimulus, with another stimulus presumed to come from the same category, and with a third stimulus presumed to come from a different category; in between-subjects designs, some infants are tested with a new stimulus from the same category, and they are compared with others tested with a new stimulus from a different category. In the differential approach, the habituation behavior of infants who see instances of different categories intermixed over trials is compared with the behavior of infants who see one or several instances of the same category repeatedly. (Both paradigms require experimental attention to physical as well as psychological differences among category members in stimulus selection.) The more common habituation-test paradigm relies on infants' generalization of habituation to same-category stimuli and dishabituation to between-category stimuli to give evidence of categorization. The less common differential habituation paradigm assesses infants' more rapid, efficient, and complete habituation to within- vs. between-category variation.

Referent Equivalence Categories

In this category type, the source or referent physical stimulus is a constant, phenomenal manifestations of it vary, but infants treat the different appearances of the stimulus as equivalent. There are at least three kinds of referent equivalence categorization. In one, babies categorize different perspectives of the same stimulus as similar, as in shape or size constancy. Two examples: McGurk (1972) found that babies as young as 3 months who were habituated to different orientations of a single stick figure later generalized habituation to a novel orientation of the same figure; likewise, Fagan (1979) found that 5- to 7-month-old babies who were familiarized with different poses of a face afterward generalized habituation to a novel pose of the same face. In the second kind of referent equivalence, babies categorize as similar different representations of the same object perceived in different numbers of dimensions. Two examples: Dirks and Gibson (1977) found that 5-month-olds who were habituated to a three-dimensional live face later treated a two-dimensional photographic slide of the same face as similar; in the same vein, Rose (1977) found that 6-month-olds who were familiarized with three-dimensional geometric objects later treated pictures of the same objects as similar. In the third kind of referent equivalence, babies categorize information about single properties or objects that comes from different sensory modalities. Two examples: Lewkowicz and Turkewitz (1980) found that newborns who had habituated heart-rate deceleration to the repetition of a light absolutely matched deceleration at the presentation of an equally intense noise; similarly, Rose, Gottfried, and Bridger (1981) found that 6-month-olds looked less at a shape with which they had had extended tactual experience. In every test of referent equivalence, babies discriminated a novel stimulus.

Perceptual Equivalence Categories

Perceptual equivalence categorization taps the infant's similar treatment of physically different, perceptually discriminable stimuli, usually drawn from different points along a single physical dimension. Hues in vision and stop-consonant phonemes in speech are examples. For instance, Bornstein, Kessen, and Weiskopf (1976) examined whether infants' perceptions of physical variation in wavelength were random or organized into correlate categories of hue as is perception in adults. Their Study 1 used a habituation-test design. Four-month-olds were divided into three kinds of groups—boundary groups, category groups, and controls—each of which habituated to a different spectral light. Following habituation, babies in boundary and category groups were probed for their recognition of the familiar habituation light and for their response to two new spectral lights that were equally displaced in physical terms (nanometers) from the habituation light. For the boundary groups, the new test lights were selected so that one was from the same adult hue category as the habituation light and the other was from a different, adjacent hue category (e.g., if the habituation stimulus was "blue", one of the test stimuli was another "blue" and one was "green"). For the category groups, the two new test lights were selected from the same adult hue category as the habituation light. Babies in the boundary groups generalized habituation to a new wavelength from the same adult hue category as the habituation wavelength, and they dishabituated to a new wavelength from a different adult hue category (like Pattern B in Figure 6). Babies in category groups generalized habituation to both new test wavelengths. Babies in a control group who were shown just the habituation wavelength in the test maintained a low level of looking. Study 2 showed converging results by the differential habituation method: Babies shown a random alternation of two wavelengths selected from different adult hue categories habituated more slowly than babies shown a random alternation of two wavelengths selected from the same category, or babies in a control group who were shown only one wavelength repeatedly. Babies in the two latter groups habituated similarly. This categorization of wavelength notwithstanding, infants can be shown to discriminate among (at least some) wavelengths they group together: For example, babies habituate faster to a single wavelength in a hue category than they do to a larger variety of wavelengths in the same category (Bornstein, 1981b). Thus, differential habituation can be used to assess perceptual discrimination or categorization, depending on the stimuli employed.

Perceptual categories are found in audition as well as in vision. For example, Eimas (e.g., Eimas, 1975; Eimas, Siqueland, Jusczyk, & Vigorito, 1971) reasoned that a phenomenon so ubiquitous and important among humans as phoneme categorization may have biological foundations. Using a habituation-test procedure with frequency of high-amplitude sucking as the dependent measure, Eimas tested perception of the boundary between adult categories of voiced and voiceless bilabial stop-consonant phonemes in three groups of babies. One group tested a between-category discrimination (/b/-/p/); a second group tested a within-category discrimination (/b/-/b'/); a third group experienced no change at "test" (/b/-/b/). The results showed clear between-category discrimination, as well as clear within-category grouping. Habituation of high-amplitude sucking has been used to replicate these findings with synthetic and with natural speech stimuli, and to extend them to other voicing contrasts (e.g., /d/-/t/), as well as to other speech contrasts, like place of articulation (e.g., /d/-/g/), liquids (e.g., /r/-/l/), etc. (see Jusczyk, this volume). Furthermore, this habituation technique has been applied in diverse field investigations showing that infants in a variety of language communities, from Guatemalan Spanish (Lasky, Syrdal-Lasky, & Klein, 1975) to Kenyan Kikuyu (Streeter, 1976), perceive speech sounds in an adultlike, categorical manner.

Because essentially the same perceptual categories may be found in human infants from widely different societies, and because various animal species identify wavelength and voice-onset time differences in categorical (if species-specific) ways (Bornstein, 1979a, 1981a), there is well-founded speculation that perceptual categories may reflect underlying native psychophysiological function. That is, nonmonotonic discriminability of wavelength (e.g., Bornstein & Korda, 1984; A. A. Wright, 1972; W. D. Wright, 1947) or of formant relations (e.g., Hanson, 1977; Kuhl, 1979, 1981; Pisoni & Tash, 1974) which characterizes the sensory apparatus is thought to function in ways that have profound consequences for the origins of perceptual organization in infancy. These sensory-perceptual functions have proved accessible to investigation via habituation.

During habituation infants internalize information about a stimulus, perhaps in terms of a mental representation. When they generalize habituation to different manifestations of that stimulus, or to different stimuli that share some quality—even though they can discriminate the stimuli—infants give evidence that they categorize. One interpretation of categorizing is that during habituation infants acquire exact physical information about a stimulus and retain it in some form of internal representation, but subsequently adopt relatively liberal criteria in judging the similarity of new stimuli to that representation. An alternative interpretation is that infants lose exact physical information about a stimulus during habituation, and recode and retain only information about stimulus class. Which interpretation holds, and under what conditions, is not known. One way to gather information on this question would be to probe for the latitude of the representation during the course of habituation. That some internal or mental representation of a stimulus must be formed in habituation, and is central in terms of nervous system function, is known, however; studies of cross-modal transfer (referent equivalence) confirm that different modalities have equivalent and ready access to that representation.

Categorization approached via habituation relies partially on results of no difference, and, although obvious difficulties undermine such conclusions, categorization experiments typically include proper (e.g., no-change) controls or ancillary demonstrations of within-category discrimination. In this way, habituation procedures can be used to tap infants' similarity judgments of perceptually discriminable stimuli, and they help to delineate infants' internal representations of similarity. This application of habituation has revealed that there are facets of the infant's world view that are highly organized perceptually. The habituation paradigm has carried us far away from the opinion of the infant as foundering amidst the hue and cry of Jamesian confusion.

MEMORY

136.55

Since Ebbinghaus (1885/1964) and the beginnings of an experimental psychology of memory, memory itself has frequently been identified with verbal recoding—even when nonverbal materials are used (e.g., Glanzer & Clark, 1962). However, it is well recognized that perception and coding of nonverbal stimuli and events produce changes in the nervous system, creating memory traces. More pertinently, memory in infancy, such as is involved in object or person recognition, must reflect the *preverbal* child's encoding, processing, retention, and retrieval of information about physical properties, objects, or events in the world. If an infant looks at a stimulus the first time you show it but looks at it less the fifteenth time, the infant's loss of interest—barring artifact—strongly suggests stimulus recognition. On this basis, the process of habituation has itself been conceived by many theorists to involve memory. Students of infancy have picked up this lead; indeed, in the hands of infancy researchers, the habituation paradigm has proven to be a very versatile and powerful tool with which to investigate the ontogeny of memory.

With habituation, it is possible, first, to track the rate of infants' encoding of a stimulus; presumably, faster habituation is an index of quicker encoding. Second, it is possible to monitor the course of mental construction, since one can "probe" during habituation to assess the ongoing development or consolidation of memory structures. By habituating infants and testing them immediately afterwards with the same stimulus, it is possible, third, to study short-term recognition memory, as it is possible, fourth, to institute a delay between habituation and test to distinguish short-term from long-term recognition memory. In these two cases, a low level of looking on re-test is interpreted as "recognition," whereas recovery of looking is interpreted as "forgetting." (The possibility that infants could display renewed interest in an item which they in fact remember tends, however, to detract from the power of this design.) Similarly, a "savings method" that compares habituation at one time with later re-habituation can be used to assess short- or long-term retention capacity in infancy. Using habituation, the ontogeny of recognition memory is amenable to study, since all of the common parameters of memory studies, including age, stimulus, study time, and interference (from the same dimension as the habituation stimulus or from a different dimension), can be manipulated in this design and their effects on infant memory assayed.

The quality of infant recognition memory, as measured by habituation, varies widely and prominently with stimulus, procedure, and individual differences among infants. For example, stimulus prototypes may possess a mnemonic advantage. The internal structure of hue categories includes some colors that are prototypical of the hue and others that are less representative (i.e., there are purer blues, and there are blues alloyed with red or with green). Prototypical, so-called "focal," colors are well known to be psychologically special: Adults (from various societies) identify, learn, name, and classify them faster and more efficiently than nonfocal ones (e.g., Berlin & Kay, 1969; Bornstein & Monroe, 1980; Rosch, 1978). The same colors are special, too, early in life: Four-month-olds habituate to focal colors faster than to nonfocal colors; that is, babies achieve the same fixed criterion of habituation more quickly when they are shown focal blue or red than when they are shown nonfocal blue-green or yellow-red. Later, after a delay when their memory for color is retested, babies give evidence that they recognize focal colors, whereas they give evidence that they forget nonfocal ones (Bornstein, 1981a). Similar results obtain with faces abstracted to be prototypical of a set (Strauss, 1979).

Habituation has been used successfully to assess encoding capacity in young infants. Lasky and Spiro (1980) presented groups of 5-month-olds visual patterns for 100 msec, followed by a 100-msec pattern-masker at intervals of 0, 250, 500, and 2000 msec after the offset of the target stimulus. The target-masker pair was repeated 45 times, and infants were then shown the habituation target paired with a new stimulus in a novelty test. Only the infants in the 2000-msec condition dishabituated, suggesting that stimulus encoding is quite slow at 5 months. In testing infant memory for different stimuli via habituation, some investigators have detected effects of retroactive interference (e.g., DeLoache, 1976; Pancratz & Cohen, 1970), whereas others have not (e.g., Caron & Caron, 1969; Martin, 1975). The emergence of these effects may depend on infants' processing and storing intervening stimulation (Cohen & Gelber, 1975), or on the similarity between interference and target materials (Fagan, 1971, 1973).

Age also affects infant recognition memory tested with habituation. Martin (1975) retested 2-, 3.5-, and 5-month-olds 1.5 minutes and 24 hours after habituation to a simple geometric pattern; both older groups remembered at both delay intervals, while the youngest infants did not. Earlier, McCall et al. (1973) conducted a study that separated the effects of infant age on encoding *versus* retrieval processes; studying habituation and recognition in infants 3 and 4.5 months of age, McCall found age differences in habituation but not in recovery. Younger babies habituated more slowly than older babies, but both groups recognized the habituation stimulus equivalently. From this pattern of results, McCall concluded that age may differentially affect encoding processes more than retrieval.

Habituation raises many questions about infant memory, both small—Is the trial of maximal looking in habituation the trial of maximal encoding?—and large—How does the picture of infant memory we have distilled from habituation studies square with the phenomenon of infantile amnesia? Moreover, habituation has limitations as an assessment of memory. For example, habituation can only be used to study recognition. Further, in habituation a novelty response to a new stimulus relative to the habituation stimulus is often the central relation that implies recognition of the habituation stimulus; however, equivalent response to the habituation and novel stimuli, or recovery to the habituation stimulus, does not necessarily indicate forgetting. As a consequence, supplementary techniques to assess infant memory are in order (e.g., Sophian, 1980).

Quite clearly, we are only at the beginning of an understanding of infant memory—even of the few aspects reviewed here. Human infants do remember (in the absence of an ability to verbalize), and they do forget. Habituation has to be awarded much of the credit for as much understanding of the dawn of memory as we possess, for this technique has begun to reveal what infants remember and how well they do it. Through simple manipulations of the habituation design, it has become possible for the first time to investigate many aspects of early development of the recognition-memory system in human beings. It has also become possible to begin an assault on how the ontogeny of memory articulates with the early development of cognition.

CONCEPT FORMATION

136.92

Clearly, there are many kinds of categories. Some categories, such as those discussed earlier, are made up of members that relate to a single original referent or share a particular perceptible quality. Other categories represent perceptually unrelated groupings that arise from convention or are learned as linguistic or cultural constructs. These categories are often called concepts. Habituation has found further use in assessing the earliest abilities of children to acquire and to use such concepts.

In studies of detection and discrimination, categorization, and recognition memory in infancy, habituation is typically restricted to a single stimulus of which, we have seen, infants are believed to construct some internal or mental representation. However, it is possible to assess whether infants will habituate to physically and phenomenally different, though conceptually-related, stimuli, in the sense that they develop an overarching concept that connects those stimuli to one another. Psychological opinion about concept formation has been summarized succinctly and defined operationally by Bourne (1966, p. 1): "...a concept exists whenever two or more distinguishable objects or events have been grouped or classified together and set apart from other objects on the basis of some common feature or property characteristic of each." Translating this definition into terms of the habituation paradigm for infants is relatively straightforward: The definition requires, first, demonstration in one context that properties, objects, or events in a set are discriminable to infants; and, second, demonstration in another context that the same set of discriminable stimuli may be grouped or classified together. We have already reviewed how discrimination might be assessed. To demonstrate concept formation and use in practice, infants are presented with several instances of the (presumed) concept until they achieve an habituation criterion; they are then tested with old and new instances of the "familiar" concept and with at least one instance of a "new" concept. Maintaining habituation to the familiar instance, generalizing habituation to new instances of the familiar concept, and dishabituating to instances of a new concept together constitute evidence for concept formation and use in infants.

Several investigators have now documented acquisition and use of a variety of concepts by human infants in the first year of life. Ross (1980), for example, investigated 12-month-olds' groupings of perceptually-related and conventionally-related objects. Ross habituated infants with multiple variations of either *M*s or *O*s or variations of either food or furniture over successive trials of fixed duration; she reasoned that these two sets of stimuli differed in level of conceptual interrelatedness. Ross then presented the children with a choice between a previously unseen member of the familiar category and a new instance of the other (novel) category. In the choice test, infants consistently looked at and reached for novel category stimuli in preference to "familiar" *M*s and *O*s or "familiar" food and furniture. These test results support the conclusion that infants abstracted perceptual similarities as well as conceptual linkages among members of the two habituation sets. (A similar study in somewhat older infants is Faulkender, Wright, & Waldron, 1974.) Bornstein (1979b), Schwartz and Day (1979), Strauss and Curtis (1981), Milewski (1979), Cohen and Strauss (1979), Caron and Caron (1981), and Caron, Caron, and Myers (1982) have used the same multiple-habituation paradigm to investigate, respectively, chromaticity, angularity, numerosity, relational coding, and invariance of gender and facial expression in young babies. In brief, multiple habituation has proven to be a unique tool with which to assess conceptual ability in young infants.

As with any rich but new technique, many aspects of conceptual habituation have not yet been examined. For example, how does variation among habituation stimuli instruct a baby about a concept? Frequently, with adults, experience with only two or three instances of a category will provoke disjunctive judgments; many instances are usually required before adults engage in category abstraction. Further, what amount of experience with, say, examples of dogs and cats is required to elicit the concept "dog or cat," and what amount of experience or what variety of experience is required to elicit the higher-order concept "pet"?

The data on conceptual ability also highlight an important methodological point in habituation. Studies of concept acquisition indicate that the interpretation of habituation and test results depends in large measure on the nature of stimulus variation in habituation as well as variation among test alternatives. Experiments by Fagan (1976) and by Cohen and Strauss (1979) serve to illustrate this point. Fagan (1976) found that 7-month-old infants who were familiarized with a face discriminated a different face in preference to the original in a test that followed habituation, but those who were familiarized with one male face discriminated a female face in preference to yet a different male face; further, infants who were familiarized with one pose of a face discriminated another pose of the same face in preference to the original pose, but those were familiarized with one pose of a face discriminated another face in preference to a different pose of the original face. Cohen and Strauss (1976) habituated groups of 7.5-month-olds to a single face in a single orientation, to a single face in multiple orientations, and to multiple faces in multiple orientations, and they then tested each group with a familiar face in a novel orientation and with a novel face in a novel orientation. Babies in the first group discriminated both test stimuli; those in the second group discriminated the novel face but generalized to the familiar face; and those in the third group generalized to both familiar and novel faces. Considering all conditions in the two experiments, babies showed sensitivity to a particular face, to male qualities of a face, to a particular pose, and to generalized poses. Clearly, the answer one obtains from infants depends on the habituation question one poses: Infant behavior in the habituation paradigm reflects both variation in familiarization and available test alternatives.

With seemingly little experience, human infants can acquire and use (some) new concepts. Beyond the referent and perceptual equivalence categories they possess, this ability places the young infant across the threshold of simple learning. No doubt, natural perceptual categories are related to learned conceptual ones (Bornstein, 1981a, 1984; Caron & Caron, 1981). Together, these capacities for perceptual and conceptual organization help the child go beyond elementary units of sensing to perceiving with understanding. What habituation performance per se may indicate about the infant's mental stature or general ability to learn constitutes the final entry in this habituation taxonomy.

INDIVIDUAL DIFFERENCES IN COGNITION

Widespread use of the habituation technique has rendered basic research questions in infancy increasingly tractable, and largely on its account, in just 20 years our understanding of the perceptual and cognitive abilities of infants —including detection and discrimination, categorization, memory, and concept formation—has grown exponentially. Most habituation studies have advanced in these areas by concentrating on substantive issues and by employing groups of babies rather than individuals. But visual attending implies the beginning of information processing, and habituation of attending—and, by inference, habituation of internal processes of attention—raises questions about the relationship between habituation and cognition as well as about individual differences in habituation, their stability, and their coordination with thinking (e.g., Furby, 1974). Specifically, do some infants process stimulus information more quickly, efficiently, or completely than do others? How is habituation performance distributed in the infant population? Does habituation performance inform about concurrent perceptual or cognitive differences among infants? Is infant habituation performance related predictively to childhood cognitive capacities? What are the origins of individual differences in habituation performance? This section of the taxonomy addresses these questions seriatim.

How do infants differ in habituation performance? We have already seen that infants differ among themselves quantitatively as well as qualitatively in their habituation performance. DeLoache (1976), Pêcheux and Lécuyer (1983), Bornstein and Benasich (1983), and Bornstein and Ruddy (1984) have all found that, ceteris paribus, infants distribute themselves in terms of the numbers of trials (or looks) they require to achieve a preset habituation criterion. Some infants habituate immediately, some in just a few trials, while others take substantially more (e.g., Figure 3). The same distribution holds true for other dependent measures, such as accumulated looking time to criterion (Bornstein & Benasich, 1983). Of course, different stimuli can be expected to produce different distributions: For example, 5-month-olds who habituate to a single face wearing a single expression produce a distribution of trials-to-criterion that is unimodal and skewed to the right, whereas comparable 5-month-olds who habituate to multiple expressions on a single face produce a more normal distribution (Bornstein & Benasich, 1983).

If habituation were to proceed from a given starting point, babies could go only down, up and then down, or up-down-etc. or down-up-etc. Therefore, logically, gross patterns of habituation may vary only very little. Indeed, there appear to be only these three main qualitative patterns of habituation in infants. Beyond their "short lookers," McCall and Kagan (1970) identified "rapid habituators," "slow habituators," and an idiosyncratic type (Figure 4) among babies shown a triad of realistic stimuli; and Bornstein and Benasich (1983) identified parallel "exponential decrease," "increase-decrease," and "fluctuating" patterns of habituators (Figure 5) among babies shown a single face. Data in the latter study show that exponential-decrease babies, who constituted a majority of the sample, took approximately half as many trials and half as much exposure to the stimulus to habituate as did increase-decrease or fluctuating babies. Of course, the population of infants showing any given pattern may vary greatly, depending on the age of the infants, their health status, etc.

Is habituation performance related to perceptual discrimination capacity? An early individual-differences view posited that infants who habituate more quickly, efficiently, or completely ought afterward to show more robust discrimination of novelty; in this formulation, speed of memory trace construction, for example, was thought to predict fidelity and durability of memory. Some early studies seemed to support such an hypothesis (e.g., McCall & Kagan, 1970; McCall & Melson, 1969; Miller, 1972). However, aspects of the fixed-trials method used in those studies disallowed a fair test of the hypothesis. To wit: The fixed-trials procedure does not always permit or guarantee all babies equal study time, and, if such differentials exist, babies can hardly be

expected to remember equivalently. When infants are allowed to reach the
same habituation criterion, they show equivalent discrimination of novelty independently of how, how quickly, or how much exposure to the stimulus they
took to habituate (Bornstein & Benasich, 1983; DeLoache, 1976; McCall et al.,
1973). As the verbal learning literature had clarified years ago, speed of learning does not predict retention in any simple way (Underwood, 1954).

Is habituation in infants related to any indexes of concurrent cognitive competence? Defining "cognitive" function in infancy presents its own problems;
nevertheless, habituation performance seems only to be a marginal concurrent
correlate of performance that is accepted to be cognitive in early infancy; it
does show stronger co-relation with more standard measures of cognitive performance in early childhood. On the one hand, Ruddy and Bornstein (1982)
found no correlation between habituation performance of 4-month-olds and
their scores on the Bayley Scales of Infant Development (Bayley, 1969), and
Greenberg, O'Donnell, and Crawford (1973) found only a loose association
between habituation and preference for complexity. Sometimes outcomes are
counterintuitive: Pêcheux and Lécuyer (1983) found that slow habituators
among 4-month-olds stayed in an exploration situation for a relatively longer
time and also explored a new toy for a longer time than did fast habituators.
Still other investigators, looking at habituation and play behavior later in the
first year, have found weak support for a positive linkage between the two
(e.g., Fenson et al., 1974; Johnson & Brody, 1977). On the other hand, Riksen-
Walraven (1978) found that habituation rate correlated significantly with exploratory play in 9-month-olds; Lewis et al. (1969) found significantly greater
habituation in 44-month-olds who solved a difficult two-choice discrimination-
learning task than in children who failed; and Miller, Spiridigliozzi, Ryan,
Callan, and McLaughlin (1980) found that 51-month-olds who habituated
more performed significantly better on oddity identification, picture matching, and block configuration tasks than did children who habituated less. In
brief, habituation is not related to standardized "intelligence" test scores in
young infants, but is related to cognitive performance in older infants and in
young children. Ruddy and Bornstein (1982) hypothesized that the absence of
any early association may reflect the fact that standardized test items for younger
infants draw heavily on motor performance which is unrelated to the more
purely cognitive assessment of habituation.[5]

Is habituation performance in early infancy predictive of cognitive performance later in childhood? Standardized tests of infants, such as the Bayley
Scales, have themselves shown little internal predictive validity (McCall, 1979b),
and on this basis most investigators have concluded either that infants develop
unpredictably during their first year or that there is no "general intelligence"
factor applicable across the life span. It is possible, however, that the motor
requirements that dominate standardized tests of younger infants obscure

---

[5] For example, the Bayley Psychomotor Development Index (PDI) and Mental Development Index (MDI) correlate +.70 at 4 months; however, they correlate only +.24 at 12 months.

otherwise stable underlying cognitive competences. Habituation, which indexes information processing and is relatively free of motor requirements, shows some promise as an infant cognitive predictor. Lewis et al. (1969, p. 29), for example, reported that children's habituation performance at 1 year correlated positively with their Stanford-Binet IQ performance at 4 years. Miller and her co-workers (e.g., Miller et al., 1979; Miller, Ryan, Short, Reis, McGuire, & Culler, 1977; Miller, Sinnott, Short, & Hains, 1976; Miller et al., 1980) were among the first to investigate the predictive validity of habituation in infants in the first half-year of life for childhood cognitive functioning. She found several significant correlations between the rank orderings of 2- to 4-month-old infants on the standard amount measure of habituation (Equation 1) and later 15-, 27-, 39-, and 51-month cognitive measures of object-concept performance, operational causality, language comprehension and production, paired-associate memory, and visual discrimination. Bornstein and Ruddy (1984; Ruddy & Bornstein, 1982) conducted similar prospective studies of habituation, cognitive development, and language acquisition. In our research, both rate and amount measures of habituation at 4 months predicted speaking vocabulary size (e.g., .52 for amount) and Bayley Scale score (e.g., .46 for amount) at 12 months, and WPPSI scores for children about 4 years of age (e.g., .54 for amount). Across these different studies, habituation performance in early infancy by itself predicts between 10% and 30% of the variance in childhood cognitive competences.

Habituation was not the only predictor of cognitive differences among the babies in the Bornstein and Ruddy studies, however. Mothers who encouraged their 4-month-olds' attention more to properties, objects, or events in the environment later had 1-year-olds who possessed larger vocabularies (.55) and who tended to score higher on standardized infant tests (.27), and still later had 4-year-olds who performed better on the Wechsler series (.51). Statistical regression techniques showed that infant habituation and maternal encouragement contributed independently to eventual child cognitive performance. Thus, infants' abilities as well as their intellectual and social experiences clearly influence cognitive development.

These positive predictive relationships between infant habituation and child cognitive competence are representative of a burgeoning literature; however, the area is so new that investigators have not yet agreed upon significant aspects of experimental design, including stimulus selection, dependent measures, or the appropriateness of different predictive correlates. Measures of amount of habituation predominate, but rate, accumulated looking to criterion, or habituation pattern may be more sensitive indexes. Understanding the effects of the stimulus is equally problematical. In general, a simple stimulus (e.g., a grating) might be expected to engender rapid, efficient, or complete habituation, while a complex stimulus (e.g., a naturalistic scene) might be expected to inhibit habituation (e.g., Caron & Caron, 1969). Among babies or across ages, however, a single stimulus complexity-habituation relation cannot be guaranteed: Some babies might get all of the information from a simple stimulus upon inspection and habituate quickly, but habituate slowly to a complex stimulus which demands more processing and time; other babies might take longer to habituate to a simple stimulus and turn away from a complex stimulus sooner, "tuning out" overload rather than habituating to it.

Which mental abilities might habituation best predict? This is an open question. Infant habituation to a single stimulus might be conceptually akin to a simple memory task, while habituation to multiple stimuli and the abstraction of invariance which ensues might be conceptually like (and hence may be predictive of) semantic development (for an elaboration of this argument, see Caron & Caron, 1981). Parametric experiments on stimulus selection, choice of dependent measures, and the appropriateness of different predictive correlates are needed to clarify these associations.

What are the origins of individual differences in habituation? The significance of this question increases if habituation is a concurrent or a predictive measure of cognitive competence in infancy. Data that bear directly on the issue do not yet exist; however, bits that can be pieced together suggest an intriguing and richly textured story. Consider the following. (a) Newborns who do habituate show individual differences (Field et al., 1982; Friedman, 1975; Siqueland, 1981). (b) Habituation performance of Down's syndrome babies lags behind that of normals (Barnet et al., 1974; Cohen, 1981). (c) Obstetrical medication inhibits habituation soon after birth, and continues to do so months into postnatal life (Brackbill, 1979). (d) Newborn preterms do not typically habituate where, in matched experiments, at least some term neonates under some circumstances do (Field, Dempsey, Hatch, Ting, & Clifton, 1979); older preterm infants habituate the same as term infants matched for conceptional age (Caron & Caron, 1981; Sigman & Parmelee, 1974). (e) Three-month-old infants who had perfect Apgar scores at birth habituate more efficiently than matched normal infants who had less than perfect Apgars at birth (Lewis, Bartels, Campbell, & Goldberg, 1967). (f) Well-nourished 1-year-olds habituate more efficiently than do their malnourished confrères (Lester, 1975). (g) The distributions of trials-to-criterion between 4-month-old singletons and twins do not statistically differ (Figure 3); however, twins are deprived in their home didactic experiences relative to singletons. For example, at 4 months, mothers of twins are encouraging their babies' attention to properties, objects, and events in the environment less than half as often on average as mothers of singletons are encouraging their babies, where encouraging attention at 4 months predicts later cognitive and linguistic development (Bornstein & Ruddy, 1984). (h) Exponential habituation among 4-month-olds (classified by slightly modified habituation criteria of Bornstein & Benasich, Figure 5) is statistically associated with vocalizing and encouraging attention in mothers (Tamis, personal communication, 23 Nov. 1983). (i) Habituation amount in 3-month-olds is ordered with several maternal activities, including touching and looking, and especially with activities indicative of maternal contingent responsivity to infant vocalization and crying (Lewis & Goldberg, 1969b). (j) Habituation rate is related to some kinds of maternal stimulation at 9 months, and mothers who participated in a program to stimulate their infants between 9 and 12 months had 12-month-olds who habituated more quickly than unstimulated babies (Riksen-Walraven, 1978). (k) Finally, parental education has been tentatively associated with habituation performance by some (Lewis et al., 1969; McCall, 1972, cited in McCall et al., 1973), but not others (McCall, 1979a); unfortunately, this measure confounds nature and nurture. In overview, these data sets indicate that both biological factors and postnatal experience play important roles in determining habituation performance in infancy.

Habituation performance in early life portends continuity with some later cognitive competences. Perhaps, one day, habituation will find additional value in indexing infant cognitive functioning, in assessing cognitive deficits (actual or potential) in infants, and in evaluating infant interventions. Before that time, however, critical data on several practical aspects of habituation will have to be garnered. For example, the short-term reliability of habituation will have to be more firmly established, the determinants of habituation will have to be clarified, and interrelations of habituation with other information-processing capacities in infants will have to be determined.

HABITUATION: A GENERAL MODEL WITH SOME SPECIFIC UNKNOWNS

The essence of habituation of visual attending and, by implication, of visual attention in human infants seems as follows. On continuous or repeated presentation of a stimulus, the infant immediately or eventually declines in looking from his or her expressed initial level of interest. That is the observed behavior. Much more is inferred: The decline is believed to reflect reciprocal processes consisting of internal or mental construction and comparison—perhaps spiritually akin to Piagetian assimilation-accommodation. *Constructor* processes are thought to consist of the infant's encoding and storage of information about a stimulus toward the development of a neural trace, memory model, or schema increasingly faithful to that stimulus. Whether the infant's constructor is active or passive is unknown; whether constructor processes begin at the introduction of the stimulus or later, and whether its processes are incremental or all-or-none (independent of when they actually begin), are unknown; further, whether the mental representation in the preverbal infant is imaginal, symbolic, or propositional is also unknown. In the complementary set of *comparator* processes, successive incoming stimulation is thought to be judged against the habituation representation. To the extent that new stimulation and internal representation do not match, looking is maintained, presumably exciting the constructor toward a more faithful or more articulated representation. If stimulation and representation match, looking is inhibited. How the comparator "knows" that the habituation stimulus differs from the representation, or that the representation is still immature, is unknown; further, why looking stops, whether on account of economy of energy expenditure or on account of the desire for additional stimulus seeking on the part of the organism, is also not known. Perhaps habituation is "noumenal"—an unknown, unknowable, yet logically necessary mental operation.

Miller, Galanter, and Pribram (1960) wrestled with a larger, but conceptually similar, problem of the translation of image into behavior. Their theorizing materialized in the construction of a unit of analysis, the TOTE, organized to control behavior relative to an internal representation (Figure 7). It may be that Test-Operate-Text-Exit, their "incongruity-sensitive mechanism" describing feedback loops in the nervous system that guide future action, is functionally appropriate for habituation as well.

This general summary jibes with Sokolov's (1958/1963, 1969) neurological interpretation of habituation. Briefly, Sokolov theorized that organisms initially orient to a new stimulus. With stimulus repetition, a neuronal model, specifically a cortical representation, of the stimulus is constructed. That model continuously increases in fidelity, and in maturity it preserves several kinds of information about the stimulus, including intensity, quality, and duration. Subsequent stimulation presented to the organism is compared in memory with this neuronal model. Matches with it fail to elicit or actually inhibit orienting; mismatches elicit orienting. Thus, habituation of the response system reflects a lack of discrepancy between current stimulation and memory based on experience; significantly, novelty reevokes orienting.

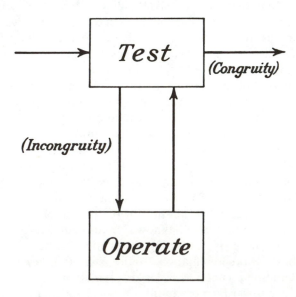

Figure 7. The TOTE unit. (After Miller, Galanter, & Pribram, 1960. Reprinted by permission.)

Several investigators have theoretically modelled habituation of visual attending in human infants. Most prominent among them are Lewis (et al., 1969), McCall (1971), Cohen (1973), Jeffrey (1976), and Olson (1976); summaries and comparisons of their different viewpoints may be found in Cohen and Gelber (1975) and in Lewis and Baldini (1979). Each basically follows Sokolov, although each makes valuable revisions, distinctions, and advances on his original theoretical position. For example, some investigators have argued that the neural traces Sokolov proposed could not copy external stimulation exactly, but rather that memory traces that develop in habituation must alternatively reflect looser active constructions that integrate multiple perspectives of external experience. Otherwise, conceptual habituation would be barred. Further, if Sokolov's model were strictly to apply, very familiar stimuli, like a mother's face, ought to lose their attraction for infants; patently, they do not.

A better theoretical understanding of habituation in infants will require answers to several questions beyond those raised already. Some questions which ought to attract the attention of researchers in the future concern the *processes of habituation*. For instance, it is mysterious why infants commonly turn away from the stimulus prior to the point at which they habituate and quit the stimulus entirely. The habituation decline in infants has not yet been accurately modelled, even though large data sets have been analyzed in an attempt to distinguish the popular linear and exponential formulations—indeed, only a proportion of infants actually shows the smooth decline widely presumed to typify habituation (44% in McCall, 1979a, and approximately 50% in Bornstein & Benasich, 1983). Processing mechanisms that characterize different styles of habituation also merit investigation. The usual definition of habituation as stimulus selective must be expanded: Habituation actually accommodates generalization over wide stimulus variation. In turn, the fact that infants categorize casts doubt on any simple match-mismatch basis of habituation. Finally, the common conception of habituation as unitary must be abandoned: Diverse stimulus-response conjunctions show nonparallel courses of habituation, and the diversity of habituation functions itself calls into question the possibility of a single underlying mediating mechanism. Clearly, there are "habituations" of many kinds.

Other questions that ought to provoke future research concern the *nature of habituation*. Studies of habituation are implicitly addressed to the subject matter of internal processes, like attention, but only have observable behaviors, like duration of looking, to go on. So, clarification of the relationships between visual scanning and information processing, such as discrimination, in infants is warranted (see Haith, Goodman, Godwyn, & Montgomery, 1982). The relationship between habituation and cognitive competence also merits pursuing beyond its present speculative and provocative stage. Habituation qua mental construction needs to be disassociated from alternative explanations, such as suppression of motor behaviors (e.g., looking or sucking). It has often been assumed that habituation reflects cortical function, but lower organisms (Kandel, 1976) and decorticate preparations, as well as single cortical cells, habituate (Hill, 1973; Marg, 1968); if habituation is so pervasive, its role in very complex cortical functioning warrants exploration.[6] Further, it has been assumed (thus far without strong justification) that the rate of decline of attending in habituation is (somehow) proportional to the rate of construction of internal representation. Moreover, the nature of internal representations inferred in infant habituation—image (Kosslyn, 1980), proposition (Pylyshyn, 1973), or whatever—required elucidation. Finally, the roles of cognition and affect in habituation merit study; that is, a relationship between habituation and "tempo" has been speculated about, but is not well understood (e.g., Johnson & Brody, 1977; Kagan, 1971). Moreover, "hedonic" versus "cognitive" components of habituation need to be disentangled. For example, Berlyne (1970) showed that adults' ratings of "pleasingness" and "interestingness" declined at different rates with repeated stimulus exposures.

It is stunning how little actually is known practically or understood theoretically about this compelling, inventive, and productive phenomenon.

CONCLUSIONS

Habituation is attention decrement to repeated stimulation; it is not sensory adaptation, effector fatigue, or change in arousal, but rather represents a primitive kind of "exposure learning" that reflects underlying brain plasticity. Habituation in infants implies mental representation, memory, internal comparison, and a variety of associated perceptual and cognitive behaviors driven by these processes. Insofar as habituation further implies selective perception (Horn, 1965), it may possess biological relevance.

---

[6] Sokolov (1958/1963, 1969) theorized that habituation consists of storing stimulus characteristics as a neuronal model *in the cortex,* an opinion in which others (e.g., Thompson & Spencer, 1966) have concurred. In this connection, several neuropsychological observations are pertinent. First, in an animal study, Monnier, Boehmer, and Scholer (1976) applied chromatic light flashes repeatedly to the eye of awake rabbits and measured electrical activity at four points along the retinogeniculostriate pathway. Responsivity of neither the retina nor the optic tract changed, whereas electrical responses recorded at the lateral geniculate nucleus and visual cortex habituated. Intriguingly, dishabituation of habituated central responses was elicited after a rest (forgetting?) and after stimulation with a complementary color (discrimination?). Second, data on cortical involvement in habituation in human infants are not clear cut. Bronshtein (1960, cited in Lipsitt, 1979) and Brackbill (1971) reported that hydrocephalic and anencephalic infants failed to habituate (see, too, Eisenberg et al., 1966); however, Graham, Leavitt, Strock, and Brown (1978) demonstrated habituation in an anencephalic infant. Third, Hutt (1968) found that brain-lesioned 4- to 7-year-olds prolonged exploration of individual objects as compared with normal children, and Schafer and Peeke (1982) have recently shown that Down's syndrome adults fail to habituate the cortical evoked potential whereas matched normals do. Unfortunately, stimulus, response, and procedural differences render these studies of habituation and human cortical deficiencies noncomparable.

Although initial orientation and attention to a stimulus may be biologically useful, continued alerting to a stimulus that has no significance for the organism would make him a victim of irrelevant environmental variability. The problem becomes vivid when one considers the limitless variety of stimuli arriving at the infant's receptors (Kessen et al., 1970, p. 340).

In certain situations, therefore, efficiency of habituation strongly implies cognitive advantage.

In this essay, I have attempted to review habituation and to bring a functional taxonomy to the literature of habituation of visual attention in human infants. This literature has burgeoned since Fantz's (1964) introduction of the technique two decades ago, and in that time habituation has proven to be one of the most versatile and fruitful techniques of infancy studies. Habituation has been applied to questions of detection and discrimination, categorization, memory, and concept formation, and to the assessment of individual differences in cognition, and habituation has provided nearly unique access to these several psychological phenomena quite early in human life.

In invoking this taxonomy, I do not mean to imply that these several capacities are specific to habituation; nor do I intend that habituation most accurately assesses the many different capacities of infants. Some questions of detection and discrimination may be addressed profitably by alternative techniques, like forced-choice preferential looking (e.g., Teller, 1979), just as understanding infant memory may be informed by complementary procedures, like conditioning (e.g., Rovee-Collier & Fagen, 1981) or search (e.g., Sophian, 1980). Minimally, cross-validation of infant abilities with multiple methodologies, and articulation of different results with those of habituation, are to be encouraged.

"Baby psychology," as James J. Gibson once called it, is still in its infancy, and *infancy* means literally deficient in language. Importantly, habituation represents a kind of mutually understandable, albeit limited and situation-specific, language that can be readily established between the developmental investigator and his or her infant subject. We are well reminded that habituation has been described by comparative psychologists as perhaps the most ubiquitous phenomenon in animal behavior (Harris, 1943) and as the simplest form of behavioral plasticity (Thorpe, 1963). In infancy studies, habituation is also proving to be the language proxy for which Jensen (1932) yearned, and the expedient, powerful metric Kessen et al. (1970) foretold.

POSTSCRIPT

135.0

Habituation is one of two common and related modes of investigation of infant mental life. The second is "familiarization." This essay has concerned itself with habituation nearly exclusively. In habituation, decrement in attention of individual infants is tracked relative to the continuous or repeated presentation of a stimulus; and often, as I have shown here, attention in habituation or afterward indexes competence. In familiarization, a stimulus or stimulus pair is presented for a fixed amount of time, and usually group-average percentages of looking are calculated; familiarization is virtually always followed by a novelty test whose results are taken to reflect stimulus processing. Interestingly, the two procedures articulate closely. Often one informs the other; consider the following examples. On the one hand, Fagan (1974) demonstrated recognition in 5- and 6-month-olds based on 10 seconds of familiarization—a much shorter time than habituation typically lasts; this result implies that decrement in habituation is a sufficient, but not a necessary, condition to infer that environmental information has been stored in memory, and that habituation of attention can continue even though some stimulus encoding has taken place. On the other hand, using familiarization, Fagan (1972) determined that 5 months was the lower age limit for discrimination of faces, whereas, using habituation, Barrera and Maurer (1981a), Bushnell (1982), and Field et al. (1982), among others, have determined that 1- to 3-month-olds discriminate faces; this comparison implies that the freedom to attend to the stimulus or not in familiarization may seriously underestimate infant capacity. Often, too, the two procedures concur: For example, Fagan and Singer (1982) have found that responsiveness to novelty following familiarization in young infants predicts later verbal intelligence, just as Bornstein and Ruddy (1984; see also Ruddy & Bornstein, 1982) found that indexes of habituation do (see the section entitled "Individual Differences in Cognition").

ACKNOWLEDGMENTS

This essay was prepared while the author held a Guggenheim Foundation Fellowship. Research reported here was supported in part by grants from The Spencer Foundation and from the National Institute of Child Health and Human Development (R01 HD17423), and by a Research Career Development Award (K04 HD00521). I thank Iona Aibel, April A. Benasich, Helen Bornstein, Sharon Krinsky, April Kuchuk, and Madeleine Tress for comments and aid in preparing the manuscript. Request reprints from Marc H. Bornstein, Infancy Studies Program, Department of Psychology, New York University, 6 Washington Place—Room 1065, New York, New York 10003.

REFERENCES

Ames, E. W., Hunter, M. A., Black, A., Lithgow, P. A., & Newman, F. M. Problems of observer agreement in the infant control procedure. *Developmental Psychology,* 1978, *14,* 507–511.

Barnet, A. B. & Goodwin, R. Averaged evoked electroencephalographic responses to clicks in the newborn. *Electroencephalography and Clinical Neurophysiology,* 1965, *18,* 441–450.

Barnet, A. B., Ohlrich, E. S., & Shanks, B. L. EEG evoked responses to repetitive auditory stimulation in normal and Down's syndrome infants. *Developmental Medicine and Child Neurology,* 1971, *13,* 321–329.

Barrera, M. E. & Maurer, D. The perception of facial expressions by the three-month-old. *Child Development,* 1981, *52,* 203–206. (a)

Barrera, M. E. & Maurer, D. Recognition of mother's photographed face by the three-month-old infant. *Child Development,* 1981, *52,* 714–716. (b)

Bartoshuk, A. K. Human neonatal cardiac acceleration to sound: Habituation and dishabituation. *Perceptual and Motor Skills,* 1962, *15,* 15–27.

Bayley, N. *Bayley scales of infant development.* New York: Psychological Corporation, 1969.

Berg, W. K. & Berg, K. M. Psychophysiological development in infancy: State, sensory function, and attention. In J. D. Osofsky (ed.), *Handbook of infant development.* New York: Wiley, 1979.

Berlin, B. & Kay, P. *Basic color terms: Their universality and evolution.* Berkeley, Ca.: University of California Press, 1969.

Berlyne, D. E. *Conflict, arousal, and curiosity.* New York: McGraw-Hill, 1960.

Berlyne, D. E. Novelty, complexity, and hedonic value. *Perception & Psychophysics,* 1970, *8,* 279–286.

Bertenthal, B. I., Haith, M. M., & Campos, J. J. The partial-lag design: A method for controlling spontaneous regression in the infant-control habituation paradigm. *Infant Behavior and Development,* 1983, *6,* 331–338.

Bogartz, R. S. The criterion method: Some analyses and remarks. *Psychological Bulletin,* 1965, *64,* 1–14.

Bornstein, M. H. Perceptual development: Stability and change in feature perception. In M. H. Bornstein & W. Kessen (eds.), *Psychological development from infancy: Image to intention.* Hillsdale, N.J.: Lawrence Erlbaum Associates, 1979. (a)

Bornstein, M. H. Effects of habituation experience on post-habituation behavior in young infants: Discrimination and generalization among colors. *Developmental Psychology,* 1979, *15,* 348–349. (b)

Bornstein, M. H. Two kinds of perceptual organization near the beginning of life. In W. A. Collins (ed.), *Minnesota symposia on child psychology.* Vol. 14. Hillsdale, N.J.: Lawrence Erlbaum Associates, 1981. (a)

Bornstein, M. H. Psychological studies of color perception in human infants: Habituation, discrimination and categorization, recognition, and conceptualization. In L. P. Lipsitt (ed.), *Advances in infancy research.* Vol. 1. Norwood, N.J.: Ablex, 1981. (b)

Bornstein, M. H. A descriptive taxonomy of psychological categories used by infants. In C. Sophian (ed.), *The origins of cognitive skills.* Hillsdale, N.J.: Lawrence Erlbaum Associates, 1984.

Bornstein, M. H. & Benasich, A. A. *Infant habituation: Assessments of short-term reliability and individual differences at 5 months.* Unpublished manuscript, New York University, 1983.

Bornstein, M. H., Ferdinandsen, K., & Gross, C. G. Perception of symmetry in infancy. *Developmental Psychology,* 1981, *17,* 82–86.

Bornstein, M. H., Gross, J., & Wolf, J. Perceptual similarity of mirror images in infancy. *Cognition,* 1978, *6,* 89–116.

Bornstein, M. H., Kessen, W., & Weiskopf, S. Color vision and hue categorization in young human infants. *Journal of Experimental Psychology: Human Perception and Performance,* 1976, *2,* 115–129.

Bornstein, M. H. & Korda, N. O. Discrimination and matching within and between hue categories measured by reaction time. *Psychological Research,* 1984, in press.

Bornstein, M. H. & Monroe, M. D. Chromatic information processing: Rate depends on stimulus location in the category and psychological complexity. *Psychological Research,* 1980, *42,* 213–225.

Bornstein, M. H. & Ruddy, M. Infant attention and maternal stimulation: Prediction of cognitive and linguistic development in singletons and twins. In H. Bouma & D. Bouwhuis (eds.), *Attention and performance X.* Hillsdale, New Jersey: Lawrence Erlbaum Associates, 1984.

Bourne, L. E. *Human conceptual behavior.* Boston, Mass.: Allyn and Bacon, 1966.

Brackbill, Y. The role of the cortex in orienting: Orienting reflex in an anencephalic human infant. *Developmental Psychology,* 1971, *5,* 195–201.

Brackbill, Y. Obstetrical medication and infant behavior. In J. O. Osofsky (ed.), *Handbook of infant development.* New York: Wiley, 1979.

Bridger, W. H. Sensory habituation and discrimination in the human neonate. *American Journal of Psychiatry,* 1961, *117,* 991–996.

Bronshtein, A. I., Antonova, T. G., Kamenetskaya, A. G., Luppova, N. N., & Sytova, V. A. On the development of the functions of analyzers in infants and some animals at the early stage of ontogenesis. In *Problems of evolution of physiological functions.* Moscow, USSR: Academy of Science, 1958.

Bushnell, I. W. R. Discrimination of faces by young infants. *Journal of Experimental Child Psychology,* 1982, *33,* 298–308.

Caron, A. J. & Caron, R. F. Degree of stimulus complexity and habituation of visual fixation in infants. *Psychonomic Science,* 1969, *14,* 78–79.

Caron, A. J. & Caron, R. F. Processing of relational information as an index of infant risk. In S. L. Friedman & M. Sigman (eds.), *Preterm birth and psychological development.* New York: Academic Press, 1981.

Caron, A. J., Caron, R. F., Caldwell, R. C., & Weiss, S. J. Infant perception of the structural properties of the face. *Developmental Psychology,* 1973, *9,* 385–399.

Caron, A. J., Caron, R. F., Minichiello, M. D., Weiss, S. J., & Friedman, S. J. Constraints on the use of the familiarization-novelty method in the assessment of infant discrimination. *Child Development,* 1977, *48,* 747–762.

Caron, R. F., Caron, A. J., & Myers, R. S. Abstraction of invariant face expressions in infancy. *Child Development,* 1982, *53,* 1008–1015.

Clifton, R. K. & Nelson, M. N. Developmental study of habituation in infants: The importance of paradigm, response system, and state. In T. J. Tighe & R. N. Leaton (eds.), *Habituation: Perspectives from child development, animal behavior, and neurophysiology.* Hillsdale, N.J.: Lawrence Erlbaum Associates, 1976.

Cohen, L. B. Observing responses, visual preferences, and habituation to visual stimuli in infants. *Journal of Experimental Child Psychology,* 1969, *7,* 419–433.

Cohen, L. B. A two-process model of infant visual attention. *Merrill-Palmer Quarterly,* 1973, *19,* 157–180.

Cohen, L. B. Examination of habituation as a measure of aberrant infant development. In S. L. Friedman & M. Sigman (eds.), *Preterm birth and psychological development.* New York: Academic Press, 1981.

Cohen, L. B., DeLoache, J. S., & Rissman, M. W. The effect of stimulus complexity on infant attention and habituation. *Child Development,* 1975, *46,* 611–617.

Cohen, L. B., & Gelber, E. R. Infant visual memory. In L. B. Cohen & P. Salapatek (eds.), *Infant perception: From sensation to cognition.* Vol. 1. New York: Academic Press, 1975.

Cohen, L. B., Gelber, E. R., & Lazar, M. A. Infant habituation and generalization to differing degrees of stimulus novelty. *Journal of Experimental Child Psychology,* 1971, *11,* 379–389.

Cohen, L. B. & Menten, T. G. The rise and fall of infant habituation. *Infant Behavior and Development,* 1981, *4,* 269–280.

Cohen, L. B. & Strauss, M. S. Concept acquisition in the human infant. *Child Development,* 1979, *50,* 419–424.

Condillac, E. B. (Bonnot Abbé de). *La logique.* Paris: l'Esprite Debure, 1780.

Cornell, E. H. Infants' discrimination of photographs of faces following redundant presentations. *Journal of Experimental Child Psychology,* 1974, *18,* 98–106.

Cornell, E. H. Infants' visual attention to pattern arrangement and orientation. *Child Development,* 1975, *46,* 229–232.

Cornell, E. H. & Strauss, M. S. Infants' responsiveness to compounds of habituated visual stimuli. *Developmental Psychology,* 1973, *9,* 73–78.

DeLoache, J. S. Rate of habituation and visual memory in infants. *Child Development,* 1976, *47,* 145–154.

Demany, L., McKenzie, B., & Vurpillot, E. Rhythm perception in early infancy. *Nature,* 1977, *266,* 718–719.

Dember, W. N. & Earl, R. W. Analysis of exploratory, manipulatory, and curiosity behaviors. *Psychological Review,* 1957, *64,* 91–96.

Dirks, J. & Gibson, E. J. Infants' perception of similarity between live people and their photographs. *Child Development,* 1977, *48,* 124–130.

Dodd, C. & Lewis, M. The magnitude of the orienting response in children as a function of changes in color and contour. *Journal of Experimental Child Psychology,* 1969, *8,* 296–305.

Ebbinghaus, H. [*Memory: A contribution to experimental psychology*] (H. A. Ruger & C. E. Bussenius, trans.). New York: Dover, 1964. (Originally published, 1885.)

Eimas, P. D. Speech perception in early infancy. In L. B. Cohen & P. Salapatek (eds.), *Infant perception: From sensation to cognition.* Vol. 2. New York: Academic Press, 1975.

Eimas, P. D., Siqueland, E. R., Jusczyk, P., & Vigorito, J. Speech perception in infants. *Science,* 1971, *171,* 303–306.

Eisenberg, R. B., Coursin, D. B., & Rupp, N. Habituation to an acoustic pattern as an index of differences among human neonates. *Journal of Auditory Research,* 1966, *6,* 239–248.

Engen, T. & Lipsitt, L. P. Decrement and recovery of responses to olfactory stimuli in the human neonate. *Journal of Comparative and Physiological Psychology,* 1965, *59,* 312–316.

Fagan, J. F. Infants' recognition memory for a series of visual stimuli. *Journal of Experimental Child Psychology,* 1971, *11,* 244–250.

Fagan, J. F. Infants' recognition memory for faces. *Journal of Experimental Child Psychology,* 1972, *14,* 453–476.

Fagan, J. F. Infants' delayed recognition memory and forgetting. *Journal of Experimental Child Psychology,* 1973, *16,* 424–450.

Fagan, J. F. Infant recognition memory: The effects of length of familiarization and type of discrimination task. *Child Development,* 1974, *45,* 351–356.

Fagan, J. F. Infants' recognition of invariant features of faces. *Child Development,* 1976, *47,* 627–638.

Fagan, J. F. The origins of facial pattern recognition. In M. H. Bornstein & W. Kessen (eds.), *Psychological development from infancy: Image to intention.* Hillsdale, N.J.: Lawrence Erlbaum Associates, 1979.

Fagan, J. F. & Singer, L. T. Infant recognition memory as a measure of intelligence. In L. P. Lipsitt (ed.), *Advances in infancy research.* Vol. 2. Norwood, N.J.: Ablex, 1982.

Fantz, R. L. Visual experience in infants: Decreased attention to familiar patterns relative to novel ones. *Science,* 1964, *146,* 668–670.

Faulkender, P. J., Wright, J. C., & Waldron, A. Generalized habituation of concept stimuli in toddlers. *Child Development,* 1974, *45,* 1002–1010.

Fenson, L., Sapper, V., & Minner, D. G. Attention and manipulative play in the 1-year-old child. *Child Development,* 1974, *45,* 757–764.

Field, T. M., Dempsey, J. R., Hatch, J., Ting, G., & Clifton, R. K. Cardiac and behavioral responses to repeated tactile and auditory stimulation by preterm and term neonates. *Developmental Psychology,* 1979, *15,* 406–416.

Field, T., Woodson, R., Greenberg, R., & Cohen, D. Discrimination and imitation of facial expressions by neonates. *Science,* 1982, *218,* 179–181.

Freedle, R. A stimulus similarity scale for temporal measures of attention in infants and children. *Developmental Psychology,* 1971, *4,* 240–247.

Friedman, S. Infant habituation: Process, problems and possibilities. In N. Ellis (ed.), *Aberrant development in infancy: Human and animal studies.* New York: Halstead Press, 1975.

Furby, L. Attentional habituation and mental retardation. *Human Development,* 1974, *17,* 118–138.

Gibson, E. J., Owsley, C. J., & Johnston, J. Perception of invariants by five-month-old infants: Differentiation of two types of motion. *Developmental Psychology,* 1978, *14,* 407–415.

Glanzer, M. & Clark, W. H. Accuracy of perceptual recall: An analysis of organization. *Journal of Verbal Learning and Verbal Behavior,* 1962, *1,* 289–299.

Graham, F. K., Leavitt, L. A., Strock, B. D., & Brown, J. Precocious cardiac orienting in a human anencephalic infant. *Science,* 1978, *199,* 322–324.

Greenberg, D. J., O'Donnell, W. J., & Crawford, D. Complexity levels, habituation, and individual differences in early infancy. *Child Development,* 1973, *44,* 569–574.

Groves, P. M. & Thompson, R. F. Habituation: A dual-process theory. *Psychological Review,* 1970, *77,* 419–450.

Haaf, R. A., Smith, P. H., & Smitley, S. Infant response to facelike patterns under fixed-trial and infant-control procedures. *Child Development,* 1983, 54, 172–179.

Haith, M. M., Goodman, G. S., Godwyn, M., & Montgomery, L. *A longitudinal study of infants' visual scanning and discrimination of form.* Paper presented at the International Conference on Infant Studies, Austin, Texas, March, 1982.

Hanson, V. L. Within-category discriminations in speech perception. *Perception & Psychophysics,* 1977, *21,* 423–430.

Harris, J. D. Habituatory response decrement in the intact organism. *Psychological Bulletin,* 1943, *40,* 385–422.

Haskins, R., Collier, A. M., Ramey, C. T., & Hirschbiel, P. O. The effect of mild illness on habituation in the first year of life. *Journal of Pediatric Psychology,* 1978, *3,* 150–155.

Hill, R. M. Characteristics of habituation displayed by mammalian visual pathway units. In H. V. S. Peeke & M. J. Herz (eds.), *Habituation.* New York: Academic Press, 1973.

Horn, G. Physiological and psychological aspects of selective perception. In D. S. Lehrman, R. A. Hinde, & E. Shaw (eds.), *Advances in the study of behavior.* Vol. 1. New York: Academic Press, 1965.

Horn, G. Neuronal mechanisms of habituation. *Nature,* 1967, *215,* 707–711.

Horowitz, F. D. Infant attention and discrimination: Methodological and substantive issues. *Monographs of the Society for Research in Child Development,* 1974, *39* (5-6, Serial No. 158).

Horowitz, F. D., Paden, L., Bhana, K., & Self, P. An infant-controlled procedure for studying infant visual fixations. *Developmental Psychology,* 1972, *7,* 90.

Hutt, C. Exploration of novelty in children with and without upper C.N.S. lesions and some effects of auditory and visual incentives. *Acta Psychologica,* 1968, *28,* 150–160.

Hutt, C., von Bernuth, H., Lenard, H. G., Hutt, S. J., & Prechtl, H. F. R. Habituation in relation to state in the human neonate. *Nature,* 1968, *220,* 618–620.

Jeffrey, W. E. The orienting reflex and attention in cognitive development. *Psychological Review,* 1968, *75,* 323–334.

Jeffrey, W. E. Habituation as a mechanism of perceptual development. In T. J. Tighe & R. N. Leaton (eds.), *Habituation: Perspectives from child development, animal behavior, and neurophysiology.* Hillsdale, N.J.: Lawrence Erlbaum Associates, 1976.

Jeffrey, W. E. & Cohen, L. B. Habituation in the human infant. In H. Reese (ed.), *Advances in child development and behavior.* Vol. 6. New York: Academic Press, 1971.

Jensen, K. Differential reactions to taste and temperature stimuli in newborn infants. *Genetic Psychology Monographs,* 1932, *12,* 363–479.

Johnson, D. & Brody, N. Visual habituation, sensorimotor development, and tempo of play in one-year-old infants. *Child Development,* 1977, *48,* 315–319.

Kagan, J. *Change and continuity in infancy.* New York: Wiley, 1971.

Kandel, E. *Cellular basis of behavior: An introduction to invertebrate neurobiology.* San Francisco, Ca.: Freeman, 1976.

Kessen, W., Haith, M. M., & Salapatek, P. H. Human infancy: A bibliography and guide. In P. Mussen (ed.), *Carmichael's manual of child psychology.* New York: Wiley, 1970.

Kosslyn, S. M. *Image and mind.* Cambridge, Mass.: Harvard University Press, 1980.

Kuhl, P. Models and mechanisms in speech perception. Species comparisons provide further contributions. *Brain, Behavior, and Evolution,* 1979, *16,* 374–408.

Kuhl, P. Discrimination of speech by non-human animals. *Journal of the Acoustical Society of America,* 1981, *70,* 340–349.

Kulig, J. W. & Tighe, T. J. Habituation in children within a behavior suppression paradigm. *Journal of Experimental Child Psychology*, 1981, *32*, 425–442.

LaBarbera, J. D., Izard, C. E., Vietze, P., & Parisi, S. A. Four- and six-month-old infants' visual responses to joy, anger, and neutral expressions. *Child Development*, 1976, *47*, 535–538.

Lasky, R. E. Serial habituation or regression to the mean? *Child Development*, 1979, *50*, 568–570.

Lasky, R. E. Length of familiarization and preference for novel and familiar stimuli. *Infant Behavior and Development*, 1980, *3*, 15–28.

Lasky, R. E. & Spiro, D. The processing of tachistoscopically presented visual stimuli by five-month-old infants. *Child Development*, 1980, *51*, 1292–1294.

Lasky, R. E., Syrdal-Lasky, A., & Klein, R. E. VOT discrimination by four to six and a half month old infants from Spanish environments. *Journal of Experimental Child Psychology*, 1975, *20*, 215–225.

Leaton, R. N. & Tighe, T. J. Comparisons between habituation research at the developmental and animal-neurophysiological levels. In T. J. Tighe & R. N. Leaton (eds.), *Habituation: Perspectives from child development, animal behavior, and neurophysiology*. Hillsdale, N.J.: Lawrence Erlbaum Associates, 1976.

Lester, B. M. Cardiac habituation of the orienting response to an auditory signal in infants of varying nutritional status. *Developmental Psychology*, 1975, *11*, 432–442.

Lewis, M. & Baldini, N. Attentional processes and individual differences. In G. A. Hale & M. Lewis (eds.), *Attention and cognitive development*. New York: Plenum Press, 1979.

Lewis, M., Bartels, B., Campbell, H., & Goldberg, J. Individual differences in attention: The relationship between infants' condition at birth and attention distribution within the first year. *American Journal of Diseases of Children*, 1967, *113*, 461–465.

Lewis, M. & Goldberg, S. The acquisition and violation of expectancy: An experimental paradigm. *Journal of Experimental Child Psychology*, 1969, *7*, 70–80. (a)

Lewis, M. & Goldberg, S. Perceptual-cognitive development in infancy: A generalized expectancy model as a function of mother-infant interaction. *Merrill-Palmer Quarterly*, 1969, *15*, 81–100. (b)

Lewis, M., Goldberg, S., & Campbell, H. A developmental study of learning within the first three years of life: Response decrement to a redundant signal. *Monographs of the Society for Research in Child Development*, 1969, *34* (9, Serial No. 133).

Lewkowicz, D. & Turkewitz, G. Cross-modal equivalence in early infancy: Auditory-visual intensity matching. *Developmental Psychology*, 1980, *16*, 597–607.

Lipsitt, L. P. Learning assessments and interventions for the infant born at risk. In T. M. Field, A. M. Sostek, S. Goldberg, & H. H. Shuman (eds.), *Infants born at risk: Behavior and development*. New York: Spectrum, 1979.

Mackworth, J. F. Vigilance, arousal, and habituation. *Psychological Review*, 1968, *75*, 308–322.

Marg, E. Receptive fields of cells in the human visual cortex. *Experientia*, 1968, *24*, 348–350.

Martin, R. M. Effects of familiar and complex stimuli on infant attention. *Developmental Psychology*, 1975, *11*, 178–185.

McCall, R. B. Attention in the infant: Avenue to the study of cognitive development. In D. N. Walcher & D. L. Peters (eds.), *Early childhood: The development of self-regulatory mechanisms*. New York: Academic Press, 1971.

McCall, R. B. Individual differences in the pattern of habituation at 5 and 10 months of age. *Developmental Psychology*, 1979, *15*, 559–569. (a)

McCall, R. B. Qualitative transitions in behavioral development in the first two years of life. In M. H. Bornstein & W. Kessen (eds.), *Psychological development from infancy: Image to intention*. Hillsdale, N.J.: Lawrence Erlbaum Associates, 1979. (b)

McCall, R. B. & Applebaum, M. I. Bias in the analysis of repeated-measures designs: Some alternative approaches. *Child Development*, 1973, *44*, 401–415.

McCall, R. B., Hogarty, P. S., Hamilton, J. S., & Vincent, J. H. Habituation rate and the infant's response to visual discrepancies. *Child Development*, 1973, *44*, 280–287.

McCall, R. B. & Kagan, J. Individual differences in the infant's distribution of attention to stimulus discrepancy. *Developmental Psychology,* 1970, *2,* 90–98.

McCall, R. B., Kennedy, C. B., & Appelbaum, M. I. Magnitude of discrepancy and the distribution of attention in infants. *Child Development,* 1977, *48,* 772–785.

McCall, R. B. & McGhee, P. E. The discrepancy hypothesis of attention and affect in infants. In I. C. Uzgiris & F. Weizmann (eds.), *The structuring of experience.* New York: Plenum, 1977.

McCall, R. B. & Melson, W. H. Attention in infants as a function of magnitude of discrepancy and habituation rate. *Psychonomic Science,* 1969, *17,* 317–319.

McGurk, H. Infant discrimination of orientation. *Journal of Experimental Child Psychology,* 1972, *14,* 151–164.

Milewski, A. E. Visual discrimination and detection of configurational invariance in 3-month-old infants. *Developmental Psychology,* 1979, *15,* 357–363.

Miller, D. J. Visual habituation in the human infant. *Child Development,* 1972, *43,* 481–493.

Miller, D. J., Ryan, E. B., Aberger, E., Jr., McGuire, M. D., Short, E. J., & Kenny, D. A. Relationships between assessments of habituation and cognitive performance in the early years of life. *International Journal of Behavioral Development,* 1979, *2,* 159–170.

Miller, D. J., Ryan, E. B., Short, E. J., Reis, P. G., McGuire, M. D., & Culler, M. P. Relationship between early habituation and later cognitive performance in infancy. *Child Development,* 1977, *48,* 658–661.

Miller, D. J., Ryan, E. B., Sinnott, J. P., & Wilson, M. A. Serial habituation in two-, three-, and four-month-old infants. *Child Development,* 1976, *47,* 341–349.

Miller, D. J., Sinnott, J. P., Short, E. J., & Hains, A. A. Individual differences in habituation rates and object concept performance. *Child Development,* 1976, *47,* 528–531.

Miller, D., Spiridigliozzi, G., Ryan, E. B., Callan, M. P., & McLaughlin, J. E. Habituation and cognitive performance: Relationships between measures at four years of age and earlier assessments. *International Journal of Behavioral Development,* 1980, *3,* 131–146.

Miller, G. A., Galanter, E., & Pribram, K.H. *Plans and the structure of behavior.* New York: Holt, Rinehart and Winston, 1960.

Monnier, M., Boehmer, A., & Scholer, A. Early habituation, dishabituation and generalization induced in the visual centres by colour stimuli. *Vision Research,* 1976, *16,* 1497–1504.

Moreau, T., Birch, H. G., & Turkewitz, G. Ease of habituation to repeated auditory and somesthetic stimulation in the human newborn. *Journal of Experimental Child Psychology,* 1970, *9,* 193–207.

Nelson, C. A., Morse, P. A., & Leavitt, L. A. Recognition of facial expressions by seven-month-old infants. *Child Development,* 1979, *50,* 1239–1242.

Olson, G. M. An information processing analysis of visual memory and habituation in infants. In T. J. Tighe & R. N. Leaton (eds.), *Habituation: Perspectives from child development, animal behavior, and neurophysiology.* Hillsdale, N.J.: Lawrence Erlbaum Associates, 1976.

Pancratz, C. N. & Cohen, L. B. Recovery of habituation in infants. *Journal of Experimental Child Psychology,* 1970, *9,* 208–216.

Pêcheux, M.-G. & Lecuyer, R. Habituation rate and free exploration tempo in 4-month-old infants. *International Journal of Behavioral Development,* 1983, *6,* 37–50.

Peeke, H. V. S. & Herz, M. J. (eds.). *Habituation.* New York: Academic Press, 1973.

Pisoni, D. B. & Tash, J. Reaction times to comparisons within and across phonetic categories. *Perception & Psychophysics,* 1974, *15,* 285–290.

Pylyshyn, Z. W. What the mind's eye tells the mind's brain: A critique of mental imagery. *Psychological Bulletin,* 1973, *80,* 1–24.

Razran, G. *Mind in evolution: An east-west synthesis of learned behavior and cognition.* New York: Houghton-Mifflin, 1971.

Riksen-Walraven, J. M. Effects of caregiver behavior on habituation rate and self-efficacy in infants. *International Journal of Behavioral Development,* 1978, *1,* 105–130.

Rosch, E. Human categorization. In N. Warren (ed.), *Studies in cross-cultural psychology*. Vol. 1. London: Academic Press, 1978.

Rose, S. A. Infants' transfer of response between two-dimensional and three-dimensional stimuli. *Child Development,* 1977, *48,* 1086–1091.

Rose, S. A., Gottfried, A. W., & Bridger, W. G. Cross-modal transfer in 6-month-old infants. *Developmental Psychology,* 1981, *17,* 661–669.

Ross, G. S. Categorization in 1- to 2-year-olds. *Developmental Psychology,* 1980, *16,* 391–396.

Rovee-Collier, C. K. & Fagen, J. W. The retrieval of memory in early infancy. In L. P. Lipsitt (ed.), *Advances in infancy research*. Vol. 1. Norwood, N.J.: Ablex, 1981.

Rubel, E. & Rosenthal, M. H. The ontogeny of auditory frequency generalization in the chicken. *Journal of Experimental Psychology: Animal Behavior Processes,* 1975, *1,* 287–297.

Ruddy, M. & Bornstein, M. H. Cognitive correlates of infant attention and maternal stimulation over the first year of life. *Child Development,* 1982, *53,* 183–188.

Ruff, H., Kohler, C. J., & Haupt, D. L. Infant recognition of two- and three-dimensional stimuli. *Developmental Psychology,* 1976, *12,* 455–459.

Saayman, G., Ames, E. W., & Moffett, A. Response to novelty as an indicator of visual discrimination in the human infant. *Journal of Experimental Child Psychology,* 1964, *1,* 189–198.

Schafer, B. W. P. & Peeke, H. V. S. Down syndrome individuals fail to habituate cortical evoked potentials. *American Journal of Mental Deficiency,* 1982, *87,* 332–337.

Schaffer, H. R., Greenwood, A., & Parry, M. The onset of wariness. *Child Development,* 1972, *43,* 165–175.

Schexnider, V. Y. R., Bell, R. Q., Shebilske, W. L., & Quinn, P. Habituation of visual attention in infants with minor physical anomalies. *Child Development,* 1981, *52,* 812–818.

Schwartz, M. & Day, R. H. Visual shape perception in early infancy. *Monographs of the Society for Research in Child Development,* 1979, *44* (7, Serial No. 182).

Siddle, D. (ed.). *Orienting and habituation*. New York: Wiley, 1983.

Sigman, M., Kopp, C. B., Parmelee, A. H., & Jeffrey, W. E. Visual attention and neurological organization in neonates. *Child Development,* 1973, *44,* 461–466.

Sigman, M. & Parmelee, A. H. Visual preferences of four-month-old premature and full-term infants. *Child Development,* 1974, *45,* 959–965.

Siqueland, E. R. Studies of visual recognition memory in preterm infants: Differences in development as a function of perinatal morbidity factors. In S. L. Friedman & M. Sigman (eds.), *Preterm birth and psychological development*. New York: Academic Press, 1981.

Siqueland, E. R. & DeLucia, C. A. Visual reinforcement of nonnutritive sucking in human infants. *Science,* 1969, *165,* 1144–1146.

Smith, E. E. & Medin, D. I. *Categories and concepts*. Cambridge, MA: Harvard University Press, 1981.

Sokolov, Y. N. [*Perception and the conditioned reflex*] (S. W. Waydenfeld, trans.). New York: Macmillan, 1963. (Originally published, 1958.)

Sokolov, Y. N. The modeling properties of the nervous system. In M. Cole & F. Maltzman (eds.), *A handbook of contemporary Soviet psychology*. New York: Basic Books, 1969.

Sophian, C. Habituation is not enough: Novelty preferences, search, and memory in infancy. *Merrill-Palmer Quarterly,* 1980, *26,* 239–257.

Stein, L. Habituation and stimulus novelty: A model based on classical conditioning. *Psychological Review,* 1966, *73,* 352–356.

Strauss, M. S. The abstraction of prototypical information by adults and 10-month-old infants. *Journal of Experimental Psychology: Human Learning and Memory,* 1979, *5,* 618–635.

Strauss, M. S. & Curtis, L. E. Infant perception of numerosity. *Child Development,* 1981, *52,* 1146–1152.

Streeter, L. A. Language perception of 2-month-old infants shows effects of both innate mechanisms and experience. *Nature,* 1976, *259,* 39–41.

Teller, D. Y. The forced-choice preferential looking procedure: A psychophysical technique for use with human infants. *Infant Behavior and Development,* 1979, *2,* 135–153.

Thompson, R. F. & Spencer, W. A. Habituation: A model phenomenon for the study of neuronal substrates of behavior. *Psychological Review,* 1966, *73,* 16–43.

Thorpe, W. H. *Learning and instinct in animals.* Cambridge, Mass.: Harvard University Press, 1963.

Tighe, T. J., & Leaton, R. N. (eds.). *Habituation: Perspectives from child development, animal behavior, and neurophysiology.* Hillsdale, N.J.: Lawrence Erlbaum Associates, 1976.

Tighe, T. J. & Powlison, L. B. Sex differences in infant habituation research: A survey and some hypotheses. *Bulletin of Psychonomic Society,* 1978, *12,* 337–340.

Underwood, B. J. Speed of learning and amount retained: A consideration of methodology. *Psychological Bulletin,* 1954, *51,* 276–282.

Weiffenbach, J. B. Sensory mechanisms of the newborn's tongue. In J. M. Weiffenbach (ed.), *Taste and development.* Bethesda, Md.: DHEW, 1977.

Welch, M. J. Infants' visual attention to varying degrees of novelty. *Child Development,* 1974, *45,* 344–350.

Wetherford, M. J. & Cohen, L. B. Developmental changes in infant visual preferences for novelty and familiarity. *Child Development,* 1973, *44,* 416–424.

Wright, A. A. Psychometric and psychophysical hue discrimination functions for the pigeon. *Vision Research,* 1972, *12,* 1447–1464.

Wright, W. D. *Researches on normal and defective colour vision.* St. Louis, Mo.: C. V. Mosby, 1947.

Young-Browne, G., Rosenfeld, H. M., & Horowitz, F. D. Infant discrimination of facial expressions. *Child Development,* 1977, *48,* 555–562.

Zelazo, P. R., Hopkins, J. R., Jacobson, S., & Kagan, J. Psychological reactivity to discrepant events: Support for the curvilinear hypothesis. *Cognition,* 1973, *2,* 385–393.

12

REACHING AS A MEASURE OF INFANTS' SPATIAL PERCEPTION

Albert Yonas
Carl E. Granrud

University of Minnesota

153.476

INTRODUCTION

The explosion of research on infant perceptual development over the last 25 years can be traced in part to the innovative use of infants' natural responses to indicate perceptual function. Eleanor Gibson (1969) has suggested that much of the advance in our knowledge has come from what she describes as the "ecological wisdom" of the researcher. Since animals have evolved perceptual sensitivity in relation to their particular environments and ways of life, "it seems wise to ask what the infant's typical environment is like and what, if anything, he can do about it" (p. 318). She describes three examples of natural behaviors characteristic of human infants: looking, reaching, and crawling. Although looking has been used extensively in the study of visual perceptual development (see Aslin's chapter, this volume), and crawling is used extensively in visual cliff studies (see Gibson & Walk, 1960), reaching has been used less as an index of spatial perception than it deserves. This chapter will explore why we believe reaching is a useful measure of the development of spatial sensitivity in humans (and perhaps in other primates). One strong reason is that this behavior occurs spontaneously. By 5 months of age, human infants demonstrate a tendency to reach for an object that is within reach, to grasp that object, if possible, and to bring that object to the mouth for further exploration and, perhaps, ingestion. While it has long been observed that infants at times will reach for objects that are beyond reach (literally reaching for the moon), we know too that, when an object is presented beyond the reach of the infant, the duration and number of reaches decrease (Gordon & Yonas, 1976). By 5 months of age (20-22 weeks), an infant, if given a choice between two objects placed at different distances, will reach consistently for the closer object. As the separation between the objects is decreased, the preference for the closer object becomes less consistent (Yonas, Sorknes, & Smith, 1983). Clearly, spatial location is important in determining whether an infant will reach for an object.

It is also clear that there is more "ecological wisdom" to be gained in understanding the natural occurrence of reaching in human infants. We know little about what sorts of things evoke reaching and what things do not. It is reasonable to guess that infants will prefer to reach for objects that are graspable (in addition to being within reach), but it is not clear what stimulus properties specify that an object can be grasped. James Gibson's (1979) concept of affordances may be useful in this context. How important is an object's rigidity? Would an infant attempt to grasp a moving object or a cloud of dust? Would an object that is glowing (giving off light) be more or less likely to elicit grasping than an object that reflects light? We do not know, but by studying the situations in which grasping occurs and does not occur in the everyday life of the infant, we may gain important insights. This discussion of what information specifies that an object is graspable has led away from our topic. The remainder of this chapter will deal with the use of reaching as a measure of sensitivity of the infant to information for spatial layout of objects.

Two aspects of spatial vision should be distinguished: one deals with sensitivity to radial direction (the x and y axes), the other with sensitivity to depth (the z axis). The development of sensitivity to visual information for radial direction would seem to be best studied using eye movements, as Aslin and Salapatek (1975) have done. They found that 1- and 2-month-olds made directionally appropriate responses to horizontally-, diagonally-, and vertically-presented stimuli. Apparently, visual sensitivity to radial direction is present very early. Unfortunately, eye movements cannot tell us whether infants are sensitive to the distance of a target. While one can study the development of a reaching system to radial direction (e.g., Bower, Broughton, & Moore, 1970), this chapter's emphasis is on the use of reaching in the investigation of infants' *depth* perception.

INFERRING SPATIAL PERCEPTION

It is difficult to make inferences about the ability of a young infant to pick up meaningful information regarding the three-dimensional layout of objects in the environment. Unlike the study of infants' detection thresholds for contrast and spatial frequency, in which any differential behavior to two stimuli indicates discrimination, the validity of our conclusion about infants' spatial perception is increased when we use spatially appropriate behaviors as indicators. However, spatial appropriateness is not a sufficient condition for positing spatial perception, since many reflex-like responses which are spatially appropriate can be accounted for in terms of responses to the proximal stimulus. For example, 1- and 2-month-old infants make directionally-appropriate saccadic eye movements to targets presented in various positions in their visual fields (Aslin & Salapatek, 1975). Although this response is spatially adapted, it involves responding to the target's retinal position rather than its location in three-dimensional space. Even some behaviors which are specific to three-dimensional space, such as the 2-month-old's ability to accommodate the lens to an object's distance (Banks, 1980), or to converge the eyes (Aslin, 1977), require responses only to the proximal stimulus and not to the distal spatial layout. Accommodation and convergence may be responses to the distal spatial positions of objects. The important question for the present discussion, however, is whether these behaviors warrant positing the construct of spatial perception. We think they do not. Spatial perception should be inferred when this construct results in the most parsiminous explanation. In explaining accommodation, for example, only a simple feedback loop which responds to maximize high spatial frequencies is required. Thus, adding the construct of spatial perception reduces the explanation's parsimony. If, on the other hand, we observe a set of spatially appropriate reaching behaviors, guided by several depth cues, we will increase the parsimony of explanation by positing that a common perception of spatial layout underlies these behaviors. Reaching, in addition to being spatially appropriate behavior, may gain inferential power from stimulus convergence and response convergence. (Stimulus convergence refers to different stimulus cues evoking the same pattern of behavior, while response convergence is used here to refer to varying responses leading to the same goal in three-dimensional space. See Garner, Hake, and Eriksen (1956) for a discussion of operationism and a concept of perception.)

Mature reaches for objects are not simply specific reflex-like responses; they have response convergence. Unlike a reflex, a reach is a complex pattern of behavior that can have enormous variability from reach to reach, yet also a great deal of commonality between reaches. For example, a 7-month-old's reaches for an object can have a large number of starting locations, have different trajectories, and involve different motor responses. Yet the hand goes to the same end point each time—the location of the object. To say that the infant reaches to the closer of two objects describes not the topography of the behavior so much as the reach's goal in distal space. In addition, as the studies discussed in this chapter demonstrate, reaching is not a response to specific cues in the proximal stimulation. Since, for example, 7-month-olds reach preferentially for the nearer of two objects when the objects' relative distances are specified by various isolated cues, it seems that preferential reaching is guided not by the proximal cues themselves, but by the information for spatial layout carried by the cues (i.e., there is stimulus convergence). A parsimonious way of interpreting this response convergence and stimulus convergence is to infer that the reaches are guided by a central registration of spatial information, the object's location in the three-dimensional space, and not by a response to some nonspatial proximal stimulus variable.

A final aspect of reaching that makes it a useful measure of spatial perception is its persistence until the goal is reached (Tolman, 1932). By 6 months of age, the infant normally continues to reach until the object is grasped and brought to the mouth. Getting the object into the mouth terminates reaching; thus, reaching appears to be intentional and goal-directed.

The usefulness of reaching as an index of depth perception is limited by the fact that reaching itself undergoes substantial changes with development. There is argument as to when the arm movements of the very young infant can be classified as reaching. While Bower (1972; see also Bower, Broughton & Moore, 1970) reported that newborns have highly coordinated reaching behaviors guided by visual information for the location of an object, earlier researchers (Gesell & Amatruda, 1964; White, Castle, & Held, 1964) had found evidence of only random thrashing of the arms in the neonate. Although careful attempts to replicate Bower's report have been carried out by DiFranco, Muir, and Dodwell (1978) and by Ruff and Halton (1978), the behavior described by Bower has not been observed. While it seems clear that the newborn is unable to reach in any functional sense (see Trevarthen, 1974), von Hofsten (1982) has found recently that when newborns are fixating an object, their arm and hand movements are aimed significantly closer to the object than are the movements that occur in the absence of fixation. Von Hofsten believes that a rudimentary form of eye-hand coordination exists in the newborn but it serves an attentional rather than a manipulative function. While his study suggests that, along with eye and head movement, arm movements provide evidence that the newborn is sensitive to radial direction, the distance of the object from the newborn has not yet been manipulated. As a result, we do not know whether the arm extensions observed by von Hofsten might be influenced by the distance of the object from the newborn. If the frequency increases as the object is placed within reach, this might suggest the presence of depth perception. On the other hand, it is possible that an increase in proximal stimulation would bring about an increase in activity level and attention to the target. A similar explanation may be applied to Bruner and Koslowski's (1972) report that somewhat older prereaching infants produced more arm and finger movement close to the mouth when presented with an object within the reach of the infant. Bruner and Koslowski concluded that the infants appreciated the distance and graspable or nongraspable nature of the object; however, the behavior observed was unlike the well-coordinated, spatially appropriate reach of the older infant. It may only be a manifestation of change in activity level rather than a response to the location of the object in three-dimensional space.

Von Hofsten (in press) recently completed a longitudinal study of the organization of prereaching movements in infants from 1 to 19 weeks of age. He presented an attractive moving object close the infants, and found an intriguing drop in the frequency of forward arm extensions and an increase in fisted forward movements at 7 weeks of age. After 7 weeks, there was a steady increase in the frequency of forward movements: from a low at 7 weeks of about 1 per minute, to about 3 per minute at 10 and 13 weeks, to about 5 per minute at 16 weeks, and to 9 per minute at 19 weeks. In our own laboratory, we have found that the ease of eliciting reaches continues to increase with age; 28-week-old infants will reach twice as often as 21-week-olds.

In addition to a change in the frequency of arm extensions in the direction of an object, there is a substantial improvement in the efficiency of these movements. Von Hofsten (1979) found that, from 15 to 24 weeks, the distance travelled by the hand, as it moves toward an object, drops by 50%. Furthermore, there is a decrease with age in the number of movements that make up a reach. As noted by von Hofsten (1979, p. 174), "the rather crude and awkward reaching at 15 weeks gives way to smooth and efficient reaching at the end of the period" (i.e., 36 weeks). One consequence of the jerky reaching behavior of young infants is that their reaching has less of the precise spatial character that makes it a convincing measure of spatial perception.

STUDIES USING REACHING AS A MEASURE
OF SPATIAL PERCEPTION

At this point, it is unclear with infants under 20 weeks of age how useful a measure of spatial perception reaching (or perhaps we should use von Hofsten's term "prereaching") will be. There are two studies that suggest that, while the arm movements of the young infant are jerky, the frequency of such movement is influenced by information for the distance of an object. In 1941, Cruikshank studied the "approach movements" of infants to a rattle positioned within and beyond the reach of infants. She found that 10- to 14-week-old infants made approximately 50% fewer "approach movements" to a rattle presented at 75 cm than to the same rattle presented at 25 cm. Older infants showed even stronger effects of distance by reaching only rarely for the out-of-reach rattle. When a larger distant rattle, that equalled the retinal size of the close rattle, was presented, the difference in approach movements was still significant, although reduced somewhat for younger subjects. The study does suggest that distance influences young infants' behavior. Cruikshank did not define "approach movements" with as much precision as we might desire, but today, more than 40 years later, her study of responsiveness to spatial information in young infants is of interest.

A recent study by Field (1976) suggests that studies using reaching with infants may be useful if the infant is not too young. Field (1976) varied object distance and contrasted the reaching behavior of a group of 8- to 13-week-old infants with a group of 18- to 22-week-old infants. He employed an explicit behavioral definition of reaching movements: an adduction movement of more than 5 cm toward the subject's median plane passing the middle of the shoulders. The reaches were scored from video tape using two cameras so that three-dimensional movements could be analyzed. Field used 60-second trials, timed from the onset of fixation, and analyzed the percentage of trials in which adduction movements occurred. He found that the older infants reached on 97% of the trials when the object was placed within reach; but when the object was beyond reach, infants reached only on 23% of the trials. In contrast, the adduction movements occurred on approximately half the trials for the 8- to 13-week-old infants regardless of the distance of the object. It would be interesting to follow up Field's study using infants between the two ages used in his study. In addition, it would be useful to vary the specific information available to the infant for the distance to the object.

Having established that very young infants respond to at least some of the spatial information available for the distance of an object, one can ask what specific information the infant is able to use to guide reaching. Spatial information can be categorized into three types: binocular, static-monocular, and kinetic. Methods for exploring the development of sensitivity to these three types of information, using reaching as an index of depth sensitivity, will be described next.

Binocular Depth Information

In our first study that used reaching, we (Gordon & Yonas, 1976) reasoned that convincing evidence for binocular depth perception would be demonstrated if reaches terminated at locations that varied systematically with the location of a stereoscopically projected virtual object. The virtual object was presented using a stereoscopic shadow caster. Polarized filters were placed over the infant's eyes, and a real object was positioned between the lamps and a rear projection screen. In such a situation, an observer with binocular depth perception sees, not a pair of shadows on the screen, but a single object at a precise location in space (specified by the convergence angle of the eyes and the disparity between the two images). In the study, stereoscopic information specified a virtual object as within or beyond the reach of 5-month-old infants. An analysis of the infants' reaches revealed that the end points of the reaches did not vary reliably with the specified distance of the virtual object. We failed to demonstrate that infants' reaches are guided precisely by binocular depth information, but we found that binocular depth information did influence reaching. Infants reached more frequently and showed more prehensile activity when binocular information specified the virtual object as within reach (15 cm) than when it specified the object as beyond reach (30 cm). This study, therefore, revealed some binocular depth perception in 5½-month-olds. In addition, it showed that reaching frequency, and not only the precise spatial endpoints of reaches, can be used as a measure for studying spatial perception.

Bechtoldt and Hutz (1979) have replicated these results using a stereo shadow caster and reaching as an index with infants from 20-36 weeks of age. By varying the filters, they contrasted reaching to a virtual object in front of the screen with reaching to a shadow of an object on the screen. A depth response was scored if one or both arms moved toward the virtual object and a hand movement appropriate to grasping or holding an object occurred. (If the hand was held open towards the screen, the reach was not scored as a depth response.) They concluded that most infants over 22 weeks of age will attempt to grasp a virtual object. They also employed this method to assess the depth perception of six strabismic infants. While 5 of the 6 infants showed no sensitivity to binocular depth information, one infant made 3 attempts to grasp the virtual object at 29 weeks of age, but no longer responded to the binocular information when tested at 36 weeks. It seems clear that reaching to virtual objects may be useful in studies of pathology as well as of normal development.

In another study of binocular sensitivity, von Hofsten (1977) analyzed the trajectories of reaches, rather than grasping responses or endpoints. His experiment evaluated infants' ability to use convergence information in locating the position of a target object. He modified the convergence angle necessary for the infant's binocular fixation of the object, and observed whether reaches were directed to apparent location of the object. Infants from 4½ to 8 months wore either 4-diopter displacing prisms, which decreased convergence, making the object look farther away than it actually was, or wore 10-diopter displacing prisms, which increased binocular convergence, making the object look closer than it actually was. Infants were tested under two lighting conditions: in the light or in the dark with only the target object illuminated. Most reaches were directed to the location of the virtual object. Von Hofsten concluded that infants use convergence as information for absolute depth by 4½ months. It could be argued, however, that the infants tested might have been using binocular disparity to localize the virtual object, making use of the relative depth information provided by their hands and the virtual object. This interpretation is strengthened by the finding that, when subjects were tested in the dark, a condition in which disparity cues relating the distance of hand and object were presumably absent, they reached infrequently. Although von Hofsten's study confounds convergence and binocular disparity, it does establish the usefulness of a fine-grained analysis of reaching trajectories in studying the development of depth perception.

Granrud and Yonas currently are using reaching as a measure to investigate the development of infants' stereopsis with convergence information eliminated. Evidence exists that infants as young as 2 months of age may detect binocular disparity in stereograms (Appel & Campos, 1977; Atkinson & Braddick, 1976). Since these studies used simple discrimination measures (fixation preference and recovery from habituation of sucking), however, they give us no indication of whether infants perceive the depth specified by binocular disparity. A study conducted by Fox, Aslin, Shea, and Dumais (1980) found stronger evidence that infants perceive depth from disparity. (For a review of research on infant stereopsis, see Aslin & Dumais, 1980; Fox, 1981). In the Fox et al. study, 3½-month-olds tracked a moving virtual object specified by binocular disparity in a dynamic random-dot stereogram. Furthermore, tracking occurred only when the amount of disparity was below the adult fusion threshold. While this result suggests that 3½-month-olds have stereopsis, the evidence would be more convincing if we observed a spatially appropriate response to the spatial layout specified by disparity.

In Granrud and Yonas' study, infants view 2 random-dot stereograms in which binocular disparity specifies a convex and a concave pyramid (see Julesz, 1971, for a detailed discussion of random-dot stereograms). The two displays are presented side by side, with the position of the pyramids randomized over trials. If infants perceive the pyramids as specified by disparity, we might expect them to reach more frequently for the convex pyramid than for the concave one. An initial study suggests that 20- to 22-week-old infants do respond to this information; a replication is now in progress.

Static-Monocular Information

A series of studies investigating infants' sensitivity to static-monocular or pictorial depth information has exploited infants' tendencies to reach preferentially for the nearer of two objects, and to reach more frequently for an object that is within reach than for one that is beyond reach. In the first such study Yonas, Cleaves, and Pettersen (1978) examined infants' sensitivity to the pictorial depth information available in an Ames trapezoidal window (Ames, 1951). When viewed monocularly by adults, this display creates a powerful illusion of a slanted rectangular window with one side several inches closer than the other. It was hypothesized that, if infants were sensitive to the depth information in the display, their reaches would be directed to the apparently nearer side.

In the first experiment, 6-month-old infants were presented with a real rectangular window rotated to bring the left or right side of the window nearer to the infant. It was established that infants directed their reaching with sufficient accuracy to demonstrate sensitivity to the different distances of the two sides of a slanted window, and that they would do so while wearing an eye-patch. Although no binocular information was available, the infants reached to the closer side of the object on 75% of the trials, indicating sensitivity to accommodation, kinetic, and/or pictorial information.

In a second experiment, a trapezoidal window photograph was presented frontally without motion to 6-month-old infants. In order to control for the possibility that infants prefer to reach for the larger side of the display without regard to depth information, a size-control display was created with one side smaller than the other but with no information that the sides were at different distances. The infants presented with the trapezoidal window reached to the larger side of the display twice as often as they reached to the smaller side (see Figure 1). The infants presented with the size-control display, in contrast, reached for the two sides with equal frequency.

A third experiment was then conducted to control for the possibility that preferential reaching was due to nonspatial proximal stimulus variables, such

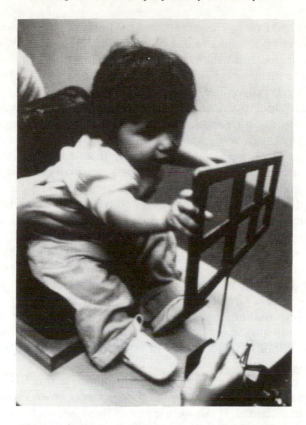

Figure 1. Infant reaching for trapezoidal window.

as acute angles, rather than to the spatial orientation of the display as specified by pictorial depth cues. Infants were randomly assigned to either binocular or monocular viewing of the trapezoidal window. It was hypothesized that, if depth information were the basis for the tendency to reach for the larger side of the trapezoidal window, it should be possible to minimize the effectiveness of pictorial depth by providing binocular depth information for the acutal frontal orientation of the window. The results from the infants who viewed the trapezoidal display monocularly replicated the results of the previous experiment; the infants preferred to reach for the larger and pictorially nearer side. The infants who viewed the display binocularly showed significantly less directionality in their reaching. The most plausible explanation for these results is that the perceived relative distances of the two sides of the window guided the infants' reaching.

The scoring of the direction of a reach can be accomplished in a highly reliable fashion from a videotape recording. Part of the video monitor screen can be masked so that scorers are blind to which side of the display is virtually closer to the infant. In the trapezoidal window studies, the side of the display that was touched first by the infant's hand was scored as the side reached for. In studies in which reaching to one of two objects is assessed, the direction of the reach is scored from the position of the hand as it crosses a line at the distance of the surface of the closer object. Inter-observer agreement for these judgments is generally greater than 85%.

After establishing that infants can respond to pictorial information for the spatial layout of a surface (the trapezoidal window), we began a series of studies designed to investigate infants' sensitivity to various pictorial cues isolated from all other spatial information. In one of these studies, Yonas, Granrud, and Pettersen (in press) explored sensitivity to the depth cue of relative size in infants from 5 to 7 months of age. In these experiments, infants viewed two different-sized objects (discs and triangles), presented side by side, suspended in front of a dark vertical surface. The two objects were always at equal distances from the infant. Seven-month-olds showed a significantly greater tendency to reach for the larger object in the monocular condition than in the binocular condition. This same pattern of reaching preferences was observed when a group of 5½-month-olds (22 to 24 weeks) was presented with a pair of discs. They reached for the larger disc on 65% of the trials with monocular presentation, but on only 50% of the binocular trials. For the youngest infants studied (20- to 22-week-olds), behavior in the monocular and binocular conditions did not differ. In both conditions, infants reached more frequently to the larger object.

Results from the binocular viewing conditions make it unlikely that 5½-and 7-month-old infants preferred to reach for the larger objects without regard to their apparent distances. If this were the case, these infants should have reached more frequently for the larger objects under both binocular and monocular viewing conditions, but no such preference was observed in the binocular condition. The results suggest, therefore, that the 5½- and 7-month-olds perceived the larger objects as closer than the smaller objects in the monocular conditions, and detected stereoscopic information which specified the objects as equidistant in the binocular conditions. In contrast, the 5-month-old infants did not give evidence of sensitivity to relative size. Unlike the older infants, these infants' results could be accounted for on the basis of a nonspatial proximal stimulus variable of retinal size.

In the previous studies, infants' preferential reaching for one of two locations was employed. With this method, an occluder is raised, making the display visible to the infant, and, in general, the infant almost immediately reaches and touches one or the other side of the display. When the display is touched, the trial is ended and the left-right position of the stimuli is interchanged before beginning the next trial. However, some depth information cannot be explored in this two-alternative fashion. As Cruikshank (1941) demonstrated, infants will reach for a single object more frequently when it is placed within reach than when out of reach. Yonas, Pettersen, and Granrud

(1982) made use of this finding in designing a study to investigate infants' sensitivity to the cue of familiar size. If the distal size of an object were known, its visual angle could be a source of information for the object's distance. A preliminary experiment tested adults in order to establish the effectiveness of the experimental displays. One group of subjects judged the apparent distances of two sets of monocularly viewed photographs of faces (a familiar class of objects). One set was larger than life-size, the other smaller. Another group judged the distances of monocularly viewed checkerboard patterns (a class of objects with no specific familar size) that were the same sizes as the faces. Adults judged the large faces to be at a distance within reach (22 cm) and the small faces to be at a distance well beyond reach (52 cm) for 5- to 7-month-old infants. Therefore, if infants viewing these displays monocularly perceive them as adults do, we would expect them to reach more to the large than to the small faces. Moreover, from the adult data we would expect no differential reaching for the large and small checkerboards when viewed monocularly. Nor would we expect differential reaching for the faces when viewed binocularly, since stereoscopic information would specify the large and small faces as equidistant. These hypotheses were tested with 5- and 7-month-old infants, using the same displays.

Seconds of reaching were scored from a video recording taken from above the infant's head. A reach was scored only when the infant was looking at the display and when one or two hands had moved forward, crossing a line placed 10 cm in front of the infant seat. (We should note that, initially, we scored both number of reaches and duration of reaching, and found that, while results with both measures were similar, the duration measure showed less variability. When only a single object is presented to the infant rather than a choice between two objects, we favor the duration measure, especially with 20- to 22-week-old infants—although with so little known about the two measures, a preference for one may only reflect superstitious behavior.)

For the 7-month-olds under monocular viewing conditions, the large face elicited more seconds of reaching than the small face. This difference was significantly larger than the analogous differences observed in the binocularly viewed face condition or in the monocularly viewed checkerboard condition. For the 5-month-olds, there were no significant differences in reaching duration among the three conditions. The results indicate that, in the monocular condition, 7-month-olds perceive the large faces as within reach and the small faces as beyond reach. As in the relative size experiments, the control conditions make it unlikely that the infants exhibited reaching preferences without regard to the displays' perceived distances. If the infants simply prefer to reach for large objects, we would expect more reaching for the large checkerboard than for the small one, but no such preference was observed. Furthermore, the infants were not simply showing a preference to reach for large faces, since binocular viewing eliminated the reaching preference observed in the monocular condition. Presumably the infants detected binocular information which specified the faces as equidistant and, therefore, they reached equally for the large and small faces.

In a final study of infants' sensitivity to pictorial depth cues, Granrud and Yonas (1984) used reaching to explore infants' perception of pictorially specified interpositon. Five- and 7-month-old infants viewed the displays pictured in Figure 2.

In the first experiment, 7-month-olds showed a significant preference to reach for the apparently nearer area in the "T" display and showed no reaching preference when viewing the "Y" display. The reaching preference when viewing the "T" display suggests that the display may have been perceived as consisting of overlapping surfaces. The lack of a reaching preference when viewing the "Y" display suggests that no section of this display was seen as nearer than the others. Five-month-olds showed no significant reaching preferences.

It could be argued, however, that the 7-month-olds simply preferred to reach for the diamond-shaped region of the display rather than for the arrowhead-shaped sections, and that this preference (based on a nonspatial proximal stimulus variable), rather than the perception of differential distance, was responsible for the results in the "T" condition. A second experiment tested this hypothesis by separating the sections of the display. If infants simply preferred to reach for the diamond-shaped section, we would expect to observe this preference even when information for overlap (T-shaped intersections) was removed from the display. Five- and 7-month-olds were presented with the "T" and "separation" displays pictured in Figure 2. Again the 7-month-olds showed a preference to reach for the side of the display that the "T" intersections specify as nearer, and showed no significant preference when viewing the

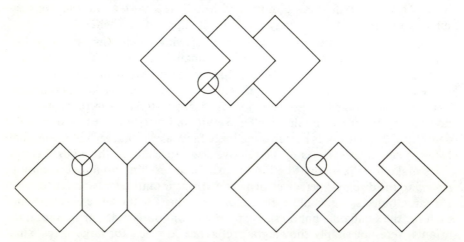

Figure 2. Schematic representation of displays used in the Granrud and Yonas (1984) investigation of infants' sensitivity to pictorially specified interposition.

"separation" display. Thus, the data support the conclusion that the 7-month-olds' reaching preference resulted from the perceived relative distances of the test displays' sections, and not to preferential reaching for a particular shape. The 5-month-olds showed a reaching preference in the "T" condition which approached significance. However, their performances in the "T" and "L" conditions did not differ significantly. Results from studies of 5-month-olds do not enable us to draw conclusions about perceived depth at this age, since nonspatial proximal stimulus variables, shape and retinal size, could account for the reaching behavior.

These studies of sensitivity to pictorial depth information are convincing in part because reaching (a spatially appropriate response) was used as a measure. However, because the precise spatial character of reaches was not examined in these studies, reaching alone is not compelling evidence of depth sensitivity. Instead, the conclusion that infants respond to depth information is justified primarily by the use of control conditions which have ruled out plausible alternative explanations for the observed reaching behavior.

Another aspect of these studies of pictorial depth information is how well the preferential reaching method does work. With this method, a trial is terminated when the infant touches the object, and this allows many trials to be run in a short period of time. Infants like to reach for real objects that they can touch, and, if the object is changed frequently, they will continue to do so for 20 or more trials before becoming bored with the game. A large number of trials is very useful in that it makes the use of within-subject designs practical.

Kinetic Information

Two studies have used reaching to study infants' sensitivity to kinetic information for depth. In the first experiment (Yonas, Granrud, & Smith, 1982), 7-month-olds viewed computer-generated random-dot displays in which accretion and deletion of texture provided the only information for contours and for depth at an edge (see Figure 3). When adults view these displays, they report seeing a textured rectangular surface moving horizontally in front of a moving textured background. We hypothesized that infants would reach more frequently for the apparently nearer surface than for the apparent background surface if they were sensitive to accretion and deletion of texture as information for depth at an edge.

We found that 48% of the infants' reaches were for the "foreground," while 35% were for the "background." The remainder of the reaches were for the edges between the foreground and background. The difference between the percentage of reaches to the foreground and the background was statistically significant, indicating that 7-month-olds are sensitive to accretion and deletion of visual texture as information for depth at an edge. There is no plausible alternative to the conclusion that the infants' reaching preference resulted from the apparent distances of the two regions. The display contained no static cues for contours or depth. Foreground and background occupied equal areas

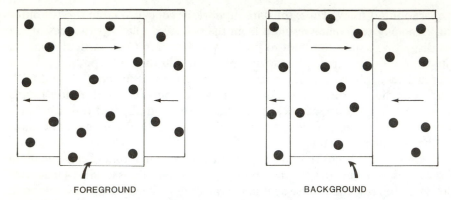

FOREGROUND   BACKGROUND

Figure 3. Schematic representation of the display used in the Yonas, Granrud, and Smith (1982) study of infants' sensitivity to accretion and deletion of texture as a cue to depth.

of the display at all times and also occupied the center of the display for equal intervals. In addition, the scoring of which half of the screen was touched was done by an observer who was blind to which portion of the screen specified the foreground.

We attempted to follow up the study with 5-month-old infants, but found that many of the infants would not complete the experiment. Moving dots on a monitor, even though they create an illusion of a surface in depth, do not evoke the same level of reaching as do real objects. In addition, the infants sat upright in a Gerry carrier infant seat. To make the infants more comfortable, we are repeating the experiment with the infant sitting in an infant seat reclined 30 degrees from the vertical and the monitor oriented at the same angle. This seems to increase the amount of reaching in 20- to 22-week-olds.

A second experiment using random dot patterns simulated a 3-dimensional surface to assess infants' sensitivity to motion parallax. Yonas, Smith, and Granrud (unpublished observation) moved an oscilloscope screen in front of 5-month-old infants; the method was similar to that first used by Rogers and Graham (1979). Two virtual surfaces, one concave and one convex, were presented to the infant, who wore an eyepatch to eliminate conflicting binocular information. Duration of reaching, in seconds, toward the screen in each condition was scored from a video recording. We found that the convex display elicited reliably longer reaching than the concave surface. This suggests that some sensitivity to motion-parallax information for depth is present by 5 months of age. Again, as in the accretion-deletion study, many infants (64%) failed to complete the experiment. Some infants arrived in inappropriate states, but many infants appeared to become distressed by the darkened room, the eye patch, the glowing oscilloscope screen, or by other factors. These infants did not attend to the display or reach a sufficient amount for their data to be included. We are repeating the study with the oscilloscope and the infant seat slanted 30 degrees from the vertical as in the accretion-deletion study. It is our hope that this more comfortable seating arrangement will produce more reaching towards a relatively uninteresting display.

COMPARING DEPTH CUES AND MEASURES OF REACHING

In addition to investigating infants' sensitivity to various depth cues in isolation, the reaching response can be used to compare the relative effectiveness of different cues in specifying spatial layout. In the first study of this type, Granrud, Yonas, and Pettersen (in press) used preferential reaching to compare monocular with binocular depth perception. A small disc was positioned within reach, and a larger disc was positioned beyond reach. The visual angles of the discs were matched. Viewing the two objects binocularly, both 5- and 7-month-olds reached for the closer object on virtually all trials; with monocular presentation, they reached to the closer object much less frequently. Since the two objects were matched for retinal size, the high degree of consistency in reaching for the near object in the binocular condition indicated that the infants perceived the objects' relative distances. The significantly weaker reaching preference for the nearer object in the monocular condition suggests that perception of relative distance was less veridical when only monocular cues were available to specify distance. This conclusion may be unwarranted in that we did not vary the amount of information provided by monocular and binocular cues. The possibility remains that monocular cues can be as effective as binocular information, if a sufficient number of these cues are provided and the salience of each cue is enhanced.

The preceding studies are demonstrations of the effectiveness of particular cues; that is, these studies explore whether a significant difference from chance exists in reaching to the apparently closer object. They do not assess the threshold of sensitivity to various types of information. To do this, one must vary the amount of information provided by each cue. For some cues, an established measure exists for describing quantitative variations, as in the case of binocular disparity measured in visual angle. For other cues, such as relative size, it is not clear how one should characterize the dimension of variation that is effective in controlling perception. As a first attempt at a parametric study of sensitivity to various depth cues, Yonas, Sorknes, and Smith (1983) systematically varied the real distance between target objects and the availability of cues specifying that distance. This was done in order to determine the minimum distance between two objects required for a reaching preference for the nearer object. It was hypothesized that the level of preferential reaching for the nearer object would be a joint function of relative distance and the information available for perceiving relative distance. Seven-month-old infants were presented with pairs of colored and patterned objects, supported invisibly in front of the seated infant by rods placed in holes in a background screen. One object of each pair was 20 cm from the infant's viewpoint; the other was 2, 4, or 8 cm farther away. There were eight conditions in the study, varying the presentation (Monocular or Binocular), whether or not relative size was available as a cue to the infants (Relative Size or Conflicting Relative Size), and whether or not accretion and deletion of texture was available (Overlap or No Overlap of objects). Infants' reaching to the objects was observed, and the percentages of reaches to the nearer object constituted the data. Thus the eight conditions varied depth information, from many cues to only motion parallax and accommodation.

Results indicated that the infants' reaching behavior was controlled by the information available for the distances of target objects. Figure 4 presents these results. It is clear that the percentage of reaches to the nearer object is related to both the depth separation between the objects and the depth information available. In all conditions, the percentage of reaches for the nearer of the two objects increased as a function of the separation in depth of the two objects. The results from the Binocular, Relative Size conditions, for example, show that 2 cm is a sufficient separation for preferential reaching to be highly consistent (approximately 80% to the nearer). A 4 cm separation is either more detectable or a more important difference than 2 cm. A comparison of the results in the Monocular and Binocular conditions reveals another interesting finding of this study. Since a 2 cm separation is sufficient for highly consistent preferential reaching with binocular presentation, it is unlikely that the less consistent reaching in the monocular condition at the same separation was due to a drop in motivation to reach for the closer object when both objects are well within reach. It seems that overall detection of differential distance was superior in the Binocular conditions. This result implies that there is an ordering of effectiveness of cues. On the other hand, monocular information can be very effective. When a sufficient amount of monocular information is available (as in the Monocular, Overlap, Relative Size condition with an 8 cm separation), monocular performance did equal binocular performance.

Because the studies described above were aimed primarily at discovering whether infants had any sensitivity to depth information, issues such as the test-retest reliability of the performance of single subjects were not addressed. Except for the study by Bechtoldt and Hutz (1979), no one has attempted to assess the sensitivity of individual infants to spatial perception. Since infants rapidly become bored with any situation including a reaching game, it is unclear just how effective reaching might be in single subject studies; on the other hand, the large number of reaches (about 20 per infant) and the very high level of consistency in reaching to the closer object by the infants in the Yonas et al. (1983) study suggest that it might be worthwhile to explore further the binocular sensitivity of strabismic infants, for example, using reaching as an index.

What we have broadly called reaching can be measured in a number of ways. Several studies have counted the number of reaches; others have scored the location contacted, the direction of the reach, the fine-grained trajectory of the reach, the duration of the reach, the presence of grasping hand movements, and even the frequency of finger movements on the midline. As in all

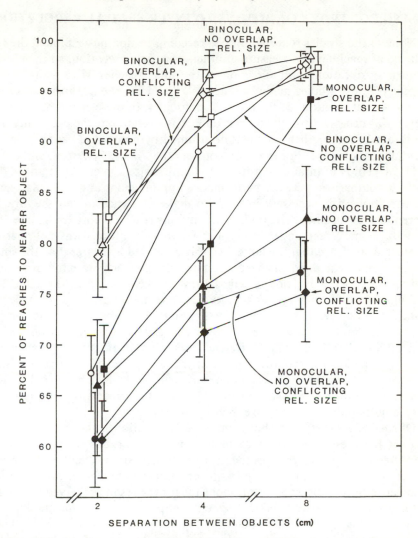

Figure 4. Results of Yonas, Sorknes, and Smith's (1983) experiment, representing percentage of reaches to the nearer object, at each of three distance separations between objects, and in each of eight conditions. The bar plotted above and below each data point indicates the standard error of each mean.

experimental work, one should choose a dependent variable that extracts the information that is needed most rapidly with the least effort. It is for that reason that we have favored a strategy of presenting two objects and scoring which object is first touched by the infant. This method is simple and quick, and the interjudge reliability for the location touched is high. We do not mean, however, to suggest that other measures might not be more appropriate for other types of studies.

USING CONTROL CONDITIONS TO INFER SPATIAL PERCEPTION

None of the studies reported in the preceding section has exploited the full richness of reaching as a measure of infants' spatial perception, since only the frequency, duration, and direction of infants' reaches were scored. The designs of these studies made it unnecessary and impractical to measure the precise spatial locations of the reaches' endpoints. In these experiments, however, it was necessary to run control conditions to eliminate the possibility that the infants' reaching behavior was determined by nonspatial variables in the experimental displays. For example, consider the Yonas, Pettersen, and Granrud (1982) study of infants' sensitivity to familiar size as a cue to depth. In this study, a comparison between performance in monocular and binocular viewing conditions was necessary in order to make inferences about the infants' perceptions of distance. The finding that infants reached more for a large face than for a small face under monocular viewing conditions was not in itself compelling evidence that the large face was perceived as nearer than the small face. It seemed equally plausible that infants simply reach more for large faces and that this preference, not perceived distance, accounted for the results. The finding of no difference in reaching for the large and small faces when viewed binocularly, however, increased the likelihood that the amount of reaching observed in the monocular condition reflected perceived distance. The additional control condition, in which no difference was found in amount of reaching for large and small checkerboard displays, further strengthened the argument that the results in the monocular condition were determined by perceived distance, since it ruled out the alternative hypothesis that infants reach more for retinally large objects only when they are wearing an eyepatch.

Of course, a variety of ad hoc alternative explanations could be proposed to account for these results. For example, one might argue that infants reach more frequently for large faces than for small faces only when they are wearing an eyepatch, and that this quirk in the infants' reaching behavior, rather than perception of distance, was responsible for the results observed by Yonas, Pettersen, and Granrud (1982). Despite the implausibility of this argument, it remains a possibility. The conclusion that infants perceive distance from familiar size therefore must be made based on parsimony of the explanation. One construct, perceived distance, can account for the results in all three conditions of the Yonas, Pettersen, and Granrud (1982) study in the following way. In the monocular condition, the large face was perceived as within reach (using familiar size as a cue for distance) and elicited much reaching, while the small face was perceived as beyond reach and elicited little reaching. In the binocular condition, the distances of both faces were perceived as equidistant due to binocular depth information; thus, no reaching preference was observed. Finally, since the checkerboard displays had no specific familiar size, the checkerboards' retinal sizes were not information for distance. Thus, the amount of reaching for large and small checkerboards did not differ. An attempt to explain these results without reference to perceived distance would require a different post hoc hypothesis to account for the results for each condition of the study.

FUTURE DIRECTIONS

The most compelling demonstration of infants' sensitivity to the spatial information carried by a given depth cue would be a reach directed to the precise location of an object. The spatial position of the object would be specified by that particular cue, isolated from all other spatial information. As we pointed out earlier, this type of demonstration was attempted unsuccessfully by Gordon and Yonas (1976). Gordon and Yonas' failure to find infants' reaches terminating at the precise distances specified by binocular depth information may have been due to the experimenter's difficulty in determining the endpoint of a reach for a virtual object. For example, it is possible that an infant could have reached precisely to the apparent location of the virtual object but continued to move his or her hand when it failed to make contact with the object. Gordon and Yonas had no way of determining whether this occurred. Recent findings by von Hofsten (1980, 1983), however, suggest a method by which the precise locations of the endpoints of infants' reaches can be used as a measure for studying spatial perception. Von Hofsten (1980, 1983; von Hofsten & Lindhagen, 1979) has found that, by 18 weeks of age, infants can catch an object which moves horizontally in front of them at a velocity up to 30 cm/second. In catching a moving object, infants do not follow and catch up to the object. Rather, they make predictive reaches, aiming their reaches ahead of the object to a predicted meeting point of the paths of the hand and object. Moreover, von Hofsten (1983) has found that infants time these predictive reaches with remarkable precision (within 1/20 second). So, at a particular time (the moment of the object's arrival at the meeting point), the infants' hand must be at a particular location (the meeting point). Since infants' reaches for a moving object are not stereotypic reflex responses but are, instead, guided by visual information combined with a flexible reaching strategy (von Hofsten, in press), von Hofsten's findings demonstrate spatial perception in 18-week-olds. In addition, this method can be used to explore further what visual depth information infants detect in perceiving spatial layout. For example, the following experiment is proposed to illustrate how reaching for moving objects could be used to determine how precisely binocular information can guide infants' reaching.

Infants will view a stereoscopic shadow-caster display similar to that used by Gordon and Yonas (1976). In this experiment, the virtual object will move horizontally across the infant's field of view at a velocity of 30 cm/sec. Binocular information in the display will specify the virtual object's path as either 15 cm or 25 cm from the infant's eyes at its nearest point. If infants are sensitive to binocular information for distance, and if they can use this information to guide reaching, they should be able to make predictive reaches for the virtual object. In order to make a predictive reach, the infant's hand must be at a specific point in space at a specified time. We can predict from the object's velocity the time at which the hand's trajectory should intercept the object. Thus, we can score the hand's spatial location at that moment. If infants perceive the precise spatial layout specified by binocular information, we should score their hands at the specified distances.

Currently, there are few studies utilizing reaching to explore spatial perception in infants younger than 5 months of age. This has been due, in part, to the belief that younger infants' reaching is not sufficiently precise to be useful as an index of perception. Several studies have reported that the reaching of infants younger than 4 months, for example, does not appear to be goal directed or guided by visual information, nor does it appear to have the sort of response convergence observed in 5-month-olds' reaching (DiFranco, Muir, & Dodwell, 1978; Ruff & Halton, 1978). Instead, very young infants' hand and arm movements appear to be random thrashing (White, Castle, & Held, 1964).

However, von Hofsten (1982) has found that newborns do make arm extensions which are aimed toward objects. While it is clear from his results that newborns' prereaching is sensitive to the radial direction of an object, it is not yet known whether or not prereaching behavior varies as a function of object distance. We could investigate whether newborns perceive depth in the following experiment. We could present very young infants (newborn to 4-months-old) with two objects matched in visual angle but at different distances, and test whether the majority of arm extensions is directed toward the nearer object. If the retinal projections of the two objects were identical, such a reaching preference would provide evidence that the infants perceived the objects' relative distances.

If we discover that prereaching behavior of neonates and/or young infants varies with spatial layout, we could then vary the distance information available to the infants. For example, as we mentioned above, results from a study by Fox et al. (1980) strongly suggest that stereopsis appears between 2½ and 3½ months of age. By 5 months, binocular depth perception seems to be superior to monocular depth perception in the guidance of spatially directed reaching (Granrud, Yonas, & Pettersen, in press). It remains unknown, however, what effect the onset of stereopsis has on infants' spatial perception. For example, perhaps the emergence of stereopsis results in a sharp increase in the veridicality of spatial perception. If this is the case, we might expect 3½-month-olds to show a reaching preference for the nearer of two objects when viewing them binocularly, but show a reduced preference (or no preference) when viewing the objects monocularly. Furthermore, 2½-month-olds might show no preference under either monocular or binocular viewing conditions, since they lack stereopsis. Whether these results would be obtained is not known. The point of this example is that prereaching could be used to answer this sort of question about infants' spatial perception, even with very young infants and, perhaps, newborns.

It is important to remember that newborn-to-4-month-olds' prereaching behavior does not necessarily have all of the characteristics that make the mature reaching of the 4- to 7-month-old a convincing index of depth perception. For example, in addition to the question of whether prereaching is spatially appropriate (i.e., whether it varies as a function of object distance), it is not clear that there is either stimulus convergence or response convergence in prereaching. Thus, it may be difficult to rule out the possibility that newborns respond to specific proximal stimulus cues rather than to distal spatial layout. These questions, however, represent interesting avenues for future research, and we hope that the reader now will agree that we have only begun to exploit the potential of reaching as a measure of infants' spatial perception.

ACKNOWLEDGMENT

The preparation of this chapter was supported by the National Institute of Child Health and Human Development grant HD-05027. The authors are indebted to Isabel Smith and Martha Arterberry for their editorial assistance, and to Kay O'Geay for typing the manuscript.

REFERENCES

Ames, A. Visual perception and the rotating trapezoidal window. *Psychological Monographs,* 1951, *65,* (1, Whole No. 324).

Appel, M. A. & Campos, J. J. Binocular disparity as a discriminate stimulus parameter for young infants. *Journal of Experimental Child Psychology,* 1977, *23,* 47–56.

Aslin, R. N. Development of binocular fixation in human infants. *Journal of Experimental Child Psychology,* 1977, *23,* 133–150.

Aslin, R. N. & Dumais, S. T. Binocular vision in infants: A review and theoretical framework. *Advances in Child Development and Behavior,* 1980, *15,* 53–94.

Aslin, R. N. & Salapatek, P. Saccadic localization of peripheral targets by the very young human infant. *Perception and Psychophysics,* 1975, *17,* 293–302.

Atkinson, J. & Braddick. O. Stereoscopic discrimination in infants. *Perception,* 1976, *5,* 29–38.

Banks, M. S. The development of visual accommodation during early infancy. *Child Development,* 1980, *51,* 646–666.

Bechtoldt, H. P. & Hutz, C. S. Stereopsis in young infants and stereopsis in an infant with congenital esotropia. *Journal of Pediatric Ophthalmology and Strabismus,* 1979, *16,* 49–54.

Bower, T. G. R. Object perception in infants. *Perception,* 1972, *1,* 15–30.

Bower, T. G. R., Broughton, J. M., & Moore, M. K. Demonstration of intention in the reaching behavior of neonate humans. *Nature,* 1970, *228,* 679–680.

Bruner, J. S. & Koslowski, B. Visually preadapted constituents of manipulating action. *Perception,* 1972, *1,* 3–14.

Cruikshank, R. M. The development of visual size constancy in early infancy. *Journal of Genetic Psychology,* 1941, *58,* 327–351.

DiFranco, D., Muir, D. W., & Dodwell, D. C. Reaching in young infants. *Perception,* 1978, *7,* 385–392.

Field, J. Relation of young infants' reaching behavior to stimulus distance and solidity. *Developmental Psychology,* 1976, *12,* 444–448.

Fox, R. Stereopsis in animals and human infants: A review of behavioral investigations. In R. N. Aslin, J. R. Alberts, & M. R. Petersen (eds.), *Development of perception: Psychobiological perspectives.* Vol. 2. *The visual system.* New York: Academic Press, 1981.

Fox, R., Aslin, R. N., Shea, S. L., & Dumais, S. T. Stereopsis in human infants. *Science,* 1980, *207,* 323–324.

Garner, W. R., Hake, H. W., & Eriksen, C. W. Operationism and the concept of perception. *Psychological Review,* 1956, *63,* 149–159.

Gesell, A. & Amatruda, C. S. *Developmental diagnosis: Normal and abnormal child development.* 2nd ed. New York: Harper & Row, 1964.

Gibson, E. J. *Principles of perceptual learning and development.* New York: Appleton-Century-Crofts, 1969.

Gibson, E. J. & Walk, R. D. The "visual cliff." *Scientific American,* 1960, *202* (April), 64–71.

Gibson, J. J. *The ecological approach to visual perception.* Boston: Houghton Mifflin, 1979.

Gordon, R. F. & Yonas, A. Sensitivity to binocular depth information in infants. *Journal of Experimental Psychology,* 1976, *22,* 413–422.

Granrud, C. E. & Yonas, A. Infants' perception of pictorially specified interposition. *Journal of Experimental Child Psychology,* 1984, *37,* 500–511.

Granrud, C. E., Yonas, A., & Pettersen, L. A comparison of monocular and binocular depth perception in 5- and 7-month-old infants. *Journal of Experimental Child Psychology,* in press.

Julesz, B. *Foundations of cyclopean vision.* Chicago: University of Chicago Press, 1971.

Rogers, B. & Graham M. Motion parallax as an independent use for depth perception. *Perception,* 1979, *8,* 125–134.

Ruff, H. & Halton, A. Is there directed reaching in the human neonate? *Developmental Psychology,* 1978, *14,* 425–426.

Tolman, E. C. *Purposive behavior in animals and men.* New York: Appleton-Century, 1932.

Trevarthen, C. The psychobiology of speech development. In E. H. Lenneberg (ed.), Language and brain: Developmental aspects. *Neurosciences Research Program Bulletin,* 1974, *12,* 570–585.

von Hofsten, C. Binocular convergence as a determinant of reaching behavior in infancy. *Perception,* 1977, *6,* 139–144.

von Hofsten, C. Development of visually directed reaching: The approach phase. *Journal of Human Movement Studies,* 1979, *5,* 160–178.

von Hofsten, C. Predictive reaching for moving objects by human infants. *Journal of Experimental Child Psychology,* 1980, *30,* 369–382.

von Hofsten, C. Eye-hand coordination in the newborn. *Developmental Psychology,* 1982, *18,* 450–461.

von Hofsten, C. Catching skills in infancy. *Journal of Experimental Psychology: Human Perception and Performance,* 1983, *9,* 75–85.

von Hofsten, C. Developmental changes in the organization of prereaching movements. *Developmental Psychology,* 1984, *20,* 378–388.

von Hofsten, C. & Lindhagen, K. Observations on the development of reaching for moving objects. *Journal of Experimental Child Psychology,* 1979, *28,* 158–173.

White, B. L., Castle, P., & Held, R. Observations on the development of visually-directed reaching. *Child Development,* 1964, *35,* 349–364.

Yonas, A., Cleaves, W., & Pettersen, L. Development of sensitivity to pictorial depth. *Science,* 1978, *200*(4337), 77–79.

Yonas, A., Granrud, C. E., & Pettersen, L. Infants' sensitivity to relative size information for distance. *Developmental Psychology,* in press.

Yonas, A., Granrud, C. E., & Smith, I. M. Infants perceive accretion/deletion information for depth. *Investigative Opthalmology and Visual Science,* 1982, *22*(3, Supplement), 124.

Yonas, A., Pettersen, L., & Granrud, C. E. Infants' sensitivity to familiar size as information for distance. *Child Development,* 1982, *53,* 1285–1290.

Yonas, A., Sorknes, A., & Smith, I. M. *Infants' sensitivity to variations in target distance and availability of depth cues.* Paper presented at the meetings of the Society for Research in Child Development, Detroit, MI., April, 1983.

13

PREFERENTIAL-LOOKING METHODS AS TOOLS FOR THE STUDY OF COGNITION IN INFANCY

/ 36.98

Elizabeth S. Spelke

University of Pennsylvania, Philadelphia

INTRODUCTION

This chapter has two themes. One is a substantive thesis: Human infants are endowed, by nature, not only with capacities to sense elementary properties of light and other stimulation, but with capacities to perceive and to conceptualize the world. Infants have perceptual and cognitive capacities that allow them to apprehend objects and to make sense of certain events. The second theme is methodological: The cognitive capacities of infants can be studied experimentally. In particular, these capacities may reveal themselves over the course of simple experiments in which two or more displays are presented to an infant and looking time to each display is recorded. Studies that use *preferential-looking methods* provide an especially valuable research tool for the study of perception and cognition in infancy.

Why focus on preferential-looking methods? One reason is practical. Stable and reliable behavioral preferences are manifest in the young of many species. Immature animals will often choose systematically to approach, to follow, or to contact one display rather than another (Gottlieb, this volume). Human infants are no exception. They systematically direct their actions toward certain kinds of displays when they reach (Yonas & Granrud, this volume) and crawl (e.g., Gibson & Walk, 1960; see Gibson & Spelke, 1983, for a review) as well as when they look. Looking preferences may be especially useful for research with human infants because these preferences emerge so early relative to other behavioral systems. To be sure, the capacity for visual exploration does not appear full-blown at birth: young infants see very poorly compared to adults (Teller, this volume), and they move their eyes and heads in a far less skilled manner (Aslin, this volume). Nevertheless, the visual behaviors of infants appear to be more advanced than any of their other directed actions. At 4 months, infants cannot yet locomote independently, and they cannot reach for and apprehend objects. Nevertheless, infants of this age and even younger ages show systematic patterns of looking under different stimulus conditions. These patterns serve to mark the events that infants detect.

The second reason for focusing on preferential-looking methods is more important. In infancy, active looking appears to be a kind of exploratory behavior. Like all exploratory behavior, it is guided by what infants already sense and know, and it is directed toward that which they seek to understand. If infants have initial conceptions of objects and events and initial abilities to enrich those conceptions through learning, then these conceptions and abilities should affect infants' patterns of visual exploration. Thus, observations of preferential looking may help to reveal both the notions with which infants begin and the problems they first attempt to solve.

This chapter will focus on two patterns of visual preference. First, infants are apt to look at an object or event that is relatively novel or surprising, in preference to an object or event that is familiar or expected. This preference appears to reflect a general tendency to explore at times and in places where there is new information to be gained. The decline of interest in a familiar event, and the renewed interest in novel events, are usually referred to as "habituation" and "dishabituation," respectively, although it is not clear whether the preference to look at a novel display is truly akin to other forms of habituation (see Tighe & Leaton, 1976; Bornstein, this volume). Second, infants are apt to look at an object or event that is accompanied by a related sound, in preference to an object or event that is accompanied by an unrelated sound. This preference may reflect a general tendency to explore one object or event at a time. Infants, like adults, may avoid attempts to follow two unrelated episodes—one visible and one audible—simultaneously.

Since the pioneering studies of Fantz (1961; see also Fantz, Fagan, & Miranda, 1975), there has developed a large body of experiments that use preferential-looking methods to investigate infants' perceptual and cognitive capacities. These experiments are too diverse to be encompassed easily in one chapter. Accordingly, this chapter will be concerned only with experiments that investigate (a) what infants know about the unity and boundaries of objects in visual scenes, (b) what infants know about relationships between visible objects and their corresponding sounds, and (c) what infants know about the persistence and the behavior of objects that move from view. The results of these experiments suggest, I believe, that patterns of preferential looking reflect more than an infant's capacity to detect color and pattern, and even more than an infant's capacity to perceive depth and motion. Looking preferences seem to reflect infants' initial perceptions and conceptions of objects and events. If this suggestion is correct, then preferential-looking methods can be used to address, through experiments, long-standing questions about the origins and the development of human knowledge.

LOOKING AT NOVEL DISPLAYS: AN INDEX OF KNOWLEDGE OF VISIBLE OBJECTS

The experiments described in this section focus on the ability to perceive visible objects as unitary and bounded. Human adults perceive the boundaries and the complete shapes of objects with an ease that is remarkable, for those boundaries are not reflected, in any simple way, in the pattern of light at the eye. The objects that we see are almost always adjacent to other objects: Objects that are fully suspended, like soap-bubbles, are rare. Adults, nevertheless, perceive each object as distinct from the things that touch it. The objects we see, moreover, are always partly hidden from view: every opaque object has a back that is hidden, and most objects have forward surfaces that are partly obscured by nearer objects as well. Adults perceive each object as complete, despite these patterns of occlusion.

The ability of adults to perceive visible objects appears to depend, in part, on conceptions about objects, their properties, and their behavior (see Spelke, 1983). For example, we appear to conceive of the world as composed of things that are relatively uniform in their shapes, colors, and textures, and this conception may lead us to group surfaces into simple, regular units in the ways that the gestalt psychologists described. We expect that these things can move and that they will move as wholes, separately from each other, in certain trajectories. This expectation may lead us to perceive objects by detecting patterns of motion. Finally, we conceive of the objects around us as instances of certain kinds, like cups and carrots, with characteristic properties and patterns of behavior. Once we can recognize what kind of thing a particular object is, our knowledge about things of its kind allows us to apprehend aspects of the object that would otherwise be obscure.

At least since the work of Piaget (1954), students of infant cognition have explored the origins and the development of conceptions of objects by focusing on infants' ability to perceive objects in visual scenes. Experiments have investigated whether, and under what conditions, infants perceive the unity of an object that is partly hidden and the boundaries of two objects that are adjacent or separated. By assessing the conditions under which infants perceive objects, such experiments promise to shed light on the origins and the development of underlying conceptions of objects.

Perception of Partly Hidden Objects

The first studies of perception of partly hidden objects, by Piaget (1954), used reaching and other manual activities as measures. These studies suggested that infants below about 7 months do not perceive the complete shapes of objects that are partly hidden. For example, Piaget's three children were able to reach for an attractive toy when it was fully in view by the age of about 4 months, but they failed to reach for the same toy when it protruded from under a cloth that partly occluded it until they were 6 to 8 months old. It appeared that the infants did not perceive the toy as complete when it was partly hidden. As a second example, one of Piaget's children readily reached for his bottle when the nipple of the bottle was oriented in his direction, but until 9 months of age, he failed to reach for the same bottle when it was rotated so that the nipple was out of view. The infant did not appear to perceive this object as having a back, or to recognize the object when it was rotated so that its visible and invisible sides were interchanged.

It is possible, however, that failures to manipulate objects appropriately derive from the infant's immature capacities to coordinate actions (see Piaget, 1952), and not from any inability to perceive and recognize objects. Infants might recognize a toy, for example, and yet fail to reach for it when it is partly covered, because they do not know how to extricate it from its cover. Infants also might recognize a rotated bottle as a bottle, and yet fail to discern how to rotate it themselves in order to get its nipple to their mouths. It is of interest, therefore, to investigate infants' perception of partly hidden objects by using preferential-looking methods.

A variety of experiments have used a familiarization/novelty-preference procedure. In these studies, 4-month-old infants were presented with a three-dimensional object whose top and bottom were visible but whose center was hidden behind a second object (Figure 1a). The object might be stationary or moving, as in this figure. This display was shown during a series of trials; each trial lasted as long as the baby looked at the object, ending when the baby looked away for 2 seconds. Infants tended to look at this display for 10 to 30 seconds on the first several trials, and then their looking times declined: Attention to the display "habituated." When looking time had decreased to half its original level, the block was removed, and infants were presented with two displays in alternation on six further trials (Figure 1b). One of these displays consisted of the two visible surfaces of the formerly occluded object, separated by a gap where the occluder had been. The other display consisted of a single connected object, created by joining together the two visible ends of the

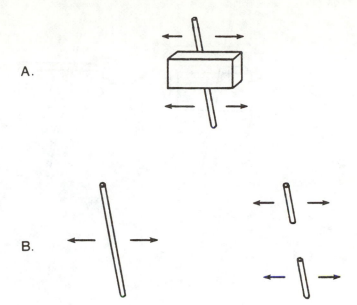

A.

B.

Figure 1. Schematic depiction of (a) the habituation display and (b) the test displays of an experiment on perception of partly occluded objects. Arrows indicate the path of motion (Kellman & Spelke, 1983).

original object. If infants perceived the visible surfaces of this partly hidden object as distinct and separate, then habituation would be expected to generalize to the display with the gap, and infants should look longer at the connected object. If infants perceived the two visible surfaces as connected behind the occluder—as parts of a single object—then habituation would be expected to generalize to the complete rod display, and the reverse preference should be observed.

Before turning to experiments that use this procedure, it is important to note that the procedure depends on certain assumptions. First, infants who are presented with a partly hidden object must attend to that object, and not only to the object in front of it. Second, the test displays of complete and broken objects must be discriminable and of roughly equal intrinsic attractiveness to the infants. Third, habituation to a configuration of two objects must generalize, to some extent, to one of those objects presented alone, and dishabituation must occur if a new object is presented. Two preliminary experiments were conducted as a check on these assumptions.

In the first experiment (Kellman & Spelke, 1983), infants were familiarized with a stationary solid black rod figure in front of the block that was to serve as the occluding object in the principal studies. Half the infants saw the complete rod and half saw the two separate rod pieces (Figure 2a). After the criterion of habituation was met, infants were shown test displays in which the rod figures appeared without the block (Figure 2b). The results indicated that

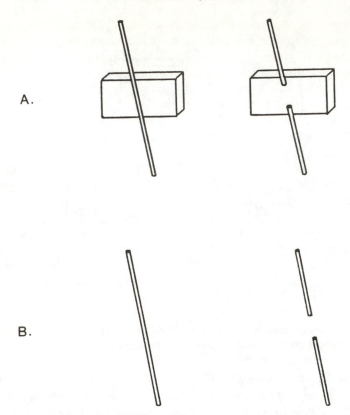

Figure 2. Schematic depiction of (a) the habituation displays and (b) the test displays of an experiment on habituation to configurations of objects (Kellman & Spelke, 1983).

the infants generalized habituation to the familiar rod figure when it was presented alone, and they dishabituated to the rod figure they had not previously seen. Averaging across the two experimental conditions, infants looked about equally at the two test displays. We may conclude that these complete and broken objects were discriminable and of about equal interest, and that habituation to these configurations of objects generalized to one of the objects presented alone and not to a new object. The habituation method can be used to investigate perception of each object in a configuration of several objects.

The second preliminary experiment (Kellman & Spelke, 1983) assessed infants' responses to changes in the visible surfaces of a partly hidden object, in order to determine whether infants perceive and attend to objects that are partly occluded. Infants in one condition were presented with a rod whose center was hidden by a block: the complete rod and block used in the former study. Infants in a second condition were presented with two rod pieces behind the same occluder, separated by a large visible gap (Figure 3a). After habituation, infants were presented, on alternating trials, with the complete test rod and with two small rod pieces separated by a large gap (Figure 3b). Thus, each

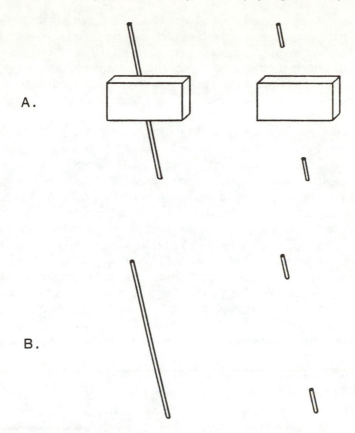

Figure 3. Schematic depiction of (a) the habituation displays and (b) the test displays of an experiment on perception of the visible surfaces of a partly occluded object (Kellman & Spelke, 1983).

test display matched the visible areas of only one of the original rod figures. Infants looked longer at the test figure that could *not* have been the figure presented during the habituation series. The experiment indicates that infants who are presented with a partly hidden rod figure attend sufficiently to its visible areas to discriminate the figure from a display that differs from it with respect to those visible areas.

Given the findings of these experiments, we may conclude that the familiarization/novelty-preference method provides a feasible means to investigate infants' perception of partly hidden objects. Therefore, a series of experiments was undertaken. In one experiment (Kellman & Spelke, 1983), infants of 4 months were presented with the black rod moving back and forth behind the occluding block, as in Figure 1, such that its center never came into view. Adults perceive the ends of this rod as connected behind the block, since the ends move together and can be joined to form an object with a homogeneous color and a regular shape. After habituating to this display, infants were presented on alternating trials with the complete rod and with the two rod pieces separated by the small gap where the block had been, moving in the same manner. In a separate experiment, infants of this age were found to look equally at these test displays when the displays were equally familiar. Nevertheless, the infants in the principal experiment looked longer at the rod with the gap. The experiment provides evidence that the infants perceived the ends of the original rod to be connected behind the block: They perceived the complete shape of this partly hidden object.

Subsequent experiments indicated that infants perceive partly hidden objects by analyzing the movements of surfaces but not by analyzing the colors and forms of surfaces. In different studies (Kellman & Spelke, 1983; Schmidt & Spelke, 1984; Termine, Hrynick, Gleitman, & Spelke, in preparation), infants have been presented with a single rod, a triangle made of rods, a solid sphere, a solid cube, and a large flat surface (Figure 4). Each object appeared without moving, behind a block that occluded its center. In all cases, habituation to these displays was followed by equal looking at complete and broken test displays. This equal looking could not have stemmed from a failure to attend to stationary objects that are partly hidden, since infants did attend to the stationary rods in the preliminary experiments. The equal looking also was not a statistical artifact of averaging together two distinct subgroups of infants, each of which dishabituated to one of the two test displays. Inspection and analysis of the distributions of looking times in the different experimental conditions revealed that the looking scores were unimodally distributed, with similar variances across conditions. It appears, therefore, that infants have no determinate perception of the complete shape of a partly hidden, stationary object.

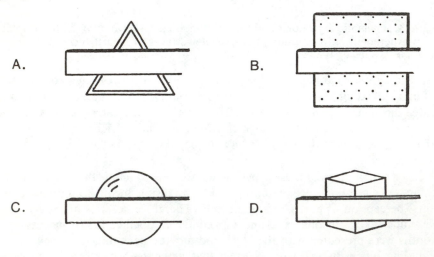

Figure 4. Schematic depiction of the occlusion displays of experiments on perception of partly hidden objects (Kellman & Spelke, 1983, display *a*; Termine, Hrynick, Gleitman, & Spelke, in preparation, display *b*; Schmidt & Spelke, 1984, displays *c* and *d*).

In a further study (Kellman & Spelke, 1983), infants were presented with a moving object with a very irregular shape. The object was composed of two surfaces of different colors and textures, with misaligned edges (Figure 5). When these surfaces moved together in a common translation behind an occluding block, infants perceived the surfaces as connected. After they became familiar with this display, they showed as strong a preference for the broken display as did infants in the original moving rod experiment. All these experiments provide evidence that infants perceive objects by detecting the movements of surfaces. Surfaces that move together rigidly are perceived to be connected in the places where they are hidden. The experiments also provide evidence that infants do not perceive the complete shapes of partly hidden objects by organizing visual displays into units of maximally regular shapes and colors. Infants appear to perceive the complete shapes of partly hidden objects under some, but not all, the conditions that are effective for adults.

In brief, 4-month-old infants' patterns of looking at displays of objects, presented successively, seem to reflect their perception of the objects and their boundaries. If infants perceive a partly hidden object as a complete object with a certain shape, habituation to the object together with its occluder will generalize to the object presented alone and fully in view. Note that this looking pattern need not have been observed, even granting that infants can perceive the complete shapes of partly hidden objects. Infants might have habituated and dishabituated to more superficial aspects of an occlusion display: to prop-

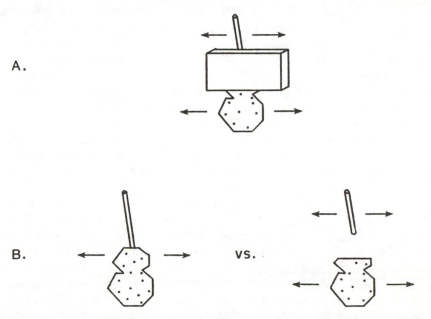

Figure 5. Schematic depiction of (a) the habituation display and (b) the test displays of an experiment on perception of partly occluded objects. Arrows indicate the path of motion (Kellman & Spelke, 1983).

erties of the visible surfaces of an object rather than to properties of the object itself. For example, infants might have perceived the original display as a unitary rod, but they might also have perceived that only two parts of the rod were visible. When the complete and broken test rods were presented, the former might have appeared more novel, because it contained a new pattern of visible surfaces, even though it contained a familiar object. In no experiment, however, was there a preference for the complete test display. Infants looked equally at the complete and broken test displays after seeing a partly hidden object that was stationary, and they looked longer at the broken display after seeing a partly hidden object in motion. In these experiments, the infants habituated to the perceived objects themselves and not to any patterns of visible surfaces.

Infants' perception of partly hidden objects can be assessed not only through multi-trial habituation procedures, but also through procedures that focus on infants' spontaneous attention to an object that is originally partly occluded and then is disoccluded. In a series of experiments (Schmidt & Spelke, 1984), 4-month-old infants were presented with a partly occluded, moving or stationary object. They were allowed to look at this display for 5 seconds, and then the occluder was moved to the side, revealing fully the object that had stood behind it (Figure 6). On half the trials, the disocclusion revealed a complete object; on the other trials, it revealed an object with a formerly hidden gap. Every time an object was disoccluded, it remained present for as long as the baby looked at it, and was removed only when the baby had looked away from the display for 2 seconds. Looking times to the complete and broken objects were then compared with each other and with the looking times of infants in baseline experiments, who viewed the complete and broken objects in alternation with no occluder. If infants perceived the object as complete while it was occluded, they were expected to look longer when the disocclusion revealed a gap, relative to the baseline preference for this broken object. Infants should perceive this display as relatively novel, puzzling, or surprising.

Experiments using this method complement those that used the standard habituation method. Infants in the baseline conditions looked about equally at the complete and broken objects. The preferences shown by infants in the experimental conditions, in contrast, depended on whether or not the partly hidden object was presented in motion. When an object was initially stationary behind the occluder, infants subsequently looked equally at the complete and broken disoccluded objects. When an object was initially seen undergoing a unitary motion behind the occluder, infants looked longer to the disoccluded object with a gap. These experiments provide converging evidence that infants perceive objects by detecting the movements, but not the colors and forms, of surfaces. Moreover, the experiments provide evidence that infants look longer at an object if the removal of its occluder reveals it to be different from the object they had perceived. Once again, infants looked longer at an object that was novel and perhaps unexpected, even though its visible surfaces matched the visible surfaces of the object in the original occlusion display.

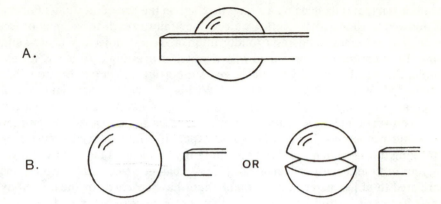

Figure 6. Schematic depiction of (a) the occlusion display and (b) the disoccluded objects of an experiment on perception of partly occluded objects (Schmidt & Spelke, 1984).

How do the findings of experiments using preferential-looking methods compare to those of the experiments using reaching methods? In one respect, these experiments support opposite conclusions. Recall that Piaget, drawing on observations of infants' reaching, concluded that young infants perceive only the visible surfaces of objects, not their complete shapes. The preferential-looking experiments, in contrast, suggest that infants never perceive just the visible surfaces of things. Depending on the stimulus conditions, infants either have no determinate perception of a partly hidden object, or they perceive the object as continuing where it is hidden. Nevertheless, the findings of the reaching experiments and the preferential-looking experiments are not in conflict, for the reaching studies were conducted with partly hidden objects that were stationary. The findings of all these experiments are consistent with the hypothesis that infants perceive partly hidden objects by detecting the movements of surfaces, and not by detecting the similarity or alignment of surfaces. Infants may perceive in accord with the conception that objects tend to move independently, as wholes. Infants evidently do not perceive in accord with the conception that objects tend to be regular in their colors and shapes.

Perception of the Boundaries of Adjacent and Separated Objects

How do infants perceive visual scenes in which objects are suspended so that they are either adjacent or separated in space? Consider first two stationary objects of different colors and textures that are adjacent in the frontal plane. Adults usually perceive such objects as distinct. The experiments on perception of partly hidden objects suggest, however, that infants will fail to perceive the boundary between the objects. Infants should perceive two stationary adjacent objects as one unit, since only their colors, textures, and shapes can serve to separate them.

The first studies of perception of adjacent objects, again, were reaching experiments. Although infants of 5 months and beyond will reach reliably for a small object that is dangled on a string, perched on the tips of an adult's fingers, or allowed to slide across another object, they fail to reach for a small object when it is stationary and rests solidly upon a second object. When 5- and 6-month-old infants are presented with a matchbox resting on a book, for example, they reach primarily for the larger, supporting object (see Bresson & de Schonen, 1976-1977; Piaget, 1954; and Wishart, 1979, for these and related observations). Piaget (1954) suggested that infants perceive two adjacent objects as a single unit when they are stationary, and as two objects when they move independently—just as one would expect if infants perceive objects by analyzing the movements and spatial contiguity of surfaces but not by analyzing the forms and colors of surfaces. It is possible, however, that reaching was unrelated to object perception. Infants might have reached for the matchbox when it moved on the book because they prefer to reach for surfaces that move, and they might have reached for the book when both objects were stationary because they prefer to reach for surfaces that are nearby. Experiments indicate that infants have such reaching preferences (e.g., Yonas, this volume). Thus, it is important to investigate infants' perception of adjacent and separated objects through observations of activities unrelated to reaching. Once again, preferential-looking methods can serve this purpose, as is illustrated by the next experiment.

In this experiment (Kestenbaum, Termine, & Spelke, in preparation), 3-month-old infants were familiarized with a display of two objects that were either adjacent or spatially separated. The displays were constructed so that the objects in one display were of the same size and distance from the baby as the objects in the other display. To accomplish this, the objects were arranged so that they were either adjacent or separated *in depth:* One object was presented in front of the other, so that they were or were not touching (Figure 7). In both displays, the objects overlapped fully at the infant's eye, however far a baby moved his or her head. Very slight head movements, however, allowed adults (and, presumably, infants) to see that the separated objects were discontinuous in depth (the sides of the nearer object ended well before the front of the further object), and that the adjacent objects were contiguous in depth (the sides of the nearer object met the front of the more distant object). After habituation, the infants were shown displays in which either one or both objects appeared in a new position closer to the infant, so that the spatial relationship of the objects was either changed or preserved. When only one of the adjacent objects was displaced, it was moved so that the objects were no longer adjacent. If infants had perceived the two objects in the original display as one unit, they were expected to look longer at the new display, in which only one object appeared in a new position. This display should now be seen as two objects, each quite unlike the object infants had perceived before. In contrast, if infants had perceived the objects in the original display as distinct, then they were expected to look equally at the two novel displays, for neither of these displays would be perceived to contain any objects that were new.

FRONT VIEW SIDE VIEW

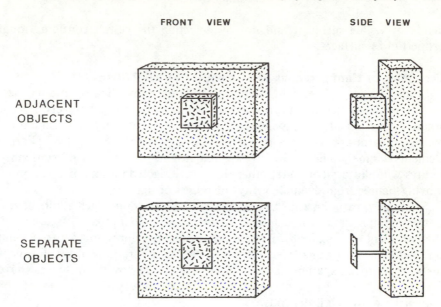

Figure 7. Schematic depiction of the displays of an experiment on perception of adjacent and spatially separated objects (Kestenbaum, Termine, & Spelke, in preparation).

The experiment used the same method as the original studies of perception of partly hidden objects. One group of infants was familiarized with the display of adjacent objects, and a second group was familiarized with the display of separated objects. Then the two test displays were presented on six alternating trials. The results were clear. The infants who had been presented with the objects that were separated in depth subsequently looked equally at the two test displays. In contrast, the infants who had been presented with the objects that were adjacent in depth looked longer at the display in which only one object appeared in a new position, changing the arrangement of the objects. The experiment provides evidence that infants perceive two adjacent objects, but not two separated objects, as one configuration.

This experiment suggests, once again, that patterns of visual preference can provide information about infants' perception of the boundaries of objects. Infants evidently looked less and less at displays in which they perceived the same objects, even if the objects were presented in a new arrangement, and they looked longer at a display in which they perceived a new object. The hypothesis that infants' looking patterns reflect their perception of objects is supported by the concordance of the results of this experiment with the results of the studies of perception of partly occluded objects, and also by the concordance of the present findings with the findings of all the reaching experiments. All these experiments provide evidence that infants perceive the unity and the boundaries of objects by detecting the spatial arrangements and the movements of visible surfaces, and not by detecting the gestalt configurational properties of surfaces.

Perception of Configurations of Elements in Visual Patterns

Studies using preferential-looking methods have investigated infants' perception of two-dimensional forms as well as three-dimensional objects. Recent studies, in particular, have focused on perception of the unity of a visual form when the form appears in a two-dimensional pattern composed of discrete elements. Some studies have investigated infants' perception of stationary figures with illusory contours; others have investigated infants' perception of moving figures from dynamic arrays of points of light.

Stationary, two-dimensional displays can be created in which adults have a powerful impression of a geometric figure, even though no such figure is actually present (see Figure 8). Perception of illusory figures appears to depend on tendencies to organize visual displays into configurations of regular, geometric patterns. Experiments using a preference-for-novelty technique have focused on the development of perception of illusory figures and of the tendencies on which it depends.

Bertenthal, Campos, and Haith (1980) presented infants of 5 and 7 months with the displays in Figure 8. These displays all consist of the same elements, but they are perceived quite differently by adults. One is perceived to contain a bright square, whereas the others are not. To investigate how infants perceive these displays, one group of infants was presented repeatedly with the illusory square and then was presented with one of the nonillusory figures. A second group of infants was presented repeatedly with a nonillusory figure, followed by the illusory square. A third group of infants was presented with the two different nonillusory figures.

At 7 months of age, infants were found to look longer at the final test display if the introduction of that display involved a change from an illusory to a nonillusory figure, or the reverse. In contrast, infants did not increase their looking when the displays changed from one nonillusory figure to another. These findings provide evidence that infants are sensitive to the configuration of elements in a display that produces an illusory figure. Infants of 7 months

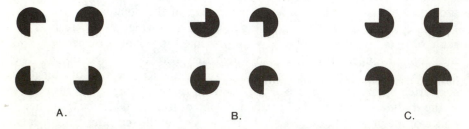

A.   B.   C.

Figure 8. Displays used in experiments on perception of illusory figures (Bertenthal, Campos, & Haith, 1980).

do not appear to respond to the individual pattern elements per se: They appear to perceive forms by organizing such elements into figures with maximally regular shapes.

The 5-month-old infants, in contrast, showed little increase in looking at any of the displays and no differential increase in looking when one of the two displays was the illusory figure display. Both in the original experiment, and in a subsequent replication and extension (Bertenthal, Haith, & Campos, 1980, cited in Lamb & Campos, 1982), 5-month-old infants appeared to be insensitive to the configuration of elements in these patterns. It appears, therefore, that infants do not tend to organize two-dimensional visual patterns into units with regular forms.

Adults also perceive unitary, structured forms when they are presented with kinetic, two-dimensional displays in which separate elements—points or circles of light—undergo certain types of movement. Adults perceive a human form when they are presented with a set of lights on the major joints of a walking human body (Johansson, 1978). Furthermore, adults perceive a human face when they are presented with a set of light-reflecting circles, painted on the face, that move and deform as the face moves expressively (Bassili, 1979). Investigators in several laboratories have now presented infants with these moving light displays (Bertenthal & Proffitt, 1982; Fox & McDaniel, 1982; Kaufmann-Hayoz & Jager, 1983; McDaniel & Odom, 1983). Their experiments, which use preferential-looking techniques, have provided evidence that infants are sensitive to the structure in both the walking and the expressive patterns of movement.

One experiment (Kaufmann-Hayoz & Jager, 1983) serves to illustrate the methods and findings. The experiment used a preference-for-novelty method. Infants of 3½ months were familiarized either with spots of light on an animately moving face, or with spots of light on an inanimately moving face mask. Then the infants were presented with the two displays, side by side. In one condition, these displays were presented upright, with the face in its canonical orientation. In the other condition, the displays were presented upside down. The inverted condition is of interest because adults do not easily recognize faces and their expressions at this orientation. The infants showed no consistent preferences between the displays in the upside-down orientation: neither motion pattern was recognizable by itself under these viewing conditions, and neither pattern was intrinsically more attractive. In the upright condition, however, the infants looked longer at the novel display. The experiment provides evidence that infants discerned the structure in the pattern of animate motion. It is possible that the presence of this structure led them to perceive the animately moving dots as a unitary human face.

In summary, these experiments suggest that infants first perceive two-dimensional patterns, as well as three-dimensional objects, under conditions involving motion. Infants do not group pattern elements into units through an analysis of static gestalt configurations, just as they do not group surfaces into objects on this basis. Studies of preferential looking appear to converge on a single description of the organization of the infant's visual world.

Perception and Knowledge of Objects of Particular Kinds

As children gain knowledge about the world, they come to consider objects as members of certain kinds, with characteristic properties and functions, and knowledge about particular kinds of objects may enhance the child's ability to perceive objects. As adults, we often perceive objects by drawing on knowledge about the properties of objects of particular sorts. Knowledge about the characteristic shapes of spoons, for example, leads us to perceive the complete shape of a spoon that is partly hidden within a bowl of cereal; knowledge about cups leads us to perceive a cup as separate from the saucer on which it rests. If an infant's perception of objects is also affected by knowledge about particular categories of objects, then studies of object perception could serve as a means to investigate the development of such knowledge.

One experiment (Schwartz, 1983) has explored that possibility. Schwartz investigated infants' knowledge of the properties of human faces by using Kellman's procedure to probe their perception of partly hidden faces. Infants were presented with a slide photograph of the face of an unfamiliar woman, projected behind a horizontal block that occluded the center of the face. After habituation, infants were shown slide photographs of the complete face, and of a face with a gap where the occluder had been. If infants can recognize a partly hidden photographed face as a face, and if they know that a face is a connected object, then they were expected to generalize habituation to the complete face and not to the broken face.

The 5-month-old infants in Schwartz's first experiment appeared to perceive the face as a connected object. These infants looked relatively longer at the broken face than did a baseline group of infants who were presented with the test displays after habituation to an unrelated object. (There was a baseline preference for the complete face.) A second experiment was then conducted to investigate whether infants' perception depended on an analysis of the features of the face, or on an analysis of the simplicity of the face's overall shape. Five-month-old infants were presented with slide displays consisting of an abstract, spotted object with the same outline shape as the face, but with no other facial features. After habituation to this display under partial occlusion, infants showed less of a preference for a broken display than did the infants in the experiment with the photographed face. It appeared that perception of the partly hidden face in the first experiment depended, at least in part, on infants' knowledge of the features of the face.

A third experiment was conducted with younger infants to investigate the development of knowledge of faces. After habituation to the partly hidden photograph of a face, 4-month-old infants showed no looking preference for the broken test face, unlike their 5-month-old counterparts. It appears that knowledge of faces comes to influence infants' perception of a partly hidden face between 4 and 5 months of age. This finding complements the findings of other experiments on face perception, which suggest that sensitivity to the configurational properties of a face increases considerably during the fifth month of life (e.g., Caron, Caron, Caldwell, & Weiss, 1973).

In summary, infants of 5 months, like adults, can use knowledge of faces as a basis for perceiving a partly occluded face as a unitary, connected object. The emergence of this ability may depend on maturation of innate mechanisms for detecting facial configurations; face recognition has been shown to have certain maturational components (Carey, 1983). The emergence of this ability may depend, as well, on learning: Since infants are able to perceive objects under conditions involving motion, they would seem to be in a position to learn about objects that are often observed in motion, such as human faces. In any case, experiments using looking-time measures hold promise as tools for investigating the development of knowledge of faces and other kinds of objects.

Some Limitations of the Methods

Although experiments using preferential-looking methods appear to have shed light on infants' perception of objects, these experiments must inevitably confront two problems of interpretation. First, what justifies the inference that the test display preferred by infants in a given experiment is the more *novel* display? Might not infants, under some conditions, look systematically at a display that is more familiar? Second, even granting that infants perceive a given test display as more novel, what justifies the inference that this display is perceived to contain novel *objects,* with different boundaries from the objects in the familiar display? Might not infants perceive the more novel display to contain the same units as the familiar display, but in a different arrangement? These problems will be considered in turn.

To begin with the first problem, many investigators have suggested that infants do not tend to look longest at the most novel of a set of displays. Responses to novelty, it is suggested, are curvilinear, with extremely novel arrangements receiving less attention than moderately novel arrangements (Kagan, 1971; McCall, Kennedy, & Appelbaum, 1977; for a recent discussion, see Kagan, Linn, Mount, & Reznick, 1979). In one experiment (McCall et al., 1977), for example, 2- and 4-month-old infants were familiarized with one of four checkerboard patterns with elements of different sizes. The infants subsequently looked longer at a new checkerboard pattern with elements of a moderately different size than they looked at a pattern with elements of a greatly different size. In a second experiment, 2-month-old infants were habituated to a line drawing in one of four orientations. They subsequently looked longer when the same drawing was presented at a moderately different orientation than when the same drawing appeared at a greatly different orientation. In both studies, infants who became familiar with one display evidently looked longest to displays that were moderately different.

Investigators using novelty-preference methods must always be alert to the possibility that infants will prefer the more familiar, and not the more novel, test display. One cannot ever conclude that a given display is more novel from the results of one experimental condition considered alone. For example, consider by itself the principal condition of the moving, partly occluded rod study by Kellman and Spelke. After habituating to the partly hidden rod, infants might have looked longer at the broken rod not because they perceived the partly hidden rod as complete but because they perceived it as broken. The broken test rod might have commanded their attention because that rod was only moderately discrepant from the habituation display, whereas the complete rod was too discrepant. It is only by comparing infants' reactions across different experimental conditions that one becomes able to interpret this difference in looking times. When one considers the results of the preliminary studies of perception of partly occluded objects, for example, one discovers that infants looked longer at the display in which a new rod figure appeared, not at the display containing the original rod figure. It is unlikely that infants would show the opposite tendency in the principal experiments, whose displays and methods were so nearly the same. Moreover, when one considers the findings of the principal experiments, one learns that the introduction of movement leads to an increase in the preference for the broken rod. If these infants were exhibiting a preference for the more familiar display, one would have to conclude that the presence of common movement *detracted* from perception of a complete rod for infants. This possibility appears remote, since common movement has the opposite effect for adults and for other animals. The total pattern of experimental findings therefore provides strong evidence that infants looked longer at the more novel of the test displays.

The usefulness of preferential-looking methods would be greatly enhanced if investigators were able to predict, in advance, when infants will prefer the more novel of two objects. One such prediction may be possible in the future, for there is one generalization that appears to be true of all the experiments using this method. After familiarization with a display of objects, infants always appear to look longer when they perceive a novel object than they will look when they perceive only objects from the original display, in familiar or novel positions. To my knowledge, all of the studies that have reported a curvilinear relation of looking time to stimulus novelty have used test objects that were either all novel, as in the case of the four distinct checkerboards, or all familiar, as in the case of the pattern at four orientations. Given a choice among several novel objects, infants may not always look longest at the object that differs the most from objects with which they are familiar. Given a choice between a novel object and a familiar object, however, infants may consistently look longer at the novel object.

Let us turn to the second interpretive problem. How does one know that infants perceive certain familiar and novel *objects,* with internal coherence and external boundaries? One challenge to this interpretation arises from an extreme empiricist stance. Perhaps infants do not perceive objects at all, but only patterns of visual sensation. In situations where adults perceive changes in the boundaries of objects, infants may experience the greatest changes in sensory patterns. For example, the sensory experiences evoked by a moving occluded rod may be more different from those evoked by the broken rod display than from those evoked by the complete rod display. Responses to sensory properties of these displays may underlie infants' looking preferences.

As many investigators have noted (see especially Gibson, 1969; Bower, 1972; Yonas & Pick, 1975), this question is not easily answered. Indeed, it will not be possible to test the sensory hypothesis fully until the sensory capacities of infants are better understood. Nevertheless, there are several ways to obtain evidence against the hypothesis. First, one can design individual experiments to be maximally biased against the hypothesis that infants perceive objects, by making the habituation display as similar as possible to the display of putatively novel objects, and as different as possible from the display of putatively familiar objects. Thus, Kellman's and Schmidt's broken test objects were designed to be nearly identical to the visible surfaces of the occluded objects. The findings of these experiments suggest, therefore, that infants responded to the objects and events themselves, and not directly to the sensory patterns to which these objects gave rise.

One can also obtain stronger evidence that infants respond to objects, and not directly to sensory patterns, by conducting a series of experiments that use different displays and that focus on a set of closely interrelated questions. Thus, the same methods have been used to investigate infants' perception of partly occluded objects, of adjacent objects, and of objects that are separated in depth. The conclusion that looking times in these experiments reflect infants' perception of objects is strengthened by the finding that all the patterns of preference can be accounted for in terms of a single, underlying tendency to group surfaces into units that are spatially connected and separately moveable. It is conceivable that all these findings could be explained in terms of a single, broad and general account of infants' sensory capacities. Such an account is difficult to imagine, however, and none has yet been proposed.

A further challenge to the interpretation of object-perception experiments arises from an extreme nativist position: How does one know that infants fail to perceive the unity of a partly hidden stationary object, or the distinctness of two stationary objects that are adjacent? Perhaps infants perceive objects under all the conditions that adults do, but they also attend to the configuration of objects in a scene, and they react to changes in this configuration. For example, infants who were habituated to two adjacent objects might have perceived two objects that were *adjacent*. When one object was displaced, these infants might have increased their looking not because they perceived a change in the boundaries of the objects, but because they perceived a change in the objects' relative positions: the objects were no longer adjacent. This last possibility has been tested through further preferential-looking experiments. Infants have been presented with a display of adjacent objects, and, in effect, they have been asked *how many units* were in the display.

When infants are presented with a visual display, they appear to enumerate the units in the display, provided that the total number of units is small. Evidence that infants are sensitive to number has come primarily from experiments using familiarization/novelty-preference methods. Infants have been presented with a succession of displays of forms, each display containing the same number of forms. After their looking time to these displays has declined, they are presented with new displays containing either the same number of forms or a different number of forms. Infants have been found to look longer at the displays that contained a new number of forms (Starkey & Cooper, 1980; Starkey, Spelke, & Gelman, 1980; Strauss & Curtis, 1981), even as newborns (Antell & Keating, 1983). This finding is of interest in itself, for it suggests that patterns of preferential looking are affected by changes in quite abstract properties of displays. For present purposes, however, the experiments are important because they provide a means to investigate infants' perception of visible objects.

One experiment (Prather & Spelke, 1982) will serve as an illustration. The experiment focused on infants' perception of adjacent and spatially separated objects. Infants of 3 months were presented with a succession of different displays of rectangular, solid objects. Although the objects in different displays were of different colors and dimensions, all the displays contained the same number of objects. For half the infants, each display contained one object; for the others, each display contained two objects that were separated in the frontal plane (Figure 9a). After looking time had declined to half its original level, infants were presented with new objects that were either adjacent, side by side, or were separated in depth (Figure 9b). The infants who had been presented with displays of one object generalized habituation to the adjacent-objects display and looked longer at the objects separated in depth. The infants who had been presented with the displays of two objects exhibited the opposite looking preference. All the infants, therefore, treated the adjacent objects as one unit, and the objects separated in depth as two units.

This experiment provides further evidence that patterns of preferential looking reflect, in part, infants' perception of objects and their boundaries. Infants perceive objects by grouping together surfaces that touch, but not by grouping together surfaces that form simple, regular configurations. Moreover, each perceived object is taken to be a unit that is countable, in some sense. All these experiments are consistent with the notion that infants have the capacity to organize the visual world into units that are internally coherent and separately moveable: the units that we as adults call "objects."

Infants may perceive objects by virtue of perceptual mechanisms that are specific to vision. Alternatively, they may perceive objects by virtue of an abstract and general conception of the material world and its organization. Infants may have the notion that the world divides into things that are spatially connected, bounded, and coherent: things that can move independently but that must move as wholes. We will return to these two possibilities after considering two more bodies of research: studies of how infants perceive objects that are sensed through two sensory modalities at once, and studies of how infants understand events in which objects move wholly from view.

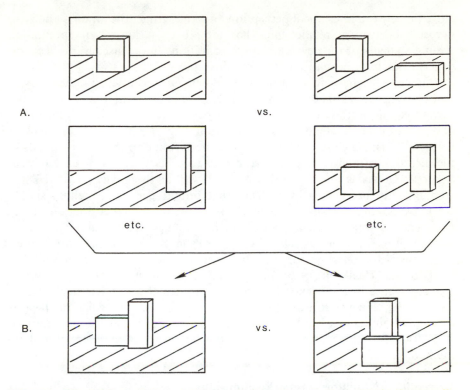

Figure 9. Schematic depiction of (a) some habituation displays and (b) the test displays of an experiment on enumeration of adjacent and spatially separated objects (Prather & Spelke, 1982).

159.3

LOOKING AT SOUNDING OBJECTS:
AN INDEX OF KNOWLEDGE OF INTERMODAL UNITY

Human adults do not live in a world of sights and sounds and tactile sensations, but a world of objects and events. When they look at an event while hearing its sound, for example, adults perceive a unitary episode. Perception of the unity of objects and events that are seen and heard depends on an ability to detect intermodal relationships: to determine when an object that is seen, and an object that is heard, are one and the same.

This ability is of considerable interest to those who study human knowledge. Since each sensory system is quite different in and of itself, the perception of intermodal relationships would seem to depend on abilities to apprehend rather abstract properties of the world. An adult's ability to perceive relationships between the diverse sounds that compose a symphony and the instruments that produce each sound, for example, appears to depend on his or her knowledge of music and its production (Pick, 1983). Because of the apparently close tie between intermodal perception and knowledge, the infant's ability to perceive intermodal relationships has long been a subject of speculation among students of the development of cognition. In the last several decades, experiments have begun to investigate this ability.

Many studies have focused on infants' tendency to orient the head, eyes, and limbs in the spatial direction of stimulation in different modalities. Under certain conditions, even newborn infants have been found to turn their eyes and heads toward a laterally positioned sound (e.g., Muir & Field, 1978; Wertheimer, 1961). Newborn infants have also been found to orient their hands in the direction of a visually presented object (e.g., Bower, 1972; von Hofsten, 1982; see Gibson & Spelke, 1983, for a review of all these experiments). These findings have been taken as evidence that infants perceive a unitary spatial world by looking, listening, and feeling. It is possible, however, that the ability to orient to events through multiple perceptual systems depends on mechanisms that are specific to each system. For example, infants may orient their heads toward a sound because of a tropistic tendency to balance the sound at the two ears (J. Gibson, 1976). Infants may extend their arms toward a visible object because of a tendency to turn so as to center the object in the visual field, and a tendency to extend the arms in the direction in which the head is turned. To investigate further the infant's sensitivity to intermodal relationships, therefore, a number of experiments have turned to preferential-looking methods.

Perception of Auditory-Visual Relationships

The first experiment of this kind, to my knowledge, investigated whether 4-month-old infants can ever determine if an event they see and an event they hear are one and the same (Spelke, 1976). When babies look and listen to one event, do they perceive what they hear as related to what they see? When they look at one event while listening to another, do they perceive that what they see is distinct from what they hear? To address these questions, infants were presented with two filmed events, side by side. One event consisted of a woman playing "peekaboo," and the other consisted of a hand holding a baton and hitting two percussion instruments in a simple rhythmic pattern. While the events were projected side by side, the soundtrack to one film was played through a central speaker. If infants perceived that the voice went with the person and the percussion music went with the instruments, they were expected to look longer at each event when its corresponding sound was played.

Why might one expect infants to explore so as to focus on one event at a time? When we as adults listen to one of several objects, we generally look at that object in preference to other objects because of two perceptual effects. First, adults usually see an event better if they can also hear it, and they hear an event better if they can also see it. This effect is apparent, for example, when one watches a symphony on television: the sound of the violins is more distinctive when the camera focuses on them than when it focuses on the wind instruments. Second, adults attend better to one audible event in a stream of sounds, avoiding distraction, if they also follow that event by looking (e.g., Reisberg, 1978). Given the apparent limits on infants' abilities to perceive and attend to events, it seemed likely that they would be especially apt to look at events to which they listen.

The results of this experiment were clear: Infants looked longer to the peek-aboo game when they heard the voice sound, and they looked longer to the percussion instruments when they heard the percussion sound. Since that study, this looking pattern has been observed by a variety of investigators using a variety of events, and it has provided evidence that infants detect a number of different auditory-visual relationships. Infants of 4½ months, for example, have been found to detect relationships between the sight and sound of a xylophone, a hand clap game, and a rattling slinky toy. When two of these events are presented side by side, infants looked longer at the event projected in sound (Bahrick, Walker, & Neisser, 1981).

How do infants determine which of two visible events is the source of an accompanying sound? Since the sounds in all the events occurred in temporal synchrony with certain movements of the visible objects, it is possible that infants perceived the sound-object relationships by detecting this pattern of synchrony. To investigate this possibility, a variety of experiments have presented infants with unfamiliar inanimate objects, each of which moved in synchrony with a different percussive sound. For example, infants have been presented with two stuffed animals that bounced on a surface, each bounce occurring at the time of a dull or a reverberant percussive sound. Infants of 4 months were found to detect this sound-object relationship: when both objects were presented, accompanied by one of the sounds, infants looked longer at the object that moved in time with the sound (Spelke, 1979). Subsequent experiments (Spelke, Born, & Chu, 1983) revealed that 4-month-old infants detect the synchrony of a sound with any change in the movement of an object, whether or not a visible impact occurs. In this respect, infants differ from adults. For example, if adults are presented with a sound, and they simultaneously see one object hitting a surface and another object stopping in midair, they perceive the sound as related to the former object. Infants, in contrast, looked equally at the impacting and the nonimpacting objects under this condition. This study and others (see Spelke et al., 1983) provide evidence that infants relate sounds to an object by detecting the object's pattern of movement. Unlike adults, they do not relate percussive sounds specifically to moments of impact.

If infants can detect the synchrony of sounds with visible object movements, they might be able to perceive a unitary object when they look and listen to a speaking person, for voices are synchronized with facial movements during human speech. A number of experiments confirm that 3- to 5-month-old infants detect the synchrony of audible speech to visible facial movements. Infants who were presented with one voice accompanied by two faces, one of which was synchronized with the voice, looked longer at the appropriately speaking face. The preference has been found both in experiments using the standard preference method, in which one voice is played between two faces that are side by side (Spelke & Cortelyou, 1981; Walker, 1982), and in experiments in which one face is presented at a time, accompanied by a synchronized or a nonsynchronized voice (Dodd, 1979).

In summary, infants can perceive the unity of many events in which objects are seen and heard. They perceive intermodal relationships, at least in part, by detecting the synchrony of visible speech and audible speaking movements. The ability to perceive intermodal relationships was revealed through infants' patterns of preferential looking: Infants tend to look at an event that corresponds to an accompanying sound, following that event by looking and listening at once. This pattern of exploration is likely to foster the development of knowledge about the perceptual world. An infant who looks and listens to an object at once is in a position to learn about the particular sounds that are characteristic of that particular object. As infants gain such knowledge, they should become able to perceive relationships between sounds and objects even under conditions in which the synchrony of sounds and movements cannot guide them. We turn now to experiments that focus on infants' knowledge of particular auditory-visual relationships. These experiments illustrate that auditory-visual preference methods can shed light on the infant's developing knowledge of objects and their characteristic sounds.

Knowledge of the Properties of Sounding Objects

The most familiar audible and visible objects in a young infant's world are probably the infant's parents. Infants often have the opportunity to look at a parent while the parent speaks to them, and the research described above suggests that infants will tend to do this systematically (see also Haith, Bergman, & Moore, 1977). It is of interest, therefore, to discover when, and under what conditions, children learn that each parent's face and voice go together.

This question has been addressed through an experiment that used a variant of the preferential-looking method described in the last section: what we have called a ''search'' method (Spelke & Owsley, 1979). When adults hear a sound very briefly, and they know what visible object is characteristically the source of that sound, they will often look for the object. Adults may look for a certain person when they hear a familiar voice or familiar footsteps, and they may look for a certain kind of animal if they hear a familiar growl. Although adults do not always look for the sources of sounds, especially in a noisy environment in which the same sounds are repeated, they generally do look for the sources of sounds that are new, sudden, or unexpected. They do this by drawing on knowledge about the sounds and the visible appearances of objects. Accordingly, the experiment with infants investigated whether infants would also turn to look at a familiar object (in this case, the mother or father) when they heard its characteristic sound (the parent's voice).

Infants of 3, 5, and 7 months of age were seated facing the mother and father, who sat side by side and faced the child without moving. After an infant's gaze was drawn between the parents, one parent's tape-recorded voice was played for a few seconds through a central speaker, and the infant's subsequent looking was observed. A series of trials were given, half with each parent's voice. The infants tended to turn to look at the parent whose voice was played: they turned first to the appropriate parent on reliably more trials than they turned to the inappropriate parent. The effects were not large: no infant turned first to the appropriate parent on every trial, and most only looked consistently to the appropriate parent on a short string of trials. (Note that when the infants turned, they encountered a motionless and unresponsive person.) Nevertheless, the looking pattern was reliable. It showed that infants as young as 3 months have learned something about the relation between each parent's voice and face.

The search method has proven useful in studies of the process of learning about intermodal relationships. Infants of 4 and 6 months have been presented with one moving, sounding object during a brief period of familiarization. Then they were shown that object and a second object, both accompanied by the sound, and their looking times to each object were recorded. Infants were found to look more at the object that corresponded to the sound (Lyons-Ruth, 1977; Lawson, 1980; Spelke, 1981). They had evidently learned, over the course of the familiarization period, that the sound and object were related.

The search method has been used to assess infants' knowledge of other properties of objects, such as their rigidity or flexibility. Bahrick (1980) presented 4½-month-old infants with either a clacking or a squishing sound, and then she presented silent films of squishing sponges and clacking blocks side by side. The sounds and films appeared on a series of brief trials. Infants tended to look first to the event that corresponded to the sound. Bahrick suggested that they perceived the rigidity or flexibility of the objects both by looking and by listening.

Similar methods have also been used to investigate infants' knowledge of the relationships between particular audible speech syllables and the particular visible gestures that produce them (Kuhl & Meltzoff, 1982; MacKain, Studdert-Kennedy, Spieker, & Stern, 1983). Infants of 4 or of 5-6 months were shown two videotapes, side by side, of a woman producing one of two syllables repeatedly. The videotapes were synchronized with each other, and both were synchronized with an accompanying speech sound that corresponded to one of the two syllables. Infants tended to look longer at the videotape of the face whose articulatory gestures corresponded to the speech sound.

Finally, preferential-looking experiments have investigated infants' sensitivity to the emotional tone of an expressive face (Walker, 1982). Infants of 5 and 7 months were presented with two films of a face expressing different emotions: happiness, sadness, anger, or a neutral expression. These films were accompanied by a voice with the same emotional tone as the expressions in one of the films. This voice, however, was not synchronized with either film, so only the common emotional tone of the face and voice tied them together. At first, infants showed no preference between the films, perhaps because they detected the asynchrony of the voice with both faces. After about 1 minute, however, infants began to look longer at the face whose expressions corresponded in tone to the voice. Infants of 5 months appear to be sensitive to information for a speaker's emotional tone.

Knowledge of Number

In the above studies, the tendency to look at an event corresponding to a sound has been used to investigate infants' perception and knowledge of events taking place around them. But this tendency can also serve to shed light on infants' knowledge of more abstract properties of the world. Wagner, Winner, Cicchetti, and Gardner (1981) present evidence that a group of infants aged 6-14 months looked preferentially at an object that adults judge to be metaphorically related to a sound; they suggest that studies of preferential looking can gauge infants' representations of figurative relations among events. Starkey, Spelke, and Gelman (1983) present evidence that 6- to 8-month-old infants look preferentially at a display of objects that corresponds numerically to a series of sounds; this evidence suggests that preferential looking can be used to investigate early representations of number. I will focus on the latter finding.

As we have noted, experiments using familiarization/novelty-preference methods have revealed that infants are sensitive to the number of objects or forms in a visual scene. These studies suggested that the infants were able to enumerate the units in the scene, arriving at a representation that captured numerical information. One could question, however, whether infants were truly sensitive to number. Since only visual displays were presented, it is possible that a visual mechanism sensitive to certain complex properties of spatial patterns underlay infants' discriminations. If this were the case, one would hesitate to grant infants any knowledge of number, for number concepts are abstract and amodal.

Accordingly, experiments were conducted to determine if 6- to 8-month-old infants are sensitive to numerical correspondences across the auditory and visual modes. The experiments used a variant of the auditory-visual preference procedure. Infants faced a screen on which two photographic slides were displayed side by side, one depicting two objects and one depicting three objects. After 2 seconds, they heard either two or three drumbeats from a central location. The slides remained in view for 10 seconds after the last drumbeat, and infants' looking preferences between them were assessed. A series of such trials were given, half with two sounds and half with three sounds. In four separate experiments, infants tended to look at the display whose number corresponded to the number of sounds (Starkey et al., 1983). It appears that infants detect number both by listening and by looking, when they are presented either with a temporally extended event or with a spatially extended array of objects.

These experiments reveal that infants are sensitive to the number of objects in a scene and to the number of events in a sound stream, and that their sensitivity to number is reflected in a pattern of preferential looking that is quite similar to that observed in studies of perception of audible and visible events. Infants tend to look at a display of forms that matches, in number, a sequence of sounds. Experiments using preferential-looking methods can be used, therefore, to assess infants' knowledge of at least one abstract property of the world.

Selective Visual Attention

This section closes with one final illustration of the usefulness of auditory-visual preference experiments for studies of infants' cognitive abilities. Such exploration has been found to shed light on the infant's capacity for selective visual attention. In studies of human adults, Neisser and Becklen (1975) first discovered a visual capacity analogous to the capacity for selective auditory attention: just as adults can attend to one of two simultaneously spoken messages, they can attend to one of two simultaneously visible events. Adult subjects were presented with two distinct events—a hand clap game and a basketball game—overlapping on a video screen. The subjects were able to follow either of these events, and they were subsequently found to be unaware of almost everything that went on in the other event.

Does selective visual attention depend on skills that children acquire slowly, or does the capacity to attend selectively emerge at an early age? To address this question, Bahrick et al. (1981) investigated "selective looking" in 4-month-old infants, using a preferential-looking technique. Infants were presented with two events—a hand clap game and a flapping toy butterfly—in full overlap. While the events were projected simultaneously, the sound track to one event was played. If infants are able to follow either of these events selectively, they were expected to attend to the event projected in sound, and thus to perceive that event better than the silent event. A subsequent test for the relative novelty of the two events was given to determine if the infants had indeed attended to the sounding event: if they had, they were expected to look longer at the event they had not followed. The experiment provided evidence that infants did attend selectively to the event projected in sound: they subsequently looked longer at the other event. This study revealed that young infants can attend selectively to one of two overlapping visual events. Once again, infants attended to the event that corresponded to an accompanying sound.

Some Limitations of the Methods

Studies of preferential looking have shed light on infants' perception of a unitary event by looking and listening, their knowledge about the properties of particular audible and visible objects, their sensitivity to number, and their capacity for selective attention. The preferential-looking methods have, however, two drawbacks. First, infants do not always exhibit a visual preference for a sound-related event, even in circumstances for which there is evidence that infants detect the auditory-visual relationship. Second, even when infants do look preferentially at an object that corresponds to a sound, one cannot be certain that they perceive a *unitary,* sounding object. We will consider each of these limitations in turn.

There are at least two different situations in which infants fail to exhibit a visual preference for a sound-related object. First, young infants do not look longer at a speaking person when presented with the mother and a female stranger. Second, infants do not look longer at one of two sounding, inanimate objects when the objects are very similar.

In a number of experiments, infants have been presented with the voices and faces of the mother and a second unfamiliar woman, and the effects of each woman's voice on looking at her face have been assessed. Cohen (1974) and Spelke and Owsley (1979) used versions of the search method to investigate whether infants would look at the mother when her own voice was played and at the stranger when the unfamiliar voice was played. Cohen obtained this pattern at 8 months of age but not at 5 months. Spelke and Owsley obtained the opposite pattern at 4 months of age: infants looked more at the mother when they heard the stranger's voice than when they heard the mother's own voice. The presence of a reverse effect in this latter study suggests, albeit weakly, that infants do know about the characteristic face and voice of the mother, and evidence in favor of this suggestion comes from studies of even younger infants, who have been shown to recognize the mother's face (Barrera & Maurer, 1981) and voice (DeCasper & Fifer, 1980). Nevertheless, infants fail to look appropriately to the mother or stranger when they hear each person's voice. Perhaps the presence of the stranger herself accounts for this failure. When she speaks, her overtures to the infants may be slightly puzzling or disturbing, and the infants may turn to the mother for reassurance. This speculation has not, however, been explored.

The second situation in which appropriate preferential looking is not consistently observed is of greater interest for the present discussion, for it harkens back to the first exploratory pattern that we have discussed. Infants may sometimes fail to look at a sounding object because they have a countervailing tendency to explore events that are new or unexpected. These tendencies may come into conflict when infants are presented with events in which simple objects behave in similar ways.

For example, a variety of experiments have investigated infants' sensitivity to the synchrony of sounds with the visible impacts of moving objects (Bahrick, 1980; Spelke, 1979, 1981; Spelke et al., 1983; see also Humphrey & Tees, 1980). In these studies, 4-month-old infants were presented with two objects differing in shape and color but composed of the same substance, such as two puppets. A different percussion sound was paired with each object: sounds were chosen so that the two sounds differed in pitch, but either could have been produced equally well by either object. While infants viewed the two objects moving out of phase, they heard the sounds in succession. Each sound was synchronized with one of the objects and not synchronized with the other object. Infants were found to detect the sound-object relationships, as evidenced by their performance on a subsequent search test: they tended to turn briefly toward each object when its synchronized sound was played. During the preference episode, however, clear and appropriate looking preferences were not always observed. There was a preference for the synchronized objects in some studies. In other studies using the same methods and displays, however, there were no reliable preferences. And in two experiments (see Bahrick, 1980; Spelke, 1981), there was a preference for the nonsynchronized object. This last effect was not replicated in subsequent research (Bahrick, in preparation; Spelke, 1981).

Why were the predicted preferences not observed? First, the events in these studies were simpler, more redundant, and less interesting than those in the studies previously described. Thus, the infants in these studies may have been prey to two conflicting tendencies: a tendency to explore one event at a time by looking and listening, and a tendency to explore two simple events at once. After discovering the auditory-visual relationship, some infants might have preferred the silent object because it was relatively new: it is not the object to which they had been listening. A tendency to seek change or novelty may then act against the tendency to look at the event one is hearing.

The results of certain studies of intermodal perception support this explanation. In a number of experiments, infants have been allowed to hear, to mouth, or to manipulate an object without seeing it, and then their visual preferences between that object and a second object were assessed. If the original period of familiarization was long, the infants in some experiments exhibited a visual preference for the novel object: the object they had not previously explored by listening or touching. This preference has been observed in studies of visual-haptic perception with infants ranging in age from 1 month (Gibson & Walker, 1982) to 1 year (e.g., Gottfried, Rose, & Bridger, 1977). It has also been observed with 4-month-old infants in studies of auditory-visual perception, in which infants were habituated to a sound and then presented with a corresponding and a noncorresponding object (Spelke, 1981). Novelty preferences are not always observed in experiments using this method (see Meltzoff & Borton, 1979, and Ruff & Kohler, 1978, for experiments in which the reverse effect was obtained). Nevertheless, the fact that a novelty preference is sometimes obtained suggests that the tendency to look at something one hears may be counteracted by a tendency to look at something new.

A second reason for the inconsistent preferences may also be offered. Inconsistent preferences have been observed only in experiments in which infants were presented with two very similar visible events, either of which could have been the source of a noise with the quality of the sound accompaniment. As the sound was played, moreover, there were occasional accidental conjunctions between its occurrence and the movements of the nonsynchronized object. If adults are given the same displays and asked to watch the nonsynchronized object, they do not perceive that object as fully independent of the sound, but report instead that the sounds and the object's movements are synchronized at some times and not synchronized at other times. This perception may reflect adults' tendency to perceive patterns of contingency among events even when no true contingency exists (e.g., Jenkins & Ward, 1965).

I suggest that the infants in the experiments with simple, synchronized objects may also have perceived each nonsynchronized object as somewhat related to the accompanying sound. Because this relationship is not perfect, it may have been especially intriguing to the infants. Along with the tendency to look at an object that moves and sounds in perfect synchrony, infants might have a competing tendency to explore an imperfectly synchronized object in order to investigate its relationship to the sound.

The results of an experiment by Bahrick and Watson (1983) are consistent with this possibility. The experiment investigated young infants' perception of the relationship between the sight and the feeling of their actively moving legs. Three-month-old infants sat facing two video screens. One screen presented a synchronized image of the infant's own moving legs and the other presented a videotaped, nonsynchronized image of another infant's moving legs, clothed so as to resemble the infant's own legs. Both visual attention and leg movements were observed. It was found that the infants moved their legs quite extensively, more than would have been expected without the visual displays. Moreover, infants showed a reliable preference for the video image of the legs that were not their own. This preference, and the increased leg movement, may reflect infants' efforts to test and discover the relation between their own movements and those of the legs that looked like their own legs, that moved in the same manner as their own legs, but that did not move in full synchrony with their own movements. The tendency to explore similar, nonsynchronized events may have prevailed over the tendency to look at an object that is perfectly synchronized with one's actions.

In brief, infants may sometimes fail to look preferentially at a sounding object because of either of two exploratory tendencies. First, infants tend to look at events that are novel, such as a moving object that differs from the sound they have been hearing. Second, infants may tend to look at events that are puzzling or problematic, such as a moving object that bears an uncertain relationship to an accompanying sound. These tendencies, of course, were the focus of the first half of this chapter: They provided the basis for all the studies of infants' perception of visible objects.

The second limitation of preferential-looking methods as a means to study infants' knowledge of intermodal relationships is more serious. Such experiments provide evidence that infants detect some relationship between a sound and a visible object, but they do not indicate *what kind* of relationship the infants perceive. I have suggested, for example, that infants perceive a unitary event when they look and listen to a speaking person. It is possible, however, that infants do not perceive one event in this case, but two separate events that are related; infants may perceive the face and the voice of a speaking person as distinct events that are correlated. Infants may look longer at an object, when they hear its sound, not because of any tendency to follow single, unitary events by looking and listening simultaneously, but because of a tendency to look at one event while listening to a second event to which it is related.

The findings of the experiments on sensitivity to number and sensitivity to metaphor lend credence to the latter possibility. It is unlikely that infants perceive three drumbeats as the same event as three stationary objects: indeed, the objects are not events at all. Infants probably perceived the objects and the drumbeats as distinct but as corresponding in number. What, therefore, do infants perceive when they look and listen to a single moving and sounding object: one object or two?

No experiment, to my knowledge, has answered this question. The question could be addressed, however, through further experiments using preferential-looking methods. Number-detection techniques might be used, for example, to investigate whether infants perceive an object that moves and makes a noise as one event or two. Alternatively, it might be possible to investigate infants' perception of visible, sounding objects by making use of a striking perceptual phenomenon experienced by adults: the "ventriloquism effect."

When adults look and listen to one event, they tend to localize the event in a single position in space, even if a sound and its corresponding object are separated. When adults watch a film or a ventriloquist's performance, for example, the sound of each object is spatially displaced from its visible source, but it is heard as coming from the direction of the appropriate object. This bias in perception occurs only when adults make the assumption that the object they see and the object they hear are one and the same (Welch & Warren, 1980). Adults tend to perceive all sources of information about an object as coming from a single position in space, but only when they believe that the sounds they hear emanate from the object they see.

It might be possible, therefore, to investigate infants' perception of the unity of an object by asking whether infants experience a ventriloquism effect. This question could be addressed, in turn, by means of a preferential-looking experiment. On a series of trials, infants could be presented with a filmed object and a sound that is displaced from the object to various extents. Their tendency to look away from the object, in the direction of the sound, could serve as an index of their ability to detect that the sound and object occupy different positions. In one condition, the sound and the filmed image would be unrelated; in the other condition, they would specify a unitary object. If infants perceive unitary objects by looking and listening, then they should be less sensitive to the spatial separation between the sound and object when they form a unitary episode. At a wider range of displacements, the unitary sound and object should be localized in the same place.

A preliminary experiment with 5-month-old infants suggests that this preferential-looking technique can be used to assess infants' localization of the displaced sound (Nachmias, Spelke, Termine, & Shepperson, unpublished observations). We do not yet know, however, whether infants experience a ventriloquism effect when they look and listen to a single object.

LOOKING AT NOVEL EVENTS: AN INDEX OF KNOWLEDGE OF PHYSICAL CAUSALITY

Human adults experience a world of material bodies that behave in conformity with physical laws. We, as adults, have knowledge about the behavior of material objects, and we use this knowledge whenever we act on objects, trace objects through time, and make predictions about an object's future states. For example, we know that objects tend to persist when they move, even if they move out of view. When an object moves freely, we predict that it will continue to exist throughout this movement. We also know that objects tend to move on certain trajectories, that they will only tend to change their pattern of movement if they come in contact with some other body, and that they are subject to gravity and will fall to the ground if they are not supported in some way. This knowledge aids us in predicting the future positions of an object, and it allows us to infer, from changes in an inanimate object's movements, what interactions with other objects have taken place.

It is again Piaget (1954) who began the systematic study of the development of these and other physical notions. Piaget focused on the ability of infants to act on objects in a systematic manner. He studied infants' developing ability to search for objects that are out of view by removing or reaching around their occluders, and infants' developing ability to apprehend distant objects by pulling toward themselves some nearer object that supports or connects with them. These abilities, Piaget found, develop quite slowly over the course of infancy. In particular, young infants do not seem to search in any way for objects that leave their view. Piaget, like many of his successors (see Harris, 1983), concluded that human notions of material bodies are constructions: Humans have no initial conceptions of objects and their behavior.

The reliance on search behaviors as indices of infants' conceptions of objects, however, has drawbacks. A young infant's failure to search for hidden objects could reflect the immaturity of the capacity for coordinated search itself, rather than the absence of a notion that objects are persisting. Two kinds of experiment provide evidence for the latter view. First, investigations of search behavior have revealed that infants come to locate objects using one kind of activity—visual tracking—before they come to locate objects in other ways, by reaching or crawling to an object (see Harris, 1983, for a review). Second, Piaget's studies of the development of coordinated activity have revealed that, in general, infants under about 8 months fail to coordinate any distinct actions into means-ends sequences (Piaget, 1952). The absence of this coordination would seem to provide a sufficient explanation for infants' failure to search for hidden objects, irrespective of infants' conceptions of those objects. Searching requires that one perform one act (e.g., removing a cover) in order to make possible the performance of future acts (e.g., obtaining an object), and this feat appears to be beyond the capacities of a young infant.

The experiments reviewed in the first section provide a further reason for questioning Piaget's theory of the development of conceptions of objects. Those experiments provide evidence that infants perceive partly hidden objects before they are capable of acting upon the objects effectively, contrary to Piaget's theory. It is important, therefore, to investigate infants' knowledge of the persistence of hidden objects using methods that do not rely on search. Recently, a number of psychologists have begun to undertake studies of infants' conceptions of the behavior of material objects by using preferential-looking techniques. These studies suggest that some conceptions of objects and of material causality are present at an early age.

Knowledge of the Causes of Object Movement

Several experiments have investigated infants' understanding that one inanimate object cannot act upon another at a distance, so as to set the second object in motion. Ball (1973) presented children ranging in age from 2 months to 2 years with two objects that moved behind an occluding screen (Figure 10a). One object approached the screen from the left, and moved behind it so that the object was fully occluded. Then the second object moved into view from behind the screen, on the right. The second object moved into view at the time, and at the speed, at which it would have moved if the first object had hit the second while it was stationary and had thereby set it in motion. Adults have been found to perceive a causal relationship between the movements of two

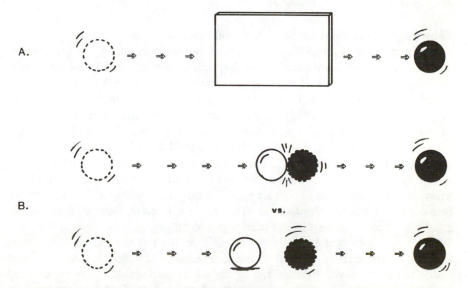

Figure 10. Schematic depiction of (a) the habituation display and (b) the test displays of an experiment on knowledge of causal relationships (Ball, 1973).

such objects: the first object is perceived to contact the second and set it in motion (see Michotte, 1963). To investigate infants' perception of this event, Ball presented the event on repeated trials, until infants' looking time had declined. Then he removed the occluder and presented two events on alternating trials. In one event, the first object hit the second, as an adult would expect. In the other event, the first object halted before making contact with the object, and the second object began to move on its own (see Figure 10b). Infants looked longer at the latter event. It appears, therefore, that they had inferred that the first object made contact with the second object behind the screen.

Ball's experiment provides evidence that infants know an inanimate object will not change its pattern of movement unless it comes into contact with other objects. Additional support for this conclusion is provided by two experiments by Leslie (1982), using a similar familiarization/novelty-preference method. Infants of 4½ and 8 months were presented with events in which a hand picked up an inanimate object, or in which one moving inanimate object set another object in motion. In different conditions, the two objects in these events either made contact or failed to make contact. Infants' looking preferences suggested that they expected the second object in each event to move only if it made contact with the first.

Ball's experiment also provides evidence that infants perceive objects to persist when they are out of view, since the infants generalized habituation from an event in which two objects were alternately visible and invisible to an event in which the two objects were visible continuously. Additional support for the latter conclusion comes from the last preferential-looking experiment to be described.

Knowledge of the Persistence of Material Bodies

Do young infants know that objects must move through space continuously, that objects are solid and cannot pass through each other, and that objects persist when they move out of view? An experiment addressed these questions by focusing on 5-month-old infants' tendency to look at events that are new or surprising (Baillargeon, 1982). In the critical events of this experiment, infants were presented with a solid box and a screen on a table (Figure 11). Initially, the screen lay flat on the table and the box stood slightly behind it. Then the screen began to rotate upward about its far edge. It completely occluded the screen by the time it had rotated 60°, and it continued rotating to the point at which it should have made contact with the box: after about 120° of rotation. One of two events occurred at this time: either the screen stopped rotating, or it continued rotating a full 180° until it rested on the table surface in the position that the block had occupied. In either case, the screen then reversed direction and returned to its original position, revealing the block once again. To an adult, the event involving the 180° rotation is impossible. This experiment focused on infants' visual attention to these events in order to determine how infants would perceive them: whether they would also represent the occluded block as continuing to exist, and whether they knew that the presence of this block should constrain the movements of the screen.

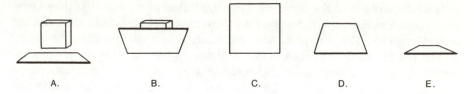

Figure 11. Schematic depiction of the test displays of an experiment on knowledge of the persistence of a hidden object. The screen moved from *a* to *d* (possible event) or from *a* to *e* (impossible event) (Baillargeon, 1982).

To assess infants' reactions to these events, the events were embedded in a familiarization/novelty-preference experiment. Infants were presented repeatedly with a display consisting only of the rotating screen. The screen rotated back and forth 180° about one of its edges. On each of a series of trials, this display was presented for as long as the infants would look at it. After looking times on successive trials had declined by half, the box was placed behind the screen in the path of its rotation. To familiarize infants with the box, it was presented behind the screen with no movement for two trials. Then infants were presented with the two events described above, in alternation, for six test trials. On each trial, an event was presented repeatedly until the infant looked away, and the infant's looking time was recorded. A subsidiary experiment had indicated that 120° and 180° rotations of the screen are of equal intrinsic interest to infants of this age, if they occur in a situation in which both events are possible.

The experimental predictions were as follows. If 5-month-old infants do not represent the existence and the location of a hidden object, then habituation should generalize more to the 180° test rotation: this was the very pattern of movement to which infants had been habituated. If, however, infants know that a hidden object persists in a definite location when it is out of view, and if they know that one object cannot pass through the space occupied by another, then they should look longer at the 180° rotation than at the 120° rotation, for two reasons. First, the 180° rotation should be seen as more novel, since the screen passed through space occupied by an object in that condition, whereas, in the habituation condition and in the 120° test conditions, the screen moved unimpeded and stopped when it hit an object or surface. Second, the 180° rotation should be seen as puzzling or surprising, since the event that it depicts is impossible: one object cannot pass freely through a place occupied by another object.

The findings were clear: infants looked longer to the impossible 180° rotation. This finding provides evidence that 5-month-old infants know that an object persists in a definite place when it is out of sight, and that the location of an invisible object limits the possible movements of a visible object. Moreover, the experiment indicates that infants reveal what they know about objects through their patterns of preferential looking to events, even at an age at which such knowledge is not revealed through their patterns of search. In this experiment, infants did not habituate and dishabituate to the surface appearance of a visual display but to the underlying configuration of objects that they knew to be present in the display. Surely, a 180° rotation is superficially more similar to itself than to a 120° rotation. After habituation to a 180° rotation, however, infants reacted to the impossible 180° rotation in the test as if it were new or surprising, and to the possible 120° rotation as if it were relatively familiar or expected. In studies of infants' knowledge of fully occluded objects, as in the earlier studies of perception of partly occluded objects, infants' looking patterns appear to be influenced most by properties of the perceived objects themselves, not by properties of the configuration of surfaces that are visible. Studies of preferential looking thus would seem to provide a promising tool for future investigations of infants' knowledge of objects and physical causality. The tendency to explore displays that are new or surprising can be used to investigate what infants perceive and know.

Limitations of These Methods

The two major problems that arise in these experiments are the same problems that arose in the experiments on infants' perception of objects. First, infants may not always look longer at the more novel or surprising of two displays. The existence of a looking preference between two events does not indicate, by itself, which event is taken to be more surprising. Second, even if one could be certain that longer looking indicated surprise, one cannot be sure that this preference reflects any systematic knowledge about material objects and their behavior. The more novel or more surprising event may be more novel or surprising for reasons that are unrelated to any conceptions about objects and pertain, instead, to sensory properties of displays.

I will not dwell on the solutions to these problems, for they are the same solutions discussed before. Both problems can only be addressed by comparing infants' reactions to a variety of stimulus displays, across a variety of experimental conditions. In the experiments described above, a number of displays were presented in order to assess the possibility that infants preferred the more familiar event and the possibility that infants reacted to sensory characteristics of the displays. Nevertheless, investigators of infants' notions of physical objects and physical causality have hardly begun to study systematically infants' diverse reactions to different causal events. This enterprise should occupy the efforts of students of infant cognition in the coming years.

CONCLUSION

In summary, infants are apt to show two patterns of visual exploration. They tend to look at events that are relatively novel and perhaps unexpected, and they tend to look at events that they also hear. Experiments that focus on these looking patterns suggest that infants have basic notions that allow them to perceive objects, events, and the causal relations within and among events. Such experiments also suggest that infants have certain capacities to perceive speech sounds, to enumerate objects, to detect expressions of emotion, and to recognize human faces. Patterns of preferential looking suggest that infants do not have all the means of perceiving and apprehending objects that we have as adults: infants do not perceive objects by analyzing their static configurational properties, for example, and they do not perceive sounding objects by relating sounds to moments of visible impact. These differences between infants and adults begin to suggest how human conceptions change with development: how concepts grow as children mature and learn.

Concerning the limitations of preferential-looking measures, the same two problems have arisen in every domain in which these methods have been applied. One problem is essentially practical: investigators cannot confidently predict, in advance, whether infants will exhibit a preference for the more novel or for the more familiar of two events, and whether infants will prefer an object that corresponds to a sound or one that does not. Until psychologists understand the conditions under which these preferences are obtained, they will need to incorporate a variety of control conditions into their experiments to determine which pattern of preference is observed in a given experimental situation.

The second problem is deeper: How can experimental psychologists discover what an infant perceives and knows? How can one ever find out whether infants perceive objects or patterns of sensation, unitary multimodal events or separate but related sights and sounds, objects interacting according to principles of physical causality or sensory patterns occurring in certain conjunctions?

To begin with the first problem, psychologists may be close to understanding some of the patterns of preference that infants exhibit. Infants may always tend to look longer at a novel object when given a choice between an object that is novel and one that is familiar, even if they do not always look longest to the most novel of several novel objects. Furthermore, infants may always tend to follow one event, by looking and listening, whenever they are given a choice between a visible object with the same properties as a sound and an object with different properties. Infants may prefer a nonsynchronized object to a synchronized object only when both objects share certain properties with the sound: for example, when both objects are composed of the same rigid substance. If these generalizations are correct, then psychologists should be able to predict the direction of the preferences that infants will exhibit in certain situations.

The second problem raises the question of what it means to ask what infants perceive and know. To some extent, "sensing," "perceiving," and "knowing" are terms with experiential content: They refer to one's conscious awareness of the world. If these terms are understood in this way, then one must conclude that every psychologist is, forever, hopelessly in the dark about the sensations, perceptions, and cognitions of other individuals, young or old. As these terms are used in science and in everyday life, however, their introspective content is rarely in the foreground. We, as ordinary humans and as scientists, will conclude that another person senses, perceives, and knows about aspects of the world whenever this hypothesis leads us to the best, most comprehensive explanation of all the person's actions. This practice, I suggest, should be the practice of psychologists who study infants.

My suggestion echoes the suggestions of several other contributors to this volume. In her discussion of infants' sensory capacities, Teller has recommended that investigators use a variety of methods to probe the same capacities. She suggested, moreover, that experimental findings be evaluated not only against each other but against the findings of experiments from neighboring disciplines. The theory that meshes best with all other scientific theories, and that accords best with all the scientific data, is the theory that sensory psychophysicists should be most ready to accept. In his discussion of infants' capacities to perceive depth and motion, Yonas also suggested that different experiments be undertaken using a variety of stimulus displays and a variety of measures. By seeking "stimulus convergence" and "response convergence" (Yonas & Pick, 1975; see also Bower, 1972) one can come to center on the best account of infants' perceptual capacities.

In sum, the same problem confronts students of infant sensation, perception, and cognition. This problem, moreover, is not specific to studies of human infancy. It is encountered in all branches of psychology, and indeed, all branches of science. The steps necessary to resolve the problem highlight why all scientific experiments need to be tied to scientific theories. When infants' diverse behaviors can be understood in terms of general theories of their mental capacities, we may be more confident that we have begun to understand those behaviors and capacities.

Psychologists now have strong grounds for drawing conclusions about infants' capacities to sense color and spatial pattern and to perceive depth, for a wealth of studies using diverse displays and methods have probed these capacities. The grounds for drawing conclusions about infants' knowledge of objects and events are weaker, because relevant studies of early cognitive capacities are far fewer in number. The burden of this discussion has been to argue, however, that infants' cognitive capacities *can* be studied. As more experiments are conducted, psychologists should come to understand the beginnings of human conceptions about the world and the ways in which those conceptions begin to change. Preferential-looking techniques can contribute to this enterprise.

ACKNOWLEDGMENTS

Preparation of this chapter was supported by a grant from the National Institutes of Health (HD-13428) and by the MIT Center for Cognitive Science under a grant from the A. P. Sloan Foundation's particular program in Cognitive Science. I thank Gilbert Gottlieb and an anonymous reviewer for helpful comments on an earlier version of the chapter.

REFERENCES

Antell, S. E. & Keating, D. P. Perception of numerical invariance in neonates. *Child Development,* 1983, *54,* 695–706.

Bahrick, L. E. *Infants' perception of properties of objects as specified by amodal information in auditory-visual events.* Unpublished doctoral dissertation, Cornell University, 1980.

Bahrick, L. E., Walker, A. S., & Neisser, U. Selective looking by infants. *Cognitive Psychology,* 1981, *13,* 377–390.

Bahrick, L. E. & Watson, J. S. *Contingency perception as a basis for early self perception.* Paper presented at the meeting of the Society for Research in Child Development, Detroit, April, 1983.

Baillargeon, R. *Object permanence in the five-month-old infant.* Paper presented at the meeting of the International Conference on Infant Studies, Austin, Texas, March, 1982.

Ball, W. A. *The perception of causality in the infant.* Paper presented at the meeting of the Society for Research in Child Development, Philadelphia, March, 1973.

Barrera, M. E. & Maurer, D. Recognition of mother's photographed face by the three-month-old infant. *Child Development,* 1981, *52,* 714–716.

Bassili, J. Emotion recognition: The role of facial movement and the relative importance of upper and lower areas of the face. *Journal of Personality and Social Psychology,* 1979, *37,* 2049–2058.

Bertenthal, B. I., Campos, J. J., & Haith, M. M. Development of visual organization: Perception of subjective contours. *Child Development,* 1980, *51,* 1072–1080.

Bertenthal, B. I. & Proffitt, D. R. *Development of infant sensitivity to biomechanical motion.* Paper presented at the meeting of the International Conference on Infant Studies, Austin, Texas, March, 1982.

Bower, T. G. R. Object perception in infancy. *Perception,* 1972, *1,* 15–30.

Bresson, F. & de Schonen, S. A propos de la construction de l'espace et de l'objet: La prise d'un objet sur un support. *Bulletin de Psychologie,* 1976–1977, *30,* 3–9.

Carey, S. The development of face perception. In G. Davies (ed.), *Perceiving and remembering faces.* London: Academic Press, 1983.

Caron, A. J., Caron, R. F., Caldwell, R. C., & Weiss, S. T. Infant perception of the structural properties of the face. *Developmental Psychology,* 1973, *9,* 385–399.

Cohen, S. Developmental differences in infants' attentional responses to face-voice incongruity of mother and stranger. *Child Development,* 1974, *45,* 1155–1158.

DeCasper, A. J. & Fifer, W. P. Of human bonding: Newborns prefer their mothers' voices. *Science,* 1980, *208,* 1174–1176.

Dodd, B. Lip reading in infants: Attention to speech presented in- and out-of-synchrony. *Cognitive Psychology,* 1979, *11,* 478–484.

Fantz, R. L. The origins of form perception. *Scientific American,* 1961, *204,* (May), 66–72.

Fantz, R. L., Fagan, J. F., & Miranda, S. B. Early visual selectivity as a function of pattern variables, previous exposure, age from birth and conception, and expected cognitive deficit. In L. B. Cohen & P. Salapatek (eds.), *Infant perception: From sensation to cognition.* Vol. 1. New York: Academic Press, 1975.

Fox, R. & McDaniel, C. Perception of biological motion in human infants. Science, 1982, *218,* 486–487.

Gibson, E. J. *Principles of perceptual learning and development.* New York: Appleton Century Crofts, 1969.

Gibson, E. J. & Spelke, E. S. The development of perception. In J. H. Flavell and E. M. Markman (eds.), *Cognitive development.* Volume 3 of P. Mussen (ed.), *Handbook of child psychology.* New York: Wiley, 1983.

Gibson, E. J. & Walk, R. D. The "visual cliff." *Scientific American,* 1960, *202* (April), 64–71.

Gibson, E. J. & Walker, A. S. *Intermodal perception of substance.* Paper presented at the meeting of the International Conference on Infant Studies, Austin, Texas, March, 1982.

Gibson, J. J. Comment on "The relation between audition and vision in the human newborn,"
Monographs of the Society for Research in Child Development, 1976, *41* (4, Serial No.
167).

Gottfried, A. W., Rose, S. A., & Bridger, W. H. Crossmodal transfer in human infants. *Child
Development,* 1977, *48,* 118–123.

Haith, M. M., Bergman, T., & Moore, M. J. Eye contact and face scanning in early infancy.
Science, 1977, *198,* 853–855.

Harris, P. Cognition in infancy. In M. M. Haith (ed.), *Infancy and biological development.*
Volume 2 of P. Mussen (ed.), *Handbook of child psychology.* New York: Wiley, 1983.

Humphrey, K. & Tees, R. C. Auditory-visual coordination in infancy: Some limitations of the
preference methodology. *Bulletin of the Psychonomic Society,* 1980, *16,* 213–216.

Jenkins, H. M. & Ward, W. C. Judgment of contingency between response and outcomes. *Psychological Monographs,* 1965, *79,* 1–17.

Johansson, G. Visual event perception. In R. Held, H. W. Leibowitz, & H.-L. Teuber (eds.),
Handbook of sensory physiology: Perception. Berlin: Springer-Verlag, 1978.

Kagan, J. *Change and continuity in infancy.* New York: Wiley, 1971.

Kagan, J., Linn, S., Mount, R., & Reznick, J. S. Asymmetry of inference in the dishabituation
paradigm. *Canadian Journal of Psychology,* 1979, *33,* 288–305.

Kaufman-Hayoz, R. & Jager, B. *Infants' perception of a face revealed through motion.* Paper
presented at the meeting of the Society for Research in Child Development, Detroit, Michi-
gan, April, 1983.

Kellman, P. J. & Spelke, E. S. Perception of partly occluded objects in infancy. *Cognitive Psychology,* 1983, *15,* 483–524.

Kuhl, P. & Meltzoff, A. N. The bimodal perception of speech in infancy. *Science,* 1982, *218,*
1138–1140.

Lamb, M. E. & Campos, J. J. *Development in infancy.* New York: Random House, 1982.

Lawson, K. R. Spatial and temporal congruity and auditory-visual integration in infants. *Developmental Psychology,* 1980, *16,* 185–192.

Leslie, A. M. The perception of causality in infants. *Perception,* 1982, *11,* 173–186.

Lyons-Ruth, K. Bimodal perception in infancy: Responses to auditory-visual incongruity. *Child
Development,* 1977, *48,* 820–827.

MacKain, K., Studdert-Kennedy, M., Spieker, S., & Stern, D. Infant intermodal speech perception is a left-hemisphere function. *Science,* 1983, *219,* 1347–1349.

McCall, R. B., Kennedy, C. B., & Applebaum, M. I. Magnitude of discrepancy in the distribution
of attention in infants. *Child Development,* 1977, *48,* 772–785.

McDaniel, C. & Odom, R. D. *Preferences for expressive patterns of movement in infancy.* Paper
presented at the meeting of the Society for Research in Child Development, Detroit, Michi-
gan, April, 1983.

Meltzoff, A. N. & Borton, R. W. Intermodal matching by human neonates. *Nature,* 1979, *282,*
403–404.

Michotte, A. *The perception of causality.* (T. R. Miles and E. Miles, trans.). London: Methuen,
1963.

Muir, D. & Field, J. Newborn infants orient to sounds. *Child Development,* 1978, *50,* 431–436.

Neisser, U. & Becklen, R. Selective looking: Attending to visually specified events. *Cognitive
Psychology,* 1975, *7,* 480–494.

Piaget, J. *The origins of intelligence in children.* New York: International Universities Press, 1952.

Piaget, J. *The construction of reality in the child.* New York: Basic Books, 1954.

Pick, A. D. *Perceiving melodies.* Paper presented at the meeting of the International Society for
the Study of Behavioral Development, Munich, August, 1983.

Prather, P. & Spelke, E. S. *Three-month-old infants' perception of adjacent and partly occluded
objects.* Paper presented at the meeting of the International Conference on Infant Studies,
Austin, Texas, March, 1982.

Reisberg, D. Visual cues and auditory attention. *Acta Psychologica,* 1978, *42,* 331–341.

Ruff, H. A. & Kohler, C. Tactual visual transfer in 6-month-old infants. *Infant Behavior and Development,* 1978, *1,* 259–264.

Schmidt, H. & Spelke, E. S. Gestalt relations and object perception in infancy. Paper presented at the meeting of the International Conference on Infant Studies, New York, April, 1984.

Schwartz, K. *Perceptual knowledge of the human face in infancy.* Paper presented at the meeting of the Society for Research in Child Development, Detroit, April, 1983.

Spelke, E. S. Infants' intermodal perception of events. *Cognitive Psychology,* 1976, *8,* 553–560.

Spelke, E. S. Perceiving bimodally specified events in infancy. *Developmental Psychology,* 1979, *15,* 626–636.

Spelke, E. S. The infants' acquisition of knowledge of bimodally specified events. *Journal of Experimental Child Psychology,* 1981, *31,* 279–299.

Spelke, E. S. *Cognition in infancy.* Occasional paper #23, MIT Center for Cognitive Science, 1983.

Spelke, E. S., Born, W. S., & Chu, F. Perception of moving, sounding objects in infancy. *Perception,* 1983, *12,* 719–732.

Spelke, E. S. & Cortelyou, A. Perceptual aspects of social knowing: Looking and listening in infancy. In M. E. Lamb and L. R. Sherrod (eds.), *Infant social cognition.* Hillsdale, NJ: Erlbaum, 1981.

Spelke, E. S. & Owsley, C. J. Intermodal exploration and perceptual knowledge in infancy. *Infant Behavior and Development,* 1979, *2,* 13–28.

Starkey, D. P. & Cooper, R. G. Perception of numbers by human infants. *Science,* 1980, *210,* 103–1034.

Starkey, D. P., Spelke, E. S., & Gelman, R. *Number competence in infants: Sensitivity to numeric invariance and numeric change.* Paper presented at the International Conference on Infant Studies, New Haven, CT, April, 1980.

Starkey, D. P. Spelke, E. S., & Gelman, R. Detection of intermodal numerical correspondences by human infants. *Science,* 1983, *222,* 179–181.

Strauss, M. S. & Curtis, L. E. Infant perception of numerosity. *Child Development,* 1981, *52,* 1146–1152.

Tighe, E. & Leaton, R. *Habituation.* New York: Academic Press, 1976.

von Hofsten, C. Eye-hand coordination in newborns. *Developmental Psychology,* 1982, *18,* 450–461.

Wagner, S., Winner, E., Cicchetti, D., & Gardner, H. "Metaphorical" mapping in human infants. *Child Development,* 1981, *52,* 728–731.

Walker, A. S. Intermodal perception of expressive behaviors by human infants. *Journal of Experimental Child Psychology,* 1982, *33,* 514–535.

Welch, R. B. & Warren, D. H. Immediate perceptual response to intersensory discrepancy. *Psychological Bulletin,* 1980, *88,* 638–667.

Wertheimer, M. Psychomotor coordination of auditory and visual space at birth. *Science,* 1961, *134,* 1692.

Wishart, J. *The development of the object concept in infancy.* Unpublished doctoral dissertation, University of Edinburgh, 1979.

Yonas, A. N. & Pick, H. L., Jr. Studies of spatial perception in infancy. In L. B. Cohen & P. Salapatek (eds.), *Infant perception: From sensation to cognition.* New York: Academic Press, 1975.

INTRODUCTION TO SECTION 4

Physiological Measures of Auditory and Visual Functions

In the initial chapter (14) in this section, Kurt Hecox and Donald Deegan describe the electrophysiological correlates of the various parameters of the acoustic signal, and the methodological significance of these issues for the measurement of changes with age in the immature auditory system. First they demonstrate the technical problems associated with the use of pure tones as stimuli, in contrast to broad-band noises: There is an inevitable confounding of signal duration, rise-fall time, and frequency with the former that does not occur with the latter. In discussing the electrophysiological auditory evoked brain stem response, the authors show the necessity of selective masking techniques to assure that the region of the basilar membrane generating the response remains the same. This is especially important when the relative contributions of peripheral and central factors are under examination. Hecox and Deegan conclude their technical presentation with a discussion of problems related to the difficulties of calibrating the auditory stimulus for the developing infant, to assure an "equivalent stimulus" at various ages when the size of the auditory canal and head are changing. Finally, they return to a discussion of the advantages of using masking noises to limit the excitatory region of the basilar membrane, so that the interpretation of changes with age can be made more specific at the anatomical level.

In the next chapter, Richard Aslin describes and evaluates visual fixation and scanning as measures of visual development, comparing their efficacy to more "global" behavioral measures such as preferential looking and habituation. Despite formidable calibration problems, Aslin finds infra-red corneal photography offering more detailed information than the global measures of preference and habituation when one is interested in the precision of visual fixation or the scanpath of the eye viewing a display. It is obvious from Aslin's review, and those of others in the present compendium, that the use of several different measures by the same investigator will be helpful in increasing the reliability and validity of findings, and that such an approach will also provide direct information on methodological problems when the findings from different laboratories are in disagreement or in doubt. Aslin's review of controversial findings on the "externality" effect and the developmental shift from narrow to broader scanpaths provides further support for the use of multiple measures by the same investigator, especially at this relatively early stage of inquiry with a not always tractable problem or organism, and where individual differences may not only be a nuisance variable but an important datum. Aslin's review reveals once again that statistically significant group trends may not really do justice to the consistency of individual differences in scanpaths, for example. Aslin concludes his chapter by noting that global measures of visual function are useful when statistically reliable differences are found, and that negative results can sometimes be clarified by the use of more microscopic measures of scanning. The latter themselves continue to be plagued with technical problems, such as the calibration of the eye-position signal and alignment of the infant with the recording apparatus. Aslin's chapter thus makes clear the empirical problems in the measurement of the development of the infant's eye movements, as well as the technical difficulties in the way of their solution.

In the final chapter, Philip Salapatek and Charles Nelson review the measurement of event-related brain potentials (ERP) in relation to visual development in the human infant. As they say, the developmental study of the electrophysiological correlates of infant sensation, perception, and cognition lags far behind the progress made using behavioral measures. Part of the problem is that recording from infants is much more difficult than recording from adults, because the infant cannot be instructed to fixate and not move its head; consequently, movement artifacts present a considerable problem. Infants also make rapid shifts in behavioral state or attention, a problem not restricted to physiological measurement. Salapatek and Nelson offer a thorough review of ERP measurement in relation to visual acuity, contrast sensitivity, spatial-temporal interaction, and accommodation. They conclude by describing how ERPs are utilized to study infant memory and attention.

14

METHODOLOGICAL ISSUES IN THE STUDY OF AUDITORY DEVELOPMENT

Kurt E. Hecox
Donald M. Deegan

University of Wisconsin, Madison

152.133

INTRODUCTION

One of the most fundamental and persistent issues in audition is the search for the mechanisms by which environmental sounds are discriminated. It has long been recognized that most biological/environmental sounds are complex in composition, potentially providing multiple acoustic cues to the observing organism. A major turning point in our understanding of this problem was the application of Fourier's theorem to the characterization of the physical properties of sound. The importance of this analytical technique, and the recognition of its implications for theories of hearing, was most articulately advanced by Helmholtz (1863). According to Fourier's theorem, all complex sounds could be adequately and completely described by knowledge of their constituent frequencies, amplitudes, and phase relations. This is demonstrated in Figure 1. From this perspective, the primary task of transducing mechanisms is the extraction of amplitude, phase, and frequency information. The principal focus of this chapter is on the issues surrounding the means by which the frequency selectivity of the auditory system is assessed. While these issues will be discussed primarily in the context of the auditory evoked potential, the principles should be applicable to any dependent variable.

Helmholtz hypothesized that the inner ear achieved Fourier analysis of complex sounds by a series of resonators (rods of Corti) sequentially arranged along the basilar membrane. The arrival of a sound would engage those reso-

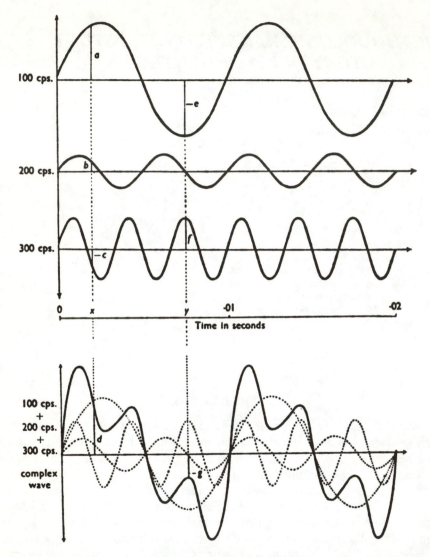

Figure 1. The production of a complex waveform (heavy line in lowest panel) from the combination of 100, 200, and 300 cps waveforms with the amplitudes, phases, and frequencies shown in the top three tracings. Note that the resultant wave bears little resemblance to its constituent frequencies whose definition is possible only through Fourier analysis. Adapted from Ladefoged (1962).

nators that corresponded to the constituent frequencies of the eliciting signal. This formulation was extremely helpful from a number of perspectives, and was highly productive from the standpoint of resulting research. However, it is now known that many of the physical requirements of such a system are not found when direct measurements are performed. Nevertheless, the fundamental notion that the ear analyzes sounds according to its constituent frequencies, and that these frequencies are laid out in a tonotopic fashion within the cochlea, has been retained as a major tenet of auditory signal processing.

This highly analytical perspective was taken by von Békésy in a series of physical measurements of basilar membrane motion, culminating in the receipt of the Nobel Prize. In these brilliant experiments, summarized in the book *Experiments in Hearing,* von Békésy (1960) demonstrated that a traveling wave is generated in response to movements of the ossicular chain of the middle ear. The vibratory motion of the most medial component of the chain, the stapes, produces this traveling wave, which is always initiated near the round window and proceeds onward to the furthermost point of the cochlear partition. As stimulus frequency decreases, the point of maximum displacement of this traveling wave proceeds from base (nearest the round window) to apex in an orderly fashion, suggesting that Helmholtz' tonotopic arrangement is mediated by the physical properties of the traveling wave.

One of the most important properties of the traveling wave, from the standpoint of the present discussion, is its dependence on the intensity of the signal. The shape of the traveling wave is asymmetrical, such that the "envelope" of displacement of the basilar membrane is characterized by a long "tail" extending from the point of maximal displacement toward the base. However, beyond the point of maximal displacement, toward the apex, there occurs a very steep reduction in the displacement envelope. With increasing intensity, especially for low frequency signals, a greater proportion of the basal extent of the basilar membrane is set into motion, due to a spread of excitation caused by the tail of the asymmetrical traveling wave. While the point of maximal displacement does not change with intensity, there is a significant increase in the basal extent of excitation. The corollary of this observation is that punctate or local excitation of the basilar membrane is achieved only at low stimulus intensities, particularly for low-frequency stimuli. This raises a major theoretical issue. How can the auditory system retain its frequency selectivity at high intensities when such a large region of the basilar membrane is sufficiently displaced to produce excitation of its attached neural elements?

Following the discovery of the cochlear microphonic potential and the eighth nerve action potential in the 1930s, there ensued a period of intense investigation of the physiological concomitants of the traveling wave. One of the major publications summarizing nearly a decade of intense research appeared in 1965 by the MIT group of investigators (Kiang, Watanabe, Thomas, & Clark, 1965). The frequency selectivity of the auditory system was reflected in the frequency specificity of the eighth nerve responses. Frequency specificity of auditory neurons was operationalized by the "tuning curve." The tuning curve is obtained by systematically changing the intensity of a stimulus until response threshold is achieved, at multiple frequencies. The point on the tuning curve requiring the minimal amount of energy for excitation is called the characteristic frequency (CF) of the particular nerve fiber. The organization of characteristic frequency along the basilar membrane exactly duplicates the tonotopic sequence of traveling wave maxima as a function of frequency. Furthermore the asymmetrical shape of the traveling wave is reflected in the tuning curves. Thus, these observations confirmed the traveling wave as the mechanism of frequency selectivity.

These electrophysiological observations also supported the concept that only a restricted region of the basilar membrane is activated at low signal intensities. In response to a high-intensity, low-frequency signal, virtually the entire basilar membrane is sufficiently activated to produce eighth nerve responses. While these responses may reflect the periodicity of the eliciting signal, they are not *place*-specific. The distinction between place specificity, meaning local activation of the basilar membrane, and frequency specificity, which refers to the fidelity with which the period of the eliciting signal is reflected in neural coding, is critical to all subsequent discussion in this article and constitutes one of the major dilemmas in achieving precision in evoked potential studies. This dilemma appears magnified in the developing system, where, paradoxically, the developmental gradients of structure and function appear diametrically opposed. Anatomical findings have supported a progression in structural development from base to apex, while electrophysiological indices have supported a progression of functional development from lower to higher frequencies.

The traditional means of assuring that frequency selectivity has been achieved is by presenting a stimulus with a very narrow acoustic spectrum. However, as discussed above, a narrow acoustic spectrum does not insure a limited region of activation on the basilar membrane when the stimulus is presented at high intensities. Thus, narrow acoustic spectra may insure frequency selectivity without achieving place specificity. In psychophysical studies using normal ears, this problem is not overwhelming, since pitch perception does not vary greatly as signal intensity is increased. Electrophysiological studies of non-human whole-nerve action potentials and cochlear microphonics, and human whole-nerve action potentials and brainstem auditory evoked potentials, require separation of place from frequency specificity. In general, the more intense an auditory signal, the more basal is the basilar membrane region from which the electrophysiological response emanates, despite the constancy of the perceptual phenomenon. This chapter addresses the need to separate the concepts of frequency and place specificity, particularly with respect to electrophysiological studies of the human auditory system. Pursuant to this goal, there follows a series of descriptions of the interaction of stimulus parameters with their respective acoustic spectra, and a discussion of the electrophysiological correlates of these manipulations, illustrating the dissociation between acoustic and electrophysiological variables. Finally, there are comments regarding the implications of these issues for the study of the immature auditory system.

SPECTRAL STIMULUS DEPENDENCIES

Most tonal signals have a finite duration. This requires that a signal (usually a sinusoid) be gated on and off. The most effective way of changing the acoustic spectra of such a signal is to change the frequency of the gated sinusoid. However, there are several potential pitfalls in such a maneuver, primarily related to the manner in which the gate is produced and its duration. Figure 2 illustrates the effect of changing stimulus duration on the resultant acoustic spectra for selected stimuli. Note that the longer the duration of a signal, the more narrow is its spectrum. The increased spectral purity is reflected in both primary node and in the magnitude and extent of the bands on both sides of the center frequency.

A second feature of gating a signal on and off is related to the shape of the resultant envelope. This is usually described in terms of the signal's rise-fall time. As shown in Figure 3, shorter rise-fall times produce a significant scatter

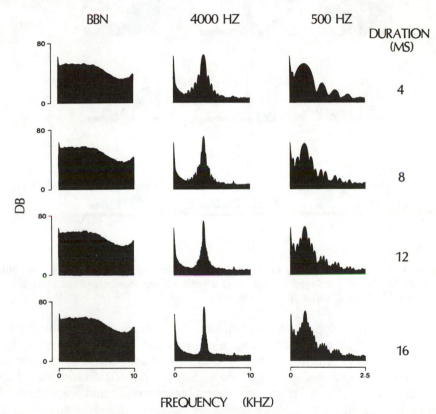

Figure 2. Acoustic spectra of a broad-band noise (BBN) burst and 4000 Hz and 500 Hz tone bursts are displayed as a function of increasing stimulus duration. Rise-fall time is constant (2 msec). Note the constancy of the noise burst spectra as a function of duration, in marked contrast to the narrowing of the spectra for tone bursts under the same conditions. In this and subsequent figures, intensities of the tone bursts and BBN burst were 94 dB peak equivalent SPL and 94 dB rms SPL, respectively. Acoustic spectra were measured in an IAC booth through a TDH-49 earphone in an MX 41/AR cushion coupled (NBS-9A) to a sound level meter (B&K 2203), the output of which was led to a spectrum analyzer (Hewlett-Packard 3582A) and averaged over 64 trials. The initial peak at extreme low frequencies is due to a sampling artifact. The noise floor is approximately 70 dB down from maximum on the relative dB axes. Note the scale change in frequency for the 500 Hz tone burst in this and subsequent figures.

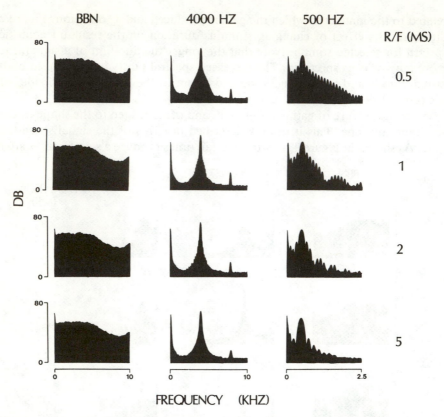

Figure 3. Acoustic spectra of a broad-band noise (BBN) burst and 4000 Hz and 500 Hz tone bursts are displayed. Duration of all stimuli was held constant at 10 msec with variable rise-fall times (R/F) as shown.

of energy in the side-band skirts of the acoustic spectra. With essentially instantaneous rise times, there is always a transient, click-like component to the signal, regardless of the frequency of the underlying sinusoid. A description of the interaction between signal envelope and acoustic spectrum is achieved by Fourier analysis. The practical implication, of course, is that, regardless of duration, optimal spectral purity cannot be achieved without a slowly rising envelope. This presents a dilemma to the electrophysiologist seeking frequency selective signals. Responses such as the whole-nerve action potential, the brainstem auditory evoked potential, and the middle latency evoked potential are dependent upon the near-simultaneous, or synchronous, firing of neuronal populations, which is best achieved by stimuli with very brief rise times. Thus, these responses are exquisitely sensitive to the physics of the initial portion of the signal and relatively insensitive to signal duration and fall time. It has been repeatedly demonstrated that more rapid rise times produce clearer and more reliably obtained whole-nerve action potentials, brainstem, and middle latency evoked potentials (Goldstein & Kiang, 1958; Hecox & Deegan, 1983; Hecox,

Squires, & Galambos, 1976; Vivion, Hirsch, Frye-Osier, & Goldstein, 1980). Rise-time effects have been described for the cortical auditory evoked potential, but seem to have a less profound effect on response morphology and reliability (Onishi & Davis, 1968). From this standpoint alone, it can be seen that the signals ordinarily used for audiometric studies, with their slowly rising envelopes, are inappropriate as electrophysiological probes.

Signal repetition rate can, in principle, change the resultant spectra also. The spectral shifts are primarily in the frequency region corresponding to the repetition rate of the signal, until the ability of the transducer to reproduce such stimulation is surpassed. For example, changing stimulus repetition rate from 30 to 90 Hz would change the associated spectrum primarily in the frequency region below 100 Hz. However, there are no clinical measures, whether behavioral or electrophysiological, designed to detect pathology in that frequency region. Therefore, repetition rate must be considered a secondary variable with respect to its impact on the acoustic spectra for both behavioral and evoked potential studies.

As shown in Figure 4, stimulus intensity has no effect on the center frequency or -3 dB bandwidth of the stimulus. This is true for both the 500 Hz and 4000 Hz stimuli in the illustration. Any spread of energy associated with increases in intensity is limited to the skirts of the acoustic spectra.

Adding to the difficulty in achieving stimulus frequency selectivity are the interactive effects of these various signal parameters. Figure 5 demonstrates acoustic spectra for selected stimuli as a function of simultaneous increases in duration and rise time. These stimuli have no plateau. Thus, the overall duration is given by twice the rise-fall time shown on the right hand side of the figure. It is readily apparent that changes in both signal duration and rise-fall time produce more dramatic effects on signal spectrum than changes in either signal parameter alone. Further, it is clear that the change in spectral purity with increasing duration and rise-fall time is greater for the 500 Hz than the 4000 Hz stimulus. If one calculates the percentage of total energy included within a half octave above and below the nominal center frequency, the improvement in spectral purity is much greater for the 500 Hz signal. In essence, the lower the frequency of a tone burst, the more difficult it is to achieve a narrow spectrum.

One of the important advantages of broad-band noise as a stimulus can be appreciated by its constant spectrum throughout major changes in both duration and rise-fall time, as seen in Figures 2, 3, and 5. If the goal of an experiment is to study the impact of rise-fall time or duration keeping spectrum constant, then the ideal signal would be a noise burst as opposed to a tone burst. As shown by these figures, the interactions between signal rise-fall time, duration, and frequency are sufficiently important that distinguishing the independent effects of these variables can be quite difficult for tone-burst stimuli.

These subtle interactions have forced investigators using tonal signals to search for the optimal combination of signal parameters, to ensure a constancy of frequency selectivity. Various solutions have been offered, including Gabor's

Kurt E. Hecox and Donald M. Deegan

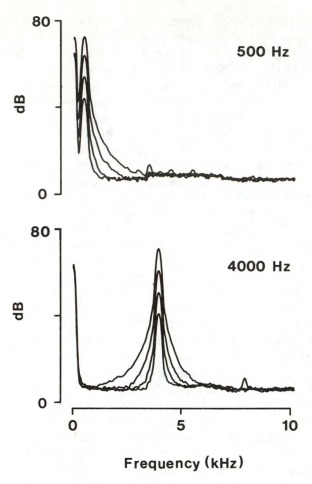

Figure 4. Acoustic spectra of 500 Hz and 4000 Hz tone buirsts are shown at stimulus intensities of 64, 74, 84, and 94 dB p.e. SPL. Stimuli were 10 msec in duration, with rise-fall times of 5 msec. Note the lack of effect on spectral bandwidth despite the varied absolute energy at each frequency.

logon and the use of a fixed number of cycles in the rise and fall times of the signal envelope (Eggermont, Spoor, & Odenthal, 1976; Gabor, 1947). While ensuring adequate frequency selectivity, such approaches confound the variables of signal duration, rise-fall time, and frequency. For example, the logon for a 500 Hz signal would consist of a 4 msec rise (twice the period of 500 Hz signal), a 4 msec fall time, and a total duration of 8 msec, while the logon for a 4000 Hz signal would consist of a 0.5 msec rise, a 0.5 msec fall, and a total duration of 1.0 msec. Clearly, comparisons across signals are confounded by duration, rise-fall time, and frequency. It would seem then, that there is no simple way of matching for acoustic frequency selectivity without confounding multiple acoustic parameters, when using tone-burst signals.

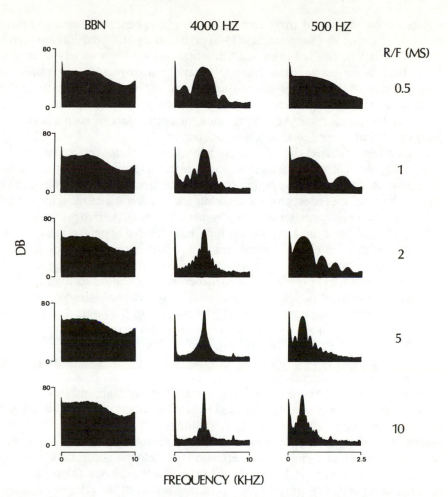

Figure 5. Acoustic spectra are displayed as duration and rise-fall time are covaried. Total duration for each condition is twice the rise-fall time (R/F). Again, note the constancy of the noise burst spectra compared to that of the tone bursts.

ELECTROPHYSIOLOGICAL STIMULUS DEPENDENCIES

The examples used in this section will be based primarily on the brainstem auditory evoked potential. This response consists of seven vertex positive deflections representing the activation of the eighth nerve and subsequent brainstem auditory nuclei and tracts. The primary dependent variable in most brainstem auditory evoked potential studies is the latency and/or amplitude of the Wave V component of the response, which is presumed to emanate primarily, but not exclusively, from the midbrain region contralateral to the stimulated ear. The second most commonly used response component is Wave I, which is the surface recorded reflection of eighth nerve activation. Systematic effects on the latency of these responses have been repeatedly demonstrated (Picton, Stapells, & Campbell, 1981) as a function of signal intensity, frequency, duration, rise-fall time, and presentation rate for a variety of stimuli (i.e., clicks, noise bursts, tonal signals). There are many candidate sources of latency shifts in all evoked potential studies. For instance, latency shifts can be attributed to peripheral factors such as an increasing traveling wave delay from basal to apical regions of the cochlea, or central factors such as synaptic delays and finite nerve conduction velocities.

In an effort to dissect the relative contributions of peripheral versus central mechanisms which might mediate latency shifts, selective masking strategies have been used to control the region of activation along the basilar membrane. Two such techniques are high-pass masking and notched-noise masking. In the high-pass masking paradigm, originally used by Teas, Eldredge, and Davis (1962), a broad-band masking noise is high-pass filtered at octave-interval cutoff frequencies in an effort to eliminate any contribution to the response that may be caused by spread of excitation of the asymmetrical traveling wave. If sufficient hardware is present, the experimenter may choose to digitally subtract the responses obtained in the presence of successive high-pass maskers. This allows the investigator to "derive" the amount of the unmasked response which is attributable to the activation of restricted regions along the cochlear partition. Thus, the "derived-band response" reflects the response emanating from the region of the basilar membrane delimited by the cutoff frequencies used in the digital subtraction.

Similarly, broad-band noise may be simultaneously high and low-pass filtered at octave-interval cutoff frequencies, leaving an octave-wide "notched" region of no noise. This technique, first implemented by Picton, Ouellette, Hamel, and Smith (1979), does not require digital subtraction techniques and provides a direct and immediate reflection of activity occuring within the notched region along the basilar membrane. Such methods (high-pass and notched-noise masking) provide place-specific indices of the relative contribution of the response-generating activity emanating from successive regions of the cochlear partition. We will make considerable use of the high-pass masking paradigm (with and without digital subtraction) in the remainder of this chapter. We have selected the high-pass technique over the notched-noise procedure primarily because of the difficulties in controlling the basal spread of energy from the low-pass section of the notched-noise into the no-noise region of the notch.

Evidence supportive of the validity of inferences based on high-pass masking techniques can be found in Figure 6. Here, the latencies of the derived-band responses have been used to estimate traveling wave velocities in the cochlea. Estimates of the anatomical distance between adjacent derived-band center frequencies (CFs) along the basilar membrane were obtained from human temporal bone material (von Békésy, 1963). The change in latency between Wave V of the responses emanating from adjacent bands provides a measure of the

4 msec DURATION

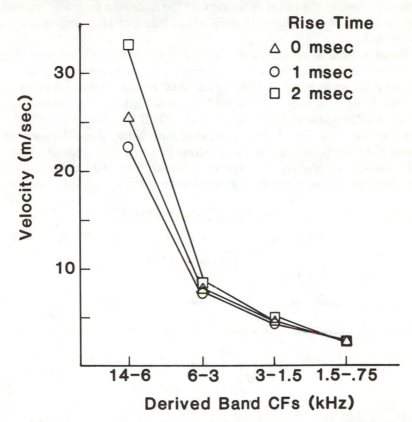

Figure 6. Traveling wave velocities are displayed as a function of derived band center frequency (CF). Velocities were calculated by obtaining anatomic estimates of the distance between adjacent pairs of CFs along the abscissa, and dividing that distance by the corresponding change in wave V latency observed between those CFs. Stimulus was a 4 msec noise burst of varying rise-fall time, presented at 50 dB re normal threshold.

time delay required for the traveling wave to progress between adjacent CFs. The ratio of the anatomical distance over the change in latency taken between successive pairs of derived bands provides an accurate approximation of the traveling wave velocity as it progresses from base to apex. As shown in Figure 6, results of these calculations demonstrate that traveling wave velocity decreases exponentially from values as high as 33 msec at the basal, high-frequency region, to values as low as 1 msec at the apical, low-frequency region. These values are in remarkable agreement with velocity estimates from more direct eighth nerve recordings, and from psychophysical measures (Eggermont & Odenthal, 1974; Elberling, 1974; Zerlin, 1969). The place specificity of derived-band responses is further validated by determining whether the individual derived-band responses summate to equal the unmasked response. This is essentially a test of the additive linearity of the high-pass subtractive masking procedure, and this condition is fulfilled, at least for click and broad-band noise stimuli.

The application of ordinary high-pass masking (without digital subtraction) to the study of the peripheral effects of varying stimulus center frequency and intensity is shown in Figure 7. 1000 Hz and 4000 Hz tone bursts were presented at 70 and 30 dB HL, with and without high-pass masking. Note that in the no masking (NM) condition, the latencies of the 70 dB HL, 1000 Hz and 4000 Hz signals are quite similar. This is somewhat surprising, given the time delay necessary for the traveling wave to progress between these regions along the basilar membrane, leading to the speculation that, despite differences in signal center frequency, the responses originate from approximately the same area of

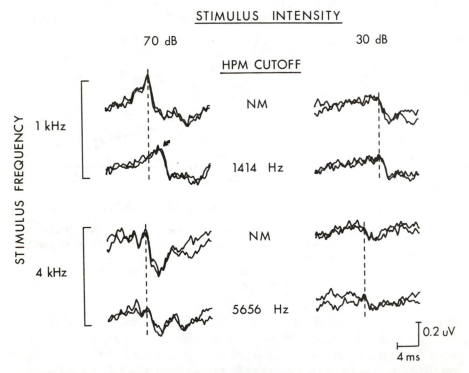

Figure 7. Auditory brain stem responses elicited by 1000 Hz and 4000 Hz tone bursts at 70 dB and 30 dB HL are displayed, with high-pass masking (HPM) and without (NM = no masking). HPM cutoffs of 1414 Hz and 5656 Hz represent the half-octave intervals above stimulus center frequency, and were selected to equalize the anatomical distance between HPM edge and stimulus center frequency. Note that the addition of HPM to a 1000 Hz stimulus at 70 dB increases latency, while at 30 dB there is little HPM effect. The addition of HPM to a 4000 Hz stimulus at either intensity produced no effect. Tone bursts were of 5 msec duration, with 2 msec rise-fall times. In this and subsequent figures, vertex positivity is up. Each trace represents the average of 2048 stimulus presentations.

the cochlear partition. This spread of excitation hypothesis is confirmed when high-pass masking is introduced with cutoff frequencies at fixed percentages above the nominal center frequency of each stimulus. The response elicited by the 1000 Hz tone burst, presented at 70 dB HL simultaneously with high-pass masking, is characterized by a significantly prolonged Wave V (indicated by arrow) when compared to the response elicited by the same signal without high-pass masking. This implies that the unmasked response to the 1000 Hz tone burst at 70 dB HL is arising from a region basal to the 1000 Hz area of the basilar membrane, since, when this region is eliminated with high-pass masking, the response latency increases. In contrast, the introduction of a high-pass masker to the 4000 Hz signal at 70 dB HL had little effect on response latency, suggesting that the unmasked response to this stimulus is in fact place specific.

As expected on the basis of traveling wave theory, the unmasked response elicited by the 1000 Hz tone burst at 30 dB HL is prolonged in latency when compared to the unmasked response evoked by the 4000 Hz tone burst at the same intensity. In addition, the introduction of high-pass masking produced very little change in the latency of Wave V of the responses to either stimulus frequency. The absence of a masking effect suggests that the 30 dB HL responses were already place specific. These findings confirm those of others, and demonstrate that presenting a signal at moderate intensities and above can activate broad regions of the cochlear partition, regardless of the nominal center frequency of the stimulus (Eggermont & Don, 1980; Kileny, 1981; Picton et al., 1979).

A similar circumstance arises in the study of derived-band responses to broad-band signals such as the click. As seen in Figure 8, the cochlear distribution of activity contributing to the evoked potential obtained in the unmasked condition is intensity dependent. The response elicited by a click presented at 60 dB HL contains activity throughout the extent of the cochlear partition, as indicated by the presence of derived-band responses (indicated by arrows) at each location along the basilar membrane. In contrast, the regional distribution of energy in response to a 30 dB HL click is somewhat more limited, with maximal derived-band response amplitude observed in the 4-2 kHz region corresponding to the frequency content of the click. These shifts in the distribution of activity along the cochlear partition are present despite a relative constancy of the click acoustic spectra as a function of intensity. Assurance of constant spectrum does not imply that the region of the basilar membrane responsible for generating a response has remained constant. It is only at relatively low intensities that place specificity can be assured without the use of selective masking techniques.

In addition to frequency and intensity, changes in signal rise time produce consistent effects on the latency of the brainstem auditory evoked potential. As signal rise time increases, so does response latency. The contribution of traveling wave phenomena to the observed latency shifts as a function of stimulus rise time has been examined through the use of high-pass masking and derived-band responses (Hecox and Deegan, 1983). As seen in Figure 9, in-

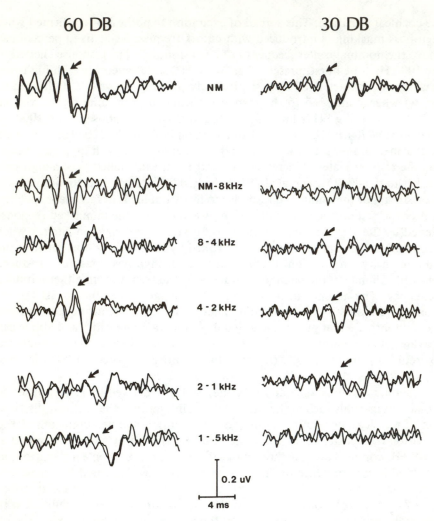

Figure 8. Click-evoked brainstem responses are shown at two intensities (HL). Derived-band responses were obtained by digitally subtracting responses elicited under successive high pass masker cutoff frequencies. Thus, the derived-band response emanates from the region of the cochlear partition delimited by the cutoff frequencies listed in the middle. Arrows indicate the presence of Wave V. NM = no masking. Note the presence of a response in all derived bands at 60 dB stimulus intensity, but only in the "mid" derived bands at 30 dB intensity.

creasing stimulus rise time results in a consistent increase in Wave V latency of the derived-band response. The amount of latency shift apparent within each derived-band is essentially the same as that observed in the unmasked waveforms. Furthermore, for the signal conditions illustrated in Figure 9, the latency shift introduced by varying rise time within each derived band is relatively constant throughout several derived-band locations along the basilar membrane.

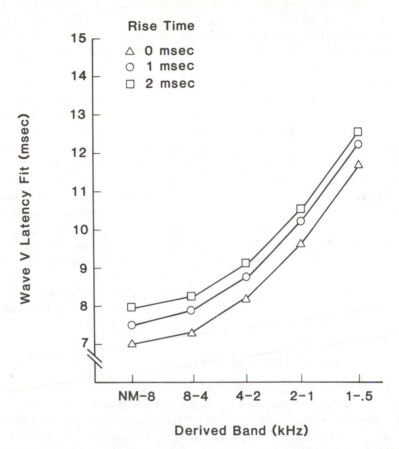

4 msec DURATION

Rise Time
△ 0 msec
○ 1 msec
□ 2 msec

Wave V Latency Fit (msec)

Derived Band (kHz)

Figure 9. Wave V latency is displayed as a function of derived-band frequency, with stimulus rise-fall time as the parameter. These exponential functions represent the best fit obtained through regression analysis of the latency data. Intercept comparisons revealed a significant increase in latency as a function of increasing stimulus rise-fall time ($p < .05$). Slope comparisons revealed these functions to be parallel, suggesting a constant effect of stimulus rise time on response latency regardless of the peripheral origin of the response. Peripheral location is assumed to be contained between the high-pass masking cut-off frequencies used to obtain the derived band. Stimulus was a 4 msec duration noise burst presented 50 dB above normal threshold.

These findings rule out spread of excitation associated with changes in signal rise time as a mechanism for the observed latency shifts, and suggest that more central (neural) factors are likely mediators of the rise time effect. In this manner, the relative contribution of the peripheral versus central factors that mediate the electrophysiological stimulus dependencies may be determined.

Changes in Wave V latency of the brainstem auditory evoked potential as a function of increasing stimulus duration have been studied systematically

noise burst signals by Hecox et al. (1976), without the use of masking procedures. By separately manipulating signal on-time and off-time, Hecox et al.
(1976) demonstrated that most of the duration effect for noise burst signals
was due to changes in signal off-time (interstimulus interval) and not on-time.
These results may be explained on the basis of forward masking, or the ability
of a given signal to mask the signal that follows it.

Several principles should be apparent from the above studies. First, selective masking strategies can be used to great advantage in quantifying traveling
wave phenomena, and distinguishing between peripheral and central influences
on response dependencies, in a manner heretofore impossible in the intact
human subject. Second, achieving some degree of frequency selectivity in stimulus acoustic spectra in no way guarantees that the response elicited by that
stimulus originates from the region of the basilar membrane reflected in the
nominal center frequency of the signal. In particular, as stimulus intensity
moves further above threshold there is an increasing likelihood that the observed response emanates from a more basal region of the cochlear partition
than expected on the basis of the stimulus frequency. Other stimulus variables,
such as duration, which can have a profound effect on acoustic spectrum, may
produce relatively little effect on a response which is onset in nature. Most importantly, it is possible to dissociate stimulus frequency specificity from electrophysiological place specificity. It is critical for the investigator to keep in
mind the difference between place and frequency specificity.

IMPLICATIONS FOR DEVELOPMENTAL STUDIES

This section begins with a consideration of some of the calibration issues in
specifying an effective stimulus as a function of age. This is then followed by a
brief discussion of structure-function relations in ontogeny, particularly as
they relate to place and frequency specificity as discussed in the previous sections. Finally, there follows a discussion of the implications of recent anatomical and physiological studies on the design and analysis of future investigations
in auditory development. These implications are synthesized from an integration
of the theoretical problems defined in the previous acoustical and physiological discussions with known principles of auditory development. The separation
or exclusion of any of these perspectives from the development of improved
methodologies can only weaken the analytical strength of future studies.

Calibration of Stimulus Delivery

As in other areas of the hearing sciences, the careful specification of signal
acoustics is the first step in the study of auditory development. However, this
goal is not easily achieved. To strictly define age-dependent differences in
responsivity, an equivalent stimulus should be used at all ages. "Equivalent
stimulus" is dependent upon the selected point of reference, such as the external auditory meatus, tympanic membrane, basilar membrane, or the eighth

nerve. Selecting any reference other than the external auditory meatus forces the investigator to face a number of significant technical calibration issues. For example, canal length and diameter have significant effects on standing wave frequencies and resonant peaks in the canal. Higher resonance frequencies will be evident in younger patients in whom the external auditory canal is shorter. Open or closed ear canal measurements, using standard microphone probe assemblies, can also interact with age, since the distance of the probe from the tympanic membrane, and the volume of the probe in relation to that of the whole canal, will vary with normal development.

The increased compliance of the infant tympanic membrane, its oblique plane with respect to a cross section of the canal, and the altered ratio of tympanic membrane size relative to stapes footplate size could all significantly influence the transfer function of the middle ear in the immature organism.

Standard models of the impact of such developmental variables on stimulus transduction do not yet exist. The typical approach has been to measure and then allow correction for variables which are known to influence the peripheral transfer function. Calibrations such as this must be performed on each subject, and vary significantly with age. Presently, age-stimulus equivalence can only be achieved with certainty at the external auditory meatus.

Ontogeny of Structure and Function

The mechanical properties of the basilar membrane impose a frequency-to-place, or tonotopic organization along the organ of Corti, such that basal regions are activated by high frequencies, and apical regions by low frequencies. The frequency to which a particular nerve fiber is maximally sensitive is dependent upon its site of attachment along the cochlear partition. This base-to-apex, high-to-low frequency tonotopic representation of the cochlea is preserved in the afferent target populations within the major nuclei of the ascending auditory system. Clear tonotopic organization has been demonstrated in the cochlear nucleus complex (Rose, Galambos, & Hughes, 1959), medial and lateral superior olivary nuclei (Goldbert & Brown, 1968; Tsuchitani & Boudreau, 1966), the ventral and dorsal muclei of the lateral lemniscus (Aitkin, Anderson, & Brugge, 1970), the central nucleus of the inferior colliculus (Merzenich & Reid, 1974; Beyerl, 1978), the principal division of the medial geniculate body (Aitkin & Webster, 1971), and the primary auditory cortex (Brugge & Merzenich, 1971).

In the developing organism, most anatomical studies reveal a general base-to-apex gradient to structural development. This gradient occurs in the cochlea, and is paralleled in most of the central auditory nuclei (Altman & Bayer, 1979, 1980a, 1980b, 1981; Kikuchi & Hilding, 1965, 1966; Pujol & Marty, 1970; Rubel, 1978; Rubel, Smith, & Miller, 1976; Ruben, 1967; Streeter, 1906). However, a variety of electrophysiological indices from several species have usually supported a functional development gradient from lower-to-higher frequencies (Aitkin & Moore, 1975; Brugge, Javel, & Kitzes, 1978; Carlier, Abonnec,

& Pujol, 1975; Hecox, 1975; Moore & Irvine, 1975; Pujol, 1972; Pujol & Hilding, 1973; Romand, 1971; Taguchi, Picton, Orpin, & Goodman, 1969; Wolf & Goldstein, 1980). Thus, it appears that there is a remarkable dissociation between structural and functional ontogeny. Anatomical studies suggest a base-to-apex structural gradient, while most physiological studies suggest a low-to-high frequency functional gradient, which is opposite to that expected on the basis of adult tonotopic relationships.

Functionally, the selective impairment of high frequency regions can be likened to, and therefore modelled as, a variable low-pass filter, as shown in Figure 10. The acoustic output of a 500 Hz tone burst and a 4000 Hz tone burst were passed through a low-pass filter at various cutoff frequencies. It is evident that, at cutoff frequencies of 4 kHz (and above), both tonal spectra are relatively unaffected. However, as the cutoff frequency of the low-pass filter is lowered (corresponding to greater immaturity of the auditory system), the high frequency stimulus is attenuated relative to the low frequency stimulus, particularly with steeper slopes to the filter cutoffs. This simple model allows a "visualization" of the functional decrease in high-frequency responsivity relative to low-frequency responsivity in the immature system. Note also that the same spectral output can be achieved with various combinations of filter cutoffs and slopes. For example, the resultant spectra from the 2 kHz cutoff, 48 dB/octave slope is nearly the same as the 0.5 kHz cutoff, 12 dB/octabe slope. Therefore, one cannot easily move from resultant spectra to filter cutoffs without consideration of the filter slopes. Understanding where and how such low-pass filter characteristics might be effected during development is a complex task. Peripheral factors, such as regional immaturities along the cochlear partition, and central factors, a partial list of which includes regional changes in myelination, nerve diameter, neuronal and synaptic density, could all serve to "filter" the output of the periphery.

The recent work of Rubel and Ryals (1983) and Lippe and Rubel (1983) suggests that developmental changes at the periphery may account for the "low-pass filter" characteristics described in the functional studies, but the contribution of central mechanisms is largely unassessed. These exciting findings are discussed in Rubel's chapter in this volume. Recent work by Teas, Klein, and Kramer, (1982) provides the first attempt to simultaneously assess the relative contribution of peripheral and central factors to these developmental phenomena. As expected on the basis of anatomical data, Wave I (auditory nerve) demonstrates a developmental gradient from high-to-low frequencies. However, Wave V (contralateral midbrain) progresses in the opposite direction, from low-to-high frequencies. This represents the first demonstration in humans that mechanisms of auditory development may differ for peripheral and central pathways.

Methodological Implications

A number of decisions must be made when selecting an auditory stimulus. This section will discuss the implications of the above described developmental phenomena for the selection of signal parameters. The traditional means of

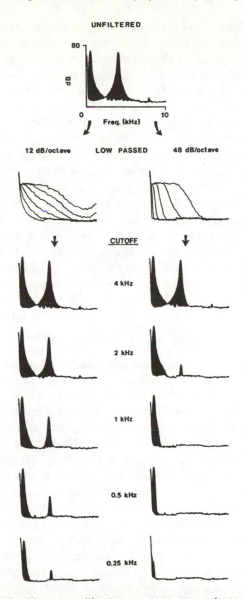

Figure 10. The effects of low-pass filtering on 4000 Hz and 500 Hz tone bursts are displayed. The two stimuli are affected differently at successive low-pass cutoffs. The magnitude of effect is dependent upon the filter slope characteristics, and is greater at 48 dB/octave (right column) than at 12 dB/octave (left column). Note that nearly identical spectral results can be obtained at different combinations of masker cutoffs and slopes.

assuring either frequency or place specificity is the presentation of a narrow spectrum signal at or near threshold. These conditions are required, in large part, by the mechanical aspects of basilar membrane motion and the spread of energy away from the traveling wave maxima as a function of intensity. Thus,

assurance of place specificity is achieved only when the effective level of stimulation results in a limited region of activation of the basilar membrane. This
can be achieved by intensities near mechanical threshold, or by using masking
paradigms which restrict the basilar membrane regions free to respond.

Threshold must be very carefully defined in this context. If, for example, a
developmentally immature subject yields elevated thresholds, as reflected by a
measure of brain activity, this still leaves undefined the relationship between
mechanical and neural thresholds. If eighth nerve thresholds are elevated, it
may be secondary to immaturity of the external, middle, or inner ear, or even
of the eighth nerve. If thresholds are elevated by 40 dB secondary to middle ear
immaturity, then cochlear and neural thresholds should coincide. Alternatively,
if the 40 dB threshold elevation occurs at the synaptic level (hair cell-eighth
nerve junction), then the stimulus intensities required for excitation of eighth
nerve fibers could activate broad regions of the basilar membrane. In fact, only
when a pathological process or immaturity is secondary to middle or external
ear changes can there be any assurance that place specificity is preserved at any
neural "threshold." Therefore, place specificity cannot be assumed without
prior knowledge of the locus of immaturity, and, when that immaturity is not
conductive in origin, simultaneous band-pass masking must be used.

As we can see from the work of Rubel and colleagues, achieving place spe-
cifity with tone bursts (or tones) does not assure that the same cochlear place is
studied at each age. Recently, stimuli presented with band-passed masking
have been used in place of unmasked tone bursts to achieve greater place and
frequency specificity. These procedures have proven quite powerful. As discussed previously, band-passed noise is presented at levels sufficient to eliminate the contribution of selected portions of the basilar membrane. However,
to obtain the same amount and extent of masking across ages, it must be assumed that response properties do not interact with masker intensity, masker
slope at the cutoff frequency, and masker bandwidth as a function of age. At
present, these assumptions are unproven. The overall implication of these
issues is that methods used to assure place or frequency specificity cannot be
developed separately from an intimate understanding of the anatomical and
physiological features of auditory development.

Most of this discussion has been centered on electrophysiological investigations, although the fundamental nature of the problems addressed hold implications for any methodology. Often, suprathreshold signals have been used to
evaluate differential sensitivity across and within ages, using behavioral methods.
The startle response, blink reflex, middle ear reflexes, and respiratory rate
changes are all examples of response measures elicited by stimuli presented far
above subjective thresholds. While each of these measures has been used in the
assessment of auditory sensitivity, considerable caution must be exercised in
the interpretation of changes in these measures as a function of age, and in implying frequency specificity under these signal conditions. For example, intensities of at least 80 to 90 dB SPL may be required to induce a blink reflex or
startle response to a 500 Hz tone in newborns. A change in this threshold as a

function of age (for example, a decrease to 70 dB) cannot be assumed to reflect improving function in the 500 Hz region of the cochlea. At these intensities, virtually the entire extent of the basilar membrane may be set into motion. Responses could therefore be generated from any portion of the basilar membrane, and the region producing the response could shift with age. If, however, a continuous high-pass masker with a cutoff of 1000 Hz is presented simultaneously with the response-eliciting tone, the "excitatory" region of the basilar membrane will be more limited. In this situation, changes in response threshold as a function of age could reflect improved sensitivity in the 500 Hz region, or might be due to decreased spread of energy away from the masker cutoff frequency. Thus, there are also ambiguities in the interpretation of developmental changes for masking paradigms.

From the methodological standpoint, high priority must be given to (a) the definition of the anatomical locus of auditory immaturity to determine the appropriateness of tone burst stimuli, and (b) the quantification of the mechanical properties of the basilar membrane as a function of age prior to using band-pass masking with assurance. Once these methodologic issues have been addressed, the many questions regarding the multifactorial nature of the auditory development can be investigated with greater validity and depth.

REFERENCES

Aitkin, L. M., Anderson, D. J., & Brugge, J. F. Tonotopic organization and discharge characteristics of single neurons in nuclei of the lateral lemniscus of the cat. *Journal of Neurophysiology*, 1970, *33*, 421–440.

Aitkin, L. M. & Moore, D. R. Inferior colliculus. II. Development of tuning characteristics and tonotopic organization in central nucleus of the neonatal cat. *Journal of Neurophysiology*, 1975, *38*, 1208–1216.

Aikin, L. M. & Webster, W. R. Tonotopic organization and discharge characteristics of single neurons in nuclei of the lateral lemniscus of the cat. *Journal of Neurophysiology*, 1971, *33*, 421–440.

Altman, J. & Bayer, S. A. Development of the diencephalon in the rat. IV. Quantitative study of the time of origin of neurons and the intranuclear chronological gradients in the thalamus. *Journal of Comparative Neurology*, 1979, *188*, 973–994.

Altman, J. & Bayer, S. A. Development of the brain stem in the rat. III. Thymidine-radiographic study of the time of origin of neurons of the vestibular and auditory nuclei of the upper medulla. *Journal of Comparative Neurology*, 1980, *194*, 877–904. (a)

Altman, J. & Bayer, S. A. Development of the brain stem of the rat. IV. Thymidine-radiographic study of the time of origin of neurons in the pontine region. *Journal of Comparative Neurology*, 1980, *194*, 905–929. (b)

Altman, J. & Bayer, S. A. Time of origin of neurons of the rat inferior colliculus and the relations between cytogenesis and tonotopic order in the auditory pathway. *Experimental Brain Research*, 1981, *42*, 411–423.

Beyerl, B. D. Afferent projections to the central nucleus of the inferior colliculus in the rat. *Brain Research*, 1978, *145*, 209–223.

Brugge, J. F., Javel, E., & Kitzes, L. M. Signs of functional maturation of peripheral auditory system in discharge patterns of neurons in anteroventral cochlear nucleus of kitten. *Journal of Neurophysiology*, 1978, *41*, 1557–1579.

Brugge, J. F. & Merzenich, M. M. Representation of frequency in auditory cortex in the macaque monkey. In Sachs, M. B. (ed.), *The physiology of the auditory system*. Baltimore, Md: National Educational Consultants, 1971.

Carlier, E., Abonnec, M., & Pujol, R. Maturation des réponses unitaires à la stimulation tonale dans le nerf cochléaire du chaton. *Journal of Physiology* (Paris), 1975, *70,* 129–138.

Eggermont, J. J. & Don, M. Analysis of the click-evoked brainstem potentials in humans using high-pass noise masking. II. Effects of click intensity. *Journal of Acoustical Society of America,* 1980, *68,* 1671–1675.

Eggermont, J. J. & Odenthal, D. W. Frequency selective masking in electrocochleography. *Revue Laryngologie Otologie Rhinologie* (Bordeaux), 1974, *95,* 489–496.

Eggermont, J. J., Spoor, A., & Odenthal, D. W. Frequency specificity of tone-burst electrocochleography. In R. Ruben, C. Elberling, & G. Salomon (eds.), *Electrocochleography*. Baltimore, Md: University Park Press, 1976, pp. 215–246.

Elberling, C. Action potentials along the cochlear partition recorded from the ear canal in man. *Scandanavian Audiology,* 1974, *3,* 13–19.

Gabor, D. Acoustical quanta and the theory of hearing. *Nature,* 1947, *159,* 591–594.

Goldberg, J. M. & Brown, P. B. Functional organization of the dog superior olivary complex: An anatomical and electrophysiological study. *Journal of Neurophysiology,* 1968, *31,* 639–656.

Goldstein, M. H. & Kiang, N. Y. S. Synchrony of neural activity in electric responses evoked by transient acoustic stimuli. *Journal of Acoustical Society of America,* 1958, *30,* 107–114.

Hecox, K. E. Electrophysiological correlates of human auditory development. In L. Cohen & P. Salapatek (eds.), *Infant perception*. Vol. 2. New York: Academic Press, 1975, 151–191.

Hecox, K. E. & Deegan, D. M. Rise-fall time effects on the brainstem auditory evoked response: Mechanisms. *Journal of Acoustical Society of America,* 1983, *73*(6), 2109–2116.

Hecox, K. E., Squires, N. K., & Galambos, R. Brainstem auditory evoked responses in man. I. Effect of stimulus rise-fall time and duration. *Journal of Acoustical Society of America,* 1976, *60,* 1187–1192.

Helmholtz, H. L. F. *Die Lehre von den Tonempfindungen als physiologische Grundlage fur die Theorie der Musik*. Braunschweig, Germany: Viewig u. Sohn, 1863.

Kiang, N. Y. S., Watanabe, T., Thomas, E. C., & Clark, L. F. *Discharge patterns of single fibers in the cat's auditory nerve*. Cambridge, Mass.: M.I.T. Press, 1965.

Kikuchi, K. & Hilding, D. The development of the organ of Corti in the mouse. *Acta Otolaryngolica* (Stockholm), 1965, *60,* 207–202.

Kikuchi, K. & Hilding, D. The development of the stria vascularis in the mouse. *Acta Otolaryngologica* (Stockholm), 1966, 277–291.

Kileny, P. The frequency specificity of tone-pip evoked auditory brain stem responses. *Ear and Hearing,* 1981, *2,* 270–275.

Ladefoged, P. *Elements of acoustics phonetics*. Chicago: University of Chicago Press, 1962.

Lippe, W. & Rubel, E. W. Development of the place principle: Tonotopic organization. *Science,* 1983, *219,* 514–516.

Merzenich, M. M. & Reid, M. D. Representation of the cochlea within the inferior colliculus of the cat. *Brain Research,* 1974, *77,* 397–415.

Moore, D. R. & Irvine, D. R. F. The development of some peripheral and central auditory responses in the neonatal cat. *Brain Research,* 1979, *163,* 49–59.

Onishi, S. & Davis, H. Effects of duration and rise time of tone bursts on evoked V potentials. *Journal of Acoustical Society of America,* 1968, *44,* 582–591.

Picton, T. W., Ouellette, J., Hamel, G., & Smith, A. D. Brainstem evoked potentials to tonepips in notched noise. *Journal of Otolaryngology,* 1979, *8,* 289–314.

Picton, T. W., Stapells, D. R., & Campbell, K. B. Auditory evoked potentials from the human cochlea and brainstem. *Journal of Otolaryngology,* 1981, *10,* Suppl. 9, 1–41.

Pujol, R. Development of tone-burst responses along the auditory pathway in the cat. *Acta Otolaryngologica* (Stockholm), 1972, *74,* 383–391.

Pujol, R. & Hilding, D. Anatomy and physiology of the onset of auditory function. *Acta Otolaryngologica* (Stockholm), 1973, *76,* 1–10.

Pujol, R. & Marty, R. Postnatal maturation of the cochlea of the cat. *Journal of Comparative Neurology,* 1970, *139,* 115–125.

Romand, R. Maturation des potentiels cochléaires dans la période périnatale chez le chat et chez le cobaye. *Journal of Physiology* (Paris), 1971, *63,* 763–782.

Rose, J., Galambos, R. & Hughes, J. R. Microelectrode studies of the cochlear nucleus of the cat. *Johns Hopkins Hospital Bulletin,* 1959, *104:* 211–251.

Rubel, E. W. Ontogeny of structure and function in the vertebrate auditory system. In M. Jacobson (ed.), *Handbook of sensory physiology.* Vol. 9. New York: Springer-Verlag, 1978.

Rubel, E. W & Ryals, B. M. Development of the place principle: Acoustic trauma. *Science,* 1983, *219,* 512–514.

Rubel, E. W, Smith, D. J., & Miller, L. C. Organization and development of brain stem auditory nuclei of the chicken: Ontogeny of N. magnocellularis and N. laminaris. *Journal of Comparative Neurology,* 1976, *166,* 469–490.

Ruben, R. J. Development of the inner ear of the mouse: A radioautographic study of terminal mitosis. *Acta Otolaryngologica* (Stockholm), 1967, Suppl. 220: 1–44.

Streeter, G. L. On the development of the membranous labyrinth and the acoustic and facial nerves in the human embryo. *American Journal of Anatomy,* 1906, *6,* 139–166.

Taguchi, K., Picton, T. W., Orpin, J., & Goodman, W. Evoked response audiometry in newborn infants. *Acta Otolaryngologica* (Stockholm), 1969, *252,* 5–17.

Teas., D. C., Eldredge, D. H., & Davis, H. Cochlear responses to acoustic transients: An interpretation of whole-nerve action potentials. *Journal of Acoustical Society of America,* 1962, *34,* 1438–1459.

Teas, D. C., Klein, A. J., & Kramer, S. An analysis of auditory brainstem responses in infants. *Hearing Research,* 1982, *7,* 19–54.

Tsuchitani, C. & Boudreau, J. C. Single unit analysis of cat superior olive S segment with tonal stimuli. *Journal of Neurophysiology,* 1966, *29,* 684–697.

Vivion, M. C., Hirsch, J. L., Frye-Osier, H., & Goldstein, R. Effects of stimulus rise-fall time and equivalent duration on middle components of AER. *Scandinavian Audiology,* 1980, *9,* 223–232.

von Békésy, G. Hearing theories and complex sounds. *Journal of Acoustical Society of America,* 1963, *35,* 588–601.

von Békésy, G. *Experiments in hearing.* New York: McGraw-Hill, 1960.

Wolf, K. & Goldstein, R. Middle component AERs from neonates to low-level tonal stimuli. *Journal of Speech and Hearing Research,* 1980, *23,* 185–201.

Zerlin, S. Traveling-wave velocity in the human cochlea. *Journal of Acoustical of America,* 1969, *46,* 1011–1015.

15

OCULOMOTOR MEASURES OF VISUAL DEVELOPMENT

Richard N. Aslin

Indiana University, Bloomington

INTRODUCTION

The use of ocular fixations as a dependent measure of the detection, discrimination, and recognition of visual stimuli has completely transformed the study of human perceptual development in the past 25 years. In particular, the two-choice preference technique developed by Robert Fantz in the late 1950s and the infrared corneal photography technique developed in William Kessen's laboratory in the mid-1960s provided two new and powerful means of assessing visual functioning in human infants. As a result of these developments, a large body of descriptive data has now been collected on infants' fixational behaviors while viewing a wide variety of visual stimuli. Unfortunately, many researchers are now so wedded to the use of visual fixations as an assessment of infant vision that the theories offered as explanations of visual development rarely consider the assumptions underlying specific dependent measures. In fact, most researchers would find it difficult to imagine a world in which visual fixations were not a reliable and valid indicator of visual processing.[1] In con-

---

[1] The term *processing* is used throughout this chapter to refer to transmission of information to a level of the central nervous system that can affect behavior (e.g., perception), but without any connotation that the information reached a conscious level.

trast, researchers studying the development of the nonvisual sensory modalities have by and large struggled along without the availability of such a robust dependent measure. The potential danger facing the study of infant vision is that a single measure or paradigm may completely dominate the area, and researchers may conclude implicitly that a description of visual development can be based entirely on the findings from only one methodological approach.

From time to time, it is useful for researchers enmeshed in the details of their empirical work to step back and reevaluate the overall goals of their research program and the potential limitations of existing methodologies. To that end, I would like to cover three major topics in this chapter. First, I will review the three primary measurement techniques used in the study of infant vision, paying particular attention to scanning measures of visual fixation. I will discuss the advantages and disadvantages of both global and detailed measures of visual fixations, including the assumptions made when interpreting data gathered from infants with these techniques. Second, I will review several recent technological advances that now offer significant improvements over recording systems used in the past. These advances do not solve all the problems associated with calibrating the accuracy of visual fixations, but they do open up the area to more detailed measures and more rapid data analyses. Finally, I will summarize several findings from the literature on infant scanning and eye-movement control. This summary will highlight what we already know about the usefulness of visual fixations in assessing visual development, and what directions these lines of research are likely to take in the future.

MEASURES OF VISUAL FIXATION

Preferential Looking

The essence of all measures of visual fixation in human infants is the fortuitous fact that infants tend to look at certain types of visual stimuli over others. This tendency to fixate preferentially[2] is present immediately after birth, and remains robust throughout development despite the absence of any system of external rewards. Fantz's (1958) contribution was to place this innate preferential-fixation behavior in the context of a simple two-choice paradigm. Although *absolute* preferences for specific stimuli may wax and wane during development, the technique relies on the presence of a *relative* preference for one of two stimuli presented simultaneously to the infant. Any evidence for preference implies that the visual system of the infant must be capable of discriminating between the two stimuli. More recent modifications of Fantz's technique (see review by Teller, 1979) have placed preferential looking within a psychophysical context which maximizes the reliability of fixation behavior obtained from an individual infant, as well as assessing stimulus *detection* rather than stimulus *discrimination*. In this latter paradigm, the two-choice task becomes one of

---

[2] The term *preference* is used throughout this chapter in a purely descriptive manner, and not as an indication of conscious or intentional choice behavior on the part of the infant.

detecting the presence of a stimulus when paired with a no-stimulus control. This detection paradigm simplifies, but does not eliminate, the main interpretive problem surrounding the preference technique; namely, the failure to show a preference for one of two stimuli may result either from the failure to detect the difference between the stimuli, or from the failure to exhibit a preference. Although psychophysical procedures minimize this interpretive difficulty by anchoring each infant's performance at both 100% and 50% correct along a simple stimulus dimension, threshold estimates must still be taken as conservative estimates of the infant's true capacity for stimulus detection.

These interpretive difficulties are even greater when both stimuli are suprathreshold. The infant may have discriminated the two stimuli, but not shown a criterion level preference based on the measure of visual fixation. Alternatively, the infant may have shown a preference for one of the two stimuli, but the basis for this discrimination may not correspond to the underlying dimension assumed by the researcher. For example, it might be tempting to conclude that an infant who prefers to fixate its mother's face over the face of another female has perceived the mother's face as a familiar configuration of features. However, it is also possible that the infant's preference was based on some salient local attribute or feature of the mother's face (e.g., her hairline), without any global processing of the entire facial stimulus. Thus, for pairs of complex stimuli such as those illustrated in Figure 1, the infant may only fixate a limited region of the two patterns, thereby basing pattern discrimination on a relatively low-level detection of a difference in contour density or luminance. Similarly, the absence of a preference may result from a failure to fixate the critical regions of the two patterns that contain the discriminative information. In summary, the preference technique provides useful data as long as the infant shows a preference. In this case, we can infer that discrimination of the two stimuli has occurred, and with a systematic manipulation of stimulus pairings we can often tease apart which stimulus parameter(s) provided the basis for this discrimination. In the absence of a preference for one of the two stimuli, however, there are three possible interpretations: (a) the infant did not prefer to

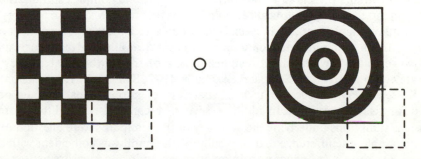

Figure 1. A schematized pattern-preference display illustrating how fixation of a local region of the two patterns (the two dashed squares) could account for discrimination based solely on differences in luminance or contour density. Reprinted from Aslin (1982).

fixate one of the stimuli, even though discrimination was present; (b) the infant was incapable of discriminating any difference between the two stimuli; or (c) the infant was capable of discrimination, but failed to fixate the critical regions of the two stimuli containing differential visual information.

These interpretive difficulties associated with the preference technique also apply to the habituation-dishabituation or response-to-novelty technique (see, for example, Cohen & Gelber, 1975). The essence of this technique is that infants typically prefer to fixate a novel visual stimulus over a familiar stimulus (cf. the chapters by Bornstein and Spelke, this volume). Thus, if an initially novel stimulus is presented repeatedly to the infant, the number and/or duration of fixations will tend to habituate as the stimulus becomes more familiar. Following habituation, a change in the stimulus tends to elicit greater fixation, and this resultant dishabituation indicates that the two stimuli were discriminated by the infant. Failure to show evidence of dishabituation, however, could indicate that (a) the "novel" stimulus was not sufficiently different from the "familiar" stimulus to elicit increased fixation, even though discrimination had occurred; (b) the critical attributes or features of the "familiar" stimulus were not encoded during the habituation phase, thereby making discrimination impossible; (c) the infant was capable of discriminating the two stimuli, but failed to fixate the critical aspects of the stimuli that provided differential visual information; or (d) the infant was in fact incapable of discriminating any difference between the two stimuli.

Scanning

Both the preference and habituation techniques rely on global measures of visual fixation to assess stimulus discrimination. Partially as a result of our knowledge of adult fixation strategies, such as those present in reading, investigators have been interested in the individual fixations made by infants while viewing a visual stimulus. The development of infrared corneal photography enabled a small group of researchers to gather detailed records of the scanpaths made by infants presented with a variety of simple and complex stimuli. Since adults tend to direct the foveal region of the retina to view specific features of a complex visual stimulus, it seemed reasonable to expect that scanpaths obtained from young infants would tell us a great deal about visual processing. However, after several initial demonstrations of the newborn's tendency to fixate contours (Kessen, Salapatek, & Haith, 1972; Salapatek, 1968; Salapatek & Kessen, 1966), it became unclear what further implications scanning data had for visual perception. In addition, several researchers realized that certain basic assumptions underlying the accuracy of the scanpaths were questionable. For example, the inference that the center of the pupil was coincident with the fovea was shown to be incorrect in many cases, inducing measurement errors as large as 8° to 10° (Slater & Findlay, 1972). Thus, it was not even clear that the infant's scanpaths based on corneal photography were an accurate representation of the details of individual fixations of the visual stimulus.

As researchers in the area of visual scanning grappled with these method-ological problems, a number of more basic interpretive issues emerged to challenge further the users of this technique. For example, the fact that a scan-path represents the translation of the fovea over a visual stimulus suggested to some investigators that no other portion of the retina was involved in visual processing. This "tunnel vision" view of scanpaths is clearly unwarranted in light of many studies of adult perception, which document that pattern pro-cessing can occur across a fairly large extrafoveal region of the retina (e.g., Day, 1957). Since acuity in adults is so much greater in the foveal area, it seemed natural to assume that this relation would also apply to infants. But, in fact, there are no data from infants on visual acuity as a function of retinal eccen-tricity. Based on the infant's poor acuity (see review by Dobson & Teller, 1978), it would appear reasonable to conclude that the proportional falloff in acuity from the fovea to the periphery is greater in adults than in infants. However, we have no data on the size of the region surrounding the line of sight (foveal or extrafoveal) which is involved in the processing of visual information dur-ing a fixation.

Another interpretive problem with the scanning technique is the assumption that a fixated stimulus is actually processed and encoded. Again, it is seductive to draw parallels between adult and infant fixations. Faced with a task like reading, in which acuity limits the retinal region within which letters can be recognized, adults systematically move the fovea to encompass the entire se-quence of words in the text (Rayner, 1978). However, in the case of an infant viewing a large two-dimensional shape or a photograph of a face, it is not at all clear that visual processing necessarily occurs during each individual fixation. Clearly, adults can recognize familiar stimuli without an extensive scanpath (e.g., in t-scope studies) by relying on extrafoveal areas of the retina (Sperling, 1960). If asked to search for details in a complex stimulus, however, adults will produce a comprehensive scanpath in an attempt to process all of the visual in-formation present in the stimulus (Noton & Stark, 1971; Yarbus, 1967).

The interpretive issues facing users of scanning as a measure of visual pro-cessing in infants can be summarized as follows. First, we do not know the size of the area surrounding the line of sight which performs visual processing and/or encoding. It seems likely that this area is of variable size, depending on the type of stimulus presented to the subject and the task demands of the situa-tion. Second, we do not know whether a currently fixated stimulus region is in fact being processed, and we do not know whether stimulus information, once processed during a fixation, is encoded for later recognition. Finally, we do not know if a scanpath is even necessary for visual processing and/or encoding of the stimulus. In adults, there are circumstances in which eye movements are unnecessary, since the critical information can be processed in a single fixa-tion. Thus, there are certainly situations, at least for adults, in which scanning of the stimulus is not a prerequisite for visual processing. This raises the possi-bility that large portions of a scanpath are unrelated to the specific characteris-tics of the stimulus.

This rather pessimistic view of the scanning technique should not be taken as an argument for its abandonment. On the contrary, there are some circumstances in which scanning data can provide important information concerning visual processing by infants (e.g., the externality effect; see "Scanning and Saccadic Eye Movements" below). In addition, researchers have only recently begun to tackle the interpretive problems underlying the use of the scanning technique. These interpretive issues have been addressed both in interactive studies of scanning, in which the stimulus undergoes a change, and in basic studies of eye movement control. In addition, the strategy of incorporating both global and detailed measures of visual fixation in the same experiment would seem to be a fruitful avenue for balancing the two methodological approaches. Before turning to these topics, however, there are a number of technical issues related to the recording of eye movements and visual fixations that demand careful evaluation. The following section is intended as a primer for the uninitiated and a review for the expert.

EYE POSITION RECORDING TECHNIQUES

Calibration

There are many trade-offs involved in choosing eye-monitoring equipment (see surveys of adult and infant eye-movement techniques by Young & Sheena, 1975, and Maurer, 1975, respectively). The single overriding issue facing investigators of infant eye movements is how to calibrate the raw eye position signal. Whether one chooses a technique such as electrooculography (EOG) that measures eye position relative to head position, or a technique such as corneal photography that measures eye position relative to fixed light sources, one must relate the resultant data to the actual line of sight. The line of sight in normal adults refers to the extension of a line from the fovea through the optics of the eye into the visual field. Because the location of the fovea cannot be specified objectively with an online recording device, it is necessary to calibrate the signal from the eye monitor by having the subject fixate specified locations in the stimulus display, and by assuming fixation with the fovea.

In adults, calibration is facilitated by two facts: (a) the line of sight is coincident with the fovea, and it does not vary within a subject across time; and (b) the adult can be instructed to foveate known positions in the stimulus display, thereby mapping the recorded eye signal onto a stimulus-display coordinate system. In contrast, the line of sight in infants may not always correspond to the anatomical center of the fovea; infants, like some adults, may prefer to fixate a target with a consistent but extrafoveal region of the retina. In addition, perhaps in part because nonverbal subjects cannot be instructed to fixate, young infants exhibit a considerable dispersion of fixations when presented with a small, stationary target (see Haith, 1980). Typical fixational variances while viewing a small visual target are illustrated in Figure 2 for an infant and an adult. The larger variance in the infant's record implies one or more of the

6-WEEK-OLD   **ADULT**

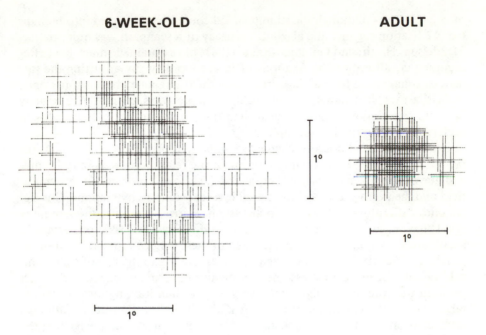

Figure 2. Distributions of fixations (60-Hz sampling rate) to a small (1°) target by a 6-week-old and by an adult .

following: (a) that the infant's visual system is incapable of accurately specifying the relative retinal location of the fixation stimulus, (b) that the infant's neuromuscular system is unable to exhibit fine control of eye position, (c) that infants have both a sensory and a motor deficit in oculomotor control, or (d) that the task confronting the infant is not compelling enough to engage precise control over fixational behavior. These constraints may be the result of higher-level neural mechanisms, low-level anatomical deficits associated with the structure of the retina (see Abramov, Gordon, Hendrickson, Hainline, Dobson, & LaBossiere, 1982), or attentional and motivational factors.

Initial applications of corneal photography (e.g., Salapatek & Kessen, 1966) and subsequent use of infrared video technology (Haith, 1969) skirted the calibration issue by assuming that the line of sight was coincident with the center of the pupil. A set of six or more infrared lights, aligned with the stimulus display and directed toward the infant's eye, created discrete reflections on the corneal surface. Human observers scored the distance from pupil center to each reflection to provide an estimate of the presumed line of sight with respect to the fixed array of lights and their known positions relative to the stimulus display. This scoring procedure has been criticized for failing to adjust the data for the discrepancy (up to 8-10° in newborns) between the center of the pupil (optic axis) and the line of sight (visual axis), as well as various parallax errors (see Slater & Findlay, 1972, 1975a; and reply by Salapatek, Haith, Maurer, & Kessen, 1972). As a result, the accuracy of these initial studies was in the range of ±2–6°. Thus, although the stimulus field could be partitioned into perhaps 6 or 12 fixation regions, the absolute accuracy of a scanpath was quite coarse. Mendelson, Haith, and Goldman-Rakic (1981) have obtained somewhat better accuracy in calibrating the fixations of infant monkeys by adjusting the raw data to compensate for parallax errors and the discrepancy between the optic and visual axes. In summary, despite calibration problems, corneal photography data are considerably more detailed than the global measures obtained with preference or habituation techniques.

An alternative calibration scheme used more recently involves an adult-like procedure that makes no assumptions about the relation between pupil center and line of sight. A small target is presented in various locations of the stimulus field and the average eye position signal is recorded, thereby mapping this signal onto a stimulus-display coordinate system. Harris, Hainline, and Abramov (1981) have argued that, although the dispersion of infants' fixations around a small target is large, a statistical treatment of these calibration data can usually generate a likely point (or small region) corresponding to the line of sight. This calibration procedure must assume that the infant actually fixated each target position with the line of sight (or fovea), rather than looking away from the target during the collection of some or all of the calibration data. Although such an assumption is impossible to verify with currently available techniques, this scheme has the advantage of generating within-subject calibrations and known accuracies based on a particular infant's dispersion of fixations.

A variation of the foregoing calibration scheme consists of replacing the stationary calibration target with a moving target. The rationale for this substitution is that infants appear to be more attentive to a moving than to a stationary target, thus optimizing the likelihood that the line of sight will be directed toward the target during the collection of calibration data. This calibration scheme has been used by Aslin (1981) in a study of smooth-pursuit eye movements, and by Bronson (1982) in a study of scanning. The disadvantage of this calibration scheme is the fact that during target movement the line of sight typically lags behind the actual target position. Thus, both Aslin and Bronson based their calibration data on fixations collected just after cessation of target movement, thereby allowing time for the line of sight to "catch" the target. Again, however, this calibration scheme must assume that the line of sight was actually directed to the position of the target during the collection of calibration data.

Resolution and Accuracy

Once calibration data have been collected, the raw eye position signal can be rescaled to estimate fixation locations on the stimulus display. The accuracy of the eye-position signal refers to the precision with which the recording technique estimates the absolute position of the line of sight. Accuracy is a function of the resolution of the recording system and the calibration of the eye-position signal. Resolution refers to the minimum change in fixation that is reliably detected by the recording system. An important advantage of recent video-based systems for recording corneal reflections (e.g., Aslin, 1981; Bronson, 1982; Hainline, 1981) is that a measure of the uncalibrated eye position signal (horizontal and vertical coordinates) is provided at a rate of 30 or 60 Hz. Thus, the temporal resolution of these recording systems is considerably greater than the 2-to-6-Hz sampling rate used to score corneal reflections gathered on film. However, because saccades typically occur at a maximum rate of 4 or 5 Hz in adults, many of the individual data points provided at higher sampling rates represent either movements of the eye or steady fixations lasting from 200 msec to several seconds. For adults, computer programs have been used to collapse these individual data points into a mean fixation position and its duration (e.g., Kliegl & Olson, 1981). Harris et al. (1981) have devised a similar procedure for use with infants. The advantage of the 60-Hz sampling rate is that fixation durations can be determined more accurately. The disadvantage is that an algorithm must be established to determine what constitutes a steady fixation and what constitutes a series of small changes in fixation around a stationary target. At present, a number of video-based systems have been able to improve the accuracy of eye position recordings to approximately ± 1-$2°$. This level of accuracy is superior to the original studies using corneal photography, but quite crude when compared to several techniques used with adults (see below).

One major reason for the increased accuracy of video-based systems is their use of the so-called "white pupil" technique (Sheena, 1976). As shown in Figure 3A, the original multiple–marker-light technique created an array of reflections on the cornea. Although the coordinates on the film plane of these reflections could be judged very accurately by an observer, the limiting factor was the accuracy of the judgment of pupil center. Figure 3B illustrates a video frame from a corneal reflection system using the white pupil technique. By placing a light source coaxial with the lens of the video camera, the image of the pupil is filled with light reflected back from the retina. The resultant white pupil greatly enhances the contrast between the normally black pupil and the slightly lighter iris.

The final step in improving the accuracy of these new video-based systems is the addition of online scoring by digital and analog circuitry. These analysis systems compute the location of the center of the pupil in the video image, as well as the location of the corneal reflection from the light source, and compensate for errors associated with lateral shifts of the pupil within the camera's field of view and parallax errors that occur as the eye rotates away from the position of the camera. Finally, and of considerable significance, these online analysis systems greatly facilitate the scoring of tremendous amounts of data. Hand-scoring a single frame (film or video), which consists of judging the x- and y-coordinates of the corneal reflections and the pupil center, takes approximately 1 minute. At a sample rate of 4 Hz, which guarantees that all fixations will be captured, 30 seconds of data collection in each of 5 stimulus conditions

A

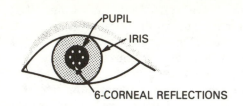

B

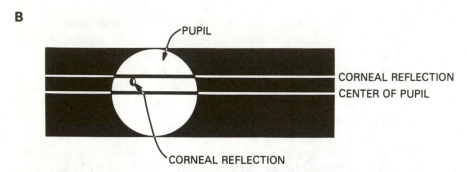

Figure 3. (A) A schematized film frame illustrating the reflections on the cornea created by six infrared-filtered lights. (B) A schematized video image from the Applied Sciences Laboratories Model 1994 eye monitor illustrating the white pupil and the single corneal reflection. The large black bar delimits the pupil diameter, and the two horizontal lines indicate the center of the pupil and the position of the corneal reflection.

across 20 infants would take up to 200 hours of scoring. Clearly, the time required for data collection and analysis has been greatly reduced as a result of technical advances in the past 5 years.

Unfortunately, the corneal reflection recording technique, even with online analysis, is not without problems. The most significant difficulty is the fact that resolution is proportional to image size. That is, as the image of the pupil within the video frame becomes larger, the analysis system can detect a smaller change in eye position. To maximize resolution, therefore, most systems use a set of lenses that fill approximately ⅓ to ½ of the video frame with the image of the pupil. The resultant 2-cm-square field of view demands quite precise alignment of the infant's eye. Since most infants will not tolerate the kind of head restraint typically used with adults, a fairly large proportion of a trial may consist of no signal at all because the infant has moved out of the camera's field of view. Pacifiers, head slings, and holding techniques have been devised to reduce this alignment problem, but as yet no system appears to work well with more than about half of all infants tested.

One potential solution to this alignment problem is to employ a servo-controlled mirror that follows the image of the pupil as the head moves. Such a system is commercially available (Sheena & Borah, 1981), but its use with infants does not as yet appear promising despite several recent attempts. One problem is that the online algorithm which attempts to maintain the image of the pupil in the center of the video frame cannot respond to rapid head movements if the image of the pupil suddenly disappears from the video frame. Since most head movements in infants are rapid and fairly large in amplitude, the usefulness of this head-tracking system appears limited. However, it might be possible to use a second camera with a larger field of view to track the head movements, rather than relying on the same high-resolution camera used to record eye position. This potential solution has not as yet been implemented.

Despite the foregoing measurement problems with the corneal reflection technique, interpretation of the resultant eye-position data is less problematic than with the other major recording technique used with infants, electrooculography (EOG). EOG consists of recording the electrical potential between the cornea and the retina from surface electrodes placed near the orbit of one or both eyes. Rotation of the eye within the orbit alters the corneal-retinal potential with respect to the fixed electrodes. As shown in panels A and B of Figure 4, if the head remains stationary and the eyes rotate to fixate a target on the subject's right, the EOG signal will change accordingly. However, as shown in panel C of the figure, if the eyes remain fixed in the head but the head rotates to the left, no change in the EOG signal will occur despite a shift in the line of sight to the left. Finally, as shown in panel D of the figure, a leftward rotation

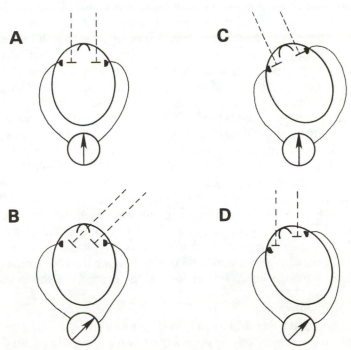

Figure 4. Schematic illustration of the EOG signal, represented by the arrow, recorded from a subject whose head is directed either straight ahead (A and B) or to the left of midline (C and D).

of the head, in combination with the maintenance of fixation on a stationary target, will result in a change in the EOG signal. Thus, the EOG signal can provide an accurate indication of the line of sight only if head movements are eliminated.[3] Since a lateral shift in head position as small as 1 or 2 cm can lead to errors as large as 10° or more, EOG appears to be a poor technique for estimating the absolute position of the line of sight. However, relative shifts in gaze, such as those in optokinetic nystagmus (OKN), can certainly be recorded with EOG.

In contrast to EOG, the corneal-reflection technique is not confounded by small head movements as long as the pupil remains in the field of view of the camera. One could imagine a large rotation of the head in combination with a counter-rotation of the eye that kept the pupil in the camera's field of view. In this situation, an EOG signal would indicate a large change in fixation because the signal is referenced to the position of the eye in the head. Because the corneal-reflection technique is based on the relation between the pupil and the fixed light source that creates the corneal reflection, small head movements are not a serious problem.

To this point, we have only considered the recording of monocular eye position. Separate recordings of the position of the two eyes create additional problems. If EOG is used, electrodes must be placed on each side of both orbits. This has proven nearly impossible with infants because of the small area between the nasal orbit and the bridge of the nose. Obviously, head movements are still a problem in recording binocular eye position with EOG. The corneal-reflection technique eliminates the head-movement artifact, but adds several other difficulties. First, if both eyes are recorded with the same camera, the resolution of eye position is reduced in proportion to the reduction in image size. Second, if two cameras are used, one for each eye, alignment of the infant within the two fields of view is more difficult, particularly if the infant's head tilts right or left from midline. Finally, calibration of the eye-position signal is more complicated because young infants are known to show poor evidence of convergence (Aslin, 1977; Slater & Findlay, 1975b). As a result, fixation of a calibration target may be accurate in one eye but not in the other, because of an inability to rotate one eye inward (or outward) to fixate the target simultaneously with both foveas. Attempts to calibrate each eye separately under monocular viewing conditions prior to collection of binocular data have been plagued by the distracting influence of various monocular patching devices. Thus, at present, no highly accurate binocular fixation data have been collected from infants using the improved versions of the corneal-reflection technique.

Systems Used with Adults

Before concluding this section on recording techniques, it might prove beneficial to place the resolution and accuracy of current techniques used with in-

---

[3] Another solution consists of accurately recording head position and subtracting the head movement signal from the EOG signal (see Regal & Salapatek, 1982).

fants in the context of current techniques used with adults. This comparison provides a goal for future developments in the recording of eye movements from young infants. There are basically three systems that have been used with adults but not (as yet) with infants. The first system consists of a pair of infrared detecting photocells, which are aligned in front of one or both eyes at a distance of approximately 1 cm to record the level of light reflected from the front of the eyeball. An infrared emitting diode is also placed in front of the eyeball to bathe the front of the eye with light invisible to the subject. The two photocells are aligned at the nasal and temporal edges of the iris so that, as the eye rotates to the left or right, the amount of reflected light picked up by the two photocells changes from a high signal (when the white or sclera of the eye is present) to a lower signal (when the iris or pupil of the eye is present). As the eye rotates, the signal in one photocell increases as the signal in the other decreases, and the difference in this signal is proportional to the position of the eye with respect to the fixed photocells. Typically, the photocells are mounted on a pair of spectacle frames and the subject is positioned in a bitebar or chinrest to minimize head movement artifacts. The resolution of these systems is less than 10 ' of arc, with an accuracy after calibration of approximately ½ °. As with EOG, however, this photocell system cannot easily be adapted for recording vertical eye movements.

The second system used with adults employs a small coil of wire embedded in a contact lens (Collewijn, 1977). A small current is passed through the coil and the subject wears the contact lens within a magnetic field. Rotation of the eye within the magnetic field induces a change in the current passing through the coil. By careful control of the magnetic field and precise measurement of the induced current changes in the coil, this technique can measure eye position with a resolution of less than 1 ' of arc and an accuracy of 1–5 ' of arc. Horizontal and vertical eye position can be recorded by using two orthogonally oriented magnetic fields, and head position can be recorded by adding a third magnetic field. While this system is extremely accurate and capable of recording both eye and head position, it demands the placement of a contact lens on the eye, and thus is not as yet feasible for use with infants or naive adult subjects.

The final system used with adults (Crane & Steele, 1978) is based on a combination of the corneal reflection technique and the fact that the posterior surface of the lens in the eye also reflects light. A light source creates four reflections from the eye, one each from the front and back surface of the cornea and from the front and back surface of the lens. These reflections are called the *Purkinje images* and are labeled "one" through "four," starting at the front surface of the cornea. Because the back surface of the lens is concave rather than convex, rotation of the eye creates a movement of the fourth Purkinje image which is opposite in direction from the movement of the first Purkinje image. However, as the head translates laterally, both the first and fourth Purkinje images move in the same direction. This system uses a dual infrared light source and can record both eye position and head position (within limited fields of view) with a resolution and accuracy nearly equal to the contact-lens technique described above. Two important advantages of this system are the fact that (a) no attachments to the subject's eyes are required; and (b) the head need not be severely restrained, because the system tracks the image of the eye with servo-controlled mirrors. The primary disadvantages of this system for use with infants are: (a) the field of view is restricted to about $\pm 10°$; (b) the pupil must be quite large to detect the fourth Purkinje image (located in the plane behind the pupil); and (c) the infrared light source must be more intense than in other techniques, because the fourth Purkinje image is greatly attenuated by the optic media.

In summary, the corneal reflection technique has been the primary technique used to record eye movements and visual fixations from infants. Both the resolution and ease of data analysis have improved markedly in the past five years with the development of online, video-based, computer-controlled systems. Calibration remains a serious problem, because the infant cannot be instructed to accurately fixate known points in the stimulus field. In addition, alignment of the infant's eye(s) within the field of view of the camera requires a docile and attentive subject. Improvements in image resolution, particularly for gathering data on binocular eye position, will undoubtedly occur in the future, along with creative means for tracking the eyes as the infant makes small head movements.

SCANNING AND EYE MOVEMENT CONTROL

Scanning and Saccadic Eye Movements

One of the key questions raised above with respect to the use of scanning in infants is whether visual processing occurs during each fixation and, if so, what area surrounding the line of sight is involved. An answer to this question will not come from a measure of scanning itself. Rather, an additional dependent measure will be needed to assess whether the stimulus information currently fixated is processed and encoded. Unfortunately, there have been no direct attempts to record simultaneously both scanning and some complementary index of processing such as preference, habituation, or conditioning. However, there are several indirect lines of evidence which support the hypothesis that a fairly limited region surrounding the line of sight is involved in stimulus encoding.[4]

Salapatek (1975) reported that 1-month-olds presented with a complex two-dimensional pattern containing both external and internal elements scanned predominantly the external elements. In contrast, 2-month-olds presented with

---

[4] Because of the sequential nature of information processing in the preference, habituation, and conditioning (HAS) techniques, they require at least a minimal level of stimulus encoding. Thus, we have no *direct* measure of online stimulus processing (i.e., what the infant perceives), but only a measure of stimulus recognition (i.e., what the infant remembers about what was perceived) based on information stored during preceding fixations.

these same complex patterns scanned both the internal and external elements, but predominantly the internal ones. This developmental shift raised the possibility that differences in scanning might result in a failure of the younger infants to process the internal elements. Of course, the younger infants may have processed the entire pattern, including the shape and configuration of all elements, without fixating every element with the line of sight. The role of peripheral vision in pattern processing has simply not been extensively explored in infants. However, there are a number of other studies of face-scanning which have also found this developmental shift from external to internal scanning (Hainline, 1978; Haith, Bergman, & Moore, 1977; Maurer & Salapatek, 1976). Thus, the phenomenon seems quite characteristic of infant scanning in general, and some other dependent measure was needed to assess visual processing in infants within these two age groups.

Milewski (1976) performed the necessary measurements by using the same two-dimensional geometric patterns which Salapatek (1975) had used in his earlier scanning studies. Milewski employed a conditioned habituation technique called *high-amplitude sucking* (HAS; see Jusczyk, this volume) to assess discrimination of a change in either internal or external pattern elements. One-month-olds discriminated a change in the external element, but did not show evidence of discriminating a change in the internal element when it was surrounded by a larger external element. In contrast, 4-month-olds discriminated a change in either the internal or external elements. A simple acuity explanation could not account for the younger infants' failure to discriminate the smaller internal element, since 1-month-olds discriminated a change in an element of this size when it was presented without the surrounding external element. Thus, infants beyond 2 months of age, who typically fixate both the internal and external elements, discriminated changes in either element, whereas infants under 2 months of age, who fixate predominantly the external element, discriminated changes only in the external element and not in the internal element. These findings suggest that pattern discrimination, at least as assessed by the HAS technique, is closely linked to the general characteristics of scanning during stimulus encoding and recognition.

A follow-up study by Milewski (1978) using the HAS technique and a study by Bushnell (1979) using the visual habituation technique have clarified the developmental shift from external to internal scanning. Milewski (1978) reported that 1-month-olds also failed to discriminate a change in a small pattern element when it was located adjacent to, rather than inside of, a larger pattern element. Thus, the so-called "externality" effect in younger infants is more likely the result of a bias to fixate and/or attend to the larger of two pattern elements. Another experiment by Milewski (1978) showed that, if a change in a small element occurred adjacent to another small element, rather than adjacent to a larger element, only about half of the infants showed evidence of pattern discrimination. Thus, it seems likely that (a) infants tend to select one pattern element for fixation, and (b) the predominantly fixated pattern element is typically the larger one, unless both elements are the same size. In contrast to

Milewski (1978), Bushnell (1979) reported that 1-month-olds did discriminate a change in a small element located adjacent to a larger element. This finding supports the "externality" effect in young infants. Bushnell also reported, however, that 1-month-olds discriminated a change in an internal element if it was either flashed or oscillating within the external element. Thus, the general tendency of young infants to ignore small elements inside larger elements can be overridden by maximizing the attention-getting attributes of the internal elements. Interestingly, 1-month-olds discriminated a change in the external element even if the unchanged internal element flashed or oscillated. Thus, the more salient internal element did not preclude attention to the change in the external element. Unfortunately, we have no scanning data for these complex stimuli which contain a flashing or oscillating internal element.

These findings on the scanning and discrimination of internal, external, and adjacent pattern elements also have implications for the development of oculomotor control. For example, what guides the initial fixation of a pattern element and the subsequent scanning sequence? Two alternatives seem feasible: (a) the direction and extent of changes in fixation are not related to the stimulus, except for a general tendency to maintain fixation of contours (Haith, 1980); or (b) the initial and subsequent fixations are controlled by pattern-processing mechanisms. If scanning is essentially a random walk around adjacent contours, then the probability of detecting a pattern change is a function of the size and number of pattern elements and the dispersion of fixations. However, if scanning is controlled by pattern-processing mechanisms, then the ability to detect pattern changes via the *peripheral* retina will determine the probability of fixating a given pattern element. To solve this dilemma (does scanning enable visual processing, or does visual processing guide scanning?) a number of investigators have used a simplified stimulus-situation to study the development of eye movements to a single target. Unfortunately, these studies are not directly relevant to scanning, because a single stimulus element does not contain the same attentional possibilities as a complex, multi-element pattern. Nevertheless, these studies of eye-movement control (see below) have answered some elementary questions about the role of peripheral processing in infant vision.

It is very difficult to look at an infant's scanpath and judge whether it results from spontaneous changes in fixation or from control by peripheral retinal processing. It is a fact, however, that even newborns move their line of sight to fixate the contours of large two-dimensional patterns. Since these patterns are usually presented within a central viewing area where spontaneous eye movements might stumble onto a contour, all one needed to assume was a random walk with a contour-fixation holding mechanism. Contour fixation in the infant, of course, might consist of small fixational eye movements within the foveal and parafoveal regions (i.e., $+/- 5$ deg). However, this random-walk model seemed particularly inefficient in view of the exquisite control of saccadic eye movements in adults (Robinson, 1973). Saccades are rapid changes in the line of sight that are programmed in direction and extent based on the location of a target goal on the peripheral retina. Programming is ballistic in the sense that initiation of the neural command to the extraocular muscles necessitates completion of the change in fixation before any corrective movement can occur. There are now a number of studies in newborns and older infants confirming that the initial saccade is consistently in the direction of a small target originally located on the peripheral retina (Aslin & Salapatek, 1975; Harris & MacFarlane, 1974; Lewis, Maurer, & Kay, 1978). Thus, the infant saccadic system does not appear to operate according to the random-walk model. However, Aslin & Salapatek (1975) documented the fact that young infants grossly undershoot the location of the peripheral target on this initial saccade. These undershoots may suggest that visual processing does not occur during each fixation, since many fixations are only brief stops on the way to peripheral pattern elements (see discussion below).

An additional finding from studies of single-target localization is relevant to the control of infant scanning. The initial report on peripheral target detection in infants (Tronick, 1972) employed a central fixation stimulus that remained present when the peripheral target was introduced. Thus, the infant was already fixating and presumably attending to the central stimulus. As a result, the change in fixation to the peripheral target presumably was preceded by a shift in attention away from the central stimulus. The studies of peripheral-target localization reviewed above removed the central stimulus when the peripheral target was introduced. In two studies (Aslin & Salapatek, 1975; Harris & MacFarlane, 1974) these two conditions of central stimulus remaining and central stimulus disappearing were compared directly. There was a much greater likelihood of peripheral-target localization when the central stimulus was removed. Since there is almost always a "central stimulus" in an episode of scanning (i.e., the currently fixated pattern element), the results from the situation in which the central stimulus remained in the field of view may be more relevant to scanning data. Nevertheless, infants did reliably direct their first saccade toward the peripheral target, even when the central stimulus remained. Thus, the random-walk model of infant scanning does not appear to be viable.

In light of this evidence for the semi-guided nature of scanning in infants, it is of interest to consider another developmental finding on the scanning of simple visual patterns. Salapatek (1975) reported that newborns and 1-month-olds tend to scan large geometric patterns with a tighter dispersion of fixations than older infants. This developmental shift from a narrow or single-element scan to a broader scanpath has also been reported by Leahy (1976) and Haith, Goodman, Goodwyn, and Montgomery (1982). However, a recent nonreplication study by Hainline and Lemerise (1982) raised a number of serious questions regarding the robustness of this effect. Hainline and Lemerise suggested that the earlier data from Salapatek might have been subject to a number of artifacts, including the presence of a faint red glow from the infrared marker lights, the use of pacifiers, and a nonquantitative analysis of the characteristics of the scanpaths. Hainline and Lemerise used an automated video-based corneal-reflection system to record the scanpaths of 1-, 2-, and 3-month-olds who viewed circles, squares, and triangles of varying size (5°, 20°, and 30°). Their results indicated that the scanpaths of all ages of infants decreased in size as stimulus size decreased. This result indicates that the infants were capable of altering their scanpath to conform to the characteristics of the stimulus. Unfortunately, the remainder of Hainline and Lemerise's results were ambiguous. First, they wanted to determine if infants concentrated their fixations within a limited region of the stimulus field. However, they collapsed the data across infants within each age group. Thus, the fact that no one quadrant was fixated more frequently than any other ignores the likely possibility that individual infants may have fixated different quadrants. Their analysis of the age change in breadth of scanning was also uninformative, because the stimulus field was divided into only four areas, and the dispersion of fixations for individual infants was not presented, either in tabular form or in a plot of the actual scanpaths. In addition, Hainline and Lemerise did not calibrate the raw eye-position signal for individual infants. As a result, the accuracy of their recordings was approximately ±4°. Thus, this reputed nonreplication of the developmental shift from a narrow to a broad scanpath did not clarify the original claims made by Salapatek (1975).

The most recent attempt at investigating the scanning of young infants is an extensive monograph by Bronson (1982). He measured the individual scanpaths and fixation durations of a small sample of 2-to-5-month-olds while they repeatedly viewed an array of stimulus elements. Bronson used a video-based corneal reflection system, a small moving target as a calibrating device, and a semi-automated analysis system to record the infants' fixations. Bronson presented three stimuli on each of several 5-sec trials, and changed the shape of one of the stimuli on intermittent trials. The stimulus that changed in shape was located either 5° or 15° in the peripheral visual field at the beginning of the trial. The infants consistently directed their first postchange fixation to the novel stimulus if it was located 5° from the line of sight, but the likelihood of fixating the novel stimulus located 15° in the periphery was not above baseline responding. In addition, although infants oriented toward the nearer changed stimulus and fixated it for a longer period of time, the *duration* of individual fixations did not increase to this novel stimulus. This does not necessarily imply that fixation duration is unrelated to visual processing. For example, Bronson found that saccadic movements terminating on a contourless area of the stimulus field had very short fixation durations. In addition, Bronson argued that extremely long fixation durations were associated with the absence of visual processing, as in a "blank stare." This inference was based in part on the significant correlation between saccades of large amplitude and subsequent short fixation durations. In other words, alert infants seemed to scan more broadly, and fixate individual contours of the stimulus more briefly, than inattentive infants. This hypothesis may also account for the reported developmental shift from a narrow to a broad scan if younger infants are in general less alert than older infants. Bronson also reported that infants under 3 months of age limited 86% of their fixations to a single stimulus within the visual field, whereas older infants limited only 48% of their fixations to a single stimulus.

A final intriguing aspect of Bronson's report is his characterization of scanpaths in many of the infants as *recursive*. That is, the sequence of fixations within the stimulus array appeared to follow the same pattern on repeated presentations of the stimuli, unless one of the stimuli underwent a change in shape. Thus, one infant might initiate a scanpath at the top of the stimulus array and proceed to fixate the bottom-right stimulus followed by the bottom-left stimulus. In contrast, another infant might begin at the bottom left and proceed to the top followed by the bottom right. Bronson hypothesized that these recursive scanpaths assisted the infant in rapidly determining whether the array of stimuli was the same or different from the previously presented set of stimuli. Of particular interest was the finding that the first stimulus fixated in a scanpath was not completely determined by stimulus salience (e.g., luminance or contour density). However, averaged across infants, this salience effect became statistically reliable. In short, there were characteristic individual differences in scanpaths that occasionally violated a model of fixation control based simply on peripheral target salience.

Bronson's study of scanning in infants raises a number of interesting questions regarding the usefulness of visual fixations as an index of visual processing. First, the significance of the duration of an individual fixation is apparently to process (and/or encode) some limited region of visual pattern. Very brief fixations presumably are not accompanied by visual processing, and extremely long fixations do not necessarily provide the infant with additional visual information. Second, the significance of a *change* in fixation is apparently to move the region of the retina that processes visual information to another location within the stimulus array. The factors which control changes in fixation include (a) peripheral-target salience, (b) familiarity with the stimulus array, (c) stimulus novelty, and (d) random error.

Data from adults reported by Findlay (1982) suggest a tentative hypothesis regarding the control of fixations during infant scanning. Findlay showed that saccadic amplitudes are correlated in an interesting way with saccadic latencies. For long latencies, the saccade directs fixation to the details of the eliciting target, whereas, for short latencies, the saccadic amplitude is determined by global stimulus attributes. Bronson (1982) found that longer fixations were associated with small saccadic amplitudes, whereas shorter fixations were associated with larger saccadic amplitudes. Thus, the majority of infants (short fixations and long saccades) may have been guided primarily by *global* stimulus attributes, and only a limited processing of stimulus detail may have occurred during the brief fixations. Other infants (showing longer fixations and shorter saccades), characterized by Bronson as inattentive, may in fact have been guided by the *details* of peripheral stimuli. Thus, these infants may have made smaller saccades to fixate nearby regions of the stimulus (regions that can be processed by near-foveal areas), and they may have fixated each region longer in an attempt to process this detailed information, rather than just the more global stimulus attributes. If the resolution of central, or foveal, vision is superior to peripheral vision in infants, then changes in fixation provide clarity of detail to initially degraded patches of visual pattern. Thus, scanning movements may be essential in initially specifying and subsequently verifying that a specific visual pattern is located in a specific spatial position within the stimulus array. Clearly, many of these issues will remain unanswered until measures of scanning are gathered with other measures of visual processing, such as preference, habituation, or conditioning.

Pursuit and Vergence Eye Movements

Up to this point we have only considered the relation of visual fixations and saccadic eye-movement control to the processing of stationary, two-dimensional patterns. In the remainder of this chapter, we will consider two additional types of eye movements, smooth-pursuit and vergence, and their relation to the visual processing of moving patterns and three-dimensional stimuli. Smooth-pursuit movements are interesting because of their potential contribution to studies of neuromuscular development and to the perception of stimulus movement. If infants cannot smoothly follow a moving target with the line of sight, then their processing of that target's details may be degraded by the resultant extra-foveal viewing. In addition, inaccurate following could lead to errors in the perception of the spatial position of the target. Until recently, studies of smooth pursuit movements in infants were limited by inaccurate recording techniques, such as the observation of global film records (McGinnis, 1930) and EOG (Dayton & Jones, 1964). One recent EOG study by Kremenitzer, Vaughan, Kurtzberg, and Dowling (1979) reported that newborns show some brief instances of smooth pursuit, but in general all past studies have concluded that smooth following movements do not emerge until the end of the second postnatal month. These older studies provided evidence that infants under 8 weeks of age employ only saccades to follow a smoothly moving target. As a result, the line of sight is only intermittently aligned with the target.

In a more recent study of the development of pursuit movements, Aslin (1981) recorded monocular eye position with a video-based corneal-reflection system and a computer-controlled video target display. The results of this study replicated the earlier findings that smooth following emerged in the 6-to-8-week age range (see Figure 5). However, the accuracy of tracking, indicated by the ability to maintain the line of sight on the target, was quite poor in 2-month-olds, even for very slow target movements. During the third postnatal month, the lag between the line of sight and the location of the moving target was greatly reduced. Thus, the saccadic-pursuit system characteristic of very young infants is gradually replaced in the second and third postnatal months by a smooth-pursuit control system. It remains unclear at the present time whether the early absence of smooth pursuit is the result of sensory limitations (poor acuity, temporal resolution, and/or velocity analysis) or motor immaturities. In addition, the relation between the accuracy of following eye movements and motion perception remains unclear without another dependent measure of the perception of target movement. It seems clear, however, that any falloff in acuity as a function of retinal eccentricity is likely to degrade the young infant's processing of the pattern details of a moving target if only saccadic-pursuit movements are present.

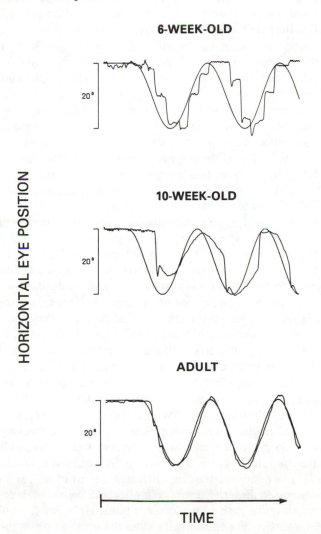

Figure 5. Pursuit eye movement records from a 6-week-old, a 10-week-old, and an adult, illustrating the emergence of smooth tracking after the sixth postnatal week. The smooth sinusoidal tracing represents the position of the moving target. Redrawn from Aslin (1981).

The final type of eye movement relevant to visual processing is the control of binocular alignment with vergence eye movements. In adults, the failure to align the two foveas accurately on a target results either in the perception of double images (diplopia) or suppression of one eye's input. As a result of this ocular misalignment, binocular depth perception (stereopsis) is lost or degraded. Several initial attempts at specifying the accuracy of binocular alignment reported that infants were exotropic (wall-eyed) until at least 2 months of age (Maurer, 1974; Wickelgren, 1967). However, these studies did not compensate for the discrepancy between the center of the pupil and the line of sight. As discussed earlier, the location of the fovea on the temporal retina results in an overestimation of the actual divergence of the two lines of sight in young infants. Two more recent attempts at specifying the ability of young infants to fixate targets binocularly abandoned absolute measures of estimating the line of sight in favor of measuring relative changes in eye position to a target presented at different viewing distances. Slater and Findlay (1975b) and Aslin (1977) reported that, in newborns and 1-month-olds, the change in binocular alignment is not sufficient to indicate binocular fixation of a target at all viewing distances within 50 cm of the infant. In particular, infants in this age range did not converge their eyes to fixate a target binocularly at a near (12–15 cm) viewing distance. Two- and 3-month-olds, however, showed convergence to near targets, although a temporal delay was present in the binocular alignment of the 2-month-olds as the target was moved from 50 cm to 15 cm.

These results indicate that young infants do not maintain consistent binocular fixation and, as a result, they may at times experience double vision or monocular suppression. An interesting correlate of the development of consistent binocular fixation is the emergence of stereopsis during the third postnatal month. Three separate studies using random-element stereograms and the preferential-looking technique (Fox, Aslin, Shea, & Dumais, 1980), line stereograms and the preferential-looking technique (Held, Birch, & Gwiazda, 1980), and random-element stereograms and visual evoked potentials (Petrig, Julesz, Kropfl, Baumgartner, & Anliker, 1981) have reported that stereopsis is not present until after the third postnatal month (see Figure 6). Of course, it is possible that infants younger than 3 months of age have the neural mechanism for stereopsis but fail the testing procedure because of attentional or oculomotor deficits. Although an attentional explanation cannot be conclusively ruled out, younger infants do perform well when presented with a monocularly visible stimulus under conditions identical to the test for stereopsis. Birch, Gwiazda, and Held (1982) have argued that the different age of onset for stereopsis in crossed and uncrossed disparity displays implicates a neural basis for the emergence of stereopsis rather than an oculomotor basis. However, it is quite possible that younger infants cannot consistently align the eyes to extract the binocular information from the stereogram. As the control of vergence movements improves, infants may begin to exhibit stereopsis for crossed disparities, but fail on uncrossed disparities, because the visual system may analyze uncrossed dis-

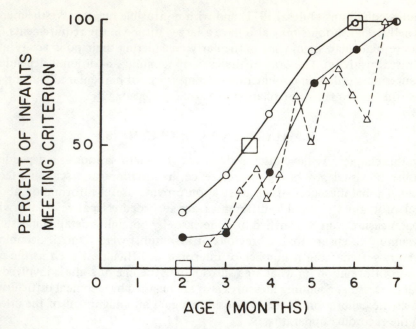

Figure 6. Summary of the results of three studies of stereopsis in human infants showing the percentage of infants tested that provided evidence of stereopsis as a function of age. ○ crossed disparity of 58′ arc and ● crossed disparity of 1′ arc from Birch, Gwiazda, and Held (1982); □ from Petrig, Julesz, Kropfl, Baumgartner, & Anliker (1981); △ from Fox, Aslin, Shea, & Dumais (1980) and additional data from Shea, Fox, Aslin, & Dumais (1980). Reprinted from Teller (1982).

parities with a somewhat different neural mechanism. The later emergence of stereopsis for uncrossed disparities, therefore, would be the result of neural development, whereas the emergence of stereopsis for crossed disparities would be the result of an improvement in the control of vergence eye movements.

A variety of questions concerning the importance of binocular eye movements for the processing of three-dimensional patterns remain unanswered. For example, (a) what region of the retina is involved in binocular fusion and stereopsis, (b) how do disparity and accommodative stimuli guide binocular alignment during early infancy, and (c) what role does early visual experience play in the development of the control of vergence eye movements? Perhaps the greatest impediment to progress in this area is the absence of an accurate measure of binocular alignment in infants. Corneal-reflection techniques work well with infants, but the resolution of binocular alignment is in the 1–2° range. Since significant changes in fusion and stereopsis can occur with misalignments as small as 15′ of arc in adults (Ogle, 1962), current eye movement techniques are simply inadequate to resolve many key issues in binocular development. In addition, the presence of binocular misalignments may not result in the absence of fusion or stereopsis. Adults can perceive relative depth under degraded

stimulus conditions (Julesz, 1971) and with nonfusible targets (Westheimer & Mitchell, 1969). Infants may also have a large latitude in the requirements for accurate binocular alignment, particularly considering their poor acuity and contrast sensitivity. Thus, as in the case of scanning, additional dependent measures are needed, in conjunction with measures of binocular alignment, to assess the consequences of fixation for visual processing.

SUMMARY AND CONCLUSIONS

In this chapter, we have discussed the use of visual fixations as a dependent measure of visual processing in preference, habituation, and scanning techniques. Global measures of visual fixation provide useful information about visual processing if reliable differences are recorded. Negative results with global measures can be clarified in some cases by obtaining detailed measures of scanning to ensure that subregions of a stimulus were fixated. Scanning, however, suffers from a number of interpretive difficulties, such as the absence of information on what area surrounding the line of sight is involved in visual processing. Scanning measures also are plagued by technical difficulties, such as the calibration of the eye-position signal and alignment of the infant with the recording apparatus.

We have also discussed the role of individual fixations in pattern perception and the control of changes in fixation. Stimulus salience (e.g., luminance or contour density) appears to control the young infant's changes in fixation, perhaps because peripheral-pattern processing is initially quite poor. Scanning in older infants is less constrained by stimulus salience and is broader in extent during the viewing of a multi-element stimulus. Individual fixation durations do not appear to provide a good index of visual processing, primarily because not all fixations appear to involve visual processing and some long fixations are characterized by inattention. Finally, the control of saccadic, pursuit, and vergence eye movements may constrain the visual processing that occurs during stimulus fixation. These issues of concurrent visual processing during fixation, and the control of changes in fixation, remain important topics for future research in the study of visual development.

REFERENCES

Abramov, I., Gordon, J., Hendrickson, A., Hainline, L., Dobson, V., & LaBossiere, E. The retina of the newborn human infant. *Science,* 1982, *217,* 265–267.

Aslin, R. N. Development of binocular fixation in human infants. *Journal of Experimental Child Psychology,* 1977, *23,* 133–150.

Aslin, R. N. Development of smooth pursuit in human infants. In D. F. Fisher, R. A. Monty, & J. W. Senders (eds.), *Eye movements: Cognition and visual perception.* Hillsdale, N.J.: Erlbaum, 1981.

Aslin, R. N. Commentary. In G. Bronson, The scanning patterns of human infants: Implications for visual learning. *Monographs on infancy,* Whole No. 2. Norwood, N.J.: Ablex, 1982.

Aslin, R. N. & Salapatek, P. Saccadic localization of visual targets by the very young human infant. *Perception and Psychophysics,* 1975, *17,* 293–302.

Birch, E., Gwiazda, J., & Held, R. Stereoacuity development for crossed and uncrossed dispari- ties in human infants. *Vision Research,* 1982, *22,* 507-514.

Bronson, G. The scanning patterns of human infants: Implications for visual learning. *Mono- graphs on Infancy,* Vol. 2. Norwood, N.J.: Ablex, 1982.

Bushnell, I. W. R. Modification of the externality effect in young infants. *Journal of Experimental Child Psychology,* 1979, *28,* 211-229.

Cohen, L. B. & Gelber, E. R. Infant visual memory. In L. B. Cohen & P. Salapatek (eds.), *Infant perception: From sensation to cognition.* Vol. 1. New York: Academic Press, 1975.

Collewijn, H. Eye and head movements in freely moving rabbits. *Journal of Physiology* (London), 1977, *266,* 471-498.

Crane, H. D. & Steele, C. M. Accurate three-dimensional eye tracker. *Applied Optics,* 1978, *17,* 691-705.

Day, R. H. The physiological basis of form perception in the peripheral retina. *Psychological Review,* 1957, *64,* 38-48.

Dayton, G. O. & Jones, M. H. Analysis of characteristics of fixation reflexes in infants by use of direct current electrooculography. *Neurology,* 1964, *14,* 1152-1156.

Dobson, V. & Teller, D. Y. Visual acuity in human infants: A review and comparison of behavioral and electrophysiological studies. *Vision Research,* 1978, *18,* 1469-1483.

Fantz, R. L. Pattern vision in young infants. *Psychological Record,* 1958, *8,* 43-47.

Findlay, J. M. Global visual processing for saccadic eye movements. *Vision Research,* 1982, *22,* 1033-1045.

Fox, R., Aslin, R. N., Shea, S. L., & Dumais, S. T. Stereopsis in human infants. *Science,* 1980, *207,* 323-324.

Hainline, L. Developmental changes in visual scanning of face and nonface patterns by infants. *Journal of Experimental Child Psychology,* 1978, *25,* 90-115.

Hainline, L. An automated eye movement recording system for use with human infants. *Behavior Research Methods and Instrumentation,* 1981, *13,* 20-24.

Hainline, L. & Lemerise, E. Infants' scanning of geometric forms varying in size. *Journal of Ex- perimental Child Psychology,* 1982, *33,* 235-256.

Haith, M. M. Infrared television recording and measurement of ocular behavior in human infants. *American Psychologist,* 1969, *24,* 279-282.

Haith, M. M. *Rules that babies look by.* Hillsdale, N.J.: Erlbaum, 1980.

Haith, M. M., Bergman, T., & Moore, M. J. Eye contact and face scanning in early infancy. *Science,* 1977, *198,* 853-855.

Haith, M. M., Goodman, G. S., Goodwyn, M., & Montgomery, L. *A longitudinal study of in- fants' visual scanning and discrimination of form.* Paper presented at the biennial meeting of the International Conference on Infant Studies, Austin, Texas, March, 1982.

Harris, C. M., Hainline, L., & Abramov, I. A method for calibrating an eye-monitoring system for use with infants. *Behavior Research Methods and Instrumentation,* 1981, *13,* 11-17.

Harris, P. & MacFarlane, A. The growth of the effective visual field from birth to seven weeks. *Journal of Experimental Child Psychology,* 1974, *18,* 340-348.

Held, R., Birch, E., & Gwiazda, J. Stereoacuity of human infants. *Proceedings of the National Academy of Science,* 1980, *77,* 5572-5574.

Julesz, B. *Foundations of cyclopean perception.* Chicago: University of Chicago Press, 1971.

Kessen, W., Salapatek, P., & Haith, M. M. The visual response of the human newborn to linear contour. *Journal of Experimental Child Psychology,* 1972, *13,* 9-20.

Kliegel, R. & Olson, R. K. Reduction and calibration of eye-monitor data. *Behavior Research Methods and Instrumentation,* 1981, *13,* 107-111.

Kremenitzer, J. P., Vaughan, H. G., Kurtzberg, D. and Dowling, K. Smooth-pursuit eye move- ments in the newborn infant. *Child Development,* 1979, *50,* 442-448.

Leahy, R. L. Development of preferences and processes of visual scanning in the human infant during the first three months of life. *Developmental Psychology,* 1976, *12,* 250-254.

Lewis, T. L., Maurer, D., & Kay, D. Newborns' central vision: Whole or hole? *Journal of Ex- perimental Child Psychology,* 1978, *26,* 193-203.

Maurer, D. The development of binocular convergence in infants. (Doctoral dissertation, University of Minnesota, 1974). *Dissertation Abstracts International, 35,* 6136–B. (University Microfilms No. 75-12,121).

Maurer, D. Infant's visual perception. In L. B. Cohen & P. Salapatek (eds.), *Infant perception: From sensation to cognition.* Vol. 1. New York: Academic Press, 1975.

Maurer, D. & Salapatek, P. Developmental changes in the scanning of faces by young infants. *Child Development,* 1976, *47,* 523–527.

McGinnis, J. M. Eye movements and optic nystagmus in early infancy. *Genetic Psychology Monographs,* 1930, *8,* 321–430.

Mendelson, M. J., Haith, M. M., & Goldman-Rakic, P. S. Monitoring visual activity in infant rhesus monkeys: Method and calibration. *Behavior Research Methods and Instrumentation,* 1981, *13,* 709–712.

Milewski, A. Infant's discrimination of internal and external pattern elements. *Journal of Experimental Child Psychology,* 1976, *22,* 229–246.

Milewski, A. Young infants' visual processing of internal and adjacent shapes. *Infant Behavior and Development,* 1978, *1,* 359–371.

Noton, D. & Stark, L. Eye movements and visual perception. *Scientific American,* 1971, *224,* 34–43.

Ogle, K. N. The optical space sense. In H. Davson (ed.), *The eye.* Vol. 4. New York: Academic Press, 1962.

Petrig, B., Julesz, B., Kropfl, W., Baumgartner, G., & Anliker, M. Development of stereopsis and cortical binocularity in human infants: Electrophysiological evidence. *Science,* 1981, *213,* 1402–1405.

Rayner, K. Eye movements in reading and information processing. *Psychological Bulletin,* 1978, *85,* 618–660.

Regal, D. & Salapatek, P. Eye and head coordination in human infants. *Supplement to Investigative Ophthalmology and Visual Science,* 1982, *22,* 85(12).

Robinson, D. A. Models of the saccadic eye movement control system. *Kybernetik,* 1973, *14,* 71–83.

Salapatek, P. Visual scanning of geometric figures by the human newborn. *Journal of Comparative and Physiological Psychology,* 1968, *66,* 247–258.

Salapatek, P. Pattern perception in early infancy. In L. B. Cohen & P. Salapatek (eds.), *Infant perception: From sensation to cognition.* Vol. 1. New York: Academic Press, 1975.

Salapatek, P., Haith, M. M., Maurer, D., & Kessen, W. Error in the corneal reflection technique: A note on Slater and Findlay. *Journal of Experimental Child Psychology,* 1972, *14,* 493–497.

Salapatek, P. & Kessen, W. Visual scanning of triangles by the human newborn. *Journal of Experimental Child Psychology,* 1966, *3,* 155–167.

Shea, S. L., Fox, R., Aslin, R. N., & Dumais, S. T. Assessment of stereopsis in human infants. *Investigative Ophthalmology and Visual Science,* 1980, *19,* 1400–1404.

Sheena, D. Pattern-recognition techniques for extraction of features of the eye from a conventional television scan. In R. A. Monty & J. W. Senders (eds.), *Eye movements and psychological processes.* Hillsdale, N.J.: Erlbaum, 1976.

Sheena, D. & Borah, J. Compensation for some second order effects to improve eye position measurements. In D. F. Fisher, R. A. Monty, & J. W. Senders (eds.), *Eye movements: Cognition and visual perception.* Hillsdale, N.J.: L. A. Erlbaum Associates, 1981.

Slater, A. M. & Findlay, J. M. The measurement of fixation position in the newborn baby. *Journal of Experimental Child Psychology,* 1972, *14,* 349–364.

Slater, A. M. & Findlay, J. M. The corneal reflection technique and the visual preference method: Sources of error. *Journal of Experimental Child Psychology,* 1975, *20,* 240–247. (a)

Slater, A. M. & Findlay, J. M. Binocular fixation in the newborn baby. *Journal of Experimental Child Psychology,* 1975, *20,* 248–273. (b)

Sperling, G. The information available in brief visual presentations. *Psychological Monographs,* 1960, *74,* (Whole number 498).

Teller, D. Y. A forced-choice preferential looking procedure: A psychophysical technique for use with human infants. *Infant Behavior and Development,* 1979, *2,* 135–153.

Teller, D. Y. Scotopic vision, color vision, and stereopsis in infants. *Current Eye Research,* 1982, *2,* 199–210.

Tronick, E. Stimulus control and the growth of the infant's effective visual field. *Perception and Psychophysics,* 1972, *11,* 373–376.

Westheimer, G. & Mitchell, D. E. The sensory stimulus for disjunctive eye movements. *Vision Research,* 1969, *9,* 749–755.

Wickelgren, L. Convergence in the human newborn. *Journal of Experimental Child Psychology,* 1967, *5,* 74–85.

Yarbus, A. L. *Eye movements and vision.* New York: Plenum Press, 1967.

Young, L. R. & Sheena, D. Survey of eye movement recording methods. *Behavior Research Methods and Instrumentation,* 1975, *7,* 397–429.

16

EVENT-RELATED POTENTIALS AND VISUAL DEVELOPMENT

Philip Salapatek

University of Minnesota

Charles A. Nelson

Purdue University

153.931

INTRODUCTION

In the present chapter we discuss the methodological issues involved in recording electrical activity from the brain of the human infant. Such a review seems necessary, particularly as the developmental study of the electrophysiological correlates of infant sensation, perception, and cognition lags far behind the progress made using behavioral indices. We begin by briefly discussing the history and uses of the electroencephalogram (EEG). This is followed by a general review of the methodology involved in recording Event-Related Potentials (ERPs). A selective review of the infant ERP literature as it relates to visual development is then provided, in which discussion is primarily restricted to acuity and the contrast sensitivity function (CSF), spatial-temporal interactions, and accommodation, while largely ignoring the binocularity and color vision literature. We conclude by reviewing how ERPs have been utilized to study infant memory and attention, and then offer recommendations for future research.

THE ELECTROENCEPHALOGRAM (EEG)

Hans Berger was the first to publish an extensive account of the recording of electrical activity from the human scalp (Berger, 1929; see Gloor, 1969, and Lindsley & Wicke, 1974, for summaries of his work). His report was followed by a flurry of activity on the topic during the 1930s (e.g., Adrian & Mathews, 1934; Gibbs, Davis, & Lennox, 1935; Jasper & Carmichael, 1935; Lindsley,

1936). On the basis of these studies, the form of the EEG was found to correlate with a variety of factors, such as psychological and physiological variables (e.g., sleep, hypnosis, age, temperature, drugs, fatigue, oxygen consumption, blood sugar level, and metabolism), and neurological pathology (e.g., epilepsy, brain tumors, and brain trauma).

For our purpose, it is noteworthy that the EEG provides irrefutable evidence that the electrophysiological basis of psychological functioning can be studied in the intact human. The EEG observed consisted of wave-like patterns (e.g., alpha and beta waves) that varied with the mental task performed (e.g., mental arithmetic vs. a relaxed state). Fifty years after Berger's discovery, the intracranial origin of the EEG is stil not precisely known, but its waves (e.g., alpha), are found to occur over all regions of the head, albeit with diminished amplitude in some locations. The EEG of the infant has received considerable attention (e.g., see Dreyfus-Brisac, 1979, for a review), so we shall not consider it in detail here.

THE EVENT-RELATED POTENTIAL (ERP)

The EEG consists of changes in electrical potential that are large enough to be detected by scalp electrodes. EEG waves are also typically spontaneous, in that they continue to occur under a constant set of physical or psychological conditions. ERPs, on the other hand, are any potentials *elicited* by a physical stimulus, or associated with the execution of a motor, cognitive, or psychophysical task (Goff, Allison, & Vaughan, 1978). ERPs, unlike the typical EEG, are associated with discrete physical or psychological events. They are also much smaller in amplitude than those potentials found in the EEG. Thus, to enhance the exact waveform of an ERP, Dawson's (1951) suggestion is followed: Potentials regularly elicited by a repetitive stimulus are discriminated from strong, irregularly occurring EEG potentials by summating or averaging all electrical activity subsequent to the stimulus. This enhances any activity that is "time-locked" to the event, and cancels out electrical activity inconsistently related to the event.

Examples of averaged visual ERPs are provided in columns 1 and 4 of Figure 1. It may be seen that a characteristic pattern of peaks and troughs in electrical potential follows stimulus onset. Those highly identifiable deflections that probably reflect distinct neural subprocesses are termed "components." They probably are the sum of graded IPSPs and EPSPs, of action potentials, and of volume conduction from various regions of the brain.

ERPs may occur to transient or steady-state stimulation. Figure 1 illustrates ERPs to transient stimulation. The stimulus eliciting the ERP was not presented a second time within 500 msec, so that deflections less than 500 msec following the stimulus were able to be expressed, especially after averaging. If the stimulus is re-presented a number of times with a very short intertrial interval (e.g., sinusoidally at 12 Hz), individual deflections become obscure and the ERP tends to track the stimulus presentations.

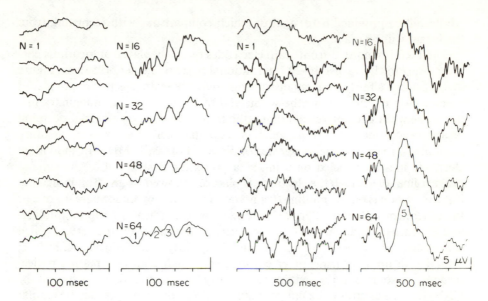

Figure 1. Comparison of single poststimulus EEG records (1st and 3rd columns) and averages of increasing numbers of repetitions (2nd and 4th columns) from parietal scalp. The 100 msec records are an expansion of the first part of the 500 msec records, to provide better resolution. Positivity is upwards. Stimulus is a right-median nerve shock delivered at start of records. (From Goff, 1974).

Components in the ERP waveform that begin shortly after the onset of a stimulus and last for less than approximately 250 msec, and that appear not to be highly influenced by cognitive or state variables, are said to be exogenous or evoked (Donchin, Ritter, & McCallum, 1978). Such components, which are essentially constant in amplitude, latency, and scalp distribution, and which are chiefly affected by the physical parameters of the stimuli, differ markedly from endogenous components. The latter components have a longer latency and are often elicited in the absence of external stimulation, and may be only slightly related to the physical parameters of the stimulus itself. As will be discussed shortly, late components are usually associated with the subject's prior experience, the instructions given the subject, or the subject's intentions. According to Donchin et al. (1978, p. 355), to be labeled "endogenous," components must meet at least some of the following criteria: (a) They must be nonobligatory responses to stimuli, (b) the amplitude, latency, and scalp distribution of the potentials are often invariant to changes in the physical parameters of the stimuli, and (c) the variance of the components is normally accounted for by variation in the tasks assigned to the subjects.

Recording of the ERP

A large number of excellent sources exist regarding the methodology of ERP and EEG recording (e.g., Goff, 1974; John, Ruchkin, & Vidal, 1978; Lindsley & Wicke, 1974). Therefore, only a cursory sketch of recording from adults will be provided here, against which comparisons with recording from the infant will be made.

The ERP is recorded from scalp electrodes typically placed at locations corresponding to the Jasper 10-20 International System (Jasper, 1958; see Figure 2). To achieve a fairly uniform distribution over the scalp, electrodes are placed a percentage of the distance between, and to each side of, an imaginary line drawn between two reference points (the inion, which is an external occipital protuberence, and the nasion, which is the point where the nasofrontal suture is cut across the median anteroposterior plane [Thomas, 1973]). The individual electrode sites are labeled by using as a prefix the first initial of the general brain region over which the electrode is placed, followed by a suffix, indicating if the electrode is on the midline (using the suffix "z") or somewhere on one or the other hemisphere (e.g., 1, 2, 3, etc.). Thus, Oz indicates occipital midline, and Pz, parietal midline, etc. (One exception to the rule is for the vertex, which is indicated by the letter "C"). The most frequently used electrodes are silver, coated with nonpolarizing silver chloride, although gold and platinum electrodes are also used (it is essential, particularly for d.c. recording, such as of the CNV, that the electrodes be nonpolarizing). Electrode montages may be bipolar or monopolar, with the ear mastoid often serving as a reference and the forehead or some other suitable site (e.g., the nose) serving as a ground. Electrode impedances should be in the order of 5 kilohms (5KΩ) or less. The amplification of the signals should be in the range of 15-20,000:1. For very low frequency ERP components, d.c. amplifiers should be employed with high-frequency filtering (40 Hz and above). For most purposes, amplification of signals from 1 to 50 or 60 Hz will be sufficient to allow detection of ERP deflections. Eye movements are typically recorded by means of miniature (silver) electrodes

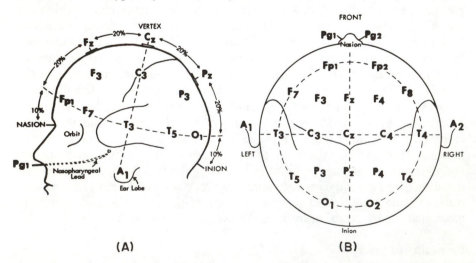

(A)   (B)

Figure 2. International electrode placement system (From Jasper, 1958, and Stevens, 1974).

placed above and below the orbit of one eye. Both ERP and EOG signals are time-locked and recorded directly onto paper, magnetic tape, or into a computer. Trials in which there is eye activity that may interfere with subsequent resolution of the ERPs may be rejected online or offline. After editing for such artifacts, ERPs are usually averaged to improve the signal-to-noise ratio, and then labeled. The labeling of deflections is done by stating if the deflection is positive (P) or negative (N), followed by the latency to occurrence; for example, P200 indicates a positive-going wave beginning 200 msec after the onset of the stimulus. (Rather than specify latency, it is also common simply to use a single digit to reflect whether the deflection is the second, third, etc., major deflection. Thus, for example, P3 would indicate the third major positive deflection.)

Recording from the infant subject can depart appreciably from recording from the adult. First, because the infant cannot be instructed to fixate a point and not move his or her head, eye movement artifacts present a considerable problem. (This is usually compensated for by using short-duration stimuli that minimize scanning, and by presenting many trials.) Similarly, because infants are more prone than most adults to rapid shifts in behavioral state or attention, compensatory measures must be invoked (e.g., testing infants between or even during feedings; using pacifiers; using research assistants who can redirect the infant's attention to the stimulus display; taking short breaks; etc.). Third, a persistent problem of testing infants concerns the distinct possibility of the electrodes slipping or falling off. (This can be corrected, however, by using collodion, foam pads, or headbands to hold the electrodes in place with only a minimum of discomfort.) Fourth, one must compensate for the fact that interelectrode distances are shorter for the infant than for the adult. Fifth, because of the thinner skull and nature of the infant's brain, many ERP components are three to four times greater in amplitude than in the adult, and appropriate compensatory measures must be employed. Finally, because infants cannot be verbally instructed to attend to a particular dimension of a stimulus or task, alternate forms of instruction become necessary (e.g., a familiarization period with certain stimuli to increase the salience of other infrequent stimuli).

The Adult ERP

Evoked, Exogenous or Early Potentials. Figure 3 is a schematic summary of the adult averaged ERP to a reversing patterned field. Of the labeled components (P60, N75, P100 or P1, N140 or N1, and P180 or P2), only P1, N1, and P2 have received any attention by investigators studying the human infant. At least for the adult, these components are all elicited or evoked by the stimulus; they may represent various reliable stages in the processing of the stimulus; they are generally observed in the averaged ERP to patterned stimuli; and the amplitude of and/or latency to these components may vary as a function of the physical characteristics of the stimulus. Additional work is necessary to

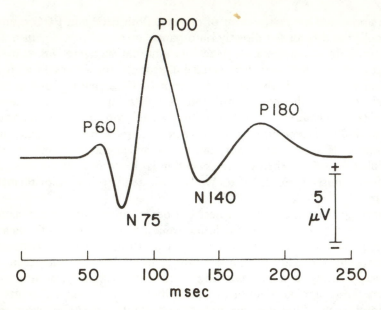

Figure 3. Schematic summary of the occipital ERP to full-field pattern reversal stimulation. Recording conditions and age affect the latencies of components. (From Goff, Allison, & Vaughan, 1978).

determine whether the processes underlying exogenous components in the infant are the same as those in the adult.

Invoked, Endogenous, or Late Potentials. As stated previously, endogenous components are typically invoked by an event or the absence of an event. Several such components have been studied in the older child and adult subject, and four of these components have been studied in infants.

The Contingent Negative Variation (CNV) is a slow negative wave that can often precede the expected time of onset of an event. It is an accurate index of "when" a subject expects an event to occur. Although there are presently no published data concerned with infant CNVs, one conference paper does exist (Hofmann, Karmel, & Lester, 1975).

The Processing Negativity (Pn) component (e.g., Näätänen, 1982) is a short latency (50 to 150 msec from stimulus onset) negative wave that appears to reflect an early stage of selective attention, and may have its locus somewhere in the central sensory system, presumably in the secondary sensory areas (Näätänen, 1982, p. 636).

The N200 (or N2) component is a negative-going wave that typically occurs approximately 200 msec after the onset of a stimulus that has been delivered a number of times at a constant rate, or at times when a stimulus has been deleted from a train of identical stimuli (Donchin et al., 1978). In agreement with Donchin et al. (1978), Ritter, Simson, Vaughan, and Macht (1982) have recently noted that the N200 component reflects discrimination and classification of stimuli. Citing several sources (e.g., Ford, Roth, & Kopell, 1976), these authors have noted that the peak latency of N200 varies as a function of the difficulty of discrimination, and precedes and correlates with the timing of discriminative behavioral responses (Ritter et al., 1982, p. 909). The N200 component, and an earlier and related negative component, Na (possibly associated with pattern recognition processes; e.g., Ritter, Simson, & Vaughan, 1983), have not yet been studied in infants.

The next major endogenous component, P300 or P3, or LPC (Late Positive Component), has been studied in both adults and infants. The P300 response is a positive-going peak with a latency in adults of about 300 to 500 msec following stimulus onset. The P300 is perhaps the most robust of the endogenous components, and has certainly been the best studied (i.e., well over 2,000 adult studies have been reported; see Pritchard, 1981, for a recent review of this literature). While many variables have been associated with the P300 response, those receiving most attention have been concerned with unattended events that produce orienting, attended events that are low probability, and stimulus salience. Several subcomponents of the P300 have also been identified in the adult's ERP (e.g., P3a and P3b; see Pritchard, 1981).

The final two major endogenous components that have been identified across the life span are the Nc and Pc waves, both reported by Courchesne (e.g., 1978; Courchesne, Ganz, & Norcia, 1981). Interestingly, more may be known about these components in infants than in adults. The Nc component in infants is a negative-going wave that peaks at about 700 msec following stimulus onset, while the Pc component is a positive-going wave peaking at about 1360 msec (Courchesne, 1984; Courchesne et al., 1981). Both components appear to be invoked by events similar to those invoking the P300. The Nc, Pc, and P300 components will receive particular attention in this chapter.

The Infant ERP

Exogenous Potentials. *a. Visual Acuity.* The recording of the visual ERP is now a well-established technique for assessing the development of infant pattern vision. Since this technique involves measurement of early visual evoked deflections of the ERP, such components have also been referred to as visual evoked potentials (VEPs) or visual evoked cortical potentials (VECPs). As Harter, Deaton, and Odom (1977a) point out, ERPs are particularly appropriate for investigating vision in infants, as no motor response is required, they are relatively easy to obtain without harm or discomfort to the infant, and they can be related to neurophysiological data from animals and perceptual data from adults. While it is possible to elicit an ERP by flashing an unpatterned light (e.g., Ellingson, 1958, 1960), much more useful information is gained by flashing patterned stimuli in the form of checkerboards or gratings. This allows the determination of not only visual acuity, but also the CSF.

Dobson and Teller (1978), Harter, Deaton, and Odom (1977b), and Sokol (1982) provide recent reviews of the literature on the development of infant acuity using the ERP. Amplitude and peak latency (or phase) of the sustained pattern ERP serves as the dependent measure. Most investigators agree that, by about 6 months, either sustained or steady-state ERP amplitude yields near-adult levels of acuity. Sokol and Dobson (1976) phase-alternated a checkerboard at 12 alt/second. By 6 months, the peak of the amplitude-checksize function occurred at 15 min of arc, similar to adults. Harter et al. (1977b) and Sokol (1978) used an extrapolation technique, similar to one described by Campbell and Mafffei (1970), to show that infant acuity reches 20/20 Snellen by 6 months. A straight line is extrapolated from the peak of the amplitude-checksize function to zero microvolts. Figure 4 is an illustration of how the tech-

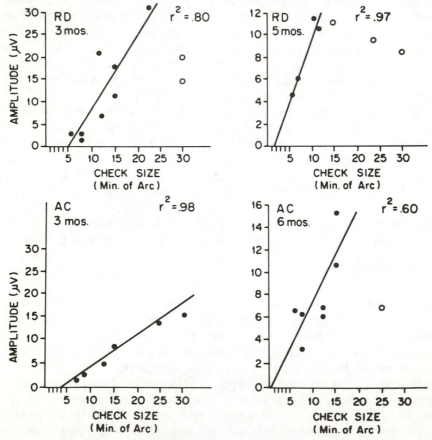

Figure 4. Amplitude of the checkerboard pattern ERP (micro-volts) as a function of check size for 2 infants between 3 and 6 months of age. Using the method of least squares, regression lines were fit to the data points shown by the closed circles; data shown by the open circles were not included in the regression analysis. Note how the X-axis intercept shifts toward smaller checks as each infant gets older. (From Sokol, 1978).

ique was used to estimate the acuity of two infants between 3 and 6 months. For subject RD, there was a shift in the peak of the amplitude-checksize function from 24 min at 3 months to 12 min at 5 months. When a straight line was extrapolated from each peak to zero microvolts, there was a shift in threshold acuity from 5 min (20/100) to 1.5 min (20/30). Subject AC shows similar results. Harris, Atkinson, and Braddick (1976), using extrapolation, found that one 6-month-old's Snellen acuity was 20/20. Pirchio, Spinelli, Fiorentini, and Maffei (1978) used ERP extrapolation to 100% contrast with infants between 2 and 10 months of age. They found that acuity increased rapidly until the fifth or sixth month and more slowly until the twelfth month, at which time it had still not reached an adult value.

In reviewing the literature on infant acuity, Dobson and Teller (1978) concluded that the three basic measures used to assess early visual acuity—optokinetic nystagmus, preferential looking, and ERP—tended to yield similar age norms during the first months of life, although ERP functions tended to indicate generally better acuity at a given age (particularly the 4- to 6-month range) than preferential looking. These authors speculated that the generally higher acuity yielded by ERPs vs. preferential looking measures could be due to three factors. First, the two techniques typically employ different stimuli (i.e., ERP stimuli are modulated temporally, while preferential looking stimuli are not). This explanation appears unlikely to account for much of the discrepancy, however, as Dobson, Teller, and Belgum (1978) found no difference in 2-month-olds' acuity using preferential looking and phase-alternating checkerboards vs. static square-wave gratings. A second explanation for the discrepancy, therefore, may lie in the fact that ERP and behavioral measures employ different scoring procedures. For example, while 75% correct responding is often required in preferential looking studies, ERP studies often use as a criterion the spatial frequency for which ERP amplitude will be at or slightly above zero. As Banks and Salapatek (1983) note, the use of more generous scoring criteria in preferential looking studies might increase the acuity estimates by 1 to 1.5 octaves, bringing them more in line with ERP estimates.

A methodological concern related to the above is the fact that the higher acuity shown by the ERP may in part be a function of response averaging. Because an infant must respond in an all-or-none fashion on a trial-by-trial basis in a behavioral experiment, subthreshold stimuli cannot be summed together. In contrast, these same subthreshold stimuli may be detected within the confines of an ERP experiment, as the infant's responses are averaged together, thus yielding a potentially higher acuity estimate. As Dobson and Teller (1978, p. 1481) note, it is an open question as to whether an infant can be said to "see" stimuli which can be detected in the averaged ERP but which cannot be used by the infant behaviorally.

Finally, the most likely and, as well, intriguing, explanation for the differences between the procedures is that the ERP may be tapping into a different level of the nervous system than behavioral measures (see Banks & Salapatek, 1983, for an extended discussion of this point). For example, Regan (1978) has shown that temporal frequency influences ERP estimates of acuity in the adult. While temporal frequency also affects psychophysical estimates in the adult (Robson, 1966), it does not do so in the same manner as occurs in ERP studies. This evidence suggests that the ERP and preferential looking procedures do, as Dobson and Teller (1978) suggest, tap into different mechanisms. Further assessment of this proposal in infants appears warranted.

A second concern in the ERP literature on acuity is the disparity among ERP studies themselves. Marg, Freeman, Peltzman, and Goldstein (1976) estimated infant acuity by examining the amplitude of the pattern onset-offset transient ERP. For each infant, they increased the spatial frequency of a square wave grating until the ERP was similar to that evoked by a subthreshold defocussed pattern of 1 min stripes. Marg et al. (1976) found that acuity was equivalent to 20/20 Snellen by 5 months, earlier than the age reported by Sokol (1978). However, Sokol (1982) points out that the fundamental spatial frequency component of checkerboards is higher by a factor of two than the individual checks, and higher than the stripe width of a rectangular bar grating. When appropriate corrections are made to equate stimuli, the Marg et al. and Sokol data are in much closer agreement.

Overall, the ERP has been shown to be a useful, reliable, and valid means of assessing infant acuity. The procedure is ideally suited to both normal and atypical populations, an advantage over certain behavioral measures. On the other hand, additional research is required to determine how ERPs relate to infants' behavior, and to what level of the nervous system they correspond.

b. Contrast Sensitivity. The CSF provides a threshold measure of the sensitivity of the visual system to contrast at any frequency. Within the confines of a behavioral task, the 70% or 75% contrast detection level at a particular spatial frequency is regarded as threshold. The frequency that results in 75% detection at the 100% contrast level is the high frequency cut-off, or visual acuity. The high frequency cut-off is typically found by linear extrapolation through frequency thresholds below 100% contrast.

Visual acuity, or the high frequency cut-off, is obviously of considerable clinical significance. Moreover, it is often predictive of what can be resolved at lower spatial frequencies, although this is not always the case. For example, Regan, Silver, and Murray (1977) report that multiple sclerosis patients often show normal Snellen acuity, but mid-range deficits in spatial frequency sensitivity that lead to reading difficulties. Hess and Howell (1977) found that about one-half of strabismic amblyopes showed a relatively depressed sensitivity to lower spatial frequencies in the amblyopic eye. Bodis-Wollner (1972) has reported loss of mid-range spatial frequency sensitivity in a case of traumatic cortical damage. These data make it clear that one cannot infer the form of the CSF from visual acuity. It also raises the question of whether the form of the CSF changes as the infant develops.

Salapatek (1982) summarizes the available data on infant CSFs. In four studies (Atkinson, Braddick, & Braddick, 1974; Atkinson, Braddick, & Moar, 1977a,b; Banks & Salapatek, 1978), the preferential looking technique was used as a dependent measure. We shall not focus on these behavioral studies here, and will turn instead to reviewing those studies using ERPs.

Pirchio et al. (1978) assessed the CSF in three infants longitudinally, and in 12 infants cross-sectionally, using ERP recordings and vertical sinusoidal gratings, phase-reversed at 8 Hz. Figure 5 depicts the CSFs for a single infant tested at 2½, 3½, and 6 months. In general, the functions are very similar at early ages to those obtained behaviorally. The curves are smoother than typical behavioral ones, perhaps due to the higher number of sweeps (50 or more) at each data point in the ERP study. Contrast sensitivities, in absolute terms, tend to be somewhat lower in general than in behavioral studies for corresponding age points, but are actually higher relative to the empirical adult values provided in the study. Optimal spatial frequency and high cut-off frequencies in this study are similar and not obviously higher than in behavioral studies in general.

Figure 6 illustrates the development of maximum contrast sensitivity, optimal spatial frequency, and visual acuity across the first year for all infants in the Pirchio et al. (1978) study. Most development takes place during the first 6 months, but has not reached full adult values even at 1 year, especially in the case of visual acuity. Growth functions, derived *across subjects,* are not that smooth, indicating individual differences in growth, or across-age errors of measurement.

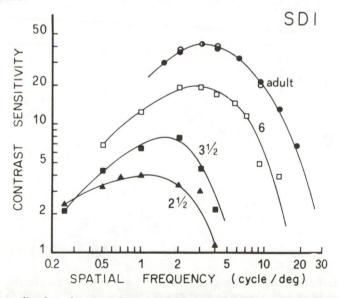

Figure 5. Amplitudes of an ERP for an infant (S.D.I.) 2.5 months old (triangles), 3.5 months old (full squares), and 6 months old (open squares) at various spatial frequencies. The points are relative amplitudes of the second harmonic of the averaged ERP, obtained with a constant contrast and normalized to the contrast sensitivity at 1 cycle/degree. Each point is the mean of several records. Data from an adult subject are reported for comparison: Full points are normalized ERP amplitudes (stimulus contrast 25%), and open points are extrapolated contrast sensitivities. (From Pirchio, Spinelli, Fiorentine, & Maffei, 1978).

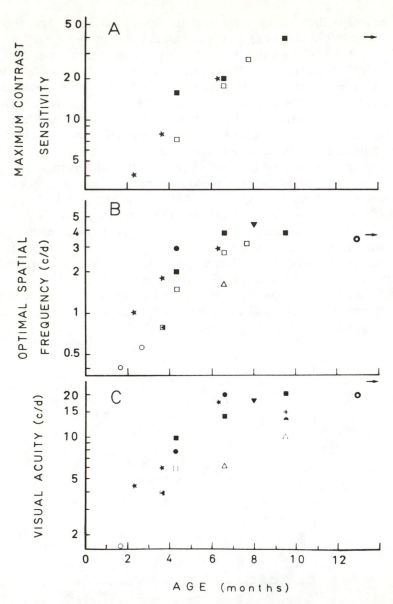

Figure 6. Maximum contrast sensitivity (A), optimal spatial frequency (B), and visual acuity (C) of 12 infants plotted against age in months. Different symbols have been used to indicate different infants. The arrows indicate ordinate values relative to a normal adult subject. (From Pirchio et al., 1978).

Figure 7 provides the only CSF data so far collected from newborns (Atkinson, Braddick, & French, 1979). Clearly there is no low-frequency turndown at birth, which one would expect if lateral inhibition were present in the visual system. Contrast sensitivity and acuity are also considerably poorer at birth

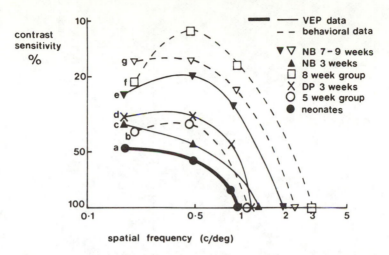

spatial frequency (c/deg)

Figure 7. Contrast-sensitivity functions for infants of different ages. Solid curves refer to sensitivities estimated from ERP measurements; dotted curves to sensitivities estimated behaviorally from fixation preference. (a) Group data from ERP measurements on 97 neonates (1-10 days); 10 Hz phase-reversing stimulus. (b) Mean behavioral data from 5-week-old infants (N = 9); 3 Hz drifting stimulus. (c) ERP data on subject NB at 3 weeks; 10 Hz phase-reversing stimulus. (d) ERP data on subject DP at 3 weeks; 10 Hz phase-reversing stimulus. (e) ERP data on subject NB at 7 weeks; 10 Hz phase-reversing stimulus. (f) Mean behavioral data from 8-week-old infants (N = 9); 3 Hz drifting stimulus. (g) Behavioral data from subject NB at 9 weeks; 10 Hz phase-reversing stimulus. Curves (b) and (g) combine data from a number of experiments. (Adapted from Atkinson, Braddick, & French, 1979).

than at 1 month. In general, the data are orderly in terms of age-related growth of the CSF, although infant DP at 3 weeks seems unusually advanced.

Harris et al. (1976) are the only researchers who have determined both a behavioral and a ERP CSF in the same infant at the same age. Figure 8 shows CSF functions for their 6-month-old infant, and for an adult, in their apparatus. The comparisons are quite remarkable. Infant and adult functions differ as one would expect in terms of overall sensitivity, maximum or peak sensitivity, optimal frequency, and cut-off frequency. As was stated previously, the ERP CSF also yielded a slightly higher estimate of sensitivity than the behavioral measure (e.g., Dobson & Teller, 1978).

By and large, the ERP has been shown to be a somewhat more efficient means of assessing the CSF than behavioral measures. As Salapatek (1982) has noted, while a behavioral choice is a simple and efficient way of determining cutoff frequency, it is too slow for assessing a complete CSF. In contrast, the ERP can deliver up to 20 trials per second, as compared to ⅓ to ⅕ trial per second using preferential looking. However, neither the ERP nor other techniques of assessing the infant CSF yet meet the necessary criteria for clinical, developmental relevance. Within- and between-subject variances, between-age reliability, and norms have not been established. The considerable individual differences so far observed leave open the question as to whether unique CSFs

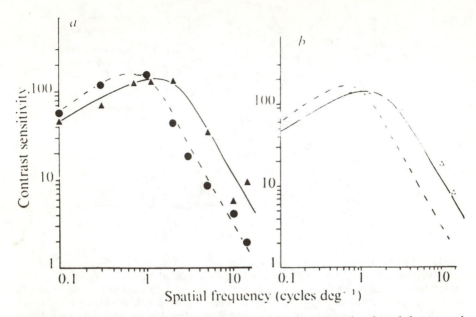

Figure 8. (a) Comparison of the contrast-sensitivity functions for the adult (▲) and infant (●), as derived from the amplitude of the event-related potential. The curves are fitted by eye. Each point is an average of several runs. (b) Comparison of the psychophysical contrast-sensitivity function for the adult (△), and the behaviorally determined contrast-sensitivity function for the infant (○). The curves from Figure 8 are repeated in this figure to aid comparison between psychophysical and event-related potential measures. (Adapted from Harris, Atkinson, & Braddick, 1976).

may be indicative of later pathology, or whether certain early deviations are inconsequential.

c. Methodological issues concerning ERPs and infant pattern perception. Sokol (1982) has argued convincingly that there are decided advantages to using latency rather than amplitude of the pattern ERP for both adults and children. He argues that the variance of the absolute latency to some early ERP components is small, both within subjects and between subjects matched for age. On the other hand, although two individuals may have identical peak latencies and equally normal vision, one may have an ERP amplitude three or four times greater than the other. This problem does not apply to interocular comparisons within individuals, where amplitude variance is small and conditions such as amblyopia can therefore be diagnosed.

In adults, the latency of early components of the ERP varies inversely with check size or directly with spatial frequency (Jones & Keck, 1978; Parker & Salzen, 1977). In Figure 9 this effect is illustrated during infancy (Sokol & Jones, 1979). At 1 month of age, the latency of P1 for 30 min checks is nearly 65 msec longer than for 240 min checks. With increasing age, there is a shift in the latency-checksize function toward shorter latencies and smaller checks. Although by 40 weeks of age mean P1 latency for large checks equals adult

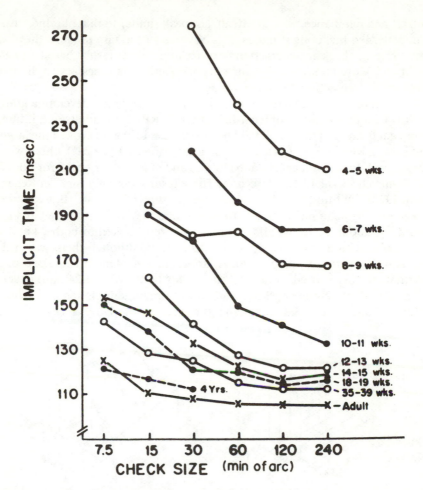

Figure 9. Mean P1 latency (msec) as a function of check size for infants, 4-year-old children, and adults. (From Sokol & Jones, 1979).

values, infant P1 latency for small checks is still longer than for adults. For checks 15 min and smaller, the latency to pattern-reversed P1 continues to decrease up to 3 years of age, and, indeed, Spekreijse (1978) has found a continued decrease in latency for onset-offset ERPs to 9 min checks up to 10 years of age. Thus, latency to principal early components is already demonstrably a useful developmental and between-subject index of visual functioning.

d. Spatial-temporal Interactions. In adults, ERP amplitude depends on an interaction between check size and pattern reversal rate (Regan, 1973, 1978; Regan & Richards, 1973). Regan found that reversal rates of 5-7 alt/sec (2.5-3.5 Hz) produce the largest ERP steady-state amplitude for small checks (< 15 min), while ERPs to large checks show two peaks, one at 5-7 alt/sec and the other at 10 alt/second. The large check ERPs are supposedly the result of both contrast and luminance, with the 10 alt/sec peak similar to that obtained using an unpatterned flickering stimulus. It is obviously necessary to know the alternation rate by checksize interaction in order to interpret results based on ERP amplitude. More important for our purposes here, it is necessary to discover whether this interaction changes with age.

To determine the alternation rate by checksize interaction developmentally, Moskowitz and Sokol (1980) recorded pattern ERPs from adults and infants. For an adult exposed to a small field (6°×6°), 12 min checks evoked the largest amplitude ERPs at 5-7 alt/second. For a large field (17°×22°), there was a sharper peak for 12 min checks at 6 alt/sec, and much larger peaks for both 12 and 48 min checks at 10-12 alt/second. These results basically confirm Regan's (1973, 1978) adult findings. The infant data are shown in Figure 10. ERPs were evoked only by 48 min checks at 7-10 weeks, and the function peaked at 4 alt/second. At about 3 months of age, potentials were elicited to both 24 and 48 min checks, with a temporal peak at 8-10 alt/sec (although there was still a peak at 4 alt/sec for 48 min checks). At approximately 4 months, peak evoked potentials further shifted toward 10 alt/sec for large (48 and 24 min) checks, and now-evident 12-min checksize potentials were bimodal in temporal distribution at 4 and 12 alt/second. At 5-6 months, this bimodality at 12 alt/sec for

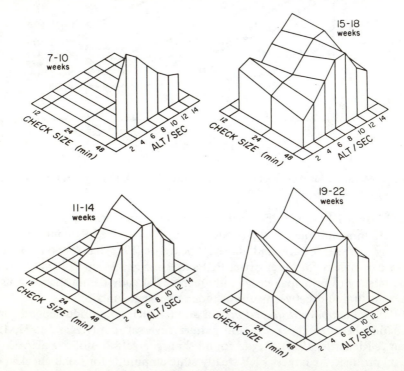

Figure 10. Three-dimensional surface representation of the effect of the interaction of alternation rate (x-axis) and check size (y-axis) on the amplitude (z-axis) of the pattern reversal ERP in infants from 7 to 22 weeks of age. Amplitude is expressed in relative (Z-score) units. (Figure from Sokol, 1982; data from Moskowitz & Sokol, 1980).

12 min checks became more distinct, while the response to 48 min checks peaked only at 10 alt/second.

The spatial-temporal findings from human infants are not identical to those obtained from the adult. For example, 19- to 22-week-old infants have a lower contrast-specific temporal peak (4 alt/sec) than adults (6 alt/sec). Thus, Sokol (1982) suggests that pattern ERP studies of infants 12 weeks or older (when recordable signals are first obtained to checks smaller than 20 min) should be conducted using rates between 3 and 5 alt/second.

e. Latency Measurements of Infant Accommodation. If an adult subject's accommodation to a reversing checkerboard is sufficiently degraded by the use of minus lenses, the peak latency of P1 remains constant as long as the subject compensates for the lens by increasing his or her accommodation. However, as soon as the total amplitude of the subject's accommodation has been reached and there is no longer sufficient plus-power to neutralize the minus lens, the target becomes blurred. At this point (8 diopters for the adult) the latency to P1 increases by nearly 10 msec (Sokol, 1982; Sokol & Moskowitz, 1981). Figure 11 shows wave-forms obtained from 2 infants and one adult, using a series of minus lenses and 30 min checks reversing at 3.75 alt/sec. It may be seen that P1 latency and amplitude were affected for the infants, but not for the adult.

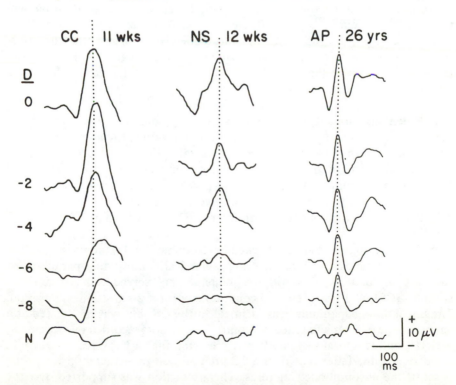

Figure 11. Pattern-reversal binocular ERPs recorded from 2 infants and one adult, using lenses of increasing amounts of minus sphere. Thirty-min checks alternating at 3.75 reversals/sec were used to evoke cortical potentials. (From Sokol, 1982).

In a larger sample, 3-month-old infants whose peak latency to P1 fell within the 95% confidence limits for the no-lens condition were categorized as seeing clearly. Infants categorized as "blurred" had P1 peak latencies beyond the 95% confidence limits for the no-lens condition. Seventy-five percent of the infants tested could compensate -3.33 diopters by accommodation. Only 50% could compensate for -5.33 and -7.33 diopters, and fewer than 20% to -9.33 diopters. This probably does not matter to the emmetropic infant, but significantly hyperopic infants may have difficulty in accommodation, since they may not be able to compensate for significant error.

The pattern ERP indicates rapid development of the visual system during the first year and slower development thereafter. Transient and steady-state ERP studies suggest that adult acuity and contrast sensitivity are reached not before 5 months, and perhaps beyond 12 months of age. However, we know very little regarding individual differences in this development. Peak latency of transient pattern ERPs and spatial-temporal ERP interactions change up to 2-3 years of age, and even up to 10 years. Hickey (1977) has found evidence for growth of cells in the lateral geniculate nucleus until at least 2 years of age. Magoon and Robb (1981) have similarly found evidence for marked development of myelinization over the first 2 years. Finally, children with a history of strabismus have shown that the critical period for the development of binocularity continues until 2-3 years of age (Banks, Aslin, & Letson, 1975; Hohmann & Creutzfeld, 1975). These studies collectively suggest that the visual system matures significantly until at least 2 to 3 years of age (Sokol, 1982), and possibly until 10 years (Spekreijse, 1978), a development that can be chronicled by the ERP.

Late Potentials. In contrast to the work on early potentials, the study of late potentials in the human infant has received remarkably little attention. This is unfortunate, given the advantages ERP recording often holds over behavioral tasks (e.g., the ability to present many trials over a short period of time), and the plethora of behavioral data on infant perception and memory with which to compare the ERP data. Recently, however, five studies have been reported that examined late potentials in infants ranging in age from 7 weeks to 12 months.

a. CNV. Hofmann et al. (1975; cited in Hofmann, 1981) studied the CNV in a group of 3-month-old infants, using a classical conditioning paradigm. A checkerboard pattern paired with the phoneme "ba" served as the conditioned stimulus (CS), and was presented continuously for a 2-sec stimulus duration. The unconditioned stimulus was identical to the CS, but was modulated at a temporal rate of 6 Hz and lasted 4 seconds. The authors recorded over occipital, parietal, and temporal regions. It was predicted that a CNV response would occur during the latter part of the CS presentation immediately prior to the onset of the unconditioned stimulus. This prediction was supported over the occipital region, but not over the parietal or temporal regions.

Unfortunately, the details of the Hofmann et al. study were sketchy, and no interpretation of the findings was offered. The findings minimally suggest that it is possible to record the CNV in young infants. However, while the paradigm used to elicit the response was similar to that used in adults, it is not clear how the response compares in function and form to the adult's. Moreover, why the response occurred only at Oz and not at more central processing regions is not clear (although one could argue that Oz would be the most mature of the three scalp regions from which recordings were made).

b. P300, Nc, and Pc. The P300, or LPC, is invoked in adults by low-frequency, task-relevant, novel and/or attended events (Pritchard, 1981). The three infant studies to have examined the P300 (or P300-like) response did so by utilizing low-frequency events. These studies, while not contradictory, do not yet provide a full picture of the form, latency, and origin of components invoked by low-probability events.

Courchesne et al. (1981) attempted to find evidence of Nc and Pc components in ten 6-month-old infants (mean age 6.2 months; range 4.0 to 7.2 months) who provided at least 70 successful ERP trials (26 infants were initially tested). Nc was designated as the maximum negative peak at Fz that occurred between 300 and 1200 msec. Pc was designated as the maximum positive peak following Nc between 500 and 1800 msec. Each trial consisted of a 100 msec presentation of a female face, with an intertrial interval of between 1800 and 2800 msec. Eighty-eight per cent of the time, a particular female face was presented. On the remaining 12% of trials, randomly interspersed among the 88% trials, a different female face was shown. The authors recorded from Fz and Pz and, in addition, analyzed for the occurrence of Nc and Pc waves from the upper and lower eye leads used to record blinks (UpE and LoE). Two hundred msec of the average pre-event EEG tracing served as baseline. P1 and N1 waves, presumably from the Pz lead, were discernible in only five of the ten infants. Nc (approximately 700 msec latency) and Pc (approximately 1360 msec latency) waves were observed for both frequent and infrequent faces in all ten infants, principally at Fz (Pc was indistinguishable at UpE and Pz). However, Nc amplitudes were larger and latencies longer for the infrequent events (Figure 12) at LoE, UpE, Fz, and Pz. On the other hand, Pc amplitudes and latencies did not differ significantly for the frequent and infrequent events, although the Pc amplitudes to the infrequent events were maximal at UpE. Finally, the investigators stated that P300 waves were not observed, although it must be noted that the authors also did not analyze for positive waves prior to 500 msec.

Since Nc and Pc amplitudes were found to be uncorrelated, and since no P300 wave was found, Courchesne et al. concluded that Nc, Pc, and P300 index separate developmental brain processes. Specifically, Courchesne et al. proposed that Nc may indicate early detection of events rather than categories, with infrequent events given unusual prominence. Nc waves may also be invoked by both frequent and infrequent events in infants, but not in children, because infants' memory traces for even familiar events may be more unstable

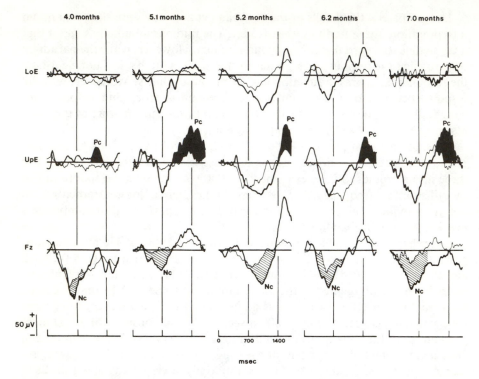

Figure 12. ERPs at LoE, UpE, and Fz to frequent events (thin lines) and to infrequent, discrepant events (thick lines) from five representative infants. The age of each infant is shown next to his or her ERP responses. ERP traces to frequent events represent averages of 5 to 20 responses; ERP traces to discrepant events represent averages of 5 to 15 responses. (From Courchesne, Ganz, & Norcia, 1981).

at a young age. Also, only unexpected, discrepant events may elicit selective attention in infants. Finally, the longer latencies to Nc for infrequent events may indicate that infants, rather than engaging in a feature-by-feature comparison of frequent and infrequent events, may be spending more time processing a less clear memory trace for the infrequent event.

The Courchesne et al. study indicates that late components are present during infancy, and that one component, Nc, is invoked by infrequent events and thus involves some sort of memory. Their data also indicate that the late components have latencies well beyond 500 msec, and that the polarity of the component indicative of infrequency and memory is opposite to that found in adults. However, one must be cautious about making too much of these results. First, what was particularly surprising about their study was that in the paradigm they used, infants had not only to discriminate the two faces, but also had to decipher the task asked of them. That is, since no instructions could be given and no familiarization to the frequent face was offered, infants had to figure out in as few as 5 to 20 trials (amounting to a possible total of 2 sec of exposure) what the investigator was asking of them (i.e., that the two faces were not only different, but that the probability of their occurring also differed within the task). This seems remarkable, and, if replicated, would call into question many behavioral data that indicate that memory for faces typically requires at least 16 to 22 sec of continuous viewing (Fagan, 1974). Second, only a very small number of infants was tested, and these infants ranged in age from 4 to 7 months (i.e., there were no more than 2 or 3 infants tested at a given age). Third, the averaged invoked responses were based on very few trials (5 to 20), each infant contributed a different number of trials to the averages, and the number of trials averaged differed for the frequent (5 to 20) vs. infrequent (5 to 15) faces. Thus, it is not clear how stable and reliable the data were within and between subjects, and to what degree noise may have contributed to the findings. Additionally, while Courchesne (1984) has speculated that an adult-like P300 response is not possible before adolescence, Courchesne et al. (1981) failed to record from more mature brain sites (e.g., Oz), and also neglected to inspect their data for positive waves prior to 500 msec, the time at which a P300 response would be expected to occur in adults. Finally, the fact that early components (e.g., P2) were present in fewer than half the infants raises questions as to exactly how clearly visible the stimuli were.

In contrast to Courchesne et al. (1981), two recent infant studies provide evidence for an endogenous component, sensitive to infrequency, that has a latency shorter than 500 msec and a positive polarity. In a first study, Hofmann, Salapatek, and Kuskowski (1981) presented 13 cooperative 3-month-olds with a random interlace of two stimuli. One was a vertical square wave grating of one spatial frequency presented 80% of the time, while the other was a square wave grating of a second spatial frequency presented 20% of the time. Each grating was presented for 500 msec, with an interstimulus interval of 500 msec. Prior to the presentation of the interlaced gratings, the 80% grating was presented for about 40 trials (100% condition). The sampling epoch for the ERP was 600 msec. Recording was from Oz and Opz. Figure 13 illustrates the results of Study 1 at Oz. Prior to 300 msec (i.e., for early exogenous components) there was no statistically significant difference in polarity between the 100% condition and trials on which the infrequent (20%) grating was delivered. Between 300 and 600 msec, there was a sustained positive increase in polarity for the 20% with respect to the 100% trials. Thus, an LPC was observed to the infrequent event. Similar results were found at Opz. As would be predicted, no LPC was found when the 100% condition was compared to the 80% condition.

A second experiment was conducted: (a) to determine whether an LPC could be found at Fz prior to 600 msec for infrequent events, and (b) to rule out the possibility that the LPC observed in Study 1 was a subcortical artifact due to adaptation of peripheral visual receptors or receptive fields. Other than the fact that the stimuli used in Study 2 were a horizontal and a vertical square wave grating, the procedure was identical to that of Study 1.

STUDY I

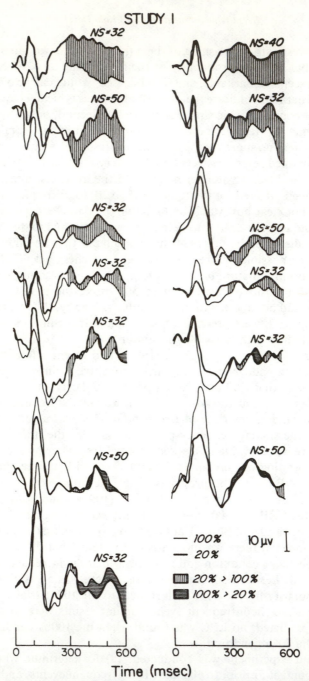

Figure 13. Data from Oz are plotted for the 13 infants in Study 1. The averaged ERP from the familiarization phases (100%) and the ERP from the low-probability trials (20%) are superimposed with respect to initial baseline. The darker trace is the ERP from the low-probability trials (20%). Vertical shading indicates greater positive voltage in the 20% ERP relative to the 100% ERP. Horizontal shading indicates greater negative voltage. Area shading extends from 300 to 600 msec. NS refers to the number of sweeps (trials) used in the average. Each ERP plot consists of at least 32 trials. For each infant, an equal number of trials is included in both the 100% and the 20% traces. Positivity is up. (From Hoffman, Salapatek, & Kuskowski, 1981).

The results of the 16 infants observed in Study 2 are provided in Figure 14. Once again, no differences of note were found at Oz, Opz, or Fz between the 20% vs. 100% or the 100% vs. 80% conditions prior to 300 msec. As in Study 1, a strong LPC was found at Oz and Opz between 300 and 600 msec for the 20% vs. 100% but not for the 80% vs. 100% comparison. Weaker evidence was found for an LPC effect at Fz. Therefore, while the LPC effect observed by Hofmann et al. appears to be due to cortical processing, at least until 600 msec this effect seems to be confined mainly to the occipital pole.

STUDY 2

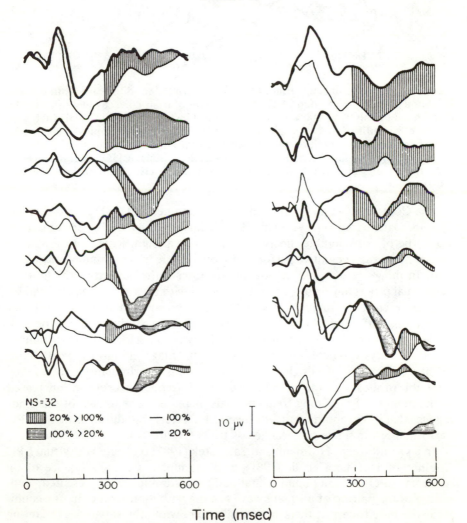

NS = 32

▦ 20% > 100%   — 100%
▤ 100% > 20%   — 20%

10 µv

Time (msec)

Figure 14. Data from Oz are plotted for the 16 infants in Study 2. Details are identical to Figure 13. (From Hofmann et al., 1981).

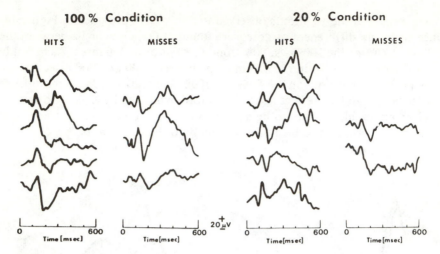

Figure 15. Examples of single-trial ERPs from the 100% condition are plotted in the left-hand portion for an infant. HITS are instances of trials correctly identified by the discriminant analysis as 100% trials. MISSES are instances of 100% trials that were incorrectly identified as 20% trials. The right portion shows examples of single trial ERPs from the 20% condition for the same infant. HITS are instances of trials correctly identified by the discriminant analysis as 20% trials. MISSES are instances of 20% trials that were incorrectly identified as 100% trials. (From Hofmann et al., 1981).

The Courchesne et al. (1981) and the Hofmann et al. (1981) results thus far described are based on averaged ERPs utilizing many trials per subject. It would be of considerable theoretical and clinical significance to be able to assess the infant's cognitive performance on a single trial or stimulus presentation. In this way, it would be possible to observe the pattern of the infant's perceptual processing as he or she is presented with a series of frequent and infrequent events. Hofmann et al. (1981) attempted such an analysis. To render the data free of noise, they selected only trials from Studies 1 and 2 for each subject on which a clear P2 was present. They then performed a discriminant function analysis to determine ERP waveforms that were most typical of frequent vs. infrequent trials (Figure 15). Using this discriminant analysis, they were able to show that the probability of an "infrequent waveform" increased as the number of preceding frequent trials increased. The impact of this finding was that it corroborated the *averaged* LPC effect, but did so using the LPC performance for single subjects across trials (Figure 16).

In a second study, Hofmann and Salapatek (1981) replicated the visual LPC findings of Hofmann et al. (1981), and attempted to find evidence of an auditory LPC. A compound visual-auditory stimulus was presented, consisting of the pairing of a square wave grating with a pure tone. In one condition, the pure tone was the same on all trials, while the square wave grating changed in spatial frequency on infrequent (20%) trials (visual condition). In a

Discriminant Prediction of Single Trials
in the 20% Condition for One Infant

20% Trials from First Test Phase in Order of Presentation									
HIT	X	X		X		X	X		X	X	X
MISS	X		X	X	X	X		X		

20% Trials from Second Test Phase in Order of Presentation										
HIT		X	X	X	X	X	X	X	X	X	X	X
MISS	X										

Figure 16. Artifact-free single trials from the 20% condition are provided for a subject who did not show a strong LPC effect in the averaged ERP analysis. Trials are ordered in the sequence in which they occurred. Note the pattern of consecutive HITS in the second test phase as compared to the first. (From Hofmann et al., 1981).

second condition, the square wave grating was the same on all trials, while the pure tone was of a different frequency on infrequent (20%) trials (auditory condition). Finally, in the visual-auditory condition, both the square wave grating and the pure tone changed on infrequent (20%) trials (visual-auditory condition). Electrodes recorded ERPs from Oz, Pz, and Cz. Evidence of an auditory LPC was expected to be maximal over Cz, while a visual LPC was expected over Oz and Pz. Experimental conditions were otherwise similar to those in the Hofmann et al. (1981) studies. A significant LPC between 300 and 600 msec was obtained at Oz, Pz, and Cz for the visual change condition, replicating earlier results. The Oz data are provided in Figure 17. For the visual-auditory change condition, a significant LPC effect was found at Oz and Pz. However, no LPC effect was found at any electrode site for the auditory change condition. Hofmann and Salapatek speculated that the onset of the visual stimulus on all trials masked the less-dominant auditory stimulus.

Of potential clinical interest was a discriminant-concordance analysis Hofmann and Salapatek applied to the foregoing data. Khrizman and her associates (reviewed by Livanov, 1977; Khrizman & Zaitseva, 1978) have proposed that, with development, the number of functional linkages among different areas of the brain increases during mental tasks. Hofmann and Salapatek applied the discriminant-function analysis mentioned earlier to ERPs from Oz, Pz, and Cz on given trials and from the three experimental conditions. They then examined the extent to which processing for infrequency was concordant across different electrode sites for the different stimulus conditions. It was found that the discriminant concordances among the combinations of scalp sites were different for each experimental condition. This resulted in a unique spatial representation of the infant's brain responses in the different experimental conditions. This analysis also provided some evidence that infants had processed the auditory changes in the study.

The Hofmann et al. (1981) and Hofmann and Salapatek (1981) studies provided the first evidence of an adult-like P300 response in human infants. In addition, the single-trial analysis performed on the Hofmann et al. data represented a promising means of examining individual differences in infants. Fi-

Visual Change
Oz

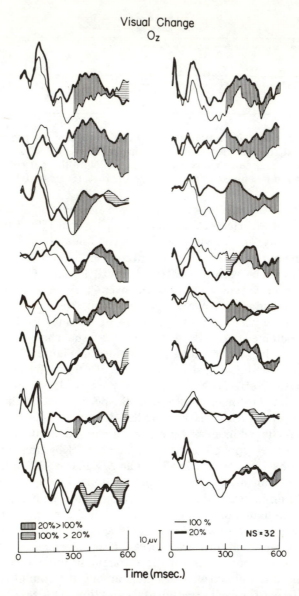

Figure 17. Data from Oz are plotted for the 16 infants in the Visual Change condition. Details are similar to those in Figure 13. (From Hofmann & Salapatek, 1981).

nally, the concordance analysis performed on the Hofmann and Salapatek data indicated that, in infants as young as 3 months, the processing involved in particular tasks may be associated with particular (albeit general) regions of the brain. Both procedures may prove useful in complementing standard averaging procedures, and in assessing clinical populations.

However, there are two potentially troublesome aspects of both studies that should be mentioned. To rule out the possibility that the results of Study 1 of Hofmann et al. (which used changes in spatial frequency) were due to subcortial adaptation effects, a second study was conducted using changes in orientation. This presumably "pushed" the task up higher in the nervous system. However, there still remained the possibility that *cortical* adaptation effects were occurring. Harter, Conder, and Towle (1980) have recently demonstrated orientation-specific adaptation in the ERPs of adults. Their effect was most prominent in the early components (principally 110 msec and 200 msec) following stimulus onset. Therefore, although the response was still cortical in nature, it is possible that the rare spatial frequency (Study 1) or rare orientation (Study 2) was not adapted and was, therefore, perceived as having higher contrast than the frequent adapted grating. Somewhat mitigating against this possibility is the fact that Hofmann et al. found no differences between the 100% and 20% conditions for the first 300 msec. It is also not clear if such adaptation effects occur in young infants. Nevertheless, such cortical adaption effects remain a possibility and require direct examination. The use of more "complex" stimuli (e.g., random checkerboards, faces) would also help in this regard (cf. Nelson & Salapatek, 1984).

A second potential shortcoming of the Hofmann et al. and Hofmann and Salapatek studies concerns the use of a 500 msec stimulus presentation. Five hundred msec would be time enough for infants to accommodate to the stimulus. Given that infants can be astigmatic (e.g., Mohindra, Held, Gwiazda, & Brill, 1978), there is the possibility that infants could have accommodated to a grating of one orientation but could have been unable to accommodate to a grating in a different orientation. Thus, the P300 response could have been due to changes in image sharpness, and may not have been related to memory per se. While such an explanation of the findings seems feasible, there is direct evidence to question it and indirect evidence to rule against it. While not questioning whether individual infants are astigmatic, the evidence for a high percentage of astigmatism occurring in the general population is equivocal. Although it is entirely possible that relatively large astigmatic errors are present in the first year, the possibility that measurement errors have inflated these figures must be entertained. As Banks (1980) points out, one must consider, in the assessment of early astigmatic errors, the varying refractive states in noncyclopegic retinoscopy and the infant's large angle alpha. So too must we consider the lack of accurate fixation controls in measuring refractive state. Thus, it would be premature to assume that, because of the age of Hofmann's subjects, all his infants were astigmatic and, therefore, would evidence differential accommodation to vertical vs. horizontal gratings.

There is also indirect evidence to "rule against" the possibility of differential accommodation to the two gratings. While in principal an astigmatic infant would find it easier to accommodate to a vertical vs. a horizontal grating, there is behavioral evidence to suggest that infants show no preference for one orientation over the other (Bornstein, 1978), and that the orientation of a grating has no bearing on infant acuity, which would in principle be affected by changes in accommodation (e.g., Teller, Morse, Borton, & Regal, 1974). Thus, while infants may be astigmatic (and it is now known how many of Hofmann's were), such astigmatism appears not to influence their behavior toward vertical or horizontal stripes. It seems unlikely that changes in accommodation could have accounted for the results. Nevertheless, it would be wise to test this claim directly, or rule out the possibility of it accounting for the results by using shorter stimulus durations or more complex stimuli (cf. Nelson & Salapatek, 1984).

Schulman-Galambos and Galambos (1978) have provided some evidence that it is possible to observe late potentials in infants 7 weeks through 12 months exposed to a variety of salient stimuli. The stimuli were 2-sec exposures of slides of Disneyland characters, a baby in various poses with his or her mother and father, and children's art class drawings. Additional stimuli consisted of a light flashed on the experimenter's face, a Raggedy Ann doll, and a television screen containing a cartoon. Recordings were from C3 and C4. Infant ERPs, regardless of age, showed a characteristic pattern of a small positive deflection at about 200 msec, followed by a large negative deflection peaking between 500 and 650 msec for most of the subjects. Schulman-Galambos and Galambos interpreted the short latency positive deflection as indicating registration of the stimulus, and the large negative deflection as a response to the novel events (perhaps an Nc component). Finally, they showed that the negative component generally disappeared with repeated stimulus presentations, and reappeared if a new stimulus was introduced.

A most thorough and ambitious longitudinal study was conducted by Barnet, Friedman, Weiss, Ohlrich, Shanks, and Lodge (1980) to chronicle the development of various components of the ERP during infancy and early childhood. Although this study used unpatterned flashes of light, and sleeping infants, and was not conducted within an LPC paradigm, we shall consider it here, since it provides such extensive data on the development of both early and late components.

The authors reported data on 16 infants tested between 7 and 17 times every 2 weeks up to 3 months of age, every 3 months until 1 year, and then every 6 months until age 3. During each test session, a sleeping infant was presented with 100 light flashes produced from a stroboscope, with the flash rate set at 1 per 2.5 seconds. Figure 18 is a schematic composite by age of the ERPs. It may readily be seen that components become more distinct and shorter in latency with age. Within-subject stability was highest for the early prominent ERP components N3, N4, P4, and N6, and least for the long latency components P6, N6, and P7. Individual subjects tended to produce consistently either high- or low-amplitude responses over the years of the study. There were also stable individual differences in the total number of components and the particular components that were present. This study emphasizes the fact that latency shifts may be expected as a function of age for ERP components. Early com-

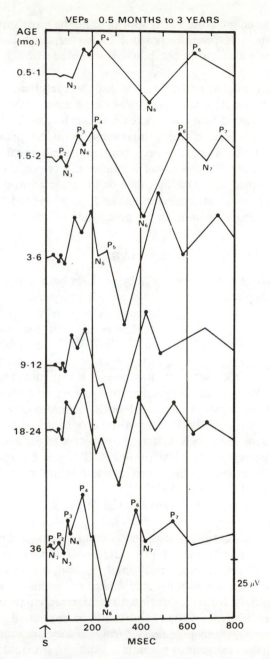

Figure 18. Schematic representation of the occipital (Oz) ERP, demonstrating maturation of the response from the neonatal period to 3 years of age. The peaks marked with dots appeared in more than 50% of the ERPs at that age. (From Barnet, Friedman, Weiss, Ohlrich, Shanks, & Lodge, 1980).

ponents in this paradigm would also appear to be the most stable and to have clinical significance. It remains possible, however, that later components would show more within-subject stability if presented within a patterned LPC paradigm.

A final study (Vaughan, 1975) points out the usefulness of the ERP for studying the sequence of neurobehavioral development within the brain. In general, Vaughan found that early potentials can be evoked by visual, auditory, and tactile stimuli from both primary and secondary projection areas by 30 weeks of conceptional age, although marked development of these potentials occurs postnatally. Frontocentral responses can be evoked shortly after 30 weeks of conceptional age. On the other hand, association-cortex potentials did not become evident until early childhood, as evidenced by responses to "missing" or "omitted" stimuli in a regular train of stimuli.

SUMMARY

The ERP has been used during infancy to study both sensory and cognitive processing. Although it is not easy to draw a simple sensory-cognitive dichotomy either with respect to ERP components or with respect to experimental paradigms, it seems reasonable to conclude at this point that the study of exogenous components in simple, nonmemory (usually sensory) tasks has far outstripped the investigation of endogenous components in paradigms involving a variety of cognitive processes, including memory, vigilance, temporal processing, and novelty. Many of the exogenous components have been well-described from prematurity onwards, in terms of both form and origin on the scalp. There are stable individual differences in the exogenous components that can persist for considerable periods of time. Parameters of the exogenous components, such as latency to P1 or amplitude of P2, can be reliably related to meaningful psychological variables such as visual acuity or preference for contour density (Karmel & Maisel, 1975).

The ERP appears to be a more sensitive clinical tool for assessing visual sensory functioning than most other techniques (e.g., visual preference). It would thus seem that research on the exogenous components can most profitably proceed along three general lines. First, more longitudinal data on the stability of individual differences should be collected. Second, the deviation of clinical populations from these norms must continue to be examined. Finally, the difficult, but potentially fruitful, continuation of research relating exogenous potentials to specific areas of the brain should be continued.

The study of endogenous potentials during infancy presents quite a different story from that of exogenous potentials. And yet, it would appear imperative to learn whether higher cognitive functions are developing normally. In contrast to the considerable literature on early potentials, there are only four published studies on late potentials during infancy (Courchesne et al., 1981; Hofmann & Salapatek, 1981; Hofmann et al., 1981; Schulman-Galambos &

Galambos, 1978). Because of differences among these studies in the paradigms employed, the brain sites sampled, the sample size of infants, and the epochs analyzed, it is not yet possible to conclude whether there exists any agreement among these studies beyond the fact that infants have memory, respond to novelty, and exhibit these abilities in one late potential or another. Hofmann et al. (1981) and Hofmann and Salapatek (1981) found a P300 between 300 and 600 msec in an infrequent-event task. It is unclear whether their P300 relates directly to the P3 found in adults for the same task (although recent evidence collected by Nelson & Salapatek, 1984, suggests that it does). Schulman-Galambos and Galambos (1978) found a negative wave indicating a response to novelty. But their wave was longer in latency than that of the Hofmann et al. and Hofmann & Salapatek studies, and occurred when interesting, but not necessarily infrequent, events were given. Courschesne et al. (1981) found a late negative wave (Nc) and an even later positive wave (Pc) to both frequent and infrequent events (although Nc amplitude was greater to infrequent vs. frequent events). Courchesne (1978, 1984) suggests that Nc decreases in latency, and shifts in polarity, to become, or to be replaced by, P3 beyond infancy. However, Courchesne et al. (1981) did not report infant data prior to 600 msec for any lead, and did not record from Oz at all, while Hofmann and Salapatek (1981) and Hofmann et al. (1981) did not analyze for late components beyond 600 msec at Fz. Thus, it is possible that the early P300, Nc, and Pc are all present in an infant infrequent-event task, but with different latencies at different scalp sites.

The first recommendation, then, for infant studies on endogenous components is to urge investigators to replicate studies, to record for longer epochs, and to sample more extensively a variety of scalp sites. When more knowledge is accumulated regarding the sequencing of late components in simple, two-stimulus, infrequent-event tasks, then it becomes possible to look for within-subject stability and between-subject differences, and to extend this analysis to clinical populations. The nature of the cognitive tasks may then be varied to study the exact capabilities of individual infants. For example, it should be possible to study temporal and event perception in a stimulus-omission paradigm where an "expected" stimulus fails to occur. Alternatively, one might examine at what age and in what populations infrequent categories of stimuli result in an LPC, rather than simply whether a particular infrequent stimulus does so.

More attention should be paid to the single-trial discriminant-function analysis technique employed by Hofmann and Salapatek (1981) and Hofmann et al. (1981). At present, this technique appears to be the most efficient way to examine the nature of an individual infant's ERP response in the fewest possible trials. It can allow us to determine the times during a task at which the infant is successfully processing the events. Finally, almost nothing is known regarding the scalp distribution, by age, of late components in infants successfully engaged in LPC paradigms. Multiple recording, with attention to the presence and concordance of components, is necessary to tease apart the functional significance of the different areas of the brain and of the ERP components.

ACKNOWLEDGMENTS

Preparation of this chapter was supported by grants from NSF (NSF-P2BI389) to the Center for Research in Human Learning, University of Minnesota, NICHD (HD-01136 and HD-17970) to the Institute of Child Development and the first author at the University of Minnesota, and NICHD (1F32HD06231-01) to the second author. The editorial assistance of Joanne Bergman, Judith Reisman, and Julie Wellman is greatly appreciated.

Philip Salapatek died unexpectedly 4 March 1984 while this chapter was in press. He will be sorely missed by all those who knew him personally, and by those who knew his work.

REFERENCES

Adrian, E. D. & Mathews, B. H. C. The Berger rhythm: Potential changes from the occipital lobes of man. *Brain,* 1934, *57,* 355–385.

Atkinson, J., Braddick, O., & Braddick, F. Acuity and contrast sensitivity of infant vision. *Nature,* 1974, *247,* 403–404.

Atkinson, J., Braddick, O., & French, J. Contrast sensitivity of the human neonate measured by the visual evoked potential. *Investigative Ophthalmology & Visual Science,* 1979, *18,* 210–213.

Atkinson, J., Braddick, O., & Moar, K. Contrast sensitivity of the human infant for moving and static patterns. *Vision Research,* 1977, *17,* 1045–1047. (a)

Atkinson, J., Braddick, O., & Moar, K. Development of contrast sensitivity over the first 3 months of life in the human infant. *Vision Research,* 1977, *17,* 1037–1044. (b)

Banks, M. S. Infant refraction and accommodation. *International Opthalmology Clinics,* 1980, *20,* 205–232.

Banks, M. S., Aslin, R. N., & Letson, R. D. Sensitive periods for the development of human binocular vision. *Science,* 1975, *190,* 675–677.

Banks, M. S. & Salapatek, P. Acuity and contrast sensitivity in 1-, 2-, and 3-month-old infants. *Investigative Opthalmology & Visual Science,* 1978, *17,* 361–365.

Banks, M. S. & Salapatek, P. Infant visual perception. In P. Mussen (general ed.), *Handbook of child psychology.* Vol. 2. *Infancy and developmental psychobiology* (M. Haith & J. Campos, volume eds.). New York: Wiley, 1983.

Barnet, A. B., Friedman, S. L., Weiss, I. P., Ohlrich, E. S., Shanks, B., & Lodge, A. VEP development in infancy and early childhood. A longitudinal study. *Electroencephalography and Clinical Neurophysiology,* 1980, *49,* 476–489.

Berger, H. Über das Elektrenkephalogramm des Menschen. *Archiv für Psychiatrie und Nervenkrankheiten,* 1929, *87,* 527–570.

Bodis-Wollner, I. Visual acuity and contrast sensitivity in patients with cerebral lesions. *Science,* 1972, *178,* 769–771.

Bornstein, M. H. Visual behavior of the young human infant: Relationships between chromatic and spatial perception and the activity of underlying brain mechanisms. *Journal of Experimental Child Psychology,* 1978, *26,* 174–192.

Campbell, R. W. & Maffei, L. Electrophysiological evidence for the existence of orientation and size detectors in the human visual system. *Journal of Physiology,* 1970, *207,* 635–652.

Courchesne, E. Neurophysiological correlates of cognitive development: Changes in long-latency event-related potentials from childhood to adulthood. *Electroencephalography and Clinical Neurophysiology,* 1978, *45,* 468–482.

Courchesne, E. Cognitive components of the event-related brain potential: Changes associated with development. In A. W. K. Gaillard & W. Ritter (eds.), *Tutorials in ERP research: Endogenous components.* Amsterdam: North-Holland Publishing Company, 1984.

Courchesne, E. Ganz, L., & Norcia, A. M. Event-related brain potentials to human faces in infants. *Child Development,* 1981, *52,* 804–811.

Dawson, G. D. A summation techique for detecting small signals in a large irregular background. *Journal of Physiology* (London), 1951, *115,* 2-3P.

Dobson, V. & Teller, D. Y. Visual acuity in human infants: A review and comparison of behavioral and electrophysiological studies. *Vision Research,* 1978, *18,* 1469–1483.

Dobson, V., Teller, D. Y., & Belgum, J. Visual acuity in human infants assessed with stationary stripes and phase-alternated checkerboards. *Vision Research,* 1978, *18,* 1288–1238.

Donchin, E., Ritter, W., & McCallum, W. C. Cognitive psychophysiology: The endogenous components of the ERP. In E. Callaway, P. Tueting, & S. H. Koslow (eds.), *Event-related brain potentials in man.* New York: Academic Press, 1978.

Dreyfus-Brisac, C. Neonatal electroencephalography. In E. M. Scarpelli & E. V. Cosmi (eds.), *Reviews in perinatal medicine.* New York: Raven Press, 1979.

Ellingson, R. J. Occipital evoked potentials in human newborns. *Electroencephalography and Clinical Neurophysiology,* 1958, *10,* 189.

Ellingson, R. J. Cortical electrical responses to visual stimulation in the human infant. *Electroencephalography and Clinical Neurophysiology,* 1960, *45,* 351–356.

Fagan, J. F. Infant recognition memory: The effects of length of familiarization and type of discrimination task. *Child Development,* 1974, *45,* 351–356.

Ford, J. M., Roth, W. T., & Kopell, B. S. Auditory evoked potentials to unpredictable shifts in pitch. *Psychophysiology,* 1976, *13,* 32–39.

Gibbs, F. A., Davis, H., & Lennox, W. G. The electro-encephalogram in epilepsy and in conditions of impaired consciousness. *Archives of Neurology and Psychiatry,* 1935, *34,* 1133–1148.

Gloor, P. Hans Berger on the electroencephalogram of man. *Electroencephalography and Clinical Neurophysiology,* 1969, Suppl. 28.

Goff, W. R. Human average evoked potentials: Procedures for stimulating and recording. In R. F. Thompson & M. M. Patterson (eds.), *Bioelectric recording techniques. Part B. Electroencephalography and human brain potentials.* New York: Academic Press, 1974.

Goff, W. R., Allison, T., & Vaughn, H. G., Jr. The functional neuroanatomy of event-related potentials. In E. Callaway, P. Tueting, & S. H. Koslow (eds.), *Event-related brain potentials in man.* New York: Academic Press, 1978.

Harris, L., Atkinson, J., & Braddick, O. Visual contrast sensitivity of a 6-month-old infant measured by the evoked potential. *Nature,* 1976, *264,* 570–571.

Harter, M. R., Conder, E. S., & Towle, V. L. Orientation-specific and luminance effects: Interocular suppression of visual evoked potentials in man. *Psychophysiology,* 1980, *17,* 141–145.

Harter, M. R., Deaton, F. K., & Odom, J. V. Maturation of evoked potentials and visual preferences in 6—45-day-old infants: Effects of check size, visual acuity, and refractive error. *Electroencephalography and Clinical Neurophysiology,* 1977, *42,* 595–607. (a)

Harter, M. R., Deaton, F. K., & Odom, J. V. Pattern visual evoked potentials in infants. In J. E. Desmedt (eds.), *Visual evoked potentials in man: New developments.* Oxford: Clarendon Press, 1977. (b)

Hess, R. F. & Howell, E. R. The threshold contrast sensitivity function in strabismic amblyopia: Evidence for a two type classification. *Vision Research,* 1977, *17,* 1049–1055.

Hickey, T. L. Postnatal development of the human lateral geniculate nucleus: Relationship to a critical period for the visual system. *Science,* 1977, *198,* 836–838.

Hofmann, M. J. *Young infants' event-related potentials (ERPs) to high probability and low probability visual and auditory events in a recognition memory task.* Unpublished doctoral dissertation, University of Minnesota, 1981.

Hofmann, M. J., Karmel, B. Z., & Lester, M. *Infants' electrophysiological response in a classical conditioning paradigm.* Paper presented at the annual meeting of the Society for Neuroscience, New York, 1975.

Hofmann, M. J. & Salapatek, P. Young infants' event-related potentials (ERPs) to familiar and unfamiliar visual and auditory events in a recognition memory task. *Electroencephalography and Clinical Neurophysiology,* 1981, *52,* 405–417.

Hofmann, M. J., Salapatek, P., & Kuskowski, M. Evidence for visual memory in the averaged and single evoked potentials of human infants. *Infant Behavior and Development,* 1981, *4,* 401–421.

Hohmann, H. & Creutzfeld, O. D. Squint and the development of binocularity in humans. *Nature,* 1975, *254,* 613–614.

Jasper, H. H. The ten twenty electrode system of the International Federation. *Electroencephalography and Clinical Neurophysiology,* 1958, *10,* 371–375.

Jasper, H. H. & Carmichael, L. Electrical potentials from the intact human brain. *Science,* 1935, *81,* 51–53.

John, E. R., Ruchkin, D. S., & Vidal, J. J. Measurement of event-related potentials. In E. Callaway, P. Tueting & S. H. Koslow (eds.), *Event-related brain potentials in man.* New York: Academic Press, 1978.

Jones, R. & Keck, M. J. Visual evoked response as a function of grating spatial frequency. *Investigative Ophthalmology & Visual Science,* 1978, *17,* 652–659.

Karmel, B. & Maisel, E. B. A neuronal activity model for infant visual attention. In L. B. Cohen & P. Salapatek (eds.), *Infant perception: From sensation to cognition. Vol. 1. Basic visual processes.* Academic Press: New York, 1975.

Khrizman, T. P. & Zaitseva, L. M. Role of neocortical association structures in the spatiotemporal organization of brain potentials of children during perception of sensory stimuli of different modalities. *Human Physiology,* 1978, *4,* 538–545.

Lindsley, D. B. Brain potentials in children and adults. *Science,* 1936, *84,* 354.

Lindsley, D. B. & Wicke, J. D. The electroencephalogram: Autonomous electrical activity in man and animals. In R. F. Thompson & M. M. Patterson (eds.), *Bioelectric recording techniques. Part B. Electroencephalography and human brain potentials.* New York: Academic Press, 1974.

Livanov, M. N. *Spatial organization of cerebral processes.* New York: Halsted Press, 1977.

Magoon, E. H. & Robb, R. M. Development of myelin in human optic nerve and tract: A light and electron microscopic study. *Archives of Ophthalmology,* 1981, *99,* 655–659.

Marg, E., Freeman, D. N., Peltzman, P., & Goldstein, P. J. Visual acuity development in human infants: Evoked potential measurements. *Investigative Ophthalmology,* 1976, *15,* 150–153.

Mohindra, F., Held, R., Gwiazda, J., & Brill, S. Astigmatism in infants. *Science,* 1978, *202,* 329–331.

Moskowitz, A. & Sokol, S. Spatial and temporal interaction of pattern-evoked cortical potentials in human infants. *Vision Research,* 1980, *20,* 699–707.

Näätänen, R. Processing negativity: An evoked-potential reflection of selective attention. *Psychological Bulletin,* 1982, *92,* 605–640.

Nelson, C. A. & Salapatek, P. *Infants' recognition of briefly presented faces as indexed by the Late Positive Component (LPC) of the event-related potential.* Paper presented at the International Conference on Infant Studies, New York, 1984.

Parker, D. M. & Salzen, E. A. Latency changes in the human visual evoked response to sinusoidal gratings. *Vision Research,* 1977, *17,* 1201–1204.

Pirchio, M., Spinelli, D., Fiorentini, A., & Maffei, L. Infants contrast sensitivity evaluated by evoked potentials. *Brain Research,* 1978, *141,* 179–184.

Pritchard, W. S. Psychophysiology of P300. *Psychological Bulletin,* 1981, *89,* 506–540.

Regan, D. Evoked potentials specific to spatial patterns of luminance and color. *Vision Research,* 1973, *13,* 2381–2402.

Regan, D. Assessment of visual acuity by evoked potential recording: Ambiguity caused by temporal dependence of spatial frequency selectivity. *Vision Research,* 1978, *18,* 439–443.

Regan, D. & Richards, W. Brightness contrast and evoked potentials. *Journal of the Optical Society of America,* 1973, *63,* 606–611.

Regan, D., Silver, R., & Murray, T. J. Visual acuity and contrast sensitivity in multiple sclerosis—hidden visual loss. *Brain,* 1977, *100,* 563–579.

Ritter, W., Simson, R., Vaughan, H. G., & Macht, M. Manipulation of event-related potential manifestations of information processing states. *Science,* 1982, *218,* 909–911.

Ritter, W., Simson, R., & Vaughn, H. G. Event-related potential correlates of two stages of information processing in physical and semantic discrimination tasks. *Psychophysiology,* 1983, *20,* 168–179.

Robson, J. G. Spatial and temporal contrast-sensitivity functions of the visual system. *Journal of the Optical Society of America.* 1966, *56,* 1141–1142.

Salapatek, P. Behavioral and electrophysiological evaluation of the infant contrast sensitivity function. In E. Jampolsky & L. Proenza (eds.), *Applications of psychophysics to clinical problems.* New York: Cambridge University Press, 1982.

Schulman-Galambos, C. & Galambos, R. Cortical responses from adults and infants to complex visual stimuli. *Electroencephalography and Clinical Neurophysiology,* 1978, *45,* 425–435.

Sokol, S. Measurement of infant visual acuity from pattern reversal evoked potentials. *Vision Research,* 1978, *18,* 33–39.

Sokol, S. Infant visual development: Evoked potential estimates. In I. Bodis-Wollner (ed.), *Annals of the New York academy of sciences,* 1982, *388,* 514–525.

Sokol, S. & Dobson, V. Pattern reversal visually evoked potentials in infants. *Investigative Ophthalmology & Visual Science,* 1976, *15,* 58–62.

Sokol, S. & Jones, K. Implicit time of pattern evoked potentials in infants: An index of maturation of spatial vision. *Vision Research,* 1979, *19,* 747–755.

Sokol, S. & Moskowitz, A. Effect of retinal blur on the peak latency of the pattern evoked potential. *Vision Research,* 1981, *21,* 1279–1286.

Spekreijse, H. Maturation of contrast EPs and development of visual resolution. *Archives Italiennes de Biologie,* 1978, *116,* 358–369.

Stevens, J. R. The electroencephalogram: Human recordings. In R. F. Thompson & M. M. Patterson (eds.), *Biolelectric recording techniques. Part B. Electroencephalography and human brain potentials.* New York: Academic Press, 1974.

Teller, D. Y., Morse, R., Borton, R., & Regal, D. Visual acuity for vertical and diagonal gratings in human infants. *Vision Research,* 1974, *14,* 1433–1439.

Thomas, C. L. (ed.). *Taber's encyclopedic medical dictionary.* Philadelphia: F. A. Davis, 1973.

Vaughan, H. G., Jr. Electrophysiologic analysis of regional cortical maturation. *Biological Psychiatry,* 1975, *10,* 513–526.

SECTION 5

Epilogue

The preceding 16 chapters have covered measurement problems in the areas of infant auditory and visual sensation, perception, and cognition in some considerable detail. While this coverage makes it apparent that the study of the sensory and perceptual side of the infant's functioning is just beginning, there is also evidence of some progress, especially in the delineation of the major problems to be solved and the difficulties that lie in the way of their solution. The problems in the first 6 months of postnatal life mostly revolve about engaging and sustaining the infant's interest and attention for sufficient periods of time to allow reliable measurement. At present, measurement of an individual infant's capacities is difficult, if not impossible, so many of the findings come from data that have been pooled across a number of babies. This is a particularly difficult barrier to a developmental psychophysics of infancy, where measurement of the thresholds of individual babies is deemed essential. Somewhat better results (or cooperation) are observed where socially meaningful, as opposed to impoverished, stimuli are employed: the voices of caretakers, human faces, and the like. The problem is two-fold: engaging the young infant's attention and sustaining it.

Research with older infants, those in the second half of the first year, becomes analytically somewhat less precise as the advanced infant's behavior is more differentiated and thus more multifaceted than before: Higher-order psychological variables may "intrude," such as looking in response to sound demanding a visual component that was not previously required or, more generally, the presence of intermodal congruences of some sort that presage or signal at least rudimentary cognitive function. While behavioral state problems become lessened somewhat in the older infant, the more multiple determination of its behavior must be taken into account.

Though not discussed to a significant degree in any of the chapters besides Elizabeth Spelke's, the rule of familiarity vs. novelty in preferential looking tasks sorely needs some theoretically motivated experimental attention. Do younger infants, by and large, prefer familiarity over novelty, while older infants prefer novelty over familiarity? Do infants of all ages prefer slight novelty over major novelty? Are these trends (if there are any) the same for auditory

455

and for visual stimuli? The familiarity/novelty question may not be unrelated to another question: Do ecologically relevant stimuli more readily engage and sustain the infant's attention and interest than artifical stimuli when both are matched for physical complexity?

The unspoken themes of the present volume are the respective concerns for what infants *can* do and what infants *do* do. It may ultimately prove detrimental to our understanding if we continue to dissociate these questions. For the present, perhaps we just need to remain alert to this dissociation and be optimistic about ultimately being able to relate the former to the latter.

AUTHOR INDEX

Italics indicate bibliographic citations.

A

Abahazi, D.A., 116, *124*
Aberger, E., Jr., 263, 285, *298*
Abonnec, M., 384, *388*
Abraham, W., 181–183, 185, 190, *193, 194*
Abramov, I., 397–399, *414, 415*
Abramson, A.S., 200, *222*
Adrian, E.D., 419, *450*
Aitkin, L.M., 62, *86,* 383, *387*
Albin, S., 176, 177, *193*
Albrecht, D.G., 33, 34, *49*
Allen, J., 142, *143*
Allison, T., 420, 424, *451*
Als, H., 176, 177, *192*
Altman, J., 383, *387*
Amatruda, C. S., 304, *322*
Ames, A., 308, *321*
Ames, E.W., 258, 271, *292, 299*
Anderson, D.J., 383, *387*
Anggaard, L., 60, 62, *86*
Anliker, M., 412, 413, *416*
Anson, B.J., 54, 55, *86*
Antell, S.E., 342, *361*
Antonova, T.G., 116, 117, *124,* 254, *294*
Appel, M.A., 307, *321*
Applebaum, M.I., 259, 272, *297, 298,* 339, *362*
Armitage, S.E., 25, *27*
Aslin, R.N., 26, *27,* 123, *125,* 131, *143,* 223, 235–237, *249,* 301–303, 307, 320, *321, 322,* 324, 393, 398, 399, 402, 407, 410–413, *414, 415, 416,* 436, *450*
Atkinson, J., 42, 43, *49, 50,* 307, *321,* 427, 428, 430–432, *450, 451*

B

Baccaro, P., 226, *250*
Bahrick, L.E., 345, 347, 349–352, *361*
Baillargeon, R., 356, 357, *361*
Baldini, N., 255, 289, *297*
Baldwin, B.A., 25, *27*
Ball, W.A., 355, *361*
Banks, M.S., 35, 42–46, *50,* 130–131, *143,* 303, *321,* 427, 428, 436, 445, *450*
Barlow, H.B., 37, *50*
Barnet, A.B., 268, 286, *292,* 446, 447, *450*
Barnett, R.K., 22, *29*
Barrera, M. E., 271, 292, *293,* 350, *361*

Barrière, M., 26, *28*
Bartels, B., 286, *297*
Bartlett, M., 25, *28*
Bartoshuk, A.K., 271, *293*
Bassili, J., 337, *361*
Bateson, P.P.G., 98, *106*
Baumgardt, E., 37, *50*
Baumgartner, G., 412, 413, *416*
Bayer, S.A., 383, *387*
Bayley, N., 284, *293*
Bechtoldt, H.P., 306, 316, *321*
Becklen, R., 349, *362*
Beecher, M.D., *27*
von Békésy, G., 65, 68, *90,* 369, 376, *389*
Belgum, J., 427, *451*
Bell, R.Q., 268, *299*
Benasich, A.A., 262, 266–268, 273, 283, 284, 286, 289, *293*
Berg, K. M., 123, *124,* 268, *293*
Berg, W.K., 116, 117, *124,* 256, 268, *293*
Berger, H., 419, *450*
Bergman, T., 346, *362,* 405, *415*
Berlin, B., 279, *293*
Berlyne, D.E., 260, 272, 290, *293*
Bernard, J., 25, *28*
Bernstein, A.S., 115, *124*
von Bernuth, H., 268, *296*
Berry, R.C., 116, *125*
Bertenthal, B.I., 259, 273, *293,* 336, 337, *361*
Bertoncini, J., 26, *28,* 201, 205, 208–212, 214, 217, *221, 222*
Beyerl, B.D., 383, *387*
Bhana, K., 257, *296*
Bijeljac-Babic, R., 209, 211, 214, 217, *221*
Birch, E.E., 131, *143,* 412, *415*
Birch, H.G., 39, *51,* 116, *126,* 172, *194,* 261, *298*
Birns, B., 116, *124*
Black, A., 258, *292*
Blank, M., 116, *124*
Blough, D., 118, *124*
Blough, P., 118, *124*
Bock, G.R., 77, *89*
Bodis-Wollner, I., 428, *450*
Boehmer, A., 290*n, 298*
Bogartz, R.S., 259, *293*
Borah, J., 400, *416*
Born, D.E., 78–80, *86*

SUBJECT INDEX